THE
BOOK OF
RESOLUTIONS
OF THE UNITED METHODIST CHURCH
2016

THE
BOOK OF
RESOLUTIONS
OF THE UNITED METHODIST CHURCH
2016

The United Methodist Publishing House
Nashville, Tennessee

THE BOOK OF RESOLUTIONS OF THE UNITED METHODIST CHURCH 2016

PREFACE

The *Book of Resolutions* has been published after each General Conference since 1968. This edition includes all resolutions that are currently valid. Resolutions that have been rescinded or superseded have been removed from this 2016 edition.

When approved by the General Conference, resolutions state the policy of The United Methodist Church on many current social issues and concerns. Only the General Conference speaks for The United Methodist Church (*Book of Discipline,* ¶ 509).

The 2000 General Conference approved a rule stating: "Resolutions are official expressions of The United Methodist Church for eight years following their adoption, after which time they shall be deemed to have expired unless readopted. Those that have expired shall not be printed in subsequent editions of the *Book of Resolutions*" (*Book of Discipline,* ¶ 510.2*a*). This edition has been prepared in accordance with that rule.

This 2016 edition presents the resolutions in seven sections: (I) The Natural World, (II) The Nurturing Community, (III) The Social Community, (IV) The Economic Community, (V) The Political Community, (VI) The World Community, and (X) Other Resolutions. The first six section titles match the sections of the Social Principles, United Methodism's foundational statement on social issues found in *The Book of Discipline of The United Methodist Church, 2016,* ¶¶ 160-166, pages 105-146. These same paragraphs appear before each section of resolutions in this volume so that users may easily connect the principles to the resolutions.

1 11111111111111111111111

To assist readers in study and use of the Social Principles and their related resolutions, this edition repeats from previous editions:

—User's Guide

—Index

—Date of General Conference adoption and date of amendment and readoption

—Relocation of the Social Principles to make comparisons with the resolutions easier

—Resolution numbering system matching the first digit with the Roman numeral of the Social Principles' six section numbers (I = 1, II = 2, III = 3)

—Revised and updated section titles

—Resolution numbers from preceding volumes to make research easier

—Running heads with the resolution numbers on each page

—Thumb indexing of the Social Principles

—Alphabetical list of resolution titles

—Scripture references in resolutions

—List of new resolutions

—List of deleted and expired resolutions

Errata can be found at Cokesbury.com, word search for *Errata*.

The 2016 *Book of Resolutions* is published by The United Methodist Publishing House—the Rev. Brian K. Milford, publisher and book editor of The United Methodist Church. Brian O. Sigmon, editor of United Methodist Resources, The United Methodist Publishing House, served as the principal editor. The late Carolyn D. Minus, former General Board of Church and Society staff member, wrote the User's Guide.

CONTENTS

¶ 160
THE NATURAL WORLD

Energy

Environment

7

CONTENTS

¶ 161
THE NURTURING COMMUNITY

¶ 162
THE SOCIAL COMMUNITY

CONTENTS

Church and Community Development

Cultural Issues

Ecumenical Issues

Organization Memberships:

Education

CONTENTS

Mental Health

Native Americans

Church Relations:

Culture and Tradition:

Health Care:

Population

Racism

Rural Issues

Urban Issues

Violence

Women

Young People

¶ 163
THE ECONOMIC COMMUNITY

CONTENTS

Workers' Rights

¶ 164
THE POLITICAL COMMUNITY

Church and State

Criminal Justice

Political Responsibility

United States Legislative Issues

¶ 165
THE WORLD COMMUNITY

Education

Global Interreligious Relations

CONTENTS

Justice and Law

US Power and Responsibility in the World

Asia:

Caribbean:

Pacific Islands:

Western Hemisphere:

Nations and Cultures

Africa:

CONTENTS

CONTENTS

War and the Military

X. OTHER RESOLUTIONS

Mission and Ministry:

Request for Study:

United Methodist Guidelines:

Worship and Liturgy:

CONTENTS

CONTENTS

USER'S GUIDE

WHAT'S THE PURPOSE OF THE *BOOK OF RESOLUTIONS*?

The Book of Resolutions, 2016, published by The United Methodist Publishing House, collects in one volume all current and official social policies and other resolutions adopted by the General Conference of The United Methodist Church. These resolutions are:

• *Official policy statements* for guiding all the work and ministry of The United Methodist Church on approximately 200 subjects;
• *Educational resources* for The United Methodist Church on important issues affecting the lives of people and all God's creation;
• *Guides* and models for helping United Methodist members and groups relate a lively biblical faith to action in daily life;
• *Resource materials* for persons preparing public statements about United Methodist concerns on current social issues.

The Book of Resolutions, 2016 is primarily a reference tool for church members and leaders. It is not a book that you will sit down to read from cover to cover.

You might not get acquainted with these resolutions until you are in the midst of some controversy in your congregation, or something happens regarding a particular subject in your community (or state, or nation). You may find that your denomination's policies give you more "food for thought." Maybe you will agree with the denomination's position. On the other hand, you may disagree. Individuals or groups in the congregation can seek to change policy with which they disagree by petitioning the General Conference to amend, replace, or delete resolutions.

Furthermore, you may look to some of the statements in this book for spiritual guidance as you make an important decision in your life about work, home, family life, or use of money and other resources.

21

CAN YOU ANSWER SOME OF MY QUESTIONS?

Why do we have all these social policies and resolutions?

The resolutions say, "We care!" Delegates to the General Conference of The United Methodist Church believe that we each need and deserve the guidance of the whole denomination as we face daily hopes, struggles, joy, or pain. The resolutions and Social Principles express our Church community's beliefs and give us evidence that the Church means for God's love to reach into situations faced each day, not just on Sunday mornings. Not all of us are intimately involved with each issue, but someone, somewhere, is.

Isn't the *Book of Discipline* enough?

The *Book of Discipline* establishes a framework for each part of United Methodism. The General Conference decided in 1968 that for reasons of length, these resolutions should be published in a volume separate from the *Discipline*. While the *Book of Resolutions* is not legally binding, it is an official guide from our denomination to be used responsibly for reference, encouragement, study, and support. (Note Judicial Council Decision 671 holds that in some circumstances resolutions do have authority of law.)

Why do the Social Principles appear in both the *Discipline* and in the *Book of Resolutions?*

The United Methodist Church puts the Social Principles in the *Discipline* (¶¶ 160–166) as one of our denominational foundation statements suggesting how faith is translated into action. Its broad principles (guides, not rules) are declarations to help us be in dialogue with one another about how faith motivates us to "get off the fence" and act.

The United Methodist Church puts the Social Principles in the *Book of Resolutions* to help us relate the broad strokes of the Social Principles to more specific exploration and applications in resolutions.

Where do these policies and resolutions come from? How do they get adopted by General Conference?

They are sent in as petitions to General Conference every four years by general agencies, annual conferences, local churches, individual members, and groups. Once submitted as petitions, most of them are worked on by delegates in a legislative committee. The legislative committees accept, reject, or amend the petitions, then report their recommendations to the General Conference plenary; all delegates then vote on their recommendations.

Can I trust the statistics and data in these resolutions?

General source references are usually given when statistics are used in a resolution. Because such data may change during the years the resolution is valid, sometimes the resolution will provide more general descriptions of social conditions that make it urgent for the church to speak on a particular topic. Resolutions will take on more meaning when you secure local statistics and data on relevant topics.

Why do church social policies and US government policies or positions seem so far apart on some of these issues?

The United Methodist Church membership extends beyond the US boundaries; it is global. So, in many cases we are speaking to, from, or with more than one national government. Further, the Christian church must never be a mirror image of any government, whether Democrat or Republican, totalitarian or democratic. We know that Christians are obligated to be responsible and participating citizens under any governmental system, but that response and participation is to be interpreted in light of our faith.

As the Social Principles state, "Our allegiance to God takes precedence over our allegiance to any state" (¶ 164). And our church's public witness is first and foremost to be judged by God by whether it supports justice, love, and mercy, particularly for the poor and powerless.

Why can't the church just let us make up our own minds on these matters after it presents us neutral information on both sides of an issue?

Most importantly, The United Methodist Church believes God's love for the world is an active and engaged love, a love seeking justice and liberty. We cannot just be observers. So we care enough about people's lives to risk interpreting God's love, to take a stand, to call each of us into a response, no matter how controversial or complex. The church helps us think and act out of a faith perspective, not just respond to all the other "mind-makers-up" that exist in our society.

No information is truly neutral. This is true even of the most "hard scientific" data secured from the most advanced technology. These resolutions do strive for objectivity, not neutrality. There are usually more than "two sides" in important social controversies. Dialogue between different sides is critical in taking a stand. Faithfulness requires favoring what best demonstrates God's love and being willing to change when new perspectives or data emerge.

Is this something new in United Methodism?

Taking an active stance in society is nothing new for followers of John Wesley. He set the example for us to combine personal and social piety. Ever since predecessor churches to United Methodism flourished in the United States, we have been known as a denomination involved with people's lives, with political and social struggles, having local to international mission implications. Such involvement is an expression of the personal change we experience in our baptism and conversion.

Is there a difference between a social policy and a resolution?

The terms are used almost interchangeably in The United Methodist Church. Most social issue resolutions refer to public policy matters, such as local, state, and federal government programs and legislation. Other statements focus on conditions affecting the church and the church's programs or funding.

HOW DO PEOPLE USE THIS *BOOK OF RESOLUTIONS*?

• An ordained minister went to console neighbor parents after their son committed suicide. At home later that evening, the pastor and his own family struggled in their grief to apply their faith to this troubling situation. What did the church say about suicide? How should a Christian act? The pastor found the 1980 *Book of Resolutions* absolutely silent on this topic. During the six years after that first personal encounter with ministry after a suicide, the pastor wrote letters and articles and talked with seminary faculty and national church staff. As a result, the 1988 General Conference adopted its first resolution on suicide. Instead of merely wishing for guidance from our church on this most difficult subject, this pastor gave constructive leadership in the church, and we now can find helpful perspectives in the *2016 Book of Resolutions*.

• Clergy writing their sermons, Sunday school teachers planning lessons, and church leaders preparing presentations for any purpose can use the new scripture index to the resolutions to find and add informative and persuasive language to their work. The mission of the church can be extended by presenting its social vision to make disciples for Jesus Christ in the world.

• A bishop and an annual conference board of church and society wanted to share a United Methodist position against the death penalty with their governor, who had to consider clemency for a death row inmate. They visited the governor and delivered a letter stating their own views of this particular situation and describing why The United Methodist Church opposes the death penalty. They used the resolution on capital punishment in the *Book of Resolutions* as the official policy of The United Methodist Church to support their plea for clemency.

• An adult church school group studied the foreign policy discussion topics called "Great Decisions," issued annually by the Foreign Policy Association. They compared its resources with positions in the relevant United Methodist policies from the *Book of Resolutions* for several evenings of lively study.

• Another adult class meeting on Sunday morning always studied faith and contemporary issues. For nearly six months, the members used the *Book of Resolutions* to guide their study and discussion. Different members made presentations on some aspect of the resolutions; then they used the study questions provided on page 34 to stimulate some challenging discussion. Occasionally, they had guest speakers or used an audiovisual resource from their conference media center to amplify the subject.

• A nurse who is an active church member found the resolutions on "Health Care for All in the United States" and "Ministries in Mental Illness" to be helpful as she reflected on the strains in her job. She found it more possible to connect her faith to her discussions with coworkers about some of the major issues facing her profession in a big city hospital.

• A local church's outreach work area asked its church council to approve a congregational statement to the county zoning board favoring the construction of several low-income housing units. As part of their homework, the work area members reviewed the "Housing in the USA" resolution in the *Book of Resolutions*. That resolution then served as a basis for their initiative; they even quoted from it when they testified at the zoning board.

HOW DO I USE THE *BOOK OF RESOLUTIONS*?

Read the preface. ——————→ It provides an orientation to the whole book.

Skim through the ——————→ Note: Resolutions are table of contents. listed under the section of the Social Principles to which they most closely relate.

Check index for ——————→ Key words will help you specific references locate resolutions

Example: If you want to know whether our denomination has spoken about AIDS or HIV, you look for those entries in the index. These subjects are referred to in a number of resolutions.

Example: What is there on "racism"? The index includes a number of references. You may also choose to look under "African Americans," "Native Americans," or "White Privilege."

Find the text of the   • Note that the Social Principles include
Social Principles.   broad, fundamental statements grouped in six topical sections. Immediately following this study guide you will find "Our Social Creed" and a new "Companion Litany" designed for worship use. Following that, come the Social Principles Preface and the Preamble, then ¶ 160, the first of the Social Principles. The remaining Social Principles can easily be found by using the thumb index on the outer edge of the pages. The Resolutions are placed after the Social Principles to which they relate.
                          • Review the "How can I understand the Social Principles?" section in this User's Guide. Use the diagrams in this section to help interpret and look for meaning in the Social Principles.

HOW CAN I UNDERSTAND THE SOCIAL PRINCIPLES?

the *Book of Resolutions* organizes almost all resolutions into the six areas of concern that form the major sections of the Social Principles. You may find it helpful to consider these six areas of concern as you explore specific resolutions.

One way of understanding the Social Principles is to consider the six sections as areas of concern: (1) the natural world, (2) the nurturing community, (3) the social community, (4) the economic community, (5) the political community, and (6) the world community.

The Natural World, the starting point for the areas of concern, provides the essential resources of life for all humankind.

THE NATURAL WORLD

Then add to the natural world the people of the world—of the World Community. All of us live in community, oftentimes becoming part of several communities. Together we make up the world community.

THE NATURAL WORLD

The World Community

All of us also become a part of the Nurturing Community. Through the people with whom we interact most often—family, friends, local church, and others—we shape our lives and the way we relate to other communities.

Three other communities impact both the nurturing community and the world community.

THE NATURAL WORLD

Nurturing

The World Community

The Social Community (or cultural community) provides the arena where we live out our responsibilities, and rights in our treatment of others.

The Economic Community, in which each of us functions, establishes production, distribution, and employment systems; it creates both wealth and poverty.

The Political Community determines whether our rights are guaranteed and our basic freedoms are upheld. Directions and goals of our social and economic communities are debated and decided in this arena.

Decisions in all these communities have an impact on the natural world and vice versa.

THE NATURAL WORLD

Social
Nurturing
Economic   Political

The World Community

Our Social Creed

"Our Social Creed" (Section VII of the Social Principles) is a summary of the foregoing sections of the Social Principles in the form of a creed. While it is recommended by the general church for separate use in worship services, "Our Social Creed" is an integral part of the Social Principles. The Companion Litany was approved by General Conference 2008 and is also intended for use in worship.

Another way of considering the six sections of the Social Principles (the six areas of concern) is to look at: (1) the role of each section, (2) the predominant faith statement in each section, (3) our responsibility defined in each section, and (4) the issues discussed in each section. The chart on the next two pages summarizes the Social Principles in this way.

The Social Principles

CATEGORY	I The Natural World	II The Nurturing Community	III The Social Community	IV The Economic Community	V The Political Community	VI The World Community
ROLE	Provides for sustenance of all creation to be used with integrity	Provides the potential to nurture human beings into the fullness of their humanity.	Provides the means for determining the rights and responsibilities of the members toward one another	Provides directions for influencing economic policies.	Provides for the ordering of society.	Provides the setting for the interaction of nations.
FAITH STATEMENT	All creation is God's.	All persons are important and loved by God.	All persons are equally valuable in the sight of God.	All economic systems are under God's judgment.	All political systems are under God's judgment.	All of God's world is one world.

OUR RESPONSIBILITY	To value and conserve all natural resources.	To innovate, sponsor, and evaluate new forms of community.	To work toward societies in which social groups and individual values are recognized, maintained, and strengthened.	To ensure that sound policies are developed that provide for full employment, adequate income, and so forth.	To take active responsibility for our government.	To work to develop the moral and spiritual capacity to achieve a stable world of love.
ISSUES	Water, air, soil, plants, energy utilization, animal life, space.	Family, marriage, human sexuality, abortion, death.	Rights of minorities, children, youth and young adults, the aging, women, men, immigrants, people with disabilities; alcohol/drugs, rural life.	Property, collective bargaining, work/leisure, consumption, poverty, foreign workers, gambling.	Basic liberties, political responsibility, freedom of information, civil obedience and civil disobedience, crime and rehabilitation, military service.	Nations and cultures, national power and responsibility, war and peace, justice and law.

HOW CAN I BETTER UNDERSTAND THE RESOLUTIONS?

Each resolution shows:

- the rationale or reasons for the resolution;
- the Social Principles paragraph to which that resolution relates (found at the conclusion of any resolution);
- the biblical references and/or theological concerns identified in that resolution;
- the major actions called for in that resolution for churches; individuals; church agencies; local, state, or national governments;
- the date the resolution was passed or amended and readopted by General Conference.
- the resolution number from preceding volumes.

The Natural World

Resolution	Social Principles Paragraph	Biblical References Theological Concerns	Actions called for	Dates of adoption and readoption
1034. Environmental Health	¶ 160A	• God gave us a good and complete earth, and we are meant to live in a way that acknowledges the interdependence of human beings with one another and with the world around us. The natural world is a place where a faithful, loving, just Creator's handiwork can be seen. • God's covenant with humanity affirms that God is involved in the healing of individuals (Proverbs 3:7-8) and includes the mandate to protect the community from dangers that threaten the health and safety of the people.	• Ask governments to enact policies that protect human beings from environmentally toxic products and by-products • Churches to become places of Christian education that teach about the products we buy and their inherent dangers. • Church must provide for the safety and health of persons in their meeting spaces and work places, and become educators and advocates for public and environmental health. • Church must educate itself on public health initiatives and advocate for them.	Adopted 2016.

The Natural World

Resolution	Social Principles Paragraph	Biblical References Theological Concerns	Actions called for	Dates of adoption and readoption
1003. Nuclear Safety in the United States	¶ 160F	The God-given charge to humans to "farm . . . and take care" of the earth (Genesis 2:15). To ensure that God's creation is protected for present and future generations.	• Urge general United Methodist agencies to assist annual conferences in all aspects of information and action strategies on this issue. • Advocate for public policy, particularly regarding nuclear power, reviewing safety of operating plants, researching designs for plant safety, phasing out nuclear weapons production, establishing uniform safety standards for civilian and military nuclear operations, reevaluating US nuclear waste policy, and conserving energy and enhancing alternative energy sources.	Adopted 1988 Amended and readopted 1992, 2004, 2012

The Social Community

Resolution	Social Principles Paragraph	Biblical References Theological Concerns	Actions called for	Dates of adoption and readoption
3024. Mission and Aging of the Global Population	¶ 162 *and* ¶ 165	• From Scripture, the stories of our faith have looked realistically but positively. Old age (carries troubles (Ecclesiastes 12:1), but age brings wisdom (Exodus 12:21, Acts 20:17) and specific pleasures such as grandchildren (Proverbs 17:6). • Old age is to be honored and re-spected, and it is a sign of God's favor on individuals and the community of God's people. • Christian tradition accords dignity to persons in old age.	• Local churches to involve older adults and learn from other cultures and countries in their understanding and appreciation of older persons. • Annual conferences to involve older adults in the full range of conference programs and learn about ways to support older persons locally and throughout the world. • General program agencies and episcopal leadership of the Church to support older persons through specific named actions.	Adopted 2004 Readopted 2008 Amended and readopted 2016

WHAT DO I DO NEXT?

Consider these questions for study and response to any of the resolutions:

• How familiar am I with the situation(s) described in this resolution?

• What are my reactions to this call for action by our church?

• How might reactions be different if we lived in another part of this country? lived in another country? were of a different economic class? attended a different church? if members of my family were present (or not present)?

• How could our local congregation creatively respond to the calls for action in the resolution?

• Are there groups in my area or state at work on this issue where I could join in action or learn more?

• What have I communicated to our congressional members or state legislators about our church's position on an issue of great importance?

• Who could we contact for more information or resources? Write to or call: Communications, General Board of Church and Society, 100 Maryland Avenue, N.E., Washington, DC 20002; (202) 488-5600 (www.umc-gbcs.org).

SOCIAL CREED

¶ 166. VII. OUR SOCIAL CREED

We believe in God, Creator of the world; and in Jesus Christ, the Redeemer of creation. We believe in the Holy Spirit, through whom we acknowledge God's gifts, and we repent of our sin in misusing these gifts to idolatrous ends.

We affirm the natural world as God's handiwork and dedicate ourselves to its preservation, enhancement, and faithful use by humankind.

We joyfully receive for ourselves and others the blessings of community, sexuality, marriage, and the family.

We commit ourselves to the rights of men, women, children, youth, young adults, the aging, and people with disabilities; to improvement of the quality of life; and to the rights and dignity of all persons.

We believe in the right and duty of persons to work for the glory of God and the good of themselves and others and in the protection of their welfare in so doing; in the rights to property as a trust from God, collective bargaining, and responsible consumption; and in the elimination of economic and social distress.

We dedicate ourselves to peace throughout the world, to the rule of justice and law among nations, and to individual freedom for all people of the world.

We believe in the present and final triumph of God's Word in human affairs and gladly accept our commission to manifest the life of the gospel in the world. Amen.

(It is recommended that this statement of Social Principles be continually available to United Methodist Christians and that it be emphasized regularly in every congregation. It is further recommended that "Our Social Creed" be frequently used in Sunday worship.)

A COMPANION LITANY TO OUR SOCIAL CREED

God in the Spirit revealed in Jesus Christ,
calls us by grace
>*to be renewed in the image of our Creator,*
>*that we may be one*
>*in divine love for the world.*

Today is the day
God cares for the integrity of creation,
>wills the healing and wholeness of all life,
>weeps at the plunder of earth's goodness.

And so shall we.

Today is the day
God embraces all hues of humanity,
>delights in diversity and difference,
>favors solidarity transforming strangers into friends.

And so shall we.

Today is the day
God cries with the masses of starving people,
>despises growing disparity between rich and poor,
>demands justice for workers in the marketplace.

And so shall we.

Today is the day
God deplores violence in our homes and streets,
>rebukes the world's warring madness,
>humbles the powerful and lifts up the lowly.

And so shall we.

Today is the day
God calls for nations and peoples to live in peace,
>celebrates where justice and mercy embrace,
>exults when the wolf grazes with the lamb.

And so shall we.

Today is the day
God brings good news to the poor,
>*proclaims release to the captives,*
>*gives sight to the blind, and*
>*sets the oppressed free.*

And so shall we.

SOCIAL PRINCIPLES

PREFACE

The United Methodist Church has a long history of concern for social justice. Its members have often taken forthright positions on controversial issues involving Christian principles. Early Methodists expressed their opposition to the slave trade, to smuggling, and to the cruel treatment of prisoners.

A social creed was adopted by The Methodist Episcopal Church (North) in 1908. Within the next decade similar statements were adopted by The Methodist Episcopal Church, South, and by The Methodist Protestant Church. The Evangelical United Brethren Church adopted a statement of social principles in 1946 at the time of the uniting of the United Brethren and The Evangelical Church. In 1972, four years after the uniting in 1968 of The Methodist Church and The Evangelical United Brethren Church, the General Conference of The United Methodist Church adopted a new statement of Social Principles, which was revised in 1976 (and by each successive General Conference).

The Social Principles, while not to be considered church law,[1] are a prayerful and thoughtful effort on the part of the General Conference to speak to the human issues in the contemporary world from a sound biblical and theological foundation as historically demonstrated in United Methodist traditions. They are a call to faithfulness and are intended to be instructive and persuasive in the best of the prophetic spirit. The Social Principles are a call to all members of The United Methodist Church to a prayerful, studied dialogue of faith and practice. (See *Discipline*, ¶ 509.)

1. See Judicial Council Decisions 833, 1254.

PREAMBLE

We, the people called United Methodists, affirm our faith in God our Creator and Father, in Jesus Christ our Savior, and in the Holy Spirit, our Guide and Guard.

We acknowledge our complete dependence upon God in birth, in life, in death, and in life eternal. Secure in God's love, we affirm the goodness of life and confess our many sins against God's will for us as we find it in Jesus Christ. We have not always been faithful stewards of all that has been committed to us by God the Creator. We have been reluctant followers of Jesus Christ in his mission to bring all persons into a community of love. Though called by the Holy Spirit to become new creatures in Christ, we have resisted the further call to become the people of God in our dealings with each other and the earth on which we live.

We affirm our unity in Jesus Christ while acknowledging differences in applying our faith in different cultural contexts as we live out the gospel. We stand united in declaring our faith that God's grace is available to all, that nothing can separate us from the love of God in Christ Jesus.

Grateful for God's forgiving love, in which we live and by which we are judged, and affirming our belief in the inestimable worth of each individual, we renew our commitment to become faithful witnesses to the gospel, not alone to the ends of earth, but also to the depths of our common life and work.

¶ 160. I. THE NATURAL WORLD

All creation is the Lord's, and we are responsible for the ways in which we use and abuse it. Water, air, soil, minerals, energy resources, plants, animal life, and space are to be valued and conserved because they are God's creation and not solely because they are useful to human beings. God has granted us stewardship of creation. We should meet these stewardship duties through acts of loving care and respect. Economic, political, social, and technological developments have increased our human numbers, and lengthened and enriched our lives. However, these developments have led to regional defoliation, dramatic extinction of species, massive human suffering, overpopulation, and misuse and overconsumption of natural and nonrenewable resources, particularly by industrialized societies. This continued course of action jeopardizes the natural heritage that God has entrusted to all generations. Therefore, let us recognize the responsibility of the church and its members to place a high priority on changes in economic, political, social, and technological lifestyles to support a more ecologically equitable and sustainable world leading to a higher quality of life for all of God's creation.

A) Water, Air, Soil, Minerals, Plants—We support and encourage social policies that serve to reduce and control the creation of industrial byproducts and waste; facilitate the safe processing and disposal of toxic and nuclear waste and move toward the elimination of both; encourage reduction of municipal waste; provide for appropriate recycling and disposal of municipal waste; and assist the cleanup of polluted air, water, and soil. We call for the preservation of old-growth forests and other irreplaceable natural treasures, as well as preservation of endangered plant species. We support measures designed to maintain and restore natural ecosystems. We support policies that develop alternatives to chemicals used for growing, processing, and preserving food, and we strongly urge adequate research into their effects upon God's creation prior to utilization. We urge development of international agreements concerning equitable utilization of the world's resources for human benefit so long as the integrity of the earth is maintained. We are deeply concerned about the privatization of water resources, the bottling of water to be sold as a commodity for profit, and the resources that go into packaging bottled water. We urge all municipalities and other governmental organizations to develop processes for determining sustainability of water resources and to determine the environmental, economic, and social consequences of privatization of water resources prior to the licensing and approval thereof.

B) *Energy Resources Utilization*—The whole earth is God's good creation and as such has inherent value. We are aware that the current utilization of energy resources threatens this creation at its very foundation. As members of The United Methodist Church we are committed to approaching creation, energy production, and especially creation's resources in a responsible, careful and economic way. We call upon all to take measures to save energy. Everybody should adapt his or her lifestyle to the average consumption of energy that respects the limits of the planet earth. We encourage persons to limit CO_2 emissions toward the goal of one tonne per person annually. We strongly advocate for the priority of the development of renewable energies. The deposits of carbon, oil, and gas resources are limited and their continuous utilization accelerates global warming. The use of nuclear power is no solution for avoiding CO_2 emissions. Nuclear power plants are vulnerable, unsafe, and potential health risks. A safe, permanent storage of nuclear waste cannot be guaranteed. It is therefore not responsible to future generations to operate them. The production of agricultural fuels and the use of biomass plants rank lower than the provision of safe food supplies and the continued existence for small farming businesses.

C) *Animal Life*—We support regulations that protect and conserve the life and health of animals, including those ensuring the humane treatment of pets, domesticated animals, animals used in research, wildlife, and the painless slaughtering of meat animals, fish, and fowl. We recognize unmanaged and managed commercial, multinational, and corporate exploitation of wildlife and the destruction of the ecosystems on which they depend threatens the balance of natural systems, compromises biodiversity, reduces resilience, and threatens ecosystem services. We encourage commitment to effective implementation of national and international governmental and business regulations and guidelines for the conservation of all animal species with particular support to safeguard those threatened with extinction.

D) *Global Climate Stewardship*—We acknowledge the global impact of humanity's disregard for God's creation. Rampant industrialization and the corresponding increase in the use of fossil fuels have led to a buildup of pollutants in the earth's atmosphere. These "greenhouse gas" emissions threaten to alter dramatically the earth's climate for generations to come with severe environmental, economic, and social implications. The adverse impacts of global climate change disproportionately affect individuals and nations least responsible for the emissions. We therefore support efforts of all governments to require mandatory reductions in greenhouse gas emissions and call on individuals, congregations, businesses, industries, and communities to reduce their emissions.

E) *Space*—The universe, known and unknown, is the creation of God and is due the respect we are called to give the earth. We therefore reject any nation's efforts to weaponized space and urge that all nations pursue the peaceful and collaborative development of space technologies and of outer space itself.

F) *Science and Technology*—We recognize science as a legitimate interpretation of God's natural world. We affirm the validity of the claims of science in describing the natural world and in determining what is scientific. We preclude science from making authoritative claims about theological issues and theology from making authoritative claims about scientific issues. We find that science's descriptions of cosmological, geological, and biological evolution are not in conflict with theology. We recognize medical, technical, and scientific technologies as legitimate uses of God's natural world when such use enhances human life and enables all of God's children to develop their God-given creative potential without violating our ethical convictions about the relationship of humanity to the natural world. We reexamine our ethical convictions as our understanding of the natural world increases. We find that as science expands human understanding of the natural world, our understanding of the mysteries of God's creation and word are enhanced.

In acknowledging the important roles of science and technology, however, we also believe that theological understandings of human experience are crucial to a full understanding of the place of humanity in the universe. Science and theology are complementary rather than mutually incompatible. We therefore encourage dialogue between the scientific and theological communities and seek the kind of participation that will enable humanity to sustain life on earth and, by God's grace, increase the quality of our common lives together.

G) *Food Safety*—We support policies that protect the food supply and that ensure the public's right to know the content of the foods they are eating. We call for rigorous inspections and controls on the biological safety of all foodstuffs intended for human consumption. We urge independent testing for chemical residues in food, and the removal from the market of foods contaminated with potentially hazardous levels of pesticides, herbicides, or fungicides; drug residues from animal antibiotics, steroids, or hormones; contaminants due to pollution that are carried by air, soil, or water from incinerator plants or other industrial operations. We call for clear labeling of all processed, genetically created, or genetically altered foods, with premarket safety testing required. We oppose weakening the standards for organic foods. We call for policies that encourage and support a gradual transition to sustainable and organic agriculture.

H) *Food Justice*—We support policies that increase access to quality food, particularly for those with the fewest resources. We affirm local, sustainable, and small-scale agriculture opportunities that allow communities to feed themselves. We decry policies that make food inaccessible to the communities where it is grown and the farmworkers involved in its growth.

THE NATURAL WORLD
THE RESOLUTIONS

ENERGY

1001. Energy Policy Statement

Humankind enjoys a unique place in God's universe. We are created in the very image of God, with the divine Spirit breathed into us, and entrusted to "take charge of" God's creation (Genesis 2:7; 1:26, 28; see Psalm 8:6). Yet, we are simply one of God's many finite creatures, made from the "topsoil of the fertile land," bound in time and space, fallible in judgment, limited in control, dependent upon our Creator, and interdependent with all other creatures. We are simultaneously caretakers with all creation and, because of the divine summons, caretakers with God of the world in which we live.

The Values Involved in Energy Policy

The decisions that humans make will either enhance or degrade the quality of life on the planet. We live in an era of energy interdependence. Confronting global issues such as climate change, energy inequity, and pollution will require international solutions based upon the values of justice and sustainability.

Scripture provides an imperative for our action and lays the foundation for the values that we seek to realize. These values underlying the policies we advocate are justice and sustainability.

1. *Justice.* As God's covenant people, with Noah, Abraham, Jacob and the prophets, we bear a special responsibility for justice.

> "Let justice roll down like waters,
>   and righteousness like an ever-flowing stream" (Amos 5:24)

is a cry echoed in hundreds of contexts throughout the Old and New Testaments. Biblical righteousness includes a special concern for the least and the last: the poor, the prisoner, the oppressed (Luke 4:18; Isaiah 61:1-2). As people of the Christian covenant, we support energy policies that seek to actualize the multifaceted biblical vision of justice. Just energy policies: close the gap dividing wealth and poverty, rich nations and poor; liberate and do not oppress; fairly distribute the benefits, burdens, and hazards of energy production and consumption, taking into consideration the living and those not yet born; and give priority to meeting basic human needs such as air, water, food, clothing, and shelter.

2. *Sustainability.* We recognize that creation entails limits to the resources entrusted to us as stewards of the earth. While God has created an economy of abundance with sufficient resources to meet all human need, our inclinations toward greed and overuse too often have transformed sufficiency into scarcity. In addition, we recognize limits to nonrenewable fuel sources available for our consumption and limits to our environment's capacity to absorb poisonous wastes. Energy policy decisions must be measured by sustainability as a criterion in addition to justice. In terms of energy policy, sustainability means energy use that will: ensure adequate resources and opportunity for present and future generations to enjoy a healthy quality of life; enhance local environmental and economic vitality while minimizing impacts on the health of both human and non-human creation; and promote social and intergenerational equity.

Technological advances have created an increasingly sophisticated and industrialized world community. As we pursue an energy policy that is just and sustainable, it is not a realistic option to ask all global citizens to return to an era where wood and candles provided the only sources of heat and light. Also, we should be aware of the tragic effects that steadily increasing energy costs will have, especially upon the aged and those living in poverty. Furthermore, some cleaner energy options available to wealthier nations are not available to peoples in all parts of the world; hence, we should endeavor to develop just and equitable energy policies.

We must creatively explore all sustainable energy options available to us. There are environmental and social problems connected with certain energy options. We believe that the economic, environmental, and social implications of each energy source should be fully assessed.

Today, the leading source of global energy consumption is fossil fuels including oil, coal, and natural gas. From extraction to end-use, the life cycle of energy produced from fossil fuels has led to severe strain on both the local and global environment.

Underground mining of coal, in addition to operational accidents, causes disabling illness or death from black lung. Strip-mining and mountaintop removal despoil lands and ruin them for further use if restoration measures are not practiced. Hydraulic fracturing, commonly called "fracking," has opened vast new deposits of oil and gas for exploration but with serious consequences for communities' water quality and geological stability. Deep sea extraction presents consequences and risks we do not yet fully understand, including destruction of aquatic ecosystems and pollution from leaks and spills. The burning of fossil fuels causes large-scale pollution and seriously alters the environment by increasing the carbon dioxide content of the atmosphere, contributing to climate change.

In addition to fueling regional instability, the use of oil resources poses significant environmental dangers. Tankers and offshore wells have created spills that have devastated seacoast areas often with long-lasting or permanent ecological damage. The emissions produced from the use of oil as fuel are a leading source of air pollution, particularly in centers of dense population.

Hydroelectric dams, particularly those in areas with considerable seismic activity, pose dangers to nearby communities and the environment. Furthermore, the building of hydroelectric dams and reservoirs destroys communities, wildlife habitats, and natural scenic beauty.

There are considerable concerns with regard to the nuclear energy option. The destructive potential of a catastrophic accident involves a great risk of irreversible damage to the environment and all living species. Nuclear waste remains active and dangerous for thousands of years. Additionally, the development of nuclear energy possibly has masked ambitions for nuclear armament.

Today, cleaner alternatives to traditional energy sources are available and increasingly cost-competitive. Harnessing solar and wind power can produce energy with far fewer net emissions. Facing increased global demand for energy resources and ever-increasing strain on the global environment, we must chart a new course rooted in our shared principles of justice and sustainability. To this end:

1. We support strenuous efforts to conserve energy and increase energy efficiency. A transition to energy efficiency and renewable energy sources will combat global warming, protect human health, create new jobs, and ensure a secure, affordable energy future. Economists have concluded that a greater increase in end-use energy can be gained through conservation and energy efficiency than through any single new source of fuel. Furthermore, conservation is nonpolluting and job producing. We include under conservation: insulation, co-generation, recycling, public transportation, more efficient motors in appliances and automobiles, as well as the elimination of waste, and a more simplified lifestyle. The technology for such steps is already known and commercially available; it requires only dissemination of information and stronger public support, including larger tax incentives than are presently available.

2. We will be models for energy conservation. United Methodists, including churches, annual conferences, general boards and agencies will model energy conservation by doing such things as: installing dampers in furnaces, insulating adequately all church properties, heating and lighting only rooms that are in use, using air circulation, purchasing energy efficient appliances, and exploring alternative energy sources such as solar energy. Local churches, camps, and agencies are urged to become involved in programs such as the Energy Stewardship Congregation and Interfaith Power and Light programs, thereby witnessing our shared values of justice and sustainability.

3. We will model sustainable and just energy values. United Methodist Church programs and mission projects must model our sustainable and just energy values. We particularly urge the United Methodist Committee on Relief (UMCOR) and the General Board of Global Ministries (GBGM) to support and fund renewable and energy efficient mission projects; and we urge the Church Architecture Office of the General Board of Global Ministries to make energy conservation and the use of renewables a prime design feature in new building design and renovations.

4. We support increased government funding for research and development of renewable energy sources and elimination of fossil fuel subsidies. We encourage the development and deployment of renewable energy technologies and government incentives to speed the application of the resulting technolo-

gies to our energy needs. The greatest national and international effort should be made in the areas of conservation and renewable energy sources.

5. We support local, regional, and national efforts to provide transition assistance for communities currently dependent on old energy fossil fuel economies. Honoring the contributions and sacrifices these communities and workers have made, often for generations, The United Methodist Church commits to being in ministry with and supporting these individuals, families, and communities as we seek a healthier and more equitable energy future.

6. We encourage international lending institutions and aid agencies to promote sustainable and just energy policies.

7. We oppose any energy policy that will result in continuing exploitation of indigenous peoples' lands. Oil exploration, hydroelectric projects, the mining of coal, and the milling of uranium despoil indigenous peoples' lands and increase health and socioeconomic problems.

8. We support national energy programs that do not increase the financial burden on the poor, the elderly, and those with fixed incomes. Energy policies must guarantee universal service to all consumers, protecting low-income and rural residents.

9. We support full cooperation of all nations in efforts to ensure equitable distribution of necessary energy supplies, the control of global warming, and rapid development and deployment of appropriate technologies based on renewable energy resources such as solar, wind, and water energy generation.

10. We urge transparency in global energy market transactions. Market manipulation can disrupt pricing and access causing harm, particularly to poor and marginalized countries and communities.

11. We exhort The United Methodist Church at all levels to engage in a serious study of these energy issues in the context of Christian faith, especially the values of justice and sustainability.

ADOPTED 1980
AMENDED AND READOPTED 2000, 2008, 2016
RESOLUTION #1001, 2008, 2012 *BOOK OF RESOLUTIONS*
RESOLUTION #5, 2004 *BOOK OF RESOLUTIONS*
RESOLUTION #6, 2000 *BOOK OF RESOLUTIONS*

See Social Principles, ¶ 160B.

1002. US Energy Policy and United Methodist Responsibility

Resolved:

God our Creator entrusts humankind with the responsibility to care for creation (Genesis 1:28; Psalm 8:6). Just as the Israelites moved in and out of obedience to God's covenant, we too have neglected our covenantal ties to God, each other, and the earth (Genesis 9:9-10). The prophetic voices condemn abuse of creation and mistreatment of our neighbors, calling us back into our covenantal responsibilities. Jesus embodied this prophetic spirit in his ministry to all people and creation. He is the reconciler of all creation. We are invited to participate in the preservation and renewal of God's good creation (Colossians 1:19-20).

Grounded in a commitment to justice and sustainability, United Methodists the world over are called to pursue lifestyles that reflect our concern for God's people and planet. Historically the world's largest user of energy resources, the United States and its residents have a unique responsibility to take actions based on sound scientific and ethical principles of respect for and justice within the World Community. The United States should focus its efforts on managing demand through conservation and efficiency and developing renewable, cleaner alternative sources of energy. Specifically, the United States must:

- move beyond its dependence on high carbon fossil fuels that produce emissions leading to climate change,
- adopt strong global commitments to emission reductions within the United Nations Framework Convention on Climate Change,
- concentrate on reducing carbon dioxide emissions within the United States and not rely on mechanisms such as emission trading with other countries to meet our targets for emission reductions under international agreements,
- reduce our reliance on nuclear power, a technology for which there are still unresolved problems such as the safe disposal or safe storage of high level waste of nuclear reactors,
- manage demand through a high priority on conservation and energy efficiency,
- shift federal resources (both tax incentives and appropriated dollars) away from fossil fuels and toward renewable energy sources such as solar, wind, and biomass,

- support development and utilization of appropriate technologies for small-scale, decentralized energy systems,
- support expansion of the infrastructure needed for cleaner energy vehicles, public transportation and ride-sharing, and
- provide necessary support for individuals, families, and communities adversely affected by a transition away from fossil fuels, nuclear power, and large-scale hydro in order to allow for alternative economic development, retraining, relocation, etc.

While national leadership is necessary, so too is the commitment of individuals, churches, and church leaders. As a reflection of our call to be caretakers of God's good earth, United Methodists should:

- educate our congregants on energy production and usage in relation to global warming,
- conduct an energy audit of our homes, church facilities, and camp structures to identify sources of energy waste and the potential financial savings of energy-related improvements,
- replace incandescent light bulbs with the most efficient alternative available,
- expand our use of public transportation, ride-sharing, teleconferencing, and other work and meeting technologies that reduce fossil fuel consumption,
- choose a cleaner vehicle and properly maintain its engine and tires for maximum fuel efficiency,
- study the consequences of our consumer choices and take action to lessen our impact on the environment, and
- advocate for policies that respond to the growing threat of climate change.

ADOPTED 2004
AMENDED AND READOPTED 2012
RESOLUTION #1002, 2008, 2012 *BOOK OF RESOLUTIONS*
RESOLUTION #6, 2004 *BOOK OF RESOLUTIONS*

See Social Principles, ¶ 160B.

1003. Nuclear Safety in the United States

Theology

God has given humans a special charge to "farm . . . and to take care of" the earth (Genesis 2:15). Nuclear technology presents a special challenge to our call to be stewards of God's creation (Psalm 8:6-8) because of the risks involved in the production, handling, and disposal of long-lived nuclear byproducts (such as plutonium) in the energy and weapons-production cycles. Until society discontinues the use of nuclear power to produce energy and weapons, we have a special responsibility to ensure that God's creation be protected for present and future generations by insisting that the entire production cycle be as safe as possible.

The problem of nuclear safety is of worldwide concern. It is the responsibility of the church to use its influence internationally to prevent the devastation that could result from nuclear disasters.

United Methodist Policy

Through its Energy Policy Statement, The United Methodist Church affirmed the need to explore all sustainable energy options while highlighting the environmental risks posed by certain options including nuclear power. "The hazards in storing radioactive wastes for thousands of years and the destructive potential of a catastrophic accident involve a great risk of irreversible damage to the environment or to the human genetic pool."[1] Furthermore, the Church has reiterated its opposition to "the production and testing of weapons designed to destroy or harm God's creation, such as . . . nuclear weapons. We urge the abolishment of chemical, biological, and nuclear weapons and urge the cleanup of sites contaminated by chemical, biological, and nuclear weapons waste."

Background

Nuclear Power

Although there has been a pause in construction of new nuclear capacity in the United States—no nuclear plants have been ordered since 1978 and none has come online since the Tennessee Valley Authority's Watts Bar 1 reactor ordered in 1970 and licensed to operate in 1996—the waste generated by current nuclear operations continues to pile up and policy-makers are debating the merits of encouraging construction of new nuclear reactors. In the United States there are currently 103 licensed reactors operating

1. Ohio Valley Environmental Coalition.

at 65 plants in 31 states. Worldwide, nearly 433 reactors generate roughly 17 percent of global electricity.

In March 2011, the earthquake and tsunami that devastated the coastal communities of Japan highlighted the vulnerability of nuclear reactors to natural disasters. In the hours and days following the natural disaster, three reactors at the Fukushima-Daiichi plant experienced meltdowns, unleashing a human-made disaster of radiation into the surrounding region. These major global disasters and other smaller safety breaches, including incidents at Three Mile Island and the Davis-Beese nuclear plant near Toledo, Ohio (USA), further increases concerns raised after the September 11, 2001 terrorist attacks that the Nuclear Regulatory Commission's oversight is insufficient and additional security and safety measures are needed.

Department of Energy Reactors

The Department of Energy (DOE) operates more than 200 nuclear facilities. Among its main responsibilities are the production and testing of the United States nuclear weapons program. The DOE facilities are generally more antiquated than civilian plants and are not subject to review by outside agencies. Five of these facilities are the main nuclear weapons production reactors. Four are located on the Savannah River in South Carolina; the fifth is the "N-Reactor" at Hanford, Washington (a complex where poor disposal of wastes in the past has created a radioactive landfill known as "one of our largest contaminated areas"). The containment systems in these plants have been criticized as being inadequate and not capable of meeting minimum civilian standards. In 1986, the DOE agreed to submit its five weapons reactors to state and federal waste disposal rules and shut down the Hanford "N-Reactor" for safety improvements. The cleanup of the Hanford site alone could cost over $100 billion. Yet most DOE plants continue to be exempt from the far more rigorous examination of commercial reactors by the Nuclear Regulatory Commission.

Emergency Planning and State Rights

After the Three Mile Island accident, rules were instituted to improve public safety in case of a nuclear accident. The new rules required the participation, in emergency planning exercise, of local and state officials. In 1986, the Nuclear Regulatory Commission, in response to two state governors' challenge to the viability of utility-produced emergency plans, requested that it be allowed to approve utility emergency evacuation plans in the event that state and local officials refuse to participate in the emergency-planning process. This rule change would ease the licensing of future nuclear reactors and seriously diminish public participation and review of safety measures, as well as increase the dangers of a serious accident.

Nuclear Wastes

One of the most controversial and costly components of the nuclear fission process is the creation of radioactive byproducts. The Nuclear Regulatory Commission divides wastes into two different categories according to the level and duration of radioactivity: high-level and low-level wastes. Each reactor produces an annual average of 20 tons of highly radioactive spent nuclear fuel and 50-200 cubic meters of low-level radioactive waste. Since the 1950s, the Department of Energy has been searching for a viable way to dispose of the wastes created by commercial nuclear reactors (irradiated fuels) and high-level wastes from weapons production. These wastes are highly radioactive and will remain radioactive. Presently, these wastes are stored within nuclear facility sites, creating what one member of Congress called hundreds of "de facto nuclear waste dumps." Over the past six decades, these by-products have been accumulating at storage sites throughout the country, including an estimated 45,000 tons of spent nuclear fuel at civilian nuclear power plants with another 2,000 tons generated annually.

The Nuclear Waste Policy Act of 1982 (NWPA) set a schedule for the location, construction, and operation of two high-level waste geologic repositories, one in the east, and one in the west. Amendments to NWPA in 1987 restricted the repository site studies to one location: Yucca Mountain. This site is located in Nevada, a state which itself has no nuclear reactors, and on land considered sacred to the Western Shoshone and Paiute. To a large extent, political considerations have taken precedence over safety and scientific considerations, and there has been improper and inadequate consultation and cooperation with state governments and Native American tribes. In 2002, Yucca Mountain was designated as the nuclear fuel repository over the objections of

Nevada's elected officials, tribal representatives, and environmental advocates. Proponents of the site highlighted the area's geological stability despite the occurrence of an earthquake registering 4.3 on the Richter scale the month of the Congressional vote.

Construction of the Yucca Mountain repository will not be completed for years and shipments of the radioactive waste—raising deep safety concerns for the millions of residents living along shipment routes—will take decades. While billed as creating a "central repository" for waste, spent nuclear fuel must remain for years on site before it is "cool" enough to transport, so this process would merely create a new, larger storage site in addition to the 100-plus on-site storage facilities that would continue to store nuclear waste.

Recommendations

The United Methodist Church expresses its deep concern over the use of a technology with severe environmental and health impacts without appropriate and extensive safety measures in the production, handling, and disposal processes. We also reiterate our opposition to the use of nuclear technology for the production of weapons.

We recommend:

1. *Reviewing the safety of operating plants.* Each of the 107 operating commercial plants in the US should be reviewed by the Nuclear Regulatory Commission and the Office of Technology Assessment of the US Congress to identify design deficiencies and weaknesses that could contribute to or cause an accident.

2. *Instituting improvement programs.* Improvement programs should be instituted in areas of demonstrated weak performance such as management, personnel performance, equipment reliability, and contractor accountability.

3. *Researching new designs for plant safety.* New designs for existing and future nuclear plants should be researched and developed so as to eliminate the potential of a core meltdown accident.

4. *Phasing out nuclear weapons production.* We urge the closing down of the five weapons-producing reactors and the Rocky Flats Plutonium Processing Plant, a thorough cleanup of any remaining nuclear wastes at these sites, and no more nuclear arms testing.

5. *Establishing uniform safety standards for civilian and military nuclear operations.* We support having all nuclear operations in the US subject to uniform basic safety provision. All Department of Energy nuclear operations should be licensed and reviewed by an independent agency such as the Nuclear Regulatory Commission or the Environmental Protection Agency. Department of Energy contractors should be held accountable to the same standards as civilian facility contractors and operators.

6. *Protecting neighboring populations.* We urge that due attention be given to the protection of populations living near nuclear power plants or along routes used to transport nuclear materials by ensuring the communities' participation in emergency evacuation plans. We support maintaining evacuation planning zones for all areas within ten miles from a nuclear facility, and engaging the full participation of state and local officials in the planning process. We believe that the safety of all potentially exposed populations should be the guide in safety improvements to nuclear power plants, not narrow cost-benefit analysis.

7. *Instituting full liability and compensation.* We hold that those corporations and governments responsible for nuclear accidents should be liable for cleanup and restitution to all victims of an accident.

8. *Reevaluating the US nuclear waste policy:*
   a. We urge a moratorium on DOE's proposed nuclear waste repository program;
   b. We urge Congress to establish an independent commission to review DOE's nuclear waste repository and Monitored Retrievable Storage Programs and to provide increased funding for the development of waste management technologies that will allow prolonged storage at the reactor site;
   c. We urge that full public participation and consultation in any future nuclear waste repository siting and transportation routing be guaranteed through provision of grants to affected localities, states, and Native American tribes; and
   d. We urge a moratorium of the building of nuclear power facilities until an adequate national plan is developed and implemented for the permanent disposal of nuclear waste products.

9. *Decommissioning.* We urge that the full cost of decommissioning (the dismantling and disposing of obsolete or closed power plants) be paid by the entities responsible for the construction and operation of nuclear facilities, not ratepayers or taxpayers.

10. *Conserving energy and finding alternative energy sources.* The greatest national effort should be made in the areas of conservation and renewable energy sources. We support increased government funding for research and development of technologies that would decrease dependence upon nuclear energy as an electricity source and urge the development of incentives, including tax and appliance standards, to speed the adoption of these technologies.

11. *Cooperating with annual conferences.* We urge the general church agencies of The United Methodist Church to assist central and annual conferences in their efforts to learn more about nuclear safety. Specifically, we urge general agencies of The United Methodist Church to assist annual conferences who have identified nuclear safety problems related to nuclear facilities, waste sites, and transportation routes within the bounds of those annual conferences.

We particularly urge the General Board of Church and Society to identify qualified nuclear safety experts who could assist annual conferences to understand and respond to nuclear waste and nuclear safety concerns in their areas.

ADOPTED 1988
AMENDED AND READOPTED 1992, 2004, 2012
RESOLUTION #1003, 2008, 2012 *BOOK OF RESOLUTIONS*
RESOLUTION #15, 2004 *BOOK OF RESOLUTIONS*
RESOLUTION #15, 2000 *BOOK OF RESOLUTIONS*

See Social Principles, ¶ 160F.

ENVIRONMENT

1025. Environmental Racism in the US

Theological Background

"If you do away with the yoke of oppression, / with the pointing finger and malicious talk / and if you spend yourselves on behalf of the hungry / and satisfy the needs of the oppressed, /

then your light will rise in the darkness, / and your night will become like the noonday."

—Isaiah 58:9-10 NIV

We are further called both in Leviticus and by our Lord Jesus Christ to love our neighbors as ourselves. When we turn from this divine will, we as a broken people promote systems that are unjust and inequitable. One manifestation of these injustices is the persistent problem of environmental racism, defined as the disproportionate toxic and industrial contamination in neighborhoods where people of color live, work, worship, and play.

The United Methodist Church (UMC) is committed to understanding and eliminating environmental racism. In the United States, the extraction, production, storage, treatment, and disposal processes of hazardous materials and wastes are too often zoned within close proximity to where people of color live. Yet, African American, Hispanic-Latino North Americans, Asian Americans, Native Americans, and non-citizens in the US are usually the least able—politically and economically—to affect the political institutions that make the decisions that allow this to happen. People of color also disproportionately suffer from the lack of public health protections in the current economy. From the founding of the United States, people of color were seen as less entitled to healthy work and environment than those of European descent. European culture, with its domesticated animals, exploitative resource extraction, mono-cropping, and mass production, was perceived as the only way America could advance. And the rich tradition of Native Americans' stewardship of their environment was demolished in the quest for land ownership.

US cities grew during a time of extreme racial inequity; zoning policies were put into place where waste dumps, rail yards, industrial centers, ports, and sewer systems developed out of proportion around communities of color.

The birth of the environmental justice movement can be traced to the 1982 historic protest in Warren County, North Carolina. More than 500 people were arrested for blocking a shipment of toxic waste (PCBs) to a landfill located in the predominantly African American county. This action was followed in 1987 by the United Church of Christ, Commission for Racial Justice's landmark report, *Toxic Wastes and Race in the United States*. This report established that race—rather than poverty, land value, or home ownership—is the most reliable predictor of proximity to hazardous waste sites in the United States. In 1992, the National Law Journal published *"Unequal Protection,"* a study that uncovered racial disparities in the enforcement of environmental protection laws. It highlighted a "racial divide in the way the US government cleans up toxic waste sites and punishes polluters." According to the report, "white communities see faster action, better results and stiffer penalties than communities where blacks, Hispanics and other minorities live. This unequal protection often occurs whether the community is wealthy or poor."

In 2007, *Toxic Wastes and Race at Twenty: 1987-2007* was published by the United Church of Christ, Justice and Witness Ministries. This report recognized that significant racial and socioeconomic disparities persisted in the distribution of the nation's commercial hazardous waste facilities. In fact, people of color are found to be more concentrated around hazardous waste facilities than previously shown in the 1987 report.

Here are some of the 2007 report's statistics:

- "20.2 percent of those living within one kilometer of a hazardous waste facility are African American while only 11.5 percent of those who live beyond five kilometers (3.1 miles) of a hazardous waste facility are African American."
- "23.1 percent of those who live within one kilometer of a hazardous waste facility are Latino; yet, only 7.8 percent of those who live beyond those five kilometers are Hispanic."
- "When facilities are clustered together, as in urban areas, African Americans comprise 29 percent of the surrounding population, and 16 percent of the population when there is a single facility."
- "Hispanics make up 33 percent of the population where there are multiple hazardous waste facilities and 25 percent of the population where there is a single facility."
- "Host neighborhoods of commercial hazardous waste facilities are 56 percent people of color whereas non-host areas are 30 percent people of color. Percentages of African Americans, Hispanics/Latinos and Asians/Pacific Islanders in host neighborhoods (vs. non-host areas) are 1.7, 2.3, and 1.8 times greater. Poverty rates in the

host neighborhoods are 1.5 times greater than non-host areas. (Statistics are from *Toxic Wastes and Race at Twenty: 1987-2007*. *Toxic Race and Waste at 20, 1987-2007* can be found at: http://d3n8a8pro7vhmx.cloudfront.net/united churchofchrist/legacy_url/491/toxic-wastes-and-race -at-twenty-1987-2007.pdf?1418423933).

Since then, more reports have come to emphasize that race matters when it comes to a community's environmental health.

People of color and persons of low socioeconomic status are still disproportionately impacted and are particularly concentrated in neighborhoods and communities with the greatest number of toxic and hazardous facilities. A growing body of research suggests that maternal exposure to environmental toxicants poses a risk not only to the mother's health but to fetal and child health and development, too. These same persons often have substandard health care. Without adequate healthcare, communities of color are at even more risk.

Not only are people of color differentially impacted by toxic wastes and contamination, they can expect different responses from the government when it comes to building resilience after an environmental disaster or remediation. This can be clearly seen during and after Hurricane Katrina and Hurricane Sandy, and in the toxic waste remediation efforts in Dickson County, Tennessee. People of color and communities of color receive sluggish attention to their concerns. It appears that neither existing environmental, health, and civil rights laws, nor local land use controls have been adequately applied or adapted toward the reduction of health risks or the mitigation of various adverse impacts to families living in or near toxic "hot spots," which disproportionately house people of color.

Despite the clear evidence and growing awareness of the consequence to everyone's health from toxic dumping, our society's attitude toward the production and disposal of hazardous products is one of "out of sight, out of mind." But "out of sight, out of mind" is most often where the poor and those rendered powerless live and work. These communities have thus become toxic "sacrifice zones." In short, environmental protection systems are broken, extraordinarily slow to respond and/or fail to provide equal protection to people of color and low-income communities.

While the focus here is on communities of color in the United States, we are aware that environmental racism is a global phenomenon. The displacement of native peoples—be it in Canada, Peru, or Ecuador—in the drive for oil and minerals has destroyed their land, water, and livelihoods; it also threatens to undermine their culture. Communities, regions and entire nations are all impacted by climate changes that have led to typhoons, hurricanes, drought, or rising waters. Nations of the Global South are already more impacted and less prepared to respond to these climate changes. One positive development is an expanding climate justice movement that links the concerns of US communities of color with leaders of international communities of color in resistance to environmental racism.

Therefore,

We urge The UMC to make sure that those who have historically experienced environmental racism are at the center of decision making and employment for a just, sustainable, healthy prosperity, and we request that:

- The Council of Bishops and all boards and agencies, conferences, local churches, and United Methodist (UM) faith communities address environmental racism as a key dimension when addressing either racism or environmental concerns.

- The General Board of Pension and Health Benefits increase their shareholder activism to hold companies accountable for environmental abuse and unsustainable production practices particularly in those instances where people of color are disproportionately impacted.

- Annual conferences, districts, local churches, UM faith communities, and general agencies to become more involved with community groups working to end environmental racism, particularly those organizations led by and for those who are directly impacted by the injustices. We urge UM faith communities to increase their support of actions and social movements led by those most impacted by pollutants.

- The UMC through its Act of Repentance in Annual Conferences and in the Church with native peoples develop respectful, honoring relationships with native peoples and ask the Church to repent of the ways its well-intentioned followers devalued and disrespected native peoples' deep spirituality and care for the land that sustains us all. It was this deep disrespect that justified the genocide of hundreds of thousands of native peoples in the name of Christianity. We ask that when native peoples' lands are hurt today by power plants, mining (including coal, gold, copper, coltan, uranium), and garbage dumps (including nuclear waste) or access to clean water that the Church diligently work to reverse the damage and work to ensure that the right of indigenous populations to free, prior and informed consent (FPIC) are transparently honored.

- The UMC to create sustainable practices throughout all boards, agency offices, and events in order to minimize waste and energy use as a response to injustice in neighborhoods which are in close proximity to incineration plants, garbage dumps, toxic chemical plants, industrial manufacturing, and power plants.
- The UMC to advocate for jobs in low income areas that are good for the environment and that help eliminate pollutants, toxins, untested chemicals, and greenhouse gasses. Jobs should also maximize energy efficiency and renewable forms of energy. We call on the UMC to ensure that communities currently suffering from economic deprivation be among the first that are hired and trained for these jobs.
- The GBCS, GBOD, GBGM, and UMW to develop educational resource programs that help annual conferences, districts and local churches respond to these concerns.

We urge the people called United Methodists to

- Advocate comprehensive legislation that remedies these injustices and adequately protects all citizens and the environment;
- Stand in solidarity with environmental justice movements led by people of color and native peoples who have been adversely impacted by environmental toxins in their neighborhoods;
- Develop a program of sustainability such as United Methodist Women's "13 Steps to Sustainability" which measures our adherence to both social justice and environmental justice principles; and
- Urge the US government to further develop and close loopholes on mandatory industry-wide standards for environmental accounting and auditing procedures that are publicla shared. Urge governments to hold industry

officials responsible—legally, criminally, and financially—
for toxic disasters when they erupt from negligence.

ADOPTED 1992
AMENDED AND READOPTED 2004, 2008, 2016
RESOLUTION #1025, 2008, 2012 *BOOK OF RESOLUTIONS*
RESOLUTION #9, 2000, 2004 *BOOK OF RESOLUTIONS*

See Social Principles, ¶ 160, *Book of Discipline*; Resolution 1023, "Environmental Justice for a Sustainable Future" (2012 *Book of Resolutions*); and Resolution 3371, "A Charter for Racial Justice Policies in an Interdependent Global Community."

1028. Law of the Sea

We recognize that "All creation is the Lord's, and we are responsible for the ways in which we use and abuse it" (¶ 160).

We are called to repent of our devastation of the physical and nonhuman world, because this world is God's creation and is therefore to be valued and conserved.

Nowhere is this need greater than in relation to the sea. In 1970 the United Nations agreed that those areas of the seabed beyond national boundaries were the "common heritage" of humankind. This means that the resources belong to everyone.

The best hope for global cooperation is through the United Nations, where representatives of the nations of the world developed the Law of the Sea.

The Law of the Sea conference worked to produce a fair and just law for the ocean, in which all nations will benefit. No one nation will have all of its interests satisfied, but mechanisms will be set up to maintain order and peace, and both developed and developing countries will have worked on the regulations.

The Law of the Sea Treaty is concerned with protecting this "common heritage" of humanity. It would:

- guarantee unimpeded access to over 100 straits, facilitating commercial transportation;
- prevent conflicts over fishing waters;
- enforce environmental regulations forbidding countries to dump harmful wastes that spoil the ocean waters;
- share equitably the ocean resources, oil, fish, minerals, and prohibit unjust exploitation of these resources by the powerful;

- regulate access to the waters of coastal countries to permit research of the marine environment;
- limit the continuing extension of national sovereignty over international waters and settle legal disputes arising therefrom;
- prevent the division of the world into competing camps depending on powerful navies; and
- create an international agency to manage cooperatively the international seabed resources.

We also affirm our support for the evolution of effective "commons" law, such as the treaties for the Antarctic, climate, biodiversity, and outer space, which support our obligations of stewardship, justice, and peace.

Further, we urge all United Methodists to become informed about the Law of the Sea and to call upon their governments to commit themselves to just and equitable implementation of the Law of the Sea and to the ratification of the treaty.

ADOPTED 1980
AMENDED AND READOPTED 1996
READOPTED 2004, 2008, AND 2016
RESOLUTION #1028, 2008, 2012 *BOOK OF RESOLUTIONS*
RESOLUTION #12, 2000, 2004 *BOOK OF RESOLUTIONS*

See Social Principles, ¶ 160A.

1029. Protection of Water

In the Bible, water in both its physical and spiritual dimensions is a gift. God covenants with God's people and invites them to experience fullness of life. A measure of this abundant life is God's offer of water as a free gift without cost or price (Isaiah 55:1). Water as an element and as a healing agent are God's gift to everyone who thirsts. "The Spirit and the bride say, 'Come!' Let everyone who hears this also say, 'Come!' Let the thirsty man come, and let everyone who wishes take the water of life as a gift" (Revelation 22:17 Phillips). Further, the Bible offers examples of God and humans intervening in people's water crises and providing water (Genesis 21:19; Genesis 24:15-21; Numbers 20:9-11). Water is an integral part of God's radical expression of God's love to all humanity. Water cannot be monopolized or privatized. It is to be shared like air, light, and earth. It is God's elemental provision for the survival of all God's children on this planet.

The problem is:

- Clean and plentiful water is the cornerstone of a prosperous community. But as we make our way through the twenty-first century, industrial and population demands are increasing as well as changing climate patterns draining rivers and aquifers. Pollution threatens the quality of what remains. (National Resource Council, found at http://www.nrdc.org/water/)
- Despite strong overall progress in worldwide access to clean drinking water, 748 million people still did not have access to improved drinking water in 2012. Wealth is the key factor to whether or not one can access an improved water supply. (World Health Organization and UNICEF, "Progress on Drinking Water and Sanitation: 2014 Update," May 2014, available: www.who.int/water _sanitation_health/publications/2014/jmp-report/en)
- The progress or lack of progress toward just and affordable distribution of clean water for all starts with a principled acknowledgment of water as a human right. This right to water needs to be coupled with strong political accountability that adequately monitors the just implementation of the right to water. This requires political will from communities and governments.
- The world uses approximately 70 percent of Its water for irrigation, 20 percent for industry, and 10 percent for domestic use. Roughly 75 percent of all industrial water usage is for energy production. It is estimated that by 2030, humanity's demand for water could outstrip sustainable supply by as much as 40 percent due to rising energy needs and continued population growth. Water policy that takes into consideration the water used in energy production and industrial agriculture must be implemented. (From http://www.unwater.org/statis tics-detail/en/c/211818/; and http://www.unwater .org/statistics-detail/en/c/211820/)
- Current global water shortages are due to a multiplicity of reasons. Fossil fuel extraction and energy production account for over half of the water use in the

United States. (http://www.ucsusa.org/clean_energy /our-energy-choices/energy-and-water-use/energy -and-water.htm1#.VdRw1HyFM9U). Industrial practices pollute water sources through chemical and toxic leaks, drainage, (http://www.ucsusa.org/clean_energy/our -clean-energy-choices/energy-and-water-use/energy -and-water.htm1#VdRw1HyFM9U) dumping, and runoff into rivers, lakes, and aquifers, which then require more sophisticated water sanitation facilities. The result is the privatization of water sanitation and distribution, as well as higher water prices. Ultimately, water becomes inaccessible to those who are impoverished.

- In addition, climate change is exacerbating drought and flooding. Flooding further pollutes water sources. When water availability and sanitation practices are compromised, community safety and security are threatened.
- Many persons who are able to afford it have turned to bottled water, and bottled water is often shipped into communities that are suffering from industrialized pollution of their water sources. And yet, bottled water takes water from one community, packages it in petroleum-based plastic (a product that uses water in every part of its extraction, production, and waste cycles), and then sells it for a profit to those who can afford it elsewhere.

The complications of the lack of clean, fresh water for communities result in the following:

Food Security:
- Many of the 840 million individuals who lack adequate food live in water-scarce regions.
- Diarrhea is the world's leading form of death affecting 2.5 million persons; 88 percent of those deaths are due to poor water quality. (Found at: http://www.who.Int /water_sanitation_health/publications/factsfigures04 /en/) Without clean water and adequate sanitation, hygiene is compromised and overall health is affected.

Safety and Security:
- When water and sanitation are threatened, community safety and security are threatened. Many countries are already experiencing violent conflict because of water shortage.

Quality of Life:

- The world's cumulative pollution of aquifers, rivers, lakes, and the oceans disturb the quality of life. Biodiversity of fresh water ecosystems has been more degraded than any other ecosystem. (Found at http://www.cbd .Int/waters/problem)

Therefore be it resolved, the people called United Methodists

- Shall affirm, educate, and advocate for clean, accessible, affordable water as a basic human right. It is to be shared and enjoyed by all God's people; policy cannot favor the rich over the poor when it comes to accessing clean water.
- Shall work to ensure that the access to fresh water by human communities preempts industrial, energy, or industrial agriculture usage of the water supply.
- Shall work to ensure that watersheds be protected for their essential role in human survival, and recognize the transboundary nature of watersheds (between communities, states, and nations) and work to cooperate across those boundaries for everyone's benefit.
- Shall work to require transnational trade agreements mandate corporations protect water supplies, and governments develop and maintain mechanisms of regulation and accountability.
- Shall encourage and develop strategies for guiding principles protecting our water supplies.
- Shall advocate that companies and corporate entities that pollute water supplies provide funds and services to clean the polluted waters.
- Shall urge all governments to make transparent, community-centered decisions about water use.
- Shall implement practices that minimize and make sustainable their own use of water in the church and at events.
- Shall advocate for federal subsidies for both the development and implementation of renewable wind and sun and geothermal energy.
- Shall develop practices that reduce the use of individual bottled water.
- Shall observe World Water Day (March 22).

Other resolutions:

Book of Resolutions, 1996, page 90, "Reduction of Water Usage"

Book of Resolutions, 1996, page 78, "Environmental Stewardship: Water"

Resolution #1033, "Caring for Creation: A Call to Stewardship and Justice"

ADOPTED 2004
READOPTED 2008
AMENDED AND READOPTED 2016
RESOLUTION #1029, 2008, 2012 *BOOK OF RESOLUTIONS*
RESOLUTION #13, 2004 *BOOK OF RESOLUTIONS*

See Social Principles, ¶ 160A.

1032. Principles for Just and Sustainable Extraction and Production

John Wesley proclaimed the following guiding principles as core to faithful action: Do no harm. Do all the good you can. Obey the ordinances of God.

Scientists have confirmed that some practices based largely on industrial extraction, production, and waste are not only harmful to many local ecologies and those who depend on them, but is harmful to the climate that humans depend on. Industrial extraction, production, and waste facilities compromise air, land, and water. Because of this, the health and well-being of surrounding communities are compromised. Yet communities who are wronged by extraction, industrial production, and waste are often under assault and militarized security forces often guard the industries from those who protest for just redress.

Because of industrial extraction, production, and waste, some people's lives are destroyed while others profit. This is harmful and is neither sustainable nor just.

These four guiding principles and questions can form the architecture for a local community's advocacy work as people of faith in the Wesleyan tradition. They can provide a principled framework in which to advocate when industries seek to establish themselves or expand themselves in local communities. They can be a road forward to development that seeks to be just, sustainable, and responsible in its extraction, production, and waste practices.

1. First, do no harm:
   • Will or does the extractive, production, or waste industry effectively prohibit practices that result in toxic expo-

sure, environmental degradation, and/or human rights violations?

2. Eradicate the root causes of poverty:
   - Will or does the extractive, production, or waste industry increase the most impoverished people's capabilities, choices, security, and power necessary for the full enjoyment of their human rights?

3. People as rights-holders:
   - Will or does the extractive, production, or waste industry guarantee people's rights to participate, including transparent access to information, freedom of expression and assembly, self-determination, and effective remedy for harms committed?

4. Sustainability:
   - Will or does the extractive, production, or waste industry adequately protect the land, water, and air for the rights of future generations and our planet?

These four guiding principles and questions should be asked by the church of any extractive, production, or waste facility, and land use or water use ordinance in any town, city, or nation.

ADOPTED 2016

See Social Principles, ¶ 160*A, B.*

1033. Caring for Creation: A Call to Stewardship and Justice

Our Call to Stewardship and Justice

Our covenant with God calls us to steward, protect, and defend God's creation. The psalmist proclaims, "The earth is the Lord's and everything in it" (Psalm 24:1) reaffirming our charge to care for creation as a trustee of God's handiwork (Genesis 1:28). We are to delight in and praise God for the abundance and diversity of creation (Psalm 148) and honor God's covenant established with all living creatures (Genesis 9:9).

The story of the garden (Genesis 2) reveals the complete and harmonious interrelatedness of creation, with humankind designed to relate to God, one another, and the rest of the created order. God's vision of "shalom" invites all of creation to know wholeness and harmony, and the good news that we are called to proclaim includes the promise that Jesus Christ came to redeem all creation (Colossians 1:15-20).

Violating the integrity of our relationship with creation is sinful. Our failure to serve as faithful caretakers of creation has local and global consequences. Our inability to share the abundance that God has entrusted to us has given rise to ecological crises and extreme poverty. Our unchecked consumption and unsustainable patterns of development have exacted a toll on creation and are increasing inequality of opportunity around the world.

Confronted with the massive crisis of the deterioration of God's creation and called to a ministry of reconciliation between God, humankind, and creation, we ask God's forgiveness and commit ourselves to a new way of being that integrates environmental, economic, and social justice. As United Methodists we therefore are called to participate in God's healing of creation through acts of personal, social, and civic righteousness. Proclaiming and modeling a new lifestyle rooted in stewardship and justice we work toward the day when all God's children respect and share in the goodness of creation.

Our Methodist Tradition and Witness

John Wesley taught a holistic view of salvation that included the deliverance of the created world in the creation of a new heaven and a new earth.

In the sermon "The New Creation" (#64) Wesley speaks imaginatively about what the new heavens and the new earth will be like, imagining into the scriptural promises of an end to death and suffering (Revelation 21:1-7), and an end to present environmental catastrophes like storms, polluted water, and animal suffering. This is all part of the promise of God's "greater deliverance" from sin. "And, to crown all, there will be a deep, an intimate, an uninterrupted union with God; a constant communion with the Father and his Son Jesus Christ, through the Spirit; a continual enjoyment of the Three—One God, and of all the creatures in him!"

Early Methodists worked toward this hoped-for view by addressing environmental concerns, such as open sewers, impure water, unplanned cities, and smoke-filled air. In response to squalor and filth in the mines and mills, Methodists advocated for a wider knowledge of concepts of basic health. The substantial decline in the death rate in England from 1700 to 1801 can be traced to this work.

Wesley's eschatological vision for the deliverance of all creation led him to respect and care for the created world here and now. "They may encourage us to imitate him whose mercy is over all of his works. They may soften our hearts towards the meaner creatures, knowing that the Lord cares for them. It may enlarge our hearts towards those poor creatures to reflect that, as vile as they appear in our eyes, not one of them is forgotten in the sight of our Father which is in heaven. . . . . Yea, let us habituate ourselves to look forward, beyond this present scene of bondage, to the happy time when they will be delivered therefrom into the liberty of the children of God" (Sermon 60, The Great Deliverance).

Our Vision

We believe clean air is a basic right and necessity for all life. Air pollution puts at risk the health of our communities and threatens to forever alter the climate. To ensure that future generations inherit a legacy of clean air:

We advocate the adoption and strict enforcement of adequate standards to control both indoor and outdoor air pollutants. These standards must be developed to protect vulnerable populations including children and the elderly. We advocate measures to prohibit smoking and the provision of adequate ventilation for indoor facilities as well as ambitious standards to limit harmful emissions from stationary and non-stationary sources.

We support efforts to protect our shared atmosphere by reducing emissions that contribute to ozone depletion, acid rain and climate change. Through bilateral and international frameworks, we advocate ratification and enforcement of agreements to reduce harmful emissions with particular emphasis and accountability by the most developed and historic emitters.

We believe water is a sacred gift from God. We further believe water is a basic human right and not a commodity to be traded for profit. To ensure that water remains pure and available to all:

We support the right of native peoples to the first use of waters on their lands.

We advocate integrated, sustainable management to reduce or eliminate factors contributing to limited water quantity and poorer water quality. We call for measures to preserve groundwater sources, to address polluted runoff that threatens water quality and safety and for effective enforcement against illegal pollution.

We support the public's right to know that water is safe for drinking, swimming, and fishing and disclosure of any pollutants discharged by industries and municipalities.

We are to tend God's land and care for all creation's creatures as faithful trustees with a commitment to preserve its goodness and diversity for future generations.

We encourage economic and agricultural practices that conserve and promote the improvement of land resources, production of healthful foods, and preservation of a clean environment.

We call on governments to support careful management of agricultural lands, protection of forests, and preservation of biodiversity among both plants and animals. We support national and international efforts to protect endangered species and imperiled habitats.

We believe that natural resources, outside the control of different nations, from the genes that form life to the air and outer space, are the common heritage of all humanity and therefore must be developed and preserved for the benefit of all, not just the few, both today and for generations to come. We believe God's whole earth has inherent value and our use of these precious gifts, including energy resources, must balance the needs of human development with the needs of non-human creation and future generations.

We support the concept of common heritage guaranteeing that people have the right to enough of the resources of the universe to provide for their health and well-being.

We support policies that encourage energy conservation and a shift toward cleaner, renewable sources of energy. We advocate for just and sustainable energy policies that prioritize the needs of those individuals and communities with the fewest resources.

We advocate for equivalent environmental standards among countries entering into trade agreements so that creation and communities are not sacrificed in the name of "free trade."

We oppose the use of creation as a means of warfare or economic oppression and urge the abolition of chemical, biological, and nuclear weapons and the cleanup of sites contaminated with the waste byproducts of militarization.

We encourage measures to minimize the use of toxic and hazardous substances, strengthen right-to-know policies so that individuals and communities can understand threats from pollution, and support policies that hold polluters responsible for the cost of cleanup and health impacts.

We acknowledge the constantly imperfect state of our knowledge regarding the impacts of new technologies and urge the development of those technologies most in accord with God's plan of wholeness for all creation.

Our Commitment

As The United Methodist Church we understand our responsibility to address and our complicity in the challenges facing God's creation. We urge all United Methodists, local faith communities, agencies, and institutions to examine their roles as caretakers of creation and to study, discuss, and work to implement this resolution.

Specifically, The United Methodist Church:

• Designates one Sunday each year, preferably the Sunday closest to Earth Day or World Environment Day, as a Festival of God's Creation incorporating creation care into the church's worship and study.

• Promotes an environmentally sound lifestyle mindful of consumption amid a culture that encourages overconsumption and waste.

• Commits to reducing, reusing, and recycling goods and to the use of recycled and "processed chlorine free" paper by United Methodist boards, agencies, and publishers.

• Encourages all institutions to perform energy audits, improve energy efficiency, and utilize clean, renewable energy sources where available.

In addition, we call for the following:

Council of Bishops:

• Communicate to the denomination the urgency of reducing our individual and corporate impact on God's creation.

• Model for the Church a "ministry of witness" by practicing "social and environmental holiness" as recommended in "God's Renewed Creation: A Call to Hope and Action."

• Support the efforts of annual conferences to form teams of United Methodists committed to creation care.

Connectional Table:

• Request that each quadrennial report to General Conference include an evaluation of creation care efforts and steps taken by the reporting body to integrate sustainable environmental practices into its ministry.

Commission on General Conference:

• Request that the meetings of General Conference model sustainable practices and report on efforts to reduce waste and consumption.

General Board of Church and Society (GBCS):

• Develop resources highlighting opportunities for personal engagement and advocacy for individuals, local churches, annual conferences, and the general Church to understand and respond to our call to be caretakers of God's creation.

• Organize teams of United Methodists to engage in concrete actions including advocacy to address locally identified challenges to creation.

General Board of Discipleship (GBOD):

• Develop curriculum and programs for all ages, in consultation with GBCS, GBGM, and UMW, that emphasize ecological responsibility as a key element of discipleship.

General Board of Global Ministries (GBGM):

• Join with GBCS, United Methodist Women (UMW), and other agencies in working with mission partners to participate in the ongoing global dialogue on sustainability through the United Nation's Commission on Sustainable Development.

• Explore and implement tangible ways to incorporate creation care into the mission, ministries, training programs, operations, and administration of GBGM.

General Board of Higher Education and Ministry (GBHEM):

• Include a greater awareness in clergy education and training of the global ecological crises.

United Methodist Communications (UMCom):

• Produce programs that stress Christian responsibility for the future of creation and include models of The United Methodist Church's involvement in creation care.

General Council on Finance and Administration (GCFA):

• Assist the denomination in its effort to be ecologically responsible in its own use of resources by collecting statistics on local churches' and general agencies' use of energy, water, paper, local purchasing efforts, minimization of toxics, and recycling to monitor the progress of the denomination in these aspects of stewardship.

General Board of Pension and Health Benefits (GBPHB):

• Develop investment guidelines, in consultation with agencies, to evaluate its securities on adherence to high standards of environmental accountability as evidenced by the adoption of an environmental code of conduct and a practice of transparency in public environmental reporting.

United Methodist Women (UMW):

• Develop educational, missional, and policy initiatives surrounding climate justice, and environmental health and their impacts on women, children, and youths.

Local Faith Communities:

• Develop programs to incorporate the concerns of ecological justice into their work in evangelism, social concerns, mission activities, stewardship, trustees, and worship.

• Endorse the Clergy Letter Project (www.theclergyletter project.org) and its reconcilatory program between religion and science, and urge United Methodist clergy to participate.

ADOPTED 2016

See Social Principles, ¶ 160.

1034. Environmental Health

God gave us a good and complete earth. We must care for that which is around us in order that life can flourish. We are meant to live in a way that acknowledges the interdependence of human beings not just on one another but the world around us, the mountains and lilies, the sparrows and the tall pine which all speaks of the nature of God.—As Jesus declared, "If these were silent, the stones would shout out" (Luke 19:40), or "consider the lilies" (Luke 12:27) or the sparrows" (Matthew 10:31), for they tell us of God's love. The psalmists declare praise for the natural world because nature reveals God's steadfast love, justice, and faithfulness. Not only are we dependent and interdependent on the ecosystems around us, but we also recognize that the natural world is a place where a faithful, loving, just Creator's handiwork can be seen.

Since the onset of industrialization and globalization, we've lost our sense of interdependence with the natural world. Though some of us go away to the beaches, forests, and lakesides to find rest and respite, we've forgotten that everything around us is made from the natural world: the houses we live in, the food we eat, the technology we use, the air we breathe, and the water we drink. The manufacturing of those products that have made our lives what they are today are made by taking the natural world, working with chemicals, and producing that which we use in daily life.—Almost everything that is manufactured uses chemicals. Some of those chemicals have proven to be troublesome to our health. When these chemicals and the chemical by-products of production meet with rivers and streams, earth, and air, toxins result.—Those who work closest to the extraction and production often are exposed to toxins at unsafe levels. We get hurt, we get sick, and our quality of life diminishes. This hurt needs careful attention and healing in order for us to have the healthy quality of life God intended.

God's covenant with humanity affirms that God is involved in the healing of individuals (Proverbs 3:7-8) and includes the mandate to protect the community from dangers that threaten the health and safety of the people. At the beginning of Methodism, John Wesley provided medicine and medical treatment at no cost to the poor in London and Bristol. In addition to pioneering free dispensaries in England, Wesley emphasized illness prevention. In *Primitive Physick*, Wesley wrote of the importance of nutrition and hygiene, as well as treatment of the sick. The first Social Creed, adopted by the 1908 General Conference of The Methodist Episcopal Church, declared that workers must be protected "from dangerous machinery, occupational disease, injuries, and mortality," and that working conditions must be regulated to safeguard the physical and moral health of the community. Today, the church is called to declare that the health of every individual is part of community health, including safe and healthy work conditions. The church has a responsibility to pronounce clearly the implications of God's law of love for human health. Where human life and health are at stake, economic gain must not take precedence.

Since Wesley's days the rapid growth of chemical usage in our industrialized extraction, production, agricultural, and waste cycles have significantly altered our environments. In industrialized zones, chemical sludge and dangerous airborne particles exist in concentrated form with significant health impacts on the communities that live and work closest to them.—Throughout the globe, industrial extraction, production, and waste happen closest to populations that are already experiencing economic inequities and injustice.—In rural areas, agricultural pesticides and chemical fertilizers disproportionately hurt not only farmworkers on large farms but small farmers who work mainly with hand tools.— Those who live downstream or close to where those chemicals have been applied are also at risk.—The Rotterdam Convention was created so that the problem of known harmful chemicals would not be traded internationally without prior knowledge of the receiving country.

According to the United Nations, there are approximately 70,000 known chemicals, and approximately 1,500 new chemicals come onto the market every year.—Although the Basel, Stockholm, and Rotterdam conventions seek to regulate the most dangerous of these chemicals, in reality, there is little knowledge about almost all of those 70,000 chemicals and their effects on human health.— Around forty chemicals are regulated when it comes to international trade. Sickness often happens years after exposure and so is difficult to trace.

Toxicology research suggests that certain chemicals such as dioxin, mercury, polychlorinated biphenyls (PCBs), or other persistent organic pollutants (POPs) that are used in production or discarded as by-products of manufacturing and/or agricultural practices can be linked to cancer, reproductive aberrations, developmental disorders, blood and muscle growth abnormalities, disease of the liver and kidney, obesity, hormone disruptions, and behavioral concerns.—Many of these chemicals are often transgenerational, where the exposure might be in one generation but the effects of that exposure are transmitted to children and grandchildren.—Toxins also seep into the environment from our everyday products, including beauty products, household cleaners, drugs, fire retardants, food and beverage containers, pesticides, pharmaceuticals for both human and animals, and industrial effluent.—When these everyday products are thrown away, in dumps or sewers, they enter water sources.— Even in regions of the world where water treatment plants exists, toxins are often still present.

Reproductive, Maternal, and Child Health

According to the United Nations Development Program (UNDP), there are three types of chemicals that affect men and women differently: (1) endocrine disrupting chemicals; (2) chemicals that are persistent (meaning they remain a long time in the environment), bio accumulative (meaning they accumulate through the food chain), and toxic; and (3) heavy metals (such as mercury, lead, and cadmium). (Found at www.undp.org /content/dam/aplaws/publication/en/publications/environ ment-energy/www-ee-library/chemicals-management/chemi cals-and-gender/2011%20Chemical&Gender.pdf <http://www

.undp.org/content/dam/aplaws/publication/en/publications/environment-energy/www-ee-library/chemicals-management/chemicals-and-gender/2011%20Chemical&Gender.pdf>.)

Endocrine disruptors are chemicals that interrupt hormonal activity. These chemicals, which include POPs, are usually bio accumulative. Though men are affected, women seem to be particularly vulnerable to chemical toxins. This could be because of their higher percentage of body fat in addition to their rapid physiological changes during pregnancy, lactation, and menopause. In addition, women's exposure to toxic chemicals can be transmitted through the placenta to the developing fetus. Children also seem to be more vulnerable to toxins in the environment. Their fast growth and proportionately high-intake needs might be reasons for this.

POPs are widely used in products because of their long half-life and their stability. They are now used almost everywhere. They are of particular concern because of their ability to affect the endocrine and immune systems, the liver, cognitive abilities, and the reproductive system (including low birth weight). They have also been linked to cancer.

Heavy metals used in high volume in industrial processes, mining, or paint are highly toxic. They affect the reproductive organs, kidneys, brain, bones, and cardiovascular function. Mercury and lead are of most concern in the international community because they are known to cause birth defects and underweight infants.

In 2013, the American Congress of Obstetricians and Gynecologists released an opinion that called for reduced exposure to toxic environmental agents, citing evidence that shows preconception and prenatal exposure to certain toxins, chemicals, and pesticides can lead to myriad reproductive health consequences, including increased risk of childhood cancer, sterility and infertility, and interference with developmental stages of reproductive function. (Found at: http://www.acog.org/Resources-And-Publications/Committee-Opinions/Committee-on-Health-Care-for-Underserved-Women/Exposure-to-Toxic-Environmental-Agents.)

In addition, harmful chemicals in our environments multiply and intersect in ways that disproportionately affect vulnerable and underserved populations. When the poor and underserved live in sacrifice zones, or are close to incinerators or garbage dumps, or are farmworkers or subsistence farmers, the harmfulness of chemicals evident in everyday products multiplies and causes adverse effects such as debilitating sickness, infant sickness, and abnormal brain, hormone, and growth development. This disproportionately affects women, and policy consideration must understand the role of women as caregivers. Future policies must also understand the disproportionate impact on families and communities when family members get sick and are underserved by health care. Healthcare providers who work in low income areas—and especially those who work in reproductive, infant, and children's health—must be educated on these ubiquitous toxins in their neighborhoods and their associated risks. And the church needs to be part of that education.

In the United States, the National Institute of Environmental Health Sciences (NIEHS) asserts that the environment may play some role in as much as 85 percent of all disease and that exposure to chemicals can have great impact on human growth and development. Some of these chemicals, along with other pollutants, may even have a long-lasting impact on a developing fetus, the effects of which could persist into adulthood and the reproductive cycle.

There are many everyday chemicals and exposures that are identified by UNDP or the Basel, Stockholm, and Rotterdam conventions as linked to various medical, behavioral, or reproductive disorders. Some of the effects of exposure may manifest in childhood, while some may emerge in adulthood.

- Air pollution: May contribute to intellectual delays, anxiety, depression, and attention problems.
- Arsenic: Leads to higher rates of liver, lung, and kidney cancers and is linked to increased mortality rates in liver and skin cancers.
- Dioxins: Greater rate of recurrent ear infections and incidents of chicken pox, and can cause developmental abnormalities.
- Endocrine disrupters (bisphenol A [BPA], pesticides, and phthalates): Increased aggression in young children, early onset of puberty, changes in mammary gland development, decrease in testosterone and sperm production, increased risk of breast cancer, abnormalities in genital development, and enlarged breast tissue in prepubescent boys.
- Flame retardants: Studies have shown growth of cancerous tumors in laboratory settings and they may alter

hormones that are essential to reproductive and neurological development.

- Lead: Increased risk of hypertensions, cardiovascular disease, diabetes, schizophrenia, and neurodegenerative changes later in life.
- Maternal smoking: Results in low infant birth weight as well as increased risk of childhood obesity.
- Mercury: Exposure before birth can cause disruptions in neurobehavioral and cognitive development.

Public health and safety is dependent on effective prevention and active protection before illness or injury have occurred. To fulfill God's commandment to love our neighbor as ourselves, we should support action that protects each individual's health and preserves the health of the community. To this end, we declare:

1. Every individual has a right to a safe and healthful environment un-endangered by a polluted natural world, a hazardous workplace, an unsanitary community, dangerous household products, unsafe drugs, and contaminated food. This human right must take precedence over considerations of cost analysis, capital investment, and financial return. It is unconscionable that anyone should profit or have their lives based on products that lead to the disease, disability, or death of themselves or another.

2. Public health hazards based on the lack of the wise use of chemicals must be prevented in order to avoid the serious individual and community consequences of injury, illness, and untimely death, including disability, physical pain, mental anguish, lost human potential, family stress, and the diversion of scarce medical resources to today's generation or future generations.

3. We must invest in research on the correlations between environmental concerns and cancer clusters, genetic defects, reproductive health issues, liver and kidney diseases, blood disorders, and brain disease. This research must include gender specific data and analysis which results in public policy.

4. The public health risks of technological development and waste must be fully researched and openly assessed before new technologies are introduced into the home, the workplace, the community, and the environment.

Consumers and workers have the right to know what technologies and substances are used in the workplace, in foods, and other products and must know the health consequences of the same.

5. The preservation and protection of human life from public and environmental health hazards is a fundamental responsibility of government that must be maintained by active public support and adequate public funds. All levels of government must enforce public and environmental health and safety laws.

6. Preventive health care should be taught in educational institutions to persons in every age group at every level of society. Health professionals in all branches of medicine and public health, and those in related fields, should be encouraged to practice preventive medicine, implement community preventive health strategies, and assist patients in the adoption of healthy lifestyles. Programs should be implemented that educate and inform consumers and workers about physical, chemical, biological, and radiological hazards of products, services, working conditions, and environmental contaminants.

7. The right to a healthy and safe workplace is a fundamental right. Employers must assume responsibility to eliminate hazards in their workplaces which cause death, injury, and disease. Employers should work together with their employees and employee organizations to achieve this objective.

The Church asks of governments to enact policies that protect human beings from environmentally toxic products and by-products:

1. The by-products, products, and/or waste of any consumer goods should be safe for the communities, families, and individuals who live or work near extraction, production, and waste sites. Industry must be held to account for its contributions to environmental degradation anywhere in the world, and environmental protections must be enacted through both national governments and international trade agreements.

2. Funding must be made available for the research of the safest possible extraction, production, consumption, products, and waste procedures. Tax incentives, penalties,

and environmental regulations must be enacted to protect people rather than profit.

3. The burden of proof for the harmlessness of particular manufacturing or agricultural method must be with the corporations who are economically benefitting from the product. Safe disposal of products must be seen as part of the cost of production.

4. Consumers have a right to know and this right needs to be respected and protected by government. Consumers must know what's in their food, their hair and skin lotions, their cosmetics, their furniture, construction materials of their homes, buildings, and furniture, as well as their lawn and garden products. Many of the most dangerous known chemicals are continuing to find their way into hair coloring, makeup, food, and water. Transparency must be required for the use of chemicals in manufacturing processes.

5. As impacts of both the use and discontinuance of chemical toxins occur to workers and their communities, economic and health safety nets must be implemented.

Church actions need to consist of the following:

1. Churches can become places of Christian education that teach about the products we buy and their inherent dangers. It is important that the church provides information on the chemicals we encounter so that those we buy are as safe as possible and our disposal of the same is least harmful to the environment.

2. The United Methodist Church must provide for the safety and health of persons in their meeting spaces and work places; and as they actualize this provision we need to become educators and advocates for public and environmental health and safety in the community as indicated in the declarations above. As a church, we have a responsibility to make sure the spaces that we are creating for our children and families within the church have undergone a thorough evaluation including evaluating cleansers, lawn chemicals, carpets, paint and furniture, and even the food we serve.

3. The church must educate itself on public health initiatives and advocate for those which concretely address the disproportionate health impacts of our current extraction,

manufacturing, agricultural, and waste economies on impoverished peoples, communities, and nations.

ADOPTED 2016

See Social Principles, ¶ 160A.

1035. Climate Change and the Church's Response

The natural world is a loving gift from God, the creator and sustainer, who has entrusted it in all its fullness to the care of all people for God's glory and to the good of all life on earth now and in generations to come. The image of God in us (Genesis1:27) is reflected in our abilities, responsibilities, and integrity, and with the power of the Holy Spirit we are called as God's coworkers in dialogue and covenant to live and serve for the good of creation.

We confess that we have turned our backs on our responsibilities in neglect, selfishness, and pride. And yet Christ's redeeming and restoring work through his death and resurrection embraces all of creation. Even in the face of destruction and disaster, we believe that God's vision for the world is of peace and wholeness and that God offers to us a future filled with hope (Jeremiah 29:11). This vision has a present and a future in the promise of a new heaven and a new earth (Revelation 21:1-8).

One manifestation of our neglect, selfishness, and pride is our sinful disregard for creation that has given rise to the injustice of climate change. Human-induced climate change is caused by the emission of CO_2 and other greenhouse gases, for which the strong economies of this world carry the vast responsibility. Those economies that have benefited from fossil-fuel development rightly bear the responsibility to rapidly reduce emissions and support less wealthy economies in their journey toward sustainable and climate resilient development.

Unless we change our ways, the average global temperature by the end of the twenty-first century is on course to increase by 4 degrees Celsius resulting in sea level rise, shrinking glaciers, extreme weather, droughts, and flooding. The United Nations' World Food Program estimates that climate change will place 20 percent more people at risk of hunger by 2050.

Leaders in some developed nations continue to debate, from places of comfort and privilege, the "reality" of a changing climate in order to perpetuate their polluting ways. As the church we witness firsthand the consequences of climate disruption in our communities and in the lives of those Christ calls us to be with in ministry. Recognizing our complicity and responsibility, we seek to chart a new path rooted in economic and ecological justice. We understand climate justice not simply as an environmental or economic concern but rather as a deep ethical and spiritual concern that the Church must address so that abundant life is ensured for our children and future generations.

As we continue to call for bold leadership and advocate for policies rooted in justice and sustainability, we understand that God is calling each of us to respond and that as a denomination we cannot hope to transform the world until we change our way of being in it.

Therefore, we call on United Methodists to:

Study the pastoral letter from the Council of Bishops entitled "God's Renewed Creation: Call to Hope and Action." Clergy and laity should use the letter and accompanying resources to preach and teach on the care for creation as part of our discipleship;

Prayerfully explore lifestyle changes as individuals and faith communities that would reduce greenhouse gas emissions and support a cleaner, healthier future;

Support communities impacted by climate change as well as those currently dependent on fossil fuel extraction and production as they transition to a new energy economy;

Challenge all United Methodist institutions, organizations, and local churches to incorporate climate stewardship, reducing the use of fossil fuel, into the design of facilities and reduce the carbon footprint of meetings;

Utilize resources available through the General Board of Church and Society, the General Board of Global Ministries, the General Board of Discipleship, and United Methodist Women to support locally-appropriate climate actions;

Advocate for national policies that shift resources, including subsidies, away from high-carbon development and toward alternative, cleaner energy sources; and

Advocate for a fair, ambitious, and binding international agreement to address climate change built on nationally appropriate commitments to both mitigation and adaptation.

ADOPTED 2016

See Social Principles, ¶ 162.

¶ 161. II. THE NURTURING COMMUNITY

The community provides the potential for nurturing human beings into the fullness of their humanity. We believe we have a responsibility to innovate, sponsor, and evaluate new forms of community that will encourage development of the fullest potential in individuals. Primary for us is the gospel understanding that all persons are important—because they are human beings created by God and loved through and by Jesus Christ and not because they have merited significance. We therefore support social climates in which human communities are maintained and strengthened for the sake of all persons and their growth. We also encourage all individuals to be sensitive to others by using appropriate language when referring to all persons. Language of a derogatory nature (with regard to race, nationality, ethnic background, gender, sexuality, and physical differences) does not reflect value for one another and contradicts the gospel of Jesus Christ.

A) Culture and Identity—We believe that our primary identity is as children of God. With that identity comes societal and cultural constructions that have both positive and negative impacts on humanity and the Church. Cultural identity evolves through our history, traditions, and experiences. The Church seeks to fully embrace and nurture cultural formation and competency as a means to be fully one body, expressed in multiple ways. Each of us has multiple identities of equal value that intersect to form our complete self. We affirm that no identity or culture has more legitimacy than any other. We call the Church to challenge any hierarchy of cultures or identities. Through relationships within and among cultures we are called to and have the responsibility for learning from each other, showing mutual respect for our differences and similarities as we experience the diversity of perspectives and viewpoints.

B) The Family—We believe the family to be the basic human community through which persons are nurtured and sustained in mutual love, responsibility, respect, and fidelity. We affirm the importance of loving parents for all children. We also understand the family as encompassing a wider range of options than that of the two-generational unit of parents and children (the nuclear family). We affirm shared responsibility for parenting where there are two parents and encourage social, economic, and religious efforts to maintain and strengthen relationships within families in order that every member may be assisted toward complete personhood.

C) Marriage—We affirm the sanctity of the marriage covenant that is expressed in love, mutual support, personal commitment, and shared fidelity between a man and a woman. We believe that God's blessing rests upon such marriage, whether or not there are children of the union. We reject social norms that assume different standards for women than for men in marriage. We support laws in civil society that define marriage as the union of one man and one woman.

D) Divorce—God's plan is for lifelong, faithful marriage. The church must be on the forefront of premarital, marital, and post marital counseling in order to create and preserve healthy relationships. However, when a married couple is estranged beyond reconciliation, even after thoughtful consideration and counsel, divorce is a regrettable alternative in the midst of brokenness. We grieve over the devastating emotional, spiritual, and economic consequences of divorce for all involved, understanding that women and especially children are disproportionately impacted by such burdens. As the Church we are concerned about high divorce rates. It is recommended that methods of mediation be used to minimize the adversarial nature and fault-finding that are often part of our current judicial processes, encouraging reconciliation wherever possible. We also support efforts by governments to reform divorce laws and other aspects of family law in order to address negative trends such as high divorce rates.

Although divorce publicly declares that a marriage no longer exists, other covenantal relationships resulting from the marriage remain, such as the nurture and support of children and extended family ties. We urge respectful negotiations in deciding the custody of minor children and support the consideration of either or both parents for this responsibility in that custody not be reduced to financial support, control, or manipulation and retaliation. The welfare of each child is the most important consideration.

Divorce does not preclude a new marriage. We encourage an intentional commitment of the Church and society to minister compassionately to those in the process of divorce, as well as members of divorced and remarried families, in a community of faith where God's grace is shared by all.

E) *Single Persons*—We affirm the integrity of single persons, and we reject all social practices that discriminate or social attitudes that are prejudicial against persons because they are single. This also includes single parents, and we recognize the extra responsibilities involved.

F) *Women and Men*—We affirm with Scripture the common humanity of male and female, both having equal worth in the eyes of God. We reject the erroneous notion that one gender is superior to another, that one gender must strive against another, and that members of one gender may receive love, power, and esteem only at the expense of another. We especially reject the idea that God made individuals as incomplete fragments, made whole only in union with another. We call upon women and men alike to share power and control, to learn to give freely and to receive freely, to be complete and to respect the wholeness of others. We seek for every individual opportunities and freedom to love and be loved, to seek and receive justice, and to practice ethical self-determination. We understand our gender diversity to be a gift from God, intended to add to the rich variety of human experience and perspective; and we guard against attitudes and traditions that would use this good gift to leave members of one sex more vulnerable in relationships than members of another.

G) *Human Sexuality*—We affirm that sexuality is God's good gift to all persons. We call everyone to responsible stewardship of this sacred gift.

Although all persons are sexual beings whether or not they are married, sexual relations are affirmed only with the covenant of monogamous, heterosexual marriage.

We deplore all forms of the commercialization, abuse, and exploitation of sex. We call for strict global enforcement of laws prohibiting the sexual exploitation of children and for adequate protection, guidance, and counseling for abused children. All persons, regardless of age, gender, marital status, or sexual orientation, are entitled to have their human and civil rights ensured and to be protected against violence. The Church should support the family in providing age-appropriate education regarding sexuality to children, youth, and adults.

We affirm that all persons are individuals of sacred worth, created in the image of God. All persons need the ministry of the Church in their struggles for human fulfillment, as well as the spiritual and emotional care of a fellowship that enables reconciling relationships with God, with others, and with self. The United Methodist Church does not condone the practice of homosexuality and considers this practice incompatible with Christian teaching. We affirm that God's grace is available to all. We will seek to live together in Christian community, welcoming, forgiving, and loving one another, as Christ has loved and accepted us. We implore families and churches not to reject or condemn lesbian and gay members and friends. We commit ourselves to be in ministry for and with all persons.[1]

H) Family Violence and Abuse—We recognize that family violence and abuse in all its forms—verbal, psychological, physical, sexual—is detrimental to the covenant of the human community. We encourage the Church to provide a safe environment, counsel, and support for the victim and to work with the abuser to understand the root causes and forms of abuse and to overcome such behaviors. Regardless of the cause or the abuse, both the victim and the abuser need the love of the Church. While we deplore the actions of the abuser, we affirm that person to be in need of God's redeeming love.

I) Sexual Abuse—Violent, disrespectful, or abusive sexual expressions do not confirm sexuality as God's good gift. We reject all sexual expressions that damage the humanity God has given us as birthright, and we affirm only that sexual expression that enhances that same humanity. We believe that sexual relations where one or both partners are exploitative, abusive, or promiscuous are beyond the parameters of acceptable Christian behavior and are ultimately destructive to individuals, families, and the social order. We deplore all forms of the commercialization and exploitation of sex, with their consequent cheapening and degradation of human personality. To lose freedom and be sold by someone else for sexual purposes is a form of slavery, and we denounce such business and support the abused and their right to freedom.

1. See Judicial Council Decision 702.

We call for strict global enforcement of laws prohibiting the sexual exploitation or use of children by adults and encourage efforts to hold perpetrators legally and financially responsible. We call for the establishment of adequate protective services, guidance, and counseling opportunities for children thus abused.

J) Sexual Harassment—We believe human sexuality is God's good gift. One abuse of this good gift is sexual harassment. We define sexual harassment as any unwanted sexual comment, advance, or demand, either verbal or physical, that is reasonably perceived by the recipient as demeaning, intimidating, or coercive. Sexual harassment must be understood as an exploitation of a power relationship rather than as an exclusively sexual issue. Sexual harassment includes, but is not limited to, the creation of a hostile or abusive working environment resulting from discrimination on the basis of gender. Contrary to the nurturing community, sexual harassment creates improper, coercive, and abusive conditions wherever it occurs in society. Sexual harassment undermines the social goal of equal opportunity and the climate of mutual respect between men and women. Unwanted sexual attention is wrong and discriminatory. Sexual harassment interferes with the moral mission of the Church.

K) Abortion—The beginning of life and the ending of life are the God-given boundaries of human existence. While individuals have always had some degree of control over when they would die, they now have the awesome power to determine when and even whether new individuals will be born. Our belief in the sanctity of unborn human life makes us reluctant to approve abortion.

But we are equally bound to respect the sacredness of the life and well-being of the mother and the unborn child.

We recognize tragic conflicts of life with life that may justify abortion, and in such cases we support the legal option of abortion under proper medical procedures by certified medical providers. We support parental, guardian, or other responsible adult notification and consent before abortions can be performed on girls who have not yet reached the age of legal adulthood. We cannot affirm abortion as an acceptable means of birth control, and we unconditionally reject it as a means of gender selection or eugenics (see Resolution 3184).

We oppose the use of late-term abortion known as dilation and extraction (partial-birth abortion) and call for the end of this practice except when the physical life of the mother is in danger and

¶ 161

no other medical procedure is available, or in the case of severe fetal anomalies incompatible with life. This procedure shall be performed only by certified medical providers. Before providing their services, abortion providers should be required to offer women the option of anesthesia.

We call all Christians to a searching and prayerful inquiry into the sorts of conditions that may cause them to consider abortion. We entrust God to provide guidance, wisdom, and discernment to those facing an unintended pregnancy.

The Church shall offer ministries to reduce unintended pregnancies. We commit our Church to continue to provide nurturing ministries to those who terminate a pregnancy, to those in the midst of a crisis pregnancy, and to those who give birth.

We mourn and are committed to promoting the diminishment of high abortion rates. The Church shall encourage ministries to reduce unintended pregnancies such as comprehensive, age-appropriate sexuality education, advocacy in regard to contraception, and support of initiatives that enhance the quality of life for all women and girls around the globe.

Young adult women disproportionately face situations in which they feel that they have no choice due to financial, educational, relational, or other circumstances beyond their control. The Church and its local congregations and campus ministries should be in the forefront of supporting existing ministries and developing new ministries that help such women in their communities. They should also support those crisis pregnancy centers and pregnancy resource centers that compassionately help women explore all options related to unplanned pregnancy. We particularly encourage the Church, the government, and social service agencies to support and facilitate the option of adoption. (See ¶ 161M.) We affirm and encourage the Church to assist the ministry of crisis pregnancy centers and pregnancy resource centers that compassionately help women find feasible alternatives to abortion.

Governmental laws and regulations do not provide all the guidance required by the informed Christian conscience. Therefore, a decision concerning abortion should be made only after thoughtful and prayerful consideration by the parties involved, with medical, family, pastoral, and other appropriate counsel.

L) Ministry With Those Who Have Experienced an Abortion—We urge local pastors to become informed about the symptoms and behaviors associated with post-abortion stress. We commit our Church to continue to provide nurturing ministries to those who terminate a pregnancy, to those in the midst of a crisis pregnancy, and to those who give birth. We further encourage local churches to make available contact information for counseling agencies that offer programs to address post-abortion stress for all seeking help.

M) Adoption—Children are a gift from God to be welcomed and received. We recognize that some circumstances of birth make the rearing of a child difficult. We affirm and support the birth parent(s) whose choice it is to allow the child to be adopted. We recognize the agony, strength, and courage of the birth parent(s) who choose(s) in hope, love, and prayer to offer the child for adoption. In addition, we also recognize the anxiety, strength, and courage of those who choose in hope, love, and prayer to be able to care for a child. We affirm and support the adoptive parent(s)' desire to rear an adopted child as they would a biological child. When circumstances warrant adoption, we support the use of proper legal procedures. When appropriate and possible, we encourage open adoption so that a child may know all information and people related to them, both medically and relationally. We support and encourage greater awareness and education to promote adoption of a wide variety of children through foster care, international adoption, and domestic adoption. We commend the birth parent(s), the receiving parent(s), and the child to the care of the Church, that grief might be shared, joy might be celebrated, and the child might be nurtured in a community of Christian love.

N) Faithful Care for Dying Persons—While we applaud medical science for efforts to prevent disease and illness and for advances in treatment that extend the meaningful life of human beings, we recognize that every mortal life will ultimately end in death. Death is never a sign that God has abandoned us, no matter what the circumstances of the death might be. As Christians we must always be prepared to surrender the gift of mortal life and claim the gift of eternal life through the death and resurrection of Jesus Christ. Care for dying persons is part of our stewardship of the divine gift of life when cure is no longer possible. We encourage the use of medical technologies to provide palliative care at the end of life when life-sustaining treatments no longer support the goals of life, and when they have reached their limits. There is no moral or religious obligation to use these when they impose

¶ 161

undue burdens or only extend the process of dying. Dying persons and their families are free to discontinue treatments when they cease to be of benefit to the patient.

We recognize the agonizing personal and moral decisions faced by the dying, their physicians, their families, their friends, and their faith community. We urge that decisions faced by the dying be made with thoughtful and prayerful consideration by the parties involved, with medical, pastoral, and other appropriate counsel. We further urge that all persons discuss with their families, their physicians, and their pastoral counselors, their wishes for care at the end of life and provide advance directives for such care when they are not able to make these decisions for themselves. Even when one accepts the inevitability of death, the Church and society must continue to provide faithful care, including pain relief, companionship, support, and spiritual nurture for the dying person in the hard work of preparing for death. We encourage and support the concept of hospice care whenever possible at the end of life. Faithful care does not end at death but continues during bereavement as we care for grieving families. We reject euthanasia and any pressure upon the dying to end their lives. God has continued love and purpose for all persons, regardless of health. We affirm laws and policies that protect the rights and dignity of the dying.

O) Suicide—We believe that suicide is not the way a human life should end. Often suicide is the result of untreated depression, or untreated pain and suffering. The church has an obligation to see that all persons have access to needed pastoral and medical care and therapy in those circumstances that lead to loss of self-worth, suicidal despair, and/or the desire to seek physician-assisted suicide. We encourage the church to provide education to address the biblical, theological, social, and ethical issues related to death and dying, including suicide. United Methodist theological seminary courses should also focus on issues of death and dying, including suicide.

A Christian perspective on suicide begins with an affirmation of faith that nothing, including suicide, separates us from the love of God (Romans 8:38-39). Therefore, we deplore the condemnation of people who complete suicide, and we consider unjust the stigma that so often falls on surviving family and friends.

We encourage pastors and faith communities to address this issue through preaching and teaching. We urge pastors and faith communities to provide pastoral care to those at risk, survivors, and their families, and to those families who have lost loved ones to suicide, seeking always to remove the oppressive stigma around suicide. The Church opposes assisted suicide and euthanasia.

P) Sexual Assault—Sexual assault is wrong. We affirm the right of all people to live free from such assaults, encourage efforts of law enforcement to prosecute such crimes, and condemn rape in any form. It does not matter where the person is, what the person is wearing, whether or not he or she is intoxicated, if he or she is flirtatious, what is the victim's gender, or any other circumstance.

Q) Pornography—Scripture teaches that humans are created in God's image and that we are accountable to God through right relationship. Sexual images can celebrate the goodness of human sexuality through positive depiction in art, literature, and education. We deplore, however, images that distort this goodness and injure healthy sexual relationships.

We oppose all forms of pornography and consider its use a form of sexual misconduct. Pornography is sexually explicit material that portrays violence, abuse, coercion, domination, humiliation, or degradation for the purpose of sexual arousal. Pornography sexually exploits and objectifies both women and men. Any sexually explicit material that depicts children is abhorrent and victimizes children. Pornography can ruin lives, careers, and relationships.

We grieve the pervasiveness of Internet pornography, including among Christians, and especially its impact on young people and marriages.

The Church is called to transformation and healing for all persons adversely affected by pornography. Congregations should send a clear message of opposition to pornography and commitment to safe environments for everyone. We encourage strategies to eradicate pornography, to support victims, and to provide open and transparent conversation and education around sexuality and sexual ethics. We also believe that people can be rehabilitated and should have the opportunity to receive treatment; therefore, churches should seek ways to offer support and care for addressing issues of addiction. Further, all churches are encouraged to review and update appropriate child, youth, and adult protection policies to reflect The United Methodist Church's position that the use of pornography is a form of sexual misconduct. By encouraging education, prevention, and pathways to recovery for all affected by pornography, we live out our Wesleyan understanding of grace and healing.

R) Bullying—Bullying is a growing problem in parts of the connection. It is a contributing factor in suicide and in the violence we see in some cultures today. We affirm the right of all people regardless of gender, socioeconomic status, race, religion, disability, age, physical appearance, sexual orientation and gender identity to be free of unwanted aggressive behavior and harmful control tactics.

As the Church, we can play a pivotal role in ending this problem. We urge churches to seek opportunities to be trained in responding to the needs of those who have been bullied, to those who perpetrate bullying, and to support those in authority who may witness or be called to intervene on behalf of those who have been bullied. Churches are urged to connect with community associations and schools in this outreach.

We encourage churches to adopt a policy of zero tolerance for bullying, including cyberbullying, within their spheres of influence; stand with persons being bullied; and take a leadership role in working with the schools and community to prevent bullying.

THE NURTURING COMMUNITY
THE RESOLUTIONS

CHRISTIAN EDUCATION

2001. Christian Education

WHEREAS, every elder, at ordination covenants to "preach the word of God, lead in worship, read and teach the Scriptures and engage the people in study and witness and to ensure faithful transmission of the Christian faith" (2004 *Discipline* ¶ 340.1); and every deacon at ordination covenants to "create opportunities for others to enter into discipleship" (2004 *Discipline*, ¶ 329.1); and

WHEREAS, the early Methodist movement was guided by the educational genius of John Wesley, who crafted an ecology of faith formation and leadership development for making disciples; and

WHEREAS, question number fourteen of the Historic Examination for Admission into Full Connection is "Will you diligently instruct the children in every place?" (2012 *Discipline*, ¶ 336);

Therefore, be it resolved, that the 2016 General Conference affirm the imperative to engage in the work of Christian education and direct United Methodist seminaries and colleges, collegiate ministries, the General Board of Higher Education and Ministry, the General Board of Discipleship, The United Methodist Publishing House, annual conferences, and local churches to assess and expand how they advance the work of Christian education in the church. This includes promoting the professional, para-professional, and undergraduate certification in camp/retreat ministry, children's ministry, Christian education, collegiate ministry, evangelism, ministry with the poor, ministry with people with disabilities, music ministry, ministry with older adults, spiritual formation, urban ministry, youth ministry, and, where appropriate, monitoring all approved seminary M.Div. programs to ensure that future leaders are being trained in the ministries of Christian education.

ADOPTED 2008
AMENDED AND READOPTED 2016
RESOLUTION #2001, 2008, 2012 *BOOK OF RESOLUTIONS*

See Social Principles, ¶¶ 161 and 162.

2004. Collegiate Ministry as a Priority of the Church

WHEREAS, collegiate ministry is a term that fully includes campus ministries (Wesley Foundations and the like), college/university chaplains, ecumenical ministries, and church-based ministry with college students; and

WHEREAS, collegiate ministry is the missional expression of The UMC on the college and university campuses of the world; and

WHEREAS, these campuses, many of them cities unto themselves, require their own unique faith communities; and

WHEREAS, those communities require called, gifted, trained, equipped, and supported collegiate ministers, who order the life of these unique ministries; and

WHEREAS, collegiate ministries actively offer the good news of Jesus Christ and the opportunity to belong to an authentic Christian community on every university and college campus; and

WHEREAS, collegiate ministries provide substantive opportunities for students to become growing, serving, learning, and leading disciples of Jesus Christ in the United Methodist tradition; and

WHEREAS, collegiate ministries are communities that are intentionally and radically open, welcoming, and inclusive to all people, seeking to be communities that authentically reflect the diversity and unity of the kingdom of God; and

WHEREAS, collegiate ministries help all students hear God's call to serve and lead in the church and world, including both lay vocations and ordained ministry in the Church; and

WHEREAS, collegiate ministries are incubators for new and effective ways for doing ministry as United Methodists, particularly with young adults; and

WHEREAS, collegiate ministries embody hope for the future of The United Methodist Church, as we raise up a new generation of disciples of Jesus Christ, for the transformation of the world;

Therefore, be it resolved, that every annual conference shall make collegiate ministry a priority; the bishops and appointive cabinets take seriously the recruitment, appointment, and certification of missionally minded, called, gifted, trained, equipped, and supported collegiate ministers; and conferences develop necessary funding to ensure the effectiveness of these ministries;

And be it further resolved, that every annual conference have a fully functioning Board of Higher Education and Campus Ministry (¶ 634) that shall fulfill its role in supporting, funding, and evaluating the effectiveness of each collegiate ministry.

ADOPTED 2016

See Social Principles, ¶¶ 161 and 162.

FAMILY

2022. Support for Adoption

The Social Principles of The United Methodist Church, in the section on "The Nurturing Community," ¶ 161A) "The Family," state: "We believe the family to be the basic human community through which persons are nurtured and sustained in mutual love, responsibility, respect, and fidelity." They further acknowledge that the family encompasses a wide range of options. One of those options is the family that includes adopted children.

Throughout the biblical texts, references are made to the importance of parenting children. We can find story after story in the Old Testament of how God expresses love and care for children, including orphans. Jesus' life reflects that same level of commitment: He was a voice for those widowed or orphaned, poor and oppressed. We affirm that God is our ultimate parent, and persons who choose to raise a family are called to be loving parents, whether they gave birth to or adopted their children.

Clinical and social service agencies that relate professionally to adoption issues look for and encourage the same attitudes and behaviors that should apply for birth children. These attitudes and behaviors include: parental love; parental responsibility; encouragement of identity development of the child; physical, emotional, and economic security of the child; educational growth of the child; and socialization of the child.

Studies done by a variety of clinical and educational agencies and institutions concur that the six factors mentioned above, expressed in various forms, are vital for a sense of stability and dependability experienced by children in a family system.

Some of the most recent studies of families and children have been done by the Search Institute of Minneapolis, Minnesota, which has identified forty developmental assets that help children grow in a healthy, caring, and responsible environment.

External assets include: support (e.g., the family provides a high level of love and support; the child experiences caring neighbors); empowerment (e.g., children are valued by being placed at the center of family life; the parent(s) serve(s) others in the community); boundaries and expectations (e.g., the parent(s) and other adults model positive, responsible behavior; the parent or parents have realistic expectations for children's growth and development); and constructive use of time (e.g., the parent(s) expose(s) children to a variety of creative activities; the parent(s) provide(s) positive, supervised time at home).

Internal assets include: commitment to learning (e.g., family members are motivated to do well in school, work, and community; the parent(s) enjoy(s) learning and demonstrate(s) this through personal learning activities); positive values (e.g., the family values caring, helping behaviors; the family values honesty); social competencies (e.g., parental planning and decision-making behaviors are modeled and observed; peaceful conflict resolution is modeled and observed); and positive identity (e.g., the family models high self-esteem; the family has a positive view of the future).

It has been observed that as the above-mentioned assets are experienced, children and families demonstrate stability and growth regardless of whether children are of birth origin or adopted.

Therefore, The United Methodist Church supports and encourages adoption by all persons who demonstrate these attitudes, behaviors, and assets. The United Methodist Church also rejects any form of coercion, deception or profiteering associated with adoption, and affirms the use of reputable, certified agencies when engaging in the adoption process.

ADOPTED 2004
AMENDED AND READOPTED 2012
RESOLUTION #2022, 2008, 2012 *BOOK OF RESOLUTIONS*
RESOLUTION #21, 2004 *BOOK OF RESOLUTIONS*

See Social Principles, ¶ 161M.

2023. Support for Clergy Families

Over the past several years, clergy, whether single or married, and their families have continued to express serious concerns for the stresses they bear in their congregations. This phrase, "life in the fishbowl," describes how pastor and staff therapist Frank J. Stalfa sees the lives of clergy and their spouses and family members in our local congregations. The image is painfully accurate about the situation filled with unrealistic expectations, virtually nonexistent boundaries for privacy and personal time, disrupted lives, crises in careers and educational programs, unending demands of congregational needs, and pressure for spouse and preacher's kids (PKs) to be persons without personal or professional needs as well as perfect, "model" Christians.

PK syndrome is documented in research on children and youth in clergy families, and it names the pressure on clergy children to set a high standard for other children to follow (the perfect student, the model son/daughter, the high-achieving youth), potentially limiting their individuality and development. Support, encouragement, and opportunities for PKs to share their pressures and joys are being addressed through annual conference PK retreats, blogs (www.preacherkids.com <http://www.preacherkids.com>) and growing recognition among congregations that they are pivotal people in the health and well-being of preacher's kids.

The 2009 Clergy Spouse and Family Survey, conducted by the General Commission on the Status and Role of Women, in collaboration with the General Board of Higher Education and Ministry, the General Board of Pension and Health Benefits, and the General Board of Discipleship, received over 3100 responses from United Methodist clergy spouses. This survey echoed many of the responses to the Leadership survey conducted in 1992 as to the contributors for marital stresses among clergy families: insufficient time together, use of money, income level, communication difficulties, differences over leisure activities, difficulties in raising children, pastor's anger toward spouse, and differences over ministry career and spouse's career. A significant and troubling finding from the Leadership survey was that 80% of clergy reported that they believed their pastoral ministry negatively affected their families. The 2009 Clergy Spouse and Family Survey revealed similar reflections from spouses and as well as several changes occurring among clergy spouses.

Although the majority of clergy spouses are female, a growing number of these spouses are male. This challenges how the "role" of clergy spouse may be related more to gender than the "position" as a spouse to a clergyperson. Noteworthy among the differences in how men married to women clergy are treated include: rather than being called the clergy spouse, they are the "men married to a minister," and the expectations placed on female clergy spouses are not placed on these male clergy spouses such as providing child care, being in a choir, teaching a children's church school, or attending worship services. Their development of a separate personal and professional identity may not be the struggle it is for many female spouses who fight to keep a career or family time or educational opportunities. This suggests that expectations of clergy spouses may not only be traditional but also gender-related. Further research could guide the Church in how to minister effectively to spouses of clergy and congregations as these roles continue to transition.

Also changing is the "traditional" supportive ministerial role identity among clergy spouses. In previous generations, the pastor's spouse was generally available to provide additional local church leadership. However, the 2009 survey revealed a very different set of life commitments as clergy spouses are now employed full-time (55%), part-time (17%), with only 12% able to be a stay-at-home parent/homemaker; 30% of clergy spouses have college degrees and 43% have graduate degrees, representing being one of the most highly educated groups in the denomination; among those surveyed, 78% were female and 21.7% were male; 70% believed their children are satisfied being a "preacher's kid" and 18% of parents indicated they didn't know how their children would assess their experience; 80% of spouses are in their first marriage and rated their marital satisfaction as very high (note that this survey was not able to reach divorced spouses of UMC clergy); and 49% are in the 51-64 age range with a combined total of 38% being younger than age 50. The changing nature of the clergy spouse role has yet to alter many expectations from many of our congregations. ("The Clergy Spouses and Families in the United Methodist Church Survey," 2009, <http://www.gcsrw.org/ClergyFamilyandSpouseSurvey/aspx>.)

Although the 2009 survey showed that the clergy spouse roles and expectations are changing, it also revealed that the experiences of being invisible, lonely, recipients of parishioner gossip and hostilities, frequent disregard to clergy family needs of adequate, safe, and efficient housing and for honoring spouses' professional careers and development, and chronic distrust from the consequences of seeking professional marital and/or family counseling for fear of how the Church (local and annual conference) may perceive them as "troubled" remain far too common among our clergy spouses.

It is unthinkable to believe that congregations intentionally wish the stress and pain that living life in a "fishbowl" can cause. Certainly, many parishioners would find it unacceptable that their expectations and demands (spoken and unspoken) would cause additional pain and hardship on their clergy family.

Christian Community for All Our Families

As United Methodists we envision churches and congregations in which all of God's children are welcome at the Table, all are nurtured and respected for their own gifts and talents, and are transformed to be Christ to others in the world. We are a Church of disciples, each to be fully engaged in transforming the world regardless of family status.

Our Church places high value on our families, yet the needs and crises of our clergy families may go unnoticed, unidentified and unaddressed. Clergy families are like every other family with strengths and stresses similar to all families. They need privacy and boundaries that protect life just as other families have.

What Can Be Done?

The roles of clergy spouse and family are unique and frequently taken for granted. These roles are, nonetheless, critical to the well-being and success of the clergy's ministry. Sustaining the emotional, spiritual, physical, and economic health of our clergy families is a ministry to be recommended to every congregation and annual conference. Recognizing that clergy have families that come in different forms and have different needs, congregants can:

1. Examine their own attitudes, perceptions, and expectations and identifying where they are unrealistic;

2. Ask themselves the questions that will identify any sexism or racism in their expectations and assumptions: If this clergy spouse/family member were another gender or another race, would I have the same expectations? Would I make the same assumptions? Would I react differently if they were a congregational family member?
3. Remember clergy and their families are human and have their own personal and professional lives;
4. Provide safe and honest sharing for clergy families when stress mounts;
5. Encourage clergy families to seek help, even taking the initiative to provide resources and support;
6. Regularly clarify and keep their expectations realistic, recognizing that pedestals are for statues;
7. Reserve family time and protect family life boundaries;
8. Provide adequate, healthy, clean, safe and efficient parsonages (which clergy families are to also treat with respect and care), with the understanding that this is the home for the clergy and family, not an extension of church property.

Congregations can share the effective and renewing models working in the episcopal areas and conferences around the Church, including but not limited to these:

1. Iowa Conference's *"What Do I Do If . . .?" Basic Information Handbook for Clergy Spouses,* distributed to clergy spouses upon the commission or ordination of their spouse.
2. Florida Conference's program of nurture, healing, and preventative care to clergy and their families, *Shade and Fresh Water.* (The three-part approach includes a therapeutic presence for families in crisis or need, including professional counseling and safe space; a preventative program for clergy families in transition in appointments; and a sustaining program encouraging healthy modeling of well-balanced lives.)
3. Varied programs, guidance, and initiatives of organizations like The Center for Ministry, the Center for Pastoral Effectiveness and Spiritual Direction, and websites like "Desperate Preacher's Site," PreachersKids.com and spouseconnect.blogspot.com.
4. www.gcsrw.org/Clergyspouse <http://www.gcsrw.org/Clergyspouse> website for postings of articles, events, retreats and resources for clergy spouses and families.

5. The book, *How the Other Half Lives: The Challenges Facing Clergy Spouses and Partners*, by Johnna Fredrickson & William A. Smith. Published by The Pilgrim Press, Cleveland, Ohio, 2010.

6. *Clergy Housing Handbook: Parsonages* available at www.gcsrw .org/clergyspouse <http://www.gcsrw.org/clergyspouse>: a collection of best practices from annual conferences with housing recommendations and checklists, designed to facilitate open, healthy and caring communication among clergy, clergy spouses and families, and parishioners.

7. Ongoing collaboration between the General Commission on the Status and Role of Women, the General Board of Higher Education and Ministry, the General Board of Pension and Health Benefits, the General Board of Discipleship, and the General Commission on Religion and Race.

Therefore, be it resolved, that the General Conference of The United Methodist Church calls on each of the following groups to address this growing crisis among our clergy families:

1. The General Commission on the Status and Role of Women will work collaboratively with the General Board of Higher Education and Ministry, the General Board of Pension and Health Benefits, and the General Board of Discipleship to convene a summit to research issues affecting clergy spouses and families, to identify and promote existing relevant and effective resources, plan the development of needed additional resources to address these concerns, and make any legislative recommendations to the 2016 General Conference.

2. Bishops, cabinets, and boards of ordained ministry will promote specific conference resources, training and orientation models, and counseling assistance programs to all clergy and families.

3. Staff-parish relations committees will use strategies and training resources for their members in these specific concerns of clergy and families.

4. District superintendents and their spouses may be called on to provide modeling and leadership for their clergy families in successful strategies. Superintendents will prioritize this issue as they work with local congregations in transitions and ongoing appointments.

5. Annual conference commissions on the status and role of women will survey spouses and families of clergy to assist annual conferences, bishops and cabinets, and general agencies in gathering data and developing resources and strategies in response to the challenges of life in the clergy family.

6. The General Commission on the Status and Role of Women will host a page on the www.gcsrw.org <http://www.gcsrw.org> website dedicated to posting available resources, links and conference events related to clergy spouse and family support ministries.

7. The General Commission on the Status and Role of Women will post on www.gcsrw.org <http://www.gcsrw.org> the *Clergy Housing Handbook: Parsonages* for easy availability and free accessibility to local church and conference boards of trustees, staff-parish councils, bishops, cabinets, boards of ordained ministry, and commissions on the status and role of women.

8. The research and data from the summit findings from GCSRW and other collaborating general church boards and agencies will be published in a summary document and made available for use by United Methodist annual conferences and other denominations and religious bodies.

ADOPTED 2004
AMENDED AND READOPTED 2012
RESOLUTION #2023, 2008, 2012 *BOOK OF RESOLUTIONS*
RESOLUTION #22, 2004 *BOOK OF RESOLUTIONS*

See Social Principles, ¶ 161*B*.

2024. May as Christian Home Month

WHEREAS, many families throughout our world suffer because of poverty, inequities in society, financial struggles, inadequate health care, violence in the home, violence in their communities, lack of knowledge for developing healthy relationships, and inadequate resources for times of transition or crisis; and

WHEREAS, according to the Social Principles of The United Methodist Church, "We believe the family to be the basic human community through which persons are nurtured and sustained in mutual love, responsibility, respect, and fidelity"; and

WHEREAS, we recognize that support from a faith community can help every family, no matter what its configuration, to more effectively provide safety, nurture growth, and sustain healthy relationships;

Therefore be it resolved, that General Conference declare the month of May Christian Home Month, with emphasis on ways congregations can support families within the congregation and within their communities, encourage worship and faith formation in the home, participate in prayer on behalf of all families, and provide ministries for forming and strengthening healthy relationships in the home.

We call upon pastors and congregations to offer classes and opportunities for forming and maintaining healthy relationships, parenting, communication skills, marriage preparation and enrichment, faith formation in the home, and coping with crises.

We call upon annual conferences to assist congregations through the development, identification, and promotion of ministries and resources in support of families and of faith formation in the home.

We call upon the General Board of Higher Education and Ministry to offer resources for clergy in marriage preparation and marriage enrichment, as well as resources to aid clergy in developing and maintaining healthy relationships within their own families.

We call upon seminaries to train clergy in forming and maintaining healthy relationships within the family, in marriage preparation, marriage counseling, and marriage enrichment.

We call upon The United Methodist Publishing House to continue publication of materials in support of healthy relationships within the family, parenting, sexuality education, and family life.

We call upon the General Board of Discipleship to produce resources for the support of Christian Home Month for use in the congregation and in the home, as well as to continue to develop, identify, and promote resources and materials for forming and sustaining healthy relationships in the home, as well as for faith formation in the home.

ADOPTED 1992
AMENDED AND READOPTED 2004, 2012
RESOLUTION #2025, 2008, 2012 *BOOK OF RESOLUTIONS*
RESOLUTION #24, 2004 *BOOK OF RESOLUTIONS*
RESOLUTION #21, 2000 *BOOK OF RESOLUTIONS*

See Social Principles, ¶ 161*B*.

2026. Gender-Selective Abortion

Gender-selective abortion—choosing abortion solely or primarily because of not preferring the unborn child's sex—is often practiced in several places in the world. Due to cultural biases, female fetuses are generally targeted for abortion in such cases much more often than males.

In the November 9, 2001, cover story of the Indian magazine, *Frontline*, Nobel Laureate Amartya Sen wrote that "sex-selective abortion" is "particularly prevalent in East Asia, in China and South Korea in particular, but also in Singapore and Taiwan, and it is beginning to emerge as a statistically significant phenomenon in India and South Asia as well."[1]

A 1998 study published by the Alan Guttmacher Institute, which was founded as a division of the Planned Parenthood Federation of America, also lists Thailand among the nations in which "sex selection is believed to play a role in abortion."[2]

Jyotsna Patro, an Indian delegate to the Asian Church Women's Conference and former president of the Church of North India Women's Fellowship, has recently reported that "[t]he callousness in allowing female feticide is worsening," with "[p]arents hav[ing] no qualms about aborting female fetuses."[3]

The widespread practice of sex-selective abortion is believed to be a main cause of the extremely skewed sex ratios at birth in India, where it was recently estimated that only 882 girls are born for every 1,000 boys, and China, where 832 girls are born for every 1,000 boys.[4]

While precise estimates vary, there are now tens of millions of "missing women" in the world thanks to sex-selective abortions. In India alone, about 10 million female fetuses are estimated to

1. Amartya Sen, "Many Faces of Gender Inequality," *Frontline*, 9 November 2001; available from <http://www.flonnet.com/fl1822/18220040.htm>; Internet; accessed 20 August 2007.

2. Akinrinola Bankole, Susheela Singh and Taylor Haas, "Reasons Why Women Have Induced Abortions: Evidence from 27 Countries," *International Family Planning Perspectives* 24, no. 3 [September 1998]; available from: <http://www.guttmacher.org/pubs/journals/2411798.html>; accessed 20 August 2007.

3. Anto Akkara, "Indian Christian Women Warn of Female Extinction from Feticide," Ecumenical News International, 26 July 2007; available from <http://www.eni.ch/featured/article.php?id=1077>; Internet; accessed 20 August 2007.

4. Raekha Prasad and Randeep Ramesh, "India's Missing Girls," *Guardian* [London], 28 February 2007; available from: <http://www.guardian.co.uk/india/story/0,,2022983,00.html>; Internet; accessed 20 August 2007. Cf. "China Riots Rooted in Child Policy, Financial Woes," Turkish Daily News, 2 June 2007.

have been selectively aborted in the last two decades.[5] The Voice of America news service recently reported that "by the year 2020," China is expected to "have 30 million more men than women, making it difficult for many men to find wives."[6] Chinese population expert Chu Junhong has reported that "[p]renatal sex selection was probably the primary cause, if not the sole cause, for the continuous rise of the sex ratio at birth" in China since the implementation of that country's one-child policy. These growing gender imbalances are believed to exacerbate such problems as prostitution and human trafficking.[7] Furthermore, according to Dr. Therese Hesketh, a researcher at the University College London Institute of Child Health and co-author of a recent study on societal gender imbalances, this emergence of large numbers of young men unable to find wives "could lead to increased levels of antisocial behavior and violence."[8]

At the March 2007 meeting of the United Nation's Commission on the Status of Women, in New York, a resolution supported by South Korea, the United States, and others would have condemned sex-selective abortion and infanticide and encouraged steps to eliminate them. However, the resolution was ultimately not adopted.[9]

The United Methodist Social Principles affirm "[o]ur belief in the sanctity of unborn human life" and "unconditionally reject" abortion being used "as a means of gender selection" (¶ 161K). While

5. Prasad and Ramesh; Cf. Neil Samson Katz and Marisa Sherry, "India: The Missing Girls," Background Facts and Links, PBS FRONTLINE/World "Rough Cut," 26 April 2007; available from: <http://www.pbs.org/frontlineworld/rough/2007/04/the_missing_gir.html>; Internet; accessed 20 August 2007.

6. Daniel Schearf, "China Acknowledges Family-planning Policy Affects Sex-Ratio Imbalance," Voice of America news, available from: <http://www.voanews.com/english/archive/2007-01/2007-01-23-voa18.cfm>; Internet; accessed 20 August 2007. Cf. Katharine Mieszkowski, "Millions of Lonely Would-Be Grooms in China," Salon.com, 12 January 2007; available from <http://www.salon.com/mwt/broadsheet/2007/01/12/china/index.html>; Internet; accessed 20 August 2007.

7. Eric Baculinao, "China Grapples with Legacy of its 'Missing Girls': Disturbing Demographic Imbalance Spurs Drive to Change Age-Old Practices," NBC News, 14 Sept 2004; available from <http://www.msnbc.msn.com/id/5953508>; Internet; accessed 17 August 2007. Cf. Prasad and Ramesh; Isabelle Attane, "The Boys Are Wanted, The Girls Aborted: Asia's Missing Women," trans. Krystyna Horko, *Guardian Weekly* [London], 11 August 2006, Le Monde Diplomatique section, p. 6.

8. "GENDER RESEARCH: Too Many Men Could Destabilize Society," *Biotech Week*, 20 September 2006, expanded reporting, p. 564. Cf. Baculinao; Prasad and Ramesh.

9. Andrea Mrozek, "A Recipe for Social Disaster," *Calgary Herald* [Alberta], 28 March 2007, p. A16.

the members of our denomination are not of one mind over the precise conditions in which abortion can be supported, we cannot support abortion for such trivial reasons as not preferring the gender of the fetus.

The widespread practice of sex-selective abortion horribly treats females as inferior before they are even born. This is absolutely contrary to The United Methodist Church's long history of championing the biblical principle of gender equality.

Therefore, be it resolved, that the General Conference of The United Methodist Church strongly condemns sex-selective abortion as a particularly lamentable and violent expression of sexism. We call on religious, government, and community leaders to proactively pursue humane means for stopping the practice of sex-selective abortion. The General Board of Church and Society is encouraged to seek out and take advantage of opportunities to make this concern of our Church known to national leaders of the United States and of other nations.

ADOPTED 2008
AMENDED AND READOPTED 2016
RESOLUTION #2027, 2008, 2012 *BOOK OF RESOLUTIONS*

See Social Principles, ¶ 161K.

2027. Putting Children and Their Families First

Paragraph 161 of the Social Principles affirms that "We believe the family to be the basic human community through which persons are nurtured and sustained in mutual love, responsibility, respect, and fidelity," and ¶ 162 affirms that children are "acknowledged to be full human beings in their own right, but beings to whom adults and society in general have special obligations" and that "children have the rights to food, shelter, clothing, health care, and emotional well-being as do adults, and these rights we affirm as theirs regardless of actions or inactions of their parents or guardians. In particular, children must be protected from economic, physical, emotional, and sexual exploitation and abuse."

The Problem

Growing up whole and healthy is increasingly difficult for children. They face weakening support systems throughout society, from home to school to church, at the very time they are struggling with unprecedented stresses. They are forced to grow up too quickly, to make significant life choices at a younger and younger age.

The percentage of children in poverty is the most widely used indicator of child well-being. Growth in the ranks of poor children in the United States during the past few decades is attributed to the growing ranks of the working poor. The number of children living in extreme poverty (income below 50 percent of the poverty level) rose from 8 percent in 2006 to 18 percent in 2008, and continues to rise (*2010 Kids Count Data Book*).

Globally, children are increasingly at risk from the effects of poverty. In its State of the World's Children Report, UNICEF reported the Gross National Income of households in the least developed countries in the world as 1.43 percent of the Gross National Income of households of industrialized countries. Nearly 9 million children under the age of five die each year from common illnesses and malnutrition associated with poverty. Poverty undermines the health, abilities, and potential of millions more children.

Public Policy Implications

Too often we engage in public policy debate, make new laws and cut budgets and programs without putting the highest priority on how any change or policy will affect children and their families. In light of the critical nature of this issue, The United Methodist Church should press for public policies that:

1. Guarantee basic income for all families that include children;

2. Provide basic support services for families in economic crisis, including food and nutrition programs, crisis respite care, and home care services;

3. Mandate full and complete access to health and medical care, including health maintenance, prenatal care, well-baby services, care for minor children, and mental health services for all family members;

4. Assure safe and affordable housing for families without regard to number and ages of children; and

5. Safeguard protective services for children at risk of all forms of abuse.

Church Program and Policy Implications

Churches must strengthen and expand their ministry and advocacy efforts on behalf of children and their families. Every church and community needs a coordinated ministry that serves families with children in the congregation and in the larger community that works hand-in-hand with human service providers and ecumenical colleagues and that addresses the public policy concerns listed above.

The church has traditionally emphasized the integrity of the institutions of marriage and family and the responsibilities of parenthood. While these emphases should be maintained, a holistic ministry with families must, of necessity, be based on the broadest possible definition of family so that the great variety of structures and configurations will be included. Grandparents often function as parents, and many families are headed by single parents or "blended" through divorce and remarriage. Adoption, fostering, and extended family structures are among those that need the church's ministry.

Churches need to understand that all the problems described here happen to individuals and families inside the congregation as well as in the community. It is critically important that each congregation deal openly with the needs of its members and its community, and develop appropriate ministry responses for children and their families.

A network of child-serving institutions and agencies, from community centers to residences for at-risk children and youth, exists across the church. Many are local expressions of national or international mission, and others are related to annual conferences. These agencies meet critical needs and urgently require the financial, volunteer, and prayer support of congregations.

We call upon The United Methodist Church to:

1. Generate a plan in every local church for assessing ministry with children (in the congregation and in the community) and implementing a vision for ministry with children and their families that takes seriously the facts and perspectives presented above. This plan is to be overseen by the official decision-making body of each local church.

2. Celebrate the Children's Sabbath in every local church each October. Utilize the resource manual developed annually by the Children's Defense Fund (www.childrensdefense.org).

3. Continue and strengthen a task force formed of persons from general Church agencies who work on issues of child and family advocacy, in order to coordinate work. The task force is convened

annually by the Office of Children's Ministries of the General Board of Discipleship.

ADOPTED 2004
AMENDED AND READOPTED 2012
RESOLUTION #2028, 2008, 2012 *BOOK OF RESOLUTIONS*
RESOLUTION #26, 2004 *BOOK OF RESOLUTIONS*

See Social Principles, ¶ 161B.

2028. Nurturing Marriage and Family

WHEREAS, according to the Social Principles of The United Methodist Church, "We believe the family to be the basic human community through which persons are nurtured and sustained in mutual love, responsibility, respect, and fidelity"; and

WHEREAS, we recognize that support from a faith community can help every family, no matter what its configuration, to more effectively provide safety, nurture growth, and sustain healthy relationships; and

WHEREAS, many families throughout our world today suffer because of poverty, inadequate health care, violence in the home, violence in their communities, lack of knowledge for developing healthy relationships, and inadequate resources for times of transition or crisis; and

WHEREAS, we recognize that healthy marriages have a positive impact on all members of a family; and

WHEREAS, we believe that United Methodist general agencies, annual conferences, and congregations can join together to strengthen and support marriages and families;

Therefore, be it resolved, that the 2012 General Conference of The United Methodist Church support efforts to nurture families and marriages.

1. We call upon pastors to take seriously the importance of premarital counseling for those seeking marriage.

2. We call upon congregations to offer classes and programs related to parenting, relationships, faith formation in the family, communication skills, conflict management, marriage preparation, marriage enrichment, and coping with crisis.

3. We call upon pastors and congregations to offer support and resources for single persons and families in all their various configurations.

4. We call upon annual conferences to assist congregations through the development, identification, and promotion of programs and resources for single persons and families in all their various configurations.

5. We call upon the General Board of Higher Education and Ministry to offer resources for clergy in marriage preparation and marriage enrichment and in developing healthy relationships within their own families.

6. We call upon seminaries to train clergy in marriage preparation, marriage counseling, and marriage enrichment.

7. We call upon the General Board of Church and Society to study state and federal legislation (both proposed and already in effect) related to strengthening marriages and families and to make recommendations to Boards of Church and Society in annual conferences regarding the possible impact of such legislation.

8. We call upon The United Methodist Publishing House to continue publication of materials in support of marriage, parenting, and family life.

9. We call upon the General Board of Discipleship to continue to develop, identify, and promote resources and materials for ministry to single persons and families in all their various configurations.

ADOPTED 2004
AMENDED AND READOPTED 2012
RESOLUTION #2029, 2008, 2012 *BOOK OF RESOLUTIONS*
RESOLUTION #27, 2004 *BOOK OF RESOLUTIONS*

See Social Principles, ¶ 161B.

HUMAN SEXUALITY

2043. Response Team Ministry for Sexual Misconduct

Introduction: Misconduct of a sexual nature committed by laity and clergy is an ongoing problem throughout the Church. Three percent of women attending church in any given month reported being sexually harassed or abused by a clergyperson at some point in their adult lives according to a nationwide study (Diana Garland, "The Prevalence of Clergy Sexual Misconduct with Adults: A Research Study Executive Summary, 2009"; <http://www

.baylor.edu/clergysexualmisconduct/index.php?id=67406>, accessed 16 July 2010). Continued revelations about mishandlings of religious leaders across all faith communities offer a sobering reminder to United Methodists to face our own abuse crisis (M. Garlinda Burton, "United Methodists Need to Face Abuse Crisis: A UMNS Commentary," umc.org 2010; <http://www.umc.org /site/apps/nlnet/content3.aspx?c=1wL4KnN1LtH&b=5259669 &ct+8437677&tr=y&auid=6486686>, accessed 14 June 2010). The United Methodist Church averages between 140 and 500 known cases of clergy sexual misconduct annually in the US alone (Sally Badgley Dolch, *Healing the Breach: Response Team Intervention in United Methodist Congregations,* Doctor of Ministry, Wesley Theological Seminary, 2010, pp. 131-32). The most recent Sexual Harassment survey in The United Methodist Church revealed significant increases in sexual harassment perpetrated by laypersons (Gail Murphy-Geiss, "Sexual Harassment in the United Methodist Church," Chicago: General Commission on the Status and Role of Women, 2005). The responsibility for handling these complaints rests with our judicatory leaders.

Bishops and district superintendents are responsible for ensuring that the church responds to allegations of sexual misconduct by either a lay or clergy person within a ministerial relationship, attending to both procedural justice or pastoral concern. In the church's response to misconduct, there can be no true procedural justice in the absence of pastoral concern just as there can be no true pastoral concern without procedural justice. The dual needs of procedural justice and pastoral concern are far better met by team effort than by one individual. A full account of justice-making requires the involvement of different persons in distinct roles throughout a process of disclosure, adjudication, and healing. A trained Response/Intervention/Care Team is a group of persons with expertise in specific areas of trauma ready to be deployed by the bishop or bishop's designee to facilitate the process of healing mandated by the *Book of Discipline.*

Definition: Response Teams are called into a situation of trauma in order to promote the possibility of healing for the congregation and the individuals involved. Response Team ministry provides a way for judicatory leaders to enable effective assessment, intervention, training and resourcing of congregations experiencing events affecting congregational health by enlisting a group of persons with training, expertise, and resources in specific areas of ministry. Members may be paid or unpaid. The Response Team is not called to any judicial or disciplinary processes for legal resolution of a situation. The Response Team is called into action by the bishop or bishop's designee, often a district superintendent, and is accountable to the bishop.

Disciplinary Mandate to Provide for Healing: The bishop and cabinet are mandated to "provide a process for healing within the congregation" or other ministry context as part of the supervisory response (¶ 363.1*f*, *Book of Discipline* 2012) and judicial process (¶ 2701.4.*c*). The *Discipline* also allows for the use of a Response Team to provide pastoral care when handling and following-up on a complaint: the bishop may select "persons with qualifications and experience in assessment, intervention, or healing" to assist during the supervisory response (¶ 363.1*b*, *Book of Discipline* 2012). These persons may perform distinct roles, such as individual support for the accused and individual support for the congregation and families affected. These roles are in addition to any interim appointment made in accordance with the *Book of Discipline* 2012, ¶ 338.3. In all cases, the bishop initiates and guides the church's response to ministerial sexual abuse.

Effective use of a Response Team can lessen legal liability and promote justice. When victims feel that the church is attending to their needs and seeking a thorough process for justice-making, they are more likely to continue engaging the church in problem-solving and resolution rather than reactively pursuing civil procedures (e.g., suing the conference). Spreading the work of pastoral care and justice-making among several persons, each with a distinct role, also reduces real and perceived conflicts of interest. A trained and ready Response Team, assembled in a timely manner, can assist the bishop with the holistic task of justice-making.

The United Methodist Church commends the use of Response Teams in cases of sexual misconduct by ministerial leaders and urges judicatory leaders to train and employ them. Only 18 annual conferences in the US maintain an active, trained Response Team ("Active" is defined as having responded to more than one congregation within a three-year period. Six additional conferences used a Response Team once between 2007 and 2009. Sally B. Dolch, *Healing the Breach*). Between 2007 and 2009, these teams responded to 156 incidents, averaging nearly three cases per conference per year. Extrapolating this data to all jurisdictions, we estimate that an additional 112 cases of ministerial sexual misconduct are handled by annual conferences in the US every year without the assistance of a Response Team. We urge bishops, district superintendents, chancellors, and other conference leaders in The UMC to seek out training in the use of a Response Team, to organize and provide for training Response Team personnel, and to employ these teams as partners in the healing ministry required when someone in leadership violates the sacred trust of ministry through sexual misconduct.

For more information on how judicatory leaders and Response Teams may collaborate in promoting congregational healing, see *When a Congregation Is Betrayed: Responding to Clergy Misconduct* by Beth Ann Gaede and Candace Reed Benyei (Herndon, VA: Alban Institute, 2006, pp. 102-16) and the "Guide to Using a Response Team," http://umsexualethics.org/ConferenceLeaders/Response Teams.aspx.

ADOPTED 2012
RESOLUTION #2043, 2012 *BOOK OF RESOLUTIONS*

See Social Principles, ¶ 161J.

2044. Sexual Misconduct Within Ministerial Relationships
See page 775.

2045. Eradication of Sexual Harassment
in The United Methodist Church and Society

Since the mid 1970s when the term "sexual harassment" was first recognized, the world has seen an evolution in awareness, laws and litigation, policies, advocacy, and international collaboration to eradicate sexual harassment in the workplace. In our own communities we have moved from debating whether or not sexual harassment is even a problem to witnessing women and men join together across national boundaries to address it in global settings, churches and ministries, and multinational workplaces.

Since the 1990s, sexual harassment is a recognized form of sexual violence and misconduct in our societies and in The United Methodist Church. The Church declared sexual harassment a sin against individuals and communities, and a chargeable offense against our clergy or laity. Critical to our understanding of the impact of harassment is the recognition that it is certainly an abuse of power over another, not only inappropriate sexual or gender-directed conduct.

Definitions

Beginning with the continuum of behaviors that includes sexual harassment: Sexual misconduct within ministerial relationships is a betrayal of sacred trust. It is a continuum of unwanted sexual or gender-directed behaviors by either a lay or clergy person within a ministerial relationship (paid or unpaid). It can include child abuse, adult sexual abuse, harassment, rape or sexual assault, sexualized verbal comments or visuals, unwelcome touching and advances, use of sexualized materials including pornography, stalking, sexual abuse of youth or those without capacity to consent, or misuse of the pastoral or ministerial position using sexualized conduct to take advantage of the vulnerability of another. It includes criminal behaviors in some nations, states, or communities.

Sexual harassment is a form of sexual misconduct. The Social Principles define it as "any unwanted sexual comment, advance or demand, either verbal or physical, that is reasonably perceived by the recipient as demeaning, intimidating, or coercive. Sexual harassment must be understood as an exploitation and abuse of a power relationship rather than as an exclusively sexual issue. Sexual harassment includes, but is not limited to, the creation of a hostile or abusive working environment resulting from discrimination on the basis of gender" (¶ 161J).

To clarify further, it is unwanted sexual or gender-directed behavior within a pastoral, employment, ministerial (including volunteers), mentor, or colleague relationship that is so severe or pervasive that it alters the conditions of employment or volunteer work or unreasonably interferes with the employee or volunteer's performance. It can create a hostile, offensive environment that can include unwanted sexual jokes, repeated advances, touching, displays, or comments that insult, degrade, or sexually exploit women, men, elders, children, or youth.

Generally, anyone can be a target and anyone can harass—women, men, youth, interns, volunteers, all racial/ethnic groups, any level of employee, clergy, or laity. In the learning place, it affects any student of either gender, any grade, any teacher or professional, or any volunteer.

Businesses, governments, congregations, and organizations lose significant human and financial resources when harassment is permitted to devastate workers, customers, or members. It damages self-esteem, productivity, and ability to minister or earn wages. It can result in illness, absenteeism, poor performance, loss of promotions and opportunities. For students it can result in failure, absenteeism, isolation from peers, loss of self-esteem and learning potential, withdrawal from teams and groups, and illness. Families of the harassed and others in work, worship, and learning places are also victims of the hostile, intimidating environment harassment creates.

Harassment in the Church

In the church, harassment can occur between a staff person, pastor, committee or council chairperson, church school teacher or helper, student, camper, counselor, youth worker, volunteer, or chaperone, paid or unpaid. It can happen on the bus to camp, in a youth group or Bible study, on a church computer or in choir rehearsal. The devastating effects on persons when it happens in a faith community jeopardize spiritual life, theological meaning, and relationships. For some, the loss of a sense of safety and sanctuary can be permanent.

In 1990, the General Council on Ministries released the study mandated by General Conference in 1988 examining sexual harassment in The UMC. Then, half of the clergy, 20 percent of laity, nearly half of students, and 37 percent of church staff had had an experience of harassment in a church setting. Nearly 20 years ago we had much work to do to eradicate this form of sexual misconduct and violence.

Four quadrennia later, good work has been done toward the elimination of sexual harassment in the Church. Thirty-five annual conferences now assign oversight of harassment issues to a "team," and many conferences require sexual misconduct awareness training for all clergy. Since the General Conference mandated sexual harassment policies in 1996, more and more churches of every size continue to report policies in place (in 2007: 34 percent of smallest and 86 percent of largest membership congregations have policies—up from 9 percent and 36 percent, respectively, in 1995). The General Commission on the Status and Role of Women has provided support and counsel to victims and church officials in hundreds of cases.

But the most recent surveys of our progress in eradicating sexual harassment (2005 and 2007[1]) are very troubling: sexual harassment remains a significant problem for women and men, lay and clergy in our church settings, programs, and with church property (including computers and the Internet):

1. Awareness of the denomination's policy on sexual harassment is relatively high (higher among clergy than laity), but awareness of the resources for victims and congregations is much lower.

2. While every local congregation is required to have a policy and procedure on sexual misconduct, including sexual harassment, in 2007 only 34 percent of small and 86 percent of largest membership churches report that they do.

3. Ninety percent of pastors have attended at least one sexual ethics training, but only one of four pastors has attended supplementary training.

4. More than three-fourths of the clergywomen and half of the laywomen had experienced sexual harassment in the Church (only a third of laymen had); the most commonly reported settings were church meetings and offices, and workplaces and social gatherings at seminary.

5. Perpetrators are most often men and increasingly laypersons in the local church. Clergy commit over a third of reported offenses. A significant change since the 1990 study was significant increases in the number of laity harassing laity, and laity harassing clergy.

6. Local churches were most likely to trivialize reports/complaints while seminaries and UM offices were more likely to move toward action against offenders.

7. Personal friends and relatives were most helpful to victims, while district superintendents, personnel officers, and seminary administrators were among the least helpful.

8. The most lasting negative effects were inability to work with the offender, emotional impacts, and worsened feelings about self and the church.

9. Smaller membership churches need resources and training specifically developed for their unique settings and dynamics.

1. "Sexual Harassment in The United Methodist Church 2005," and the "Quadrennial Local Church Survey 2007," by the General Commission on the Status and Role of Women," Chicago, Illinois, Gail Murphy-Geiss, Principal Investigator.

In The United Methodist Church, constant vigilance is needed to keep effective, updated policies and procedures in all places in the church. Regular training of our lay and clergy leaders is a critical ongoing ministry of our church, with focus on the troubling use of "cyber-sex" (sexualized material in telecommunications) in church programs, with church property, or on church premises.

In 2006, a significant national symposium addressing sexual misconduct in The United Methodist Church, "Do No Harm," was held. At that critical event, participants asked episcopal leaders to focus on clergy training, lay leadership training, and early intervention with problem clergy. Advocacy and intervention teams have been working in many conferences but not all, and every episcopal area needs to maintain working, effective channels and procedures. We need and are grateful for strong episcopal leadership across the Church who maintain our achievements and forcefully address existing barriers to a harassment-free denomination.

A Vision of God's Hospitable Community

Sexual harassment destroys community. This alienating, sinful behavior causes brokenness in relationships—the opposite of God's intention for us. From the first biblical stories of human community in the garden to the letters of Paul to the first Christian communities, we learn that all of us, both female and male, are created in the image of God, and thus have been made equal in Christ. We are called to be stewards of God's community of hospitality where there is not only an absence of harassment, but also the presence of welcome, respect, and equality.

Therefore, the General Conference calls for intensified efforts worldwide to eradicate sexual harassment in the denomination and its institutions including these strategies:

1. Episcopal leaders implement plans to address and eradicate sexual harassment in each episcopal area including regular, updated training of clergy, early intervention with problem clergy, and regular training of lay men and women, especially in smaller membership churches;

2. The General Commission on the Status and Role of Women, in collaboration with appropriate agencies (including the General Board of Discipleship's Safe Sanctuaries ministry), continue to develop and distribute resources to reduce the risk of abuse

in local churches and increase United Methodists' understanding and action on sexual harassment in church and society;

3. The General Board of Higher Education and Ministry, in collaboration with appropriate agencies, develop and distribute resources on sexual harassment specific to those in ordained ministry and to lay leaders, students, faculty, and administrators of United Methodist-related educational institutions;

4. Annual conferences throughout the connection will encourage their local and national governments to collect accurate data on the incidence and nature of sexual harassment in their workplaces, and encourage their national governments to adopt laws, policies, and procedures for eradicating sexual harassment;

5. The General Commission on the Status and Role of Women continue to monitor and assess the Church's progress in eradicating sexual harassment and will seek ways to report its findings to the Church on the specific areas to be strengthened within the life of the Church including policy development, prevention, education, and training;

6. The General Board of Church and Society and the General Board of Global Ministries advocate for laws that prohibit sexual harassment in US workplaces, and continue to provide resources to the denomination on international initiatives to eradicate harassment and other forms of violence against women;

7. The Office of Christian Unity and Interreligious Relationships work cooperatively with the World Council of Churches "Decade to Overcome Violence" (2001-2010); and

8. The General Commission on the Status and Role of Women continue to conduct assessments of The United Methodist Church's progress to eradicate this behavior from the Church worldwide.

For more information and resources, see *The Book of Resolutions, 2012,* "Sexual Misconduct Within Ministerial Relationships" (#2044) and the original text of this resolution in *The Book of Resolutions, 2004,* p. 155.

ADOPTED 1992
REVISED AND ADOPTED 2000, 2008, 2016
RESOLUTION #2045, 2008, 2012 *BOOK OF RESOLUTIONS*
RESOLUTION #37, 2004 *BOOK OF RESOLUTIONS*
RESOLUTION #31, 2000 *BOOK OF RESOLUTIONS*

See Social Principles, ¶ 161J.

2046. Sexual Ethics as Integral Part of Formation for Ministerial Leadership

Background: A 2005 survey conducted by the General Commission on the Status and Role of Women (henceforth, GCSRW), "Sexual Harassment in The United Methodist Church," found a high number of incidents of sexual harassment in local churches and seminary settings (Gail Murphy-Geiss, "Sexual Harassment in The United Methodist Church," Chicago: General Commission on the Status and Role of Women, 2005). A 2009 study, "Sex and the Seminary: Preparing Ministers for Sexual Health and Justice" by the Religious Institute, found that few seminaries offer comprehensive courses in sexuality issues for religious professionals and most seminarians can graduate without taking a course in sexuality. Furthermore, tenure-track faculty are the least likely to teach sexuality-related courses. One of the report's key recommendations is that seminaries require coursework on human sexuality and healthy professional boundaries (Kate M. Ott, "Sex and the Seminary: Preparing Ministers for Sexual Health and Justice," New York: Religious Institute, 2009).

Since 1996, The United Methodist Church has called for "United Methodist-related schools of theology to provide training on the prevention and eradication of sexual harassment, abuse, and misconduct within the ministerial relationship" (*Book of Resolutions* 2008, p. 139; see also *Book of Resolutions* 1996, p. 131). The United Methodist Church has also urged seminaries to address issues of pornography and pornography addiction (*Book of Resolutions* 2008, pp. 155-56). Some schools have done well in teaching professional ethics and sexual ethics for ministry, and some faculty members work very hard to attend to the ethical aspects of the ministerial profession. These efforts, however, often depend on the passionate commitment of individual faculty members and administrators and are not yet integrated into the institutional structures of expectation in seminary education. (This dynamic goes beyond United Methodist theological education. In a 400-page, landmark study of clergy education by the Carnegie Foundation for the Advancement of Teaching, issues of sexual ethics and interpersonal boundaries are mentioned only three times, briefly. Charles Foster, Lisa E. Dahill, Lawrence A. Golemon, and Barbara Wang Tolentino, *Educating Clergy: Teaching Practices and Pastoral Imagination*, San Francisco:

Jossey-Bass, 2006, pp. 173, 315 and 338.) The United Methodist Church desires that professional ethics go beyond a special emphasis of lone faculty members and become an integral and intentional part of the fabric of ministerial formation. The United Methodist Church calls for seminaries and Course of Study schools to strengthen existing curricular coverage and training in professional ethics for United Methodists preparing for roles of ministerial leadership.

A multidisciplinary, multiethnic, racially diverse, ecumenical group of scholars, clergy, and consultants has unanimously agreed on the fundamental need to improve the structures of professional education for clergy. Many persons and groups have been included and consulted in developing a strategy to improve training in professional ethics for United Methodists preparing for roles of ministerial leadership. In April 2010, GCSRW convened a full-day seminar of seminary faculty, administrators, and consultants, with the participation of the General Board of Higher Education and Ministry, to examine the issue of ministerial preparedness and sexual misconduct and to develop recommendations for addressing this need. (Details of this seminar, along with resources and updates on this project have been made available online throughout the development and testing of these guidelines: http://umsexualethics.org/Education/SeminaryCurriculumDevelopment.aspx.) Two seminar participants from different United Methodist seminaries committed to offering a pilot course in sexual ethics for ministry in the fall semester of 2010. The success of these elective courses was reported back to GCSRW in January 2011. Meanwhile, GCSRW conducted listening sessions and pedagogical workshops with two additional United Methodist seminaries during the academic year 2010-2011. Plans are also being made for meeting with each United Methodist Seminary faculty by 2014. GCSRW collaborated in January 2011 with the FaithTrust Institute and the Religious Institute to present a panel and pedagogy workshop for the Society of Christian Ethics on "Teaching Sexuality from a Professional Ethics Perspective." (This session was made possible, in part, by a grant from the Wabash Center for Teaching and Learning in Theology and Religion, which is funded by the Lilly Endowment Inc. and located at Wabash College in Crawfordsville, Indiana.) GCSRW also presented its work in this area to participants of "Do No Harm 2011," a national sexual ethics

5. best practices of ministry (including topics such as: cyber-safety, Safe Sanctuaries [Joy T. Melton, *Safe Sanctuaries: Reducing the Risk of Child Abuse in the Church*, Nashville: Discipleship Resources, 1998]; healthy communications, clergy self-care; life-long sexuality education; ministering with sex offenders).

This common core of expectations will provide a baseline of preparation for ministerial leaders in The UMC. The regular, up-to-date sexual ethics training currently required of all clergy under appointment can build upon this shared foundation instead of having to start with the basics every time (*Book of Resolutions* 2008, p. 139). District committees on ordained ministry and conference boards of ordained ministry can expect clergy candidates to have a working knowledge and understanding of these facets of professional ethics and sexuality in ministry before they are appointed to serve a church. The continued training for clergy during residency can also build on this common core.

Be it further resolved, GCSRW will continue its work to improve training in professional ethics for United Methodists preparing for roles of ministerial leadership. Specifically, GCSRW will continue the four-stage plan described above.

Second Stage: GCSRW will continue to encourage and equip all faculty members to address these issues as they pertain specifically to their academic discipline. GCSRW will work with faculty groups to develop a series of curricular models and resources for each core MDiv course, tailored to each discipline of study: theology, ethics, evangelism, biblical studies, field education, etc. (including each of the basic graduate theological studies required for UM ordination, *Book of Discipline* 2008, ¶ 324.4a).

Third Stage: concurrent with the second, GCSRW will work with seminaries to address co-curricular and extra-curricular formation of seminary students. Specifically, GCSRW will create guidelines for intentionally utilizing the implicit curriculum (e.g., plagiarism policies and student honor codes) to model professional ethics, policies, procedures, and adjudication of misconduct.

Fourth Stage: GCSRW will develop strategies for greater ongoing collaboration among UM seminaries, and between seminaries, GCSRW and other general agencies, and boards of ordained ministry. GCSRW has already begun this work by participating in a roundtable discussion, "Improving the Gatekeeping Function by Seminaries and Denominations," convened by the FaithTrust Institute in March 2011.

Measuring Our Accountability: Seminaries have a great deal of flexibility to contextualize the ways in which these learning goals are reached. Each seminary has the freedom to shape its curricula and courses in ways that best suit the structures of the particular seminary. These guidelines do not specify an additional three-semester-hour course for ordination (although this is one possible way to meet the objectives listed above) but rather that the objectives be achieved throughout the entire professional degree (MDiv) or five-year Course of Study. It is intended that seminary administrators will coordinate how these topics will be covered across different academic courses and how each of these competencies and goals will be achieved throughout either track.

Be it further resolved, The United Methodist Church calls for:

1. District committees and conference Boards of Ordained Ministry to expect seminary and Course of Study graduates, beginning with the entering class of 2013, to have met the goals, achieved the competencies, and covered the content areas as outlined;

2. each seminary to report to GCSRW, by January 2014, its plan for meeting the above objectives;

3. Directors of Course of Study programs to report the same to GCSRW by September 2014;

4. GCSRW to assist the academic dean or other administrator at each seminary in interpreting these objectives, reporting the plan for compliance, and measuring the program's success; and

5. GCSRW to report the results of this effort to General Conference 2016.

ADOPTED 2012
RESOLUTION #2046, 2012 *BOOK OF RESOLUTIONS*

See Social Principles, ¶ 161J.

PORNOGRAPHY

2081. Pornography and Sexual Violence

Throughout the Bible, themes exist that highlight the imperfect nature of humanity and the hope for redemption through our relationship as God's children held in God's loving arms. The Old Testament laws of purity invite an understanding of the body created in God's image and accountable to God through right relationship. Christ shared with us a vision of the world that confirms our vulnerability and affirms sacred personhood. Jesus Christ provides a path to a loving and protective relationship with God and with others; treating our neighbors and families with love thereby fostering healthy physical and emotional relationships. John Wesley described the path to right relationship with God toward achieving invitation into God's kingdom as a journey toward Christian perfection. We struggle mightily throughout life to move toward that vision of Christian perfection in an imperfect world.

In the midst of our imperfect world we grieve at actions of sexual exploitation and pornography. Our Social Principles declare that, "We deplore all forms of the commercialization, abuse, and exploitation of sex. We call for strict global enforcement of laws prohibiting the sexual exploitation of children and for adequate protection, guidance, and counseling for abused children. All persons, regardless of age, gender, marital status, or sexual orientation, are entitled to have their human and civil rights ensured and to be protected against violence. The Church should support the family in providing age-appropriate education regarding sexuality to children, youth, and adults" (¶ 161F *The Book of Resolutions*, 2012).

The issue of pornography has undergone a dramatic change over the past two decades, one that shifts the definition, increases the complexity, and requires a new level of discussion. The use of violent, aggressive themes accompanying sexually explicit material has continued to increase. Television, the Internet, and emerging wireless technologies have made sexually aggressive media widely available, particularly to children and youth. Pornography is frequently relied upon as a source of information about sexuality. The Church is called to lead society in articulating an ethic that affirms God's good gift of human sexuality and that protects the vulnerable from sexual violence and coercion.

Common understandings of pornography no longer serve us well. Some believe pornography is a social evil because it is sexual, while others may defend pornography as a universal right to freedom of expression because it is sexual. Yet the truth is that pornography is not only about sex; it is often about violence, degradation, exploitation, and coercion.

While there is not widespread agreement on definitions, the following are suggested as the basis for dialogue:

Pornography is sexually explicit material intended primarily for the purpose of sexual arousal that often portrays violence, abuse, coercion, domination, humiliation, or degradation. In addition, any sexually explicit material that depicts children is pornographic.

The impact of pornography on behavior is difficult to measure. While there is little evidence that consuming pornography causes an individual to commit a specific act of sexual aggression, several studies suggest that such consumption is addictive and may predispose an individual to sexual offenses, and that it supports and encourages sexual offenders to continue and escalate their violent and abusive behavior. Few dispute the fact that a society that supports multibillion dollar industries promoting sexual violence as entertainment and portraying the abuse and torture of women and children in a sexual context is a society in trouble.

"Pornography, by its very nature, is an equal opportunity toxin. It damages the viewer, the performer, and the spouses and the children of the viewers and the performers. It is a distortion of power and fosters an unhealthy understanding about sex and relationships. It is more toxic the more you consume, the "harder" the variety you consume and the younger and more vulnerable the consumer. The damage is both in the area of beliefs and behaviors. The belief damage may include Pornography Distortion, Permission-Giving Beliefs and the attitudes about what constitutes a healthy sexual and emotional relationship. The behavioral damage includes psychologically unhealthy behaviors, socially inappropriate behaviors and illegal behaviors."[1]

The vast majority of pornography is inextricably linked to oppression of women. Its appeal will continue as long as sexual arousal is stimulated by images of power and domination of one person over another, most often male over female. Pornography is also linked to racism; women of color are invariably portrayed in the most violent and degrading ways. The destructive power of pornography lies in its ability to ensure that attitudes toward sexuality will continue to be influenced by images that negate human dignity, equality, and mutuality. Pornography contributes

1. Layden, Dr. Mary Anne, Co-Director, Sexual Trauma and Psychopathology Program, Center for Cognitive Therapy University of Pennsylvania, Testimony, The Science Behind Pornography Addiction, US Senate Committee on Commerce, Science and Transportation Web site, (expert witness testimony), http://commerce.senate.gov/hearings/witnesslist.cfm?id=1343 (18 May 2005).

to alienation in human relationships and distorts the sexual integrity of both women and men.

The expansion of pornography onto the Internet in recent years has made access easier for providers and consumers of pornography, and especially for adults who sexually abuse children. There is mounting evidence that pedophiles routinely use the Internet to lure children into their hands. A staggering number of chat rooms promote rape, incest, sex with children, child prostitution, and other criminal and violent behaviors.

Pornographic materials are being transmitted in cyberspace on a global scale, permitting access by both adults and children. Disclaimers warning of graphic materials on these sites have not prevented children from viewing them. Most sites offer free "previews" of graphic, obscene, and violent images and are linked to other sites. According to the United States Commission on Pornography, 12- to 17-year-old adolescents are among the largest consumers of pornography.

Those portrayed in Internet pornographic images are typically women, especially women of color. Female bodies are treated as objects and commodities, and female body parts are dismembered and magnified for pornographic effect and cyber-sexual consumption. The global nature of the Internet and its lack of regulation enables such materials that may be legal in one country to be accessed in a country where they may be illegal. National boundaries are easily crossed, and there is no international code of conduct to monitor pornographic material.

Care should be taken that children and youth are protected from pornographic materials. The supervision and love of Christian parents and other caring adults, supported by the extended church family, are the primary source of sex education. A comprehensive approach to sex education offers an additional basis for countering pornography. Children, youth, and adults need opportunities to discuss sexuality and learn from quality sex education materials in families, churches and schools. An alternative message to pornography, contained in carefully prepared age-appropriate sex education materials that are both factual and explicit and portray caring, mutually consenting relationships between married adults, is needed. Materials should be measured by the intentions expressed and the goals served, not by the degree of explicitness of sexual imagery. If we fail to provide such materials, accompanied by parental and adult supervision, we risk reliance of children and youth on pornography as the primary source of information about sexuality.

Our position on pornography is clear: We oppose all forms of pornography. We support laws that protect women and children and incarcerate those who are purveyors in the "industry" that instigates and expands child and adult pornography activities.

Addiction to adult pornography affects marital relationships, familial relationships, and may lead to criminal behavior. The addict must be treated with the best practices toward complete and total recovery and rehabilitation to ensure the best chance at future healthy relationships. Where rehabilitation and recovery fail we stand ready to support the spouses and families of addicts with love and care.

Addiction to child pornography is a deviant and criminal behavior that must be addressed through rehabilitation and legal means. We deplore the use of the criminal justice system as the sole means to address addiction; however, when the pornography addict resorts to criminal behavior that harms or hurts another person, especially children, or should rehabilitation not succeed, we support legal means by which the person with the addiction is held accountable and monitored by the legal system so as to protect the addict and the victims from future harm.

The United Methodist Church is already on record naming sexual violence and abuse as sins and pledging to work for their eradication ("Domestic Violence and Sexual Abuse," 2000 *Book of Resolutions;* "Violence Against Women and Children," 2008 *Book of Resolutions*) and stating that "children must be protected from economic, physical, emotional, and sexual exploitation and abuse" (Social Principles, ¶ 162C).

Understanding pornography to portray violence, abuse, and humiliation in a sexual setting, and understanding any sexually explicit depiction of children to be pornographic, we affirm that The United Methodist Church is opposed to pornography. We further affirm our commitment to quality sex education. To address pornography at its root causes we encourage United Methodists to join in:

1. action toward developing effective societal and governmental policies that eradicate child pornography, adult exploitation and enslavement;

2. education to encourage healthy relationships and behaviors;

3. compassion and encouragement for rehabilitation and recovery of addicts, their families, and victims;

4. sensible laws that focus on a restorative justice model; and encourage incarcerated persons to pursue rehabilitation and recovery.

We call upon The United Methodist Church, its general agencies, annual conferences and local churches, to:

1. educate congregations about the issue of pornography, especially Internet pornography, and enact strict policies that provide oversight of church-owned computers and sexual ethics education and training;

2. seek strategies to reduce the proliferation of pornography;

3. work to break the link between sex and violence by encouraging healthy human relationships;

4. monitor and prevent access by children and youth to pornography and sexually explicit material;

5. participate in efforts to ban child pornography and protect child victims;

6. promote the use of United Methodist and other quality sex education materials that help children and youth gain an understanding of and respect for mutually affirming sexuality;

7. provide educational sessions for parents on minimizing the risk to children from Internet usage. Encourage parents to establish rules for teenagers and children; encourage parents to utilize screening technology;

8. call for social responsibility in all media, including the Internet and in all public libraries, and work with local, national, and international groups that advocate for global media monitoring of images of women, men and children; and

9. participate in ecumenical and/or community efforts that study and address the issue of pornography.

ADOPTED 1988
REVISED AND ADOPTED 2000
REVISED AND READOPTED 2008, 2012
RESOLUTION #2081, 2008, 2012 *BOOK OF RESOLUTIONS*
RESOLUTION #42, 2004 *BOOK OF RESOLUTIONS*
RESOLUTION #36, 2000 *BOOK OF RESOLUTIONS*

See Social Principles, ¶ 161Q.

SPIRITUALITY

2101. Support Chrysalis at All Levels of the Church

WHEREAS, this is a ministry given to us from the Upper Room; and

WHEREAS, this brings a spiritual awareness of Jesus Christ to our youth in a unique, loving, patient, and kind way; and

WHEREAS, we rejoice in the truth which is revealed in this effort to involve our youth in a very important ministry in the Chrysalis movement; and

WHEREAS, youth may return to their local churches and be present and future leaders of the church,

Therefore, be it resolved, that:

1. The General Conference urge all annual conferences to increase their efforts and resources in the Chrysalis movement so that the youth of our churches know and are in touch with Christ; and

2. The General Conference encourage churches to enlist and involve their youth, girls and boys, in the life and work of Chrysalis so that they may return and be leaders within their own congregations.

Furthermore, General Conference encourages the General Board of Discipleship and Upper Room ministries to continue their emphasis on Chrysalis.

ADOPTED 2000
AMENDED AND READOPTED 2008
READOPTED 2016
RESOLUTION #2101, 2008, 2012 *BOOK OF RESOLUTIONS*
RESOLUTION #38, 2004 *BOOK OF RESOLUTIONS*
RESOLUTION #33, 2000 *BOOK OF RESOLUTIONS*

See Social Principles, ¶ 161*B*.

2102. Support the Walk to Emmaus at All Levels of the Church

WHEREAS, the Walk to Emmaus is given to us from the Upper Room; and

WHEREAS, this ministry brings a spiritual awareness of Jesus Christ to all adults in a unique, loving, patient, and kind way; and

WHEREAS, we rejoice in the truth which is revealed in this effort; and

WHEREAS, this ministry involves our members in a very important ministry; and

WHEREAS, this ministry enables members to return to their local churches and be present and future leaders of the church,

Therefore, be it resolved, that General Conference:

1. urges all annual conferences to increase their efforts and resources in the Walk to Emmaus so that the adults of our churches know and are in touch with Christ;

2. encourages churches to enlist and involve their adult members, men and women, in the life and work of the Walk to Emmaus so that they may return and be leaders within their own congregations; and

3. encourages the General Board of Discipleship and Upper Room ministries to continue their emphasis on Walk to Emmaus.

ADOPTED 2000
READOPTED 2008 AND 2016
RESOLUTION #2102, 2008, 2012 *BOOK OF RESOLUTIONS*
RESOLUTION #39, 2004 *BOOK OF RESOLUTIONS*
RESOLUTION #34, 2000 *BOOK OF RESOLUTIONS*

See Social Principles, ¶ 161.

2103. Lay Responsibility for Growth of the Church

WHEREAS, The United Methodist Church has steadily lost membership for many years in its country of origin; and,

WHEREAS, in the most recent year's totals, The United Methodist Church lost 70,000 members, thus exceeding the previous year's losses of 60,000 members; and,

WHEREAS, the historic strength of The United Methodist Church lay in well-equipped laity who were passionate in their beliefs; and,

WHEREAS, the clergy of The United Methodist Church continue to equip the laity for the task of winning commitments for Christ through witness, service, and transforming ministry; and,

WHEREAS, too many of our laity no longer claim that core responsibility of every Christian to find those who are lost and lead them into a church home,

Therefore, be it now resolved, that we, the laity, working with the clergy, accept primary responsibility for the growth and vitality of The United Methodist Church.

ADOPTED 2008
READOPTED 2016
RESOLUTION #2105, 2008, 2012 *BOOK OF RESOLUTIONS*

See Social Principles, ¶ 161.

2104. Encourage Supplemental Women's Ministries

WHEREAS, the needs of women today are complex, dynamic, and unique in every congregation and studies show that a variety of women's ministry programs is the most effective means of enabling and encouraging women to grow deeper in their relationship with Jesus Christ, to serve in their local church, and to serve passionately in mission outreach and justice advocacy in a lost and hurting world;

Therefore, be it resolved, that the 2016 General Conference of The United Methodist Church encourages the local church to provide women's ministry programs that fit the unique needs of the women in the church and are consistent with our values, theology, and social principles of The United Methodist Church.

ADOPTED 2016

See Social Principles, ¶ 161*F*.

¶ 162. III. THE SOCIAL COMMUNITY

The rights and privileges a society bestows upon or withholds from those who comprise it indicate the relative esteem in which that society holds particular persons and groups of persons. We affirm all persons as equally valuable in the sight of God. We therefore work toward societies in which each person's value is recognized, maintained, and strengthened. We support the basic rights of all persons to equal access to housing, education, communication, employment, medical care, legal redress for grievances, and physical protection. We deplore acts of hate or violence against groups or persons based on race, color, national origin, ethnicity, age, gender, disability, status, economic condition, sexual orientation, gender identity, or religious affiliation. Our respect for the inherent dignity of all persons leads us to call for the recognition, protection, and implementation of the principles of *The Universal Declaration of Human Rights* so that communities and individuals may claim and enjoy their universal, indivisible, and inalienable rights.

A) Rights of Racial and Ethnic Persons—Racism is the combination of the power to dominate by one race over other races and a value system that assumes that the dominant race is innately superior to the others. Racism includes both personal and institutional racism. Personal racism is manifested through the individual expressions, attitudes, and/or behaviors that accept the assumptions of a racist value system and that maintain the benefits of this system. Institutional racism is the established social pattern that supports implicitly or explicitly the racist value system. Racism, manifested as sin, plagues and hinders our relationship with Christ, inasmuch as it is antithetical to the gospel itself. In many cultures white persons are granted unearned privileges and benefits that are denied to persons of color. We oppose the creation of a racial hierarchy in any culture. Racism breeds racial discrimination. We define racial discrimination as the disparate treatment and lack of full access and equity in resources, opportunities, and participation in the Church and in society based on race or ethnicity.

Therefore, we recognize racism as sin and affirm the ultimate and temporal worth of all persons. We rejoice in the gifts that particular ethnic histories and cultures bring to our total life. We commit as the Church to move beyond symbolic expressions and representative models that do not challenge unjust systems of power and access.

We commend and encourage the self-awareness of all racial and ethnic groups and oppressed people that leads them to demand their just and equal rights as members of society. We assert the obligation of society and people within the society to implement compensatory programs that redress long-standing, systemic social deprivation of racial and ethnic persons. We further assert the right of members of historically underrepresented racial and ethnic persons to equal and equitable opportunities in employment and promotion; to education and training of the highest quality; to nondiscrimination in voting, access to public accommodations, and housing purchase or rental; to credit, financial loans, venture capital, and insurance policies; to positions of leadership and power in all elements of our life together; and to full participation in the Church and society. We support affirmative action as one method of addressing the inequalities and discriminatory practices within the Church and society.

B) Rights of Religious Minorities—Religious persecution has been common in the history of civilization. We urge policies and practices that ensure the right of every religious group to exercise its faith free from legal, political, or economic restrictions. We condemn all overt and covert forms of religious intolerance, being especially sensitive to their expression in media stereotyping. We assert the right of all religions and their adherents to freedom from legal, economic, and social discrimination.

C) Rights of Children—Once considered the property of their parents, children are now acknowledged to be full human beings in their own right, but beings to whom adults and society in general have special obligations. Thus, we support the development of school systems and innovative methods of education designed to assist every child toward complete fulfillment as an individual person of worth. All children have the right to quality education, including full sex education appropriate to their stage of development that utilizes the best educational techniques and insights. Christian parents and guardians and the Church have the responsibility to ensure that children receive sex education consistent with Christian morality, including faithfulness in marriage and abstinence in singleness. Moreover, children have the rights to food, shelter, clothing, health care, and emotional well-being as do adults, and these rights we affirm as theirs regardless of actions or inactions of their parents or guardians. In particular, children must be protected from economic, physical, emotional, and sexual exploitation and abuse.

D) Rights of Young People—Our society is characterized by a large population of young people who frequently find full participation in society difficult. Therefore, we urge development of policies that encourage inclusion of young people in decision-making processes and that eliminate discrimination and exploitation. Creative and appropriate employment opportunities should be legally and socially available for young people.

E) Rights of the Aging—In a society that places primary emphasis upon youth, those growing old in years are frequently isolated from the mainstream of social existence. We support social policies that integrate the aging into the life of the total community, including sufficient incomes, increased and nondiscriminatory employment opportunities, educational and service opportunities, and adequate medical care and housing within existing communities. We urge social policies and programs, with emphasis on the unique concerns of older women and ethnic persons, that ensure to the aging the respect and dignity that is their right as senior members of the human community. Further, we urge increased consideration for adequate pension systems by employers, with provisions for the surviving spouse.

F) Rights of Women—We affirm women and men to be equal in every aspect of their common life. We therefore urge that every effort be made to eliminate sex-role stereotypes in activity and portrayal of family life and in all aspects of voluntary and compensatory participation in the Church and society. We affirm the right of women to equal treatment in employment, responsibility, promotion, and compensation. We affirm the importance of women in decision-making positions at all levels of Church and society and urge such bodies to guarantee their presence through policies of employment and recruitment. We support affirmative

¶ 162

action as one method of addressing the inequalities and discriminatory practices within our Church and society. We urge employers of persons in dual career families, both in the Church and society, to apply proper consideration of both parties when relocation is considered. We affirm the right of women to live free from violence and abuse and urge governments to enact policies that protect women against all forms of violence and discrimination in any sector of society.

G) Rights of Men—Because we affirm women and men to be equal in every aspect of their common life, we also affirm the rights of men. We affirm equal opportunities in employment, responsibility, and promotion. Men should not be ignored or lose opportunities or influence because they are men.

We recognize that men are also victims of domestic violence and abuse. We encourage communities to offer the same policies and protection as provided for women in similar situations. We affirm the right of men to live free from violence and abuse and urge governments to enact policies that protect men against all forms of violence and discrimination in any sector of society.

We recognize that men's role in raising children is in equal importance to women's and call for equal rights as women in opportunities for parental leave. When parents divorce, men often have less contact with their children. We call for equal access to child-custody, but emphasize that the best interest of the child always is the most important.

H) Rights of Immigrants—We recognize, embrace, and affirm all persons, regardless of country of origin, as members of the family of God. We affirm the right of all persons to equal opportunities for employment, access to housing, health care, education, and freedom from social discrimination. We urge the Church and society to recognize the gifts, contributions, and struggles of those who are immigrants and to advocate for justice for all. We oppose immigration policies that separate family members from each other or that include detention of families with children, and we call on local churches to be in ministry with immigrant families.

I) Rights of Persons with Disabilities—We recognize and affirm the full humanity and personhood of all individuals with mental, physical, developmental, neurological, and psychological conditions or disabilities as full members of the family of God. We also affirm their rightful place in both the church and society. We

¶ 162

affirm the responsibility of the Church and society to be in ministry with children, youth, and adults with mental, physical, developmental, and/or psychological and neurological conditions or disabilities whose particular needs in the areas of mobility, communication, intellectual comprehension, or personal relationships might make more challenging their participation or that of their families in the life of the Church and the community. We urge the Church and society to recognize and receive the gifts of persons with disabilities to enable them to be full participants in the community of faith. We call the Church and society to be sensitive to, and advocate for, programs of rehabilitation, services, employment, education, appropriate housing, and transportation. We call on the Church and society to protect the civil rights of persons with all types and kinds of disabilities.

J) Equal Rights Regardless of Sexual Orientation—Certain basic human rights and civil liberties are due all persons. We are committed to supporting those rights and liberties for all persons, regardless of sexual orientation. We see a clear issue of simple justice in protecting the rightful claims where people have shared material resources, pensions, guardian relationships, mutual powers of attorney, and other such lawful claims typically attendant to contractual relationships that involve shared contributions, responsibilities, and liabilities, and equal protection before the law. Moreover, we support efforts to stop violence and other forms of coercion against all persons, regardless of sexual orientation.

K) Population—Since the growing worldwide population is increasingly straining the world's supply of food, minerals, and water and sharpening international tensions, the reduction of the rate of consumption of resources by the affluent and the reduction of current world population growth rates have become imperative. People have the duty to consider the impact on the total world community of their decisions regarding childbearing and should have access to information and appropriate means to limit their fertility, including voluntary sterilization. We affirm that programs to achieve a stabilized population should be placed in a context of total economic and social development, including an equitable use and control of resources; improvement in the status of women in all cultures; a human level of economic security, health care, and literacy for all. We oppose any policy of forced abortion or forced sterilization.

¶ 162

L) Alcohol and Other Drugs—We affirm our long-standing support of abstinence from alcohol as a faithful witness to God's liberating and redeeming love for persons. We support abstinence from the use of any illegal drugs. Since the use of illegal drugs, as well as illegal and problematic use of alcohol, is a major factor in crime, disease, death, and family dysfunction, we support educational programs as well as other prevention strategies encouraging abstinence from illegal drug use and, with regard to those who choose to consume alcoholic beverages, judicious use with deliberate and intentional restraint, with Scripture as a guide.

Millions of living human beings are testimony to the beneficial consequences of therapeutic drug use, and millions of others are testimony to the detrimental consequences of drug misuse. We encourage wise policies relating to the availability of potentially beneficial or potentially damaging prescription and over-the-counter drugs; we urge that complete information about their use and misuse be readily available to both doctor and patient. We support the strict administration of laws regulating the sale and distribution of alcohol and controlled substances. We support regulations that protect society from users of drugs of any kind, including alcohol, where it can be shown that a clear and present social danger exists. Drug-dependent persons and their family members, including those who are assessed or diagnosed as dependent on alcohol, are individuals of infinite human worth deserving of treatment, rehabilitation, and ongoing life-changing recovery. Misuse or abuse may also require intervention, in order to prevent progression into dependence. Because of the frequent interrelationship between alcohol abuse and mental illness, we call upon legislators and health care providers to make available appropriate mental illness treatment and rehabilitation for drug-dependent persons. We commit ourselves to assisting those who suffer from abuse or dependence, and their families, in finding freedom through Jesus Christ and in finding good opportunities for treatment, for ongoing counseling, and for reintegration into society.

M) Tobacco—We affirm our historic tradition of high standards of personal discipline and social responsibility. In light of the overwhelming evidence that tobacco smoking and the use of smokeless tobacco are hazardous to the health of persons of all ages, we recommend total abstinence from the use of tobacco. We urge that our educational and communication resources be utilized to support and encourage such abstinence. Further, we recognize the

¶ 162

harmful effects of passive smoke and support the restriction of smoking in public areas and workplaces.

N) Medical Experimentation—Physical and mental health has been greatly enhanced through discoveries by medical science. It is imperative, however, that governments and the medical profession carefully enforce the requirements of the prevailing medical research standard, maintaining rigid controls in testing new technologies and drugs utilizing human beings. The standard requires that those engaged in research shall use human beings as research subjects only after obtaining full, rational, and uncoerced consent.

O) Genetic Technology—The responsibility of humankind to God's creation challenges us to deal carefully with and examine the possibilities of genetic research and technology in a conscientious, careful, and responsible way. We welcome the use of genetic technology for meeting fundamental human needs for health and a safe environment. We oppose the cloning of humans and the genetic manipulation of the gender of an unborn child.

¶ 162

Because of the effects of genetic technologies on all life, we call for effective guidelines and public accountability to safeguard against any action that might lead to abuse of these technologies, including political or military ends. We recognize that cautious, well-intended use of genetic technologies may sometimes lead to unanticipated harmful consequences. The risks of genetic technology that can hardly be calculated when breeding animals and plants and the negative ecological and social impacts on agriculture make the use of this technology doubtful. We approve modern methods of breeding that respect the existence of the natural borders of species.

Human gene therapies that produce changes that cannot be passed to offspring (somatic therapy) should be limited to the alleviation of suffering caused by disease. Genetic therapies for eugenic choices or that produce waste embryos are deplored. Genetic data of individuals and their families should be kept secret and held in strict confidence unless confidentiality is waived by the individual or by his or her family, or unless the collection and use of genetic identification data is supported by an appropriate court order. Because its long-term effects are uncertain, we oppose genetic therapy that results in changes that can be passed to offspring (germ-line therapy). All the genetic procedures must be accompanied by independent, ethically oriented measures of testing, approval, and control.

P) Rural Life—We support the right of persons and families to live and prosper as farmers, farm workers, merchants, professionals, and others outside of the cities and metropolitan centers. We believe our culture is impoverished and our people deprived of a meaningful way of life when rural and small-town living becomes difficult or impossible. We recognize that the improvement of this way of life may sometimes necessitate the use of some lands for nonagricultural purposes. We oppose the indiscriminate diversion of agricultural land for nonagricultural uses when nonagricultural land is available. Further, we encourage the preservation of appropriate lands for agriculture and open space uses through thoughtful land use programs. We support governmental and private programs designed to benefit the resident farmer rather than the factory farm and programs that encourage industry to locate in nonurban areas.

We further recognize that increased mobility and technology have brought a mixture of people, religions, and philosophies to rural communities that were once homogeneous. While often this is seen as a threat to or loss of community life, we understand it as an opportunity to uphold the biblical call to community for all persons. Therefore, we encourage rural communities and individuals to maintain a strong connection to the earth and to be open to: offering mutual belonging, caring, healing, and growth; sharing and celebrating cooperative leadership and diverse gifts; supporting mutual trust; and affirming individuals as unique persons of worth, and thus to practice shalom.

Q) Sustainable Agriculture—A prerequisite for meeting the nutritional needs of the world's population is an agricultural system that uses sustainable methods, respects ecosystems, and promotes a livelihood for people that work the land.

We support a sustainable agricultural system that will maintain and support the natural fertility of agricultural soil, promote the diversity of flora and fauna, and adapt to regional conditions and structures—a system where agricultural animals are treated humanely and where their living conditions are as close to natural systems as possible. We aspire to an effective agricultural system where plant, livestock, and poultry production maintains the natural ecological cycles, conserves energy, and reduces chemical input to a minimum.

Sustainable agriculture requires a global evaluation of the impact of agriculture on food and raw material production, the

the goal of universal access to telephone and Internet services at an affordable price.

U) Persons Living with HIV and AIDS—Persons diagnosed as positive for Human Immune Virus (HIV) and with Acquired Immune Deficiency Syndrome (AIDS) often face rejection from their families and friends and various communities in which they work and interact. In addition, they are often faced with a lack of adequate health care, especially toward the end of life.

All individuals living with HIV and AIDS should be treated with dignity and respect.

We affirm the responsibility of the Church to minister to and with these individuals and their families regardless of how the disease was contracted. We support their rights to employment, appropriate medical care, full participation in public education, and full participation in the Church.

We urge the Church to be actively involved in the prevention of the spread of AIDS by providing educational opportunities to the congregation and the community. The Church should be available to provide counseling to the affected individuals and their families.

V) Right to Health Care—Health is a condition of physical, mental, social, and spiritual well-being. John 10:10b says, "I came so that they could have life—indeed, so that they could live life to the fullest." Stewardship of health is the responsibility of each person to whom health has been entrusted. Creating the personal, environmental, and social conditions in which health can thrive is a joint responsibility—public and private. We encourage individuals to pursue a healthy lifestyle and affirm the importance of preventive health care, health education, environmental and occupational safety, good nutrition, and secure housing in achieving health. Health care is a basic human right.

Providing the care needed to maintain health, prevent disease, and restore health after injury or illness is a responsibility each person owes others and government owes to all, a responsibility government ignores at its peril. In Ezekiel 34:4a, God points out the failures of the leadership of Israel to care for the weak: "You don't strengthen the weak, heal the sick, bind up the injured, bring back the strays, or seek out the lost." As a result all suffer. Like police and fire protection, health care is best funded through the government's ability to tax each person equitably and directly fund the provider entities. Countries facing a public health crisis

¶ 162

such as HIV/AIDS must have access to generic medicines and to patented medicines. We affirm the right of men and women to have access to comprehensive reproductive health/family planning information and services that will serve as a means to prevent unplanned pregnancies, reduce abortions, and prevent the spread of HIV/AIDS. The right to health care includes care for persons with brain diseases, neurological conditions, or physical disabilities, who must be afforded the same access to health care as all other persons in our communities. It is unjust to construct or perpetuate barriers to physical or mental wholeness or full participation in community.

We believe it is a governmental responsibility to provide all citizens with health care.

We encourage hospitals, physicians, and medical clinics to provide access to primary health care to all people regardless of their health-care coverage or ability to pay for treatment.

W) Organ Transplantation and Donation—We believe that organ transplantation and organ donation are acts of charity, *agape* love, and self-sacrifice. We recognize the life-giving benefits of organ and other tissue donation and encourage all people of faith to become organ and tissue donors as a part of their love and ministry to others in need. We urge that it be done in an environment of respect for deceased and living donors and for the benefit of the recipients, and following protocols that carefully prevent abuse to donors and their families.

X) Mental Health—The World Health Organization defines mental health as "a state of well-being in which the individual realizes his or her own abilities, can cope with the normal stresses of life, can work productively and fruitfully, and is able to make a contribution to his or her community." Unfortunately, mental health eludes many in our world resulting in considerable distress, stigma, and isolation. Mental illness troubles our relationships because it can affect the way we process information, relate to others, and choose actions. Consequently, mental illnesses often are feared in ways that other illnesses are not. Nevertheless, we know that regardless of our illness we remain created in the image of God (Genesis 1:27) and that nothing can separate us from the love of God (Romans 8:38-39).

No person deserves to be stigmatized because of mental illness. Those with mental illness are no more violent than other persons are. Rather, they are much more likely to be victims of violence or preyed on by others. When stigma happens within the church, mentally ill persons and their families are further victimized. Persons with mental illness and their families have a right to be treated with respect on the basis of common humanity and accurate information. They also have a right and responsibility to obtain care appropriate to their condition. The United Methodist Church pledges to foster policies that promote compassion, advocate for access to care and eradicate stigma within the church and in communities.

THE SOCIAL COMMUNITY
THE RESOLUTIONS

ACCESSIBILITY/EQUAL ACCESS

3001. Accessibility Grants for Churches

WHEREAS, it is essential that The United Methodist Church as a denomination find a way to assist local churches to find grant money to assist them in becoming more accessible by removing architectural barriers; and

WHEREAS, our denomination establishes many programs around specific groups of people, whether they be ethnic groups or age-targeted groups; and

WHEREAS, each of the groups that the church claims an interest in and sets priorities for includes persons with disabilities. There are more than one billion people living with disabilities in the world, of which 56 million live in the United States, according to United Nations data. The United Nations recently focused on the issue of disability by calling for institutions to become more accessible; and

WHEREAS, the *Book of Discipline* calls the Church to inclusiveness, and states: "A further mark of inclusiveness is the setting of church activities in facilities accessible to persons with disabilities;" and

WHEREAS, since 2000, more than 140 churches in the United States have received grants to help them increase their accessibility;

Therefore be it resolved, that The United Methodist Church set aside funds to again provide accessibility grants to churches in the annual conferences, and that the program be administered from within the General Board of Global Ministries.

ADOPTED 2000
READOPTED 2008

AMENDED AND READOPTED 2016
RESOLUTION #3001, 2008, 2012 *BOOK OF RESOLUTIONS*
RESOLUTION #44, 2004 *BOOK OF RESOLUTIONS*
RESOLUTION #38, 2000 *BOOK OF RESOLUTIONS*

See Social Principles, ¶ 162*I*.

3002. United Methodist Implementation of the United Nations' Standard Rules on the Equalization of Opportunities for Persons With Disabilities and the Americans With Disabilities Act

WHEREAS, the General Board of Global Ministries three decades ago called "United Methodists to a new birth of awareness of the need to include, assimilate, receive the gifts, and respond to the needs, of those persons with intellectual, physical, psychological and/or neurological disabilities, including their families"; and

WHEREAS, the General Conference resolved in 1980 to take major steps in adapting facilities, new and existing, such as "church sanctuaries, educational buildings, parsonages, camps, colleges, or other church-related agencies or facilities" so that they meet minimum guidelines for "barrier-free construction" (see "Barrier-Free Construction for People with Disabilities," 2008 *Book of Resolutions* #3304); and

WHEREAS, the Americans with Disabilities Act (ADA) has now been in existence for more than 20 years; and

WHEREAS, the United Nations adopted the Standard Rules on the Equalization of Opportunities for Persons with Disabilities (Standard Rules) in 1993; and

WHEREAS, the ADA's and the Standard Rules' primary goal is to promote access to all aspects of social interaction including education, employment, commerce, recreation, government, and transportation, and

WHEREAS, the Lord Jesus Christ set the example of ministering to those with disabilities as a priority of his earthly ministry; and

WHEREAS, we as United Methodists have a policy of "Open Hearts, Open Minds, and Open Doors;" and

WHEREAS, people around the world are affected by disabilities caused by land mines, war, disasters, and natural causes, and one in five Americans has one or more disabilities;

Therefore, be it resolved, that the assembled delegates to this General Conference of The United Methodist Church 2012 affirm our support of the full implementation of the provisions of the United Nations' Standard Rules and the Americans with Disabilities Act including Title I, which states that employers "may not discriminate against qualified individuals with disabilities" and will "reasonably accommodate the disabilities of qualified applicants or employees unless undue hardship would result."

Be it further resolved, that the General Conference of The United Methodist Church 2012 urge all our congregations and agencies to implement and enforce the provisions of the Standard Rules, ADA, and all disability-related programs within every area that members of The United Methodist Church reside with the same vigor and interest as they would any other law affecting their able-bodied constituency. This includes, but is not limited to the provision of accessible buildings, bathrooms, and parking; telephone access; hymnals and literature in large print and other alternative formats; closed captioning of all audiovisual media; amplification, assistive listening devices, and/or professional American Sign Language interpretation or other indigenous sign language interpretation and real-time captioning when needed.

Be it further resolved, that the General Conference of The United Methodist Church will show its adherence to the Standard Rules and the ADA by meeting in an accessible location and budgeting for accommodations needed by delegates and non-delegates, including but not limited to: providing large print and alternative format materials for visually impaired delegates and non-delegates; and providing professional American Sign Language interpretation or other indigenous sign language interpretation and real-time captioning for delegates and non-delegates to General Conference, including remote viewers. This is to be coordinated by the General Board of Global Ministries.

ADOPTED 2012
RESOLUTION #3002, 2012 *BOOK OF RESOLUTIONS*

See Social Principles, ¶ 162I.

3004. The Church and Deaf Ministries Steering Committee

Persons who are Deaf, late-deafened, hard of hearing or deaf-blind desire to serve the church and become a resource for the whole connection.

Structure

1. There shall be a steering committee composed of ten (10) members recruited by an assigned staff member of GBGM as follows: two persons who are Deaf, two late-deafened, two hard of hearing, one deaf-blind, one deaf institutional ministry professional, and two clergy with experience in ministry with persons who are Deaf, late-deafened, hard of hearing, or deaf-blind.

2. The committee shall be inclusive with regard to gender, ethnicity, jurisdictions, and different sign language and hearing abilities.

3. The steering committee members shall elect their own officers: president, vice-president, and secretary.

Tasks and Objectives of the Steering Committee

The Committee shall set an overall agenda utilizing allocated funds for the quadrennium and be charged with responsibilities including . . .

- providing resources for the general church, annual conferences, faith communities, and local churches; and working with general boards and agencies, and engaging in interagency cooperation especially with the older adult division and the task force on disability ministries.
- developing Christian leadership among the community of persons who are Deaf, late-deafened, hard of hearing and deaf-blind. This includes having the ability to attend seminaries or other credentialing systems for entering the pastoral ministry when God calls.
- encouraging and nurturing young people who are Deaf, late-deafened, hard of hearing or deaf-blind to engage in this ministry
- creating new places for worship with people who seek to worship with other people who are Deaf, late-deafened and deaf-blind
- engaging in ministry with persons who have been historically undereducated and underemployed
- improving global health through mission including communication in sign language or other means of communication such as assistive listening devices

Accountability

The Committee will be accountable to an assigned section of the General Board of Global Ministries sharing yearly progress reports and evaluation. The steering committee shall also report to The United Methodist Congress of the Deaf for discussion, sharing information, and plans for implementation.

Summary

In The United Methodist Church, the ministry with people who are Deaf, late-deafened, hard of hearing, and deaf-blind is a vital part of our four focus areas, developing leaders and creating new places for worship, including people that have not been included in worship, improving global health and engaging in ministry with the poor.

ADOPTED 2000
READOPTED 2008
AMENDED AND READOPTED 2012
RESOLUTION #3004, 2012 *BOOK OF RESOLUTIONS*
RESOLUTION #3009, 2008 *BOOK OF RESOLUTIONS*
RESOLUTION #111, 2004 *BOOK OF RESOLUTIONS*
RESOLUTION #101, 2000 *BOOK OF RESOLUTIONS*

See Social Principles, ¶ 162I.

AGING

3023. Older Adult Recognition Day

Whereas, special observances in The United Methodist Church are intended to illustrate the nature and calling of the church and are celebrated annually; and

Whereas, special observances are placed on the calendar to make clear the calling of the church as the people of God; and

Whereas, both the population in the United States and throughout the world is increasingly aging and growing older as more people are living longer; and

Whereas, the average age of the membership in The United Methodist Church is comprised of persons 60 years of age and older; and

WHEREAS, older adults make significant and important contributions in the life of The United Methodist Church and to the spreading of the gospel throughout the world; and

WHEREAS, the scripture commands us to "honor your father and your mother";

Therefore, be it resolved, that The United Methodist Church observe an annual Older Adult Recognition Day; and

Be it further resolved, that an Older Adult Recognition Day may be observed annually, preferably during the month of May. The day is to recognize and celebrate the gifts, talents, and contributions older adults make within and beyond the local church. The day should also provide congregations with the opportunity to learn more about the issues and concerns related to aging and older adulthood. The Committee on Older Adult Ministries will have responsibility for the supervision and promotion of the observance of this special day.

ADOPTED 2008
READOPTED 2016
RESOLUTION #3023, 2008, 2012 *BOOK OF RESOLUTIONS*

See Social Principles, ¶ 162E.

3024. Mission and Aging of the Global Population

Throughout the world, many older persons look to religion for meaning in life, for opportunities to serve, and for a way to address human suffering. The achievement of long life among increasing numbers of global citizens holds possibilities for an invigorated ministry by, for, and with older persons. In taking action, older people challenge discriminatory perceptions of the aged and reveal abundant talents and capacities.

From the earliest days reported in our Scripture, the stories of our faith have looked at aging realistically but positively. Ecclesiastes 12 catalogues the physical miseries of old age with the warning to "remember your creator in your prime, before the days of trouble arrive" (12:1). Nevertheless, the patriarchal stories, depicting individuals who lived hundreds of years, expressed the belief that life itself was good and, therefore, extended life was very good. Age was presumed to bring wisdom, and the elders of Israel were looked to for guidance (Exodus 12:21, etc.), as were, later, the elders of the church (Acts 20:17). Age brings its own pleasures, including grandchildren (Proverbs 17:6), and is marked by the beauty of gray hair (Proverbs 20:29). A life well lived, that is righteous in the sight of God, gives purpose to our aging; Psalm 92 vividly pictures the righteous elderly, who "will spring up like a palm tree . . . they will bear fruit even when old and gray; they will remain lush and fresh" (92:12, 14). Those who survive to old age are, therefore, to be honored, especially one's father and mother (Deuteronomy 5:16; Mark 10:19). It can be assumed that when Paul spoke of giving "honor [to] those you should honor" (Romans 13:7), he meant to include respect for older persons. A sign of the coming of the Lord is that not only young but also old shall be merry (Jeremiah 31:13). Zechariah's vision of a truly restored Jerusalem was one in which not only would once again the streets be full of boys and girls playing, but of old men and old women, who "will have a staff in their hand because of their great age" (Zechariah 8:4-5).

Through the centuries, the church has held varying attitudes toward older persons, but the prevailing tradition accords dignity to persons in old age. This tradition underpins our United Methodist Social Principles statement on rights of the aging, in which social policies and programs are called for "that ensure to the aging the respect and dignity that is their right as senior members of the human community" (¶ 162E).

Advances in public health and education, as well as control of infectious diseases, have contributed to these changes. Nevertheless, the extreme conditions of poverty, war and hunger, and the HIV/AIDS pandemic prevent realization of the biblical hope for a blessed old age. In situations of armed conflict, combatants increasingly target older persons. All too frequently, families and other caregivers abuse older persons in domestic and institutional settings. Income support and access to health care in old age apply only to a small minority in many countries. Age and gender discrimination often blocks access to the participation and involvement throughout the world. In these challenging situations, a greater proportion of older persons now take their own lives.

Many older persons live in vulnerable situations. They live in rural areas, working the land, and are predominantly female. Older persons are heavily concentrated in agriculture, with manufacturing jobs ranking a distant second. Women outlive men in virtually all countries. Most women past age sixty-five are widows, a trend likely to continue. They suffer low incomes and chronic illnesses. Less than 10 percent of older women in many poor societies read or write. Across the globe, traditional social support based on family structures continues to erode, leaving many elders in isolation with no one to care for them in their last years.

In some developing countries, older persons attract love and respect precisely because of their experience and their place as wise leaders and survivors within the community. Contrast this love and respect with some attitudes in the United States and other Western nations that deprecates old age because it is less "productive," or because physical energy and commercial images of beauty replace spiritual energy and the beauty of the inner soul. For this reason, the United States and other developed societies can learn much from other societies.

The United Methodist Church therefore calls upon

A. Local churches to:

    1. involve older adults intergenerationally and in ways that empower and encourage them to use resources for skills, knowledge, experience, and spiritual insight; and

    2. use resources from general agencies of The United Methodist Church that suggest actions and models for learning from other cultures and countries in their understanding of and appreciation of older persons.

B. Annual conferences to:

    1. involve older adults in the full range of programs of the conference, including Volunteer in Mission (VIM) projects; health ministries in which able older adults care for the frail elderly; public advocacy; and use of resources and action suggestions from the Committee of Older Adult Ministries of The United Methodist Church;

    2. ask itinerating missionaries to speak to constructive ways churches in the United States can: (a) learn from the customs, values, and practices of churches in other countries and cultures; and (b) support older persons in other countries and cultures through Advance Specials, VIM projects, and mission support; and

3. study the United Nations International Plan of Action on Ageing adopted in 2002 as a basis for action initiatives and guide to programming.

C. All general program agencies of The United Methodist Church to:

1. develop resources and programs that support and undergird the faith development of older adults and encourage their full participation in ministry;

2. identify specific actions in their ongoing programs and ministries by which families on a global basis can be assisted in caring for their frail elderly;

3. include older persons in training for care-giving in relation to mission and ministry globally; and

4. provide analysis and advocacy training to equip older adults to defend and expand public policies and programs that serve all elders.

D. The General Board of Church and Society and the General Board of Global Ministries to:

1. advocate support for older persons' needs and capacities in governmental and nongovernmental organizations, including the United Nations, the US government, and ecumenical and other nongovernmental international organizations; and

2. study and share with the whole Church pertinent issues related to the well-being of older persons, such as allocation of governmental resources for support and care, end-of-life issues, and avoidance of age discrimination in employment and community life.

E. The General Board of Global Ministries to include in mission education:

1. positive images of older persons in all countries and cultures, along with images realistically depicting the difficulties many of these persons have under conditions of poverty and isolation;

2. information about the "double bind" in which many poor societies find themselves by virtue of the demands of a growing young population and the demands of a growing older population; and

   3. resources for annual conferences and local churches that provide models for appropriate mission and ministry on the local level, and specific action and program suggestions.

  F. All general agencies and all episcopal leadership to:

   1. include older persons as full participants in programs and ministries from planning through decision making and evaluation;

   2. seek opportunities by which The United Methodist Church can affirm its aging members, and offer ways that older members can collaborate with younger persons in evangelism and renewal of the whole church, to the end that persons of all ages are called to the discipleship of Jesus Christ; and

   3. lift the prophetic voice of Christian faith to proclaim a vision of human community in which older persons are accorded respect and dignity as those made in the image of God and part of the human family.

ADOPTED 2004
READOPTED 2008
AMENDED AND READOPTED 2016
RESOLUTION #3024, 2008, 2012 *BOOK OF RESOLUTIONS*
RESOLUTION #313, 2004 *BOOK OF RESOLUTIONS*
RESOLUTION #297, 2000 *BOOK OF RESOLUTIONS*

See Social Principles, ¶¶ 162 and 165.

ALCOHOL AND OTHER DRUGS

3041. Alcoholic Beverage Advertising at Sporting Events

The United Methodist Church strongly protests the advertising of beer or any other alcoholic beverage at or near Olympics games and other sporting events. We consider it scandalous for any alcoholic beverage to be listed as a sponsor of the Olympics or any other national or international sports organization or event.

The Bible tells us that our bodies are "temples of the Holy Spirit" (1 Corinthians 6:13-20). Because we are created in God's own image, we should strive to perfect our bodies in God's image.

United Methodism has a long history of passionate, committed action against alcohol use and abuse, and encouraging people to abstain from alcohol. Susannah Wesley in a letter to John Wesley urged piety with these words: "Take this rule: Whatever weakens your reason, impairs the tenderness of your conscience, obscures your sense of God, or takes off the relish of spiritual things; in short, whatever increases the strength and authority of your body over your mind, that thing is sin to you, however innocent it may be in itself." John Wesley in his sermon on the use of money advised: "Neither may we gain by hurting our neighbor in his body. Therefore we may not sell anything which tends to impair health. Such is, eminently, all that liquid fire commonly called 'drams' or spirituous liquor."

Sports events receive great public attention and attract thousands of fans who attend or watch on television. Advertising of alcoholic beverages at these events is an attempt to increase the sale and consumption of alcohol by the viewing audience, many of whose members are underage. Abuse of alcoholic beverages contributes to many problems in society such as automobile accidents; violence, especially against women and children; risky behavior; and tragic deaths.

General Conference calls for these actions to be taken:

1. The General Board of Church and Society should provide advocacy, education, and resources about the harmful effects of alcohol marketing practices and engage United Methodists in action campaigns prioritizing public health. Further, that the General Board of Church and Society communicate with government leaders, public health organizations, elected officials, and sports organizations to achieve effective policies that protect public health and guard against predatory practices of the alcohol industry.

2. The General Board of Pension and Health Benefits continue its long-standing exclusion of alcohol manufacturers from its investment portfolio, and asks the board to challenge public media in its portfolio not to carry promotions of alcohol products;

3. All United Methodist agencies and related institutions should take into account the church's Social Principles and alcohol concerns and, specifically, consider the role of alcohol producers and their advertising and marketing practices as a factor in any decision concerning purchasing food products manufactured by them;

4. All United Methodist general agencies communicate, interpret, and advocate for this concern with their affiliated institutions.

ADOPTED 2000
AMENDED AND READOPTED 2004, 2012
RESOLUTION #3041, 2008, 2012 *BOOK OF RESOLUTIONS*
RESOLUTION #82, 2004 *BOOK OF RESOLUTIONS*
RESOLUTION #72, 2000 *BOOK OF RESOLUTIONS*

See Social Principles, ¶ 162L.

3042. Alcohol and Other Drugs

As God's children and participants in the gift of abundant life, we recognize the need to respond to those who know brokenness from the widespread abuse of alcohol and other drugs in our world. The experience of God's saving grace offers wholeness to each individual. In light of the reality of alcohol and other drug abuse, the church has a responsibility to recognize brokenness and to be an instrument of education, healing, and restoration. First, we must be committed to confronting the denial within ourselves that keeps individuals and nations from overcoming their struggle with alcohol and other drug abuse. Second, the alcohol and other drug problem must be understood as a social, economic, spiritual, and health problem. Third, the church has a fundamental role in reorienting the public debate on alcohol and other drugs by shifting the focus from punishment to prevention and treatment. This is rooted in the Christian belief in the ongoing possibilities for transformation in the life of each individual and in our world.

The alcohol and other drug crisis has reached global proportions. More alcohol and other drugs are produced and consumed than ever before. In consuming countries, with their attendant problems of poverty, racism, domestic violence, hopelessness, and material despair, alcohol and other drug abuse is a part of a continuing cycle of economic and spiritual turmoil.

Abuse of legal drugs (alcohol, tobacco, and pharmaceuticals) remains a leading cause of disease and death around the world. While recreational use of illegal drugs in the United States has declined, the use of drugs remains socially acceptable as levels of addiction and abuse continue to rise.

Growing numbers of cities, small towns, and rural areas around the world are caught in a web of escalating alcohol and other drug-related violence. As the findings of the regional hearings in the United States stressed: "Drug addiction crosses all ethnic, cultural, and economic backgrounds." Social systems are dangerously strained under the heavy weight of alcohol and other drug-related health and social problems. Meanwhile, the supply of drugs from developing countries continues to grow in response to high demand from the developed countries.

International strategies should reflect the need for balanced, equitable economic growth and stable democratic governments in drug-producing developing countries. Most importantly, any alternative strategy must be rooted in local communities. The most creative and effective approaches to the present crisis begin at the local level.

The United States policy response to the drug crisis has focused almost exclusively on law enforcement and military solutions. This policy, in some cases, has led to erosion of precious civil liberties and human rights, especially for poor and minority communities.

The United Methodist Church has long opposed abuse of alcohol and other drugs. In 1916, the General Conference authorized the formation of a Board of Temperance, Prohibition, and Public Morals "to make more effectual the efforts of the church to create public sentiment and crystallize the same into successful opposition to the organized traffic in intoxicating liquors."

During the 1988-92 quadrennium, The United Methodist Church launched a comprehensive Bishops' Initiative on Drugs and Drug Violence, which, through regional hearings across the United States, deepened the denomination's awareness of alcohol and other drug problems. The report of these hearings concluded: "Therefore, The United Methodist Church must play a key role in confronting drug and alcohol addiction. . . ." Today, The United Methodist Church remains committed to curbing drug traffic and the abuse of alcohol and other drugs.

In response to the alcohol and other drug crisis, The United Methodist Church commits itself to a holistic approach, which emphasizes prevention, intervention, treatment, community organization, public advocacy, and abstinence. Out of love for God and our neighbors, the church must have a positive role by offering a renewed spiritual perspective on this crisis. We commend local congregations, annual conferences, and general agencies and seminaries to take action in the areas of alcohol, tobacco, and other drugs.

I. Alcohol

Alcohol is a drug, which presents special problems because of its widespread social acceptance. We affirm our long-standing conviction and recommendation that abstinence from alcoholic beverages is a faithful witness to God's liberating and redeeming love.

This witness is especially relevant because excessive, harmful, and dangerous drinking patterns are uncritically accepted and practiced. Society glamorizes drinking, and youthful immaturity can be exploited for personal gain. The costs associated with alcohol use/abuse are more than the costs associated with all illegal drugs combined. Worldwide, millions of individuals and their families suffer as a result of alcoholism. The medical consequences of alcohol abuse include fetal alcohol syndrome—which is a preventable cause of mental retardation, cardiac defects, and pre- and postnatal growth retardation. Chronic alcohol consumption can have a damaging effect on every body organ, including brain, liver, heart, stomach, intestines, and mouth. Alcohol is a factor in many other social problems such as crime, poverty, and family disorder. The societal costs of alcohol abuse include lost productivity, increased health-care costs, loss of lives in vehicular accidents, and criminal activity.

Thus, The United Methodist Church bases its recommendation of abstinence on critical appraisal of the personal and societal costs in the use of alcohol. The church recognizes the freedom of the Christian to make responsible decisions and calls upon each member to consider seriously and prayerfully the witness of abstinence as part of his or her Christian commitment. Persons who practice abstinence should avoid attitudes of self-righteousness that express moral superiority and condemnatory attitudes toward those who do not choose to abstain. Because Christian love in human relationships is primary, abstinence is an instrument of love and sacrifice and always subject to the requirements of love.

Our love for our neighbor obligates us to seek healing, justice, and the alleviation of the social conditions that create and perpetuate alcohol abuse.

Therefore:

1. We urge individuals and local congregations to demonstrate active concern for alcohol abusers and their families. We encourage churches to support the care, treatment, and rehabilitation of problem drinkers.

2. We urge churches to include the problems of alcohol and the value of abstinence as a part of Christian education.

3. We encourage individuals and local congregations to develop prevention education for family, church, and community. We encourage sound empirical research on the social effects of alcohol.

4. We oppose the sale and consumption of alcoholic beverages within the confines of United Methodist Church facilities and recommend that it be prohibited.

5. We ask individuals and local congregations to study and discuss the problem of driving while intoxicated and impaired by alcohol or other drugs, and we support legislation to reduce such activity.

6. We direct the General Board of Discipleship and The United Methodist Publishing House to incorporate educational material on alcohol and other drug problems, including the material on prevention, intervention, treatment, and the value of abstinence throughout its graded literature.

7. We expect United Methodist-related hospitals to treat the alcoholic person with the attention and consideration all patients deserve. We urge the worldwide health-care delivery system to follow this example.

8. We urge all legislative bodies and health-care systems and processes to focus on and implement measures to help meet the special needs of those disproportionately affected by alcohol use.

9. We favor laws to eliminate all advertising and promoting of alcoholic beverages. We urge the General Board of Church and Society and local churches to increase efforts to remove all advertising of alcoholic beverages from the media. We urge special attention to curbing promotions of alcoholic beverages on college campuses as well as racial minority communities.

10. We urge the US Federal Trade Commission and agencies of other governments to continue developing better health hazard warning statements concerning the use of alcohol.

11. We urge the United States government to improve interagency coordination of drug and alcohol abuse efforts so that

there are uniform policies and regulations, and we urge the cooperation of all governments in these areas.

II. Tobacco

The use of tobacco is another form of drug abuse, even though it is legal. Overwhelming evidence links cigarette-smoking with lung cancer, cardiovascular diseases, emphysema, and chronic bronchitis. In addition, cigarette-smoking can negatively affect a developing fetus, and secondary smoke is a known carcinogen. The United Methodist Church discourages all persons, particularly children, youths and young adults, from using any form of tobacco.

We commend the suspension of cigarette advertising on radio and television. We are concerned about other advertisements that associate smoking with physical and social maturity, attractiveness, and success, especially those targeted at youth, racial minorities, and women. We support the rules of the US Federal Trade Commission and agencies of other governments requiring health warning statements in cigarette packaging. We are also concerned that the tobacco industry is marketing tobacco in developing countries.

Therefore:

1. We recommend that tobacco use be banned in all church facilities.

2. We recommend a tobacco-free environment in all public areas.

3. We recommend the prohibition of all commercial advertising of tobacco products.

4. We support expanded research to discover the specific mechanisms of addiction to nicotine. We urge the development of educational methods that effectively discourage the use of tobacco and methods to assist those who wish to stop using tobacco.

5. We urge the Department of Agriculture and other government agencies to plan for and assist the orderly economic transition of the tobacco industry—tobacco growers, processors, and distributors—into industries more compatible with the general welfare of the people.

6. We support comprehensive tobacco control policies and legislation that includes provisions to: a) support The Framework Convention on Tobacco Control (FCTC), the Global Tobacco

Treaty and its provisions; b) reduce the rate of youth smoking by increasing the price of cigarettes; c) protect tobacco farmers by helping them shift from tobacco to other crops; d) give the US Food and Drug Administration full authority to regulate nicotine as a drug in the United States; and e) fund anti-tobacco research and advertising, as well as education and prevention campaigns.

III. Drugs

Pharmacologically, a drug is any substance that by its chemical nature alters the structure or function of any living organism. This broad definition encompasses a wide range of substances, many of which are psychoactive and have the potential for abuse. These include marijuana, narcotics, sedatives and stimulants, psychedelics, and hallucinogens. Additionally, commonly used products such as glue, paint thinners, and gasoline have the potential to be abused as inhalants. The United Methodist Church grieves the widespread misuse of drugs and other commonly used products that alter mood, perception, consciousness, and behavior of persons among all ages, classes, and segments of our society.

A. Marijuana

Like alcohol and tobacco, marijuana is frequently a precursor to the use of other drugs. The active ingredient is THC, which affects the user by temporarily producing feelings of euphoria or relaxation. An altered sense of body image and bouts of exaggerated laughter are commonly reported. However, studies reveal that marijuana impairs short-term memory, altering sense of time and reducing the ability to perform tasks requiring concentration, swift reactions, and coordination. Some countries permit the use of marijuana in medicines. Recently, some states in the United States have passed legislation permitting the medical use of marijuana. Some studies indicate circumstances in which marijuana can have an important palliative medicinal effect unavailable through other means. The medical use of any drug, however, should not be seen as encouraging recreational use of it. We urge all persons to abstain from all use of marijuana, unless it has been legally prescribed in a form appropriate for treating a particular medical condition.[1]

1. Performance Resource Press, Inc., Troy, Michigan.

B. Sedatives and Stimulants

Sedatives, which include barbiturates and tranquilizers, are prescribed appropriately for treatment of anxiety. These legally prescribed drugs need to be taken only under appropriate medical supervision. The use of this class of drugs can result in dependence.

Severe physical dependence on barbiturates can develop at doses higher than therapeutic doses, and withdrawal is severe and dangerous. The combination of alcohol and barbiturates is potentially lethal.

Stimulants range from amphetamines such as methamphetamine ("crystal meth") to mild stimulants such as caffeine and nicotine. Prescribed for obesity, sleep disorders, hyperactivity, fatigue, and depression, stimulants produce a temporary sense of vitality, alertness, and energy.

Unlike other stimulants, cocaine has limited medical uses. When the powder form is inhaled, cocaine is a highly addictive central nervous system stimulant that heightens the body's natural response to pleasure and creates a euphoric high, and has the potential to be extremely lethal. "Crack," a crystallized form of cocaine, is readily available because of its lesser cost. Addiction often comes from one use of the substance.

C. Psychedelics or Hallucinogens

Psychedelics or hallucinogens, which include LSD, psilocybin, mescaline, PCP, and DMT, produce changes in perception and altered states of consciousness. Not only is medical use of psychedelics or hallucinogens limited, if present at all, but the use of these drugs may result in permanent psychiatric problems.

D. Narcotics

Narcotics are prescribed for the relief of pain, but the risk of physical and psychological dependencies is well documented. Derived from the opium plant, natural narcotics include heroin, morphine, codeine, and Percodan, while synthetic narcotics include oxycodone, methadone, and meperidine.

Therefore, as The United Methodist Church:

1. We oppose the use of all drugs, except in cases of appropriate medical supervision.

2. We encourage the church to develop honest, objective, and factual drug education for children, youths, and adults as part of a comprehensive prevention education program.

3. We urge the church to coordinate its efforts with ecumenical, interfaith, and community groups in prevention, rehabilitation, and policy statements.

4. We encourage the annual conferences to recognize the unique impact of drugs and its related violence upon urban and rural areas and provide appropriate ministries and resources.

5. We strongly encourage annual conferences to develop leadership training opportunities and resources for local church pastors and laity to help them with counseling individuals and families who have alcohol- and other drug-related problems; counseling those bereaved by alcohol- and other drug-related deaths and violence; and teaching stress management to church workers in communities with high alcohol and other drug activity.

6. We support comprehensive tobacco control policies and legislation that includes provisions to: a) reduce the rate of youth smoking by increasing the price of cigarettes; b) protect tobacco farmers by helping them shift from tobacco to other crops; c) give the US Food and Drug Administration full authority to regulate nicotine as a drug in the United States; d) fund anti-tobacco research and advertising, as well as education and prevention campaigns.

7. We urge redevelopment of more effective methods of treatment of drug abuse and addiction.

8. We support government policies that restrict access to over-the-counter drugs such as ephedrine derivatives that can be converted to illegal and addictive drugs; for example, "crystal meth."

9. We support government policies concerning drugs that are compatible with our Christian beliefs about the potential transformation of all individuals.

10. We urge all United Methodist churches to work for a minimum legal drinking age of twenty-one years in their respective states/nations.

11. We support strong, humane law-enforcement efforts against the illegal sale of all drugs, and we urge that those arrested for possession and use of illegally procured drugs be subject to education and rehabilitation.

12. We note with deep concern that law enforcement against possession and use of illegally procured drugs has resulted in a

dramatic increase in jail and prison populations, often consisting disproportionally of poor, minority, young persons, often due to huge sentencing disparities between possession of "crack" cocaine (the cheaper form, used more by poor minorities, where possession of only 5 grams is subject to a five-year mandatory minimum sentence) and possession of powder cocaine (the more expensive and purer form where possession of 500 grams or more is necessary to invoke a five-year mandatory minimum sentence), even though the two forms are pharmacologically identical, and therefore call for fairness in sentencing through reform of sentencing guidelines governing the possession and use of powder and crack cocaine

ADOPTED 1996
AMENDED AND READOPTED 2000, 2004, 2008, 2012, 2016
RESOLUTION #3042, 2008, 2012 *BOOK OF RESOLUTIONS*
RESOLUTION #83, 2004 *BOOK OF RESOLUTIONS*
RESOLUTION #73, 2000 *BOOK OF RESOLUTIONS*

See Social Principles, ¶ 162L.

3043. Keep Children and Youth Free From Alcohol and Other Drugs

Our Christian faith calls us to teach and lead children and youth through Jesus' example. By his example, we are called to give children special attention enabling them to be free from harm (Matthew 19:13-15 NRSV). Alarming statistics make it clear that the United States and many other countries have not given the proper attention to the use of alcohol and other drugs by children and youth and that as a society, we tolerate access to alcohol and other drugs by underage young people. For example, it is illegal in most US states to sell or give alcoholic beverages to those under 21, and illicit use and sale of controlled substances is a crime at any age, yet more than a third of children begin using alcohol before they are teens and one in ten young teens is a regular user of marijuana and other drugs. Research shows that alcohol and other drugs bring harm to growing bodies and minds. Young people with inner stamina, self-esteem, and a strong and vital faith can more readily say, "no" to alcohol and other drugs. To address this critical problem, many schools have instituted programs on alcohol and other drugs. However, the Justice Department reports that many school programs aimed to help young people have not deterred their use of alcohol and other drugs. Inattention to this critical issue and the failure of many school programs demonstrates the importance of a comprehensive action plan among faith communities to address this crisis.

Therefore, be it resolved, that The United Methodist Church supports efforts to keep children and youth alcohol free, drug free, and safe from access to illicit drug use. By following a comprehensive approach to this issue young people can understand the importance of avoiding use of alcohol and other illicit drugs to ensure that they live full and healthy lives.

An Action Plan for the Church to Combat the Use of Alcohol and Other Illicit Drugs Among Children and Youth

1. We call upon individual families to pray for their children and to teach their children by precept and example the preference of avoiding beverage alcohol and illicit drugs and resisting peer pressures as a commitment to a healthy life and faith.

2. We call upon all people to pray and give moral and financial support to community, church, and other efforts to discourage children and teens from the use of alcohol and other drugs.

3. We call upon our local congregations to include in their Christian education programs and their worship services resources, studies, and seminars that emphasize to children and youth the detrimental effects of alcohol and other drugs.

4. We call upon local congregations to observe an annual Drug and Alcohol Awareness Sunday, and to prioritize this issue within the life of the congregation as a way to challenge young people and their elders to say "no" as an aspect of their commitment to grow in their Christian faith.

5. We further call upon local congregations to create a substance abuse ministry incorporating education, resources, and support for prevention and recovery which emphasizes our commitment to healing and love that is free of judgment, particularly as it relates to children and youth.

6. We call upon our fellow citizens and countries to support legislation that will help to curtail availability of alcoholic beverages to youth and to support public programs that help to instill values in young people that will help them to have drug-and-alcohol-free lives.

7. We call upon other religious bodies to join us in adopting resolutions and supporting efforts to curtail alcohol and drug abuse in our communities, states, and nation.

8. We direct the General Board of Church and Society and the General Board of Discipleship to develop and promote resource materials to implement this concern within the connection.

ADOPTED 2000
REVISED AND READOPTED 2008 AND 2016
RESOLUTION #3043, 2008, 2012 *BOOK OF RESOLUTIONS*
RESOLUTION #84, 2004 *BOOK OF RESOLUTIONS*
RESOLUTION #74, 2000 *BOOK OF RESOLUTIONS*

See Social Principles, ¶ 162L.

BLACK AMERICANS

3061. Black Family Life

Our Social Principles state that "we believe the family to be the basic human community through which persons are nurtured and sustained in mutual love, responsibility, respect, and fidelity" (¶ 161B).

Families of all types in the United States are vulnerable to social and economic change.

Black families today face a myriad of challenges including violence within their geographical community, higher than average high school drop-out rates, single parent households, Black males serving jail and prison terms, health problems, higher than average unemployment rates, and economic stress that contribute to many of our families living without a future of hope.

We call upon GBOD (General Board of Discipleship) to identify resources and materials to assist local churches. These resources will be posted on the GBOD website and promoted at meetings, events, and conferences. We call upon local churches to develop programs of mentoring, counseling, conflict resolution or strategies to strengthen Black family life germane to the community in which it resides.

ADOPTED 1992
AMENDED AND READOPTED 2000, 2004, 2012

RESOLUTION #3061, 2008, 2012 *BOOK OF RESOLUTIONS*
RESOLUTION #57, 2004 *BOOK OF RESOLUTIONS*
RESOLUTION #51, 2000 *BOOK OF RESOLUTIONS*

See Social Principles, ¶ 162A.

3062. African American Methodist Heritage Center (AAMHC)

The history, heritage and hopes of United Methodists of African American descent are inextricably intertwined with the history, heritage, and hopes of John Wesley's Methodism since its beginnings in North America. Yet, the whole church has been slow to celebrate that linkage, perhaps due to a lack of knowledge and understanding of the story of trials and triumphs.

It is not widely known that:

- In 1760 the first person of African heritage to be converted to Methodism was Peter Denis;
- In 1765 when Robert Strawbridge preached in Baltimore one of the speakers was a man of African heritage, Caleb Hyland, who later became a member of Sharp Street Methodist Church, one of Methodism's oldest African American Churches;
- The first Methodist class meeting in New York City included a Black woman named Betty, a servant of Barbara Heck;
- John Wesley himself chided a group at Fells Point in Baltimore for failing to include a group of Black persons as full participants; and
- Black Harry Hosier was a great preacher and colleague of Francis Asbury and, along with Richard Allen, was among the attendees at the Christmas Conference of 1784 when the Methodist Church in North American was organized.

The full and rich history of African Americans in Methodism is still unfolding. It is the vision of the African American Methodist Heritage Center to facilitate the revelation of that history so that it informs the present and builds hope for the future. Through the Heritage Center, African American United Methodists are seeking to recover and preserve the stories and the artifacts of the celebrations and the calamities, the accomplishments and the adversities, the connection and separation, and the whole gamut of experiences encountered over the nearly three hundred years of the church's journey in America. Methodism, as well as the American society in general, struggled with the sin of racism and segregation. African American Methodists as well as non-African American Methodists dared to be proactive in the long pursuit of justice and equality and full personhood under God.

Failure to remember the full story of the depths from which the journey started will doom those who fail to remember to the fate of not recognizing that history oft repeats itself. Even in the twenty-first century vestiges of racial bigotry overshadow the claims of some persons that racism is in the past and is not impacting the dream that we can be "one people under God".

The American Poet Langston Hughes raised the question in his poem "Harlem," ". . . . What happens to a dream deferred? Does it dry up like a raisin in the sun? . . . . or does it just explode?" The question is very relevant to the ministry of the African American Methodist Heritage Center should there not be adequate support from the total denomination to implement the dream and to maintain the Heritage Center.

We know that God "Makes a way out of no way," and reality out of dreams. An African American Methodist Heritage Center that is affirmed, supported, and sustained by ALL of United Methodism, is a living testimony to how those who were victimized and those who caused their victimization have been able, with God's help, to make of trials and tribulations, everlasting triumph! The Heritage Center is telling the story of the rocky road Methodism has travelled, and it also is an expression of how a people who believed and trusted when there was no reason to believe and trust sustained themselves and made visible the "Amazing Grace" of God.

As people with a memory and as people of hope, the General Conference of The United Methodist Church affirms the need to remember the past and to live through the present into a future that is richer and stronger because of our journey together. Therefore:

WHEREAS, Black Methodists for Church Renewal (BMCR) and other interested United Methodists had the vision that there be an African American Methodist Heritage Center to recover, preserve, and share the rich history and invaluable contributions of African Americans in The United Methodist Church and its predecessor denominations; and

WHEREAS, the initiative was taken to create a Board of Trustees that established the African American Methodist Heritage Center, which is properly organized and incorporated as a not-for-profit organization under the law of the state of New Jersey and approved as a 501(c) (3) tax exempt organization by the Internal Revenue Service; and

WHEREAS, the 2004 General Conference of The United Methodist Church approved a resolution, "African American Methodist Heritage Center" [#71, *The Book of Resolutions, 2004*], that affirmed the concept of the Heritage Center and authorized the Board of Trustees to pursue funding through the United Methodist Development Fund (now The United Methodist Development Center); and

WHEREAS, the General Commission on Archives and History has partnered with the board of trustees in the development and ministry of the African American Methodist Heritage Center by officially accepting the Heritage Center to be housed in the Archives Building where the collection is protected by proper scientifically controlled systems for the preservation, cataloguing and maintenance by staff to enable research into the story of African Americans in Methodism; and

WHEREAS, the Heritage Center has implemented many aspects of its Strategic Plan for Ministry, that include providing workshops and some resources; and

WHEREAS, The United Methodist Church in its entirety, desires more effective fulfillment of the ministry of the Heritage Center; and

WHEREAS, the fund-raising efforts to date have yielded limited resources for adequately addressing the resource and information needs expressed by the constituency;

Therefore, be it resolved, that permission is continued for fund raising by the African American Methodist Heritage Center and for the continued development of an endowment through the United Methodist Church Foundation; and

Be it further resolved, that the General Conference recognize that Discipleship Ministries, Higher Education and Ministry, Global Ministries, the General Commission on Archives and History, and the General Commission on Religion and Race have cooperated in the undergirding of the ministry of the Heritage Center and encourage all of the general agencies to determine ways and means whereby they too, can support this ministry; and

Be it further resolved, that the Heritage Center will be intentional in reaching out to the Pan-Methodist Commission membership to encourage the identification, preservation, and sharing of artifacts and memorabilia of our common Methodist heritage that will benefit the seven individual denominations, and Methodism as a whole, in telling the full story of Methodism in regard to the African American experience (The African Methodist Episcopal Church, The African American Methodist Episcopal Zion Church, The Christian Methodist Episcopal Church, The Union American Methodist Episcopal Church, The American Union Methodist Protestant Church, The Free Methodist Church).

Be it further resolved, that all United Methodists work, study, support, and pray for the recovery, preservation, and sharing of the unique story of African Americans in Methodism, recognizing that to do so is embracing and remembering the WHOLE story of Methodism.

ADOPTED 2008
AMENDED AND READOPTED 2016
RESOLUTION #3062, 2012 *BOOK OF RESOLUTIONS*
RESOLUTION #3063, 2008 *BOOK OF RESOLUTIONS*

See Social Principles, ¶ 162*A*.

3063. Resourcing Black Churches in Urban Communities

WHEREAS, the struggle for social, economic, and political survival of Black people in the United States is manifested in their historical migration to urban centers; and

WHEREAS, the problems that have evolved through the decades now face this population of people, isolated from access to the material resources needed to unleash its power and creativity in a manner that will build rather than destroy communities; and

WHEREAS, United Methodist Black churches in urban communities have historically been centers of spiritual nurture and social and political action that have cared for the youth and offered viable alternatives to the negative aspects of decaying urban centers; and

WHEREAS, there is a demonstrated need in all urban com-munities in this country for strong, vital Black congregations to reach into the hurts and pains of the community and provide the spiritual revival that is needed in order to reclaim individuals and communities and manifest the healing power of God to combat drugs, violence, and a growing sense of hopelessness; and

WHEREAS, the gospel mandates that we "promote the welfare of the city where I have sent you into exile. Pray to the LORD for it, because your future depends on its welfare" (Jeremiah 29:7); and

WHEREAS, United Methodist Black congregations in urban communities are called, as are all churches, to minister to the needs of persons in the communities where the church is located; and

WHEREAS, while the conditions in urban communities for the Black diaspora continue to worsen, including anti-Black violence, and the need for grounding in a faith and reliance on the power of God for the strength and vision to reclaim and rebuild strong, proud, faith-centered communities grows daily, the resources and persons in Black urban congregations decrease;

Therefore, be it resolved, that the General Conference direct the General Board of Discipleship to develop resources, programs, and strategies that will enable the development of Black leadership, such as the Convocation for the Pastors of Black Churches, and specific programs and strategies that will foster financial self-sufficiency, such as launching a stewardship education program.

Be it further resolved, that the training events designed and implemented by the General Board of Discipleship and General Board of Global Ministries (School of Congregational Development, Path1 trainings, Convocation for the Pastors of Black Churches, and others) include training components that address the needs of Black churches and communities.

Be it further resolved, that the General Board of Global Ministries work with emerging and existing Black churches in urban communities to develop and maintain vital congregations providing practical ministries and missions that address the spiritual, social, and economic decline in these communities.

Be it further resolved, that the General Board of Global Ministries and the General Board of Discipleship coordinate their work in relation to strengthening urban Black congregations with the annual conferences and urban ministry units of annual conferences, and the Strengthening the Black Church for the Twenty-First Century initiative.

ADOPTED 1992
AMENDED AND READOPTED 2004
READOPTED 2008
AMENDED AND READOPTED 2016
RESOLUTION #3063, 2012 *BOOK OF RESOLUTIONS*

RESOLUTION #3064, 2008 *BOOK OF RESOLUTIONS*
RESOLUTION #59, 2004 *BOOK OF RESOLUTIONS*
RESOLUTION #53, 2000 *BOOK OF RESOLUTIONS*

See Social Principles, ¶ 162A.

3065. Observance of Martin Luther King Jr. Day

The prophetic witness of Dr. Martin Luther King, Jr. for justice and peace embodies the spirit of the Social Creed, the Social Principles of The United Methodist Church and the inclusiveness of our denomination. His words continue to inspire and guide our commitment to the whole Gospel:

"We cannot be truly Christian people so long as we flaunt the central teachings of Jesus: brotherly love and the Golden Rule." —Martin Luther King, Jr.

"Was not Jesus an extremist for love—'Love your enemies, bless them that curse you, pray for them that despitefully use you.' Was not Amos an extremist for justice—'Let justice roll down like waters and righteousness like a mighty stream.' Was not Paul an extremist for the gospel of Jesus Christ—'I bear in my body the marks of the Lord Jesus.' Was not Martin Luther an extremist— 'Here I stand; I can do none other so help me God.' Was not John Bunyan an extremist—'I will stay in jail to the end of my days before I make a butchery of my conscience.' Was not Abraham Lincoln an extremist—'This nation cannot survive half slave and half free.' Was not Thomas Jefferson an extremist—'We hold these truths to be self-evident, that all men are created equal.' So the question is not whether we will be extremist but what kind of extremist will we be. Will we be extremists for hate or will we be extremists for love? Will we be extremists for the preservation of injustice—or will we be extremists for the cause of justice? In that dramatic scene on Calvary's hill, three men were crucified. We must not forget that all three were crucified for the same crime— the crime of extremism. Two were extremists for immorality, and thusly fell below their environment. The other, Jesus Christ, was an extremist for love, truth and goodness, and thereby rose above his environment."—Martin Luther King, Jr.

The observance of Martin Luther King Jr. Day enriches and strengthens our social witness today.

Therefore, be it resolved, that each annual conference in the United States observe Martin Luther King Jr. Day with appropriate services of commemoration in recognition of Dr. King; and on that day we strongly recommend that in the United States we close the bishops' office, all conference offices, all district offices, all local church offices, and, where feasible, business offices of church-related institutions; and that we support local activities surrounding the celebration of Dr. King's life and ministry; that we encourage local school districts in the United States not to hold classes on Martin Luther King Jr. Day; and that if local school districts hold classes, we encourage them to use Martin Luther King Jr. Day to celebrate Dr. King's work and address the need for the continuing struggle for justice.

ADOPTED 1992
AMENDED AND READOPTED 2004, 2008, 2016
RESOLUTION #3065, 2012 *BOOK OF RESOLUTIONS*
RESOLUTION #3066, 2008 *BOOK OF RESOLUTIONS*
RESOLUTION #61, 2004 *BOOK OF RESOLUTIONS*
RESOLUTION #55, 2000 *BOOK OF RESOLUTIONS*

See Social Principles, ¶ 162A.

3066. Support Reparations for African Americans

WHEREAS, the General Conference acknowledges and profoundly regrets the massive human suffering and the tragic plight of millions of men, women, and children caused by slavery and the transatlantic slave trade; and

WHEREAS, at the conclusion of the Civil War, the plan for the economic redistribution of land and resources on behalf of the former slaves of the Confederacy was never enacted; and

WHEREAS, the failure to distribute land prevented newly freed Blacks from achieving true autonomy and made their civil and political rights all but meaningless; and

WHEREAS, conditions comparable to "economic depression" continue for millions of African Americans in communities where unemployment often exceeds 50 percent; and

WHEREAS, justice requires that African American descendants of the transatlantic slave trade be assured of having access to effective and appropriate protection and remedies, including the right to seek just and adequate reparation or satisfaction for the legacy of damages, consequent structures of racism and racial discrimination suffered as a result of the slave trade; and

WHEREAS, Isaiah 61:1-3 provides a model for reparations: "He has sent me . . . to bind up the brokenhearted, to proclaim release for the captives, . . . to proclaim the year of the LORD's favor, . . . to provide for Zion's mourners, to give them a crown in place of ashes, oil of joy in place of mourning, and a mantle of praise in place of discouragement"; and,

WHEREAS, January 5, 1993, Congressman John Conyers Jr. (D-Mich.) introduced H.R. 40 to the House of Representatives, calling for the establishment of the Commission to Study Reparation Proposals for African Americans, "acknowledging the fundamental injustice, cruelty, brutality and inhumanity of slavery in the United States from 1619 to the present day," for the purpose of submitting a report to Congress for further action and consideration with respect to slavery's effects on African American lives, economics, and politics;

Therefore, be it resolved:

1. that we support the discussion and study of reparation for African Americans;

2. that we petition the President, the Vice President, and the United States House of Representatives to support the passage and signing of H.R. 40;

3. that a written copy of this petition be delivered to the President and Vice President of the United States, the United States Senate Majority Leader, the House Speaker, and House Member John Conyers Jr.;

4. that the General Commission on Religion and Race and the General Board of Church and Society develop a strategy for interpretation and support of passage of H.R. 40;

5. That the appropriate general boards and agencies of The United Methodist Church develop and make available to its members data on the history of slavery and the role of theology in validating and supporting both the institution and the abolition of the slave trade; and

6. That we call upon The United Methodist Church to acknowledge the memory of the victims of past tragedies and affirm that, wherever and whenever these tragedies occur, they must be condemned and their recurrence prevented.

ADOPTED 1996
AMENDED AND ADOPTED 2004
READOPTED 2012
RESOLUTION #3066, 2012 *BOOK OF RESOLUTIONS*
RESOLUTION #3067, 2008 *BOOK OF RESOLUTIONS*

RESOLUTION #62, 2004 *BOOK OF RESOLUTIONS*
RESOLUTION #56, 2000 *BOOK OF RESOLUTIONS*

See Social Principles, ¶ 162A.

CHILDREN

3081. Childcare and the Church

Our Call

As people of faith, we are called to teach children through scripture, our tradition as Methodists, the Social Principles, the ritual of baptism, and our concern for families. In responding to the call set before us, we will provide environments for children to be nurtured in the faith and to grow as children of God.

Scripture tells us to teach children the words of God (Deuteronomy 4:10; 6:7) and not to prevent them from discovering Jesus (Matthew 19:14; Mark 10:14; Luke 18:16). We can also help children to grow as Jesus grew, "strong . . . filled with wisdom; and God's favor was on him" (Luke 2:40*b*).

John Wesley set the example for us as Methodists as he began health clinics and schools for the children to learn to read and encouraged the pastors to meet with the children regularly. His call to meet the needs of people where they were stands as a marker for us today. Using our buildings that otherwise might sit empty six days a week to meet the physical, mental, and emotional needs of children and their families clearly meets Mr. Wesley's expectations.

Our Social Principles (¶ 162C) state, "Once considered the property of their parents, children are now acknowledged to be full human beings in their own right, but beings to whom adults and society in general have special obligations. . . ." This Social Principle calls us to take responsibility for meeting the needs of children, including education and protection. Additionally, it calls us to meet the needs of not just our children but all children.

In our service of infant baptism in The United Methodist Church, we promise to "surround these persons with a community of love and forgiveness, that they may grow in their service to others . . ." (*The United Methodist Hymnal*, page 40). In recognition of this promise and in response to the sacredness of all children as set forth in scripture, through the teachings of John Wesley, and in our Social Priniciples, our vision for childcare must include a vision of services available to all families on an equitable basis. Through the particular ministry of childcare, we extend the nurturing ministry of the church and proclaim justice to children, families, and communities.

The church has important responsibilities in initiating, encouraging, and participating in the highest quality of childcare for children and families, not only in the local community and beyond.

Therefore, we recommend the following:

1. *See childcare as planned ministry.*

Each congregation of The United Methodist Church that maintains any childcare ministry program must intentionally assess its understanding of discipleship as it relates to weekday ministry. Each childcare ministry program may encompass one or all of the following expressions of ministry: nurture, outreach, and witness by asking three questions. What are the congregation's gifts for ministry with children? What is the mission of childcare? How is intentional ministry a part of the daily operation of the program?

Congregations must determine how the childcare program embraces the church's mission.

a. Nurture includes Christian education, stewardship, and worship. In a program that focuses on nurture, spiritual development through Christian education is central. When children are cared for, they learn to care for others and for their world. An intentional part of the curriculum and resources should be the selection of stories (biblical and secular) and methods, and the integration of "God talk" and Christian values into daily conversations, worship opportunities, and interactions. In our childcare ministry programs, we reflect our commitment to being God's stewards in the ways we use and allocate our physical and ecological resources.

b. Outreach includes the areas of advocacy, safety, health, welfare, and equity, and how well they are addressed in our communities. Embracing outreach as a part of a weekday ministry program follows our traditional roots of caring for the needs of the community. As a congregation responds to the needs of people in the community through weekday ministry, the community and the congregation discover many blessings Each congregation should determine the unmet needs of their surrounding community by providing specialty childcare for children and families with special needs, striving to meet needs specific to the community, and advocating for the needs of children and families. Congregations should make every effort to work collaboratively with other community agencies and groups to assure that needs are being met without duplication of efforts and in support of each other.

c. Witness includes the areas of evangelism, membership care, and spiritual formation. In embracing witness as our particular expression of ministry, we proclaim God active in our lives. A witness to our faith speaks clearly through the actions of weekday ministry boards, through the caring love of the staff, the use of developmentally appropriate practices, gentle and caring words, curriculum and resources, the environment of the facilities, and the attitude of the congregation.

Every congregation of The United Methodist Church needs to define its ministry through childcare and include a statement of this ministry through weekday ministry programs as part of employee handbooks, parent handbooks, community statements, and church reports.

2. *Uphold the quality of childcare in the Church.*

Any time a child enters a childcare ministry program housed in a church, expectations are raised regarding quality of the program, behavior of the childcare staff and church staff, and adherence to the Christian doctrines of love and justice. Since the program is in the church, families have different expectations than if they are taking their child to a commercial childcare facility, So a church cannot divorce itself, either morally or legally, from what takes place in its building through childcare ministry programs. The childcare ministry program shall include developmentally appropriate curriculum and resources, the involvement of the congregation with the program, pastoral availability to families and staff involved in childcare, safe and clean buildings and equipment, and the highest quality in staff and staff support in each of the following areas:

a. Program Reviews: An annual review of the childcare ministry program should take place with joint participation of childcare staff, church personnel, and informed, interested laity.

b. Licensing: Congregations should strive to meet and surpass licensing standards in their state. The regulations of basic health and safety conditions in a building/program that serves children are the appropriate responsibility of the state and do not interfere with the free exercise of religion. Congregations should seek to be actively informed about such licensing procedures and requirements and should work to reform such regulations when they do not mandate standards that serve the best interests of children.

c. Self-Study: Through a self-study process, every childcare facility can look for ways to evaluate and assess the effectiveness of the care provided. Churches should follow a process of self-study for their childcare ministry programs on a regular basis. These self-studies are available through some annual conferences, the National Association for the Education of Young Children, and the United Methodist Association of Preschools—Florida.

d. Personnel: As congregations seek to support childcare ministry programs, competitive salaries, benefits, and support of the staff of these programs should be of concern and subject to review and discussion to insure the best for the children and families involved. Congregations have a responsibility to advocate for higher pay and benefits for childcare workers. These professional caregivers should maintain excellence and integrity in the important job they do, and they should be appropriately compensated for it. Appropriate screening protects the children, the childcare providers, and the congregation. It is important to meet any government regulations and the Safe Sanctuaries® policies of your local church regarding the screening of childcare workers as appropriate. A yearly plan for comprehensive continuing education should be part of the congregation's support for childcare providers.

3. *Be advocates for quality childcare.*

Going beyond the congregation, United Methodists should be diligent advocates for childcare nationwide.

a. Stay informed about childcare conditions existing today and the issues involved in the design of an adequate public policy for childcare.

b. Use the appropriate councils and agencies of the church to monitor public policy at federal, state, and local levels of government.

c. Become involved in church conferences and meetings, and in the larger arena of childcare through the Children's Defense Fund, the National Association for the Education of Young Children, and other research-based advocates of quality childcare.

d. Call upon staff at the General Board of Church and Society to monitor, serve as an advocate for, raise issues concerning, and bring the voice of the Church to bear on childcare policy development.

e. Call upon the staff of the General Board of Discipleship and The United Methodist Publishing House to express arising needs as they relate to program support, needed curriculum and resources, and policies regarding church and childcare center relationships.

f. Call upon the General Board of Global Ministries to assist churches in responding to childcare needs in their communities with appropriate programs and resources.

g. Call upon the General Board of Discipleship in consultation with the General Council on Finance and Administration to make available to local congregations resources that address legal aspects and procedures to follow in establishing childcare facilities and/or programs.

ADOPTED 2000
REVISED AND READOPTED 2008, 2016
RESOLUTION #3081, 2008, 2012 *BOOK OF RESOLUTIONS*
RESOLUTION #63, 2004 *BOOK OF RESOLUTIONS*
RESOLUTION #57, 2000 *BOOK OF RESOLUTIONS*

See Social Principles, ¶ 162C.

3082. Church Support of Caregivers of Children

We believe that children are the most vulnerable and precious resource of our societies, and they need loving adult support to flourish. Adult caregivers of children need parenting support systems as well. Today, children are being raised in a variety of household structures headed by various caregivers; and children in these families are in our communities, schools, and congregations. To flourish, families need a support system that embraces their household's structure, and church ministry programs should reflect that changing dynamic.

We call upon each local United Methodist Church to:

1. make a conscious effort in its ministry action, as well as in its words, to nurture children by supporting their family unit and its caregivers, regardless of that family structure;

2. examine the structure of existing ministries to determine if they can be more effective and inclusive by changing titles, timing of events, group expectations, or other norms;

3. determine if new ministries are needed to help non-traditional caregiver groups, and create them as appropriate; and

4. prayerfully consider opportunities to minister and love children and their caregivers without limit.

ADOPTED 2008
AMENDED AND READOPTED 2016
RESOLUTION #3082, 2008, 2012 *BOOK OF RESOLUTIONS*

See Social Principles, ¶ 162C.

3084. Reducing the Risk of Child Sexual Abuse in the Church

Jesus said, "Whoever welcomes one such child . . . welcomes me" (Matthew 18:5). Children are full participants in the life of the church and in the realm of God.

Jesus also said, "As for whoever causes these little ones who believe in me to trip and fall into sin, it would be better for them to have a huge stone hung around their necks and be drowned in the bottom of the lake" (Matthew 18:6). Our Christian faith calls us to offer both hospitality and protection to the little ones, the children. The Social Principles of The United Methodist Church state that "children must be protected from economic, physical, emotional, and sexual exploitation and abuse" (¶ 162C).

Tragically, churches are not always safe places for children. Child sexual abuse, exploitation, including online, and ritual abuse occur in congregations of all sizes and geographical locations. The problem cuts across all economic, cultural, and racial ethnic lines. Most annual conferences can cite specific incidents of child sexual abuse and exploitation within churches. Virtually every congregation has among its members adult survivors of early sexual trauma.

Such incidents are devastating to all who are involved: the child, the family, the local church, and its leaders. Churches are torn apart by the legal, emotional, and monetary consequences of litigation following allegations of abuse.

1. "Ritual abuse" refers to abusive acts committed as part of ceremonies or rites.

2. God calls us to make our congregations safe places, protecting children and other vulnerable persons from sexual and ritual abuse. God calls us to create communities of faith where children and adults grow safe and strong. In response to this churchwide challenge, the following steps shall be taken to reduce the risk of child sexual abuse:

A. Local churches should:

1. develop and implement an ongoing education plan for the entire congregation and its leaders on the reality of child abuse, risk factors leading to child abuse, and strategies for prevention;

2. adopt comprehensive screening procedures (use of application forms, interviews, reference checks, background clearance, and so forth) for all adults directly or indirectly involved in the care of children and youth;

3. develop and implement safety procedures for church activities such as having two or more nonrelated adults present in classroom or activity; leaving doors open and installing half-doors or windows in doors or halls; providing hall monitors; instituting sign-in and sign-out procedures for children ages ten or younger; and so forth, that meet or exceed Safe Sanctuaries® policies;

4. advise children and young persons of an agency or a person outside as well as within the local church whom they can contact for advice and help if they have suffered abuse;

5. carry liability insurance that includes sexual abuse coverage;

6. assist the development of awareness and self-protection skills for children and youth through special curriculum and activities; and

7. be familiar with annual conference and other church policies regarding clergy sexual misconduct.

B. Annual conferences should:

1. develop safety and risk-reducing policies and procedures for all conference-sponsored events and activities where children, youth, and/or vulnerable adults are present; and

2. develop guidelines and training processes for use by church leaders who carry responsibility for prevention of child abuse in local churches. Both sets of policies shall be developed by a task force appointed by the cabinet in cooperation with appropriate conference agencies. These policies shall be approved by the annual conference and assigned to a conference agency for implementation. It is suggested that the policies be circulated in conference publications and shared with lay professionals and clergy at district or conference seminars.

C. *The General Board of Discipleship and the General Board of Global Ministries should:*

1. cooperatively develop and/or identify and promote the following resources;

2. sample policies, procedures, forms, and so forth for reducing the risk of sexual abuse and exploitation of children and youth in local churches, both in relation to their own sponsored programs and to any outreach ministries or other programs for children or youth that use church space;

3. child abuse prevention curriculum for use in local churches;

4. training opportunities and other educational resources on child sexual abuse and exploitation and on ritual abuse; and

5. resources on healing for those who have experienced childhood sexual trauma.

ADOPTED 1996
READOPTED 2004, 2008
AMENDED AND READOPTED 2016
RESOLUTION #3084, 2008, 2016 *BOOK OF RESOLUTIONS*
RESOLUTION #65, 2004 *BOOK OF RESOLUTIONS*
RESOLUTION #59, 2000 *BOOK OF RESOLUTIONS*

See Social Principles, ¶ 162C.

3085. Child Soldiers

"Jesus loves the little children. All the children of the world. Red and yellow, black and white, they are precious in his sight. Jesus loves the little children of the world."

"Allow the children to come to me. Don't forbid them, because God's kingdom belongs to people like these children" (Luke 18:16).

The use of children as soldiers is abhorrent and unacceptable. Children represent the future of human civilization and the future of every society. To permit them to be used as pawns of warfare, whether as targets or perpetrators, is to cast a shadow on the future.

As armed conflict proliferates around the world, an increasing number of children are exposed to the brutalities of war. In numerous countries, boys and girls are recruited as child soldiers by armed forces and groups, either forcibly or voluntarily. Reports by the United Nations and nongovernmental organizations such as Amnesty International and the Coalition to Stop the Use of Child Soldiers reveal:

- The majority of the world's child soldiers are involved in a variety of armed political groups. These include government-backed paramilitary groups, militias, and self-defense units operating with government support in many conflict zones. Others include armed groups opposed to central government rule, groups composed of ethnic, religious, and other minorities; and clan-based or factional groups fighting governments and each other to defend territory and resources.

- Most child soldiers are aged between 14 and 18. Some children as young as 8 years of age, however, are being forcibly recruited, coerced, and induced to become combatants. The children most likely to become soldiers are from impoverished and marginalized backgrounds or separated from their families.

- Hundreds of thousands of under-18-year-olds are estimated to have become a part of armed forces in at least 60 countries. While thousands were recruited, others were forcibly conscripted in military roundups to replenish numbers in unpopular armies. Still others were enlisted in countries where the lack of a functioning birth registration system made it impossible to verify the age of recruits and ensure protection of under-18-year-olds from active military service. Forced abductions, sometimes of large numbers of children, continue to occur in some countries.

- Sometimes, children become soldiers in order to survive. A military unit can be something of a refuge, serving as a kind of surrogate family. Children may join if they believe that this is the only way to guarantee regular meals, clothing, or medical attention. Parents may encourage their daughters to become soldiers if their marriage prospects are poor.

Much has been achieved to stop the use of child soldiers since the General Conference adopted a resolution on the matter in 2000. Substantial progress has been made in establishing an international legal and policy framework for protecting children from involvement in armed conflict. The Optional Protocol to the UN Convention on the Rights of the Child on the involvement of children came into force in 2002. It sets 18 as the minimum age for direct participation in hostilities, for compulsory recruitment by governments, and for all recruitment into armed groups. The International Criminal Court defines all recruitment of children under the age of 15, by governments and armed groups, and their active participation in hostilities as a war crime in both international and noninternational armed conflict. Central conferences in Africa, such as the Liberia Conference, have initiated programs to rehabilitate and integrate ex-combatant children for productive and peaceful life in their families and communities.

The General Conference of The United Methodist Church urges the General Board of Church and Society and the General Board of Global Ministries to:

- Encourage partnership and collaboration among international organizations, including faith-based groups that monitor governments and armed groups in the recruitment and mobilization of children for military purposes, and ensuring adherence to international norms and agreements prohibiting child soldiers.
- work with international organizations, faith groups, and other nongovernmental organizations to ban the use of child soldiers;
- urge governments to sign the Optional Protocol to the UN Convention on the Rights of the Child on the involvement of children in armed conflict;
- promote and advocate for government funding of demobilization, disarmament and reintegration programs specifically aimed at child soldiers, taking particular account of the needs of former girl soldiers; and

- provide financial assistance to central conferences for programs to rehabilitate and reintegrate former child soldiers into their families and communities.

ADOPTED 2000
REVISED AND READOPTED 2008, 2012
RESOLUTION #3085, 2008, 2016 *BOOK OF RESOLUTIONS*
RESOLUTION #66, 2004 *BOOK OF RESOLUTIONS*
RESOLUTION #60, 2000 *BOOK OF RESOLUTIONS*

See Social Principles, ¶¶ 162C and 164I.

3087. Prohibit Corporal Punishment in Schools and Childcare Facilities

Some schools and childcare facilities around the world permit striking another person for the purpose of causing physical pain.

Corporal punishment is humiliating and degrading to children, causing emotional and sometimes physical injury.

It is difficult to imagine Jesus Christ condoning any action that is intended to hurt children physically or psychologically. Jesus' teachings on loving our neighbor and living in peace with one another are foundational for opposition to corporal punishment in institutions in ministry with and to children.

Corporal punishment sends a message that hitting smaller and weaker people is acceptable.

As people of faith who value children and who are committed to nonviolent conflict resolution, we are called to identify effective alternatives to corporal punishment that teach children to be self-disciplined rather than to submit out of fear.

Schools and childcare centers should inspire children to enjoy learning, and school and childcare personnel should be able to encourage positive behavior without hitting children.

Therefore, be it resolved, that The United Methodist Church calls upon all governments and educational institutions to enact laws prohibiting corporal punishment in schools and day and residential childcare facilities.

ADOPTED 2004
AMENDED AND READOPTED 2012
RESOLUTION #3087, 2008, 2012 *BOOK OF RESOLUTIONS*
RESOLUTION #69, 2004 *BOOK OF RESOLUTIONS*

See Social Principles, ¶ 162C.

3088. Discipline Children Without Corporal Punishment

WHEREAS, corporal punishment models aggressive behavior as a solution to conflict,

WHEREAS, some research has associated corporal punishment with increased aggression in children and adults, increased substance abuse, increased risk of crime and violence, low self-esteem, and chronic depression,

WHEREAS, it is difficult to imagine Jesus of Nazareth condoning any action that is intended to hurt children physically or psychologically,

WHEREAS, time-outs and deprivation of privileges are as effective as corporal punishment in stopping undesirable behavior,

WHEREAS, the effectiveness of corporal punishment decreases with subsequent use and therefore leads caretakers to hit children more severely,

WHEREAS, children must eventually develop their own conscience and self-discipline, which are fostered by a home environment of love, respect, and trust,

Therefore, be it resolved, that The United Methodist Church encourages its members to adopt discipline methods that do not include corporal punishment of their children.

And be it further resolved, that The United Methodist Church encourages congregations to offer opportunities for dialogue and education on effective discipline of children.

ADOPTED 2004
READOPTED 2012
RESOLUTION #3088, 2008, 2012 *BOOK OF RESOLUTIONS*
RESOLUTION #70, 2004 *BOOK OF RESOLUTIONS*

See Social Principles, ¶ 162C.

CHURCH AND COMMUNITY DEVELOPMENT

3101. National Cooperative Ministry Leadership

WHEREAS, the effectiveness of cooperative projects, ministries, and parishes for the purposes of congregational nurturing, outreach to communities of the poor and marginalized, and witnessing to Christian commitments in rural, urban, and suburban communities has long been recognized; and

WHEREAS, in fulfillment of the mandate from the 2008 General Conference "to plan and carry forward a national cooperative parish consultation in order to facilitate broader use of existing cooperative forms and the incorporation of new patterns and processes that continue to emerge throughout the church," an event known as "Soaring High: Cooperative Ministries Changing Lives, Congregations and Communities" was held in Huntsville, AL in 2009. Under the coordination of the Rural Chaplains Association, this gathering reaffirmed the need and potential for bringing people together for training, networking and celebration;

Therefore, be it resolved, that the General Board of Global Ministries, the General Board of Discipleship, the General Board of Higher Education and Ministry, and the Office of Christian Unity and Interreligious Relationships be called upon to provide encouragement, financial support and work with constituencies that are at the forefront of cooperative ministries. This will include training events that expand the effective use of cooperative patterns and processes within the Church and ecumenically;

Be it further resolved, that the annual conferences, districts, and local churches of The United Methodist Church be called on to implement processes that will result in understandings of how to initiate needed cooperative projects, ministries, and parishes and to facilitate their movement toward local and global mission and ministry.

ADOPTED 2004
REVISED AND READOPTED 2008, 2012
RESOLUTION #3101, 2008, 2012 *BOOK OF RESOLUTIONS*
RESOLUTION #51, 2004 *BOOK OF RESOLUTIONS*

See Social Principles, ¶ 162P.

3102. Support for Multicultural and Global Churches

WHEREAS, a truly multicultural congregation is more than "token" participation of racial/ethnic persons, but grounded in racial equity that incorporates into the worship style, leadership, and entire ministry cultural and language elements of the different racial/ethnic/tribal groups present in the congregation thus ensuring that everyone has a place at the table where power is shared (resources and decision-making) and where conflict is managed in a culturally proficient way; and

WHEREAS, congregations thrive where everyone brings gifts to the mutually "owned table," and where the entire congregation is shaped by all in an equitable manner and not by one dominant group; and

WHEREAS, ethnically/culturally specific ministries have historically been a source of strength, encouragement, and empowerment for people of color, and have enabled people to move outside of their local congregations to participate in the larger church and world and have contributed greatly to the global nature of the church; and

WHEREAS, it is important that the church be culturally proficient in seeking to understand the context of all people and reaching people where they are; and racial/ethnic/cultural/tribal diversities have been a reality in God's creation from the very beginning; and

WHEREAS, mobility, advanced technology, war, political instability, and socioeconomic realities have brought the diversity of the world into neighborhoods, churches, and communities creating a challenge for homogenous churches, shifting demographics; and multicultural ministries have sometimes been placed in opposition to the continued development and strengthening of racial/ethnic local churches and historically marginalized communities; and multicultural ministries are often being used to dismiss the uniqueness of the different groups and/or simply as a superficial face make-up (a few different faces in the congregation) that does not impact the life, language, leadership style, and decision-making of the congregation; and in these cases, multiculturalism can be a disguised form of racism and ethnocentrism; and

WHEREAS, the General Commission on Religion and Race is mandated by the Church to ensure the equal participation of all believers as members of the same body that is the body of Christ and the question of multicultural congregations or ethnic/culturally specific congregations is not an either/or proposition but rather two distinct paths needed to achieve the inclusive spirit revealed to us at Pentecost, when people understood each other, not through a common language, but through the power of the Spirit who affirmed and embraced everyone; and

WHEREAS, one of the principles of inclusiveness is self-determination and people of color in their continued quest for empowerment in the midst of a racist church and society benefit from the power to determine if their cultural and spiritual needs are best met in an ethnic specific congregation or in a multicultural one; and in many occasions an "ethnic specific" congregation can be the beginning of becoming a multicultural church and multicultural ministries should be looked upon as one of the models of the inclusive and multicultural church; and

WHEREAS, there are many ways in which the Church can be multicultural and inclusive without being together in the same worship service such as community work, mission, children and youth, church governance, etc.;

Therefore, be it resolved, that The United Methodist Church's commitment to inclusiveness and racial equity affirms the continued development and strengthening of the racial/ethnic congregations as well as the development and strengthening of congregations that are culturally aware, modeling racial equity and becoming truly multicultural congregations as defined above; and the Council of Bishops provides direction to annual conferences on matters of multicultural and ethnic specific ministries so that local churches are provided with resources and guidance in their efforts to respond to diverse communities; and

Be it further resolved, that the General Commission on Religion and Race will partner with the General Board of Global Ministries, the General Board of Higher Education and Ministry, the General Board of Church and Society, and the General Board of Discipleship in the development of resources within current budgetary resources that undergird the creation and the strengthening of multicultural and ethnic specific ministries; and United Methodist seminaries and schools of theology will incorporate into their curriculums cross-racial and cross-cultural competencies needed to prepare students who will be able to minister in diverse settings.

ADOPTED 2012
RESOLUTION #3102, 2012 *BOOK OF RESOLUTIONS*

See Social Principles, ¶ 162A.

3103. Facilitation of Cooperative Ministry
Throughout the Church

WHEREAS, cooperative forms of ministry have proven to enhance the ministries of laity, certified lay ministers, and to provide greater support and peer accountability among clergy, and to further connectional awareness and increased resourcing from the connectional church; and,

WHEREAS, cooperative ministry is an intentional style of team ministry that enables groups of congregations and their pastors and laity and networking groups of church and community persons focused around a common passionate missional interest to work together in nurture, outreach, and witness for the purpose of transformation of the world;

Therefore, be it resolved, that cooperative ministry be affirmed and undergirded by:

1. all boards and agencies of The United Methodist Church by collaborating around matters concerning cooperative ministries;

2. bishops and cabinets giving priority to cooperative ministries in the appointment making process, including ecumenically cooperative ministries;

3. cabinets, conference staff, and other conference leaders giving special attention to cooperative work in rural, urban, declining, growing, stable, racial/ethnic, multicultural, and large and small membership charges and churches.

ADOPTED 2008
AMENDED AND READOPTED 2012, 2016
RESOLUTION #3103, 2012 *BOOK OF RESOLUTIONS*
RESOLUTION #3105, 2008 *BOOK OF RESOLUTIONS*

See Social Principles, ¶ 162.

3104. Church and Community Workers

WHEREAS, current social and economic needs across the USA continue to call upon the church for attention and action in accordance with Christ's teachings; and

WHEREAS, developing contacts and linkages between local church/cooperative ministries and community groups is key to the understanding of and response to human hurt and need and responding to justice issues, and is a primary strength of the church and community ministry program; and

WHEREAS, for over half a century church and community workers have worked effectively in mission outreach with The United Methodist Church in town and rural, urban, and specialized settings; and

WHEREAS, the goals of church and community ministry programs are closely aligned with the four mission initiatives of The United Methodist Church; and

WHEREAS, church and community workers are an effective cadre of missionaries serving within the bounds of the USA who are employed and assigned by the General Board of Global Ministries;

Therefore, be it resolved, that the General Board of Global Ministries continue to recruit, enlist, train, and deploy church and community workers and provide joint funding with other partners; and

Be it further resolved, that the funding partnership continue between the local area, annual conference, and the General Board of Global Ministries in order to place church and community workers in economically depressed areas.

ADOPTED 1992
REVISED AND READOPTED 2000, 2008, 2016
RESOLUTION #3104, 2012 *BOOK OF RESOLUTIONS*
RESOLUTION #3106, 2008 *BOOK OF RESOLUTIONS*
RESOLUTION #53, 2004 *BOOK OF RESOLUTIONS*
RESOLUTION #45, 2000 *BOOK OF RESOLUTIONS*

See Social Principles, ¶ 162R.

3109. Volunteers in Mission

WHEREAS, the United Methodist Volunteers in Mission (UMVIM) movement is one of the most dynamic mission outreach programs of the denomination today; every conference has a UMVIM Coordinator in place; and

WHEREAS, some jurisdictions have a paid full-time UMVIM coordinator who, because of the time commitment, is able to assist their respective conferences more effectively than those coordinators who are part-time; and

WHEREAS, although United Methodist Volunteers in Mission is a major mission outreach now, with thousands of United Methodists participating annually, the potential is much greater; and

WHEREAS, the church needs to invest in ways which will enhance the program, involve even more United Methodists, and bring Christ's love to people and churches in need around the world; and

WHEREAS, full-time jurisdictional coordinators will be a great help in the expansion of this effective, hands-on mission and service outreach of The United Methodist Church,

Therefore, we recommend that every jurisdiction include in its budget a line item to cover the salary, professional expenses, and office expenses for a jurisdictional United Methodist Volunteers in Mission coordinator.

In addition, we request that the General Board of Global Ministries continue to work with the central conferences and autonomous churches to support the Volunteers in Mission programs in those regions.

ADOPTED 2000
READOPTED 2008
AMENDED AND READOPTED 2016
RESOLUTION #3109, 2012 *BOOK OF RESOLUTIONS*
RESOLUTION #3111, 2008 *BOOK OF RESOLUTIONS*
RESOLUTION #55, 2004 *BOOK OF RESOLUTIONS*
RESOLUTION #49, 2000 *BOOK OF RESOLUTIONS*

See Social Principles, ¶ 162.

CULTURAL ISSUES

3121. Affirming the Use of Diverse Languages in the United States and Opposing a Constitutional Amendment Making English the Official Language

The United States is a country whose inhabitants are enriched by diverse traditions, languages, and cultures. While English is the most commonly used or "primary" language of the country, other languages have been used throughout the history of the nation. For example, Native American languages and Spanish were already spoken when the first English colonists arrived. Throughout that same history, there have been various efforts to prescribe the use of English and to proscribe the use of other languages. These efforts sometimes resulted in legislation that had the effect of legalizing discrimination against various language minority groups, as was the case for German, Swedish, French, Greek, and Italian immigrants who came to this country in great numbers during the nineteenth century. Such legislative attempts were eventually overcome by the constitutional principles of equal rights. The acknowledgment of English as the primary language of the United States does not deny the right and contribution of other languages or the inherent right of people to retain and speak their native language.

The attempt to remove bilingual education is one particular area of concern. Education has played a very important role in the development of this nation. To have access to it and to receive a sound education are considered inalienable rights of all children. Bilingual education has been and continues to be a critical tool to ensure these rights for non-English-speaking children living now in the United States. It has been an instrument of education for children to make the transition from their native languages to English (without abandoning their native languages) while at the same time staying at the level correspondent to their age. Bilingual education does work. There are thousands of living examples of bilingual education successes. Students who learned English in bilingual classrooms and who continue to achieve to the highest of academic and professional standards are living examples of bilingual education successes.

Over the years, there have been consistent efforts in different parts of the country to make English the official language of the United States. Notwithstanding their unsuccessful attempts to pass a constitutional amendment, we are now seeing concerted efforts to bring the same policy to state and local levels. The movement to declare constitutionally English as the official language of the nation is not based upon any real need but, in fact, may be motivated by an effort to deny the pluralistic foundation of the country and to deny the dignity and wholeness of persons from different racial and ethnic groups who rightly considered their languages an integral part of their cultures. We fear the real purpose of some may be not so much to make English the *official* language of the US as to make English the *exclusive* language of the nation.

The English-only "movement" includes efforts to pass a constitutional amendment making English the official language of the United States, opposition to federal legislation for bilingual education, voting-rights bills, and the FCC licensing applications for Spanish-language broadcasts.

This movement is another manifestation of the systemic racism that has infected this country for generations. The English-only movement blames the deterioration of the American fabric on immigration and the use of languages other than English. It contends that the nation's unity rests upon the use of an official language. It defines multiculturalism and multilingualism as "anti-unity." Consequently, the movement, if successful, could further discriminate against and segregate the racial and ethnic population of the United States. Essential information such as: numbers for the 911 emergency, hospital emergency rooms, police, firefighters; and medical and legal forms, language services, bilingual education, and interpreters in the judicial system might be denied.

As Christians, we believe that we are children of God, created in God's image, and members of the family of God.

We believe that diversity is a gift of the creative genius of God and that languages are an expression of the wisdom of God.

We believe that competence in the English language is important to participate fully in the life of the United States, but we also acknowledge the fact that we live in a global context, the global family of God, where people and nations experience interdependency at all levels and where the acquisition of a second language represents a better understanding of other people's cultures, hopes, and dreams.

We believe that our nation should maximize the rich contributions that the ethnic/language groups bring to this country by preserving those languages and encouraging people living within the United States to learn other languages.

We believe that it is the will of God that each human being is affirmed as a whole person and that it is in the acceptance and interchange of our uniqueness that we find a witness of God's *shalom*.

We oppose the attempt to rob a person of his or her language as dehumanizing and as a denial of that person's wholeness.

We oppose the English-only movement as a manifestation of the sin of racism.

Therefore, be it resolved, that

1. the Council of Bishops, annual conferences, and members of local churches contact their local, state, and federal representatives urging support for practices and policies that permit provision of information in languages appropriate to the residents of communities and opposition to any movement that seeks to make English the only language of the United States; and

2. the General Board of Church and Society make this resolu-

tion an urgent item in their agenda for lobbying, constituency education, and advocacy.

ADOPTED 1988
AMENDED AND ADOPTED 2000
AMENDED AND READOPTED 2008, 2016
RESOLUTION #3121, 2008, 2012 *BOOK OF RESOLUTIONS*
RESOLUTION #72, 2004 *BOOK OF RESOLUTIONS*
RESOLUTION #64, 2000 *BOOK OF RESOLUTIONS*

See Social Principles, ¶ 162.

3122. Expansion of Inclusive Language

WHEREAS, we live in an ever-changing global community with a diversity of multi-racial identities where racial/ethnic identification is not limited to one category and much of the world bases identity on ethnic nationality rather than racial/ethnic categories; and

WHEREAS, the United Nations and countries other than the US have varying racial/ethnic classifications; and

WHEREAS, the inclusion and naming of persons with more than one racial or ethnic identity gives visibility to people who often are excluded; and

WHEREAS, many of our own forms within our church are exclusive requiring the growing population of biracial/multiracial people to choose between one identity or another, by requiring people to identify themselves by selecting only one of the six dominant racial options: Asian, Black, Hispanic/Latino(a), Native American, Pacific Islander, and White;

Therefore, be it resolved, that The United Methodist Church expand its inclusive language in all aspects of the church to include biracial/multiracial persons by offering racial identification options that are not limiting but embracing of persons with more than one racial or ethnic background.

ADOPTED 2012
RESOLUTION #3122, 2012 *BOOK OF RESOLUTIONS*

See Social Principles, ¶ 162A.

3123. Support for Ethnic Ministry Plans

WHEREAS, ¶ 140 of *The Book of Discipline, 2012* states "As a diverse people of God who bring special gifts and evidences of

God's grace to the unity of the Church and to society, we are called to be faithful to the example of Jesus' ministry to all persons"; and

WHEREAS, ¶ 162A of The Social Principles affirms the ministry to all persons and states, "We rejoice in the gifts that particular ethnic histories and cultures bring to our total life"; and

WHEREAS, six ethnic ministry plans (Asian Language Ministry, Hispanic, Korean, Native American, Pacific Islander, and Strengthening the Black Church) have affirmed and have made significant contributions to the growth and strengthening of major ethnic ministries; and

WHEREAS, continuing needs for the six ethnic ministry plans (Asian Language Ministry, Hispanic, Korean, Native American, Pacific Islander, and Strengthening the Black Church) are clearly demonstrated by their successes in making disciples of Christ; and

WHEREAS, funding for these ethnic national plans are essential and critical in order to continue ministry to ethnic people;

Therefore, be it resolved, that this General Conference of The United Methodist Church expresses its support for continuing existence and funding of the ethnic national plans.

ADOPTED 2004
READOPTED 2008
AMENDED AND READOPTED 2016
RESOLUTION #3123, 2012 *BOOK OF RESOLUTIONS*
RESOLUTION #3124, 2008 *BOOK OF RESOLUTIONS*
RESOLUTION #80, 2004 *BOOK OF RESOLUTIONS*

See Social Principles, ¶ 162A.

3124. The Church's Response to Ethnic and Religious Conflict

If only you knew . . . the things that lead to peace.
—Jesus of Nazareth (Luke 19:42)

The tragic conflicts in so many places around the world today reveal the deep potential for hatred, fear, and religious belief to stir up violence in humankind. These conflicts pose a great challenge to all faith traditions and especially to the Christian church as the mediator of Jesus' gospel of love and reconciliation in the world. The church's pain is only made greater by the fact that so many of these violent conflicts pit one religious group against another.

When the disciples James and John saw this, they said, "Lord, do you want us to call fire down from heaven to consume them [a Samaritan village]?" But Jesus turned and spoke sternly to them. (Luke 9:54-55)

We confess that as Christians we too have responded to religious and ethnic differences out of fear, ignorance and even hatred. We have too quickly resorted to violence as a means of resolving conflicts.

The rising tide of violence in the world threatens to engulf communities, nations, and world civilizations. It is time for the church to become proactive in resolving conflict nonviolently and developing alternatives to violence. Specifically:

- we call upon the General Board of Global Ministries to continue partnerships with Christian Peacemakers, the Ecumenical Accompaniment Program in Palestine & Israel, Witness for Peace, International Solidarity Movement, and other nonviolent movements that provide a Christian presence in situations of international, interreligious, and interethnic conflict, to explore the possibility of including United Methodists on teams that serve in areas of conflict;
- we call upon the General Board of Global Ministries to incorporate the principles of nonviolent conflict resolution and interethnic and interreligious dialogue in mission training and other mission programming;
- we call upon the General Board of Church and Society, together with the General Commission on Religion and Race and the Office of Christian Unity and Interreligious Relationships, to promote and participate in interreligious dialogues to develop new approaches to mutual understanding, respect, and cooperation, and to develop, for use in local church and community settings, guidelines on how to set up local dialogues and how to develop and implement alternatives to violence;
- we call upon our seminaries and United Methodist-related colleges and universities to offer courses on alternatives to violence and to sponsor local community initiatives to diffuse ethnic and religious conflict. We also call on our seminaries to encourage the study of the theological roots of violence and of Jesus' teachings on nonviolence and resisting evil; and
- we call upon all governments, working with the United Nations, to give leadership by redirecting funds from mil-

itary exercise training programs to the UN High Commission for Human Rights and other international human rights organizations for the tasks of human rights training, peacemaking, peacekeeping, reconstruction, and rehabilitation. This means reallocating funds from building weapons to building communities, from teaching to kill to teaching to protect life. Modest beginnings in such an effort can be seen in community policing initiatives in many cities, in international peacekeeping forces, and in the nonviolent transition to democracy in South Africa;

- we call upon the General Board of Discipleship, together with the General Board of Global Ministries, to address our growing multi-faith contexts in developing church school curriculum by utilizing resources from ecumenical and interfaith organizations;
- we call upon local churches to be engaged in multicultural and multi-faith dialogue and cooperative events that seek to prevent violence;
- we call upon annual conferences to organize high school and adult trips through United Methodist Seminars (a program offered by United Methodist Women and the General Board of Church and Society) or United Methodist Volunteers in Mission to study Ethnic and Religious Conflicts and alternatives to violence.

ADOPTED 1996
AMENDED AND READOPTED 2004
READOPTED 2008
AMENDED AND READOPTED 2016
RESOLUTION #3124, 2012 *BOOK OF RESOLUTIONS*
RESOLUTION #3126, 2008 *BOOK OF RESOLUTIONS*
RESOLUTION #81, 2004 *BOOK OF RESOLUTIONS*
RESOLUTION #71, 2000 *BOOK OF RESOLUTIONS*

See Social Principles, ¶ 162A, B.

3125. Holocaust Memorial Day *(Yom HaShoah)*

In recent years, Jewish communities have honored the custom of remembering the Holocaust *(Shoah)* on 27 Nisan of the Jewish calendar. This observance has become a powerful means of educating people about this heinous crime against humanity and sensitizing them to present and potential violence rooted in racial hatred.

WHEREAS, "In the twentieth century there is particular shame in the failure of most of the church to challenge the policies of governments that were responsible for the unspeakable atrocities of the Holocaust" ("Building New Bridges in Hope," *Book of Resolutions* 2008); and

WHEREAS, the same document observes, "[t]he Christian Church has a profound obligation to correct historical and theological teachings that have led to false and pejorative perceptions of Judaism and contributed to persecution and hatred of Jews";

Therefore, be it resolved, that the General Conference calls The United Methodist Church to contrition and repentance of its complicity in "the long history of persecution of the Jewish people" and asks the Office of Christian Unity and Interreligious Relationships to give special programmatic emphasis to Holocaust awareness and to prepare resources for use in local churches, annual conferences, and their Conference Commissions on Christian Unity and Interreligious Concerns or equivalent structures to enable them to become more aware of the Holocaust and its impact, and

Be it further resolved, as a sign of our contrition and our solidarity with the Jewish community, the General Conference urges the observance of *Yom HaShoah,* Holocaust Memorial Day each spring (The date of *Yom HaShoah* may be calculated for each year by using a Hebrew date converter.) in United Methodist local churches and urges the Office of Christian Unity and Interreligious Relationships, in cooperation with other agencies of The United Methodist Church, in a time of increasing anti-Semitism, to work within the structure of our own Church to find ways to support the work against anti-Semitism in the world today and to prepare resources for local churches to use in observing *Yom HaShoah.*

We continue to pray for God's grace to speak in Jesus' name against bigotry, hatred, genocide, or other crimes against humanity whenever and wherever they are perpetrated.

ADOPTED 2000
REVISED AND READOPTED 2008, 2012
RESOLUTION #3125, 2012 *BOOK OF RESOLUTIONS*
RESOLUTION #3127. 2008 *BOOK OF RESOLUTIONS*
RESOLUTION #75, 2004 *BOOK OF RESOLUTIONS*
RESOLUTION #66, 2000 *BOOK OF RESOLUTIONS*

See Social Principles, ¶ 162.

3126. Prejudice Against Muslims and Arabs in the USA

Today across the world there are increased incidents of violence and prejudice against Muslims, and against non-Muslim Arabs. Arab organization offices, mosques, and Islamic centers have been bombed and torched. Muslims and persons whose garb appears Islamic (particularly Sikhs) are being detained in airports and other places without justification. They are continually subjected to harassment and discrimination. Though discriminatory acts against Arabs and Muslims do not stand in isolation from similar acts perpetrated against other racial and ethnic persons around the world, their existence and effects upon Arabs and Muslims have been little acknowledged in society, with concomitant deleterious effect on perceptions in primarily non-Muslim parts of the world, as they touch upon relations with predominantly Arab and Muslim nations and organizations.

Therefore, The United Methodist Church, in the knowledge that Jesus calls us to the blessings of peacemaking and reminds us that the highest law is to love God and neighbor, calls its members and its leaders:

1. To oppose demagoguery, manipulation, and image making that seeks to label Arabs and Muslims in a negative way;

2. To counter stereotypical and bigoted statements made against Muslims and Islam, Arabs and Arabic culture;

3. To increase knowledge of neighbor by study and personal contact that yield a greater appreciation of the Muslim and Arabic contributions to society;

4. To act decisively to include Arabs and Muslims in interfaith and community organizations;

5. To pray for the perfection of community among us and to participate fully in the process of bringing it into being; and

6. To publicly denounce through statements from the Council of Bishops and the General Board of Church and Society current practices that discriminate against this community.

In order to aid United Methodists to respond to this call, all boards, agencies, and institutions of The United Methodist Church are requested to provide resources and programs and, where appropriate, to act in advocacy.

ADOPTED 1988
AMENDED AND READOPTED 2000, 2004

READOPTED 2008
AMENDED AND READOPTED 2016
RESOLUTION #3126, 2012 *BOOK OF RESOLUTIONS*
RESOLUTION #3128, 2008 *BOOK OF RESOLUTIONS*
RESOLUTION #78, 2004 *BOOK OF RESOLUTIONS*
RESOLUTION #69, 2000 *BOOK OF RESOLUTIONS*

See Social Principles, ¶ 162*B*.

ECUMENICAL ISSUES

3142. Guidelines for Cooperation in Mission

WHEREAS, the World Methodist Council has recommended the following be adopted by its member churches:

People of the Wesleyan heritage look upon the whole world as their parish. They feel committed to preach the gospel of Jesus Christ to all people.

Many of the churches in that Methodist tradition are responding anew to the call for mission in the whole world. There are changing patterns of migration and increasing movements of peoples, both geographically and spiritually. As a result new Methodist missions are started in areas where there are already communities and churches of the Wesleyan tradition working. In places, this has created confusion and unhealthy competition and has been an offense to the gospel. Sometimes, both clergy and laity seek to move from one church to another.

It is natural to those who are in the tradition of John Wesley to seek out and respond to new opportunities and to respond to requests for help. We want to stretch out our hand to all whose heart is as our heart and to work closely together. Our instinct is to share as fully as possible with all who share with us in the same mission. We are therefore committed to support each other in our work and to do nothing that would undermine each other.

In this fluid situation the World Methodist Council finds it necessary for the sake of its common mission to ask its member churches to agree on some principles and guidelines on this matter.

Three basic principles should apply especially to all such Methodist work being done by different member churches in the same area.

- Respect
- Courtesy
- Communication and consultation

Two consequences follow:

1. When any member churches of the WMC are intending to support and endorse new work in an area of the world, before agreeing officially:

- Other member churches should be notified.
- Advice should be sought in order to minimize, or prevent, any duplication of resources.

We are aware that the needs of people of particular languages or cultures may make new mission work necessary. But the principles of respect, courtesy, and communication should ensure that all our traditions can delight in new manifestations of the work of God's Spirit. The Holy Spirit often works beyond our own boundaries and limitations. At the same time, whenever possible, we would encourage those involved in "new" Methodist movements to link with an existing church. We believe it is possible to order our relationships in a cooperative way and to help new fellowships to seek the most appropriate church to join.

2. The same principle should apply where member churches presently find themselves working alongside each other in various countries:

- Different Methodist traditions should be encouraged to join together, or at least to work in a spirit of consultation and cooperation.
- Different Methodist traditions should communicate fully with each other, and thereby share resources and experience for the furtherance of God's kingdom.

No member churches should be working in competition with each other, because this implies the breakdown of respect, courtesy, and communication. Good practice would be to develop regular meetings and clear protocols governing the relationship of churches together in particular areas.

The World Methodist Council, through its officers, offers its good services to provide a platform and the channels necessary for information and consultation between its member churches on these matters.

Therefore, be it resolved, that The United Methodist Church adopts these guidelines in its commitment to the pursuit of Christ's call to Christian unity and in a spirit of solidarity with other member churches of the World Methodist Council.

ADOPTED 2004
READOPTED 2012
RESOLUTION #3142, 2008, 2012 *BOOK OF RESOLUTIONS*
RESOLUTION #94, 2004 *BOOK OF RESOLUTIONS*

See Social Principles, ¶162.

3143. Encounter With Christ in Latin America and the Caribbean

WHEREAS, the 2008 General Conference established a Coordinating Group for the Holistic Strategy on Latin America and the Caribbean Special Program in order to develop a mission partnerships with Methodist and United Churches throughout Latin America and the Caribbean; and

WHEREAS, the Coordinating Group, constituted by bishops of The United Methodist Church, bishops/presidents of the Methodist and United Churches within the Latin America/Caribbean region, the program related United Methodist general agencies and representatives of MARCHA (Methodists Associated Representing the Cause of Hispanic Americans) have affirmed the growing importance of our shared mission and ministry; and

WHEREAS, the Encounter with Christ permanent fund (025100) administered by the General Board of Global Ministries is a primary source of financial support for our mission partnership, with interest monies of some three hundred and seventy-five thousand dollars having already supported around fifty joint mission projects in Methodist and United churches in twenty-one countries and four regional entities of the region; and

WHEREAS, a unique dimension of Encounter involves a process of shared decision making regarding the utilization of interest monies on behalf of mission among the leadership of CIEMAL (Council of Evangelical Methodist Churches in Latin America and the Caribbean) and MCCA (Methodist Church in the Caribbean and the Americas) and the General Board of Global Ministries; and

WHEREAS, the bishops/presidents and other leadership of CIEMAL and MCCA conveyed to the Conference of Methodist

Bishops meeting in Panama in November, 2010 the critical importance of Encounter for our mission partnership, and

WHEREAS, the process of globalization and immigration has brought us ever more closer together with sister and brother Methodists of Latin America and the Caribbean; and

WHEREAS, MARCHA, along with a host of other United Methodists has supported the development of the Encounter permanent fund 025100 and the Encounter Advance Special 14729 A from the beginning of the mission effort:

Therefore, be it resolved, that General Conference celebrate the achievement of reaching the amount of 1.5 million dollars in the Encounter permanent fund 025100 and call upon annual conferences, local churches and individuals to renew and increase their commitment to Encounter as a primary mean of expressing our solidarity together in mission and ministry with Latin America and the Caribbean.

ADOPTED 2004
READOPTED 2008
AMENDED AND READOPTED 2012
RESOLUTION #3143, 2012 *BOOK OF RESOLUTIONS*
RESOLUTION #3144, 2008 *BOOK OF RESOLUTIONS*
RESOLUTION #96, 2004 *BOOK OF RESOLUTIONS*

See Social Principles, ¶ 162.

3144. Resolution of Intent: With a View to Unity

In 1750, John Wesley wrote the sermon "Catholic Spirit," in which he presented his views on mutual tolerance among those seeking to unite in love:

"... And 'tis certain, so long as 'we know' but 'in part', that all men [sic] will not see all things alike. It is an unavoidable consequence of the present weakness and shortness of human understanding that several men will be of several minds, in religion as well as in common life. So it has been from the beginning of the world, and so it will be 'till the restitution of all things.'

"Nay farther: although every man necessarily believes that every particular opinion which he holds is true (for to believe any opinion is not true is the same thing as not to hold it) yet can no man be assured that all his own opinions taken together are true.

Nay, every thinking man is assured they are not, seeing *humanum est errare et necire*—to be ignorant of many things, and to mistake in some—is the necessary condition of humanity. This therefore, he is sensible, is his own case. He knows in the general that he himself is mistaken; although in what particulars he mistakes he does not, perhaps cannot, know.

"Every wise man therefore will allow others the same liberty of thinking which he desires they should allow him; and will no more insist on their embracing his opinions than he would have them to insist on his embracing theirs. He bears with those who differ from him, and only asks him with whom he desires to unite in love that single question. 'Is thine heart, as my heart is with thy heart?' " (*The Works of John Wesley*, Volume 2, Sermons II, "Catholic Spirit," 83-85).

In 1970 the General Conference adopted a resolution of intent. It was offered to the conference by Albert Outler on behalf of the Theological Study Commission on Doctrine and Doctrinal Standards. Engaged in the debate, among others, were Harold A. Bosley, Robert E. Cushman, and Georgia Harkness. The resolution was adopted as presented (*Journal of the 1970 General Conference, The United Methodist Church*, 255). However, the resolution was not included in, or was mistakenly deleted from, *The Book of Resolutions of The United Methodist Church*, 1970.

At the General Conference of 1992, a new resolution, "Ecumenical Interpretations of Doctrinal Standards," offered by the General Commission on Christian Unity and Interreligious Concerns (now the Office of Christian Unity and Interreligious Relationships), was received, adopted, and subsequently printed in *The Book of Resolutions of The United Methodist Church*, 1992 (245-46). Although grounded in the Study Commission's resolution of intent, this document is not as comprehensive in its scope as was the original, with specific reference to our current understanding of the composition of our Doctrinal Standards.

The original resolution of intent is resubmitted as a substitute for "Ecumenical Interpretations of Doctrinal Standards":

WHEREAS, it is common knowledge that the context of the original Thirty-Nine Articles (1563—and specifically Articles XIV, XIX, XXI, XXII, XXIV, XXV, XXVIII, XXX) was bitterly polemical, it is of prime importance in an ecumenical age that they should be reconsidered and reassessed. They were aimed, deliberately, at the Roman Catholic Church in a time of reckless strife, and were a mix of the theological and nontheological convictions of embattled schismatics fighting, as they believed, for national survival and evangelical truth. John Wesley's hasty abridgement (1784) of the original Thirty-Nine Articles (down to twenty-four) retained seven out of the ten of these anti-Roman references (XIV, XV, XVI, XVIII, XIX, XX, XXI) in his enumeration. This reflects his conviction as to their applicability to the Roman Catholic Church as he perceived it at the time. This much must be recognized and acknowledged as belonging to our inheritance from our Anglican-Wesleyan past.

It is, however, one of the virtues of historical insight that it enables persons, in a later age, to recognize the circumstances of earlier events and documents without being slavishly bound to their historical evaluation, especially in a subsequent epoch when relationships have been radically altered. Such a transvaluation will enable us freely to relegate the polemics in these articles (and the anathemas of Trent, as well) to our memories "Of old, unhappy, far-off tales / And battles long ago" and to rejoice in the positive contemporary relationships that are being developed between The United Methodist Church and the Roman Catholic Church, at levels both official and unofficial.

Therefore, be it resolved, that we declare it our official intent henceforth to interpret all our Articles, Confessions, and other "standards of doctrine" in consonance with our best ecumenical insights and judgment, as these develop in the light of the Resolution of the 1968 General Conference on "The Methodist Church and the Cause of Christian Unity" (*Book of Resolutions 1968*, 65-72). This implies, at the very least, our heartiest offer of goodwill and Christian community to all our Roman Catholic brothers and sisters, in the avowed hope of the day when all bitter memories (ours and theirs) will have been redeemed by the gift of the fullness of Christian unity, through our common Lord, Jesus Christ (*Journal of the 1970 General Conference, The United Methodist Church*, 255).

ADOPTED 2000
READOPTED 2008
AMENDED AND READOPTED 2016
RESOLUTION #3144, 2012 *BOOK OF RESOLUTIONS*
RESOLUTION #3145, 2008 *BOOK OF RESOLUTIONS*
RESOLUTION #97, 2004 *BOOK OF RESOLUTIONS*
RESOLUTION #86, 2000 *BOOK OF RESOLUTIONS*

See Social Principles, ¶ 162.

3148. Affirm and Implement a Full Communion Relationship Between The Uniting Church of Sweden and The United Methodist Church

The Uniting Church of Sweden and The United Methodist Church agree that in their legislative bodies there shall be one vote to accept or reject, without separate amendment, the resolution that follows. If adopted by both churches, each church agrees to take the following measures to establish a relationship of full communion:

WHEREAS, Jesus Christ calls us to unity so that the world may believe; and

WHEREAS, The Uniting Church of Sweden and The United Methodist Church are united in the wish to deepen our witness and work together for the sharing of the love of Christ in the world and its communities,

Therefore, be it resolved, that The Uniting Church of Sweden and The United Methodist Church hereby:

1. recognize each other as constituent members of the one, holy, catholic, and apostolic church, the body of Christ, as described in the Holy Scriptures and confessed in the church's historic creeds;

2. recognize the authenticity of each other's sacraments and welcome one another to partake in the Eucharist;

3. affirm the authenticity of each church's Christian ministry;

4. recognize the validity of each other's offices of ministry.

5. actively commit to working together as partners in mission and co-laborers in the ministry of Christ Jesus, and as a visible witness to the unity of Christians in sharing the love of God among all peoples and throughout Creation.

To facilitate growing into this relationship of full communion, the two churches will appoint a coordinating committee with members from The Uniting Church of Sweden and from the Northern Europe Central Conference.

This agreement will take effect upon an affirmative vote by the General Conference and a concurring vote by The Uniting Church of Sweden.

ADOPTED 2016

See Social Principles, ¶ 162.

3149. Affirm and Implement a Full Communion Relationship Between the Moravian Church (Northern and Southern Provinces) and The United Methodist Church

The Moravian Church (Northern and Southern Provinces) and The United Methodist Church agree that in their legislative bodies there shall be one vote to accept or reject, without separate amendment, the resolution that follows. If adopted by these churches, each church agrees to take the following measures to establish a relationship of full communion:

WHEREAS, Jesus Christ calls us to unity so that the world may believe; and

WHEREAS, the Moravian Church (Northern and Southern Provinces) and The United Methodist Church find that we have deep historic ties and many parallels in the life and ministries of our two churches, and that we are united in the wish to deepen our witness and work together for the sharing of the love of Christ in the world and its communities;

Therefore, be it resolved, that the Moravian Church (Northern and Southern Provinces) and The United Methodist Church hereby:

1. Affirm that a relationship of full communion exists between our churches and that we commit ourselves to working actively and faithfully together.

2. For the purposes of this relationship, full communion is understood to entail

    2.1. recognizing and valuing the diverse gifts present in each church;

    2.2. respecting each other as part of the one holy catholic and apostolic church as affirmed in the Apostles' Creed and the Nicene Creed;

    2. 3. committing each church to cooperate in common ministries of evangelism, witness, and service;

    2.4. recognizing the validity of each other's sacramental life and ministerial orders, allowing for the transfer of membership between churches as within each church and the orderly exchange of clergy (subject to the regulations of church order and practice of each church); and

    2. 5. committing each church to continue to work for the unity of the church, recognizing that this relationship of full communion is but a step toward the unity to which we are called.

3. To facilitate growing into this relationship of full communion, the two churches appoint a coordinating committee consisting of no fewer than three representatives each (that is, three representatives of The United Methodist Church and three representatives of the Moravian Church (Northern and Southern Provinces)). This committee shall make policy recommendations to the two churches to aid in the reception of the relationship and shall explore opportunities for common ministries of evangelism, witness, and service. Both The United Methodist Church and the Moravian Church, Northern and Southern Provinces, commit to urging central conferences of The United Methodist Church and other provinces of the Unitas Fratrum to explore formal relationships of full communion, especially in Africa and Europe, where these do not already exist.

This agreement will take effect upon an affirmative vote by the General Conference and concurring votes of approval by the synods of the Northern and Southern Provinces of the Moravian Church.

ADOPTED 2016

See Social Principles, ¶ 162.

ORGANIZATION MEMBERSHIPS

3156. Pan-Methodist Full Communion

Implementing Resolution for Full Communion Among the African Methodist Episcopal Church, the African Methodist Episcopal Zion Church, the African Union Methodist Protestant Church, the Christian Methodist Episcopal Church, the Union American Methodist Episcopal Church, and The United Methodist Church

The African Methodist Episcopal Church (AMEC), The African Methodist Episcopal Zion Church (AMEZC), The African Union Methodist Protestant Church (AUMPC), The Christian Methodist Episcopal Church (CMEC), The Union American Methodist Episcopal Church (UAMEC), and The United Methodist Church (UMC) hereby agree that in their legislative bodies there shall be one vote to accept or reject, without separate amendment, the resolutions which follow. If adopted by all churches, each church agrees to take the following measures to establish a relationship of full communion:

WHEREAS, Jesus Christ calls us to unity so that the world may believe; and

WHEREAS, The African Methodist Episcopal Church, The African Methodist Episcopal Zion Church, The African Union Methodist Protestant Church, The Christian Methodist Episcopal Church, The Union American Methodist Episcopal Church, and The United Methodist Church share a common heritage of faith and a commitment to mission; and

WHEREAS, The United Methodist Church has expressed in its General Conference through a formal Act of Repentance its apology for the injury it inflicted on its African American brothers and sisters through its racist position and policies that led to the formation of the historically African American Methodist churches;

Therefore, be it resolved, that The African Methodist Episcopal Church, The African Methodist Episcopal Zion Church, The African Union Methodist Protestant Church, The Christian Methodist Episcopal Church, The Union American Methodist Episcopal Church, and The United Methodist Church hereby:

1. recognize in one another the one, holy, catholic, and apostolic faith as it is expressed in the Scriptures, confessed in the Church's historic creeds, and attested to in the common doctrinal standards of the six churches;

2. recognize the authenticity of each other's Baptism and Eucharist, and extend sacramental hospitality to one another's members;

3. recognize the validity of our respective ministries, including:
   - each other's ordination of persons to the Ministry of Word and Sacrament;
   - the authentic diaconal service of deaconesses, home missioners, and ordained deacons in the six churches; and
   - each other's polity and ministries of oversight (including the interpretation of church doctrines, discipline of members, authorization of persons for ordained and lay ministries, and provision for administrative functions);

4. recognize the full interchangeability and reciprocity of all ordained ministers of Word and Sacrament, subject to the constitutionally approved invitation for ministry in each other's churches;

5. applaud one another's ecumenical conversations with other church bodies acknowledging that each church remains free to pursue additional full communion agreements as each deems appropriate, so that the world may believe.

This agreement will be actualized upon an affirmative vote by the General Conference.

ADOPTED 2012
RESOLUTION #3150, 2012 *BOOK OF RESOLUTIONS*

See Social Principles, ¶ 162A.

EDUCATION

3161. Education: The Gift of Hope

WHEREAS, John Wesley was a "unique and remarkable educator (who) gave to the whole Methodist movement . . . a permanent passion for education"[1], and

WHEREAS, Wesley believed that persons develop their full God-given potential when they educate their mind as well as nurture their spirit; and

WHEREAS, the historic United Methodist concern for education is witnessed through commitment to educational opportunity for all persons regardless of gender, sexual orientation, ethnic origin, or economic or social background; and

WHEREAS, this commitment continues as United Methodist individuals, congregations, colleges, collegiate ministries, and other groups become involved in local education in their communities; and

WHEREAS, these efforts make a significant contribution to furthering access, advancing and enhancing student learning, and advocating for the continued improvement of educational opportunity; and

WHEREAS, educators, families, and communities are concerned about substance abuse and violence in our schools and communities, along with other social problems which undermine the safety of children and the quality of their lives in school and in society at large; and

---

1. *The Story of Methodism*, Halford E. Luccock, Paul Hutchinson, Robert W. Goodloe (Abingdon Press, 1926; page 361).

WHEREAS, United Methodists have a moral concern to take initiatives to support and create alliances involving educators, community leaders, and students to address the challenges of contemporary education and to work to resolve the threats to quality education;

Therefore, be it resolved, that every United Methodist congregation develop a strategy for being in partnership with local United Methodist-related educational institutions and collegiate ministries, other educators, community leaders, and students in providing a positive, safe, helpful, and hopeful environment in which students can live and learn and grow into principles Christian leaders.

ADOPTED 1996
AMENDED AND READOPTED 2000
AMENDED AND READOPTED 2008, 2016
RESOLUTION #3161, 2008, 2012 *BOOK OF RESOLUTIONS*
RESOLUTION #98, 2004 *BOOK OF RESOLUTIONS*
RESOLUTION #87, 2000 *BOOK OF RESOLUTIONS*

See Social Principles, ¶ 162C, D.

3162. The Right of All to Quality Education

The Social Principles acknowledge that children are full human beings in their own right (Social Principles, ¶ 162C). Children have a right to education, and parents and governments have an obligation to provide them with the access to an adequate education. "Thus, we support the development of school systems and innovative methods of education designed to assist every child toward complete fulfillment as an individual person of worth. All children have the right to quality education" (¶ 162C).

The United Methodist Church is committed to the "achievement of a world community that is a fellowship of persons who honestly love one another. We pledge ourselves to seek the meaning of the gospel in all issues that divide people and threaten the growth of world community" (¶ 165).

While remarkable progress has been made in the last ten years toward achieving education for all, the right to education remains one of the most widely and systematically violated of all human rights. In 2010, 72 million children of primary school age are not enrolled in school (2010 UNESCO Report). Gender disparities are still prevalent, even though the number of girls out of schools has declined. There has been little progress in helping to eradicate adult illiteracy, a condition that plagues 759 million people, two-thirds being women. Millions of children are leaving school without having acquired basic skills.

This was also true for the Israelites as for any of the peoples of the ancient world. Walter A. Elwell points out that in the Hebrew Scripture we find "repeatedly that the success of the community and the continuity of its culture were conditioned by the knowledge of and obedience to God's revealed law (Joshua 1:6-8). Thus, to ensure their prosperity, growth, and longevity as the people of Yahweh, Israel's mandate was one of education—diligently teaching their children to love God, and to know and obey his statutes and ordinances (Deuteronomy 6:1-9). Likewise, the New Testament record links the success of the church of Jesus Christ, as a worshiping community of 'salt and light' reaching out to a dark world, to the teaching of sound doctrine"[1] (see also John 13:34-35; Romans 12:1-2; Ephesians 4:14; Titus 2:1). Every additional year of schooling reduces a young man's risk of becoming involved in conflict by 20 percent, creating a safer world for us all.

Clearly, the above example highlights the importance of teaching children about the faith; however, it also illustrates the importance of educating children in general. The above illustrates the need to instill in our children values that could benefit the entire human family. Thus, we can echo the international community in asserting that education is a human right. We can also affirm that education is a social and spiritual benefit from which no one should be barred or impeded.

Unfortunately, the right to education remains one of the most widely and systematically violated of all human rights. Today, 115 million children are not enrolled in school; the majority of them girls. Forty percent (40%) of children in Africa receive no education. Another 150 million children start primary school but drop out before they have completed four years of education, the vast majority before they have acquired basic literacy skills. Unless urgent action is taken, they will join the ranks of nearly one billion illiterate adults in the world.

The benefits of an education are enormous. A good education helps people gain access to better paying jobs, thus, helping reduce

1. Elwell, Walter A. "Entry for 'Education in Bible Times'" *Evangelical Dictionary of Theology.*<http://www.biblestudytools.net/Dictionaries/BakerEvangelicalDictionary/bed.cgi?number=1218. 1997

the number of people who live in poverty. By the same token, a good education is essential for a sustained economic growth. Education provides people with skills and empowers them to take advantage of new opportunities. Completing just five years of education can increase agricultural efficiency significantly. In addition, studies have shown that educating girls not only raises their future wages, but dramatically reduces infant and maternal mortality rates.

People across the world are demanding that the right to education for all children be upheld. Governments, local communities and community-based organizations in poor countries are striving, often in spite of the most appalling adversity, to educate their children. Recent achievements to provide primary education could be derailed by the global economic crisis, newly falling aid levels, and educational challenges. In May 2010, seven million people participated in the Global Campaign for Education's week of action and called for an end to the global crisis in education. The mission of the Campaign is to make sure that governments act now to deliver the right to every girl, boy, and woman and man to a free quality public education.

In 2000 many communities around the world responded to The United Nations' call to "Education for All." In addition, the United Nations' "Millennium Development Goals" document includes a goal to achieve universal primary education by 2015. Rich countries have repeatedly promised that poor countries with credible national education plans would not be allowed to fail due to a lack of resources, but this promise has yet to be translated into action. UNESCO estimates that $16 billion will be needed each year to achieve this goal. If current trends continue, 56 million primary school age children will still be out of school by 2015. Rich countries and the World Bank must increase and improve aid for basic education.

Therefore, the General Conference of The United Methodist Church calls on the United States, the European Union, China, Japan, Brazil, Argentina, India, and other rich nations as well as the International Monetary Fund and the World Bank to deliver on their promises to the world's children by providing substantial and sustained increases in aid for basic education in poor countries, and create a Global Fund for Education. The International Monetary Fund must not press governments to cut education spending as a means to "balance" their budgets, or to stimulate the economy.

In addition, we urge United Methodists in countries around the world to advocate their governments to provide such support for their children's education.

ADOPTED 2004
AMENDED AND READOPTED 2012
RESOLUTION #3162, 2008, 2012 *BOOK OF RESOLUTIONS*
RESOLUTION #100, 2004 *BOOK OF RESOLUTIONS*

See Social Principles, ¶ 162C, *D*.

3164. DREAM Act

WHEREAS, for generations workers and their young children have come to the US without authorization to satisfy the labor needs of our nation, contributing to its economic development; and,

WHEREAS, these children are being penalized by increased college tuition and are denied the opportunity to practice their profession because of their immigration status; and

WHEREAS, the Federal DREAM Act, first introduced in Congress in 2001, is a bipartisan legislation that would open the possibility of higher education, as well as a conditional pathway to US citizenship, for undocumented students who were brought to the US as children (before their 16th birthday), and who are now caught in a situation that is not of their own making. The Act would require such students, sometimes known as "The Dreamers," to complete a college degree or two years of military service in order to be granted temporary residency and then be eligible to apply for US citizenship.

Therefore, we, the General Conference of The UMC, urge the US Congress to adopt the DREAM Act and provide for these children, who have lived most their lives in this country, access to educational opportunities and full participation in the life of the only nation they have known, and identify with, the US.

ADOPTED 2012
RESOLUTION #3164, 2012 *BOOK OF RESOLUTIONS*

See Social Principles, ¶ 162C, *D*, and *H*.

3165. United States Public Education and the Church

I. Historic Church Support for Public Education

In the past, The United Methodist Church has issued statements supportive of public education. At a time when public education has become a political battleground, the church is called to remember, first and foremost, the well-being of all God's children. Education is a right of all children and is affirmed by Scripture which calls us to "train children in the way they should go" (Proverbs 22:6). Furthermore, the Social Principles affirm that education "can best be fulfilled through public policies that ensure access for all persons to free public elementary and secondary schools and to post-secondary schools of their choice" (¶ 164E <https://www.umofficialresources.com/reader/9781426766213/>).

The public school is the primary route through which most children enter into full participation in our economic, political, and community life. As a consequence of inequities in our society, we have a moral responsibility to support, strengthen, and reform public schools. They have been, and continue to be, both an avenue of opportunity and a major cohesive force in our society, especially as society becomes more diverse—racially, culturally, and religiously—almost daily.

Historically, education has been held to contribute to the development of religious faith. To that end, the great figures of the Reformation called for the establishment of schools. Our founder, John Wesley, was dedicated to the education of poor and underprivileged children. The Sunday School Movement of the latter 18th century was an outgrowth of this ministry and largely established a model for access to public education, regardless of social or economic status. Our heritage should lead us to defend the public schools and to rejoice that they nearly reflect our country's racial, ethnic, and religious diversity now more than ever before.

II. The Larger Social Context

We welcome the fact that many public schools now teach about diversity and the role of religion in human life and history; and we applaud the schools' efforts to promote those virtues necessary for good citizenship in a pluralistic democracy. These reforms help to accommodate the constitutional rights of all students and their parents. Just as we encourage schools to ensure that all religions are treated with fairness and respect, so we urge parents and others to refrain from the temptation to use public schools to advance the cause of any one religion or ethnic tradition, whether through curriculum or through efforts to attach religious personnel to the public schools. We believe that parents have the right to select home schooling or private or parochial schools for their children. But with that personal right comes an obligation to support quality public education for all children. The long-range solution is to improve all schools so that families will not be forced to seek other educational alternatives.

At a moment when childhood poverty is shamefully widespread, when many families are under constant stress, and when schools are limited by the lack of funds and resources, criticism of the public schools often ignores an essential truth: we cannot improve public schools by concentrating on the schools alone. In this context, we must address with prayerful determination the issues of race and class that threaten both public education and democracy in America.

III. Disparities in High School Graduation Rates

The Social Principles support "the development of school systems and innovative methods of education designed to assist every child toward complete fulfillment as an individual person of worth" (¶ 162C). Unfortunately, many schools in the United States are far from achieving this goal. According to the National Center for Education Statistics, in 2012, some 3.1 million public high school students—only 81 percent, graduated on time with a regular diploma. Failure to finish high school with a diploma, with the devastating consequences this has for an individual's future prospects, is a bitter reality that disproportionately impacts minority youth. Nationally, the highest graduation rates are among Asian/Pacific Islanders (93 percent) followed by Caucasians (85 percent). Graduation rates are substantially lower for other students of all backgrounds: among Hispanics, only 76 percent of student entering the ninth grade graduate four years later, while just 68 percent of African Americans do so, with similar figures for indigenous youth. These high attrition rates have been attributed to both "drop out" and "push out"—students dropping out of school because they find no help or encouragement to overcome challenges, and to low-achieving students being pushed out into alternative programs such as GED to improve a school's test scores.

These sobering figures clearly indicate that, despite some progress in recent years, schools in the United States are largely failing to equip a large number of students, and a high percentage of minority youth, with the knowledge, understanding, and skills needed for entering college or gainful employment, as well as the exercise of citizenship responsibilities necessary for the survival of a democratic society. These failings are indicative of a crisis that is marginalizing millions of American youth (especially minority youth), consigning them to second-class citizenship, contributing to an erosion of American democracy, and leaving many members of faith communities less equipped to bear witness to issues of justice and peace.

IV. Public Funding Issues

By almost any standard of judgment, the schools our children attend can be described in contradictory terms. Some are academically excellent; others are a virtual disgrace. Some are oases of safety for their students; others are dangerous to student and teacher alike. Some teachers are exceptionally well qualified; others are assigned to areas in which they have little or no expertise. Some school facilities are a fantasy land of modern technology; others are so dilapidated that they impede learning.

The wide disparities among public schools exist largely because schools reflect the affluence and/or the political power of the communities in which they are found. Within virtually every state, there are school districts that lavish on their students three or four times the amount of money spent on other children in the same state. A new phenomenon in our society is "re-segregating of communities" which further diminishes the effectiveness of public schools. Most tellingly, the schools that offer the least to their students are those serving poor children, among which children of color figure disproportionately, as they do in all the shortfalls of our common life. Indeed, the coexistence of neglect of schools and neglect of other aspects of the life of people who are poor makes it clear that no effort to improve education in the United States can ignore the realities of racial and class discrimination in our society as a whole.

We acknowledge the debate over whether public funds might appropriately be used to remedy the lingering effects of racial injustice in our nation's educational system. We do not purport to resolve our differences over this issue, but we do affirm our conviction that public funds should be used for public purposes. We also caution that government aid to primary and secondary religious schools raises constitutional problems and could undermine the private schools' independence and/or compromise their religious message.

V. A Call to Action

In view of this crisis and the urgent need to hold our educational system accountable in providing equity in access to a high school education for all students from all social backgrounds, we call upon local, state, and federal education agencies to do the following:

1. Publicly report annual graduation and retention rates by sex, race and ethnicity;
2. Make increasing retention and graduation rates a major focus of educational reform along with equitable distribution of financial and educational resources to all school districts so that they may provide a quality education to all students.

Local churches and all communities of faith must become better informed about the needs of the public schools in their communities and in the country as a whole. Only through adequate information can we defend public education and the democratic heritage which it supports. Full knowledge of our religious and democratic traditions helps us ensure that those elected to school boards are strongly committed to both public education and religious liberty.

Therefore, we call upon local churches, annual conferences, and the general agencies of The United Methodist Church to support public education in the following ways:

1. Establish and nurture partnerships with local public schools such as providing after-school and vacation enrichment programs, adopt-a-school programs, teacher appreciation programs, updated library materials, and parenting enrichment classes.

2. Monitor reform efforts in public schools, including the creation of charter and magnet schools, of schools-within-schools, of full inclusion or appropriate placement of children who are differently-abled, and of classes sized to best serve all children;

3. Prompt local and state authorities to offer students curricula and textbooks that are rich, inviting, and include the following ideas:

- religion as an essential dimension in the development of civilization;
- basic character and civic virtues such as honesty, truthfulness, and respect for life and property;
- the role of the many ethnic, racial, and religious groups in the history and culture of the United States; and
- quality, age-appropriate comprehensive health education.

4. Reject racial- and gender-biased curricula and testing which limit career options of children and youth;

5. Advocate at the state and local level for adequate public school funding and equitable distribution of state funds; and supporting efforts to end unjust educational disparities between rich and poor communities;

6. Champion strengthened teacher training and enhanced professional development for teachers and administrators. Encourage young people in the church to consider careers in education.

7. Push for universal, early, and quality preschool education for all children.

8. Champion public education as a basic human right; and curb school districts' reliance on school fund-raising and state-alternative revenues, such as gambling, for financial support.

9. Encourage local churches to provide and/or support local nutritional initiatives, especially when schools are not in session.

ADOPTED 2000
AMENDED AND READOPTED 2004
READOPTED 2008
AMENDED AND READOPTED 2016
RESOLUTION #5051, 2008, 2012 *BOOK OF RESOLUTIONS*
RESOLUTION #263, 2004 *BOOK OF RESOLUTIONS*
RESOLUTION #246, 2000 *BOOK OF RESOLUTIONS*

See Social Principles, ¶ 162C.

GENETICS

3181. New Developments in Genetic Science

I. Foreword

The ethical implications of new developments in genetic science continue to make themselves known as new aspects of the technology are introduced in medicine, agriculture, and forensic science.

The 1988 General Conference approved a statement affirming the positive prospects and warning of the potential dangers of genetic technologies and authorized the establishment of a Genetic Science task force to:

1. review and assess scientific developments in genetics and their implications for all life;

2. take initiatives with industrial, governmental, and educational institutions involved in genetic engineering to discuss further projections and possible impact;

3. convey to industry and government the sense of urgency to protect the environment as well as animal and human life;

4. support a moratorium on animal patenting until the task force has explored the ethical issues involved;

5. cooperate with other churches, faith groups, and ecumenical bodies sharing similar concerns;

6. explore the effects of the concentration of genetic engineering research tasks and applications in a few crops; and

7. recommend to the 1992 General Conference such further responses and actions as may be deemed appropriate.

II. Our Theological Grounding

The United Methodist doctrinal/theological statement affirms that "new issues continually arise that summon us to fresh theological inquiry. Daily we are presented with an array of concerns that challenge our proclamation of God's reign over all of human existence" (1988 *Book of Discipline*, ¶ 69).

One of the concerns that merits critique in light of theological understandings is genetic science. The urgent task of interpreting the faith in light of the biotechnology revolution and evaluating the rapidly emerging genetic science and technology has only begun. The issues demand continuing dialogue at all levels of the church as persons from diverse perspectives seek to discern and live out God's vision for creation.

The following affirmations provide the theological/doctrinal foundation of the task force's work and recommendations. The task force urges the whole church to join in the urgent task of theological inquiry in what has been called the genetic age.

A. All creation belongs to God the creator

Creation has its origin, existence, value, and destiny in God. Creation belongs to God, whose power and grace bring the cosmos out of nothingness, order out of chaos, and life out of death. Creation is a realm of divine activity as God continually seeks to bring healing, wholeness, and peace. The goodness of our genetic diversity is grounded in our creation by God.

B. Human beings are stewards of creation

While human beings share with other species the limitations of finite creatures who owe their existence to God, their special creation "in the image of God" gives them the freedom and authority to exercise stewardship responsibly.

The image of God, in which humanity is created, confers both power and responsibility to use power as God does: neither by coercion nor tyranny, but by love. Failure to accept limits by rejecting or ignoring accountability to God and interdependency with the whole of creation is the essence of sin. Although the pursuit of knowledge is a divine gift, it must be used appropriately with the principle of accountability to God and to the human community and the sustainability of all creation.

C. Technology in service to humanity and God

God has given human beings the capacity for research and technological invention, but the worship of science is idolatry. Genetic techniques have enormous potential for sustaining creation and, for some, improving the quality of human life when they are applied to environmental, agricultural, and medical problems. When wisely used, they often provide positive, though limited and imperfect, solutions to such perplexing social problems as insufficient food supply, spread of disease, ecological deterioration, overpopulation, and human disease. When used recklessly, for greedy profit, or for calculated improvement of the human race (eugenics), genetic technology becomes corrupted by sin. Moreover, we recognize that even the careful use of genetic technologies for good ends may lead to unintended consequences. We confess that even our intended consequences may not be in the best interest of all.

D. From creation to redemption and salvation

Redemption and salvation become realities by divine grace as we respond in faith to God's action in Jesus Christ to defeat the powers of sin that enslave the human spirit and thwart the realization of God's purposes for creation. Having distorted God's good intention for us in creation, we now are called to be conformed to God's true image in Jesus Christ.

The community of Christ bears witness to the truth that all persons have unity by virtue of having been redeemed by Christ. Such unity respects and embraces genetic diversity, which accounts for many differences among people. Love and justice, which the Scriptures uplift and which Jesus Christ supremely expresses, require that the worth and dignity of the defenseless be preserved and protected.

III. Issues in the Development of Genetic Research and Technology

A. Genetic science affects every area of our lives

The food we eat, the health care we receive, how crimes are prosecuted, our biological traits, and the environment in which we live are all affected by research and developments in genetic science. As stewards of and participants in life and its resources, we seek to understand, to evaluate, and to utilize responsibly the emerging genetic technologies in accordance with our finite understanding of God's purposes for creation. The uses of genetic science have the potential for promoting as well as thwarting these aspects of the divine purpose.

The rapid growth of genetic science has increased our awareness of these concerns, has created new concerns, and has accelerated the theological, ethical, and pastoral challenges that genetics poses to persons of faith.

B. Scientific change now leads societal change

A major dimension of the biological revolution is genetic science. Fewer than fifty years ago, the actual genetic substance of living cells, DNA, was firmly identified. Now, altering DNA in plants and animals, even humans, in order to correct disorders or to introduce characteristics that are more desirable is being done. Genetic developments in medicine and agriculture promise to alter the very nature of society, the natural environment, and even human nature.

C. Genetic science challenges society

Extensive research has been conducted in plant and animal genetics, with significant implications for the food supply, farm policy, agricultural economics, and ecological balance. New developments in genetic engineering, collectively called synthetic biology, are allowing the re-engineering of whole organisms. Bioengineers have "printed out," from computers linked with vials of nucleic acids of DNA and RNA, whole viruses and bacteria using these synthetic biology tools. These enhanced kinds of genetic engineering are already being used to make new drugs and new foods (See "Principles for the Oversight of Synthetic Biology" available at: <http://www.synbiowatch.org/2013/05/principles-for-the-oversight-of-synthetic-biology/>). Delays in commercializing some of the new technologies may afford society and the church additional time to address the implications, but the time available for serious reflection on the consequences of these technologies prior to their implementation is brief.

IV. Questions About Biotechnology

Although genetic technologies are similar to other technologies, genetic science and technology force us to examine, as never before, the meaning of life, our understanding of ourselves as humans, and our proper role in God's creation.

Several basic questions can provide a framework within which to evaluate the effect of genetics or any other new technology on any segment of society. The questions revolve around issues of appropriateness, availability, efficacy, and accessibility.

V. The Patenting of Life Forms

The patenting of life forms is a crucial issue in the debate over access to genetic technologies. Some claim that patenting of life will give complete control to the owner and so limit access. Others insist that the scientists and funding agencies or institutions must have some return on their investment. A compromise that many societies have worked out in order to provide economic returns for those who have developed a technology while providing access, eventually, to the entire society is the patent or exclusive control of a technological invention for a period of years.

In 1984, the General Conference of The United Methodist Church declared genes to be a part of the common heritage of all peoples. Therefore, exclusive ownership rights of genes, organisms, and cells as a means of making genetic technologies accessible raises serious theological concerns and profound ethical concerns. While patents on organisms, cells, and genes themselves are opposed, process patents—wherein the method for engineering a new organism is patented—provide a means of economic return on investment while avoiding exclusive ownership of the organism and can be supported. In 2013, the US Supreme Court ruled that genes are not patentable subject matter, but still allowed copies of the genes to be patented (<http://www.supremecourt.gov/opinions/12pdf/12-398_1b7d.pdf>).

VI. Recommendations

A. Medical implications

1. Testing and treatment
   a. We support the right of all persons to health care and health-care resources regardless of their genetic or medical conditions.
   b. We support equal access to medical resources, including genetic testing and genetic counseling by appropriately educated and trained health-care professionals.
   c. We support human somatic gene therapies (recombinant DNA therapies that produce genetic changes in an individual that cannot be passed to offspring) that prevent or minimize disease and its effects. But we believe these therapies should be limited to the alleviation of suffering caused by disease. We are concerned by reports of deaths of patients in somatic-gene research programs and urge that strengthened guidelines and government regulations be developed for the use of all somatic gene therapies. We oppose human germ-line therapies (those that result in changes that can be passed to offspring) because of the possibility of unintended consequences and of abuse. We are concerned that both the US and the United Kingdom are considering approving the first experiments that would deliberately change the DNA of a human embryo. With current technology it is not possible to know if artificially introduced genes will have

unexpected or delayed long-term effects not identifiable until the genes have been dispersed in the population.

Furthermore, we urge that government regulations and professional organization guidelines be developed and effectively implemented for all gene therapies. Given the reports of deaths from somatic gene therapies and the development of genetically engineered leukemia in some patients undergoing somatic-gene therapy, we urge a careful reexamination of the appropriateness of this therapy.

d. We call on all nations to ban human cloning (the intentional production of genetically identical or essentially identical human beings and human embryos), whether such cloning is funded privately or through government research.

e. We call for a ban on medical and research procedures that intentionally generate "waste embryos" that will knowingly be destroyed when the medical procedure or the research is completed. The exception to this is when ova (eggs) are being collected for in vitro fertilization. A woman is at risk for complications each time drugs are given to stimulate ovulation and ova are removed. Obtaining and fertilizing multiple ova may be justified to avoid the necessity of multiple attempts to obtain ova. The first attempt at IVF results in a living child less than 30% of the time thus making multiple attempts necessary.

2. Privacy and confidentiality of genetic information

a. We support the privacy of genetic information. Genetic data of individuals and their families shall be kept secret and held in strict confidence unless confidentiality is waived by the individual or his or her family, or unless the collection and use of genetic identification data are supported by an appropriate court order.

b. We support wide public access to genetic data that do not identify particular individuals, but we oppose using genetic data gathered for purposes other than that to which consent was given.

c. We oppose the discriminatory or manipulative use of genetic information, such as limiting, terminating, or denying insurance or employment.

B. Agricultural implications

1. We support public involvement in initiating, evaluating, regulating, and funding of agricultural genetic research.

    a. We believe the public has an important policy and financial role in ensuring the continuation of research that furthers the goal of a safe, nutritious, and affordable food supply.

    b. We believe that the public should have input into whether a research effort, or its products, will serve an unmet need in food, fuel, fiber production and processing.

    c. We believe that the benefits of research applications should accrue to the broadest possible public, including farmers and consumers.

2. We urge that genetically modified crops and genetically engineered or cloned animal products be fully tested as new food stuff, and that they be labeled so that consumers have a choice in which kind of agricultural products they buy.

C. Environmental implications

1. As stewards of the planet Earth, we should be concerned not only with the well-being of humans, but also with the wholeness of the rest of creation.

2. We urge that genetically engineered organisms be released into the environment only after careful testing in a controlled setting that simulates each environment in which the organisms are to be used.

3. We urge the development of criteria and methodologies to anticipate and assess possible adverse environmental responses to the release of genetically engineered organisms.

4. Prior to the release of each organism, plans and procedures should be developed to destroy genetically engineered organisms that may cause adverse environmental responses.

VII. What the Church Can Do

1. We request that clergy be trained to provide pastoral counseling for persons with genetic disorders and their families as well as those facing difficult choices as a result of genetic testing. These choices might include decisions such as those related to reproduction, employment, and living wills. Churches are encouraged to

provide support groups for individuals and families affected by genetic disorders.

2. We call on the church to support persons who must make difficult decisions regarding genetic information related to reproduction. We urge that the church support efforts to improve the quality of genetic testing on embryos and fetuses so that accurate information is provided to couples and their doctors about genetic conditions. We reaffirm the United Methodist position opposing the termination of pregnancy solely for the purpose of gender selection (2012 United Methodist *Book of Discipline* ¶ 161J).

3. We urge theological seminaries to include courses and continuing education events that equip clergy to address theological and ethical issues raised by scientific research and technology.

4. We urge the church to establish and maintain dialogue with those persons working to develop or promote genetics-based technologies, including especially those working in the fields of synthetic biology. The ethical concerns of the church need to be injected into the laboratory, the factory, and the halls of government in an ongoing manner.

5. Produce resources to educate on genetics science, theology and ethics, including workshops, seminars and resource materials. General agencies of the church should develop additional interpretive resources on genetics issues.

ADOPTED 1992
AMENDED AND READOPTED 2000
AMENDED AND READOPTED 2008, 2016
RESOLUTION #3181, 2008, 2012 *BOOK OF RESOLUTIONS*
RESOLUTION #102, 2004 *BOOK OF RESOLUTIONS*
RESOLUTION #90, 2000 *BOOK OF RESOLUTIONS*

See Social Principles, ¶ 162O.

3182. Human Cloning

Cloning has sparked enormous and sustained concern in the general public, including the church. For the purposes of this document, human cloning means the intentional production of genetically identical or essentially identical human beings and human embryos. Cloning touches on many crucial questions about human nature, raises hopes and expectations, and brings to the fore uncertainties and fears. While we do not see obvious benefits of human cloning and while we recognize potential dangers of cloning, we also acknowledge the excitement that this new research generates for advances in medicine, agriculture, and other scientific endeavors.

As United Methodists, our reflections on these issues emerge from our faith. We remember that creation has its origin, value, and destiny in God, that human beings are stewards of creation, that technology has brought forth both great benefit and great harm to creation. As people of faith, we believe that our identity as human beings is more than our genetic inheritance, our social environment, or the sum of the two. We are created by God and have been redeemed by Jesus Christ. We recognize that our present human knowledge on this issue is incomplete and finite. We do not know all of the consequences of cloning (psychological, social, or genetic). It is important that the limits of human knowledge be considered as policy is made.

Therefore, we submit the following policy positions:

1. We call for a global ban on all human cloning, including the cloning of human embryos. This would include all projects, privately or governmentally funded, that are intended to advance human cloning. Transcending our concerns with embryo wastage are a number of other unresolved and barely explored concerns with substantial social and theological ramifications: use or abuse of people, exploitation of women, tearing of the fabric of the family, the compromising of human distinctiveness, the lessening of genetic diversity, the direction of research and development being controlled by corporate profit and/or personal gain, and the invasion of privacy. These unresolved concerns generate significant distrust and fear in the general public.

2. We call for a ban on therapeutic, medical, research, and commercial procedures which generate unused embryos for the purpose of cloning, including the making of embryos for experiments or stem cells. The methods of concurrent research protocols in cloning necessitate the production of excess or "unused embryos," which are ultimately destroyed.

3. We commit to the widespread discussion of issues related to cloning in public forums, including United Methodist schools, seminaries, hospitals, and churches. Given the profound theological and moral implications, the imperfection of human knowledge,

and the tremendous risks and social benefits, we urge that there be a moratorium on cloning-related research until these issues can be discussed fully by both the general public including significant participation from communities of faith, as well as by experts in agricultural and biological science, public policy, ethics, theology, law, and medicine, including genetics and genetic counseling. The psychological and social effects of cloning on individuals, families, parental relationships, and the larger society should be fully discussed. Those presently affected by in vitro fertilization, surrogacy, artificial insemination, and other reproduction technologies should be consulted to provide insight into some related psychological and social issues.

4. We call on all nations to ban human cloning, including the cloning of human embryos for research, and to identify appropriate government agencies to enforce the ban. Appropriate social and governmental bodies must monitor and guide research and developments in the field. Concern for profit and commercial advantage should be balanced by consideration for individual rights, the interest of wide constituencies, and the common good of future generations.

ADOPTED 2000
REVISED AND READOPTED 2008, 2016
RESOLUTION #3182, 2008, 2012 BOOK OF RESOLUTIONS
RESOLUTION #103, 2004 BOOK OF RESOLUTIONS
RESOLUTION #91, 2000 BOOK OF RESOLUTIONS

See Social Principles, ¶ 1620.

3184. Repentance for Support of Eugenics

Eugenics, the belief that certain "genetic" traits are good and others bad, is associated in the public mind mostly with the extreme eugenics policies of Adolf Hitler, which ultimately led to the Holocaust. The study of eugenics did not begin with Hitler or his German scientists, but rather was first promoted by Sir Francis Galton, in England. Galton, a cousin of Charles Darwin, expanded on Darwin's theories and applied them to the human population. In an article entitled "Hereditary Character and Talent" (published in two parts in MacMillan's Magazine, vol. 11, November 1864 and April 1865, pp. 157-166, 318-327), Galton expressed his frustration that no one was breeding a better human:

"If a twentieth part of the cost and pains were spent in measures for the improvement of the human race that is spent on the improvement of the breed of horses and cattle, what a galaxy of genius might we not create! We might introduce prophets and high priests of civilization into the world, as surely as we can propagate idiots by mating cretins. Men and women of the present day are, to those we might hope to bring into existence, what the pariah dogs of the streets of an Eastern town are to our own highly-bred varieties."

Galton in the same article described Africans and Native Americans in derogatory terms making it clear which racial group he thought was superior. Francis Galton, the founder of the Eugenics Society, spoke hopefully about persuading people with desirable genes to marry and have large families. Galton's successor at the helm of the Eugenics Society was Major Leonard Darwin (1850-1943), a son of Charles Darwin. Leonard Darwin, who ran the Eugenics Society until 1928, made the transition from "positive eugencis" to "negative eugenics" and promoted plans for lowering the birthrate of the unfit.

Built into the idea of natural selection is a competition between the strong and the weak, between the fit and the unfit. The eugenicists believed that this mechanism was thwarted in the human race by charity, by people and churches who fed the poor and the weak so that they survived, thrived, and reproduced.

Ironically, as the Eugenics Movement came to the United States, the churches, especially the Methodists, the Presbyterians, and the Episcopalians, embraced it.

Methodist churches around the country promoted the American Eugenics Society "Fitter Family Contests" wherein the fittest families were invariably fair skinned and well off. Methodist bishops endorsed one of the first books circulated to the US churches promoting eugenics.[1] Unlike the battles over evolution and creationism, both conservative and progressive church leaders endorsed eugenics. The liberal Rev. Harry F. Ward, professor of Christian ethics and a founder of the Methodist Federation for Social Service, writing in *Eugenics*, the magazine of the American Eugenic Society, said that Christianity and eugenics were compatible

1. George Henry Naply, *The Transmission of Life*, Philadelphia: J. Fergus, 1871 endorsed by Bishop Levi Scott and Bishop T. A. Morris, both of the Methodist Episcopal Church.

because both pursued the "challenge of removing the causes that produce the weak."[2]

Conservative Rev. Clarence True Wilson, the General Secretary of the Methodist Episcopal Board of Temperance, Prohibition, and Public Morals, and the man chosen to debate Clarence Darrow after William Jennings Bryan's death, believed that only the white Aryan race was the descendant of the lost tribes of Israel.[3] Methodists were active on the planning committees of the Race Betterment Conferences held in 1914, and 1915.[4] In the 1910s, Methodist churches hosted forums in their churches to discuss eugenics. In the 1920s, many Methodist preachers submitted their eugenics sermons to contests hosted by the American Eugenics Society. By 1927, when the American Eugenics Society formed its Committee on the Cooperation with Clergymen, Bishop Francis McConnell, president of the Methodist Federation for Social Service, served on the committee. In 1936, he would chair the roundtable discussion on Religion and Eugenics at the American Eugenics Society Meeting.[5] The laity of the church also took up the cause of eugenics. In 1929, the *Methodist Review* published the sermon "Eugenics: A Lay Sermon" by George Huntington Donaldson. In the sermon, Donaldson argues, "the strongest and the best are selected for the task of propagating the likeness of God and carrying on his work of improving the race."[6]

Both the Methodist Episcopal Church and the Methodist Episcopal Church, South promoted eugenics.[7] Most of the time, church advocates of eugenics supported "positive eugenics"—essentially careful selection of mates. Nevertheless, sterilization became an

2. Harry F. Ward, "Is Christian Morality Harmful, Over Charitable to the Unfit?" *Eugenics I* (December 1928):20.

3. Robert Dean McNeil, *Valiant for Truth, Oregonians Concerned About Addiction Problems*, Portland, (1992), pp.19,141 Prohibition was Wilson's main concern as the head of the Methodist Episcopal Board of Temperance, Prohibition, and Public Morals, but eugenics, anti-immigrant programs, anti-Catholic sentiments were a key part of his message. He believed that Indians and Negros were especially prone to alcoholism. (See his *The Pocket Cyclopedia of Temperance*, p. 252.)

4. Methodist Episcopal Bishop John Hamilton of the San Francisco Area served on the planning committee for the 1915 Conference. See *Proceedings of the Second National Conference on Race Betterment*, August 4-8, 1915.

5. American Eugenics Society, program for "Round Table Conferences and Annual Meeting," New York, 1936.

6. George Huntington Donaldson, "Eugenics: A Lay Sermon," *Methodist Review*, 112 (1929), p. 60.

7. See C. L. Dorris, "The Impending Disaster," *Methodist Review*, 75 (1926):720-724.

acceptable kind of eugenics along with marriage laws limiting marriage between whites and nonwhites. Some annual conferences supported such laws and a few opposed them.

Indiana passed the first forced sterilization law in 1907; eventually 33 states passed similar laws. Most used Harry Laughlin's model law that provided for the sterilization of "feeble minded, insane, criminalistic, epileptic, diseased, blind, deaf, deformed, and dependent" including "orphans, ne'er do wells, tramps, homeless, and paupers."[8] Virginia passed in 1924 a sterilization law based on the Laughlin model and on the same day passed a law making marriage between a white person and a nonwhite person a felony.[9]

Thirty-three US States eventually passed laws authorizing sterilization of criminals, the mentally ill, the "feeble minded." Sterilization of the allegedly mentally ill continued into the 1970s in several states, by which time about 60,000 Americans had been involuntarily sterilized. In 1933, Hitler's Nazi government used Laughlin's Model Law as the basis for its sterilization law that led to the sterilization of some 350,000 people.

State-sponsored eugenics reached an abhorrent extreme in the Nazi extermination programs of the 1930s and 1940s. Initially directed at people with similar health or social problems as were targeted by the US sterilization laws, these were eventually expanded to cover entire populations—Jews, Gypsies, Poles— judged by the Nazi regime to represent "worthless lives" (*lebensunwerte Leben*). While certain overt state policies such as the use of gas chambers have not been used recently, "ethnic cleansing" has emerged in several countries—including Bosnia, Rwanda, Cambodia, and Sudan and shows that eugenic horrors have not disappeared.

8. www.eugenicsarchive.org <http://www.eugenicsarchive.org>, Essay 8— Sterilization Laws.

9. On March 20, 1924, the Virginia Legislature passed two closely related eugenics laws: SB 219, entitled "The Racial Integrity Act[1]" and SB 281, "An ACT to provide for the sexual sterilization of inmates of State institutions in certain cases," henceforth referred to as "The Sterilization Act." The Racial Integrity Act required that a racial description of every person be recorded at birth, and felonized marriage between "white persons" and nonwhite persons. The law was the most famous ban on miscegenation in the US and was overturned by the US Supreme Court in 1967, in Loving v. Virginia. Virginia repealed the sterilization act in 1979. In 2001, the House of Delegates voted to express regret for the state's selecting breeding policies that had forced sterilizations on some 8,000 people. The Senate soon followed suit.

While Germany now has a strong sensitivity to the issues of eugenics, in the US apology for past eugenic excesses has been slow in coming. California did not repeal its law until 1979 and, in 1985, around 20 states still had laws on their books that permitted the involuntary sterilization of "mentally retarded" persons. Family planning programs around the world have included forced sterilization as a tool even recently. In 2002, Peru's Minister of Health issued an apology for the forced sterilization of indigenous women during the recent presidency of Alberto Fujimori. The state governments of Virginia, California, Oregon, and North Carolina have apologized for their support of eugenics. United Methodist General Conferences have called for an end to forced sterilization, but have not yet apologized on behalf of Methodist predecessors who advocated for eugenic polices.

Repentance for Support of Eugenics

Matthew in the opening of his Gospel (Matthew 1:1-16) reminds us that in Jesus' earthly family were not just Jews, but also four Gentile women. As Christians, we are not called because of our genetic identity; we are not called to reengineer our bodies or those of our children, or destroy those different from us, but rather to follow Christ.

The United Methodist General Conference formally apologizes for Methodist leaders and Methodist bodies who in the past supported eugenics as sound science and sound theology. We lament the ways eugenics was used to justify the sterilization of persons deemed less worthy. We lament that Methodist support of eugenics policies was used to keep persons of different races from marrying and forming legally recognized families. We are especially grieved that the politics of eugenics led to the extermination of millions of people by the Nazi government and continues today as "ethnic cleansing" around the world. We urge United Methodist annual conferences to educate their members about eugenics and advocate for ethical uses of science.

ADOPTED 2008
AMENDED AND READOPTED 2016
RESOLUTION #3184, 2012 *BOOK OF RESOLUTIONS*
RESOLUTION #3185, 2008 *BOOK OF RESOLUTIONS*

See Social Principles, ¶ 1620.

HEALTH CARE

3201. Health Care for All in the United States

Theological and Historical Statement

From our earliest days United Methodists have believed that providing health care to others is an important duty of Christians. John Wesley found ways to offer medical services at no cost to the poor in London. The first Methodist Social Creed (adopted in 1908) urged working conditions to safeguard the health of workers and community.

The provision of health care for all without regard to status or ability to pay is portrayed in the parable of the good Samaritan (Luke 10:24-35) as the duty of every neighbor and thus of every person. In a conversation that began with the question of how one might obtain eternal life, Jesus asserted that one must love God and one's neighbor. In response to the next question as to who one's neighbor is, Jesus portrayed a Samaritan, an outsider, who, coming upon a wounded traveler, provided him with health care. Jesus portrayed the duty to provide health care as (1) one that is owed regardless of the merit or ethnicity of the person in need; (2) one that is owed to the limit of one's economic capacity—the Samaritan told the innkeeper, "Take care of him, and when I return, I will pay you back for any additional costs" (v. 35); and (3) a duty that one neglects at the peril of one's eternal life. In a democracy, where citizens govern, our duty to our neighbor merges with the duties that the Hebrew Scriptures assign to government: The prophet Ezekiel denounced the leaders of ancient Israel whose failure of responsible government included failure to provide health care: "You don't strengthen the weak, heal the sick, bind up the injured, bring back the strays, or seek out the lost; but instead you use force to rule them with injustice" (Ezekiel 34:4). The United Methodist Church therefore affirms in our Social Principles (¶ 162V) health care as a basic human right, and affirms the duty of government to assure health care for all.

In the United States today, however, despite the passage and implementation of the Affordable Care Act, fulfillment of this duty is thwarted by simultaneous crises of access, quality, and cost. The result of these crises is injustice to the most vulnerable, increased risk to health care consumers, and waste of scarce public and private resources.

Access Barriers Are an Injustice to the Most Vulnerable

In today's United States, health-care access continues to be disproportionately afforded to the affluent, the employees of government and large corporations, the very poor, and many receiving adequate pensions plus Medicare. While numbers of Americans have now obtained through the Affordable Care Act (ACA) insurance they previously could not access, uneven application of the law from state to state means that many continue to be uninsured. Lack of health-care access affects minorities disparately, and the results of the devastating expense of a long-term or terminal illness, inadequate care in general, and the extraordinary cost of insurance all contribute to keeping many minorities in the poverty cycle, dependent on welfare and other forms of assistance, and imprisoned in struggling and dangerous communities. Disparities in access lead to disparities in treatment. The poor, the aging, women, children, people with disabilities, and persons of color are most at risk. The infant mortality rate in the United States is the worst among the "developed" countries. African-American women die from cervical cancer at three times the rate of Caucasian women. African Americans have a significantly lower life span than Caucasians, and Hispanics have the least access to the health-care system of any group. Native Americans, besides suffering greatly from alcoholism, have a substantially higher diabetes and tuberculosis rate than average US rates. Recent immigrants who experience health problems find the health-care system poorly equipped to meet their needs. We believe it is unconscionable and abhorrent that any human being should ever be denied access to adequate health care due to economic, racial, or class barriers (United States Bureau of the Census, Centers for Disease Control and Prevention, and US Department of Health and Human Services—Office of Minority Health).

Quality Issues Put All Patients at Risk

In the United States, the provision of health care has been transformed from a ministry to a commercial commodity measured in patient encounters, tests performed, medications dispensed, and beds filled. In the process, quality of care suffers as the primary concern is often cost, not care. The physician-patient relationship is thereby compromised. Insurance companies in their efforts to reduce costs seek to control physicians' practice of medicine, thereby interfering with the physician-patient relationship. As a result, medical decisions are often made with primary consideration for the costs to the corporation, not for the optimum health of the patient. In the current climate physicians who prescribe treatments or tests not preapproved by the insurance corporation face severe financial penalties or other disincentives to optimum patient care. Physician time is consumed with excessive paperwork, malpractice suits, and inadequate government programs (The Directives of the American Medical Association House of Delegates address these issues at each meeting).

The American claim-based system produces enormous administrative burdens as well as denial of needed care. When claims are not denied by policy, they are often denied by the sheer burden of bureaucracy that must be overcome to obtain approvals. It has been estimated that today's physician spends about one-third of his or her time satisfying these insurance company regulations and seeking approvals for treatment, time the physician could be spending with patients. Competition for premium dollars and concern for high profits have taken priority over necessary care at actual cost. It is evident that private insurance companies are prone to deny claims while continuing to receive premiums, favoring higher profit over the "health and wholeness" of the weakened, the worried, and the sick. These same companies want to limit a patient's right to sue in civil court when the company breaches its own contract to provide benefits, regardless of the suffering or death a benefit denial may cause.

In these types of cases a benefit denial is tantamount to medical malpractice. Care Management has often been taken over by funding agencies rather than physicians. Managed care companies, HMOs, PPOs, and the like, interfere with the physician's ability to develop comprehensive treatment plans for his or her patients. They require that a decision be made by the corporation about treatment cost and efficacy. Medical decisions are in effect made by persons much less qualified than the patient's physician or the specialist a physician may recommend. In fact, persons with little or no medical training often make those decisions. Many insurance companies hire nurses to review the physicians' diagnoses and treatment plans. While it is unusual for nurses to oversee doctors, it is also evident that these nurses have had no contact with the patient under review.

Hospitals are required to provide uncompensated care. As a result, patients who are unable to pay for small primary care bills are able to incur large hospital bills when their untreated illness has become life-threatening. In 2008, the estimated cost of uncompensated care included in each individual policy was $368, and in each family policy was $1051 (Hidden Health Tax: America Pays a Premium. Families USA). Hospitals can no longer stay financially sound under existing policies.

Hospital staffing, due to cost concerns, imposes burdens on patient care that compromises quality, issues reflected in unhappy staff and increased numbers of union complaints and strikes in recent years. Error rates due to overwork and other factors are a crisis; the Institute of Medicine estimates that 100,000 persons die in American hospitals each year as a result of medical errors.

Spiraling Costs Waste Scarce Resources

Per capita health care costs in the United States are more than twice the median level for the thirty industrialized nations in the Organization for Economic Cooperation and Development. The Centers for Medicare and Medicaid Services have calculated that in 2012 health-care expenditures in the United States reached $2.8 trillion (Centers for Medicare and Medicaid Services, Office of the Actuary, National Health Statistics Group).

While some of the escalating costs of health care can be attributed to advances in technology and the aging of the population, a very significant part is due to the nature of America's health insurance market, in which:

- Today's physician spends one third or more of his or her time satisfying insurance requirements and seeking approvals for service.
- Multiple insurance companies, programs, coverage, claims processes, create confusion, duplication, and unnecessary administrative costs. It has been estimated that the cost of administration of Medicare is 4 percent to 5 percent of its budget, while the Affordable Care Act limits a private company's budget for administration and profit to 20 percent. Health-care provision is managed by

a massive bureaucratic complex: more than fifty state and state-level Medicaid systems, the Department of Veterans Affairs, the Railroad Employees insurance program, Indian Health Service, federal and state employee systems, health care for retired military personnel, Medicare and countless programs of the various private insurance companies: HMOs, PPOs, Medicare Supplemental Plans, etc. These entities rarely communicate in similar terms: neither to patients, to physicians, or to hospitals, thereby complicating efforts of providers and patients to properly file and receive payments on legitimate claims.

- Premium increases are driven by requirements to show a profit rather than rises in actual costs of treatment. High premiums to support the high profit margins of private health insurance companies force people to choose between health insurance and sustenance, housing, or other needs of a family, making even basic health insurance too expansive for an average individual or family. High co-payments and uncovered costs lead to significant impoverishment.
- Costs are shifted to the consumer through increasing deductibles and co-payments for care.
- Despite the ACA, large numbers of personal bankruptcies continue to be the result of illness. In 2013 such bankruptcies affected nearly 2 million Americans.
- Despite the increased prevalence of health insurance, a study estimated that in 2013 about 56 million adults—more than 20 percent of the population between 19 and 64—would struggle with health-care related bills (Dan Mangan, "Medicare Bills are the Biggest Cause of US Bankruptcies: Study. CNBC, 25 June). Even individuals with ostensibly good insurance, let alone those who are uninsured, find themselves in situations where they must sell and/or spend all assets, including homes, financial holdings, lifetime savings accounts, etc., in order to qualify for Medicaid and restore any medical coverage at all.

Increased costs of health care inevitably impact state and federal resources available for Medicaid, often leading to reduction in the number of providers willing to participate, and ultimately to decreased access to health care for the poor and the physically or mentally challenged.

More and more annual conferences and even congregations are feeling the burden of providing health care to their clergy and their lay staff. Small churches, even multiple-point parishes, have difficulty paying for increasing health premiums for clergy. Funds going to this purpose are in effect diverted from other important ministries. Some United Methodist conferences have discontinued their own health insurance program in favor of clergy obtaining their coverage in the Health Insurance Marketplaces.

The Vision of Health Care for All

The United Methodist Church is committed to health care for all in the United States, and therefore advocates for a comprehensive health-care delivery system that includes access for all, quality care, and effective management of costs.

1. *Access for All.* In a just society, all people are entitled to basic maintenance and health-care services. We reject as contrary to our understanding of the gospel, the notion of differing standards of health care for various segments of the population. The American Health Care system must serve and be sensitive to the diversity of all people in the United States and its territories. Regional planning processes should coordinate the services rendered by all health-care institutions, including those funded by governments, to create a more effective system of health services in every area. Priorities should be established for the provision of health services, such as preventive care, mental-health services, home care, and health education. Corrective measures should be taken where there is maldistribution or unavailability of hospital beds, intermediate care and nursing home care, home-delivered care, neighbor-hood health centers, community mental-health centers, and emergency care networks.

2. *Quality Care.* Health care should be comprehensive, including preventive, therapeutic, and rehabilitative services. The American health care system should provide comprehensive and portable benefits to everyone; including preventive services, health promotion, primary and acute care, mental-health care, and extended care. It should promote effective and safe innovation and research for women and men in medical techniques, the delivery of health services, and health practices. It should assess the health impacts of environmental and occupational safety, environmental pollution, sanitation, physical fitness, and standard-of-living issues

such as housing and nutrition. Professional health-care personnel should be recruited and appropriately educated to meet the health-care needs of all persons. Especially urgent is the need for physicians trained in geriatric medicine. Special priorities should be established to secure among the professional group at least proportional representation of women and minorities who are now seriously under-represented. We encourage development of community support systems that permit alternatives to institutional care for such groups as the aging, the terminally ill and mentally ill, and other persons with special needs. We encourage medical education for laypersons that will enable them to effectively evaluate medical care they need and are receiving. Religious and other appropriate forms of counseling should be available to all patients and families when they are called upon to make difficult medical choices, so that responsible decisions, within the context of the Christian faith, may be made concerning organ transplants, use of extreme measures to prolong life, abortion, sterilization, genetic counseling, institutionalization, and death with dignity. We support the medical community in its effort to uphold ethical standards and to promote quality assurance.

3. *Effective Administration of Care and Management and Financing of Costs.* The American health-care system must incorporate an equitable and efficient financing system drawn from the broadest possible resource base. It must reduce the current rapid cost inflation through cost-containment measures. It must provide services based on equity, efficiency, and quality, with payments to providers that are equitable, cost-efficient, and easy to administer and understand. The system must be sensitive to the needs of persons working in the various components of the health-care system and give special attention to providing not only for affirmative action in the recruitment, training, and employment of workers, but also for just compensation for all workers at all levels and for retraining and placement of those displaced by changes in the health care system.

Advocacy Steps

Globally, the church has a continuing duty to provide, in many parts of the world, the ministry of health care that government is unable to provide. In the United States, however, government has the capability to assure the provision of health care for all; doing so will extend health care to many who currently have no access, and doing so without the wastefulness of the current system will represent far better stewardship of resources than at present. In the United States, The United Methodist Church therefore supports a three-tiered approach to health-care advocacy:

1. *Single Payer.* We call for swift passage of legislation that will entitle all persons within the borders of the United States to the provision of health-care services, the cost of such services to be equitably shared by American taxpayers, and the government to distribute the funds to providers in a coordinated and comprehensive manner. This concept, known as "single-payer," would extend health care to all persons in the United States. Choice of private doctor and other health-care providers would be maintained. Public funds would make payment, and these funds would be generated by individual premiums and payroll taxes. Studies have shown that this method can be achieved with no increase over what is already being spent on health care from all sources. It therefore not only accomplishes the objective, but it best exercises our stewardship of public resources (Lewin Group, "Analysis of the Costs and Impact of Universal Health Care Models for the State of Maryland: The Single-Payer and Multi-Payer models." Report to Maryland Citizens Health Initiative Educational Fund. May 2, 2000).

2. *Incremental Steps toward Single Payer.* We recognize that much of the cost savings of "single payer" flow from the virtually total elimination of the health insurance industry. We cannot wait to overcome the current barriers to a single-payer plan, and therefore support all initiatives that move segments of our population closer to a single-payer system. The Affordable Care Act represents a substantial advance in providing health coverage to many Americans, and we support its extension and refinement.

3. *Recognizing that the nation is deeply divided nationally* on the philosophical bases for addressing America's health-care delivery problems, we support state-level initiatives in which individual states, at their own initiative become laboratories for trying out varying approaches to providing health care for all. We support in particular efforts at the federal level to support state-based efforts through necessary waivers of federal regulations.

Bringing America's health-care crisis under control will call upon the efforts of every sector of society and demand both personal and social responsibility. We therefore call upon all United Methodist persons and entities to do their part:

- Individuals. We call upon United Methodist individuals and families to pursue a healthy lifestyle, preventing many health problems before they start and strengthening physical capacity to combat problems which do arise.
- Health Care Institutions. We call upon United Methodist-affiliated health-care institutions to adopt, reaffirm, and strengthen policies supporting care delivery that is Christlike, compassionate, and wholistic rather than fee-driven and compartmentalized. We call upon such institutions as a requirement of their affiliation, to develop United Methodist standards of care that distinguish them from profit-driven, secular institutions.
- Seminaries. We call upon United Methodist seminaries to develop curricula linking sound biblical theology with clergy self-care and advocacy for universal health care.
- General Agencies. We call upon all agencies, commissions, and annual conferences of The United Methodist Church in the United States to adopt principles and support policies that are consistent with this resolution.

We charge the General Board of Church and Society with primary responsibility for advocating health care for all in the United States Congress and for communicating this policy to United Methodists in the USA.

ADOPTED 2008
AMENDED AND READOPTED 2016
RESOLUTION #3201, 2008, 2012 *BOOK OF RESOLUTIONS*
RESOLUTION #108, 2004 *BOOK OF RESOLUTIONS*
RESOLUTION #95, 2000 *BOOK OF RESOLUTIONS*

See Social Principles, ¶ 162V.

3202. Health and Wholeness

Theological and Historical Statement

Health is the ultimate design of God for humanity. Though life often thwarts that design, the health we have is a good gift of God. When God created humankind, God declared it "was supremely good" (Genesis 1:31). Among Jesus' statements on the purpose of his presence is the statement that he came that we "could live life to the fullest" (John 10:10). Every account of Jesus' ministry documents how Jesus saw restoration to health as a sign of the kingdom of heaven becoming present amongst us. When John the elder wrote to Gaius (3 John 2), he wished for him physical health no less than spiritual. The biblical narrative is filled with stories of God's healing presence in the world. This includes spiritual, psychological, emotional, social, as well as physical healing.

For John and Charles Wesley, health was integral to salvation. In the Wesleyan understanding of salvation, Christ's self-giving on the cross not only freed us from the guilt of sin, but restored us to the divine image in which we were created, which includes health. John Wesley not only preached spiritual health, but worked to restore physical health among the impoverished people who heard his call. He wrote *Primitive Physick*,[1] a primer on health and medicine for those too poor to pay for a doctor. He encouraged his Methodists to support the health-care needs of the poor. Charles Wesley's hymns reflect early Methodism's awareness of spiritual health as a component of salvation.

Achieving Health

Health has, for too long been defined only as the absence of disease or infirmity. The World Health Organization took a more wholistic view when it termed health as "a state of complete physical, mental and social well-being."[2] We who are people of faith add spiritual well-being to that list, and find our best definition in the biblical concept of "shalom." Shalom conveys or expresses a comprehensive view of human well being including "a long life of happiness ending in natural death (Gen. 15:15)."[3] From the perspective of Shalom, health includes biological well-being but necessarily includes health of spirit as well. From the perspective of Shalom, health is social harmony as well as personal well-being, and necessarily presumes the elimination of violence. Thus the health that God wants for humanity both presumes and seeks the existence of justice as well as mercy, the absence of violence as

1. Wesley, John, *Primitive Physick: Or, An Easy and Natural Method of Curing Most Diseases* (London: J. Palmar, 1751).

2. World Health Organization. *Constitution of the World Health Organization*, Geneva, 1946.

3. Richardson, Alan, *A Theological Word Book of the Bible*, New York: MacMillan, 1950, p. 165.

well as the absence of disease, the presence of social harmony as well as the presence of physical harmony.

As disciples of the One who came that we might have life and have it abundantly, our first and highest priority regarding health must be the promotion of the circumstances in which health thrives. A leading health expert encourages the study of health not from the perspective of what goes wrong, but of what goes right when health is present. These "leading causes of life" include coherence, connection, agency (action), blessing, and hope.[4] Our lives are healthy when we are linked to a source of meaning, when we live in a web of relationships that sustain and nurture us, when we know we have the capacity to respond to the call God has placed on our lives, when we contribute to the affirmation of another at a deep level, and when we lean into a future that is assured, in this life and forever.

No one portion of the seven billion members of God's global family has a monopoly on the expertise of achieving health. Achieving health, therefore, assumes mutual respect among the peoples of this Earth and the sharing of lessons learned in each society among the others.

Physical and emotional health is the health of the bodies in which we live, and we are therefore urged to be careful how we live (Ephesians 5:5).

As spiritual beings, our physical health affects our spiritual health and vice versa. St. Paul has termed our bodies as "God's temples" (1 Corinthians 3:16; see also 6:16, 19-20), echoing Jesus himself (John 2:21). We therefore are stewards, custodians, managers of God's property: ourselves, our bodies, minds, and spirits. Paul urges us to present to God our bodies as a living sacrifice and this is our "appropriate priestly service" (Romans 12:1), and to do everything for the glory of God (1 Corinthians 10:31). When we honor our bodies and those of others, we are honoring God and God's good creation.

The biblical mandate has specific implications for personal care. We must honor our bodies through exercise. We must honor our bodies through proper nutrition, and reducing consumption of food products that we discover add toxins to our bodies, excess weight to our frames, and yet fail to provide nourishment. We must recognize that honoring our bodies is a lifelong process.

4. Gunderson, Gary and Larry Pray, *The Leading Causes of Life*, The Center of Excellence in Faith and Health, Methodist LeBonheur Healthcare, Memphis, TN, 2006.

The second priority must be the correction of those circumstances in which health is hindered or thwarted. The interconnectedness of life is such that those things that diminish our health are most often things beyond the control of physicians, clinics, or insurers. The Ottawa Charter for Health Promotion identified the basic prerequisites for health as peace, shelter, education, food, income, a stable ecosystem, sustainable resources, social justice, and equity.[5] One estimate of factors influencing health gives medical health delivery only 10 percent of the impact; family genetics account for 20 percent of the variability in health, environment 20 percent, and lifestyle 50 percent.[6] Thus the achievement of health requires attention to:

- Environmental Factors. Environmental factors include clean air, pure water, effective sanitary systems for the disposal of wastes, nutritious foods, adequate housing, accessible, people-oriented transportation, work for all who want to work, and hazard-free workplaces are essential to health. Environmental factors include not only the natural environment, but the spiritual environment, the social environment, and the political environment, including issues of war and peace, wealth and poverty, oppression and justice, environmental profiling and environmental racism. The best medical system cannot preserve or maintain health when the environment is illness-producing.

- Public Health Factors. Disease prevention, public health programs, and health education including sex education, appropriate to every age level and social setting are needed globally. Services should be provided in a compassionate and skillful manner on the basis of need, without discrimination as to economic status, mental or physical disability, race, color, religion, gender, age, national origin, language, or multiple diagnoses.

- Social Lifestyle Factors. Lifestyle factors detrimental to good health include inadequate education, poverty, unemployment, lack of access to food, stress-producing con-

5. Ottawa Charter for Health Promotion, cited in Dennis Raphael, "Toward the Future: Policy and Community Actions to Promote Population Health," in Richard Hofrichter, Editor, *Health and Social Justice: Politics, Ideology, and Inequity in the Distribution of Disease*. San Francisco: Jossey-Bass, 2003.

6. Daughters of Charity National Hospital System, 1994.

ditions which include such critical issues as domestic violence and other crimes and social pressures reinforced by marketing and advertising strategies that encourage the abuse of guns, tobacco, alcohol, and other drugs. Other societal pressures that affect health are overachievement, overwork, compulsion for material gain, and lack of balance between family/work responsibilities and personal renewal.[7]

- Spiritual Lifestyle Factors. A relationship with God, learning opportunities throughout life, personal renewal, recreation, green space and natural beauty add essential positive spiritual focus to life which influences health through fulfillment and positives attitudes of hopefulness and possibility.[8]

- Personal Lifestyle Factors. Those factors, which may be choices, habits or addictions destructive to good health include overeating or eating nonnutritious foods, substance abuse, including alcohol, tobacco, barbiturates, sedatives, and so forth. Failure to exercise or to rest and relax adequately is also injurious to health.

- Cultural Factors. Harmful traditional practices such as child marriage can result in serious health problems such as obstetric fistula[9] and the spread of HIV & AIDS. Other practices such as female circumcision can result in pain and

7. *Supererogation* is the technical term for the class of actions that go "beyond the call of duty, obligation, or need." *Merriam-Webster Dictionary* (2007 online version). 2004 *Book of Discipline* ¶ 103, Section 3, Our Doctrinal Standards and General Rules, Article XI, p. 62.

8. *CAM at the NIH Newsletter*, National Center for Complementary and Alternative Medicine, National Institutes of Health (US), Vol. XII, No.1, 2005. Various research and ongoing research; see www.nccam.nih.gov/health.

9. C. Murray and A. Lopez, *Health Dimensions of Sex and Reproduction*. Geneva: World Health Organization, 1998. Obstetric fistula is a rupturing of the vagina and rectum causing persistent leakage of feces and urine. It is a health risk commonly associated with child marriage because of the mother's physical immaturity at the time of childbirth. (Source: International Center for Research on Women) A majority of women who develop fistulas are abandoned by their husbands and ostracized by their communities because of their inability to have children and their foul smell. It is estimated that 5 percent of all pregnant women worldwide will experience obstructed labor. In the United States and other affluent countries, emergency obstetric care is readily available. In many developing countries where there are few hospitals, few doctors, and poor transportation systems, and where women are not highly valued, obstructed labor often results in death of the mother. (Source: The Fistula Foundation)

the spread of infection.[10] Having unprotected sex with multiple partners, a practice in many countries, has significantly increased the spread of AIDS and other diseases.[11]

The biblical view of health integrates the physical and the spiritual, and therefore both are needed in the achievement and restoration of health. In Western Protestant interpretation of health and healing, however, the union of the body and spirit is often dismissed. Cultures that respect and revere that union are often disregarded or looked upon in a condescending manner. Jesus did not make these distinctions, and the early church struggled with it. An illustrative narrative is that of the healing of the woman who suffered from a hemorrhage (Matthew 9:20-22).

She believed that touching his garment would make her well. He told her that her faith had made her whole, which includes physical wellness. We must, if we are to achieve good health, unite the body and spirit in our thinking and actions.

Restoring Health

The experience of ill health is universal to humankind. When environmental factors have contributed to ill health of body or mind, the restorative powers given to the body and spirit by God, even with the best medical care, will be severely challenged if the environmental factors themselves are not changed.

God challenges our global church, as God has challenged God's servants through the ages, to help create networks of care around the world for those who are sick or wounded. Global networks of care should emphasize:

1. health care as a human right[12];
2. transforming systems that restore health care to its identity as a ministry rather than as a commodity, and reforming those economic, financial and legal incentives to treat health care as a commodity to be advertised, marketed, sold, bought and consumed;
3. citizen leadership from the lowest levels to the highest in each society so that all can have active involvement in the

10. Hosken, Fran P., *The Hosken Report: Genital and Sexual Mutilation of Females*, 4th rev. ed. (Lexington (Mass.): *Women's International Network* News, 1994).

11. *Multiple Partners and AIDS-UNAIDS, Practical Guidelines for Intensifying HIV Prevention: Towards Universal Access*, March 2007-03-19.

12. UM Social Principles ¶ 162V, *Book of Discipline*, Nashville: United Methodist Publishing House.

citizen leadership from the lowest levels to the highest in each society so that all can have active involvement in the formulation of health-care activities that meet local needs and priorities;

4. public financing mechanisms suited to each society that assures the greatest possible access of each person to basic health services;

5. advocacy care that engages the broader community in what the Ottawa Charter for Health Promotion terms the Five Pillars of Action: building healthy public policy, creating supportive environments that promote health, strengthening community action, developing personal skills, and reorienting health services[13];

6. health promotion and community health education that enables each person to increase control over his or her health and to improve it[14] and then to be a neighbor to another, in the fashion of the good Samaritan, who took the steps that he could, simply because he was there (Luke 10:29-37);

7. primary care workers who are drawn from the community and are trained to assist with the most common illnesses, as well as educate about the impact that can be achieved by improving environmental factors, such as health and sanitation;

8. basic health services that are accessible and affordable in each geographic and cultural setting;

9. medical care when the degree of illness has gone beyond what can be assisted by primary health workers;

10. hospital care, compassionate and skilled, that provides a safe environment for surgery and healing from illness under professional care; and

11. complete and total transparency to persons (or their designees) under the care of a medical practitioner, of their medical condition, so they can be an active director in their own care.

13. Ottawa Charter for Health Promotion, cited in Dennis Raphael, "Toward the Future: Policy and Community Actions to Promote Population Health," in Richard Hofrichter, Editor, *Health and Social Justice: Politics, Ideology, and Inequity in the Distribution of Disease*. San Francisco: Jossey-Bass, 2003.

14. World Health Organization, 1986.

The Call to United Methodists

Therefore, we call upon United Methodists around the world to accept responsibility for modeling health in all its dimensions. Specifically, we call upon our members to:

- continue the redemptive ministry of Christ, including teaching, preaching, and healing. Christ's healing was not peripheral but central in his ministry. As the church, therefore, we understand ourselves to be called by the Lord to the holistic ministry of healing: spiritual, mental emotional, and physical;
- examine the value systems at work in our societies as they impact the health of people and promote the value of shalom in every sphere;
- work for programs and policies that eliminate inequities around the world that keep people from achieving quality health;
- work for policies that enable people to breathe clean air, drink clean water, eat wholesome food, and have access to adequate education and freedom that enable mind and spirit to develop;
- make health concerns a priority in the church, being careful not to neglect the special issues of gender or age, treatment or prevention;
- collaborate as the body of Christ through establishment of networks for information sharing and action suggestions; and
- work toward healthy societies of whole persons.
  a) Part of our task is to enable people to care for themselves and to take responsibility for their own health.
  b) Another part of our task is to ensure that people who are ill, whether from illness of spirit, mind, or body, are not turned aside or ignored but are given care that allows them to live a full life.
  c) A related obligation is to help society welcome the sick and the well as full members, entitled to all the participation of which they are capable.
  d) People, who are well, but different from the majority, are not to be treated as sick in order to control them. Being old, developmentally disabled,

mentally or physically disabled is not the same as being sick. Persons in these circumstances are not to be diminished in social relationships by being presumed to be ill.

e) We see this task as demanding concern for spiritual, political, ethical, economic, social, and medical decisions that maintain the highest concern for the condition of society, the environment, and the total life of each person.

In addition, we call upon specific entities within our United Methodist connection to take steps toward health and wholeness as follows:

Congregations

United Methodist congregations are encouraged to:

- organize a *Health and Wholeness Team* as a key structure in the congregation. Among the team's responsibilities would be to seek each member to develop their spiritual gifts in order that the body of Christ be healthy and effective in the world. The apostle Paul commented that "many of you are weak and sick, and quite a few have died" (1 Corinthians 11:27-30). We suggest that this may have resulted not simply from failing to discern the body of Christ present in the communion bread, but from failing to discern the body of Christ as the congregation. When church members are not allowed to use their spiritual gift, they stagnate or die spiritually and the spiritual affects the physical health of the individual. The spread of health and wholeness should be discerned clearly as a guiding factor in why it is that we make disciples;
- accept responsibility for educating and motivating members to follow a healthy lifestyle reflecting our affirmation of life as God's gift;
- become actively involved at all levels in the development of support systems for health care in the community; and
- become advocates for a healthful environment; accessible, affordable health care; continued public support for health care of persons unable to provide for themselves; continued support for health-related research; and provision of church facilities to enable health-related ministries.

Annual Conferences

We encourage annual conferences to:
- continue their support and provision of direct-health services where needed through hospitals and homes, clinics, and health centers;
- work toward a comprehensive health system which would provide equal access to quality health care for all clergy and lay employees, including retirees;
- undertake specific actions to promote clergy health, physical, mental, emotional and spiritual; and
- support the establishment of Health and Wholeness teams in every congregation.

Seminaries

We call on our United Methodist theological schools to:
- become involved in a search for Christian understanding of health, healing, and wholeness and the dimensions of spiritual healing in our congregations. Include coursework that will train clergy not only in pastoral care, but also in intentional caring of the congregation that promotes the physical and spiritual health of each church member; and
- work toward a comprehensive health system that would provide equal access to quality health care for all clergy and lay employees of seminaries, including retirees.

Educational and Health Care Institutions

We call on our United Methodist colleges, universities, hospitals, and seminaries to gain an added awareness of health issues and the need for recruitment and education of persons for health-related ministries who would approach such ministries out of a Christian understanding and commitment.

General Agencies

We call on:
- the General Board of Discipleship to develop educational and worship resources supporting a theological understanding of health and stewardship of our bodies;
- the General Board of Church and Society and General Board of Global Ministries to support public policies and

programs that will ensure comprehensive health-care services of high quality to all persons on the principle of equal access; and

- the General Board of Pension and Health Benefits to undergird the social teachings of the Church by enacting policies and programs for United Methodist employees that ensure comprehensive health-care services of high quality to all persons on the principle of equal access.

ADOPTED 1984
AMENDED AND READOPTED 2000, 2008, 2016
RESOLUTION #3202, 2008, 2012 *BOOK OF RESOLUTIONS*
RESOLUTION #109, 2004 *BOOK OF RESOLUTIONS*
RESOLUTION #96, 2000 *BOOK OF RESOLUTIONS*

See Social Principles, ¶¶ 162V and 165C.

3203. Maternal Health: The Church's Role

"I came so that they could have life—indeed, so that they could live to the fullest" (John 10:10).

Motherhood is sacred. Mothers are important figures in our biblical tradition. Women like Eve, Hagar, Sarah, Elizabeth, and Mary, the mother of Jesus, are remembered for their role as bearers of new life. But within the sacred texts, stories also tell of maternal tragedy and loss. Both Rachel (Genesis 35:16-20) and the wife of Phinehas (1 Samuel 4:19-20) died after prolonged and difficult labors.

Tragically, stories of maternal death are commonplace today. For many women, especially those living in poverty and in developing countries, giving birth is dangerous and life-threatening. Worldwide maternal mortality is a leading cause of death for women of child-bearing age. Every 90 seconds a woman dies somewhere in the world from complications during pregnancy or childbirth; for every woman who dies, another 20 suffer disability.

The main causes of maternal mortality include infection, hemorrhaging, high blood pressure, and obstructed labor. They are mostly preventable.

In the Gospel of John, Jesus tells the disciples that he came so that they could live life to the fullest. God desires that every mother, every child, and every family not only survive, but thrive.

Tragically, survival is often a daily struggle for those who lack access to basic services and care. God calls us to respond to the suffering in the world, to love our neighbors throughout the world. As followers of Christ, we are members of the same body. The loss of one member is a loss for all.

The global community is taking steps to address the tragedy of maternal mortality. Members of the United Nations established in 2000 the eight Millennium Development Goals (MDGs) that set targets for improving health, reducing disease and poverty, and ensuring human rights of all people. The fifth MDG, to improve maternal health, sets a goal of reducing maternal mortality by 75 percent by 2015.

Maternal deaths have dropped by a third since 1990. While such progress is significant, increased efforts must be implemented globally to reach the 2015 target of 75 percent reduction. Maternal deaths exist in both developed and developing countries. An example among developed countries is that maternal mortality in the United States is on the rise. US maternal deaths have doubled since 1987.

Maternal mortality is a moral tragedy. Nearly all of the more than 350,000 annual maternal deaths occur in the developing world. Many factors contribute to this vast health inequity.

Health Barriers

In the developing world many women of child-bearing age lack access to reproductive health services such as prenatal care, postnatal care, and family-planning services. This is particularly dangerous for pregnant women. With no hospital or clinic nearby, women customarily give birth at home in unsanitary conditions. This puts both the woman and her baby at risk of infection. If a woman experiences a life-threatening complication while in labor at home, she may not be able to reach emergency care in time. Situations like these could be prevented if women had access to health information and medical care.

Unintended pregnancy is also a health concern. Globally, more than 200 million women would like to avoid or delay pregnancy, but they lack access to modern contraceptive services. This results in millions of unintended pregnancies every year. Supply shortages, lack of education, misinformation, and cultural barriers all contribute to this unmet need. Without access to contraceptives, women are unable to manage the timing and birth spacing of their children. This is of particular concern to women who have given birth within the past two years and those who are HIV-positive: The former's bodies may not have fully recovered, and the latter's immunity is compromised.

Birth spacing is a key health intervention for reducing both maternal and infant mortality. When a woman spaces her pregnancies at least three years apart, she is more likely to have a healthy delivery, and her children are more likely to survive infancy. If a woman becomes pregnant too soon after giving birth, her body does not have time to recover and her risk for complications increases. To be able to space her pregnancies in the healthiest manner, a woman must have access to safe, modern family-planning services.

Providing family-planning services to a woman is inexpensive, costing approximately $2 a year. The direct and indirect benefits, however, of women planning their families are priceless and countless: smaller family size, better health for both children and mother, less economic burden on the family, and women's continued economic contribution to the greater community. By meeting all the unmet need for family planning, maternal mortality rates would drop by a third, and the need for abortion would be reduced significantly. Furthermore, the use of condoms reduces the risk of infection for HIV and other sexually transmitted infections. In particular, access to female condoms is crucial for empowering women to initiate their own protection against these infections.

Cultural Barriers

Many cultural differences complicate this issue. Having a large family is a sign of honor in many parts of the world. Having many children, especially boys, is a showcase of a man's virility. Men who expect their wives to bear many children may not consider or support birth spacing or family planning.

The expectation of giving birth to many children comes not only from the husband, but also from other family members, particularly the mother-in-law. In some areas of the developing world, the mother-in-law makes the decision regarding contraceptive use. Such societal and familial pressures often conflict with a woman's personal desires regarding her fertility and can adversely affect her health.

Marrying age also affects maternal health. Child marriage is prevalent in many cultures. Girls marry and begin giving birth in early adolescence. If these young females are not practicing family planning, they could have multiple children before their 20th birthday. Young women not fully developed physically at the time of marriage are at great risk for complications such as obstetric fistula, a birth injury that leaves them incontinent.

The Call

Women are crying out for not only their own survival but also the survival of their families and communities. They deserve access to services and care that empower their personal decision-making. As a global church, we are called to eradicate systems of oppression and marginalization that inhibit women's well-being.

Recommendations

We call upon all local congregations to:

1. Support United Methodist projects around the world working on maternal health and family planning;

2. Advocate with policy makers at all levels to increase access to maternal health and family-planning services; and

3. Support local health initiatives that expand access to information and services for women's health.

We call upon the General Board of Church and Society to continue placing a programmatic emphasis on education and advocacy for the next quadrennium on maternal health.

ADOPTED 2012
RESOLUTION #3203, 2012 *BOOK OF RESOLUTIONS*

See Social Principles, ¶ 162V.

3205. Faithful Care for Persons Suffering and Dying

Theological Statement

As Christians, we live between the certainty of death and the promise of resurrection. Jesus proclaims this paradox in John's Gospel: "I am the resurrection and the life. Whoever believes in me will live, even though they die. Everyone who lives and believes in me will never die" (John 11:25-26). In the face of loss, we pray that God may help us "to live as those who are prepared to die, and when our days here are accomplished, enable us to die as those who go forth to live, so that living or dying, our life may be in you, and that nothing in life or in death will be able to separate us from your great love in Christ Jesus our Lord" (*United Methodist Hymnal*, A Service of Death and Resurrection, p. 871). All Christians therefore have a ministry of faithful care for persons suffering and dying. As we minister to others we minister to Christ (Matthew 25:34-40). We exercise that ministry when we care for those who are closest to us as well as to those who are strangers. We exercise that ministry in a number of important ways.

Preparation for Our Own Death and Resurrection

Our ministry to persons who are suffering and dying necessarily includes ourselves. Recognizing that death faces each of us, we are called to prepare for our own death and resurrection. That includes affirming and exercising our relationship with God in Christ. It includes reconciliation with others. It includes making wills—the legal preparation for others to take on the stewardship of the material goods which God has entrusted to us. It includes obtaining social and health insurance when it is available to us so that we minimize the burden we place on others. And it includes preparation for times of illness when we are not able to speak for ourselves. Living wills and instructions provide not only clarity and guidance to care providers and loved ones, but immeasurable relief from the burden of their decision making on our behalf in times of great stress.

Assisting Others Who Face Suffering and Dying

Care for others is the calling of the whole community of faith, not only pastors and chaplains. Because Christian faith is relevant to every aspect of life, no one should be expected to cope with life's pain, suffering, and ultimate death without the help of God through other people. In care, God's help and presence are revealed. When we as the church offer care, we empathize with suffering patients and share in the wounds of their lives. When we listen as patients express their feelings of guilt, fear, doubt, loneliness, hurt, and anger we offer them a connection with others and God. When we listen as patients tell their stories of both the extraordinary and the everyday, we help them to make connections between their experiences and God's joy. We provide resources for reconciliation and wholeness and assist persons in reactivating broken or idle relationships with God and with others. We provide comfort by pointing to sources of strength, hope, and wholeness, especially Scriptures and prayer. Family and friends as well as those who are suffering and dying need care. Those who are grieving need the assurance that their feelings are normal human responses and need not cause embarrassment or guilt. Health-care workers—doctors and others who have intimate contact with dying persons—also need care.

Pastoral Care by Pastors and Chaplains

We exercise our ministry for persons suffering and dying as we support those in specialized ministries. Pastors and chaplains sustain the spiritual growth of patients, families, and health-care personnel. They bear witness to God's grace with words of comfort and salvation. They provide nurture by reading the Scriptures with patients and loved ones, by Holy Communion, by the laying on of hands, and by prayers of praise, petition, repentance, reconciliation, and intercession. They provide comfort and grace with prayer or anointing after a death. They conduct rituals in connection with a terminal illness, of welcome into the care of hospice or a nursing center, or of return to a local congregation by persons who have been absent.

Pastoral caregivers not only offer comfort and counsel, but help patients understand their illness. They can assist families in understanding and coming to grips with information provided by medical personnel. Pastoral caregivers are especially needed when illness is terminal and patients and family members have difficulty discussing this reality freely.

Medical Care

As human interventions, medical technologies are only justified by the help that they can give. Their use requires responsible judgment about when life-sustaining treatments truly support the goals of life, and when they have reached their limits. There is no moral or religious obligation to use them when the burdens they impose outweigh the benefits they offer, or when the use of medical technology only extends the process of dying. Therefore, families should have the liberty to discontinue treatments when they cease to be of benefit to the dying person.

Palliative Care

The World Health Organization has described palliative care as care that improves the quality of life of patients and their families through the prevention and relief of suffering. It provides relief from pain; it intends to neither hasten nor postpone death; it integrates the psychological and spiritual aspects of patient care. It provides support both to patient and family. It is applicable early in the course of illness, may accompany treatment, and while its intent is simply relief from distressing symptoms, it may positively influence the course of illness. Ministering to the needs of the suffering and dying includes affirming the need for palliative care, as well as the need for comfort, encouragement, and companionship. Those who are very ill and the dying especially express their needs as they confront fear and grief and loneliness.

When there is no reasonable hope that health will improve, and the rationale for treatment may diminish or cease, palliative care becomes the dominant ministry. Hospital care may be of no benefit and the family can be encouraged to take the loved one home so that the loved one can die surrounded by family and in familiar circumstances.

Patient Rights

We exercise the ministry of faithful care as we support the rights of patients. As Christians, we have a duty to provide counsel, and patients have a right to receive it. Decisions can be complex and not easily made. We affirm that:

a. Patients deserve to be told the truth.
b. Patients are entitled to a share of decision-making both before and during their illness.
c. Patients have a right to refuse nourishment and medical care.
d. Decisions are best made within a family of faith.

The complexity of treatment options and requests by physicians for patient and family involvement in life-prolonging decisions require good communication. Pastoral caregivers can bring insights rooted in Christian convictions and Christian hope into the decision-making process. When advance directives for treatment, often called "living wills" or "durable powers of attorney," are being interpreted, the pastoral caregivers can offer support and guidance to those involved in decision-making. They can facilitate discussion of treatment and palliative options, including home and hospice care. Decisions concerning faithful care for the suffering and the dying are always made in a social context that includes laws, policies, and practices of legislative bodies, public agencies and institutions, and the social consensus that supports them. The social and theological context of dying affects individual decisions concerning treatment and care and even the acceptance of death. Therefore, pastoral caregivers must be attentive to the social situations and policies that affect the care of the suffering and dying and must interpret these to patients and family members in the context of Christian affirmations of faithful care.

Affirming Life

We exercise that ministry as we affirm both life and death. In providing counsel, we affirm the Christian tradition that has drawn a distinction between the cessation of treatment and the use of active measures by the patient or caregiver which aim to bring about death. Patients and those who act on their behalf have a right to cease nourishment and treatment when it is clear that God is calling the patient home. By contrast, however, we understand as a direct and intentional taking of life the use of active measures by the patient or caregiver that aim to bring about death. This United Methodist tradition opposes the taking of life as an offense against God's sole dominion over life, and an abandonment of hope and humility before God. The absence of affordable, available comfort care can increase the pressure on families to consider unacceptable means to end the suffering of the dying.

The withholding or withdrawing of life-sustaining interventions should not be confused with abandoning the dying or ceasing to provide care. Even when staving off death seems futile or unreasonably burdensome to continue, we must continue to offer comfort care: effective pain relief, companionship, and support for the patient in the hard and sacred work of preparing for death.

Health Delivery Reform

We exercise our ministry as we advocate for the reform of structures and institutions. As Christians, we have a duty to advocate.

We advocate for patient rights, which are easily neglected, especially when patients cannot speak for themselves, and when families are overwhelmed by the stress and confusion of difficult news. This is a reason that preparation is so important.

The duty to care for the sick calls us to reform the structures and institutions by which health and spiritual care are delivered when they fail to provide the comprehensive physical, social, emotional, and spiritual care needed by those facing grave illness and death.

We advocate for health coverage for all globally. In the world today, many nations do not have universal health care and many millions of people have either no health insurance or grossly inadequate coverage, leaving them without reliable access to medical treatment. Even when basic access is provided, good quality comfort care—including effective pain relief, social and emotional support, and spiritual counsel—is often not available.

Absence of comfort care can leave people with a distorted choice between enduring unrelieved suffering and isolation, and choosing death. This choice undermines rather than enhances our humanity. We as a society must assure that patients' desire not to be a financial burden does not tempt them to choose death rather than receiving the care and support that could enable them to live out their remaining time in comfort and peace.

We charge the General Board of Church and Society to advocate, identify, and address instances where proper care for the suffering and dying is unavailable due to scarcity of resources, unhealthy ideologies, and oppressive conditions.

Proclaiming the Good News

We exercise our ministry as we teach the Christian good news in the context of suffering and dying. We call upon the General Boards of Discipleship and Higher Education and Ministry to develop and promote resources and training for clergy and laity globally that:

Acknowledge dying as part of human existence, without romanticizing it. In dying, as in living, mercy and justice must shape our corporate response to human need and vulnerability.

Accept relief of suffering as a goal for care of dying persons rather than focusing primarily on prolonging life. Pain control and comfort-giving measures are essentials in our care of those who are suffering.

Train pastors and pastoral caregivers in the issues of bioethics as well as in the techniques of compassionate companionship with those who are suffering and dying.

Educate and equip Christians through preaching resources and adult education programs to consider treatments for the suffering and the dying in the context of Christian affirmations of God's providence and hope.

Acknowledge, in our Christian witness and pastoral care, the diverse social, economic, political, cultural, religious and ethnic contexts around the world where United Methodists care for the dying.

We also call upon the General Board of Global Ministries to promote our understanding of Ministry to Persons Suffering and Dying in United Methodist health-care institutions around the globe.

ADOPTED 2004
READOPTED 2008
AMENDED AND READOPTED 2016
RESOLUTION #3205, 2008, 2012 *BOOK OF RESOLUTIONS*
RESOLUTION #115, 2004 *BOOK OF RESOLUTIONS*

See Social Principles, ¶¶ 161M and 162V.

3209. Local Church Participation in Global Health Ministry

WHEREAS, it is the responsibility of the United Methodist Global Health to "assist conference units in addressing emerging and ongoing global health issues" and further states that the United Methodist Global Health has as one of its responsibilities to "assist local churches, districts, and annual conferences to develop ministries of health, healing, and wholeness";

Therefore, be it resolved, in order to address emerging and ongoing health issues and to develop ministries on health, healing, and wholeness, each local church is encouraged to participate in at least one global health ministry each year.

ADOPTED 2016

See Social Principles, ¶ 162V.

HISPANIC AMERICANS

3222. Annual Conference Strategic, Comprehensive Plans for Hispanic/Latino-Latina Ministries

WHEREAS, God calls us to proclaim God's wonderful acts (1 Peter 2:9) and to be good stewards of God's manifold grace, serving one another with whatever gift each has received (1 Peter 4:10), and to organize ourselves for the work of ministry (Ephesians 4:7-13); and

WHEREAS, our United Methodist heritage integrates missional action with organizational support; and

WHEREAS, *The Book of Discipline, 2012* declares that "the mission of the Church is to make disciples of Jesus Christ for the transformation of the world by proclaiming the good news of God's grace and by exempifying Jesus' command to love God and neighbor, thus seeking the fulfillment of God's reign and realm in the world" (¶ 121), and that "each annual conference is responsible to focus and guide the mission and ministry of The United Methodist Church within its boundaries by envisioning the ministries necessary to live out the mission of the church in and through the annual conference; . . . providing encouragement, coordination, and support for the ministries of nurture, outreach, and witness in districts and congregations for the transformation of the world; . . . developing and strengthening ethnic ministries, including ethnic local churches and concerns. . . ." (¶ 608); and

WHEREAS, according to the 2014 United States census analysis, nearly 64 million people of Hispanic origin (who may be of any race) would be added to the nation's population between 2014 and 2060. Their numbers are projected to grow from 55.4 million to 114.8 million, an increase of just over 100 percent. Their share of the nation's population would increase from 17.4 percent to 28.6 percent. The US is the third largest Latino country in the world and Hispanics remain the largest minority group, with 55.4 million on July 1, 2014—17.4 percent of the total population; and

WHEREAS, these figures represent an undercount and do not reflect accurate information about undocumented persons; and

WHEREAS, according to the General Board of Global Ministries Office of Research's analysis of the census data, every annual conference of The United Methodist Church in the United States has within its boundaries a growing Hispanic/Latino-Latina population; and

WHEREAS, for four quadrennia the General Conference has approved the National Plan for Hispanic/Latino-Latina Ministry as a mission initiative of the whole church, and it is a comprehensive plan of evangelization with Hispanic/Latino-Latina communities by the whole church; and

WHEREAS, in direct relationship to the implementation of the National Plan for Hispanic/Latino-Latina Ministry, 900 faith communities have been established in 52 conferences; 1,400 lay missioners have been equipped and deployed; 260 pastor mentors; 150 new Hispanic/Latino-Latina congregations have been started in 35 conferences; 160 existing Hispanic/Latino-Latina churches in 35 conferences have been strengthened; and 1,500 outreach ministries have been established in 52 conferences; 53 annual conferences have been developing a comprehensive plan; more than 150 Portuguese-speaking leaders have been trained; 50 consultants already trained; more than 800 non-Hispanic/Latino leaders trained through the convocations; and

WHEREAS, according to the Office of the National Plan for Hispanic/Latino-Latina Ministry's estimates, the Hispanic/Latino-Latina membership in The United Methodist Church has increased by 40 percent from 2008 to 2012; and

WHEREAS, according to the Office of the National Plan for Hispanic/Latino-Latina Ministry's estimates, Hispanic/Latino-Latina persons represent 0.1 percent of the total membership of The United Methodist Church and Hispanic/Latino-Latina congregations represent approximately 0.1 percent of all United Methodist chartered churches; and

WHEREAS, these figures represent an undercount due to challenges in reporting the number of Hispanic/Latino-Latina members in multicultural churches and non-Hispanic/Latino-Latina congregations, and the number of Hispanic/Latino-Latina congregations sharing facilities with other ethnic and cultural churches; and due to difficulties in the challenges of reporting and collecting data from some Hispanic/Latino Latina congregations; and

WHEREAS, in spite of the National Plan for Hispanic/Latino-Latina Ministry and other missional efforts, advances and success in reaching the people group called Hispanic/Latino-Latina and the increased presence of Hispanic/Latino-Latina persons in the United Methodist connectional system, the people group in the

United States called Hispanic/Latino-Latina represents a huge mission field;

Therefore, be it resolved, that every annual conference in the United States shall develop and periodically update a strategic, comprehensive plan for Hispanic/Latino-Latina ministries within its boundaries, and this plan will include, but not be limited to, socioeconomic, cultural, and religious analysis of the Hispanic/Latino-Latina communities that will be served; and strategies to strengthen existing Hispanic/Latino-Latina ministries and congregations, to start new ministries and congregations, to identify, equip, and deploy clergy and laity leaders, and to identify and deploy material and financial resources; and

Be it further resolved, that the Council of Bishops, the National Plan for Hispanic/Latino-Latina Ministry, the General Board of Discipleship and the General Board of Global Ministries ensure that the conference comprehensive plans are in place and provide support and consultation in the development of the plans.

Source: Projections of the size and composition of the US Population: 2014–2060 <https://www.census.gov/recontent/dam/census/library/publications/2015/demo/p25-1143.pdf>

ADOPTED 2004
REVISED AND READOPTED 2008, 2016
RESOLUTION #3222, 2008, 2012 *BOOK OF RESOLUTIONS*
RESOLUTION #29, 2004 *BOOK OF RESOLUTIONS*

See Social Principles, ¶¶ 161 and 162.

HIV AND AIDS

3241. A Covenant to Care: Recognizing and Responding to the Many Faces of HIV/AIDS in the USA

United Methodists have been in ministry since the beginning of the HIV/AIDS pandemic. They have followed the way of healing, ministry, hospitality, and service shown by Jesus Christ. According to the Gospel of Luke (4:16-21), Jesus identified himself and his task with that of the servant Lord, the one who was sent to bring good tidings to the afflicted, hope to the brokenhearted, liberty to the captives, and comfort to all who mourn, giving them the oil of gladness and the mantle of praise instead of a faint spirit

(Isaiah 61:1-3). God's Word calls us to a ministry of healing, a ministry that understands healing not only in physiological terms but also as wholeness of spiritual, mental, physical, and social being.

The Context of Caring Ministry in the United States

In recent years, AIDS in the United States has received less media attention, but that does not mean the disease has gone away. Though medical drugs can prolong the life of people who have been infected, there is no cure for AIDS. Not only must our commitment to ministry continue, but it must also expand, particularly in the area of prevention education.

HIV/AIDS affects and infects a broad cross-section of people in the United States and Puerto Rico: all ages, all races, both sexes, all sexual orientations. The cumulative number of AIDS cases reported to Centers for Disease Control (CDC) through December 2008 is 1,106,391. Adult and adolescent AIDS cases total 851,974 among males and 211,804 among females.[1]

In the early 1980s, most people with AIDS were gay white men. Overall incidences of new cases of AIDS increased rapidly through the 1980s, peaked in the early 1990s, and then declined. However, new cases of AIDS among African Americans increased. By 1996, more cases of AIDS were reported among African Americans than any other racial/ethnic population. The number of people diagnosed with AIDS has also increased, with American Indians and Alaska Natives in 2005 ranking 3rd after African Americans and Hispanics.[2] In 2005, the rate of adult/adolescent AIDS cases per 100,000 population was 71.3 among African Americans, 27.8 among Hispanics, 10.4 among Native Americans/Alaska Natives, 8.8 among whites, and 7.4 among Asians/Pacific Islanders.[2] Though national surveillance data does not record the hearing status of people with HIV/AIDS, the Department of Health and Human Services believes that deaf and hard-of-hearing people have been disproportionately infected with HIV.[3]

1. Centers for Disease Control and Prevention (CDC). *HIV/AIDS Surveillance Report 2008*. http://www.cdc.gov/hiv/surveillance/resources/reports/2008 report/

2. National Institute of Allergy and Infectious Diseases (NIAID), Fact Sheet: HIV Statistics (December 2005). <http://www.niaid.nih.gov/factsheets/AIDS stat.htm> (31 January 2006)

3. Department of Health and Human Services (HRSA) "Programs: The Deaf and Hard of Hearing and HIV/AIDS." http://hab.hrsa.gov/programs/fact sheets/deaffact.htm (4 March 2003)

As of December 2006, according to CDC estimates, more than one million people in the United States were infected with HIV. One-quarter of these were unaware of their status! Approximately 56,300 new HIV infections occur each year: about 75 percent men and 25 percent women. Of these newly infected people, almost half are African Americans, 30 percent are white, 17 percent are Hispanic. A small percentage of men and women are part of other racial/ethnic groups.[4] No longer is HIV a disease of white gay men or of the east and west coast; it has not been for more than a decade. In 2007, 40 percent of persons with AIDS were living in the South, 29 percent in the Northeast, 20 percent in the West, 11 percent in the Midwest, and 3 percent in the US territories.[5]

United Methodist churches, districts, and conferences can help to stop the spread of HIV/AIDS by providing sound, comprehensive, age-appropriate and culturally sensitive preventive education, including information that abstinence from both sex and injection drug use is the safest way to prevent HIV/AIDS. In addition, the church can provide grounding in Christian values, something that cannot be done in public schools or in governmental publications on HIV/AIDS.

Youth and Young Adults: AIDS is increasingly affecting and infecting our next generation of leaders, particularly among racial and ethnic minorities. In 2007, African American blacks and Latinos/Hispanics accounted for 87 percent of all new HIV infections among 13- to 19-year-olds and 79 percent of HIV infections among 20- to 24-year-olds in the United States, even though together they represent only about 32 percent of people in these ages.[6]

Racial and Ethnic Minorities: African Americans, Hispanics and Native Americans have been disproportionately infected with HIV/AIDS. Representing only an estimated 12 percent of the total US population, African Americans make up almost half, 45 percent, of all AIDS cases reported in the country. While there were fewer new HIV infections among black women than black

4. National Institute of Allergy and Infectious Diseases (NIAID), Fact Sheet: HIV Statistics (December 2002). <http://www.niaid.nih.gov/factsheets/AIDS stat.htm> (31 January 2003)

5. Centers for Disease Control and Prevention, "US HIV and AIDS Cases Reported through December 2007 Year-end Report." <http://www.cdc.gov/hiv /resources/factsheets/geographic.htm>

6. Advocates for Youth. <http://advocatesforyouth.org/component/content /article/430-young-people-and-hiv>

men in 2006, CDC's new analysis finds that black women are far more affected by HIV than women of other races.[7]

It is critical to prevent patterns of risky behaviors that may lead to HIV infection before they start. Clear communications between parents and their children about sex, drugs, and AIDS is an important step. Church, school, and community-based prevention education is another step. Youth and young adults must be actively involved in this process, including peer education.

The large and growing Hispanic population in the United States is also heavily affected by HIV/AIDS. Although Hispanics accounted for 14.4 percent of the United States population in 2005, they accounted for 18.9 percent of persons who received an AIDS diagnosis.[8]

Women: AIDS among women has been mostly "an invisible epidemic" even though women have been affected and infected since the beginning. Women of color are especially impacted by the disease. The majority of female adults and adolescents living with an HIV diagnosis in 2008 were infected with the virus through heterosexual contact (73 percent). An estimated 15 percent of diagnosed HIV infections in 2009 among females were attributed to injection drug use.[9] Of the total number of new HIV infections in US women in 2009, 57 percent occurred in blacks, 21 percent were in whites, and 16 percent were in Hispanic/Latinas.[10] Reducing the toll of the epidemic among women will require efforts to combat substance abuse and reduce HIV risk behaviors.[10]

People who are Deaf, Late-Deafened, and Hard of Hearing: In the United States, studies on the deaf or hard of hearing are limited and it is unclear how many people in this subpopulation are living with HIV/AIDS. Estimates fall into a wide range of 8,000 to 40,000 people.[11] The National Center for Health Statistics reports that adults with hearing loss have poorer health and increased risk of engaging in health risk behaviors than adults with good

7. Centers for Disease Control and Prevention, "HIV/AIDS among African Americans." 2006. <http://www.cdc.gov/hiv/topics/aa/>

8. Centers for Disease Control and Prevention, "HIV/AIDS among Hispanics in the United States." 2006. <http://www.cdc.gov/mmwr/preview/mmwrhtml/mm5640a4.htm>

9. Avert (Averting HIV and AIDS). <http://www.avert.org/usa-transmission-gender.htm>

10. Centers for Disease Control and Prevention, "HIV/AIDS among US Women." 2009. <http://www.cdc.gov/women/pubs/std.htm>

11. US Department of Health and Human Services, HIV/AIDs Bureau 2008 <http://hab.hrsa.gov/abouthabpopulations/deafhardofhearingfacts.pdf>

hearing. The rate of substance use disorder among deaf or hard of hearing is higher than among the general population. Substance use, in turn, is linked to higher risk for HIV infections.[11] Undergraduate deaf college students scored significantly lower on the HIV/AIDS Knowledge Index than hearing undergraduate students. This lack of knowledge about HIV disease contributes to the fact that the deaf are often not diagnosed with HIV until symptomatic and die sooner than hearing individuals.[11] Many people erroneously assume that American Sign Language (ASL) users have high English proficiency, but the truth is that ASL has its own grammar and syntax and communicates in concepts. As a result, HIV prevention and treatment materials are often culturally inappropriate and linguistically incomprehensible for the deaf and hard of hearing.[11] Developing communication methods appropriate for the deaf or hard of hearing may help reduce health risk behaviors in this population and ensure equal access to health services. These methods may include peer to peer communication, as research suggests that the deaf are more likely to learn from each other rather than from formal information sources.[11]

Older Adults: The number of persons 50 years and older living with HIV/AIDS has been increasing in recent years.[12] In 2005, persons aged 50 and older accounted for 24 percent of persons living with HIV/AIDs (increased from 17 percent in 2001). Some older persons may be less knowledgeable about HIV/AIDS and therefore less likely to protect themselves.[12] Reaching this group of people with HIV prevention messages means exploring avenues such as church, widows' support groups at senior centers, and Golden Age Clubs at community centers and churches.

Drug-Associated HIV Transmission: Since the epidemic began, injection drug use (IDU) has directly and indirectly accounted for more than one-third (36 percent) of AIDS cases in the US. Racial and ethnic minorities in the US are most heavily affected by IDU-associated AIDS. In 2000, IDU-associated AIDS accounted for 26 percent of all cases among African Americans and 31 percent among Hispanic adults and adolescents, compared with 19 percent of all cases among white adults/adolescents. Noninjection drugs such as cocaine also contribute to the spread of the epidemic when users trade sex for drugs or money, or when they

12. Centers for Disease Control and Prevention, CDC HIV/Surveillance Report, 2005 <http://cdc.gov/hiv/topics/over50/resources/factsheets/over50.htm>

engage in risky sexual behavior that they might not engage in when sober.[13]

HIV prevention and treatment, substance abuse prevention, and sexually transmitted disease treatment and prevention services must be better integrated to take advantage of the multiple opportunities for intervention-first, to help uninfected people stay that way; second, to help infected people stay healthy; and third, to help infected individuals initiate and sustain behaviors that will keep themselves safe and prevent transmission to others.[13] Efforts such as needle exchange programs need to be implemented and/or expanded in order for the spread of HIV to be reduced.

The Challenge for Ministry

Across the United States, in churches large and small, pastors and laity have asked, "What can my church do?" Churches can build on areas which are already doing well; they can covenant to care. Churches and other United Methodist organizations need to continue or begin compassionate ministry with persons living with HIV/AIDS and their loved ones. In terms of prevention education, United Methodists have an opportunity to teach not only the facts about HIV transmission and how to prevent infection but to relate these facts to Christian values. Congregations can do HIV/AIDS prevention education in broader contexts, such as human sexuality and holistic health, as well as addressing societal problems, such as racism, sexism, addiction, and poverty. We call on United Methodists to respond:

1. Churches should be places of openness and caring for persons with AIDS and their loved ones. We ask congregations to work to overcome attitudinal and behavioral barriers in church and community that create stigma and discrimination of persons with AIDS and their loved ones. Congregations can offer Christian hospitality and become arks of refuge to all. We must remember that:

- the face that AIDS wears is always the face of a person created and loved by God;
- the face that AIDS wears is always the face of a person who is someone's mother or father, husband or wife, son or daughter, brother or sister, loved one or best friend;

13. Centers for Disease Control and Prevention, "Drug-Associated HIV Transmission Continues in the United States," 2002. <http://www.cdc.gov/hiv/re sources/factsheets/idu.htm>

• the face that AIDS wears is always the face of a person who is the most important person in someone else's life.

2. Each congregation and annual conference, through their church and society committees, should mobilize persons for legislative advocacy at the local, state, and national levels to support for HIV/AIDS initiatives in the United States. These advocacy efforts will be strengthened through partnerships with organizations/coalitions who are currently involved in this issue.

3. Educational efforts about AIDS should use reliable medical and scientific information about the disease, transmission, and prevention. Spiritual resources must also be included to enable people to address issues related to discipleship, ministry, human sexuality, heath and wholeness, and death and dying. Education helps to prepare congregations to respond appropriately when they learn that a member has been infected by the HIV virus or diagnosed with AIDS. It can lead to the development of sound policies, educational materials and procedures related to the church school, nurseries, and other issues of institutional participation. Prevention education can save lives.

4. Each congregation should discern the appropriate response for its context. Ministries should be developed, whenever possible, in consultation and collaboration with local departments of public health and with other United Methodist, ecumenical, interfaith, and community-based groups concerned about the HIV/AIDS pandemic. Congregations can organize to provide spiritual, emotional, physical and/or financial support to those in their community who are caring at home or elsewhere for a person who has AIDS. Projects might include observing events such as World AIDS Day (December 1) and the Black Church Week of Prayer for the Healing of AIDS (first week in March), sponsoring support groups for people with AIDS and their loved ones, developing strong general church programs for children and youth that also include AIDS education, pastoral counseling, recruiting volunteers, and offering meeting space for community-based organizations, including groups trying to overcome substance abuse and sexual addiction.

5. The United Methodist Church has a congregational HIV/AIDS ministry called the Covenant to Care Program, whose basic principle is "If you have HIV/AIDS or are the loved one of a person who has HIV/AIDS, you are welcome here." We commend those who have been in ministry through this program and recommend

"Covenant to Care" to all United Methodist organizations. More information is available on the General Board of Global Ministries' website at http://gbgm-umc.org/health/aids/.[14]

ADOPTED 2004
READOPTED 2008
AMENDED AND READOPTED 2012
RESOLUTION #3241, 2008, 2012 <i>BOOK OF RESOLUTIONS</i>
RESOLUTION #152, 2004 <i>BOOK OF RESOLUTIONS</i>
RESOLUTION #141, 2000 <i>BOOK OF RESOLUTIONS</i>

See Social Principles, ¶ 162*U*.

3243. The Church and the Global HIV/AIDS Pandemic

In response to the global HIV/AIDS pandemic, The United Methodist Church will work cooperatively with colleague churches in every region. The Bible is replete with calls to nations, religious leaders, and faithful people to address the needs of those who are suffering, ill, and in distress. Jesus Christ reached out and healed those who came to him, including people who were despised and rejected because of their illnesses and afflictions. His identification with suffering people was made clear when he said that "whatsoever you do to the least of these, you also do to me" (Matthew 25:40, paraphrased). His commandment that "you should treat people in the same way that you want people to treat you" (Matthew 7:12) is a basis for the church for full involvement and compassionate response.

The Global Impact of HIV/AIDS

The global statistics are grim. At the end of 2007, 33 million adults and children were living with HIV/AIDS in the world; of these 31 million were adults and 2 million were children.

At this time, there is no cure for HIV/AIDS. It is mainly spread through intimate sexual contact with an infected person, by needle-sharing among injecting drug users, and, less commonly, through transfusions of infected blood or blood clotting factors. HIV can also be contracted if unsterilized needles tainted with

14. For more information about the Covenant to Care Program or the Church and HIV/AIDS Ministries, contact UMCOR, General Board of Global Ministries, Room 1500, 475 Riverside Dr., New York, NY 10115; Voice Phone: 212 870 3871; Fax: 212 870 3624; TDD: 212 870 3709. <http://www.gbgm-umc.org/health/aids/>.

infected blood are used by health care workers, tattooists, and acupuncturists. Other routes of transmission are through transplantation of organs from infected individuals, donated semen, and skin piercing instruments used in cosmetic, traditional, and ceremonial practices. AIDS is not caused by witchcraft, mosquito bites, or nonsexual contact such as shaking hands or hugs.

The HIV/AIDS pandemic compounds the strain on institutions and resources, while at the same time undermining social systems that enable people to cope with adversity. In seriously affected nations, HIV/AIDS compromises education and health systems, shrinks economic output and undermines sociopolitical stability. With life expectancy falling and the labor force becoming decimated, many countries are facing low economic growth rates. In parts of southern Africa, a food shortage has added to the woes. Agricultural productivity is declining as more and more women and young people are infected and become unable to work in the fields. The ramifications of HIV/AIDS are particularly grave for societies where the extended family is the system of social security for the care of elderly people, those who are ill, and orphans.

Women and Children

Women and children have been affected in increasing numbers. Deaths from AIDS have left 15 million orphans in Africa. These children are being looked after by extended families, older siblings in child-headed households, and orphan trusts. Older relatives, especially women, have to bear an enormous burden of taking care of the orphans. In countries that are also affected by war and civil strife, children and young people are more vulnerable to becoming infected with HIV because they are at the higher risk of sexual abuse, forced military recruitment and prostitution.

This burden is increased when women are also faced with stigma and discrimination and the hardships of civil strife, war, and famine. Women often have less status and less access to education, health care, and economic security than men, which in turn affect their ability to protect themselves from infection. Many cannot say "no" or negotiate the use of condoms because they fear they will be divorced or that their husband or other male partner will respond by battering them. Pregnant women who are HIV positive may be subjected to forced sterilizations or abortions. The use of rape and sexual violence as instruments of war adds a further serious dimension. As of 2008 according to UNAIDS, 16 million of the 33 million persons infected with AIDS are women.

Health budgets and resources are being adversely affected in countries that have to care for increasing numbers of citizens afflicted with HIV/AIDS. For example, it costs approximately $200 to treat a person for a year using the cheapest form of generic antiretroviral drugs, but very few can afford this medicine in sub-Saharan Africa. Antiretroviral drugs and other medicines must be made available at an affordable cost, especially in sub-Saharan Africa. Until effective preventive strategies are implemented, helpful medicines are made universally available, and an effective vaccine is introduced, the future is bleak for deterring the spread of HIV/AIDS.

The suffering borne by individuals, families, and communities and the strain placed on health-care facilities and national economies, call for intensified cooperative efforts by every sector of society, including the church, to slow and prevent the spread of HIV, provide appropriate care of those already ill and speed the development of an effective and affordable vaccine. Those caring for AIDS patients need support too. Communities, health-care workers, and home-care programs must be equipped to meet the challenge.

Drugs and AIDS

Of the 33 million persons living with HIV, one million are injecting drug users. Many more have used, and continue to use, alcohol and other drugs.

The international drug trade knows no boundaries or frontiers and has no specific national identity. It is now worth an estimated $400 billion per year and is organized and managed like a multinational corporation. Drugs of all kinds are now produced in all regions of the world. Despite its illegality, drug production and distribution has become a major source of revenue for many countries. The most lucrative markets remain in the United States and Western Europe, but consumption is spreading fast in Eastern Europe, Southeast Asia, and throughout Africa.

In the United States, an estimated one-third of HIV/AIDS cases are related to injecting drug use. Substance abuse is directly tied to the increase in HIV/AIDS among women. Women are primarily infected with HIV through injecting drugs (48 percent) or heterosexual transmission from an infected partner, who is often himself a drug user (54 percent).

Research has shown over and over again that drug use, injected or otherwise, can affect decision-making, especially about engaging in unsafe sex, which in turn promotes the spread of AIDS.

The Role of United Methodists

The global AIDS pandemic provides a nearly unparalleled opportunity for witness to the gospel through service, advocacy, and other healing ministries. United Methodist public health specialists, health workers, social workers, teachers, missionaries, clergy, and laity live and work in areas where the AIDS pandemic is spreading. United Methodist congregations, schools, health facilities, women's, men's, and youth groups can play a major role by providing awareness, support, education, and care to those affected by HIV/AIDS.

Recommendations

In response to the HIV/AIDS crisis in the world, The United Methodist Church commits itself to a holistic approach of awareness, education, prevention, treatment, community organizing and public advocacy. Out of our love and concern for our brothers, sisters and children in our local and global communities, the following actions are strongly recommended.

A. Local congregations worldwide to:

1. be places of openness where persons whose lives have been touched by HIV/AIDS can name their pain and reach out for compassion, understanding, and acceptance in the presence of persons who bear Christ's name;

2. provide care and support to individuals and families whose lives have been touched by HIV/AIDS;

3. be centers of education and provide group support and encouragement to help men, women, and youth refrain from activities and behaviors associated with transmission of HIV infection;

4. advocate for increased levels of funding for HIV/AIDS. In the United States, persons should contact their US Congresspersons and urge adequate funding for the Global Fund for AIDS,

tuberculosis, and malaria as well as the United States' bilateral initiatives on AIDS. Additionally, funding for the United Nations Population Fund (UNFPA) must be guaranteed from the United States each year. UNFPA works diligently to provide resources for reproductive health of women and girls as well as HIV/AIDS prevention;

5. observe World AIDS Day on or around December 1 each year. Materials for World AIDS Day are available from the websites of UNAIDS (http:/www.unaids.org), the General Board of Global Ministries (http://www.umcor.org/UMCOR/Programs/Global -Health/HIV/), and the General Board of Church and Society (http:/www.umc-gbcs.org);

6. include problems of alcohol, drug abuse and unsafe sex and the value of abstinence as part of Christian education;

7. provide support, comfort, and care to those afflicted with alcohol-related problems, drug addiction and HIV/AIDS within their given mandate and work to implement needle exchange programs locally as a means of reducing the spread of AIDS;

8. make available creative programs and activities for school children, youth, and young adults that keep them away from alcohol and drug abuse; and

9. promote and make available peer education models based on empowerment and self-determination.

B. General program agencies to:

1. assist related health institutions to obtain supplies and equipment to screen donated blood and provide voluntary HIV testing;

2. support efforts by churches, projects, and mission personnel within regions to promote disease prevention and to respond to the needs of family care providers and extended families;

3. facilitate partnership relationships between institutions and personnel from region to region, as appropriate, to share models and effective approaches regarding prevention, education, care, and support for individuals and families with HIV/AIDS;

4. assist health workers to obtain regional specific, timely updates on the diagnosis, treatment, and prevention of HIV/AIDS;

5. facilitate the sharing of pastoral-care resources and materials dedicated to the care of persons and families whose lives have been touched by HIV;

6. respond to requests from the regions to develop training seminars and workshops for church-related personnel in coop-

eration with ecumenical efforts, private voluntary organizations, and programs already existing in the regions;

7. advocate national, regional, and international cooperation in the development, availability, and transport of appropriate/relevant equipment and supplies for infection control, disease prevention, and treatment;

8. support programs that focus on the enhancement of women through economic justice and education as well as programs that provide comprehensive reproductive health services, family planning, and HIV/AIDS prevention information;

9. work cooperatively with the Office of the Special Program on Substance Abuse and Related Violence (SPSARV) of the General Board of Global Ministries on issues related to drugs and AIDS; and

10. urge the federal government to improve interagency cooperation and coordination to fight the double scourge of drugs and AIDS. (General Board of Church and Society and General Board of Global Ministries).

C. Annual conferences to:

1. explore HIV prevention and care needs within their areas and to develop conference-wide plans for appropriate, effective responses;

2. promote pastoral responses to persons with HIV/AIDS that affirm the presence of God's love, grace, and healing mercies;

3. encourage every local church to reach out through proclamation and education to help prevent the spread of HIV infection and to utilize and strengthen the efforts and leadership potential of men's, women's, and youth groups.

D. Episcopal leaders to:

1. issue pastoral letters calling for compassionate ministries and the development of educational programs that recognize the HIV/AIDS epidemic as a public health threat of major global and regional significance;

2. provide a level of leadership equal to the suffering and desperation that individuals, families, and communities are experiencing; and

3. Partner with the UMC Global AIDS Fund to mobilize funding for AIDS projects around the world and in the annual conferences.

God's Unconditional Love and Christ's Healing Ministry

The unconditional love of God, witnessed to and manifested through Christ's healing ministry, provides an ever-present sign and call to the church and all persons of faith to join efforts to prevent the spread of HIV, provide care and treatment to those who are already infected and ill, uphold the preciousness of God's creation through proclamation and affirmation, and be harbingers of hope, mercy, goodness, forgiveness, and reconciliation within the world.

The United Methodist Church unequivocally condemns stigmatization and discrimination of persons with HIV/AIDS and violence perpetrated against persons who are or are presumed to be infected with HIV. The United Methodist Church advocates the full involvement of the church at all levels to be in ministry with, and to respond fully to the needs of, persons, families, and communities whose lives have been affected by HIV/AIDS. In keeping with our faith in the risen Christ, we confess our belief that God has received those who have died, that the wounds of living loved ones will be healed, and that Christ, through the Holy Spirit, is present among us as we strive to exemplify what it means to be bearers of Christ's name in the midst of the global HIV/AIDS pandemic.

ADOPTED 2004
REVISED AND READOPTED 2008, 2012
RESOLUTION #3243, 2008, 2012 *BOOK OF RESOLUTIONS*
RESOLUTION #298, 2004 *BOOK OF RESOLUTIONS*
RESOLUTION #278, 2000 *BOOK OF RESOLUTIONS*

See Social Principles, ¶¶ 165B and 162U.

3244. United Methodist Global AIDS Fund

"Come to me, all you who are struggling hard and carrying heavy burdens, and I will give you rest." (Matthew 11:28)

For over thirty years the General Conference of The United Methodist Church has spoken with prophetic compassion to the global issue of HIV & AIDS. The United Nations has declared the AIDS pandemic a "global emergency," saying human life is threatened everywhere and world security is at risk as the planet faces the worst health crisis in 700 years.

According to the World Health Organization since the beginning of the epidemic, almost 78 million people have been infected with the HIV virus and about 39 million people have died of HIV. Globally, 37 million people are living with HIV or AIDS. Approximately 7,500 people are infected daily, including 900 babies born with HIV, which is completely preventable with access to testing and anti-retroviral drugs.

The 2004 General Conference established the United Methodist Global AIDS Fund (UMGAF) (UMCOR Advance #982345) and the 2008 and 2012 General Conferences reaffirmed this global health initiative. By 2015 UMGAF had funded, in partnership with the General Board of Global Ministries, 287 church-oriented and Christ-centered HIV & AIDS projects in 44 countries plus scores of annual conference AIDS projects. UMGAF facilitates ongoing educational efforts to equip hundreds of United Methodists to respond to the AIDS crisis locally and globally. Advocacy for prevention, care, and treatment has been a consistent focus of UMGAF since 2004 through its partnership with the General Board of Church and Society, which administers the AIDS Network in The United Methodist Church.

The face of AIDS is changing in the world. More persons have access to life-saving drugs, which is reducing the number of overall deaths. But stigma inflicted by the Church and society keeps people from being tested and treated. UMGAF is the official entity in The United Methodist Church addressing these concerns as it works and prays for an AIDS-free world.

Of the total money raised in each annual conference for UMGAF, 25 percent shall be retained by the annual conference for programs combating HIV & AIDS in their region and/or in other global connectional projects. Each annual conference shall designate an appropriate agency for the promotion and distribution of these funds.

Also, of the total money raised in each annual conference for the United Methodist Global AIDS Fund, 75 percent shall be remitted by the conference treasurer to the Advance office at the General Board of Global Ministries for distribution to global projects in consultation with GBGM staff and the interagency United Methodist Global AIDS Fund Committee. UMGAF is governed by a committee comprised of one representative each from the General Board of Global Ministries, Council of Bishops, General Board of

Church and Society, Division on Ministries With Young People, Office of Christian Unity and Interreligious Relationships, United Methodist Women, and General Commission on Communications, and three persons who are not serving on any of these agencies chosen by the committee for expertise and diversity. UMGAF is staffed by the volunteer committee as well as consultants. In order to ensure United Methodist HIV and AIDS ministries, operational and programmatic funds for the United Methodist Global AIDS Fund Committee will be provided either by a special apportionment or contingency funds of The United Methodist Church. The United Methodist Global AIDS Fund Committee will faithfully:

1. assist local congregations and conferences in identifying and creating global partnerships for mutual HIV & AIDS ministry;

2. provide support for projects sponsored by local congregations or organizations related to The United Methodist Church, partner autonomous Methodist churches and the ecumenical church;

3. encourage partnerships between congregations and conferences in the United States and Methodist congregations and ecumenical organizations globally that are engaged in the struggle against HIV & AIDS;

4. advocate for social justice, particularly related to decreasing stigma and increasing governmental and nongovernmental funding for HIV & AIDS, tuberculosis, and malaria;

5. develop appropriate promotional materials and funding guidelines;

6. resource United Methodists through training and networking opportunities; and

7. explore ways to ensure sustainability both fiscally and programmatically through intentional coordination and collaboration with the global health efforts at the general church level.

As a critical global health initiative, the 2016 General Conference recommits itself to the vital ministry of the United Methodist Global AIDS Fund.

ADOPTED 2004
READOPTED 2008
AMENDED AND READOPTED 2012, 2016
RESOLUTION #3244, 2008, 2012 *BOOK OF RESOLUTIONS*
RESOLUTION #154, 2004 *BOOK OF RESOLUTIONS*

See Social Principles, ¶ 162U.

3245. Endorsing "20/20: Visioning an AIDS-Free World"

WHEREAS, The United Methodist Church has long been committed to creating an AIDS-free world, and beginning in 2005 started the United Methodist Global AIDS Fund as a global health initiative to raise funds to support church-oriented and Christ-centered HIV and AIDS ministries, and

WHEREAS, this fund successfully has raised funds for distribution for more than 175 projects in over 37 countries (including the United States), and the need for continued and increased funding for programs of HIV and AIDS education, prevention, care, and treatment is everywhere evident, and

WHEREAS, more than 30 million people are infected worldwide, almost 50 percent of whom are women, and over 15 million AIDS orphans struggle to survive, we are reminded anew that "where there is no vision, the people perish" (Proverbs 29:18 KJV) and that Jesus called his disciples to "heal every disease and every sickness" (Matthew 10:1), and

WHEREAS, our founding leader, John Wesley practiced medicine himself and called his followers to care for the sick and suffering, and to avoid stigmatization and discrimination, and

Whereas, a gift as small as $20 can stop the transmission of HIV from several mothers to their newborn babies, supply nutrients to 20 HIV-positive children suffering from dehydration, ensure nursing care for a newborn infant born with AIDS, teach young people and adults how to prevent HIV, feed an HIV-positive person for a month so they can take powerful medicines, and provide free Upper Room biblical readings and prayers for those infected and affected.

Therefore, be it resolved, that the 2012 General Conference endorses the new "20/20: Visioning an AIDS-Free World" campaign of the United Methodist Global AIDS Fund Committee, and

1. Encourages every United Methodist to contribute yearly $20, $200, or more to the United Methodist Global AIDS Fund Advance #982345 and to invite others to join in this mission of mercy. Twenty-five percent of what the annual conference raises should be used within the conference for AIDS work, either locally or in global projects.

2. Asks each church and annual conference to educate its members about the HIV and AIDS crisis and to take up at least one major annual conference offering during the quadrennium.

3. Invites local congregations and individuals to join the 2020 Club composed of those who have committed $2,020 by 2020 to the United Methodist Global AIDS Fund.

4. Requests United Methodists to pray for an AIDS-free world, remembering the words of Galatians 6:9: "Let's not get tired of doing good, because in time we'll have a harvest, if we don't give up."

Be it further resolved, that the 2012 General Conference requests that planners of the 2016 and 2020 General Conferences set aside plenary time to review the progress of this "20/20: Visioning an AIDS-Free World" campaign, evaluating and highlighting the contributions United Methodists have made to this global health initiative.

ADOPTED 2012
RESOLUTION #3245, 2012 *BOOK OF RESOLUTIONS*

See Social Principles, ¶ 162U, V.

IMMIGRATION

3281. Welcoming the Migrant to the US

The Historical Context

From the dawn of creation human beings have migrated across the earth. The history of the United States is a migration narrative of families and individuals seeking safety, economic betterment, and freedom of religious and cultural expression. The reasons for those who immigrated willingly are numerous and varied depending on the context, but what all immigrants share is the promise of what they believe lies in another land other than their own. Migrants today continue to travel to North America because of the effects of globalization, dislocation, economic scarcity, persecution, and other reasons.

The arrival of migrants to the United States from so many parts of the world has also meant that there is a diversity of cultures and worldviews. The diversity of cultures, worldviews, and languages has placed an enormous strain upon migrants. To effectively deal with this trauma and ease the process of acculturation, migrants should be encouraged to preserve strong cultural and familial ties to their culture of origin.

The arrival of new cultures has also felt threatening to US citizens, and this has too often resulted in conflict and even violence. Throughout the history of the United States, the most recently arrived group of migrants has often been a target of racism, marginalization, and violence. We regret any and all violence committed against migrants in the past and we resolve, as followers of Jesus, to work to eliminate racism and violence directed toward newly arriving migrants to the United States.

The Biblical and Theological Context

Regardless of legal status or nationality, we are all connected through Christ to one another. Paul reminds us that when "one part suffers, all the parts suffer" as well (1 Corinthians 12:26). The solidarity we share through Christ eliminates the boundaries and barriers which exclude and isolate. Therefore, the sojourners we are called to love are our brothers and sisters, our mothers and fathers, our sons and daughters; indeed, they are us.

Throughout Scripture the people of God are called to love sojourners in our midst, treating them "as if they were one of your citizens" and loving them as we do ourselves (Leviticus 19:33-34 NRSV). Love for the sojourner is birthed out of the shared experience the Israelites had as a people in sojourn searching for the Promised Land. The attitudes and actions required of God's people were to emanate from the reflection of their liberation from slavery by God's hand. As the people of God were liberated from oppression, they too were charged to be instruments of redemption in the lives of the most vulnerable in their midst-the sojourner (Exodus 22:21; 23:9; Leviticus 19:34; Deuteronomy 10:19; 16:12; 24:18, 22—all NRSV).

In the New Testament, Jesus' life begins as a refugee to Africa when he and his family flee to Egypt to escape Herod's infanticide (Matthew 2:13-18). Jesus fully identifies with the sojourner to the point that to welcome the sojourner is to welcome Jesus himself (Matthew 25:35). Jesus teaches us to show special concern for the poor and oppressed who come to our land seeking survival and peace.

In Scripture, Jesus continually manifests compassion for the vulnerable and the poor. Jesus incarnated hospitality as he welcomed people and ministered to their greatest need. Jesus' presence on earth initiated the Kingdom reality of a new social order based on love, grace, justice, inclusion, mercy, and egalitarianism, which was meant to replace the old order, characterized by nepotism, racism, classism, sexism, and exclusion. The broken immigration system in the United States and the xenophobic responses to migrants reflect the former social order. The calling of the people of God is to advocate for the creation of a new immigration system that reflects Jesus' beloved community.

The fear and anguish so many migrants in the United States live under are due to federal raids, indefinite detention, and deportations which tear apart families and create an atmosphere of panic. Millions of immigrants are denied legal entry to the US due to quotas and race and class barriers, even as employers seek their labor. US policies, as well as economic and political conditions in their home countries, often force migrants to leave their homes. With the legal avenues closed, immigrants who come in order to support their families must live in the shadows and in intense exploitation and fear. In the face of these unjust laws and the systematic deportation of migrants instituted by the Department of Homeland Security, God's people must stand in solidarity with the migrants in our midst.

In Scripture, sojourners are also identified as heralds or messengers bringing good news. This is seen in many stories of the Bible:

- Abraham welcomed three visitors and then was promised a child even though Sarah was past the age of bearing children (Genesis 18:1-11);
- Rahab hid the spies from Israel, and her family was ultimately spared (Joshua 2:1-16);
- the widow at Zarephath gave Elijah her last meal and received food and ultimately healing for her dying son (1 Kings 17:7-24); and
- Zacchaeus, upon welcoming Jesus into his home, promised to share half his possessions with the poor and repay those he stole from four times the amount owed. As Jesus entered Zacchaeus's home he proclaimed that salvation had come to his house (Luke 19:1-10).

All of these stories give evidence to the words of the writer of Hebrews who advises the listeners to "not neglect to show hospitality to strangers, for by doing that some have entertained angels without knowing it" (13:2 NRSV). God's people are called to welcome the sojourner not only because of God's commands to do so, but because God's people need to hear the good news of the gospel incarnated in their stories and in their lives. Welcoming the sojourner is so vital to the expression of Christian faith that to engage in this form of hospitality is to participate in our own salvation.

There is theologically and historically an implied nature of mutuality in migration. Both the migrant and the native are meant to benefit from migration. Welcoming the migrant is not only an act of mission; it is an opportunity to receive God's grace. The globalization of international economies and the continuing movement of migrants have created an increasingly diversified US population and should be reflected in United Methodist congregations and national church leadership.

Therefore, The United Methodist Church understands that at the center of Christian faithfulness to Scripture is the call we have been given to love and welcome the sojourner. We call upon all United Methodist churches to welcome newly arriving migrants in their communities, to love them as we do ourselves, to treat them as one of our native-born, to see in them the presence of the incarnated Jesus, and to show hospitality to the migrants in our midst, believing that through their presence we are receiving the good news of the gospel of Jesus Christ.

The Current Context

Immigration to the United States has changed in the last 20 years largely because the world has changed. Globalization has lessened the geographical distance between the poor and affluent, but it has also greatly exacerbated the chasm between those with access to resources and those denied that same access. Vast inequities between the global North and South are a continuing source of conflict and a draw of resources and people from the South to the North. Globalization has localized issues which used to be hidden or detached by geographical boundaries, but has not created forms of accountability or mediated the necessity of cross-cultural reconciliation between those victimized by international economic policies and those who benefit from them. Global media enable the poor of the global South to see the lifestyles of the affluent in the global North, while rarely seeing the intense poverty that also exists there. This creates both tensions and a draw to attain that same lifestyle.

Although unregulated trade and investment have economically benefited some, many more have been sentenced to a lifetime of poverty and marginalization. In poorer countries natural resources have been removed by transnational corporations which have no stake in the continuing welfare of the local people, the enhancement of their cultural traditions, or their ecological environment. The lack of these resources often leads to a drastic reduction in jobs, wages, and labor protections. Public social benefits are eliminated and the nation sinks deeper into debt as it turns to such institutions as the World Bank and International Monetary Fund.[1] As the affluent North continues to expand its wealth, this expansion occurs at the expense of the impoverished South. Every region in the world is affected in some way by the global economic divide. Yet, while money and products easily flow across borders, the movement of people who have been forced to migrate because of intolerable economic conditions is increasingly restricted.

When those whose livelihoods have been eradicated in favor of corporate globalization attempt to sojourn to North America to work and provide for their families, they receive a mixed message that is confusing and ultimately oppressive. Immigrants have moved into areas of the United States where there are economic opportunities that US citizens have largely ignored. Employers often prefer undocumented workers in order to increase profit margins. Until all jobs provide a livable wage employers will be able to pit US citizens against undocumented workers in a downward spiral that undermines the labor rights for all.

Because the US immigration system has not kept up with the changing pace of migration and the US economy, the population of undocumented migrants has grown dramatically. Yet, the growing population of undocumented migrants has not yet been harmful to most US workers because they are not competing for the same jobs. While the United States labor force is growing older and more educated, the need for unskilled workers remains strong. The Migration Policy Institute reports that the economic necessities for repairing the immigration system are clear, as they predict by 2030 immigrant workers will comprise between one-third and one-half of the US labor force.[2] Testifying before the

1. Moe-Lobeda, Cynthia D. *Healing a Broken World: Globalization and God.* Minneapolis, MN: Fortress Press, p. 28.
2. B. Lindsay Lowell, Julia Gelatt & Jeanne Batalove, *Immigrants and Labor Force Trends: The Future, Past, and Present.* Washington, DC: Migration Policy Institute, July 2006, p. 1.

Senate Committee on Aging in 2003, then-Chairman of the Federal Reserve Board, Alan Greenspan, called for increased numbers of migrants to sustain an aging labor force and a continued economic vacuum among low-skilled workers.

Although the economic necessity of migrant workers is clear, any immigration or economic system which calls for a perpetual class of second-class workers cannot be supported by people of faith. Undocumented migrants are exploited for their labor and economic contribution to the United States. They are denied their rights to collectively bargain for livable wages and safe working conditions, and they are shut out of access to the social services of which they support through their difficult labor. Any reform of the immigration system must also allow for the full protections of all workers which includes the opportunity to gain legal status for all migrants.

Even though migrants have proven a tremendous benefit to the United States' economy, migrants have been systematically excluded from receiving any benefits. Excluding access to health care promotes an increase in the demand on emergency rooms to provide that daily care or it forces migrants fearful of seeking medical care to live in continued pain and suffering. The United States benefits from migrant labor, but migrants have been forced to live in the shadows, unable to fully contribute or receive appropriate care.

Immigration: A Human Rights Issue

Since 9/11 the debate surrounding immigration has unfortunately been framed as an issue of national security. All of this emphasis on border security has not stemmed the flow of undocumented migration, even though the United States has poured billions of dollars into militarizing the border.

The use of local law enforcement as immigration agents should be stopped as well. When local law enforcement officials engage in immigration enforcement, migrants are often unwilling to report crimes and are forced to live in situations where they are exploited, abused, and victimized.

All nations have the right to secure their borders, but the primary concern for Christians should be the welfare of immigrants.

Between 1994 and 2009, according to the Department of Homeland Security Border Safety Initiative, more than 3,860 migrants have died crossing the border between the United States and Mexico (https://www.aclu.org/files/pdfs/immigrants/humani tariancrisisreport.pdf).

Raids of workplaces, homes, and other social places have often violated the civil liberties of migrants. Migrants should be given due process and access to adequate legal representation. Due to these raids and the ensuing detentions and deportations that follow them, families have been ripped apart and the migrant community has been forced to live in a constant state of fear.

To refuse to welcome migrants to this country—and to stand by in silence while families are separated, individual freedoms are ignored, and the migrant community in the United States is demonized by members of Congress and the media—is complicity to sin.

A Call to Action

The United Methodist Church affirms the worth, dignity, and inherent value and rights of all persons regardless of their nationality or legal status. United Methodist churches throughout the United States are urged to build bridges with migrants in their local communities, to learn from them, celebrate their presence in the United States and recognize and appreciate the contributions in all areas of life that migrants bring. We call upon all United Methodist churches to engage in the following:

- advocate for legislation that will uphold the civil and human rights of all migrants in the United States and will provide an opportunity to attain legal status for all undocumented migrants currently in the United States, as well as for those arriving in the future;
- begin English as a Second Language classes as part of a ministry to migrant communities and advocate for federal and state support of expanded ESL classes;
- denounce and oppose the rise of xenophobic, racist, and violent reactions against migrants in the United States, and support all efforts to build relationships among people, instead of building walls among diverse ethnicities and cultures;
- welcome newly arriving immigrants into our congregations;

- oppose the building of a wall between the United States and Mexico, which the communities of both sides of the border are in opposition to;
- call the United States government to immediately cease all arrests, detainment, and deportations of undocumented immigrants, including children, solely based upon their immigration status until a fair and comprehensive immigration reform is passed;
- provide wherever possible pastoral care and crisis intervention to refugees and newly arrived migrants, identifying and responding compassionately to their spiritual, material, and legal needs;
- work with civic and legal organizations to support migrant communities affected by harsh immigration laws and over-reaching national security measures;
- support those churches that prayerfully choose to offer sanctuary to undocumented migrants facing deportation;
- continue the work of the United Methodist Task Force on Immigration composed of staff from the general boards and agencies, representatives of the Council of Bishops, and members of caucuses and national plans that was created by the resolution, "Opposition to the Illegal Immigration Reform and Immigration Resolution Act" (2004 *Book of Resolutions*, #118).

Further, The United Methodist Church is urged to advocate for the comprehensive reform of the US immigration system. The executive action taken by President Obama in 2014 was a necessary temporary step that allowed certain groups of immigrants to apply for temporary legal status, though not citizenship. Therefore, we acknowledge that legislative change is the permanent step that is needed.

Any legislation to reform the US immigration system must affirm the worth, dignity, and inherent value and rights of migrants, and must also include:

- an opportunity for citizenship for all undocumented migrants. Any pathway created for undocumented migrants should have minimal obstacles, and those requirements should not be designed to preclude migrants from eligibility for legalization;
- clearing the backlogs and reunifying families separated by migration or detainment;

- an increase in the number of visas for short-term workers to come into the United States to work in a safe, legal, and orderly way. Opportunities for legalization should be available for those who wish to remain permanently;
- the protection of all workers who come to stay for a certain period of time as well as for those who stay permanently. The right to bargain for higher wages, to protest against poor working conditions, and to preserve their human rights should be maintained by all workers, documented and undocumented alike;
- elimination of for-profit detention centers;
- elimination of indefinite detention, incarceration of children, and the expanding prison population, which also benefits privately owned detention centers and prisons;
- preservation of due process and access to courts and to adequate legal representation for all migrants regardless of legal status.

ADOPTED 2008
AMENDED AND READOPTED 2016
RESOLUTION #3281, 2008, 2012 *BOOK OF RESOLUTIONS*

See Social Principles, ¶¶ 162H and 163F.

3284. Faithfulness in Response to Critical Needs

We express our utmost concern for the passage of anti-immigrant laws, which adversely affect the well-being of citizens and residents of this country as they engage in providing humanitarian aid to undocumented persons in several States.

The United Methodist Church is an open door church, where every person is invited to come in, get closer to God, and become a part of a community of faith. That community is totally committed to attaining the good for all people through social and spiritual transformation. Any policies and laws attempting to limit or restrain the church's work of responding to the needs of others is contrary to its most fundamental beliefs as stated in the Gospel: "For God so loved the world that he gave his only Son, so that everyone who believes in him [regardless of color of skin or legal immigrant status] will have eternal life" (John 3:16). Similarly, the parable of the good Samaritan invites us, as Christians, to do good to all people irrespective of their place of origin.

We want to issue a call to The United Methodist Church and all other members of the Christian community to renew their commitment and strengthen their resolve to be faithful to respond to the needs of others, particularly as we face laws, whose primary intent is to discourage Christians from fulfilling their mission: to love and help the neighbor. We remember when the apostles were faced by similar circumstances after the authorities wanted to impede the fulfillment of their mission, they firmly declared in Acts 5:29: "We must obey God rather humans!" hence the Christian mandate to engage in civil disobedience when laws and policies deem to be unjust.

We urge the General Conference of The United Methodist Church to request the US federal government to ensure the protection of the freedom of religion in the United States by stopping the promulgation of laws that penalize church members for helping immigrants in need; actions that aside from being congruent with Christian faith, are vivid examples of God's love for every person.

At the same time, we ask the various governmental entities in every community to respect, at all times, places of worship as well as all religious activities within and outside our sanctuaries or other church property.

We bid the United States government to give due legislative recognition to the legal right of every human being to exercise his or her faith without the fear of persecution, particularly while coming together to give public expression of their faith.

ADOPTED 2012
RESOLUTION #3284, 2012 *BOOK OF RESOLUTIONS*

See Social Principles, ¶ 162H.

INTERRELIGIOUS ISSUES

3291. Called to Be Neighbors and Witnesses: Guidelines for Interreligious Relationships

The emergence of religiously diverse societies and the new dynamics in old religious communities prompt many faith communities to reconsider how they relate to one another and to prevailing secular ideologies representing a great opportunity for learning and an enhanced understanding of our common concerns.

Called to Be Neighbors

The vision of a "worldwide community of communities" commends itself to many Christians as a way of being together with persons of different religious convictions in a pluralistic world. Ultimately, this is to shift the question from, "To which church do we belong?" to "Have we participated in promoting the work of the Holy Spirit?" That suggests that we United Methodist Christians, not just individually, but corporately, are called to be neighbors with other faith communities, and to work with them to create a human community, a set of relationships between people at once interdependent and free, in which there is love, mutual respect, and justice.

Called to Be Witnesses

Jesus issued his famous missionary mandate, "Therefore, go and make disciples of all nations." (Matthew 28:19) Thus, we are called to bridge geographic, sociological, racial, or cultural boundaries. We are to proclaim and witness to the God who has bound humanity together in care for one another, regardless of our differences.

As we reflect on our faith and in our witness to and encounter with our diverse neighbors, we rediscover that God is also Creator of all humankind, the "one God and Father of all, who is Lord of all, works through all, and is in all" (Ephesians 4:6 GNT).

Dialogue: A Way to Be Neighbors

Dialogue is the intentional engagement with persons who hold other faith perspectives for purposes of mutual understanding, cooperation, and transformation. A positive foundation from which to connect with persons in other faith communities is recognition of the gifts they bring. Engaging in dialogue with positive expectation offers the sharing of mutually beneficial spiritual gifts and overcoming past hostilities. Each religious community's faith offers a positive way to resolve conflict and offers resources for building community. Dialogue seeks to provide an environment allowing differences, affirms the positives, and brings a deeper relationship.

Dialogue: A Way to Witness

Dialogue can lead to a relationship of mutual acceptance, openness, and respect. True and effective dialogue requires Christians be truly open to persons of other faith communities about each other's convictions on life, truth, salvation and witness. Dialogue leads to the understanding and receiving of each other's wisdom.

Dialogue creates relationships of mutual understanding, openness, and respect. We leave to the Holy Spirit the outcome of our mutual openness. A large part of our task, and foundational to interreligious dialogue and cooperation, is to learn to discern the Spirit's work.

We must be obedient to our own call to witness and be loving and neighborly to persons of other faith communities. In dialogue, these deeply held truths encounter each other in witness and love, so that greater wisdom and understanding of truth may emerge that benefits all parties.

Neighbors and Witnesses: Into the New Millennium

The command to love one's neighbors and the call to witness to Jesus Christ to all people are inseparably linked. The profound challenge this represents for United Methodist Christians can be seen most sharply in the many diverse religious movements and to the religious nones.

The calling to be witnesses and neighbors to all people, is based on the biblical caution not to bear false witness (Matthew19:18) and the admonition to live at peace with all people (Hebrews 12:14). Love of neighbor and witness to Christ are the two primary attitudes United Methodist Christians must affirm in their relationship with persons of other faiths and those without a religious tradition.

United Methodist Christians enter a new millennium full of challenges and opportunities. We seek to learn how the Holy Spirit works among all peoples of the world, especially among those in other religious traditions and to those without a religious tradition.

Guidelines for Interreligious Relationships

These guidelines will assist United Methodists to be faithful to their call to witness and the call to be neighbors with persons of other faith communities.

1. Identify the various faith communities and familiarize your congregation with them.

2. Initiate dialogues with different faith communities, remaining sensitive to areas of historic tension. Be open to the possibilities for deepened understanding and new insight.

3. Work with persons of other faith communities to resolve economic, social, cultural and political problems in the community.

4. Plan community celebrations with an interreligious perspective together with persons of other faith traditions.

5. Develop new models of community building that strengthen relationships and allow people to dwell together in harmony while honoring the integrity of their differences.

Intent

The intent in developing interreligious relationships is not to amalgamate all faiths into one religion. In dialogue, we mutually seek insight into the wisdom of other traditions and we hope to overcome our fears and misapprehensions.

United Methodist Christians are neighbors with persons whose religious commitments are different from our own. We open ourselves to dialogue and engagement with persons of other faith communities and to other Christians whose understandings, cultures, and practices may be different from our own.

Therefore, The United Methodist Church, in the knowledge that Jesus calls us to the blessings of peacemaking and reminds us that the highest law is to love God and neighbor, calls its members and its leaders:

1. To oppose demagoguery, manipulation, and image making that seeks to label Arabs and Muslims in a negative way;

2. To counter stereotypical and bigoted statements made against Muslims and Islam, Arabs and Arabic culture;

3. To increase knowledge of neighbor by study and personal contact that yield a greater appreciation of the Muslim and Arabic contributions to society;

4. To act decisively to include Arabs and Muslims in interfaith and community organizations;

5. To pray for the perfection of community among us and to participate fully in the process of bringing it into being; and

6. To publicly denounce through statements from the Council of Bishops and the General Board of Church and Society current practices that discriminate against this community.

In order to aid United Methodists to respond to this call, all boards, agencies, and institutions of The United Methodist Church are requested to provide resources and programs and, where appropriate, to act in advocacy.

ADOPTED 1988
AMENDED AND READOPTED 2000, 2004
READOPTED 2008
AMENDED AND READOPTED 2016
RESOLUTION #3141, 2012 *BOOK OF RESOLUTIONS*
RESOLUTION #3128, 2008 *BOOK OF RESOLUTIONS*
RESOLUTION #78, 2004 *BOOK OF RESOLUTIONS*
RESOLUTION #69, 2000 *BOOK OF RESOLUTIONS*

See Social Principles, ¶162B

3292. United Methodist Guiding Principles for Christian-Jewish Relations

In order to increase our understanding of and with peoples of other living faith traditions, of ourselves as followers of Jesus Christ, and of God and God's truth, The United Methodist Church encourages dialogue and experiences with those of other faiths. For important and unique reasons, including a treasury of shared Scripture and an ancient heritage that belong to us in common but that also contain our dividedness, we look particularly for such opportunities with Jews. United Methodist participation in Christian-Jewish dialogue and relationships is based on the following understandings:

1. There is one living God, in whom both Jews and Christians believe.

While the Jewish and Christian traditions understand and express their faith in the same God in significantly different ways, we believe with Paul that God, who was in Christ reconciling the world to God's own self (2 Corinthians 5:18-19), is none other than the God of Israel, maker of heaven and earth. Above all else, Christians and Jews are bonded in our joyful and faithful response to the one God, living our faith as each understands God's call.

2. Jesus was a devout Jew, as were many of his first followers.

We know that understanding our Christian faith begins by recognizing and appreciating this seminal fact. Neither the ministry of Jesus and his apostles nor the worship and thought of the early church can be understood apart from the Jewish tradition, culture, and worship of the first century. Further, we believe that God's revelation in Jesus Christ is unintelligible apart from the story of what God did in the life of the people of Israel.

Because Christianity is firmly rooted in biblical Judaism, we understand that knowledge of these roots is essential to our faith. As expressed in a statement from the Consultation on the Church and Jewish People of the World Council of Churches: "We give thanks to God for the spiritual treasure we share with the Jewish people: faith in the living God of Abraham, Isaac, and Jacob; knowledge of the name of God and of the commandments; the prophetic proclamation of judgment and grace; the Hebrew Scriptures; and the hope of the coming Kingdom. In all these, we find common roots in biblical revelation and see spiritual ties that bind us to the Jewish people."[1]

3. Judaism and Christianity are living and dynamic religious movements that have continued to evolve since the time of Jesus, often in interaction with each other and with God's continual self-disclosure in the world.

Christians often have little understanding of the history of Judaism as it has developed since the lifetime of Jesus. As a World Council of Churches publication points out: "Bible-reading and worshiping Christians often believe that they `know Judaism' since they have the Old Testament, the records of Jesus' debates with Jewish teachers and the early Christian reflections on the Judaism of their times. . . . This attitude is often reinforced by lack of knowledge about the history of Jewish life and thought through the 1,900 years since the parting of the ways of Judaism and Christianity."[2]

As Christians, it is important for us to recognize that Judaism has developed vital new traditions. This evolving tradition has given the Jewish people profound spiritual resources for creative life through the centuries. We increase our understanding when we

1. "The Churches and the Jewish People, Towards a New Understanding," adopted at Sigtuna, Sweden, by the Consultation on the Church and the Jewish People, sponsored by the World Council of Churches, 1988.

2. "Ecumenical Considerations on Jewish-Christian Dialogue, 1993," World Council of Churches, paragraph 1.6.

learn about the rich variety of contemporary Jewish faith practice, theological interpretation, and worship, and discover directly through dialogue how Jews understand their own history, tradition, and faithful living.

4. Christians and Jews are bound to God though biblical covenants that are eternally valid.

As Christians, we stand firm in our belief that Jesus was sent by God as the Christ to redeem all people and that in Christ the biblical covenant has been made radically new. While church tradition has taught that Christianity superseded Judaism as the "new Israel," we do not believe that earlier covenantal relationships have been invalidated or that God has abandoned Jewish partners in covenant.

We believe that just as God is steadfastly faithful to the biblical covenant in Jesus Christ, likewise God is steadfastly faithful to the biblical covenant with the Jewish people, and no covenantal relationship is invalidated by the other. Further, we are mysteriously bound to one another through our covenantal relationships with the one God and Creator of us all. The covenant God established with the Jewish people through Abraham, Moses, and others continues because it is an eternal covenant. Paul proclaims that the gift and call of God to the Jews is irrevocable (Romans 11:29). Thus, we believe that the Jewish people continue in covenantal relationship with God.

5. As Christians, we are clearly called to witness to the gospel of Jesus Christ in every age and place. At the same time, we believe that God has continued, and continues today, to work through Judaism and the Jewish people.

Essential to the Christian faith is the call to proclaim the good news of Jesus Christ to all people. Through the announcement of the gospel in word and work comes the opportunity for others to glimpse the glory of God, which we have found through Jesus Christ. Yet we also understand that the issues of the evangelization of persons of other faiths, and of Jews in particular, are often sensitive and difficult.

We acknowledge that a lack of clarity on the meaning of evangelism in the context of Christian-Jewish relations is distressing to our Jewish neighbors. In the 1997 joint commentary on *Building New Bridges in Hope*, Jewish scholar Leon Klenicki said,

"The question considered by this principle is very crucial in the relationship of Christians and Jews. It reminds us of the word 'evangelism' which brings great uneasiness to Jewish hearts. Through the centuries, evangelism has been a way by which Christians tried to convert and persecute Jews in the Western world. As Jews, we need to understand the exact meaning of evangelism."

We acknowledge that as United Methodist Christians our mission is to make disciples of Jesus Christ. This mission invites us to bear witness to Christ's light. In this context, The United Methodist Church neither makes the Jews a unique focus of our witness-bearing, nor excludes Jews from our longing that all persons may of their own volition believe in Jesus Christ our Savior and Lord. We affirm our responsibility to offer the gospel of Jesus Christ to all in witness that is respectful of the culture and religious convictions of others. Even as we offer our own faith, we remain open to learn from and be enriched by those who have faith experiences different from our own.

We bear our Christian witness in a state of humility since we cannot know fully the way in which God's Spirit will work, nor can we know in whom the Spirit will be made manifest. We have always proclaimed that God spoke through the prophets of Israel and Judah and that Jesus spoke and acted in the tradition of those prophets. "God's grace is active everywhere, at all times, carrying out this purpose as revealed in the Bible. It is *expressed* in God's covenant with Abraham and Sarah, in the Exodus of Israel from Egypt, and in the ministry of the prophets" (*Book of Discipline*, ¶ 121).

We believe that God has not abandoned God's covenant with the Jews. We are indebted to our Jewish forebearers through whom the Scriptures of the Old Testament have come to us and through whom the one true God has been revealed in the world. Therefore, we reject any and all forms of evangelism that are coercive in their nature, violent in their means, or anti-Semitic in their intent.

It is our belief that Jews and Christians are coworkers and companion pilgrims who have made the God of Israel known throughout the world. Through common service and action, we jointly proclaim the God we know. Together through study and prayer, we can learn how the God we believe to be the same God speaks and calls us continually into closer relationship with one another, as well as with God.

6. As Christians, we are called into dialogue with our Jewish neighbors.

Christians and Jews hold a great deal of Scripture, history, and culture in common. And yet, we also share 2,000 painful years of anti-Semitism and the persecution of Jews by Christians. These two apparently discordant facts move Christians to seek common experiences with Jews and especially to invite them into dialogue to explore the meaning of our kinship and our differences. Our intention is to learn about the faith of one another and to build bridges of understanding.

While for Christians, dialogue will always include testimony to God's saving acts in Jesus Christ, it will include in equal measure listening to and respecting the understanding of Jews as they strive to live in obedience and faithfulness to God and as they understand the conditions of their faith.

Productive interfaith dialogue requires focused, sustained conversation based on willingness to recognize and probe genuine differences while also seeking that which is held in common. We are called to openness so that we may learn how God is speaking through our dialogue partners. As stated in the World Council of Churches' "Guidelines on Dialogue": "One of the functions of dialogue is to allow participants to describe and witness to their faith on their own terms. . . . Participants seek to hear each other in order to better understand each other's faith, hopes, insights, and concerns."[3] Fruitful and respectful dialogue is centered in a mutual spirit of humility, trust, openness to new understanding, and commitment to reconciliation and the healing of the painful wounds of our history.

7. As followers of Jesus Christ, we deeply repent of the complicity of the church and the participation of many Christians in the long history of persecution of the Jewish people.

The Christian church has a profound obligation to correct historical and theological teachings that have led to false and pejorative perceptions of Judaism and contributed to persecution and hatred of Jews. It is our responsibility as Christians to oppose anti-Semitism whenever and wherever it occurs.

We recognize with profound sorrow that repeatedly and often in the last 2,000 years, the worship, preaching, and teaching of the Christian church has allowed and sometimes even incited and directed persecution against Jews. The church today carries grave

3. "Guidelines on Dialogue," adopted at London Colney, England, by the Consultation on the Church and the Jewish People of the Unit on Dialogue and People of Living Faiths and Ideologies, World Council of Churches, 1981, paragraph 3.4.

responsibility to counter the evil done by Christians to Jews in the Crusades, the Inquisition, the pogroms, and the Holocaust carried out often in the name of Jesus Christ.

Historically and today, both the selective use and the misuse of Scripture have fostered negative attitudes toward and actions against Jews. Use of New Testament passages that blame "the Jews" for the crucifixion of Jesus have throughout history been the basis of many acts of discrimination against Jews, frequently involving physical violence. There is no doubt that traditional and often officially sanctioned and promulgated Christian teachings, including the uncritical use of anti-Jewish New Testament writings, have caused untold misery and form the basis of modern anti-Semitism.

Misinterpretations and misunderstanding of historical and contemporary Judaism continue, including the mistaken belief that Judaism is a religion solely of law and judgment while Christianity is a religion of love and grace. The characterizations of God in the Hebrew Bible (called the Old Testament by Christians) are rich and diverse; strong images of a caring, compassionate, and loving deity are dominant for Jews as well as for Christians. Further, there are parallels between New Testament Christian understandings of the "spirit of the law" and contemporaneous theological developments in first-century Jewish theology.

The church has an obligation to correct erroneous and harmful past teachings and to ensure that the use of Scripture, as well as the preparation, selection, and use of liturgical and educational resources, does not perpetuate misleading interpretations and misunderstanding of Judaism.

Finally, it is essential for Christians to oppose forcefully anti-Jewish acts and rhetoric that persist in the present time in many places. We must be zealous in challenging overt and subtle anti-Semitic stereotypes and bigoted attitudes that ultimately made the Holocaust possible, and which stubbornly and insidiously continue today. These lingering patterns are a call to Christians for ever-new educational efforts and continued vigilance, so that we, remembering and honoring the cries of the tortured and the dead, can claim with Jews around the world to be faithful to the post-Holocaust cry of "Never Again."

8. As Christians, we share a call with Jews to work for justice, compassion, and peace in the world in anticipation of the fulfillment of God's reign.

Together, Jews and Christians honor the commandment to love God with all our heart, soul, and might. It is our task to join in common opposition to those forces—nation, race, power, money—that clamor for ultimate allegiance. Together, we honor the commandment to love neighbor as self. It is our task to work in common for those things that are part of God's work of reconciliation. Together, we affirm the sacredness of all persons and the obligation of stewardship for all God has created.

Jews still await the messianic reign of God foretold by the prophets. Christians proclaim the good news that in Jesus Christ, "the kingdom of God is at hand"; yet we, as Christians, also wait in hope for the consummation of God's redemptive work. Together, Jews and Christians long for and anticipate the fulfillment of God's reign. Together, we are "partners in waiting." In our waiting, we are called to witness and to work for God's reign together.

9. As United Methodist Christians, we are deeply affected by the anguish and suffering that continue for many people who live in the Middle East region that includes modern Israel.

We commit ourselves through prayer and advocacy to bring about justice and peace for those of every faith.

Within The United Methodist Church, we struggle with our understanding of the complexity and the painfulness of the controversies in which Christians, Jews, and Muslims are involved in the Middle East. The issues include disputed political questions of sovereignty and control, and concerns over human rights and justice. We recognize the theological significance of the Holy Land as central to the worship, historical traditions, hope, and identity of the Jewish people. We are mindful of this land's historic and contemporary importance for Christians and Muslims. We are committed to the security, safety, and well-being of Jews and Palestinians in the Middle East, to respect for the legitimacy of the state of Israel, to justice and sovereignty for the Palestinian people, and to peace for all who live in the region.

As we join with others of many religious communities in wrestling with these issues and searching for solutions, we seek to work together with other Christians, Jews, and Muslims to honor the religious significance of this land and to bring about healthy, sustainable life, justice, and peace.

Conclusion

Using the foregoing foundation and principles, The United Methodist Church encourages dialogue with Jews at all levels of the church, including and especially local congregations. It is also hoped that there will be many other concrete expressions of Jewish-Christian relationships, such as participating in special occasions of interfaith observance, and joint acts of common service and programs of social transformation. These offer great opportunity to Christians and Jews to build relationships and together work for justice and peace (shalom) in our communities and in the world, serving humanity as God intends.

ADOPTED 2016

See Social Principles, ¶ 162B.

3293. Receive Guidelines for Ministering to Mormons Who Seek to Become United Methodists

Whereas, United Methodists seek to act in ways that are faithful, compassionate, and just in relationship to other faith traditions, extending hospitality toward all and charity toward those whose faith and practice differ from ours; and

Whereas, as an expression of such hospitality and charity, United Methodists need to offer the pathways into membership for persons of other faith traditions with graciousness, consistency, and clarity; and

Whereas, the Church of Jesus Christ of Latter-Day Saints presents itself as a faith tradition outside the parameters of historic, apostolic Christianity;

Therefore, we continue to recommend that United Methodist churches should receive persons from the Church of Jesus Christ of Latter-Day Saints by offering the sacrament of Christian baptism following a period of *catechesis* (a time of intensive exploration and instruction in the Christian faith); and

Further, we continue to affirm *Sacramental Faithfulness: Guidelines for Receiving People from the Church of Jesus Christ of Latter-Day Saints (Mormons)* as a study resource and guideline for pastors and congregations who seek to offer pathways to receive former Mormons who seek to become United Methodist; and

Further, we authorize the General Board of Discipleship to provide ongoing resources in accordance with *Sacramental Faithfulness: Guidelines for Receiving People from the Church of Jesus Christ of Latter-Day Saints (Mormons)* to the Church to guide pastors and congregations who receive such persons who seek to become United Methodists in ways that are faithful to our United Methodist heritage.

ADOPTED 2000
REVISED AND READOPTED 2008
READOPTED 2016
RESOLUTION #3147, 2012 *BOOK OF RESOLUTIONS*
RESOLUTION #3149, 2008 *BOOK OF RESOLUTIONS*
RESOLUTION #16, 2000 *BOOK OF RESOLUTIONS*

See Social Principles, ¶ 162.

MENTAL HEALTH

3302. The Church and People With Intellectual, Physical, Psychological, and/or Neurological Disabilities

We call United Methodists to a new birth of awareness of the need to accept, include, receive the gifts of, and respond to the concerns of those persons with intellectual, physical, psychological, and/or neurological disabilities, including their families.

Because the experience of disabilities is included in all racial, social, sexual, and age groupings, and this experience is common to every family and at some time in every life;

And because a large part of the ministry of our Lord focused on persons with conditions such as intellectual, physical, psychological, and/or neurological disabilities;

And because the body of Christ is not complete without people of all areas of life, including people with all types of disabilities;

And because there exist inadequacies in the church and in society with regard to concerns for the rights of people with disabilities, utilization of talents, and their full participation within the life of the church and society;

And believing that the church is most faithful to the teachings and example of Jesus when it expresses love in concrete ways in a mutual ministry with those who are marginalized, neglected, avoided, or persecuted by society;

And believing in the legacy of John Wesley, Phillip Otterbein, and Jacob Albright, who held that vital piety flows into compassionate ministry;

And knowing that prevailing societal norms unduly glorify the conditions of youthful beauty, mental alertness, and material affluence to the exclusion and avoidance of those whose disabilities put them outside these norms,

Therefore, we pledge ourselves to:

Accessibility:

1. Renew and increase our commitments as a church to the development of a barrier-free society, especially in the many facilities of the church and parsonages. To indicate the seriousness of our intent, we must set time limits to ensure the greatest physical accessibility in the shortest feasible periods and extend our policy of not providing funding through or approval by United Methodist agencies unless minimum guidelines are met, which include but are not limited to:

    a. providing adequate access to sanctuary pews, altars, chancel areas and pulpit, classrooms, and restrooms;

    b. providing curb cuts, ramps with at least a 1:12 inclination or platform lifts; and

    c. providing facilities with equipment and supplies to meet the needs of persons with visible and hidden disabilities, including persons with vision and/or hearing impairments.

2. All meetings of The United Methodist Church should be welcoming and accessible to people with disabilities. General church agencies, jurisdictions, annual conferences, and districts should nominate people with disabilities to their boards and committees and enable their full participation.

3. All United Methodist churches are asked to conduct an audit of their facilities to discover barriers that impede the full participation of people with disabilities. (See ¶ 2533.6, 2012 *Book of Discipline.*) Steps should then be taken to remove those barriers. The Accessibility Audit for Churches is a recommended resource available from the General Board of Global Ministries.

Awareness:

1. Sensitize and train local church pastors to the needs and opportunities for ministry with people with disabilities and their families.

2. Lead the local churches in attitudinal change, to the end that the people called United Methodists are sensitized to the gifts, needs, and interests of people with disabilities, including their families.

3. Take advantage of the great opportunities for our church to work cooperatively and ecumenically with others who are addressing these issues and extend an active invitation to work jointly where possible.

4. Suggest one Sunday each year as Disability Awareness Sunday to sensitize people to our accessibility concerns. (See ¶ 265.4, 2012 *Book of Discipline*.)

Adequate Resources:

1. Provide resources through the church at all levels, including curricula, for persons with various disabilities, so that each individual has full opportunity for growth and self-realization with the community of faith and the society at large.

2. Strongly recommend that all curriculum material be so designed that it can be adapted to meet the needs of people with disabilities; that curriculum material portray people with disabilities in leadership roles within church and society; that curriculum material reflect the Guidelines for the Elimination of Handicappist Language as produced by the General Council on Ministries.

Affirmative Action:

1. Include in all our efforts of affirmative action the concerns and interests of people with disabilities, particularly in the active recruitment and encouragement of persons with disabilities for leadership roles, both clergy and lay, within the church and its agencies, in hiring practices, job security, housing, and transportation.

2. Urge the General Board of Higher Education and Ministry to monitor annual conference boards of ordained ministry so that people with disabilities are given equal treatment in the steps to ordained ministry.

3. Strongly urge that our schools of higher education and theological training provide specialized courses for faculty and students in the awareness and appreciation of gifts, needs, and interests of people with disabilities. This includes the emphasis of accessibility and equal employment in these institutions, as well

as those in the larger society. Accreditation by the University Senate should be withdrawn from institutions where persons who are disabled are excluded, either from attendance, services, or employment.

4. Strongly urge local churches to conduct needs-assessment surveys. Such a survey would suggest to a local church what particular actions must be taken to fully include people with disabilities within the life of the church.

Advocacy Within the Church:

Implement within each annual conference methods of recruiting, sensitizing, and training persons as advocates to work with and on behalf of people with disabilities on a one-to-one basis and to enable them to achieve their human and civil rights as well as to assume their rightful place in the life of the church and community. Each annual conference should also develop the larger concern of advocacy for people with disabilities to enable them to achieve appropriate housing, employment, transportation, education, and leisure-time development.

Advocacy Within the Society:

While there is much to be done within the church to make real the gospel of inclusiveness with regard to people with disabilities, there is a world society that also must be made aware of the concerns and needs of these persons. We urge the church and its people to stand alongside people with disabilities and to speak out on their rights in society. These rights include access to jobs, public transportation and other reliable forms of transportation, adequate housing, and education. We are people under orders to minister to and with all God's children. We are all a people in pilgrimage! We have too often overlooked those of God's children who experience life in different ways from ourselves. We pledge ourselves to an inclusive, compassionate, and creative response to the needs and gifts of people with disabilities.

Barrier-Free Construction for People With Disabilities:

Be it resolved, that church monies from agencies of The United Methodist Church beyond the local church be granted, loaned, or otherwise provided only for the construction of church sanctuaries, educational buildings, parsonages, camps, colleges, or other church-related agencies or facilities that meet minimum guidelines in their plans for barrier-free construction;

That local churches utilizing their own funds or funds secured through lending agencies and institutions beyond The United Methodist Church be urged to make adequate provision in their plans to ensure that all new and remodeled church buildings shall be of barrier-free construction;

That local churches be urged to adapt existing facilities through such programs as widening doorways, installing ramps and elevators, eliminating stairs where possible, providing handrails, adequate parking facilities, and restrooms so that people with disabilities may take their appropriate place in the fellowship of the church; and

That the appropriate national agencies provide technical information for local churches to assist in providing barrier-free facilities.

ADOPTED 1984
AMENDED AND READOPTED 1996, 2004
READOPTED 2008
AMENDED AND READOPTED 2012
RESOLUTION #3304, 2008, 2012 *BOOK OF RESOLUTIONS*
RESOLUTION #122, 2004 *BOOK OF RESOLUTIONS*
RESOLUTION #110, 2000 *BOOK OF RESOLUTIONS*

See Social Principles, ¶ 162I.

3303. Ministries in Mental Illness

Theological Statement

We believe that faithful Christians are called to be in ministry to individuals and their families challenged by disorders causing disturbances of thinking, feeling, and acting categorized as "mental illness." We acknowledge that throughout history and today, our ministries in this area have been hampered by lack of knowledge, fear, and misunderstanding. Even so, we believe that those so challenged, their families, and their communities are to be embraced by the church in its ministry of compassion and love.

Our model is Jesus, who calls us to an ethic of love toward all. As Jesus proclaimed the reign of God, his words and proclamations were accompanied by "healing every disease and every sickness" (Matthew 9:35). Jesus had compassion and healed those besieged by mental illness, many of whom had been despised, rejected, persecuted, and feared by their community.

John Wesley and the founders of The United Methodist Church practiced a faith grounded in the redemptive ministry of Jesus Christ, with a focus on healing the whole person: physical, spiritual, emotional and mental. The concern for the health of those within the ministry of the church led to establishment of medical services for those in need without regard to financial means, thereby refusing no one for any reason. That spirit of all-encompassing love and compassion serves as a legacy and a model for us as we seek to respond to those challenged by mental illness.

Today, because of the achievements of the scientific and medical communities, we know more about the causes and treatment of the many disorders considered "mental illnesses." More important, we know that the gift of healing is one of the spiritual gifts received from God. The call of those baptized in Christ includes a mandate to exercise the gift of healing by the church as evidence of God's love, a precursor to the reign of God, and a sign of the presence of God's Holy Spirit through the community of the church.

We therefore commit ourselves to learning more about the causes of mental illnesses; advocating for compassion and generosity in the treatment of mental illnesses; and prayerfully leading our congregations to be in ministry, demonstrating that our church, as the body of Christ, can work to provide the means of grace that leads to wholeness and healing for all.

Challenges Facing Persons With Mental Illness and Their Congregations and Communities.

Mental illness is a group of brain disorders that cause disturbances of thinking, feeling, and acting. Research published since 1987 has underscored the physical and genetic basis for the more serious mental illnesses, such as schizophrenia, manic-depression, and other affective disorders.

All aspects of health—physical, mental, and spiritual—were of equal concern to Jesus Christ, whose healing touch reached out to mend broken bodies, minds, and spirits with one common purpose: the restoration of well-being and renewed communion with God and neighbor. Many interventions are needed to heal the often chronic conditions of the brain and nervous system, known as mental illness. The body of Christ needs deeper healing in understanding, education, compassion, and adequate ways to support the families and individuals living with mental illness. Those impacted by mental illness also need to be supported in their quest for healing, knowing that most often Jesus heals over time, using a variety of healing modalities.

Precisely because mental illness affects how we think, feel or act, it has an impact on our ability to function in community with others.

There are many reasons that explain why persons with a mental illness diagnosis exhibit difficult or disruptive behaviors. The reasons include traumatic events like war; abuse or domestic violence; a life of physical or emotional poverty; deprivation of social experiences and limited social skills; and behaviors due to loneliness, being misunderstood, being powerless, or the absence of joy in their lives.

Therefore, mental illness challenge our commitment to community. We experience this challenge in several key ways:

1. Stigma

Stigma has been with us for millennia and remains a major issue today. When the man of Gadara said his name was "Legion, . . . because we are many," his comment suggests the countless individuals in every age, whose mental dysfunction causes fear, rejection, or shame, and to which we tend to respond with the same few measures no more adequate for our time than for his: stigmatization, isolation, incarceration, and restraint. Jesus embraced and healed such persons with special compassion (Mark 5:1-34).

2. Incarceration

We believe all persons with a mental illness diagnosis should have access to the same basic freedoms and human rights as other persons in a free society. A fine line of distinction exists between criminal violation of the law and behavior that is criminalized because law enforcement agencies have had no other recourse for handling persons whose actions resulted from mental illness symptoms that affect thinking, perceptions and behavior. We oppose the use of jails and prisons for incarceration of persons who have serious, persistent mental illnesses for whom treatment in a secure hospital setting is far more appropriate. Moreover, many incarcerated persons with mental illness need psychiatric medications. Citing economic reasons as the cause for failure to provide medications to a person who needs them is unacceptable, as is imposing medication compliance as a condition of release or access to treatment and other services.

3. Deinstitutionalization

We express particular concern that while the process followed in the United States and some other nations in recent years of deinstitutionalizing mental patients has corrected a longstanding problem of "warehousing" mentally ill persons, it has created new problems. Without adequate community-based mental-health programs to care for those who are dehospitalized, the streets or prisons have become a substitute for a hospital ward for too many people. Consequently, often the responsibility, including the costs of mental-health care, has simply been transferred to individuals and families or to shelters for the homeless that are already overloaded and ill-equipped to provide more than the most basic care. Furthermore, the pressure to deinstitutionalize patients rapidly has caused some mental-health systems to rely unduly upon short-term chemical therapy to control patients rather than employ treatments that research has demonstrated are successful.

4. Misunderstanding of Faith

Sometimes Christian concepts of sin and forgiveness, are inappropriately applied in ways that heighten paranoia or clinical depression. Great care must be exercised in ministering to those whose mental illness results in exaggerated self-negation. While all persons stand in need of forgiveness and reconciliation, God's love cannot be communicated through the medium of forgiveness for uncommitted or delusional sins.

The Response We Need

John Wesley's ministry was grounded in the redemptive ministry of Christ with its focus on healing that involved spiritual, mental, emotional, and physical aspects. His concern for the health of those to whom he ministered led him to create medical services at no cost to those who were poor and in deep need, refusing no one for any reason. He saw health as extending beyond simple biological well-being to wellness of the whole person. His witness of love to those in need of healing is our model for ministry to those suffering from mental illness.

1. Healing

Effective treatment recognizes the importance of medical, psychiatric, emotional, and spiritual care, psychotherapy or professional pastoral psychotherapy in regaining and maintaining health. Congregations in every community are called to participate actively in expanding care for persons who are mentally ill and their families as an expression of their nature as the body of Christ.

Treatment for mental illness recognizes the importance of a nonstressful environment, good nutrition, and an accepting community.

2. Congregations

The church, as the body of Christ, is called to a ministry of salvation in its broadest understanding, which includes both healing and reconciliation, of restoring wholeness both at the individual and community levels. We call upon the church to affirm ministries related to mental illness that embrace the role of community, family, and the healing professions in healing the physical, social, environmental, and spiritual impediments to wholeness for those afflicted with brain disorders and for their families.

We call upon local United Methodist congregations, districts, and annual or central conferences to promote United Methodist congregations as "Caring Communities." The mission to bring all persons into a community of love is central to the teachings of Christ. We gather as congregations in witness to that mission, welcoming and nurturing those who assemble with us. Yet we confess that in our humanity we have sometimes failed to minister in love to persons and families with mental illness. We have allowed barriers of ignorance, fear, and pride to separate us from those who most need our love and the nurturing support of community.

United Methodist congregations around the world are called to join the Caring Communities program, congregations and communities in covenant relationship with persons with mental illness and their families. Caring Communities engage intentionally in:

- Education. Congregations engage in public discussion as well as responsible and comprehensive education about the nature of mental illness and how it affects society today. Such education not only helps congregations express their caring more effectively, but reduces the stigma of mental illness so that persons who suffer from brain disorders, and their families, can more freely ask for help. Such education also counters a false understanding that mental illness is primarily an adjustment problem caused by psychologically dysfunctional families.
- Covenant. Congregations through their church councils enter into a covenant relationship of understanding and love with persons and families with mental illness to nurture them. The covenant understanding may well extend to community and congregational involvement with patients in psychiatric hospitals and other mental-health care facilities.
- Welcome. Congregations extend a public welcome to persons with mental illness and their families.
- Support. Congregations think through and implement the best ways to be supportive to persons with mental illness and to individuals and families caring for them.
- Advocacy. Congregations not only advocate for specific individuals caught up in bureaucratic difficulties, but identify and speak out on issues affecting persons with mental illness and their families that are amenable to legislative remedy.

3. Communities

We call upon the communities in which our congregations are located to develop more adequate programs to meet the needs of their members who have mental illness and their families. This includes the need to implement governmental programs at all levels that monitor and prevent abuses of persons who have mental illness, as well as those programs intended to replace long-term hospitalization with community-based services.

Mental illness courts, properly established, regulated, and administered could and should be maintained to handle cases involving persons with serious mental illnesses. Such courts can ensure compassionate and ethical treatment. These courts are often able to avoid criminalizing behaviors that result from symptoms affecting thought, perceptions, and behavior. When governing bodies institute such courts, they should:

- understand and embrace an ethical understanding of the compassionate intent of the law in the establishment of mental-health courts when mental illness is a factor in law enforcement.
- respect all human rights of persons confined for the purpose of mental-illness treatment in an accredited psychiatric facility, either public or private, including their legal right to have input into their treatment plan, medications and access to religious support as state laws allow. We hold all treatment facilities, public and private, responsible for the protection of these rights.

Depending on the unique circumstances of each community, congregations may be able to

- support expanded counseling and crisis intervention services;
- conduct and support workshops and public awareness campaigns to combat stigmas;
- facilitate efforts to provide housing and employment for deinstitutionalized persons;
- advocate for improved training for judges, police, and other community officials in dealing with persons with mental illness and their families;
- promote more effective interaction among different systems involved in the care of persons with mental illness, including courts, police, employment, housing, welfare, religious, and family systems;
- encourage mental health treatment facilities, public and private, including outpatient treatment programs, to take seriously the religious and spiritual needs of persons with a mental illness; and
- help communities meet both preventive and therapeutic needs related to mental illness.

4. Clergy Support

We call upon the General Board of Higher Education and Ministry and the General Board of Pension and Health Benefits to:

- give attention to addressing issues that arise when United Methodist clergy experience mental illness; and
- promote the development of pastoral leadership skills to understand mental illness and be able to mediate with persons in their congregations and their communities concerning the issues and needs of persons who have a mental illness.

5. Legislation

We call upon the General Board of Church and Society and other United Methodists with advocacy responsibility to:

a. advocate systemic reform of the health-care systems to provide more adequately for persons and families confronting the catastrophic expense and pain of caring for family members with mental illness;

b. support universal global access to health care, insisting that public and private funding mechanisms be developed to ensure the availability of services to all in need, including adequate coverage for mental-health services in all health programs;

c. advocate that community mental-health systems, including public clinics, hospitals, and other tax-supported facilities, be especially sensitive to the mental-health needs of culturally or racially diverse groups in the population;

d. support adequate research by public and private institutions into the causes of mental illness, including, as high priority, further development of therapeutic applications of newly discovered information on the aspect of genetic causation for several types of severe brain disorders;

e. support adequate public funding to enable mental-health-care systems to provide appropriate therapy;

f. collaborate with the work of entities like the National Alliance on Mental Illness (NAMI), a US self-help organization of persons with mental illness, their families and friends, providing mutual support, education and advocacy for those persons with severe mental illness, and urging the churches to connect with NAMI's religious outreach network. We also commend to our churches globally Pathways to Promise: Interfaith Ministries and Mental Illness, St. Louis, Missouri, as a necessary link in our ministry on this critical issue; and

g. build a global United Methodist Church mental illness network at the General Board of Church and Society to coordinate mental-illness ministries in The United Methodist Church.

6. Seminaries

We call upon United Methodist seminaries around the world to provide technical training, including experience in mental-health units, as a regular part of the preparation for the ministry, in order to help leaders and congregations become more knowledgeable about and involved in mental-health needs of their communities.

ADOPTED 1992
AMENDED AND READOPTED 2004
AMENDED AND READOPTED 2012, 2016
RESOLUTION #3303, 2012 *BOOK OF RESOLUTIONS*
RESOLUTION #3305, 2008 *BOOK OF RESOLUTIONS*
RESOLUTION #123, 2004 *BOOK OF RESOLUTIONS*
RESOLUTION #111, 2000 *BOOK OF RESOLUTIONS*

See Social Principles, ¶ 162*V.*

3304. Healing of Post-Abortion Stress

WHEREAS, we recognize that there is a legal right to an abortion in many countries, we also recognize that some regret that event later in life,

WHEREAS, the church should be about offering healing ministries for all types of brokenness,

Therefore, be it resolved, that the 2012 General Conference of The United Methodist Church urge pastors to become informed about the symptoms and behaviors associated with post-abortion stress; and

Be it further resolved, that the 2012 General Conference of The United Methodist Church encourage local churches to make available contact information for counseling agencies that offer programs to address post-abortion stress for all seeking help.

ADOPTED 2004
REVISED AND READOPTED 2012
RESOLUTION #3304, 2012 *BOOK OF RESOLUTIONS*
RESOLUTION #3306, 2008 *BOOK OF RESOLUTIONS*
RESOLUTION #124, 2004 *BOOK OF RESOLUTIONS*

See Social Principles, ¶ 162*V.*

NATIVE AMERICANS

3321. Native People and The United Methodist Church

Historical Overview and Theological Foundations

We believe that Native American/American Indian (American Indian: The US government and many tribal governments use the term "American Indian." We understand the words "Native American," "Indigenous people," and "First Nations people" to be interchangeable terms.) traditions affirm the presence of Creator God, the need for right relationship with our Creator and the world around us, and a call for holy living. Through corporate and personal conviction, our people individually and tribally are led by the Spirit of God to a greater awareness of God. Traditional beliefs, consistent with the gospel and the historic witness of the Church should not be understood as contrary to our beliefs as Native Christians. The testimony of historic and contemporary Native Christians should be counted in the historic witness of the Church.

Many Native traditions were erroneously feared, rather than understood as vehicles for the grace and the knowledge of God. Such fears have resulted in persecution of traditional Native peoples (The term "Native People" in this context refers collectively to American Indians, Alaska Natives, and Native Hawaiians) and Native Christians; and,

Many Native traditions have been misinterpreted as sin, rather than varying cultural expressions leading to a deeper understanding of our Creator and the Creator's divine presence and action in our world.

God's creating presence speaks to us through our cultures, rituals, and languages. This contextual incarnational testimony is vital to the ongoing work of the Church among Native people. For hundreds of years, Native Americans, Alaska Natives, and Native Hawaiians, compelled by the gospel have chosen to become disciples of Jesus Christ. In doing so, we have affirmed that relationship with God and our brothers and sisters is contained in the gospel of Jesus Christ. We bear witness to the mercy of God through our faith, continuing in discipleship and ministry.

As Native Christians, we affirm for the Church and ourselves that many elements of our traditions and cultures are consistent with the gospel of Jesus Christ, and the teachings of the Church. We affirm that the Holy Spirit is faithful in guiding us in holy living within our Native cultures and the broader culture. We recognize that just as in the broader culture, not all expressions of traditional cultures are appropriate for all believers; God is faithful in leading us to acceptable worship and continued growth in grace, as tribal people. We further affirm that our identity as Native or tribal persons is pleasing to our Creator and vital to the body of Christ. We affirm for each other that our languages, cultures, identities, and many traditions are pleasing to God and have the potential to renew and enrich the Church and offer hope to the world. God created us as Native People; to flout how God created us is to reject the authenticity of who and whose we are.

The General Conference of The United Methodist Church affirms the sacredness of American Indian people, their languages, cultures, and gifts to the church and the world.

We call upon the world, and the people of The United Methodist Church to receive the gifts of Native Americans, including American Indians, Alaska Natives, and Native Hawaiians, as people of God. We allow for the work of the Great Spirit/God among our communities and tribes without prejudice.

In 1452, the Papal Bull Romanus Pontifix declared war against all non-Christians throughout the world, sanctioned and promoted the conquest, colonization, and exploitation of non-Christian nations and their territories. In 1453, Spain was given rights of conquest and dominion over one half of the world and Portugal the other half.

In 1823, the Christian Doctrine of Discovery was adopted into law by the US Supreme Court (*Johnson v. McIntosh*). Chief Justice Marshall observed that Christian European nations had assumed dominion over the lands of America, and upon discovery, Native American Indians had lost their rights to complete sovereignty as independent nations and retained a mere right of occupancy in their lands.

Indigenous people were once sole occupants of this continent. Scholars vary greatly in their estimates of how many people were living in the Americas when Columbus arrived in 1492; however, estimates range from 40 million to 90 million for all of the Americas. American Indian tribal populations were decimated after the arrival of the Europeans. This decimation was rationalized according to:

   a. the European belief in their "discovery" of the new world;
   b. the arrogance of Manifest Destiny;
   c. the cavalier destruction of the Native concept of tribal communal land; and
   d. lack of immunity to diseases carried by Europeans to the Americas.

During the American Revolution, American Indian tribes and confederations of tribes were recognized as sovereign indigenous nations in nation-to-nation relationships with the major European powers. Later, these relationships were maintained with the newly formed US government, which formed 371 treaties with Indian nations between 1778 and 1871.

More than five million people identify as either American Indian or Alaska Native, according to the 2010 Census;

Prior to European contact, the indigenous nations of this continent were sovereign, autonomous, and self-regulating.

The establishment, enactment, and progression of the Doctrine of Discovery influenced law and behavior, perpetuated a climate of violence against Native people through colonization, forced removals, enactment of treaties that were then regularly violated, killings and the "Indian Wars" continuing today in a subtler but in a no less violent and invasive manner.

Government and religious institutions intentionally destroyed many of our traditional cultures and belief systems. To assimilate our peoples into mainstream cultures, many of our ancestors as children were forcibly removed to boarding schools, often operated by religious institutions, including historical Methodism. The Doctrine of Discovery facilitated a climate of hostility and genocide. Native peoples were targets by those seeking land and other natural resources.

Genocide became a tool of greed and a response to fear. While attempting to erase Native people from existence, traditional cultures, rituals, and languages also fell prey to acts of genocide.

A key historical fact for United Methodists to consider, acknowledge, and address is the 1864 Sand Creek Massacre, a violent act influenced by the Doctrine of Discovery that resulted in the genocide of almost 200 persons, mostly women and children, at a US peace camp. The Sand Creek attack was led by a Methodist preacher, Colonel John Chivington.

In 2007, the United Nations adopted "United Nations Declaration on the Rights of Indigenous Peoples" that called into question the validity of the Christian Doctrine of Discovery, which for centuries served as "legal" rationale for stealing land and dehumanizing aboriginal peoples, as well as justification for the establishment of boarding schools throughout North America to "civilize" Indian children.

In 2009, President Obama pledged to Native people the United States' support of the "Declaration of Indigenous Peoples." The declaration seeks to right historical wrongs through use of the papal bulls of the Roman Catholic Church that are official decrees by the pope sanctioning the seizing of indigenous lands worldwide.

Treaties are regarded as binding, sacred, and enduring texts by American Indians and Alaska Natives, comparable to the US Constitution and Bill of Rights. Therefore, it is disturbing that the US government ignored its trust responsibilities by violating treaties and other promises.

Tribal sovereignty is an inherent international right of Native nations. It encompasses various matters, such as jurisdiction over Indians and non-Indians on tribal lands, education and language, child welfare and religious freedom. Land is both the physical and spiritual foundation of tribal identity, as stated by Kidwell, Noley, and Tinker (2001) in their book, *A Native American Theology*: "Land is today the basis upon which tribal sovereignty rests; the rights of Indian people to live upon, use and to govern in a political sense the members of the tribe who live on the land and those whose tribal membership gives them an association with it" (p. 15). Early US Supreme Court decisions support and affirm tribal sovereignty, most notably the Marshall trilogy of cases in the nineteenth century, and *Winter v. S.* (1908).

Recent Supreme Court decisions, however, have ignored previous precedent and contradicted earlier rulings, undermining tribal sovereignty.

The effects of practicing the concept of a Comity Agreement by The United Methodist Church has resulted in the failure of the Church to follow through with the biblical mandate of propagating the gospel to all nations and, further, has caused the failure of the Church to create a climate for leadership development of Native Americans. A Comity Agreement would be discriminatory that violates the right of Native Americans to associate with the denomination of their choice.

Native American Contemporary Issues

A gap in knowledge exists in The United Methodist Church, in congregations and other United Methodist entities, relative to comprehending concepts of Native American life, cultures, languages, spirit, values, contemporary issues, and such. This knowledge gap has been a consistent problem over history, with minimal effort from non-Indian entities to change their attitudes toward Native Americans until more recently. Lack of knowledge, racism, and prejudice, and the absence of Native American representation at decision-making levels of the Church contribute to misunderstanding contemporary issues that affect Native people, and a history of missteps and violations of Native protocol. Contemporary issues affecting Native people need further exploration, understanding and action.

Furthermore, the American Indian population continues to shift between rural to urban population centers. The human condition of many American Indians reflects a legacy of poverty and socioeconomic factors. A serious shortage exists of American Indian pastors and trained professionals to respond to these conditions. Native American Ministry Sunday provides an opportunity for The United Methodist Church to support American Indian ministries and communities.

Health

American Indians are the most socioeconomically deprived minority group in the United States. The poverty level for children on reservations is more than twice the national average, and unemployment rates are three times that of other Americans. American Indians continue to lead national statistics in infant mortality, suicide, alcoholism, diabetes, HIV/AIDS, and tuberculosis.

The US government is bound by treaty to provide health care for all American Indians. The US government provides medical services through Indian Health Services, United States Public Health Service, and the Department of Health and Human Services to American Indians who belong to the federally recognized tribes.

The federal government's legislative and executive branches frequently threaten to reduce funding for the Indian Health Services Program. Any funding cuts could severely curtail or cancel health care for a large number of eligible American Indians.

Leadership Development

Native American Ministries Sunday, a key United Methodist Special Sunday offering has enabled a route for Native American leadership development. Before its inception, there were fewer than five ordained elders and diaconal ministers in The United Methodist Church. As a result of the ongoing support for Native American Ministry Sunday, well over 100 Native people have been seminary trained and ordained as elders and deacons. They are serving in local churches, annual conferences, and general agency leadership positions. This program, along with laity leadership development that is culturally appropriate and carefully constructed, are key considerations in continuing to expand leadership development among Native People and in Native tribes, churches, and communities.

Education

The concept of illiteracy is unacceptable in a time when society projects a formal demeanor of progress and opportunity for all members. Dispelling myths that Native People receive unlimited funds from the government for all their needs is a key action to understanding the educational obstacles for Native individuals seeking higher education. Past support from The United Methodist Church for the participation of American Indians in higher education has been appreciated, yet it has been inconsistent and the threat to eliminate it is omnipresent. A trend of decreasing American Indian participation in higher education is beginning to appear at the national and regional levels; and the consistently rising costs of higher education contribute considerably to the decrease of American Indian participation in higher education. Recent statistics suggest an upward trend of academic success for American Indians currently participating in higher education.

Economic Development for Native American People

For more than 500 years, Native Americans have lived and survived in the context of colonialism and capitalism, and have been impacted by the economics of greed. Many have been forced to live in poverty; a small segment of the Native American population is surviving, however, through tribal economic development based on gambling. Unfortunately, tribal gambling casinos have had negative social consequences beyond and even within tribes.

The need for economic development and growth is critically acute in most Native American communities across the United

States. Economic conditions are appalling, with some reservations facing exceptionally high rates (some as high as 80-90 percent) of unemployment, well above the national average.

In fact, many reservations have very high poverty rates in the United States and rank very low in health and education indicators. There is little or no tax base on many reservations. Equity for investment is practically nonexistent or equity comes from questionable sources and at an exorbitant rate. As a result, some tribes have resorted to gambling endeavors in an effort to improve their economies. The vast majority of tribes remain in desperate need of meaningful, diversified economic development, however.

Economic development encompasses everything from job creation to reform in tax codes, from the creation of banking institutions to the expansion of tribal autonomy, development of basic physical infrastructure, such as roads and sewers; telecommunications to bridge the digital divide; fiscal literacy development for Native American people. Collectively, these basic essentials are requirements for effective economic development.

The US Department of the Interior has grossly mismanaged tribal lands. It has lost track of billions of dollars in mining, logging, and other royalties that should have gone to benefit Native American tribes. Fiscal accountability and ethical management of trust funds is an absolute necessity in the quest for tribal economic self-sufficiency.

Economic realities, such as "one world economies" and "mega-mergers," can have a negative impact on both the rich and poor of this world. Native American spirituality speaks to and challenges inequities with its understanding of how to care for the whole family of God. Native American United Methodists believe their cultural understanding of stewardship is God-given and has been distorted from its intended purpose; God's creation has been used with greed rather than care.

Journey of Repentance, Reconciliation, and Healing

The United Methodist Church desires to move forward on a journey of repentance, reconciliation, and healing with Native People. To move on this journey we commit to the following action steps and covenant together with Native People to work toward healing of their historic grief and trauma.

Confession to American Indians

The United Methodist Church (and its predecessor bodies) has sinned and continues to sin against its American Indian brothers and sisters. The denomination apologizes for its participation, intended and unintended. For the listening to begin, we must respect the traditional ways of Native People. Therefore, The United Methodist Church pledges its support and assistance in upholding the American Indian Religious Freedom Act (P.L. 95-134, 1978).

The General Conference recommends that local churches develop statements of confession as a way of fostering a deep sense of community with American Indians. The General Conference encourages the members of our Church to stand in solidarity on these important religious issues, and to provide mediation when appropriate for ongoing negotiations with state and federal agencies regarding these matters.

Action Steps and Covenant

The United Methodist Church affirms and commits to upholding these beliefs, principles, and actions:

1. We acknowledge that the intentions and politicization of Christianity distorted the gospel/good news for the purpose of colonization and must be decolonized.

2. We affirm that American Indian sovereignty:
   - is a historical fact, is significant, and cannot be disregarded in favor of political expediency;
   - American Indians have a right to self-govern;
   - preserves culture, land, religious expression, and sacred spaces; and
   - ensures survival of Native People.

3. We need to demythologize and increase our understanding of American Indians and Indian country.

4. We affirm the sacredness of humankind:
   - affirming all persons are equal in God's sight;

Natural resources are sacred and we deplore practices of exploitation.

5. We reject stereotypes and frames that depict American Indians in harmful or distorted ways.

6. We observe that the belief systems of Native American Indians and non-natives may not have commonality.

Healing Relationships With Indigenous Persons

The United Methodist Church will build bridges of respect and understanding with indigenous persons. Our churches must listen and become educated about the history of the relationship between indigenous persons and Christian colonizers in their own geographic location. Through prayer and relationship building, they will celebrate the gifts that indigenous people bring to the body of Jesus in the world.

Acts of Repentance and Healing

At the 2012 General Conference, The United Methodist Church held an Act of Repentance with Native Peoples. The Act challenged every conference and local congregation to implement actions demonstrating a genuine attitude of repentance including:

1. Encouragement and resourcing the education and training of laity and pastors by providing culturally sensitive learning environments.

2. Primacy be given to learning and prioritizing Native American United Methodists in leadership, programming, education, strategizing, and establishment of Native ministry.

3. Wherever the Church holds land and/or property in trust, give due priority and consideration to transferring a portion of the land and/or property back to the tribe(s) that are/were indigenous to the area.

Comity Agreements Affecting Development of American Indian Ministries

For the Church to consider and work in partnership with Native People to explore unique and culturally appropriate ways to be in ministry with Native People, The United Methodist Church will not be a party to any interdenominational agreement that limits the ability of any annual conference in any jurisdiction to develop and resource programs of ministry of any kind among American Indians.

Doctrine of Discovery

The United Methodist Church condemns the Doctrine of Discovery as a legal document used for the seizing of lands and abusing the human rights of indigenous peoples. The United Methodist Church will work toward eliminating the use of the Doctrine of Discovery.

American Indian Sacred and Religious Life, Practice, and Location

A. Sacredness and Solidarity

The General Conference of The United Methodist Church affirms the sacredness of American Indian people, their languages, cultures, and gifts to the church and the world.

We call upon the world and The United Methodist Church to receive the gifts of American Indians as people of God. We allow for the work of the Spirit of God among our communities and American Indian people without prejudice.

The United Methodist Church pledges its support and assistance in upholding American Indian practices including:

Traditional ceremonies and rituals,

Access to and protection of sacred sites and public lands for ceremonial purposes,

Use of religious objects (feathers, tobacco, sweet grass, bones, shells, drums, etc.) in traditional ceremonies and rituals.

United Methodists are encouraged to stand in solidarity with American Indians on these important religious issues and to provide mediation when appropriate for ongoing negotiations with state and federal agencies regarding these matters.

B. Religious Freedom

The General Board of Church and Society will make available information on the American Indian Religious Freedom Act. The General Board of Church and Society will support legislation that provides for a legal cause of action when sacred sites may be affected by governmental action; proposed legislation should also provide for more extensive notice to and consultation with American Indian tribes and affected parties.

The General Board of Church and Society may enter and support court cases relating to the American Indian Religious Freedom Act.

The General Board of Church and Society will communicate with the Senate Committee on Indian Affairs, declaring that the position of The United Methodist Church is to strengthen the

American Indian Religious Freedom Act of 1978 for American Indians and preserve the God-given and constitutional rights of their religious freedom.

C. Sacred Sites

The General Board of Church and Society shall continue to support legislation that will provide for a legal course of action when sacred sites may be affected by governmental action. Proposed legislation should also provide for more extensive notice to and consultation with tribes. On behalf of the whole United Methodist Church, the General Board of Church and Society may enter and support court cases relating to the American Indian Religious Freedom Act.

The General Board of Church and Society shall communicate with the Senate Committee on Indian Affairs, declaring that the position of The United Methodist Church is to strengthen the American Indian Religious Freedom Act of 1978 and preserve the God-given and constitutional rights of religious freedom for American Indians, including the preservation of traditional American Indian sacred sites.

D. Repatriation of Ancestors and Religious/Sacred Ritual Objects

The 1990 National Native American Graves and Repatriation Act mandated the return of human remains and ritual objects to American Indian tribes and nations. *Giving Our Hearts Away: Native American Survival* by Thomas White Wolf Fassett (a resource sponsored by United Methodist Women), *On This Spirit Walk: The Voices of Native American and Indigenous Peoples* by Henrietta Mann and Anita Phillips, and the "Return to the Earth" project of the Mennonite Central Committee are study guides to culturally relevant American Indian traditions that provide an opportunity for The United Methodist Church to engage in its commitment for Restorative Justice.

The United Methodist Church pledges its support in the following ways:

1. Use the study guides as an educational resource;
2. Engage in dialogue with American Indians in their local area;
3. Advocate when appropriate; and

4. Annual conferences and local churches consider identification of land and setting aside of land for the repatriation of American Indian remains.

American Indian History and Contemporary Culture
as Related to Effective Church Participation

The General Board of Discipleship in cooperation with the Native American Comprehensive Plan, the General Board of Higher Education and Ministry, and the General Commission on Religion and Race will develop curriculum for the training of United Methodist pastors on the history of American Indians in the United States, their relationships with The United Methodist Church and its missiology.

The annual conference boards of ordained ministry in the United States and the Council of Bishops will ensure the implementation of the training within the next quadrennium. The Native American International Caucus will develop a list of leadership/resource persons that can be used as trainers for these sessions. United Methodist seminaries should include American Indian history and theology in their curriculum.

General Conference will advocate for the development and implementation of a training policy whereby American Indian history, culture, and contemporary affairs are an integral part of ministry and administrative training for all aspects of The United Methodist Church.

The General Conference supports a policy that the concept of "American Indian preference" be used in the selection of instructors and speakers for the proposed training components. The Native American International Caucus will provide a list of qualified American Indian leaders.

Leadership Development

It is recommended that The United Methodist Church will include Native American leadership development as a component of its overall effort to develop new leaders for the present and future of the Church. Included in these efforts will be mentoring programs, peer support systems, and restoring traditional and historic ways that bring forth new leaders for Native American communities.

Native American Ministries Sunday

All annual conferences should promote the observance of Native American Ministries Sunday, and encourage local churches to support American Indian Sunday with programming and offerings.

American Indian Representation in The United Methodist Church

The United Methodist Church will develop a policy that will ensure American Indians representative of every jurisdiction will be identified, selected, and placed on pertinent boards and/or committees of general agencies. All entities of The United Methodist Church will develop a policy by which Native Americans from within all the jurisdictions will be identified to be considered to be placed on their boards and agencies.

American Indian Tribal Sovereignty

The United Methodist Church reaffirms its support for tribal sovereignty and commends the following guidance that acknowledges and affirms American Indian sovereignty as a significant fact that cannot be ignored or disregarded. American Indians have a right to self-governance.

The General Board of Church and Society will identify legislation impacting American Indians, and develop communications advocating for the obligation of the United States on its treaties with American Indians.

Missions With American Indians

The General Board of Global Ministries will identify and promote innovative and culturally appropriate mission opportunities with American Indian tribes and communities.

Economic Development

The United Methodist Church supports the efforts of American Indian tribes, communities, and economic ventures compatible with the Social Principles of The United Methodist Church to create means and methods of economic development.

The General Board of Church and Society, General Commission on Religion and Race, and the General Board of Global Ministries in collaboration with American Indians will develop educational tools for local churches and individuals as a study on contemporary American Indian economic issues.

The General Board of Church and Society will work with the National Congress of American Indians and other American Indian organizations in advocating for federal economic development programs and initiatives.

The General Board of Church and Society, General Board of Global Ministries, and United Methodist Women will facilitate participation of United Methodist American Indians in the work of the United Nations Permanent Forum on Indigenous Issues on economic development. United Methodist Women will continue to make available *Giving Our Hearts Away: Native American Survival* by Thomas White Wolf Fassett.

Education

The General Conference endorses and supports development, implementation, and assessment of a higher education recruitment/retention forum, sponsored by the General Board of Higher Education and Ministry for Native Americans throughout the denomination's regions. The forum will be organized and managed by the General Board of Higher Education and Ministry in cooperation with Native American leadership.

Be it further resolved, that the General Conference encourages The United Methodist Church to use the information and materials generated as a result of the forum for sensitizing and familiarizing non-Indian membership about Native Americans in their respective communities.

Health and Wholeness

The United Methodist Church supports access to adequate medical services to ensure a balance of physical, mental, and spiritual well-being and asks that the US Congress increase rather than decrease federal funds to operate American Indian health facilities.

The General Board of Global Ministries will support funding of economic development projects of American Indian tribes.

The General Board of Pension and Health Benefits will pursue investment of funds in American Indian financial institutions and communities.

ADOPTED 2016

See Social Principles, ¶ 162A.

3324. Trail of Repentance and Healing

WHEREAS, The United Methodist Church and its predecessors have acknowledged a historic desire to spread the good news of the gospel yet in many cases have caused indignities, cultural genocide and atrocities against tribal persons; and

WHEREAS, God has been present with all persons since creation, and through prevenient grace has been a living and moving Spirit among the world's diverse cultures; and in many parts of the world, to become a Christian may mean one is expected to abandon one's culture and traditional religion, resulting in tension and division within families and tribes, and the loss of the unique identity associated with family and clan, including in some places: the requirement to stop speaking one's own language, to change one's clothing and hair, to discontinue participation in native prayer ceremonies and many cultural activities such as music and dance; and

WHEREAS, The United Methodist Church adopted Resolution 3322 [Confession to Native Americans] in 1992 and readopted the same in 2004 and 2008 recognizing the worth and dignity of all persons and our church's participation in the destruction of Native American people, culture, and religious practices; and

WHEREAS, The United Methodist Church adopted Resolution 135 [Support Restitution to the Cheyenne and Arapaho Tribes of Oklahoma for the Sand Creek Massacre] in 1996 acknowledging the genocide of almost 200 persons, mostly women and children, at a US peace camp in an attack led by a Methodist preacher, Col. John Chivington; and

WHEREAS, The United Methodist Church adopted Petition 80158 [Sand Creek Massacre National Historic Site Support] in 2008 to contribute $50,000 toward the development of the Sand Creek Massacre National Historic Site Research and Learning Center for promoting awareness of the site and for its use for Native American services of remembrance and commemoration; and

WHEREAS, The United Methodist Church adopted Resolution 121 [Healing Relationships with Indigenous Persons] in 2000, readopted as Resolution 133 in 2004, and revised and readopted as Resolution 3323 in 2008 that recognized that the history of Christianity's spread across the world was often accompanied by actions that damaged the culture, life ways, and spirituality of indigenous persons; and

WHEREAS, Resolution 3323 (*BOR* 2008) directs the 2012 General Conference of The United Methodist Church to hold an Act of Repentance Service for the Healing of Relationships with Indigenous Persons, which would launch study, dialogue, and acts of repentance in all conferences over the following quadrennium; and

WHEREAS, an Act of Repentance service is a first step in launching a process of healing relationships with indigenous persons throughout the world in order to be the living and resurrected body of Christ in the world; and

WHEREAS, a call to repentance is followed by confession, and confession is followed by a call for a change for the better as a result of remorse or contrition for one's sins; and

WHEREAS, the Office of Christian Unity and Interreligious Relationships (OCUIR) was charged in Resolution 3323 with the responsibility of planning the 2012 General Conference event; the necessary study; development of resources, models, and guidelines for building relationships with indigenous persons in preparation for a process of listening, repentance, and healing; and making such resources available to conferences and local congregations;

Therefore, be it resolved, that The United Methodist Church begin a process of healing relationships with indigenous persons to continue throughout the quadrennium and beyond that necessarily includes such activities as using study guides and resources; self-examination, discovering the ongoing impact of historic traumas; confessing our own participation in the continuing effects of that trauma; building relationships with indigenous persons wherever we, the church, are; building those relationships through listening and being present with indigenous persons; working beside indigenous persons to seek solutions to current problems; advocating and resourcing programs that are self-determined by native and indigenous persons to be part of the healing process; and holding an Act of Repentance Service for the Healing of Relationships with Indigenous Persons in each conference; and

Be it further resolved, that every conference, and every local congregation of The United Methodist Church develop and nurture relationships with the indigenous persons of the place where that conference resides through a process of deep listening and learning; and

Be it further resolved, that every conference, and every local congregation of The United Methodist Church is encouraged to implement specific actions to demonstrate a genuine attitude of repentance such as 1) encourage and resource the education and training of indigenous leadership including laity and pastors, by providing culturally sensitive learning environments, 2) wherever the church is holding land and/or property in trust, consider transferring a portion of that land and/or property or its income to indigenous persons' projects, and 3) in conjunction with ¶ 2548.2 (*BOD* 2012), whenever a conference entity is closing a charge or holds excess land, consider transferring any land and property to an indigenous community; and

Be it further resolved, that full implementation of the recommendations in this resolution be proposed to the Council of Bishops for consideration; and

Be it further resolved, that bishops of The United Methodist Church shall provide spiritual leadership and pastoral guidance for the fulfillment of this essential work to heal the soul of our church, our people, and the land.

ADOPTED 2012

See Social Principles, ¶ 162A.

3327. Oppose Names Demeaning to Native Americans

Debate is ongoing in the United States about the appropriateness of using Native American names as mascots for sports teams, both at the professional and amateur levels. The publication *Words That Hurt, Words That Heal,* produced by The United Methodist Church, emphasizes that the use of names and language is a powerful instrument for good as well as for destructive purposes. It is demeaning to depict Native Americans as violent and aggressive by naming a sports team the "Braves" or the "Warriors." This implies that all Native Americans are aggressive and violent. The use of such names is not conducive to development of a society committed to the common good of its citizenry nor to the self-esteem of Native children.

The United Methodist *Book of Resolutions* has contained statements as far back as 1992 that urged the denomination to repent for its role in the dehumanization and colonization of our Native American brothers and sisters. Accordingly, a Repentance Service was held during the 2012 General Conference. All United Methodist boards and agencies worked before and after that Repentance Service to ensure that their work respects the culture and values of Native people.

In light of this position on repentance, we strongly believe continued use of Native American names as mascots for sports teams is demeaning and racist. We urge all United Methodist-related universities, colleges, and schools to replace any mascots that demean and offend our Native American sisters and brothers. We also support efforts throughout our society to replace such mascots and symbols.

United Methodists have not been the sole voice on this issue. Many other communities, religious groups, and secular organizations have addressed this concern through statements, articles, protests, and resolutions. In spite of these efforts, however, sports teams still employ Native American names and symbols.

WHEREAS, The United Methodist Church is committed to the elimination of racism within the Church and within society; and

WHEREAS, The United Methodist Church is equally committed to participate actively in the continued struggle of building the true community of God where reconciliation comes together with justice and peace; and

WHEREAS, The United Methodist Church rejects the use of Native American names and symbols for sports teams and considers the practice a blatant expression of racism;

Therefore, be it resolved through this action of the General Conference, The United Methodist Church calls upon all general agencies and related organizations to be intentional about raising awareness of the harm caused by some sports teams through the use of mascots and/or symbols promoting expressions of racism and disrespect of Native American people.

ADOPTED 2016

See Social Principles, ¶ 162A.

3328. United Methodist Responses to the Sand Creek Massacre

The 2016 General Conference commits The United Methodist Church to learning and teaching its own history and entering into a journey of healing in relationship with the descendants of the Sand Creek Massacre of 1864.

1. We receive with appreciation the report, *Remembering the Sand Creek Massacre: A Historical Review of Methodist Involvement, Influence, and Response,* by Dr. Gary Roberts, which was authorized by the 2012 General Conference in Petition #20767, "1864 Sand Creek Massacre." We commend this report to the Church as a resource for understanding the Sand Creek Massacre and the history of the Church's role in colonization, displacement, and destruction of indigenous cultures in every land. And we refer the report to The United Methodist Publishing House to prepare study materials for use across the connection.

2. We acknowledge that too often in the past and yet today, Christian individuals and the Church as an institution have been agents of death rather than protectors of life. Clergy and lay leaders who were trained, respected, and honored by the Methodist Episcopal Church used their influence through the church, the government, and the military, in ways that caused profound harm to Indian peoples at Sand Creek, including killing nearly 200 peaceful Indians camped under the protection of the US government and desecrating the bodies of the slain. We acknowledge that leading up to the massacre, during the massacre, and in the aftermath of the massacre, representatives of the Church utterly failed to uphold gospel values of respect for human life and all of creation, justice for all people, self-giving love, and hospitality to strangers.

3. We commit The United Methodist Church to the following actions, recommended by official Sand Creek Massacre tribal descendants' representatives:
   a. Recognize the Northern Cheyenne Tribe of Montana, the Cheyenne and Arapaho Tribes of Oklahoma, and the Northern Arapaho of Wyoming as the Federally recognized Tribes as stated in the 1865 Treaty of Little Arkansas with the US Government, and the official representatives concerning the Sand Creek Massacre.

The Council of Bishops will initiate formal negotiations with official tribal representatives to produce a Memorandum of Understanding establishing an ongoing healing relationship between these tribes and The United Methodist Church.

b. Through the General Board of Church and Society in cooperation with other agencies of the Church, support legal efforts for reparations approved in the Treaty of Little Arkansas with the Cheyenne and Arapaho people in 1865, but never paid in full (<http://digital.library.okstate.edu/kappler/vol2/treaties/che0887.htm>).

c. Through the Mountain Sky and Oklahoma Areas, where descendant tribes are located, support and encourage participation in the annual Spiritual Healing Run, commemorating the Sand Creek Massacre and promoting healing of generational trauma.

d. Through the Office on Christian Unity and Interreligious Relations of the Council of Bishops, and the General Commission on Archives and History, assist with the creation of public memorials remembering and honoring the people who were killed at Sand Creek.

e. Through the Office on Christian Unity and Interreligious Relations, in cooperation with the General Board of Church and Society, encourage the Roman Catholic Church to repeal the Doctrine of Discovery (see *The Book of Resolutions of The United Methodist Church 2012*, Resolution 3331, "Doctrine of Discovery," page 424). The Doctrine of Discovery was established by papal bulls in the 15th century and became "a principle of international law used to justify Western Europe's dominion over lands occupied for thousands of years by indigenous peoples . . . sanctioning and promoting the conquest, colonization and exploitation of non-Christian lands and peoples" (<http://www.loretocommunity.org/mission-work/justice-and-peace/papal-bull-rescission-committee/>).

f. Through the General Board of Church and Society in cooperation with the General Board of Global Ministries and the General Commission on Religion and Race and other agencies of the Church, support tribal work to strengthen the Cheyenne and Arapaho way of life by respecting traditional religious practices, protecting tribal ancestral lands and assisting with development of renewable energy projects for a healthier environment.

g. Through the Council of Bishops and the General Board of Church and Society, encourage return to the tribes Native artifacts or remains in the United States covered by the Native American Graves Protection and Repatriation Act (NAGPRA) or related to the Sand Creek Massacre.

h. Through these same agencies, to support acquisition of property and increase tribal landholdings in ancestral lands.

i. Encourage United Methodist Women to develop a MissionU study on this topic.

[See ADCA Volume 2, Section 3 for full text of the report.]

ADOPTED 2016

See Social Principles, ¶ 162A.

3331. Doctrine of Discovery

WHEREAS, in 2007 the United Nations passed the "Declaration of Indigenous Peoples" that called into question the validity of the Christian Doctrine of Discovery, which for centuries served as "legal" rationale for stealing land and dehumanizing aboriginal peoples, as well as justification for the establishment of boarding schools throughout North America to "civilize" Indian children; and

WHEREAS, in 2009 President Obama pledged to the Native people the United States' support of the "Declaration of Indigenous Peoples"; and

WHEREAS, "The Declaration of Indigenous Peoples" seeks to right the historical wrongs through the use of the papal bulls of the Roman Catholic Church that are official decrees by the pope sanctioning the seizing of indigenous lands worldwide; and

WHEREAS, in 1452 the Papal Bull Romanus Pontifix, declaring

war against all non-Christians throughout the world and sanctioning and promoting the conquest, colonization, and exploitation of non-Christian nations and their territories; and

WHEREAS, in 1453 Spain was given rights of conquest and dominion over one side of the globe and Portugal the other; and

WHEREAS, in 1823 the Christian Doctrine of Discovery was adopted into law by the US Supreme Court (Johnson V. McIntosh). Chief Justice Marshall observed that Christian European nations had assumed dominion over the lands of America—and upon discovery, Indians had lost their rights to complete sovereignty as independent nations and retained a mere right of occupancy in their lands;

Therefore be it resolved, all levels of The United Methodist Church are called to condemn the Doctrine of Discovery as a legal document and basis for the seizing of native lands and abuses of human rights of indigenous peoples; and

Be it further resolved, that The United Methodist Church will work toward eliminating the Doctrine of Discovery as a means to subjugate indigenous peoples of property and land.

ADOPTED 2012
RESOLUTION #3331, 2012 *BOOK OF RESOLUTIONS*

See Social Principles, ¶ 162A.

3333. Native American Religious Freedom Act

WHEREAS, tribal people have gone into the high places, lakes, and isolated sanctuaries to pray, receive guidance from God, and train younger people in the ceremonies that constitute the spiritual life of Native American communities; and

WHEREAS, when tribes were forcibly removed from their homelands and forced to live on restricted reservations, many of the ceremonies were prohibited; and

WHEREAS, most Indians do not see any conflict between their old beliefs and the new religion of the Christian church; and

WHEREAS, during this century the expanding national population and the introduction of corporate farming and more extensive mining and timber industry activities reduced the isolation of rural America, making it difficult for small parties of Native Americans to go into the mountains or to remote lakes and buttes to conduct ceremonies without interference from non-Indians; and

WHEREAS, federal agencies began to restrict Indian access to sacred sites by establishing increasingly narrow rules and regulations for managing public lands; and

WHEREAS, in 1978, in an effort to clarify the status of traditional Native American religious practices and practitioners, Congress passed a Joint Resolution entitled "The American Indian Religious Freedom Act," which declared that it was the policy of Congress to protect and preserve the inherent right of Native Americans to believe, express, and practice their traditional religions; and

WHEREAS, today a major crisis exists in that there is no real protection for the practice of traditional Indian religions within the framework of American constitutional or statutory law, and courts usually automatically dismiss Indian petitions without evidentiary hearings; and

WHEREAS, while Congress has passed many laws that are designed to protect certain kinds of lands and resources for environmental and historic preservation, none of these laws is designed to protect the practice of Indian religion on sacred sites; and

WHEREAS, the only existing law directly addressing this issue, the American Indian Religious Freedom Act, is simply a policy that provides limited legal relief to aggrieved American Indian religious practitioners;

Therefore, be it resolved, that the General Board of Global Ministries and the General Board of Church and Society make available to the church information on the American Indian Religious Freedom Act; and

Be it further resolved, that the General Board of Church and Society support legislation that will provide for a legal cause of action when sacred sites may be affected by governmental action; proposed legislation should also provide for more extensive notice to and consultation with tribes and affected parties; and

Be it further resolved, that the General Board of Church and Society may enter and support court cases relating to the American Indian Religious Freedom Act; and

Be it further resolved, that the General Board of Church and Society communicate with the Senate Committee on Indian Affairs, declaring that the position of The United Methodist Church, expressed through the 1992 General Conference, is to strengthen the American Indian Religious Freedom Act of 1978 and preserve the God-given and constitutional rights of religious freedom for Native Americans.

ADOPTED 1992
AMENDED AND READOPTED 2004
READOPTED 2012
RESOLUTION #3333, 2012 *BOOK OF RESOLUTIONS*
RESOLUTION #3329, 2008 *BOOK OF RESOLUTIONS*
RESOLUTION #143, 2004 *BOOK OF RESOLUTIONS*
RESOLUTION #131, 2000 *BOOK OF RESOLUTIONS*

See Social Principles, ¶ 162A.

3334. Regarding Native American Culture and Traditions as Sacred

For hundreds of years Native Americans, Native Alaskans, and Native Hawaiians, compelled by the gospel have chosen to become disciples of Jesus Christ. In doing so, we have affirmed with the voices of the saints that all that is necessary for salvation, relationship with God and our brothers and sisters, is contained in the gospel of Jesus Christ. We bear witness to the mercy of God through our faith, continuing in discipleship and ministry.

Government and religious institutions intentionally destroyed many of our traditional cultures and belief systems. To assimilate our peoples into mainstream cultures, as children many of our ancestors were forcibly removed to boarding schools, often operated by religious institutions, including historical Methodism. Historically, Native peoples have been targets by those seeking land and other natural resources. Genocide became a tool of greed and a response to fear. While attempting to erase Native people from existence, traditional cultures also fell victim to acts of genocide.

As Native Christians, we affirm for the church and ourselves that many elements of our traditions and cultures are consistent with the gospel of Jesus Christ, and the teachings of the church. We affirm that the Holy Spirit is faithful in guiding us in holy living within our cultures and the broader culture. We recognize that just as in the broader culture, not all expressions of traditional cultures are appropriate for all believers; God is faithful in leading us to acceptable worship and continued growth in grace, as tribal people. We further affirm that our identity as Native, or tribal persons is pleasing to our Creator and vital to the body of Christ.

We affirm for each other that our languages, cultures, identities, and many traditions are pleasing to God and have the potential to refresh the church and offer hope to the world. To be less is to be other than what God is asking us to be in our time.

We further believe that many of our Native traditions affirm the presence of God, our need for right relationship with our Creator and the world around us, and a call for holy living. Both through corporate and personal conviction our people individually and tribally are led by the Spirit of God to a greater awareness of God. Traditional beliefs, consistent with the gospel and the historic witness of the church should not be understood as contrary to our beliefs as Native Christians. Furthermore, the testimony of historic and contemporary Native Christians should be counted in the historic witness of the church.

WHEREAS, we believe that God's creating presence speaks to us through our languages and cultures and that such testimony is vital to the ongoing work of the church among our people; and

WHEREAS, many Native traditions were erroneously feared, rather than understood as vehicles for the grace of God, and;

WHEREAS, such fears have resulted in persecution of traditional Native peoples and Native Christians; and

WHEREAS, many traditions have been misinterpreted as sin, rather than varying cultural expressions leading to a deeper understanding of our creator;

Therefore, be it resolved, that the General Conference of The United Methodist Church affirms the sacredness of Native people, their languages, their cultures, and their gifts to the church and the world.

Be it further resolved, that we believe in the faithful leadership of the Holy Spirit in assisting us as individuals and communities in the preservation of those cultures and the continuation of their faith; that just as there are many parts of the body of Christ, there are many Native traditions, languages, customs, and expressions of faith; that in the best of Native traditions, the church, and the spirit of ecumenism, we allow for the work of the Spirit of God among our communities and tribes without prejudice.

Therefore, be it further resolved, that being justified by faith, we will honor as sacred those practices that: call us back to the sacredness of Native people; affirm as beautiful their identity among the world's peoples; lead us into right relationship with our Creator, creation, and those around us; and call us into holy living. We call upon the world, the church, The United Methodist Church, and the people of The United Methodist Church to receive the gifts of Native people as people of God.

ADOPTED 2004
READOPTED 2012
RESOLUTIION #3334, 2012 *BOOK OF RESOLUTIONS*
RESOLUTION #3331, 2008 *BOOK OF RESOLUTIONS*
RESOLUTION #147, 2004 *BOOK OF RESOLUTIONS*

See Social Principles, ¶ 162A.

3346. Support for the Indian Child Welfare Act: Education, Health Care, and Welfare

Historically, a high percentage of Indian families in comparison to the general population have been broken up by the often unwarranted removal of their children by non-tribal public and private agencies. A disturbingly high percentage of such children have been placed in non-Indian foster and adoptive homes and institutions.

Indian children have a unique political status as members of sovereign tribal governments. Congress, through the US Constitution, statutes, treaties, and the general course of dealing with Indian tribes, is charged with the responsibility for the protection and preservation of Indian tribes and their resources, including Indian children.

The special political status of Indian tribes, as well as the history of biased treatment of Indian children and families under public and non-Indian private child-welfare systems, is the basis for the enactment of the Indian Child Welfare Act (25 U.S.C. § 1901).

Recent high-profile cases underscore the importance of enforcement of the Indian Child Welfare Act and assurance that children are not illegally separated from their tribal connections.

Therefore, The United Methodist Church strongly supports the Indian Child Welfare Act and the critical connection between children and their respective tribes and tribal cultures and traditional practices.

ADOPTED 2016

See Social Principles, ¶ 162A.

POPULATION

3361. World's Population and the Church's Response

Historical and Theological Statement

The population of the world was about 300 million at the time of Christ and changed very little in the next thousand years. The population of the world reached one billion in 1804, three billion in 1960, and rose to about 6.8 billion in 2010. It is expected to reach about 9.2 billion by 2050 (US Bureau of the Census, Population Division). From a finite globe, each human being consumes air, water, food, shelter and energy, and leaves behind waste to accommodate. Though there is no agreement on what earth's capacity is, simple mathematics assert that at some point a growing population must reach the capacity of that finite globe.

Our Scriptures contain both continuous and time-limited commandments. The Great Commandment to love God and our neighbor as ourselves (Luke 10:27) is continuous; it persists forever and its validity has no beginning or ending. By contrast, God's commandment to the newly created man and woman, "Be fertile and multiply; and fill the earth . . ." (Genesis 1:28) is a time-limited commandment that ends when it has been fulfilled. For the first time in human history, humanity is faced with the challenge of determining if the commandment has been fulfilled, and if it has, whether human fruitfulness and multiplication is no longer mandated in the same way.

In Genesis 1:28, God goes on to command man and woman to "take charge," meaning to exercise stewardship responsibility on behalf of God, the world's creator and owner. As stewards of the earth, we now have the responsibility of identifying how our stewardship of human reproduction is fulfilling God's will, and how it may be thwarting it. To assist us in this stewardship, God has provided humans with methods of contraception previously unknown. In clear distinction from faiths that reject use of such methods, The United Methodist Church believes effective, safe contraception is indeed responsible stewardship.

Our stewardship responsibility for human reproduction in the context of the population challenges of the world is in the service of God's ongoing creative and re-creative concern for the universe was expressed through Jesus Christ, who has called us to find the meaning of our lives in dual love of God and neighbor. In our exercise of stewardship, we live responsibly before God, writing history by the actions of our lives. The imperative for the individual Christian and the Christian community is to seek patterns of life, shape the structures of society, and foster those values that will dignify human life for all in a world in which God's love is infinite but the earth's resources are finite.

Human Population Growth Impacts Many Issues

A review of today's major problems, such as hunger, poverty, disease, lack of potable water, denial of human rights, economic and environmental exploitation, overconsumption, technologies that are inadequate or inappropriate, and rapid depletion of resources, suggests that all are affected by continuing growth of population, which is estimated to reach 9.2 billion persons by 2050.

- Population Growth and Resources. While hunger, poverty, disease, injustice, and violence in the world cannot be simplistically blamed only on population growth, each is exacerbated by population increases, and swelling numbers of people makes addressing these issues more challenging. With each passing day we are discovering more and more connections between population and sustainable development. Population growth has an obvious impact on land use, water consumption, and air quality. Communities are called to be responsible stewards of all these resources. How can we protect God's gift of the natural environment and at the same time provide a place of sustainability for humans?

- Population Growth and Climate Change. Numerous world bodies—including the International Conference on Population & Development and the United Nations Conference on Environment & Development, as expressed in the Millennium Declaration and the 2005 World Summit Outcome Document—have affirmed the interrelationship of population growth and climate change. Environmental degradation, resource depletion, and climate change result from poverty and lack of access to resources, and also from excessive consumption and wasteful production patterns. Mountaintop removal for coal mining in Appalachia, destruction of the rain forest in Brazil, or fires to clear land in Borneo all result from population pressures, degrade the environment, and affect global climate. Slowing population growth can give countries more time to meet human needs while protecting the environment.

- Population and Aging. Population growth combined with improved health results in growing numbers of elderly, many of them are among the world's most poor. It is estimated that the number of people over 60 years old is expected to outnumber children by 2040 for the first time in history. As communities engage in sustainable development, it will be important for the needs of the aging to be considered, such as economic sustenance, health care, housing, and nutrition. We must also insure the elimination of violence against older persons and provide support and care for the many elderly who are caring for their children and grandchildren, including those affected by the HIV/AIDS pandemic. These concerns for the challenges faced by persons of different ages remind us that in our stewardship of human reproduction, parents must be concerned not only with their capacity to nurture an infant, but with the world's capacity to sustain fruitful, fulfilling lives of increasing length.

Injustice Contributes to Population Growth

- Oppression of women is a significant driver of population growth. Gender inequality in parts of the world exacerbates these complex issues. We know that in many nations, women are considered property and lack basic human rights such as protection under the law and access to education, housing, and jobs. Women comprise 70 percent of the world's poor and many are captives (knowingly or unknowingly) within patriarchal structures, policies, and practices. Numerous studies have demonstrated that when women's status is improved by the building blocks of equal rights—access to basic health care, adequate nutrition, proper sanitation, increased educational opportunities—fertility declines dramatically. (See Nafis Sadik, *Population Policies and Programmes: Lessons Learned From Two Decades of Experience* [New York: UN Family Planning Association, New York University Press, 1991], pp. 247, 267, 384.) One of the most important building blocks of equal rights is women's full partnership in marital decision-making, including their expressions of sexuality. Meeting women's unmet need for family planning would result in 150,000 fewer maternal deaths a year (Singh, Susheela, Jacqueline E. Darroch, Lori S. Ashford and Michael Vlassoff, *Adding It Up: The Costs and Benefits of Investing in Family Planning and Maternal and Newborn Health* [New York: Guttmacher Institute and UNFPA, 2009]). Child mortality would decline by 13 percent if all women could delay their next pregnancy by at least 24 months. It would decline by 25 percent if women could delay their next pregnancy 36 months (United Nations [2009]. *World population monitoring, focusing on the contribution of the Programme of Action of the International Conference on Population and Development to the internationally agreed development goals, including the Millennium Development Goals.* Report of the Secretary-General. E/CN.9/2009/3).

A Call to Action

As people of faith, we are called to educate ourselves about the interconnectedness of life's critical concerns and live as responsible stewards. The church can address these complex population-related issues on several fronts. We call on:

1. all United Methodists to access educational opportunities that focus on the issue of population and its inter-relatedness to other critical issues such as poverty, disease, hunger, environment, injustice, and violence, and to promote these opportunities in the local church;

2. United Methodist medical and mission facilities around the world to provide a full range of reproductive health and family planning information and services;

3. the General Board of Church and Society and United Methodist Women to advocate for legislation around the world that can help in upgrading the social status of women and that includes women in development planning and processes. Specifically, we call on them to continue advocating for the United States to ratify the United Nations Convention for the Elimination of Discrimination Against Women (CEDAW) and to encourage all countries to take action to ensure equal rights for women;

4. the General Board of Discipleship and the General Board of Global Ministries to develop and implement programs within The United Methodist Church that provide and/or enhance edu-

cational opportunities for girls and women, making it possible for them to achieve levels of self-sufficiency and well-being;

5. governments around the world to give high priority to addressing the malaria crisis and HIV/AIDS pandemic and urge adequate funding to eradicate and prevent these diseases;

6. legislative bodies of the developed nations to recognize the crucial nature of population growth and to give maximum feasible funding to programs of population, environment, health, agriculture, and other technological-assistance programs for developing nations. International assistance programs should be based on mutual cooperation, should recognize the diversities of culture, should encourage self-development and not dependency, and should not require "effective population programs" as a prerequisite for other developmental assistance;

7. governments and private organizations to place a high priority on research aimed at developing a range of safe, inexpensive contraceptives that can be used in a variety of societies and medical situations. Promote greater understanding of attitudes, motivations, and social and economic factors affecting childbearing; and

8. governments to implement systems of social insurance and support for older persons to ensure adequate economic sustenance and housing, and quality health care and nutrition.

ADOPTED 2004
AMENDED AND READOPTED 2012
RESOLUTION #3361, 2008, 2012 *BOOK OF RESOLUTIONS*
RESOLUTION #159, 2004 *BOOK OF RESOLUTIONS*

See Social Principles, ¶ 162K.

RACISM

3371. A Charter for Racial Justice in an Interdependent Global Community

Racism is a system of inequality based on race prejudice and the belief that one race is innately superior to all other races. In the United States, systemic race-based prejudice and misuse of power have justified the conquest, enslavement, and evangelizing of non-Europeans. During the early history of this country, Europeans used legal documents such as the Christian Doctrine of Discovery of 1823 to justify the notion that their civilization and religion were innately superior to those of both the original inhabitants of the United States and the Africans who were forcibly brought to these shores as slaves. The concepts of race and racism were created explicitly to ensure the subjugation of peoples the Europeans believed to be inferior. The myth of European superiority persisted—and persists—in every institution in American life. Other people who came, and those who are still coming to the United States—either by choice or by force—encountered and continue to encounter racism. Some of these people are the Chinese who built the country's railroads as indentured workers; the Mexicans whose lands were annexed; the Puerto Ricans, the Cubans, the Hawaiians, and the Eskimos who were colonized; and the Filipinos, the Jamaicans, and the Haitians who lived on starvation wages as farm workers.

In principle, the United States has outlawed racial discrimination; but in practice, little has changed. Social, economic, and political institutions still discriminate, although some institutions have amended their behavior by eliminating obvious discriminatory practices and choosing their language carefully. Adding to this reality, the success of some prominent people of color has contributed to the erroneous but widespread belief that America is in many ways a "post-racial" society where race is seldom a factor in the opportunities and outcomes in people's lives. The institutional church, despite sporadic attempts to the contrary, also still discriminates on the basis of race.

The damage from years of systemic race-based exploitation has not been erased and by all measurable indicators, a color-blind society is many years in the future. A system designed to meet the needs of one segment of the population cannot be the means to the development of a just society for all. The racist system in the United States today perpetuates the power and control of those who are of European ancestry. It is often called "white supremacy." The fruits of racism are prejudice, bigotry, discrimination, and dehumanization. Consistently, African Americans, Hispanics, Latinos, Asians, Native Americans, and Pacific Islanders have been humiliated by being given jobs, housing, education, medical services, transportation, and public accommodations that are all inferior. With hopes deferred and rights still denied, the deprived and oppressed fall prey to a colonial mentality that can acquiesce to the inequities.

Racist presuppositions have been implicit in US attitudes and policies toward Asia, Africa, the Middle East, and Latin America. And the fact that racism is not explicitly expressed in these policies leads many to believe that race-based prejudice in public policy is a thing of the past. While proclaiming democracy, freedom, and independence, the United States, however, has been an ally and an accomplice to perpetuating racial inequality and colonialism throughout the world. The history of The United Methodist Church and the history of the United States are intertwined. The "mission enterprise" of the churches in the United States went hand in hand with "Westernization," thus sustaining a belief in and the institutionalization of this nation's superiority. Through policies that were hyper expansionist and inherently racist, such as Manifest Destiny.

We are conscious that "we have sinned as our ancestors did; we have been wicked and evil" (Psalm 106:6 GNT). We call for a renewed commitment to the elimination of institutional racism. We affirm the 1976 General Conference Statement on The United Methodist Church and Race that states unequivocally: "By biblical and theological precept, by the law of the church, by General Conference pronouncement, and by Episcopal expression, the matter is clear. With respect to race, the aim of The United Methodist Church is nothing less than an inclusive church in an inclusive society. The United Methodist Church, therefore, calls upon all its people to perform those faithful deeds of love and justice in both the church and community that will bring this aim into reality."

Because we believe:

1. That God is the Creator of all people and all are God's children in one family;

2. That racism is a rejection of the teachings of Jesus Christ;

3. That racism denies the redemption and reconciliation of Jesus Christ;

4. That racism robs all human beings of their wholeness and is used as a justification for social, economic, environmental, and political exploitation;

5. That we must declare before God and before one another that we have sinned against our sisters and brothers of other races in thought, in word, and in deed;

6. That in our common humanity in creation all women and men are made in God's image and all persons are equally valuable in the sight of God;

7. That our strength lies in our racial and cultural diversity and that we must work toward a world in which each person's value is respected and nurtured;

8. That our struggle for justice must be based on new attitudes, new understandings, and new relationships and must be reflected in the laws, policies, structures, and practices of both church and state.

We commit ourselves as individuals and as a community to follow Jesus Christ in word and in deed and to struggle for the rights and the self-determination of every person and group of persons.

Therefore, as United Methodists in every place across the land, we will unite our efforts within the Church to take the following actions:

1. Eliminate all forms of institutional racism in the total ministry of the Church, giving special attention to those institutions that we support, beginning with their employment policies, purchasing practices, environmental policies, and availability of services and facilities;

2. Create opportunities in local churches to deal honestly with the existing racist attitudes and social distance between members, deepening the Christian commitment to be the church where all racial groups and economic classes come together;

3. Increase efforts to recruit people of all races into the membership of The United Methodist Church and provide leadership-development opportunities without discrimination;

4. Establish workshops and seminars in local churches to study, understand, and appreciate the historical and cultural contributions of each race to the church and community;

5. Raise local churches' awareness of the continuing needs for equal education, housing, employment, medical care, and environmental justice for all members of the community and to create opportunities to work for these things across racial lines;

6. Work for the development and implementation of national and international policies to protect the civil, political, economic, social, and cultural rights of all people such as through support for the ratification of United Nations covenants on human rights;

7. Support and participate in the worldwide struggle for liberation in church and community;

8. Facilitate nomination and election processes that include all racial groups by employing a system that prioritizes leadership

opportunities of people from communities that are disproportionately impacted by the ongoing legacy of racial injustice. Use
measures to align our vision for racial justice with actions that
accelerate racial equity.

ADOPTED 1980
READOPTED 2000, 2008, 2016
RESOLUTION #3371, 2008, 2012 *BOOK OF RESOLUTIONS*
RESOLUTION #161, 2004 *BOOK OF RESOLUTIONS*
RESOLUTION #148, 2000 *BOOK OF RESOLUTIONS*

See Social Principles, ¶ 162*A*.

3373. Affirmative Action

The United Methodist Church has long been committed to the
principle of social inclusiveness. That is, in keeping with the spirit
of the gospel, we affirm that all persons—whatever their racial or
ethnic identity, whatever their gender or national origin, whatever their physical state or condition—are full-fledged members
of the human community with every one of the rights and privileges that such membership entails. The implementation of "affirmative action" reflects a shared understanding that diversity is
a positive outcome of social inclusion that yields benefits for the
entire community.

In light of that commitment, the church has, in years past,
adopted a strong stand supportive of the concept of "affirmative
action." Recently, this concept has been subjected to intense opposition. While some of the particular policies adopted under that
rubric may be in need of revision—given developments that have
occurred over the course of time—we would, at this moment,
reconfirm our support for the basic concept. Inclusionary efforts
that lead to diversity yield enriched environments for our daily
living and learning.

The Declaration of the United Nations World Conference
against Racism, Racial Discrimination, Xenophobia and Related
Intolerance (Durban, South Africa, 31 August to 8 September
2001) contains the following affirmations:

- recognition of the need for special measures or positive
  actions for the victims of racism, racial discrimination,
  xenophobia and related intolerance in order to promote
  their full integration into society;

- recognition that such measures should aim at correcting the conditions that impair the enjoyment of rights;
- recognition of the need to encourage equal participation of all racial and cultural, linguistic and religious groups in all sectors of society; and,
- recognition of the need for measures to achieve appropriate representation in educational institutions, housing, political parties, legislative bodies, employment, especially in the judiciary, police, army and other civil services.

The concept of affirmative action emerged in response to the Civil Rights Movement of the 1960s as one of a set of public policies designed to overcome a tragic history of racist and sexist practices throughout this nation and to create a more equitable social system in keeping with the spirit of the gospel and in keeping with the proclaimed democratic ideals of the American people.

Affirmative action is not intended to enable class privilege for the wealthy, such as using family legacies or donor contributions to gain personal advantages. The specific intent of affirmative action, given its origins, was to bring the prestige and power of government to bear on economic and educational institutions, requiring them to put into effect carefully conceived plans to admit qualified persons who traditionally had been excluded from participating in them—women, ethnic and racial persons, and, at a later time, persons with disabilities.

Over the past three decades, programs of affirmative action have had a significant effect in the employment patterns of corporations and public agencies and in the character of the professional staff and student bodies of educational institutions, private and public. Proportionately, more women, racial and ethnic minorities, and people with disabilities have found their talents and training recognized than before such programs were instituted.

At the same time, however, many women, racial and ethnic persons, and persons with disabilities, though fully competent, have confronted obstacles in these settings, stifling their advancement in education and in employment. Unemployment of racial and ethnic persons remains appreciably higher than the national average. Women workers continue to earn less than male workers in the same or similar positions, and they continue to confront limitations in promotion to a more prestigious and responsible level of jobs. Persons with disabilities are bypassed regardless of their motivations.

Despite these persistent inequities, the concept of affirmative action is currently under severe attack. In some locations, it has been abolished as a public policy on several (somewhat different and not altogether compatible) grounds:

- that it promotes the hiring (in business) or admission (to institutions of higher education) of unqualified persons;
- that it discriminates unduly against white males;
- that it has a negative impact on the self-esteem of affirmative action candidates; and
- that its goals have been at this time fully realized and therefore it is no longer necessary.

In light of the evidence, however (except in those cases where policies of affirmative action have been badly or improperly administered), all of these alleged grounds seem specious. The implementation of affirmative action has resulted in concrete gains for people of color and women in higher education and the corporate world. However persuasive they seem on the surface, they tend to slough off or to ignore the persistence of significant and widespread inequalities of opportunity affecting women, ethnic and racial persons, and persons with disabilities throughout our social system.

From the perspective represented by The United Methodist Church, the most fundamental premise underlying the concept of affirmative action is both moral and spiritual. Concern for the disadvantaged and the oppressed is a major feature of the message of the Hebraic prophets and of Jesus. According to biblical teaching, we are mandated, in the face of inhumane discrimination—whether that discrimination is intended or unintended—to do what we can to redress legitimate grievances and to create a society in which the lives of each and all will flourish.

For this fundamental reason, we reconfirm our commitment to the concept of affirmative action. The use of numerical goals and timetables is a legitimate and necessary tool of effective affirmative action programs. This concept retains its pertinence as a means of attaining a more inclusive society in our educational systems, in our businesses and industries, and in religious and other institutions. No persons—whatever their gender, their ethnic or racial heritage, their physical condition—should be deprived of pursuing their educational or employment aspirations to the full extent of their talents and abilities.

Fairness is the rule for affirmative action, guaranteeing more opportunities for all to compete for jobs. Indeed, the purpose of affirmative action has always been to create an environment where merit can prevail.

Rather than curtail or abolish programs in affirmative action, we should instead move toward the reallocation of the resources of our society to ensure the fullest opportunities in the fulfillment of life.

At the same time, given the tenacity of many forms of racism, sexism, and ableism—both blatant and subtle—the concept of affirmative action retains its relevance as part of an overall effort to create a more just and equitable social system.

Therefore, be it resolved, that the 2016 General Conference of The United Methodist Church calls upon all its members to:

1. affirm our Judeo-Christian heritage of justice and inclusiveness as a foundation for the concept of affirmative action;

2. constitute a model for others in society by practicing and strengthening our own affirmative action policies, whatever our station in life;

3. declare our support of efforts throughout the society to sustain and, where needed, strengthen affirmative action legislation and programs;

4. collaborate with movements and initiatives seeking to ensure effective participation of ethnic and racial persons, women, and persons with disabilities in all sectors of our society; and

5. interpret the genuine meaning of affirmative action, dispelling the myths and responding to the specious appeals that would undercut and vilify affirmative action policies and programs.

Be it further resolved, that the 2016 General Conference reaffirm its mandate to implement affirmative action programs in all general church boards and agencies, annual conferences, church-related institutions, districts, and local churches.

Be it further resolved, that the General Commissions on Religion and Race and the Status and Role of Women continue to assess the progress of The United Methodist Church and related institutions and to provide assistance in helping them move toward greater conformity with the principle of inclusiveness.

ADOPTED 1996
AMENDED AND READOPTED 2004, 2008, 2016
RESOLUTION #3373, 2008, 2012 *BOOK OF RESOLUTIONS*
RESOLUTION #163, 2004 *BOOK OF RESOLUTIONS*
RESOLUTION #150, 2000 *BOOK OF RESOLUTIONS*

See Social Principles, ¶ 162A.

3374. Annual Conferences', Districts', and Local Congregations' Responsibilities for Eradication of Racism

WHEREAS, conferences, districts, and local congregations within the United States are becoming more diverse; and

WHEREAS, it is predicted that within the United States, the population of persons of European descent will be less than 50 percent before 2050; and

WHEREAS, racism has been a systemic and personal problem within the US and The United Methodist Church (UMC) and its predecessor denominations since its inception; and

WHEREAS, The UMC is committed to the eradication of racism; and

WHEREAS, it takes significant change, learning, time, and healing to eradicate racism; and

WHEREAS, it takes significant attitudinal and systemic change to learn and to incorporate the gifts and contributions of the different racial-ethnic persons within the church's ministry, structures, and mission; and

WHEREAS, since 1980 the Charter for Racial Justice Policies has served as an articulation of United Methodist understanding of the biblical imperative for the eradication of racism and a guide for action (#161 2004 *Book of Resolutions*—"A Charter for Racial Justice Policies in an Interdependent Global Community");

Therefore, be it resolved, that every annual conference, district, and local congregation within the United States develop and implement a strategy and program to educate and support systemic and personal changes to end racism and work multi-culturally, and

Be it further resolved, that an educational program which will include understanding systemic racism, a strategy for its eradication, appreciation and valuation of diversity, and guidelines for working with different groups in communities toward becoming an inclusive church be offered at least yearly within the annual conference, and

Be it further resolved, that all clergy and lay leadership be encouraged to participate in such programs and that all newly ordained clergy be required to participate in these programs, and

Be it further resolved, that United Methodist Women and the General Commission on Religion and Race continue to make available to annual conferences, districts, and local churches resources such as the Charter for Racial Justice to assist them in their efforts, and

Be it further resolved, that the General Commission on Religion and Race include as part of its review process the adherence of annual conferences, districts, and local congregations in equipping and supporting leadership to eradicate racism and work multi-culturally, and that as annual conferences, districts, and local congregations develop and implement programs, results will be forwarded by the Conference Commission on Religion and Race (or other conference structures dealing with those responsibilities) to the General Commission on Religion and Race.

ADOPTED 2000
REVISED AND READOPTED 2008 AND 2016
RESOLUTION #3374, 2008, 2012 *BOOK OF RESOLUTIONS*
RESOLUTION #164, 2004 *BOOK OF RESOLUTIONS*
RESOLUTION #151, 2000 *BOOK OF RESOLUTIONS*

See Social Principles, ¶ 162A.

3375. Membership in Clubs or Organizations That Practice Exclusivity

WHEREAS, membership held in any club or organization that practices exclusivity based on gender, race, or socioeconomic condition is clearly in violation of the stance of the United Methodist Social Principles;

Therefore, it is recommended, that United Methodists who hold memberships in clubs or organizations that practice exclusivity based on gender, race, or socioeconomic condition prayerfully consider whether they should work for change within these groups or resign their membership. If one decides to resign, we urge that the decision and reasons be made public. This reflects the intent and purpose of the Social Principles of The United Methodist Church.

ADOPTED 1992
READOPTED 2004, 2008, 2016
RESOLUTION #3375, 2012 *BOOK OF RESOLUTIONS*
RESOLUTION #3377, 2008 *BOOK OF RESOLUTIONS*
RESOLUTION #167, 2004 *BOOK OF RESOLUTIONS*
RESOLUTION #155, 2000 *BOOK OF RESOLUTIONS*

See Social Principles, ¶ 162A.

3376. White Privilege in the United States

European Americans enjoy a broad range of privileges denied to persons of color in our society, privileges that often permit them to dominate others who do not enjoy such privileges. While there are many issues that reflect the racism in US society, there are some cases where racism is the issue, such as affirmative action, housing, job discrimination, hate crimes, and criminal justice. In addition, there are many broader social issues where racism is one factor in the equation, albeit often the major one.

Poverty is a serious problem in the US, but a far greater percentage of people of color are poorer than white persons. Police brutality is also more prevalent in communities of color. Schools in predominantly white communities receive a far higher proportion of education dollars than those in predominantly non-white communities, leading to larger class size, fewer resources, and inferior facilities.

While welfare affects the entire society, it hits predominantly non-white communities hardest. Many in Congress support tax credits for families to enable middle-class parents to stay home with their children, welfare "reform" forces poor, single parents to take low-paying jobs and leave their children to inadequate or nonexistent day care. Because more and better job opportunities are open to white persons, they are leaving the welfare rolls faster than non-white persons, making non-white persons a disproportionate segment of the welfare population.

While people of color make up about 30 percent of the United States' population, they account for 60 percent of those imprisoned. The prison population grew by 700 percent from 1970 to 2005, a rate that is outpacing crime and population rates. The incarceration rates disproportionately impact men of color: 1 in every 15 African American men and 1 in every 36 Hispanic men are incarcerated in comparison to 1 in every 106 white men. According to the Bureau of Justice Statistics, one in three black men can expect to go to prison in their lifetime. Individuals of color have a disproportionate number of encounters with law enforcement, indicating that racial profiling continues to be a problem. A report by the US Department of Justice found that Blacks and Hispanics were approximately three times more likely to be searched during a traffic stop than white motorists. African Americans were twice as likely to be arrested and almost four times as likely to experience the use of force during encounters with the police (American Prospect, March 17, 2012, *The 10 Most Disturbing Facts About Racial Inequality in the U.S. Criminal Justice System*).

If only one of these areas impacted communities of color disproportionately, an explanation might be found in some sociological factor other than race. But where race is a common thread running through virtually every inequality in our society, we are left with only one conclusion: White, European Americans enjoy a wide range of privileges that are denied to persons of color in our society. These privileges enable white persons to escape the injustices and inconveniences which are the daily experience of racial ethnic persons. Those who are White assume that they can purchase a home wherever they choose if they have the money; that they can expect courteous service in stores and restaurants; that if they are pulled over by a police car it will be for a valid reason unrelated to their skin color. Persons of color cannot make these assumptions.

We suggest that the church focus not only on the plight of people living in urban or rural ghettos, but also on white privilege and its impact on white persons. For example, churches in white or predominantly white communities need to ask why there are no persons of color in their community, why the prison population in their state is disproportionately Black and Hispanic persons, why there are so few Black and Hispanic persons in high-paying jobs and prestigious universities, why schools in white communities receive more than their fair share of education dollars, and why white persons receive preferential treatment from white police officers.

We ask the General Conference to recognize white privilege as an underlying cause of injustice in our society including our church and to commit the church to its elimination in church and society.

The rights and privileges a society bestows upon or withholds from those who comprise it indicate the relative esteem in which that society holds particular persons and groups of persons.

We ask each local church with a predominantly white membership: 1) to reflect on its own willingness to welcome persons without regard to race and to assess the relative accessibility in housing, employment, education and recreation in its community to white persons and to persons of color; and 2) to welcome persons of color into membership and full participation in the church and community and to advocate for their access to the benefits which white persons take for granted.

We challenge individual white persons to confess their participation in the sin of racism and repent for past and current racist practices. And we challenge individual ethnic persons to appropriate acts of forgiveness.

Finally, we call all persons, whatever their racial or ethnic heritage, to work together to restore the broken body of Christ.

ADOPTED 2000
AMENDED AND READOPTED 2008, 2016
RESOLUTION #3376, 2012 *BOOK OF RESOLUTIONS*
RESOLUTION #3379, 2008 *BOOK OF RESOLUTIONS*
RESOLUTION #170, 2004 *BOOK OF RESOLUTIONS*
RESOLUTION #166, 2000 *BOOK OF RESOLUTIONS*

See Social Principles, ¶ 162A.

3377. Opposition to Racial Profiling in the US

WHEREAS, racial profiling in the United States, is a practice directed at people based solely on race and has been a concern of numerous civil rights organizations and The United Methodist Church for decades; and

WHEREAS, insidious racial profiling by some law enforcement practices around the country has risen; and

WHEREAS, racial profiling is a violation of the respect for human rights, an abhorrent manifestation of racism, and violation of the moral standard of the United States and The United Methodist Church; and

WHEREAS, various states have signed or attempted to sign legislation that would give local law enforcement the right to arrest anyone they suspect is in the country illegally, which violates the equal protection clause in the US Constitution; and

WHEREAS, racial profiling threatens the safety of both US citizens and immigrants;

Therefore, we call on the Council of Bishops, annual conferences, and members of local churches to contact their local, state, and federal representatives urging that they prioritize and enact legislation to end racial profiling and allocate sufficient funds for its vigorous enforcement so as to ensure:

    a. a federal prohibition against racial profiling,

    b. retraining of law enforcement officials on how to discontinue and prevent the use of racial profiling, and

    c. law enforcement agencies are held accountable for use of racial profiling.

Therefore, finally, we call on The United Methodist Church through its annual conferences, districts, and local churches and under the leadership of the General Board of Church and Society and the General Commission on Religion and Race, in coordination with the General Board of Global Ministries and United Methodist Women, to be proactive in educating the constituency about racial profiling and establishing networks of cooperation with criminal justice and law enforcement agencies.

ADOPTED 2016

See Social Principles, ¶ 162A.

3378. Racism and Economic Injustice Against People of Color in the US

Biblical and Theological Grounding

WHEREAS, the prophet Isaiah spoke out:

> *Woe to those who make unjust laws, / to those who issue oppressive decrees, / to deprive the poor of their rights / and withhold justice from the oppressed of my people (Isaiah 10:1-2a NIV); and*

WHEREAS, Jesus taught the foundation of the law and the prophets was to love God and to love your neighbor as yourself and he made clear that everyone is our neighbor; and

WHEREAS, Jesus proclaimed the essence of his ministry when he read from the scroll of the prophet Isaiah:

> *The Spirit of the Lord is upon me, / because he has anointed me / to bring good news to the poor. / He has sent me to proclaim release to the captives / and recovery of sight to the blind, / to let the oppressed go free. (Luke 4:18 NRSV); and*

WHEREAS, the prophet Isaiah proclaimed God's condemnation of economic injustice, saying:

> *Look, you serve your own interest on your fast day, / and oppress all your workers. / Look, you fast only to quarrel and to fight / and to strike with a wicked fist. / Such fasting as you do today / will not make*

*your voice heard on high. . . . / Is not this the fast that I choose: / to
loose the bonds of injustice, / to undo the thongs of the yoke, / to let the
oppressed go free, / and to break every yoke? / Is it not to share your
bread with the hungry, / and bring the homeless poor into your house;
/ when you see the naked, to cover them, / and not to hide yourself from
your own kin? (Isaiah 58:3b-4, 6-7 NRSV); and*

Background and Motivation

WHEREAS, this condemnation applies directly to the reality of
racial injustice and economic inequality in the US; and

WHEREAS, the US has the most unequal distribution of income
and wealth of all developed nations; and

WHEREAS, in 1967, when Jim Crow segregation was wounded,
but still alive, median household income was 43 percent higher for
white, non-Hispanic households than for black households, yet
by 2011, with legal segregation eliminated, that figure had risen
to 72 percent (Ned Resnikoff, "Race is the elephant in the room
when it comes to inequality," MSNBC, posted 03/13/14, updated
05/23/14. Available online at <http://www.msnbc.com/msnbc
/washingtons-silence-the-racial-wealth-gap>); and

WHEREAS, despite steadily rising overall wealth in the US, the
"wealth gap" between whites and African Americans went from
12 to 1 in 1984 to 19 to 1 in 2009 (Ibid.). Significant disparities exist
at all income levels. So, for example, in the bottom fifth of households, poor whites have an average of $24,000 in assets. Poor
black households have, on average, $57 in assets, for a ratio of 421
to 1. In the middle income level, the ratio is 5.2 to 1 and even at
the highest income level, white households have, on average 3.2
times more wealth than black households (Tim Wise, *Colorblind:
The Rise of Post-Racial Politics and the Retreat from Racial Equality*
(San Francisco: City Lights Books, 2010), 69-70); and

WHEREAS, "African Americans are twice as likely as whites to
be employed in low-wage jobs and twice as likely to be unemployed," even when the job climate is good. In addition, on average, black men remain unemployed seven more weeks than white
men and black women are out of work five more weeks than white
women (Ibid., 66-67); and

WHEREAS, while median income for Asian Americans is higher
than that of whites, Asian Americans earn less than whites at the
same educational level (Ibid., 95) and many Asian Americans still
live in poverty; and

WHEREAS, slavery, Jim Crow segregation, the sharecropping and tenant-farmer system, the convict slave-labor system (See Douglas A. Blackmon, *Slavery by Another Name: The Re-Enslavement of Black Americans from the Civil War to World War II* (New York: Anchor Books, 2008)), thousands of lynchings, KKK terror, and other historical practices prevented the accumulation of wealth and property by most African American families and the legacy of those systems of oppression still affects many families, recent studies show that ongoing mass disparities between whites and blacks in the US can be directly attributed to current racist policies and practices:

> One study showed that African Americans, Latinos, and Asian Americans have more than a one-in-three chance of suffering discrimination in any given job search, concluding that roughly 600,000 blacks, 275,000 Latinos, and 150,000 Asian Americans face job discrimination each year (Wise, 88).
>
> In studies of service-industry employment, research showed that even when researchers sent African-American testers who were more qualified, white applicants were more likely to get an interview (Ibid., 90-91).
>
> A Princeton study using black, white, and Latino test applicants who were trained to have the same communication styles, physical characteristics, and demeanor found that white applicants were far more likely than applicants of color to be called back. It also found that even white men claiming a felony record were slightly more likely to be called back than black applicants with no criminal record (Ibid., 88-89); and

WHEREAS, the deliberate de-industrialization of the US in the 1970s and '80s led to massive job losses among people of color, who had only gained access on a large scale to good-paying blue-color jobs. This is directly linked to the re-impoverishment of a large proportion of African-American households, to urban decay (as incomes and tax revenues plummeted) and the dramatic rise in the jail and prison population (starting around 1980). People of color (especially African American and Hispanic men) became an unneeded surplus labor force and mass incarceration became one of the primary solutions to that problem; and

WHEREAS, widespread discrimination against people of color continues in the US in housing, education, health care, and the policing and criminal justice system; and

WHEREAS, we need a vision of a beloved community, founded on social and economic justice and motivated by self-giving love.

This vision includes removing the power of police oversight and discipline from the police themselves; substantially reducing sentences for minor crimes and dramatically reducing the prison population; eliminating the "prisons for profit" system; providing genuinely equal education opportunities for all; creating an economic system that provides for an equitable distribution of wealth, with much larger programs to assist developing nations; reinstating and strengthening voting-rights protections; and strengthening investigation and enforcement against discrimination in employment, housing, education, and healthcare; and

WHEREAS, racial injustice and inequality still constitute the cornerstone of US economic and social policy and practice; and

WHEREAS, intense and ongoing systemic and institutional racism is still the greatest barrier in the US to building beloved community;

Therefore, be it resolved, that The United Methodist Church advocates, encourages, and will support a new multiracial, mass movement for racial and economic justice in the US; and

Be it further resolved, that every annual conference in the US support anti-racism training for every active clergy member and for all members of the conference Board of Ordained Ministry and district committees on ordained ministry, and that this training be offered as well to other key leaders among laity in each conference. We note that anti-racism training must address white privilege and focus on intentional struggle and advocacy against racism in our churches and in society at large. So-called "diversity training" or "sensitivity training" is insufficient; and

Be it further resolved, that every annual conference, district, and local church should be engaged, intentionally, in being an anti-racist church, not merely on paper, but in action. Church bodies at every level should seek to educate themselves on the extent of racism in business, education, government, housing, and healthcare and find ways to advocate for the elimination of specific instances locally and nationally.

Resources on Racism and Economic Justice for People of Color:

Tim Wise, *Colorblind: The Rise of Post-Racial Politics and the Retreat from Racial Equity* (San Francisco: City Lights Books, 2010).

Joseph Barndt, *Becoming the Anti-Racist Church: Journeying Toward Wholeness* (Minneapolis: Fortress Press, 2011).

Charles Marsh, *The Beloved Community: How Faith Shapes Social Justice, from the Civil Rights Movement to Today* (New York: Basic Books, 2005).

Douglas A. Blackmon, *Slavery by Another Name: The Re-Enslavement of Black Americans from the Civil War to World War II* (New York: Anchor Books, 2008).

ColorOfChange.org — "we keep our members informed and give them ways to act on pressing issues facing Black people in America."

ADOPTED 2016

See Social Principles, ¶ 162A.

3379. Stop Criminalizing Communities of Color in the United States

In the United States, policing policies, immigration law enforcement, and exponentially growing incarceration rates all disproportionately impact persons of color and harm families and communities. The United Methodist Church must work to dismantle policies that assume whole groups of people are criminals and encourage public acceptance of the injustices of racial profiling (2008 *Book of Resolutions*, #3378), mass incarceration, and disenfranchisement of entire communities demonized as a threatening "other."

Economic Crisis and Demonization of Communities

Globally and within nations, including the United States, there is a widening gap between rich and poor (2012 *Book of Resolutions*, #4052 and #6028). To maintain order amid this wealth and resource inequality, governments increasingly enact policies that divide workers and exploit migrant labor, as did Pharaoh in the biblical story of the Exodus. The Book of Exodus opens with Pharaoh looking over the land of Egypt and seeing a people growing in strength and number; he becomes fearful.

"He said to his people, 'Look, the Israelite people are more numerous and more powerful than we. Come, let us deal shrewdly with them, or they will increase and, in the event of war, join our enemies and fight against us and escape from the land'" (Exodus 1:9-10 NRSV).

Pharaoh did not fear other peoples or migrant labor but rather, he feared that a mixed multitude of Israelites, impoverished Egyptians, and "enemies" would unite (Exodus 12:38) and rise up to free themselves from exploitation. As in Pharaoh's day, today's governments use fear-based policies to divide and to control populations that might otherwise challenge the growing concentration of wealth and resources in the hands of a few.

Today, invoking the crises language of national security—"the war on drugs," "the war on illegal immigration," "the war on terror"—the US government, like Pharaoh, has targeted poor, racial, ethnic, migrant, and other marginalized communities of color for selective enforcement of statutes, and thus criminalized entire communities.

Waging "War" on Communities of Color

The 40-year-old "war on drugs" has had a devastating impact on communities of color in the United States. In 2012, 23.9 million Americans, ages twelve and over, and of all races and socioeconomic levels had used an illicit drug or abused a medication, according to the National Institute on Drug Abuse (National Institute on Drug Abuse, 2015). But the "war on drugs" has not been waged across all races and socioeconomic levels; it has been waged through systemic selective law enforcement targeting African Americans, Latinos, and Native Americans (2012 *Book of Resolutions* #3042, #3376, and #5033) in settings that vary from traffic stops, SWAT-type raids on homes and grocery stores, and stop-and-searches of people going about their daily tasks.

Policies like New York City's "stop and frisk" and "broken windows" policing have empowered officers to detain and search pedestrians without probable cause and make arrests for minor infractions. In 2013, 88 percent of the nearly 200,000 persons "stopped and frisked" by the New York Police Department were innocent civilians; 85 percent of those stopped were Black and Latino, and 11 percent were White (New York Civil Liberties Union, 2015). These policies subject hundreds of thousands of innocent people of color to routine abuse, public humiliation, injury, and even unprosecuted deaths for some (Harris-Perry, 2014).

Similarly, children of color are punished more severely and more frequently than their white classmates (US Department of Education, 2014), making school suspensions and expulsions "stops" on the "school-to-prison pipeline"—pushing children out of school and onto troubled streets and then off to prison.

Such over-policing erodes community trust in law enforcement and sends a clear message to police that not all Americans are equal under law, as people in targeted communities do not have the same constitutional protections other Americans enjoy (Alexander, 2010).

Targeting Migrants

This criminalization of entire communities is being expanded today in the name of a so-called "war on 'illegal' immigration" and "war on terror." As with the "war on drugs," citizens and migrants alike in "immigrant" communities are subjected to racial profiling and suspension of basic rights. Migrants are being arrested and held in prisons in a growing network of "detention centers," many private for-profit institutions.

Roundups targeting specific communities of color, such as Immigration and Customs Enforcement (ICE) raids or drift-net arrests (this refers to police sweeps within a specific community and arrests without probable cause designed to catch potential criminals) sweep up large numbers of people without probable cause often for nonviolent offenses. In the process, more than 5,000 migrant parents have permanently lost custody of their children as detention court and family court policies collide (Race Forward). When migrants who have been deported seek to reunite with their families, they face felony charges for reentering the United States. More than 25,000 migrants with these and other nonviolent convictions are detained in thirteen private prisons under the "Criminal Alien Requirement" program, costing taxpayers billions of dollars every year.

Mass Incarceration

The criminalization of communities of color includes mass incarceration. The "war on drugs" has played a critical role in the escalation of US incarceration rates. From 1970 to 2009 the US prison population grew more than 700 percent (American Civil Liberties Union, 2015) so that today, with only 5 percent of the world's population, the United States incarcerates 25 percent of all prisoners in the world. This makes the US the world's largest jailer. More than 60 percent of the people incarcerated in US prisons are people of color. Nearly half of federal prisoners (48 percent) are incarcerated for drug offenses (Federal Bureau of Prisons, 2015). Nearly half of state prisoners (47 percent) were convicted of nonviolent drug, property, or public order crimes (The Sentencing Project, 2015).

Migrant communities also find themselves in the tight grip of mass incarceration promoted by a growing prison industry, which includes the multibillion-dollar business of detention and deportation. In 2010, private companies in the United States operated more than 250 correctional facilities, housing almost 99,000 prisoners. These companies regularly lobby Congress for more detention and mandatory sentences as they profit from increased incarceration and extended sentences, even if this is not the most effective use of taxpayer dollars (Detention Watch Network, 2011). US Immigration and Customs Enforcement (ICE) detains an average of 34,000 immigrants each day, three times the number detained in 1996. In 2012, about 400,000 immigrants were detained, costing taxpayers $1.7 billion at an average of $122 a day per bed (Carswell, Sarah; Grassroots Leadership; Detention Watch Network, 2015). As of 2015, a congressionally mandated bed quota *obliged* ICE to incarcerate 34,000 immigrants in detention at any given time or pay private companies in any case (Detention Watch Network, 2015).

Both citizen prisoners and migrant detainees are frequently held in facilities far away from their families and legal counsel, placing tremendous hardship on loved ones and their ability to legally fight for their freedom.

Impact on Women and Children

Women of color—citizen and migrant—are at the crux of the mass incarceration of people of color. African American and Latina women make up the fastest-growing population in US prisons and jails (The Rebecca Project for Human Rights). Nearly 25 percent of women in state prisons are there for nonviolent drug-related offenses (Carson, 2015). Fifty-six percent of female prisoners are mothers (Glaze & Maruschak, 2015).

Women in prison and detention face sexual harassment and sexual abuse, as they struggle to keep families together. Women who face abuse in prison and detention fear speaking out and cannot flee. Both imprisoned and detained women have been chained and shackled during childbirth. Most incarcerated women were first survivors of sexual and physical abuse.

Ending the Torture of Solitary Confinement

Once incarcerated, the conditions of confinement for many people of color continue to follow a pattern of bias, as exemplified by the use of solitary confinement in jails, prisons, and immigrant detention centers. According to the Bureau of Justice Statistics, on any given day, roughly 80,000 incarcerated adults and youth are held in solitary confinement in the United States. A disproportionate number of them are people of color (Schlanger, 2013). Prolonged solitary confinement in US prisons constitutes torture and violates the Convention Against Torture and Other Cruel, Inhuman or Degrading Treatment or Punishment (CAT).

Solitary confinement also impacts immigrants confined in civil detention. Women are placed in solitary confinement in retaliation for reporting incidents of rape.

Ongoing Punishment After Incarceration

The impact of the criminalization of communities of color does not end after incarceration. Rather, upon their release from prison, people with a felony conviction begin a lifelong sentence of second-class citizenship, stripped of their right to vote, facing legal discrimination in employment and housing, and banned from accessing government services such as tuition assistance, food stamps, housing, and more. Such experiences are described in Michelle Alexander's *The New Jim Crow: Mass Incarceration in the Age of Colorblindness.*

The United Methodist Church's Response

The United Methodist Church affirms the inalienable human rights of all persons. The Charter for Racial Justice calls us to challenge institutional racism. Also, The United Methodist Church's Social Principles (¶ 164*H*) calls United Methodists to practice restorative justice, seeking alternatives to retribution and restoration of right relationships among all God's people. So, The United Methodist Church calls on local and national governments to:

- Stop the criminalization of communities of color and the cacophony of "wars" being waged against these communities.
- Make the enforcement and protection of international human rights law central to criminal justice and immigration policy.
- End racial/ethnic/religious profiling by law enforcement officers and end "zero tolerance" policies in schools.
- Suspend ICE raids, end family detention and ALL incarceration of children in compliance with the United Nations Convention on the Rights of the Child. Keep families together.
- End local police involvement in immigration enforcement (2012 *Book of Resolutions*, #3281).
- End mandatory sentencing laws and mandatory detention policies, and affirm judicial discretion in sentencing and deportation rulings.
- Restore the full citizenship rights, including the vote, to US citizens with felony convictions; remove barriers to their employment and ability to secure housing and supportive services. Provide education and job creation so they can rejoin society.
- Repeal employer sanctions and other measures that criminalize undocumented migrants seeking work.

The United Methodist Task Force on Immigration, representing the Council of Bishops, agencies, and racial/ethnic caucuses should work to:

- Affirm the humanity and inherent dignity of all who are under correctional control and examine links between criminal justice and immigrant enforcement policies as they impact communities of color.
- Challenge the criminalization of migrants in the United States and globally by engaging annual and central conferences in advocacy. Build alliances with ecumenical and secular groups.

General Board of Church and Society, General Commission on Religion and Race, the General Board of Global Ministries, and United Methodist Women should:

- Develop local church resources on this issue with US and international groups.

- Work with central conferences to deepen research, analysis, and action on global migration policies.
- Mobilize congregations to challenge private prisons and detention centers, and to advocate the release of prisoners held for nonviolent offenses.

Annual conferences and local congregations should:

- Challenge police engagement in immigration enforcement.
- Call United Methodists to discernment on these issues through use of the Wesleyan Quadrilateral, as well as the frameworks of human rights, racial justice, and restorative justice. Use a critical lens regarding mass media. (See Resolution #8016, "Proper Use of Information Communication Technologies.")
- Engage with churches and local communities in speaking out publicly for police accountability regarding racial profiling, misconduct, abuse, and killings.
- Work to end the use of solitary confinement.
- Provide reentry ministries for people released from prison.

ADOPTED 2016

See Social Principles, ¶ 162A.

RURAL ISSUES

3391. Call to the Churches for the Renewal of Rural Ministries

For 70 years the religious community has joined together through Agricultural Missions, Inc. as one way of supporting and accompanying rural communities around the world in their efforts to end poverty and injustice. For many years now rural communities in the United States and across the world have faced daunting new challenges in the wake of increasing globalization of food systems and promotion of policies that favor corporations over family farms.

Using global and regional trade agreements, corporations are controlling decisions that profoundly affect the lives of rural people. Trade regulations and treaties, both current and under negotiation, such as the Free Trade Area of the Americas (FTAA), have conferred on corporations the right to supersede national farm policies in any nation, to demand access to local markets, and to purchase and own local water distribution systems and other essential services.

The market-based model of economic development fostered by the World Trade Organization, the World Bank and the International Monetary Fund and imposed through international trade agreements, such as the North American Free Trade Agreement (NAFTA), has resulted in and/or hastened the:

1. displacement of people from the land and the decline in the culture of the family farm;

2. belief among rural residents, particularly the youth, that there is no future in agriculture, leading to the impoverishment and eventual death of many rural communities;

3. increasing rates of farmer suicides and farm worker exploitation, as well as violence in the family and the community, substance abuse and related problems; and

4. violation of the integrity of God's creation as typified by the pollution of the air, land, and water and disruption of the ecology and climate on a global scale.

It is essential that the churches stand with those who work the land in their struggles and witness to their work. As churches, we need to provide material and moral support and raise our voices, lest by our silence the structures of power assume our consent to the injustices being committed against rural peoples and communities. We bear witness that alternatives that are just and sustainable are being developed, despite enormous odds, by the shared efforts of rural communities in many countries and regions. The Church needs to renew and expand relationships with these communities and struggles and make common cause with them.

The Church possesses the lenses of the gospel and has the responsibility to bring moral and ethical scrutiny to social and economic policy. The Church must play a critical and essential role in evaluating economic policies for consistency with the Scripture and the Christian principles of justice.

Therefore, we call The United Methodist Church to respond as worshiping congregations and as institutions responsible for providing moral guidance and prophetic vision to society at large and to impoverished people, in particular:

1. At the congregational level, pastors must be better equipped to address the despair affecting rural people, by working closely with local organizers and grassroots organizations.

2. At the institutional level, The United Methodist Church should:

    a. work with universities in the United States in rural areas and reclaim land-grant colleges, including historically black and Indian tribal colleges, to promote the interests of small-scale farmers instead of agribusinesses;

    b. consider setting up an ecumenical fund to assist small farmers threatened with bankruptcy to keep their farms and assist them in engaging in sustainable farming practices;

    c. promote a culture and economy of sufficiency, conservation, and thrift for corporate and individual lifestyles as best models of stewardship of God's creation;

    d. advocate a process of public audits to call to accountability agribusinesses, banks and other financial institutions (including the international financial institutions), and transnational corporations and call on them to remedy the negative impact of their policies and activities on rural communities;

    e. strengthen its partnership with farm and rural community-based organizations and networks to educate and engage members on critical policy issues, including agricultural subsidies, food and trade policies, economic justice, and the integrity of creation;

    f. accompany farm workers in their struggles to secure healthy living conditions and living wages, obtain and maintain the right to organize, and to support rural grassroots organizations that work with them in these endeavors; and

    g. develop concrete programs to demonstrate its solidarity with and accompaniment of small-scale, minority, and indigenous producers to secure their rights to their land and the fullness of life promised by Jesus Christ.

ADOPTED 2004
READOPTED 2008
AMENDED AND READOPTED 2016
RESOLUTION #3391, 2008, 2012 *BOOK OF RESOLUTIONS*
RESOLUTION #174, 2004 *BOOK OF RESOLUTIONS*

See Social Principles, ¶ 162P.

3395. Ministries of Rural Chaplains

WHEREAS, the General Conference for the past five quadrennia has affirmed the Rural Chaplains Association and the ministries of rural chaplains, and called on The United Methodist Church to prepare and certify rural chaplains as a significant means of enabling renewal in towns/villages and rural churches and communities globally; and

WHEREAS, the Rural Chaplains Association has women, men, laity and clergy members, both United Methodist and ecumenical, in the global community; and

WHEREAS, rural chaplains are lay and clergy persons who have sensed the call to live in, work with, and advocate for town and rural persons, families, congregations and communities; and

WHEREAS, special emphasis is placed on advocacy for justice issues among all people, regardless of ethnicity, gender, age or economic status; and

WHEREAS, rural chaplains meet annually for encouragement, networking, resourcing, and support by means of focus events to enrich person-related chaplaincy-type skills, biblical understandings and experiential exposures related to issues such as immigration, migrant workers, farm works, rural businesses and communities; and

WHEREAS, rural chaplains work with other prophetic persons/groups on the local level who are committed to long-term involvement aimed at developing local and outside resources to assist with transformation of the lives of rural congregations and communities; and

WHEREAS, the Rural Chaplains Association continues to work to expand its international/global linkages in order to expose participants to cultural, economic, political, ecological, and religious life of rural people from places around the world;

Therefore be it resolved, that The United Methodist Church commend and reaffirm its commitment to the Rural Chaplains Association as rural chaplains continue to carry out their ministries of care, of justice, and of nurture with people in rural areas and town and village communities; and

Be it further resolved, that the General Board of Global Ministries be encouraged to continue an active and ongoing relationship with the Rural Chaplains Association.

ADOPTED 2008
AMENDED AND READOPTED 2012, 2016
RESOLUTION #3395, 2012 *BOOK OF RESOLUTIONS*
RESOLUTION #3396, 2008 *BOOK OF RESOLUTIONS*

See Social Principles, ¶ 162P.

URBAN ISSUES

3411. Pathways to Transformation 2016-2024

A United Methodist Urban Ministry Plan for Making Disciples of Jesus Christ for the Transformation of the World

WHEREAS, change is inevitable but transformation is optional, The United Methodist Church has the opportunity to transform and energize urban churches and communities; and

WHEREAS, the Holy Boldness: Pathways to Transformation Plan, adopted by the 2012 General Conference, has been developed to continue and strengthen the National Urban Ministry Plan adopted at the 1996 General Conference and reaffirmed in 2004; and

WHEREAS, the primary goal of the Plan calls for The United Methodist Church to provide a vision for the future: identify areas of focus and collaboration; organize and mobilize financial and human resources; and

WHEREAS, according to the "State of the World Population 2014" report, "in 2014, 54 percent of the world's population was in urban areas," and 1.8 billion children were living in urban areas, and "without proper planning, cities across the globe will face the threat of overwhelming poverty, limited opportunities for youth, and religious extremism"; and

WHEREAS, ultimately, the Pathways to Transformation Plan will be effective if annual conferences, districts, and, especially, local churches and faith-based community organizations and agencies develop strategies and carry out the agreed-upon goals and objectives; and

WHEREAS, it is also critical for the whole church (congregations in and outside urban areas, annual conferences, and general church agencies) to work in collaboration to support those working locally to transform urban congregations and the communities to meet the need of growing urban areas; and

WHEREAS, the priorities, goals, and objectives identified for this Plan were determined through a national survey of laity, pastors, faith-based community organization staff, annual conference staff, seminary presidents and deans, and bishops; and

WHEREAS, the primary goals are to accomplish the following:

1. transform existing urban congregations through training, coaching, and mentoring;
2. equip new urban churches and faith communities;
3. assist annual conferences and districts in urban strategic planning;
4. challenge and assist urban congregations to transform the communities in which they reside; and

WHEREAS, the priorities that will inform and guide these goals are:

- urban theology and leadership development;
- urban evangelism and congregational development;
- living in community with the poor;
- strengthening and developing multicultural relationships and congregations;
- eradicating racism and other forms of oppression;
- creating and developing urban/suburban collaboration and partnerships;
- community economic development;
- wholeness, healing, and health; and

WHEREAS, these goals and priorities further support the four areas of collaboration developed by the Connectional Table: 1) leadership development, 2) starting new congregations, 3) partnering with the poor, and 4) global health. This Plan is particularly synergistic with the third proposal, "partner with the poor to seek justice and address the causes of human suffering that result from poverty," which has been assigned to Global Ministries; and

WHEREAS, urban transformation will require an ecumenical and interfaith collaborative effort by local churches working in cooperation with other denominational members of the Methodist family and other denominations, community organizations, businesses, and governmental institutions; collaboration will need to occur beyond the city limits by collaborating with exurban churches that share similar challenges, and churches in suburban areas that have committed persons, resources, and relational roots in urban neighborhoods, all of which strengthen ministry; and

WHEREAS, collaboration will also need to occur at the general church level with Urban Networks and general agency teams working together to identify common strategies that they can mutually accomplish; the national strategies linking with local strategies and needs; national collaboration involving the ethnic ministry plans already adopted by our Church with a particular sensitivity to those who are poor; and finally, national collaboration involving other ecumenical and inter-faith bodies and national urban resources;

Therefore, be it resolved, that the general agencies, Urban Networks, annual conferences, districts, and, especially, local churches to take authority and responsibility to accomplish the goals and objectives of the Plan; and

Be it further resolved, that the General Board of Global Ministries Office of Networks and Constituencies or its equivalent will be responsible for the coordination and implementation of the Plan. Objectives and action steps have been developed and will be implemented as funding is made available; and

Be it further resolved, in order to facilitate this coordination and implementation, the Office of Networks and Constituencies or its equivalent will have copies of the Plan available for any who wish to partner in this effort, and that with God's help, we can reclaim our cities for United Methodism and, in the process, meet Christ on the streets walking with his people.

ADOPTED 2008
AMENDED AND READOPTED 2012, 2016
RESOLUTION #3411, 2008, 2012 *BOOK OF RESOLUTIONS*
RESOLUTION #180, 2004 *BOOK OF RESOLUTIONS*
RESOLUTION #171, 2000 *BOOK OF RESOLUTIONS*

See Social Principles, ¶ 162R.

VIOLENCE

3422. Speaking Out for Compassion: Transforming the Context of Hate in the United States

So justice is driven back, / and righteousness stands at a distance; / truth has stumbled in the streets, / honesty cannot enter. / Truth is nowhere to be found, / and whoever shuns evil becomes a prey. / The LORD looked and was displeased / that there was no justice. / [God] saw that there was no one, / [God] was appalled that there was no one to intervene; / so [God's] own arm achieved salvation . . . / and [God's] own righteousness sustained him.

—Isaiah 59:14-16 (NIV)

Therefore, put off falsehood and speak truthfully, for we are all members of one body.

—Ephesians 4:25 (NIV paraphrased)

When Isaiah observed that "truth has stumbled in the streets" and "truth is nowhere to be found," he said "God was appalled." At a time of rising vitriol, racism, hate, and violence in the world born of deep economic crisis and global shifts, it is time for the church to speak out. If we do not, God will be appalled. We feel compelled to raise a prophetic voice challenging the climate of distrust, distortion of truth and fear, shifting the conversation to our common future. In many places, the level of anger has crossed a line in terms of civility. Whatever the disagreement about policy or program, this behavior is unacceptable. It represents a spiritual crisis that calls for us to respond by deepening our understanding of God's call and filling our own deep yearnings for spiritual wholeness, that can empower us to love and compassion without giving up our responsibility to speak out for justice. The consequences of this climate of fear and hostility has been an increase in the number of reported hate crimes, particularly in the post-9/11 world. Reports of hate crimes or acts such as the following have become part of the daily lives of people in the United States:

- A Muslim Arab-American woman receives a threat from a co-worker "You and your kids will pay;
- A Catholic high school student is punched and kicked on a bus by a group of youth for looking "Chinese";
- A teenage boy is beaten with a baseball bat because of his perceived sexuality;
- Anti-Semitic graffiti is spray painted on Jewish gravestones;
- Four men attack and kill one of twelve undocumented immigrants.

These acts promote and are manifestations of bigotry based on religion, race, sexual orientation, and national origin.

If we look at these as acts of individuals or groups of individuals we will fail to recognize the systemic context of injustice that give rise to such acts.

In addition to the realities of the post-9/11 increase in hate and fear mongering, many parts of our nation are facing a deep economic crisis. More and more people in the United States are learning the harsh realities: job loss, reduction of work hours, bankruptcies, lack of affordable health care resource, resources, foreclosures, predatory lending, declining wages, budget cuts for education and critical social programs. In the United States, the overall unemployment rate in November 2014 was 5.8 percent but for Latinos and African Americans, the respective rates were 6.6 percent and 11.1 percent. We recognize that there is cause for anger among all economic and social groups. However, we are alarmed by the climate of hate in public discourse in the United States that has emerged in the wake of these difficult economic realities. We must challenge the misdirection of anger toward the most vulnerable for all are impacted by these crises.

As Christians we are called to be models of compassion. The United Methodist Social Principles affirm,

"We affirm all persons as equally valuable in the sight of God. . . . We support the basic rights of all persons to equal access to housing, education, communication, employment, medical care, legal redress for grievances, and physical protection. We deplore acts of hate or violence against groups or persons based on race, color, national origin, ethnicity, age, gender, disability, status, economic condition, sexual orientation, gender identity, or religious affiliation" (Social Principles, ¶ 162).

"The strength of a political system depends upon the full and willing participation of its citizens. The church should continually exert a strong ethical influence upon the state, supporting policies and programs deemed to be just and opposing policies and programs that are unjust" (Social Principles, ¶ 164B).

The Charter for Racial Justice states that all persons are equally valuable in the sight of God, that racism is a rejection of the teachings of Jesus Christ, that we must work toward a world in which each person's value is respected and nurtured. We remember our roots in speaking out for justice. Methodist women organized against lynching in the 1930s. The church spoke out boldly during the 1960s in support of the Civil Rights Movement. In South Africa and the United States, United Methodists were strong in the opposition to apartheid. We spoke boldly for peace and the reunification of Korea. In the 1980s we called for an end to US government funding of paramilitary groups in Central America. When the United States began bombing Afghanistan in 2003, we called for an end to the bombing as well as long term support for the United Nations and international human rights. We continue to speak out in support of migrants and immigrants who are demonized and criminalized in many countries.

We do not want God to be appalled. We confess that we have not always behaved well as a church. We have violated one another and acknowledge the need to reexamine our own behavior in following our impulse to first protect our own needs and our own security.

It is time to act boldly and, with God's grace, truth will be found and we will know justice. We call for The United Methodist Church—individuals, congregations, conferences, boards and agencies, clergy, and laity—to:

- Develop multigenerational educational resources to build understanding of the systemic nature of racism, sexism, homophobia, and other forms of marginalization.
- Provide biblically-based resources for young people and adults that address the historic and systemic roots of hate speech and all the manifestations of hate in our society;
- Enter into dialogue and action, speaking out for compassion and against hate. A faithful dialogue requires the courage to speak up without misusing privilege and power. This will include:
  - O Redefining compassion as the process of inviting and sustaining faith in full dialogue.
  - O Acknowledging the wholeness of the human family means willingness to stay in community with those whom we disagree, by embracing both patience and humility.
  - O Commitment to a lifelong journey of personal and collective discipline.
  - O Commitment to listen attentively, respectfully and never using dialogue as an excuse for talk and no action or to mask dishonesty.
  - O Encouraging United Methodists to end complicity with hate by speaking out when jokes, disparagements, and stereotypes are based on difference.
  - O Creating opportunities to hear from excluded groups about the reality and impact of hate and partner with them to act for justice;
  - O Encouraging law-enforcement personnel to maintain records on hate crimes and to bring

to justice the perpetrators of such violence and intimidation.

- We call upon the church at all levels to create sacred spaces for common prayer and community discussion as an invitation to reconciliation.
- To convene conversations in family gatherings, churches, communities, and the political arena about current realities, fears, and the need for faith-filled compassionate response;
- Work with ecumenical and interfaith partners to create workshop resources and develop community activities to unite religions in our work to end all manifestations of hate;
- Engage in efforts to enable communities to unearth the truth about past and present hate-violence, to bring perpetrators (including state actors) to justice, and to heal wounds and seek reconciliation based on justice and more equitable power relationships.
- Be active participants in civic or religious organizations that promote unity and diversity, and work to eradicate acts of hate as well as work with diverse grassroots and national organizations.
- We call upon conferences, boards, and agencies to use resources in our global church to share models and strategies for faithful dialogue and to intentionally practice words and attitudes that will help us find common ground.

We call on all annual conferences to

- Report on their work on undoing the culture of hate at their annual conference meeting;
- Include hate crimes in their annual conference report to the General Commission on Religion and Race;
- Work with the General Board of Church and Society, the General Board of Global Ministries, and United Methodist Women on this concern.

ADOPTED 2008
AMENDED AND READOPTED 2016
RESOLUTION #3422, 2008, 2012 *BOOK OF RESOLUTIONS*

See Social Principles, ¶ 162A, H, J <https://www.umofficialresources.com /reader/9781426766213/>.

3425. Prohibition of Bullying

Bullying is a behavioral expression of aggressiveness that attempts to yield power over another person(s) or people(s). This may be expressed by physical or psychological means. Bullying can result in the death of the victim. We have only to look at scripture for evidence. The Book of Esther is about the bullying of one man and the grace God expressed through God's persons. The questioning, beating, and subsequent death on the cross of Jesus the Christ is the ultimate example of expressed abuse of power over a person, even the Son of God. Stephen and a host of Christian martyrs have suffered similar personal attacks that led to death for the cause of Christ. There are persons today who suffer and die because another person(s) seek to overwhelm them by aggressive behavior.

It is hereby resolved, that

In an effort to reduce bullying in society, United Methodist congregations will:

- categorically oppose the practices of adult, youth, and child bullying, mobbing (also known as scapegoating);
- diligently work to increase societal awareness of these destructive behaviors;
- welcome teens and offer safe places for teens to gather;
- post and widely distribute materials including contacts for hotlines and other local and national resources;
- incorporate the topic of adolescent bullying into sermons, making clear the church's position;
- use language of responsibility and healing rather than blame and punishment;
- encourage family members, neighbors, and friends who suspect or know of abuse to come forward;
- provide education and training for clergy and laity on abuse prevention, detection, and intervention;
- create and nurture peer groups for adolescents to raise awareness of the stresses in their own families and issues that are risk factors for abuse;
- raise awareness about Internet bullying and peer pressure;
- organize forums, inviting outside speakers, including survivors, abusers, and representatives of local and national organizations to facilitate discussions and encourage congregants to come forth about their own risk status; and

- encourage congregant volunteers to organize and run support groups and foums.

ADOPTED 2004
AMENDED AND READOPTED 2012
RESOLUTION #3425, 2008, 2012 *BOOK OF RESOLUTIONS*
RESOLUTION #188, 2004 *BOOK OF RESOLUTIONS*

See Social Principles, ¶ 162.

3427. Eradicating Sexual and Gender-Based Violence

All of creation is sacred in God's sight. Because many women and children, along with others, are ignored, abused, and violated, we urge renewed commitment to prohibiting violence against women and children in all its forms.

Violence takes different forms and in many cases, it is about power and control. Violence is a tool used by the strong to dominate the weak and the powerful to dominate the vulnerable. Often the mere threat of violence is enough to achieve the goal of dominance and control. Human beings are especially vulnerable with respect to gender and sexuality, and therefore sexual and gender-based violence (SGBV) is particularly devastating.

Exploitation, abuse, and violence take many forms: child marriage, female genital mutilation, child soldiers, displacement of persons, family violence, polygamy, human trafficking, and rape as an act of war.

Child Marriage

In 1948 the Universal Declaration of Human Rights affirmed that marriage must be based on consent. Yet, in practice, one third of girls in the developing world are married before the age of 18 and 1 in 9 are married before the age of 15: usually without their consent and often to men they do not know (Child Marriage Facts and Figures, International Center for Research on Women, <http://www.icrw.org/child-marriage-facts-and->figures). As recently as 2010, 67 million women aged 20-24 around the world had been married before the age of 18 (Child Marriage Facts and Figures, International Center for Research on Women, http://www.icrw.org/child-marriage-facts-and-figures). Child marriage itself is an expression of power and control, and can lead to further experiences of violence.

Female Genital Mutilation

According to the World Health Organization, "female genital mutilation (FGM) comprises all procedures that involve partial or total removal of the external female genitalia, or other injury to the female genital organs for nonmedical reasons. FGM is recognized internationally as a violation of the human rights of girls and women" (Female Genital Mutilation Fact Sheet, World Health Organizationhttp://www.who.int/mediacentre/factsheets/fs241/en/). FGM is nearly always carried out on minors to keep girls and women from experiencing pleasure during sexual intercourse, rationalized that this will keep girls from straying outside of marriage. FGM "has no medical benefits" and can cause harmful medical complications including "severe pain, shock, bleeding, recurrent bladder and urinary tract infections, infertility and an increased risk of childbirth complications and newborn deaths" (Female Genital Mutilation Fact Sheet, World Health Organization, http://www.who.int/mediacentre/factsheets/fs241/en/).

Child Soldiers

UNICEF estimates that "300,000 children—boys and girls under the age of 18—are involved in more than 30 conflicts worldwide. Children are used as combatants, messengers, porters, cooks, and for forced sexual services. Some are abducted or forcibly recruited, others are driven to join by poverty, abuse, and discrimination, or to seek revenge for violence enacted against them or their families" (Fact Sheet: Child Soldiers, UNICEF, http://www.unicef.org/emerg/files/childsoldiers.pdf). Sexual violence is increasingly common in conflict situations and is perpetrated against both girls and boys.

Displaced Persons

Displaced children, women, lesbian, gay, bisexual, and transgender (LGBT) persons, and persons with disabilities are particularly at risk of sexual and gender-based violence (UN High Commissioner on Refugees). During conflict and disaster, children are easily separated from their families. Limited in their ability to protect themselves, they are vulnerable to sexual exploitation, abuse, trafficking, forced or early marriage, female genital mutilation, or other harmful traditional practices. With less access to employment than men, women and girls are often compelled to engage in sex for survival. In the developing world, they are in danger of rape, assault, and even death as they search for water, firewood, and food for the household. Added to these social and physical atrocities are the possibilities of unwanted pregnancy, HIV infection, and the transmission of the virus from the mother to her unborn child.

Family Violence

Violence and abuse exist around the world and in families in virtually every congregation; tragically, no church or community is exempt. Abuse among family members—child abuse, spouse/partner abuse, elder abuse—takes many forms: emotional, physical, verbal, sexual, and economic. It is manifested through violence, abusive language, controlling behavior, intimidation, and exploitation.

Polygamy

Some traditions observe polygamy: multiple wives of one husband. Polygamy typically places women in a subordinate role subject to the power and control of the husband, and with no legal rights to family property.

Labor and Sex Trafficking

Modern-day slavery has become the fastest-growing transnational criminal enterprise earning an estimated $150 billion (US) in illegal profits annually while enslaving 21 million people around the world (Human Trafficking, UN Office on Drugs and Crime, http://www.unodc.org/unodc/en/human-trafficking/what-is-human-trafficking.html). The United Nations underscores the role of violence in trafficking, defining it as "the recruitment, transportation, transfer, harboring, or receipt of persons, by means of the threat or use of force or other forms of coercion, of abduction, of fraud, of deception, of the abuse of power or of a position of vulnerability, or of the giving or receiving of payments or benefits to achieve the consent of a person having control over another person, for the purpose of exploitation.

"Exploitation includes . . . sexual exploitation, forced labor or services, slavery or practices similar to slavery, servitude" (Human Trafficking, U.N. Office on Drugs and Crime, http://

www.unodc.org/unodc/en/human-trafficking/what-is-human
-trafficking.html).

Rape as a Weapon of War

For centuries, women have been raped as an act of violence
and a demonstration of power—especially in times of conflict and
war. Rape has been and is sanctioned by some military organizations for the gratification of soldiers during war. For example,
during World War II "comfort women" were forced to have intercourse with soldiers. The motivation for abuse of women is also
a deliberate strategy to terrorize opposing forces and the civilians
in their territory. For example, in eastern Democratic Republic of
Congo, rape of women by warring parties has been confirmed
as "a war in the war." Many women are raped by armed groups
including the regular forces of the country. Impregnating women
and forcing them to bear children who will continue to remind
them of their violation is used as a way to destabilize opposition ethnic groups. Unfortunately, government responses tend to
focus on violence against individual women rather than violence
used as a strategic weapon. Thus, women and girls are discouraged from reporting the crime because of the stigma associated
with being a victim.

According to United Nations Women, one in three women and
girls are impacted by physical or sexual violence in their lifetimes.
Violence has immediate and residual consequences:

Psychological Trauma

Sexual and gender-based violence inflicts deep emotional and
physical wounds that can carry lifelong scars. Child brides often
show signs symptomatic of sexual abuse and post-traumatic
stress, and are therefore extremely vulnerable to domestic violence, abuse, and abandonment (Facts and Figures, International
Center for Research on Women, http://www.icrw.org/child-mar
riage-facts-and-figures). One woman who was raped as a tactic of
war stated: "[A]fter the rape, I was in pain all the time and lost all
sexual desire. Because of my chronic fatigue I could no longer work.
My husband eventually abandoned me and the children" (Child
Marriage Sexual and Gender-based Violence in the Democratic
Republic of Congo, World Health Organization, http://www
.who.int/hac/crises/cod/sgbv/sgbv_brochure.pdf). The World

Health Organization reports: "Many survivors of sexual and gender-based violence suffer from psychological trauma expressed through symptoms such as chronic fatigue, anxiety, insomnia, depression, etc. Some have even resorted to suicide. And trauma that boys and men face as witnesses or perpetrators of sexual violence is underestimated" (Sexual and Gender-based Violence in the Democratic Republic of Congo, World Health Organization, http://www.who.int/hac/crises/cod/sgbv/sgbv_brochure .pdf).

Physical Injury

Underage girls experience higher mortality during pregnancy and childbirth. Girls younger than 15 years old are five times more likely to die in childbirth than women in their 20s, making pregnancy among the leading causes of death for girls ages 15 to 19 globally (Facts and Figures, International Center for Research on Women, http://www.icrw.org/child-marriage-facts-and-fig ures). One million girls worldwide suffer from an obstetric fistula, a hole between the vagina and rectum or bladder that is caused by prolonged obstructed labor, leaving a woman incontinent of urine or feces or both. This commonly occurs among girls who are anatomically immature. As a result of the incontinence and resulting foul smell, the girl or woman is often rejected by her husband and community (What is Fistula? Fistula Foundation, https://www.fistulafoundation.org/what-is-fistula/fast-facts -faq/). Child brides, often unable to effectively negotiate safer sex, are vulnerable to sexually transmitted infections, including HIV, along with early pregnancy. Nearly 2,500 adolescents are infected with HIV daily (Opportunity in Crisis, UNICEF, http://www .unicef.org/lac/Opportunity_in_Crisis-Report_EN_052711.pdf). Other practices such as FGM can result in pain and the spread of infection (Child Marriage Female Genital Mutilation Fact Sheet, World Health Organization http://www.who.int/mediacentre /factsheets/fs241/e).

Economic Hardship

The United Nations Development Program reports that in many places women lack access to paid work or the ability to get a loan. Thus women, who make up 50 percent of the world's population, own only 1 percent of the world's wealth (Gender and Poverty Reduction, U.N. Development Program, http:// www.undp.org/content/undp/en/home/ourwork/povertyre duction/focus_areas/focus_gender_and_poverty.html). People living in poverty, and particularly women and children, are disproportionately affected by violence. Abusive interpersonal relationships and unfair treatment, cultural practices and norms, institutional policies, and business practices at every level of society, including between some nations, continue to deny women's and girls' sacred worth and perpetuate gender inequality. Sexual and gender-based violence is not only a gross human-rights violation, but fractures families and communities, and hampers development, also costing billions of dollars annually on healthcare costs and lost productivity (Estimating the Costs of Violence Against Women in Viet Nam, United Nations Women, http:// www.unwomen.org/~/media/headquarters/attachments/sec tions/library/publications/2013/2/costing-study-viet-nam%20 pdf.pdf). Child marriage limits young girls' skills, resources, knowledge, social support, mobility, and autonomy. Young married girls have little power in relation to their husbands and in-laws. Perceived as a way to provide for a daughter's future, married young she will be subjected to physical and sexual violence without education or skills to create economic opportunity for her or her children (Child Marriage Facts and Figures, International Center for Research on Women, http://www.icrw.org /child-marriage-facts-and-figures).

Stigmatizing the Victim

Many victims of sexual violence are stigmatized in society or rejected by their families. Misguided religious morality often reinforces stigma and blame regarding rape, domestic violence, gender identity, disability, and sexually transmitted infections like HIV. A significant consequence of sexual and gender-based violence is the breaking of sacred trust within society, including the Christian community, where vulnerable members are violated. When brokenness is reinforced, it can lead to new social manifestations of violence. For example, a woman's inability to bear a child, a teenager's odor from a fistula formed in prolonged labor, or her positive HIV status are grounds for divorce. At the same time, traditional beliefs such as child marriage and FGM are reinforced by traditional leadership and mandatory cultural practice.

Disempowerment

The combined effect of these many consequences of sexual and gender-based violence is decreased ability to create solutions and respond to local concerns. All of the manifestations of violence identified above limit the educational and employment opportunities for women. Girls who marry young are less likely to discuss family planning—healthy timing and spacing of pregnancies—with their husbands, increasing the chances of infant mortality and maternal death. Rather than spending time developing ideas that would generate income, enhancing the emotional and physical health of families and communities, women and children plagued by sexual and gender-based violence often focus precious resources on survival.

Sexual and Gender-Based Violence Is Not New

One thousand years before Christ, Tamar was raped by her brother Amnon (2 Samuel 13). An earlier account tells of the gang-rape of a concubine (Judges 19), and an even earlier account the rape of Dinah (Genesis 34). These are stories not only of the violence done to women, but the failure of those in power to support the victims. In Tamar's case, her father, King David, was silent, doing nothing for Tamar, the victim, but rather protecting Amnon, the perpetrator, and thus his own dynasty.

The history of our faith is the history of attempts to recover the insight of Genesis 1 that all creation is sacred in God's sight, and all human beings are creatures of sacred worth. Jesus was an advocate for the sacred worth of all. In the account of the woman caught in adultery (John 7:53–8:11), we see Jesus actively oppose violence against women. Jesus saw beyond the stigma and blame that her accusers imposed on her. Unlike King David, Jesus did not employ his power to cover the injustice, but instead recognized her dignity, interrupted the proposed violence, and sought to restore her to community. Jesus' response expresses his commitment to abundant life (John 10:10), and his call to help create the circumstances in which abundant life can thrive. Jesus' gracious response reaches for the redemption of both victim and perpetrator and stops the cycle of violence.

Our Call

United Methodists have worked to eradicate the many forms of violence that destroy the integrity of individuals, families, communities, and nations. People of faith must work to change attitudes, beliefs, policies, and practices at all levels of society that dehumanize and promote the exploitation and abuse of women and girls. Women with equal rights are better educated, healthier, and have greater access to land, jobs, and financial resources. Because women and children, along with others, are ignored, abused, and violated, we urge renewed commitment to eradicating violence against women and children in all its forms.

We call on all United Methodists, local churches, campus ministries, colleges, universities, seminaries, annual conferences, general agencies and commissions, and the Council of Bishops to:

1. Teach, preach, and model healthy masculinity and respectful relationships that reflect the sacred worth of women and girls (Principles of Healthy Masculinity, http://www.maleallies.org/principles-of-healthy-masculinity);

2. Engage men and boys as allies in the promotion of gender equality;

3. Assess resources used in local ministry settings to ensure the promotion of sacred worth of women and girls and healthy masculinity;

4. Develop theological, educational, and advocacy tools to raise public awareness of sexual and gender-based violence, and to promote a culture of nonviolence;

5. Develop and implement culturally relevant and culturally competent training focused on violence against women;

6. Advocate for an end to harmful traditional practices, such as child marriage, polygamy, and female genital mutilation;

7. Advocate for training in local contexts for people on the front lines of disaster and conflict to recognize women's and girls' increased vulnerability to opportunistic rape, sexual exploitation, and other forms of sexual and gender-based violence;

8. Advocate for full and legal access to medically safe reproductive health-care services. Violence against women undermines sexual and reproductive health, contributing to unwanted pregnancies, unsafe abortions, fistulas, sexually transmitted infections, and HIV, and their recurrence;

9. Ensure that adolescent sexual and reproductive health services address gender-based violence, including access to prompt quality care in cases of rape, emergency contraception and Post Exposure Prophylaxis to prevent HIV infection, and additional referrals (e.g., legal, specialized counseling, and support groups);

10. Provide comprehensive sexuality education so that girls and women in abusive relationships have increased understanding of their bodies and tools to protect themselves from sexually transmitted diseases and/or unwanted pregnancies;

11. Advocate for girls to have access to higher levels of education to decrease the rates of child marriage and poverty;

12. Ensure that all children have access to registration and documentation, including birth registration, to increase access to basic services. and,

13. Advocate for the reduction of war and conflict in the world to reduce conditions that increase the risk of aggression toward women and girls.

The Church must reexamine the theological messages it communicates in light of the experiences of victims of sexual and gender-based violence. We must treat with extreme care the important, but often-misused, concepts of suffering, forgiveness, and the nature of marriage and the family. Part of our call, as individuals and as a Church, is seeking to address the root causes of violence, working to eradicate it in its multiple forms, and being God's instruments for the wholeness of affected women and children. As people of faith we must become aware of how violence affects our communities, how we can end our participation in it, and what interventions will end its ongoing cycles.

ADOPTED 2016

See Social Principles, ¶ 162C, F.

3428. Our Call to End Gun Violence

Jesus' call to his followers to be peacemakers (Matthew 5:9) is tied to intimate relationship with God, and echoes God's dreams for peace for all of creation as expressed in Micah 4:1-4:

"In days to come, / the mountain of the LORD's house / shall be established as the highest of the mountains, / and shall be raised up above the hills. / Peoples shall stream to it, / and many nations shall come and say: / 'Come, let us go up to the mountain of the

LORD, / to the house of the God of Jacob; / that he may teach us his ways / and that we may walk in his paths.' / For out of Zion shall go forth instruction, / and the word of the LORD from Jerusalem. / He shall judge between many peoples, / and shall arbitrate between strong nations far away; / they shall beat their swords into plowshares, / and their spears into pruning hooks; / nation shall not lift up sword against nation, / neither shall they learn war any more; / but they shall all sit under their own vines and under their own fig trees, / and no one shall make them afraid; / for the mouth of the LORD of hosts has spoken" (NRSV).

Micah's prophetic dream points to a time when all peoples will journey to God's presence so God "may teach us his ways and that we may walk in his paths" (4:2). Micah describes God as the final judge and the nations will travel to God's presence out of their desire to live in peace without violence and bloodshed.

The stunning imagery of Micah's dream is the transformation of weapons into instruments of harvesting food that occurs after the judgments are handed down to the nations. The transformation is not complete until the nations participate in their own transformation. The work that went into creating the weapons will be matched by the human effort it will take to transform those weapons into peaceful instruments. God does not collect or hide the weapons from the nations, nor does God transform the weapons outside of human effort. The text states that the nations themselves, "shall beat their swords into plowshares, and their spears into pruning hooks."

Violence, in so many ways, is fueled by fear and self-protection. Iron plows and pruning tools can be used as weapons. Yet, in Micah's vision, genuine peace and security are given to all people by God after the weapons of violence are transformed: "they shall all sit under their own vines and under their own fig trees, and no one shall make them afraid." Culture as well as weapons will be transformed: Indeed, "neither shall they learn war any more."

Whether it happens in the towns of northeastern Nigeria, a suburb in the United States, the streets of Australia, or an office in France, gun violence has become an all-too-often frightening phenomenon. We need the reality of Micah's vision more than ever.

Small arms include assault rifles, submachine guns, light machine guns, grenade launchers, portable anti-aircraft guns and anti-tank guns, among other weapons (Small Arms Survey, <http://www.smallarmssurvey.org/weapons-and-markets

/definitions.html>). Nations encumbered with violence from small arms face the greatest obstacles to delivering social services to those who need them the most (Ibid.). Armed violence contributes to crime, human trafficking, drug trafficking, gender-based violence, racial and ethnic conflicts, systemic economic inequalities, persistent unemployment, and human rights abuses among other social maladies (Small Arms Survey, http://www.small armssurvey.org/armed-violence/social-and-economic-costs /impact-on-development.html). In many countries small arms are the greatest hindrance to food security.

One crucial step toward curbing this violence on an international scale is the Arms Trade Treaty that passed the United Nations in 2013. Its focus is to prevent arms from being traded into already dangerous situations. The treaty does not regulate the trade of small arms within nations. In adopting the treaty, the 118 nations that signed it and the 31 nations that have already ratified it are stating that gun violence is a universal problem devastating lives and creating tremendous instability in nations and entire regions in the world (<http://disarmament.un.org /treaties/t/att/deposit/asc>).

Gun violence also greatly affects families and individuals. One of the most prominent forms of gun violence is suicide. Worldwide, there are nearly one million suicides every year, which amounts to more than 3,000 per day (World Health Organization, International Association for Suicide Prevention, http://www .who.int/mental_health/prevention/suicide/suicideprevent /en/, Worldwide Suicide Prevention Day is September 10, http://www.iasp.info/wspd/). While not all of these involve firearms access to firearms makes suicide more attainable for many who attempt it. Indeed, firearms are the most frequent method for suicides in countries where firearms are common in private households (World Health Organization, <http://www.who.int /bulletin/volumes/86/9/07-043489/en/>).

When domestic violence incidents involve the use of firearms the results are often deadly. "Gender inequality, tolerance and cultural acceptance of the use of violence against women, and common notions of masculinity that embrace firearms possession (which may be supported by both men and women) all combine to create a climate that places women at risk of Intimate Partner Violence involving firearms" (Small Arms Survey, <http://www.smallarmssurvey.org/fileadmin/docs/A-Year

book/2013/en/Small-Arms-Survey-2013-Chapter-2-summary
-EN.pdf>). A US-based study of mass shootings between January
2009 and January 2013 revealed that 57 percent of the incidents
involved the killing of a family member, or a current or former
intimate partner of the shooter (<https://s3.amazonaws.com
/s3.mayorsagainstillegalguns.org/images/analysis-of-recent
-mass-shootings.pdf>).

As followers of Jesus, called to live into the reality of God's dream
of shalom as described by Micah, we must address the epidemic of
gun violence so "that he may teach us his ways and that we may
walk in God's paths." Therefore, we call upon United Methodists
to prayerfully address gun violence in their local context. Some of
the ways in which to prevent gun violence include the following:

1. For congregations to make preventing gun violence a regular
part of our conversations and prayer times. Gun violence must
be worshipfully and theologically reflected on, and we encourage
United Methodist churches to frame conversations theologically
by utilizing resources such as "Kingdom Dreams, Violent Realities: Reflections on Gun Violence from Micah 4:1-4" produced by
the General Board of Church and Society.

2. For congregations to assist those affected by gun violence
through prayer, pastoral care, creating space, and encouraging
survivors to share their stories, financial assistance, and through
identifying other resources in their communities as victims of gun
violence and their families walk through the process of grieving
and healing.

3. For individual United Methodists who own guns as hunters
or collectors to safely and securely store their guns and to teach
the importance of practicing gun safety.

4. For United Methodist congregations that have not experienced gun violence to form ecumenical and interfaith partnerships with faith communities that have experienced gun violence
in order to support them and learn from their experiences.

5. For United Methodist congregations to lead or join in ecumenical or interfaith gatherings for public prayer at sites where
gun violence has occurred and partner with law enforcement to
help prevent gun violence.

6. For United Methodist congregations to partner with local
law-enforcement agencies and community groups to identify gun
retailers that engage in retail practices designed to circumvent
laws on gun sales and ownership, encourage full legal compli-

ance, and to work with groups like Heeding God's Call that organize faith-based campaigns to encourage gun retailers to gain full legal compliance with appropriate standards and laws.

7. For United Methodist congregations to display signs that prohibit carrying guns onto church property.

8. For United Methodist congregations to advocate at the local and national level for laws that prevent or reduce gun violence. Some of those measures include:

- Universal background checks on all gun purchases
- Ratification of the Arms Trade Treaty
- Ensuring all guns are sold through licensed gun retailers
- Prohibiting all individuals convicted of violent crimes from purchasing a gun for a fixed time period
- Prohibiting all individuals under restraining order due to threat of violence from purchasing a gun
- Prohibiting persons with serious mental illness, who pose a danger to themselves and their communities, from purchasing a gun
- Ensuring greater access to services for those suffering from mental illness
- Establishing a minimum age of 21 years for a gun purchase or possession
- Banning large-capacity ammunition magazines and weapons designed to fire multiple rounds each time the trigger is pulled
- Promoting new technologies to aid law-enforcement agencies to trace crime guns and promote public safety.

ADOPTED 2016

See Social Principles, ¶ 162.

WOMEN

3441. Celebration of 150 Years of United Methodist Women

WHEREAS, the United Methodist Women's national organization is charged by the *Book of Discipline* of The United Methodist Church, 2012 to "support ministry with and advocate for the oppressed and dispossessed with special attention to the needs of women, children, and youth; . . . to build a supportive community among women; and . . . engage in activities that foster growth in the Christian faith, mission education, and Christian social involvement throughout the organization" (¶ 1902); and

WHEREAS, the United Methodist Women's national organization continues its education ministries, its outreach in the name of Christ, its work for justice, peace, human community, and its compassionate service with women, children and youth; and

WHEREAS, the outreach and service of United Methodist Women members in their local communities, districts, and conferences are a vital component of the church's public witness to God's love for all; and

WHEREAS, for over 145 years, United Methodist Women and its predecessors have persistently followed the mandates of its vision and mission in serving women, youth, and children through mission education, opportunities for spiritual growth, opportunities for Christian social involvement, and financial support for mission at home and around the world; and

WHEREAS, United Methodist Women continues to stand in solidarity with women, youth, and children by addressing issues such as violence, exploitation, and all levels of discrimination and work with other groups to address and eliminate poverty and hunger as the gospel of Jesus Christ requires; and

WHEREAS, United Methodist Women will celebrate its 150th anniversary in 2019 and continues to be at the heart of the denomination's mission movement by working with Bible Women, regional missionaries, deaconesses/home missioners, and local churches;

WHEREAS, United Methodist Women is building onto its rich legacy of compassionate dedication for the next 150 years of service in God's mission on behalf of women, children, and youth in local and global communities:

Therefore, be it resolved, that the General Conference affirms the powerful witness of United Methodist Women in our Church and our world; and celebrates the forthcoming 150th anniversary and the organization's commitment to continue service to Christ and the Church.

ADOPTED 2004
READOPTED 2008
AMENDED AND READOPTED 2016
RESOLUTION #3441, 2008, 2012 *BOOK OF RESOLUTIONS*
RESOLUTION #19, 2004 *BOOK OF RESOLUTIONS*

See Social Principles, ¶ 161 <https://www.umofficialresources.com/reader /9781426766213/>.

3442. Every Barrier Down: Toward Full Embrace of All Women in Church and Society

All of you who were baptized into Christ have clothed yourselves with Christ. There is neither Jew nor Greek; there is neither slave nor free; nor is there male and female, for you are all one in Christ Jesus.

(Galatians 3:27-28)

As the Church of Jesus Christ enters its third millennium, women continue to heed the call to transform the Church and the world in the name of the One who names us and claims us all for witness, mission and earth-shaking transformation.

As much as he was a product of his era—one admittedly marked by gender, class, religious, and community exclusion—Jesus Christ brought to us a ministry of transformational invitation. The Living Christ invited—and still invites—to a common table of grace, justice, and power, people who had never before been invited to the religious power tables, including women, cultural and religious minorities, social outcasts, and disreputable community sinners.[1] And women, in claiming their voice in the new faith movement ignited by the Messiah, became leaders in expanding that movement and in pushing further for inclusion of Gentiles in what was then viewed as Jesus' renewal of Judaism.

Women, in fact, advocated for and sought to protect the inclusive equality of discipleship called forth by Jesus. In this way, they challenged the Jesus movement to remain true to the new vision of human relationship that Jesus initiated by extending its table fellowship, sharing the message of the coming reign of God and inviting Gentiles (non-Jews) to share in that reign.[1] Jesus treated women with dignity and respect, challenged the conventional sexism of his day, and forever redefined the role of women in the church and society.

As with many expressions of the Christian faith, it took The United Methodist Church and its forebears a while to capture Christ's vision. In 1770, the first Methodist woman was appointed a class leader in the United States; in 1817, women were allowed to hold prayer meetings but denied a license to preach; in 1884 Anna Howard Shaw's ordination by the Methodist Protestant Church was ruled out of order; and full voting rights for women

1. *An End to This Strife: The Politics of Gender in African American Church* by Demetrius K. Williams, Augsburg Fortress Press, 2004.

in the Methodist tradition were not universally recognized until 1956.

Since that time, however, God's call to women as preachers, teachers, administrators, mission workers, treasurers, lay leaders, trustees, peace-with-justice advocates, voting rights' workers, Christian educators, and evangelists has blown a fresh breath across the globe and throughout the Church on the wings of the Holy Spirit, despite the rise and fall of our denominational enthusiasm for addressing sexism, gender bias, prejudice, and bad theology. God has done great things with us and, sometimes, in spite of us. Among the victories celebrated throughout our denomination's history:

- twenty-seven percent of United Methodist pastors in local churches today are women, compared with less than one in 100 in 1972;
- of the 66 active United Methodist bishops around the world, 13 are women; 11 in the US and 2 in central conferences. Of the US women bishops, nine are white and two are Latina. No other US racial-ethnic group is represented among women bishops. In 2012 the first woman bishop was elected to serve in Africa. Since 2012 there has been no black US woman among the active United Methodist US bishops;
- The United Methodist Church gave to the world the first African American (Leontine T. C. Kelly, 1984) and first Latina (Minerva Carcaño, 2004) bishops in mainline Christendom;
- women comprise half of all students enrolled in United Methodist seminaries and seeking ordination;
- United Methodist Women is the largest and most prolific mission working entity on behalf of women, children, and youth in our denomination, with ministries of education, discipleship, economic and social development, health care, advocacy, and empowerment in over 120 nations around the world.

In many ways The United Methodist Church has been a standard-bearer among Judeo-Christian faith communions in terms of full inclusion of women in the life, ministry, and witness of the institutional church and its regional and local expressions. However, if we ask, "Is The United Methodist Church a credible and reliable witness to Christ's exemplary embrace of all women as valued, respected partners in the total institutional life and global witness and impact of the Church?"—the honest answer is not yet. We still fall short when it comes to living out the challenge of Galatians 3:27-28, which declares men and women are truly one in Christ. There are still areas of leadership, of professional ministry, of decision-making, and of areas of discipleship for which the Church will not trust, value, revere, or allot resources to women to the same degree as their brothers in the faith. Some recent examples include:

- a number of United Methodist congregations in 2007 still flatly refuse to accept a woman as senior pastor and are especially opposed to receiving a woman in a cross-racial clergy appointment. In 2006, a racial-ethnic clergywoman assigned to an Anglo church was allegedly menaced by members to dissuade her acceptance of the appointment. In another instance, laity threatened to leave the congregation unless the woman pastor wore a dress instead of slacks to prove she was "a real lady";

- in a 2007 survey of local United Methodist congregations, 18 percent said they do not have women serving as ushers (an increase over 2004), and local church chairpersons of the church council, finance, and trustees are still overwhelmingly men and not women;

- United Methodist membership in the US is declining among young women (and men) and people of color, particularly among those in low-income communities;

- according to the most recent "Clergy Age Trends in The United Methodist Church 2014" report from the Lewis Center, the number of female elders under the age of 35 has increased from 38 percent in 2013 to 39 percent in 2014;

- a number of lay and clergy respondents to a survey on sexual harassment in the church mandated by the 2004 General Conference dismissed any ministries related to empowering women and addressing sexism as "political crap," which "has nothing to do with spreading the good news of Jesus Christ";

- a woman district superintendent reportedly was called a "bitch" when she disagreed with a male colleague during a meeting of the conference cabinet;

- several prominent Church leaders—including bishops— have joined with secular society in decrying "the tyranny of diversity" and retreating from the work of undoing racism and sexism;

- such things as: "We need to stop worrying about politics and focus on the gospel . . ." (that is, as long as the gospel is interpreted in a way that continues to privilege North Americans, white people, and males); and "We'll accept a woman or person of color as long as she's qualified" (Could this infer that white men are automatically assumed to be qualified and that women and people of color get their jobs because of some other criteria, not because of their gifts and talents?);
- the United Methodist Women's national organization is under attack for having too much money and too much power in the hands of a women-controlled board of directors. Proposals by opponents include reducing the number of United Methodist Women directors who can also serve on the General Board of Global Ministries in the interest of "gender balance";
- complaints of alleged sexual abuse of women by lay and clergy leaders in church settings are on the rise, according to the General Commission on the Status and Role of Women;
- women comprise 54 percent of total members of our denomination, yet account for less than 30 percent of ordained ministers, and only 27 percent of the top-paying offices in US annual conferences (treasurers, chancellors, and directors of connectional ministry);
- of 20 active bishops who oversee the work of the church in Europe, Africa, and the Philippines, only two are women.

According to United Methodist theologian and ethicist Rosetta Ross, the defining characteristic of an authentic Christian community is that we love one another as God loves us. Such love is not a passive, merely personal emotion, but requires that we constantly strive to be in right relationship with one another, that we pursue justice and well-being for all, and that we be courageous in undoing that in the community that stymies the building of God's beloved—and loving—community.[2]

2. "Blazing Trails and Transcending Boundaries Through Love: Women of Color and 'Religious Work'" by Rosetta E. Ross, Associate Professor of Philosophy and Religious Studies, Spelman College, Atlanta Georgia, 2006.

In fact, Dr. Ross asserts that agapé love in the Christian understanding is love that "affirms the dignity and value of life," and depends on the "interrelatedness of all relationships—intimate or corporate, public or private," as expressed through the actions, practices, and behaviors of individuals and the corporate Christian community.

"Whatever we love with the social love of agapé—our understanding of a particular movement; persons living in war zones or without clean drinking water; communities of which we are a part; the cause of justice; or the natural beauty of creation—is evident in our expressions of faithful attentiveness to it," concludes Dr. Ross, who is also a South Carolina United Methodist clergywomen.

The United Methodist Church, as a community conceived as a corporate expression of Christ's love for us all, has declared its belief in the full equality of women and its desire to embrace women, and has historically decried institutional sexism in all forms in every corner of the world. Yet, we are still on the journey to faithful living; to "walking our talk"; to emulating Jesus' model of turning convention on its ear in favor of doing God's new thing when it comes to engaging women as universally respected, full participants in every aspect of our corporate and congregational lives. We are still living into what it means to extend agapé love to all the daughters and sons of God, beyond the historic patriarchy and misogyny that has marred full participation of women in church and society.

Our reliability as an agency of God's love assumes that we are paying attention to one another and we are seeking to empower, to unshackle, to raise up those who are still oppressed, repressed, derided, treated as "less than." This agapé love seeks to make the world better through persistently affirming all life, and we are willing to call all people and systems—including our own denomination—to account for how we either empower or repress the children of God. Agapé love fears no risk of ridicule or of interrupting business as usual. In fact, God's love requires that we act, even if it means taking positions that are uncomfortable, unpopular, inconvenient, or even frightening. Further, it requires courage. To quote Dr. Ross, "We are behaving courageously when we have the resolve to take the actions and create the context needed for overcoming challenges we face in seeking to be faithful to what we love and are committed to."

Until we fully affirm the dignity and value, the contributions, the theological perspectives, the concerns, the hopes, the recommendations, and even the discourse of and among women, The United Methodist Church will not be adequately equipped to make of all disciples, to carry a word of hope and peace and love to a broken world, and to demonstrate our authenticity as the incarnation of the life-transforming and barrier-breaking body of Christ.

We therefore ask the General Conference to recommit The United Methodist Church to fulfilling the following recommendation as we continue our journey toward dismantling sexism in the church and inviting all women from every station to share in God's welcome table, by challenging the denomination to:

1. *Listen anew to women, with new emphasis on women of color.* The experiences of racial-ethnic women in the United States and women from The United Methodist Church in Africa and the Philippines mirror the parables and other Gospel stories of triumph over obstacles, being strangers in a strange land, reinterpreting familiar stories for new disciples, and bringing our talk about love and justice in line with our walk, especially as the Church also exists in a society that is still racist and sexist. We ask the general agencies to create evangelistic tools, programs, educational materials, networks, and opportunities to empower women in the church and society, including specific resources for and leadership opportunities offered to women under 35, racial-ethnic women in the United States, women from nations beyond the United States, women in recovery from addiction, divorced women, professional women, farm women, and skeptical-about-the-church women. We further urge church growth teams to include women from these groups in order to help the Church focus more on being a vibrant movement in people's lives instead of just a religious institution. In our leadership development at all levels, the Church must put energy, resources, skill and prayerful action into engaging new women in lay and clergy leadership.

2. *Champion economic parity and justice, beginning in our own communities.* Our largely Western-focused denomination must witness in our giving and our living to the power of agapé by working actively for the well-being of all people. This is particularly critical in our work with women around the world who, with their children, are more likely than any other demographic group to live in poverty; to lack access to adequate health care,

housing, and education; and to lack political power sufficient to transform systems. The United Methodist Church must lead the way by valuing the comparable work and worth of women in our churches, agencies, and related entities, and by championing such things as affordable child care and health care, pay equity, financial aid, and educational support for single women in Africa and the Philippines. Each agency and annual conference should report to the 2012 General Conference on how they have engaged women, including women of color, women from Africa and the Philippines, and women under 35.

3. *Evangelize and identify, recruit, and develop leaders among women.* In recent years, some church pundits have claimed that Christian churches have become "too feminized," and therefore irrelevant and unappealing to men. However, these same observers fail to consider that even with decades of male-only leadership among churches, and even in the face of narrow and misogynist misreading of the Bible to exclude and blame them for human sin, many women have continued to stay actively and joyfully involved in the life of the institutional Church. We challenge general agencies and annual conferences to include in church growth and new discipleship strategies efforts to reach women of color, young women, poor women, career women, teen girls, older women, immigrant women, women survivors of violence, women in prison, women leaving prison, women seeking, women rearing children on limited incomes, etc.

4. *Adopt a posture of "no tolerance" to sexual violence, harassment, and abuse in church and society.* According to some estimates by denominational advocates and legal experts, The United Methodist Church has paid more than $50 million from 2000 to 2004 in legal fees, counseling, mediation, and reparations related to sexual misconduct and abuse in church settings committed by lay and clergy. While sexual misconduct can impact anyone and be perpetrated by anyone, most cases involve men as offenders and women and children as victims. If women cannot trust the Church to believe them, protect them from abuse, and offer them clear justice when abuse happens, it again calls into question the authenticity of the Church's witness. It could suggest to them that the Church—and, by extension, God—does not care about, want, or value the participation of women. We call on the Council of Bishops to collaborate with the General Commission on the Status and Role of Women to continue to develop and enforce effective

policies, laws, and practices and consistent application of those policies and practices to reduce risk of misconduct and offer swift and just recompense and remediation for victims when abuse happens.

5. Engage women in theological exploration and shaping and teaching church doctrine. There is no one women's perspective or women's theology or women's view of Christianity. What is common among many women in The United Methodist Church, however, is that their participation in theological discourse is typically treated as "in addition to" the "classical" biblical and theological teachings. Feminist/womanist/mujerista perspectives are often considered subversive and treated as suspect. Discussions of gender-inclusive language, reading the Hebrew and Greek text through women's eyes, and liberation theology—especially as discussed by women—are regarded by many as a threat to the Christian faith, instead of new and perhaps even more authentic perspectives on it. Further, laywomen and clergywomen in local parishes often do not see themselves as theologians, with as much right to explore Scripture, to embrace the gospel anew, and to offer their learnings to the wider Church. We urge the denomination to affirm the importance of women's perspectives in theological discussions in the denomination, and we applaud the General Board of Higher Education and Ministry for its Women of Color Scholarship Program that empowers and engages women of color in theological education and discourse. Further, we ask that the board monitor United Methodist seminaries for inclusion of women's theological perspectives as expressed in the number of tenured faculty, etc. Also, we invite the General Commission on the Status and Role of Women to create curricula for local churches with teaching tools on inclusive language, sexism, creating a girl-friendly church, and myths about women and church leadership. And we ask active members of the Council of Bishops to study with pastors and lay leaders in their respective annual conferences on the history of women as preachers and teachers in the church, using "Women Called to Ministry," a six-part curriculum developed by the General Commission on the Status and Role of Women and the General Board of Higher Education and Ministry, and available at www.gcsrw.org.

6. Create a "report card" on overcoming sexism for each agency and annual conference. The General Commission on the Status and Role of Women shall create sufficient monitoring tools, focus-group interviews, desk audits and surveys, along with baseline standards in order to evaluate the progress of each annual conference and each general agency in terms of full participation of women, dismantling institutional sexism, and addressing sexual misconduct.

Recommended resources: www.gcsrw.org, www.umsexualethics.org; *The Journey Is Our Home: A History of the General Commission on the Status and Role of Women*, by Carolyn Henninger Oehler, 2005; 2008 Resolutions #2044, "Sexual Misconduct Within Ministerial Relationships," and #2045, "Eradication of Sexual Harassment in Church and Society."

ADOPTED 2008
AMENDED AND READOPTED 2016
RESOLUTION #3442, 2012 *BOOK OF RESOLUTIONS*
RESOLUTION #3443, 2008 *BOOK OF RESOLUTIONS*
RESOLUTION #190, 2004 *BOOK OF RESOLUTIONS*
RESOLUTION #180, 2000 *BOOK OF RESOLUTIONS*

See Social Principles, ¶ 163.

3443. Eradication of Sexism in the Church

Whereas, sexism continues to be a pervasive and systematic force within our church and our society; and

Whereas, sexism deprives the church and society of the opportunity to use the skills and talents that women have; and

Whereas, a General Commission on the Status and Role of Women 2007 survey of local churches in the United States found that only 55% of small churches and 62% of large membership churches have policies against sexual harassment; inclusive language studies are rare in local congregations with only 4% of laity and 31% of clergy indicating they use inclusive language when referring to God; and urban congregations more frequently have inclusive language studies, harassment policies, and diverse use of female lay persons (as Board of Trustees members and ushers, for example); and

Whereas, the Church remains committed to the eradication of sexual harassment against children, employees, volunteers, clergy and their families, and congregants. Yet sexual misconduct remains a serious problem in our conferences, with 1 in 33 women experiencing sexual harassment in local church meetings and worship, and an alarming number of local congregations do not have policies, procedures, or training in place for laity and clergy in stopping and preventing sexual harassment and misconduct; and

WHEREAS, women comprise 58% of the denomination's membership but hold only one-fifth of the top leadership positions in the US annual conferences and as leaders are largely relegated to committees without much financial power like women's ministry and advocacy, racial-ethnic concerns and youth ministry rather than committees that exert considerable influence and control over funding as well as the allocation of money in annual conference ministries, and women employed by general church agencies hold 77% of administrative and clerical support positions (Data from the General Council on Finance and Administration 2009; Women by the Number: issues November 2010, December 2010, January 2011, and March 2011; *THE FLYER*); and

WHEREAS, the Church continues to lose clergywomen from local church ministry into more welcoming forms of ministry, indicating a persistent, subtle, and often unchallenged sexism that denies women in The United Methodist Church the opportunity to participate fully and equally in all areas of the Church;

Therefore, be it resolved, that the General Conference continue to commit itself to eradicating sexism in the church and that it affirm the work and tasks of the General Commission on the Status and Role of Women and of the annual conference-related commissions and counterparts; and

Be it further resolved, that each annual conference commission or counterpart be given the financial backing to pursue projects that are aimed at educating the members of the local churches about the issues of sexism and at sponsoring the leadership events that enable the annual conference commission members to be better advocates for all who seek equity and inclusiveness; and

Be it further resolved, that each annual conference, United Methodist seminary, and all United Methodist-related institutions are called to have policies on sexual harassment and equal opportunity; and

Be it further resolved, that each annual conference and local congregation is called have policy, procedures, and training opportunities in place for lay and clergy in stopping and preventing sexual harassment and misconduct; and that progress to full compliance will be reported through the Episcopal Office to the General Commission on the Status and Role of Women at the Commission's request. The Commission will be responsible to report to General Conference 2016; and

Be it further resolved, that the General Conference support the General Commission on the Status and Role of Women as the advocacy and monitoring agency of women's issues for increasing opportunities for females in leadership, promoting equality in filling decision-making posts, and fostering inclusiveness in all facets of The United Methodist Church.

ADOPTED 1996
AMENDED AND READOPTED 2004, 2012
RESOLUTION #3443, 2012 *BOOK OF RESOLUTIONS*
RESOLUTION #3444, 2008 *BOOK OF RESOLUTIONS*
RESOLUTION #48, 2004 *BOOK OF RESOLUTIONS*
RESOLUTION #40, 2000 *BOOK OF RESOLUTIONS*

See Social Principles, ¶ 162F.

YOUNG PEOPLE

3461. Local Church Support for Young People

WHEREAS, The United Methodist Church supports young people and is called to minister to them; and

WHEREAS, the young people in The United Methodist Church are in need of growth and revival churchwide; and

WHEREAS, in order for young people to grow in the worldwide church, they must first grow in the local church,

Therefore, be it resolved, that each local church do all in its power to support and strengthen young people's ministries at its local level, so that they may be strengthened worldwide.

ADOPTED 2008
AMENDED AND READOPTED 2016
RESOLUTION #3461, 2008, 2012 *BOOK OF RESOLUTIONS*

See Social Principles, ¶ 162D.

¶ 163. IV. THE ECONOMIC COMMUNITY

We claim all economic systems to be under the judgment of God no less than other facets of the created order. Therefore, we recognize the responsibility of governments to develop and implement sound fiscal and monetary policies that provide for the economic life of individuals and corporate entities and that ensure full employment and adequate incomes with a minimum of inflation. We believe private and public economic enterprises are responsible for the social costs of doing business, such as employment and environmental pollution, and that they should be held accountable for these costs. We support measures that would reduce the concentration of wealth in the hands of a few. We further support efforts to revise tax structures and to eliminate governmental support programs that now benefit the wealthy at the expense of other persons.

A) Property—We believe private ownership of property is a trusteeship under God, both in those societies where it is encouraged and where it is discouraged, but is limited by the overriding needs of society. We believe that Christian faith denies to any person or group of persons exclusive and arbitrary control of any other part of the created universe. Socially and culturally conditioned ownership of property is, therefore, to be considered a responsibility to God. We believe, therefore, governments have the responsibility, in the pursuit of justice and order under law, to provide procedures that protect the rights of the whole society as well as those of private ownership.

B) Collective Bargaining—We support the right of all public and private employees and employers to organize for collective bargaining into unions and other groups of their own choosing. Further, we support the right of both parties to protection in so doing and their responsibility to bargain in good faith within the framework of the public interest. In order that the rights of all members of the society may be maintained and promoted, we support innovative bargaining procedures that include representatives of the public interest in negotiation and settlement of labor-management contracts, including some that may lead to forms of judicial resolution of issues. We reject the use of violence by either party during collective bargaining or any labor/management disagreement. We likewise reject the permanent replacement of a worker who engages in a lawful strike.

C) Work and Leisure—Every person has the right to a job at a living wage. Where the private sector cannot or does not provide jobs for all who seek and need them, it is the responsibility of government to provide for the creation of such jobs. We support social measures that ensure the physical and mental safety of workers, that provide for the equitable division of products and services, and that encourage an increasing freedom in the way individuals may use their leisure time. We recognize the opportunity leisure provides for creative contributions to society and encourage methods that allow workers additional blocks of discretionary time. We support educational, cultural, and recreational outlets that enhance the use of such time. We believe that persons come before profits. We deplore the selfish spirit that often pervades our economic life. We support policies that encourage the sharing of ideas in the workplace, cooperative and collective work arrangements. We support rights of workers to refuse to work in situations that endanger health and/or life without jeopardy to their jobs. We support policies that would reverse the increasing concentration of business and industry into monopolies.

D) Consumption—Consumers should exercise their economic power to encourage the manufacture of goods that are necessary and beneficial to humanity while avoiding the desecration of the environment in either production or consumption. Consumers should avoid purchasing products made in conditions where workers are being exploited because of their age, gender, or economic status.

And while the limited options available to consumers make this extremely difficult to accomplish, buying "Fair Trade Certified" products is one sure way consumers can use their purchasing power to make a contribution to the common good. The International Standards of Fair Trade are based on ensuring livable wages for small farmers and their families, working with democratically run farming cooperatives, buying direct so that the benefits and profits from trade actually reach the farmers and their communities, providing vitally important advance credit, and encouraging ecologically sustainable farming practices. Consumers should not only seek out companies whose product lines reflect a strong commitment to these standards, but should also encourage expanded corporate participation in the Fair Trade market.

Consumers should evaluate their consumption of goods and services in the light of the need for enhanced quality of life rather than unlimited production of material goods. We call upon consumers, including local congregations and Church-related institutions, to organize to achieve these goals and to express dissatisfaction with harmful economic, social, or ecological practices through such appropriate methods as boycott, letter writing, corporate resolution, and advertisement.

E) *Poverty*—In spite of general affluence in the industrialized nations, the majority of persons in the world live in poverty. In order to provide basic needs such as food, clothing, shelter, education, health care, and other necessities, ways must be found to share more equitably the resources of the world. Increasing technology, when accompanied by exploitative economic practices, impoverishes many persons and makes poverty self-perpetuating. Poverty due to natural catastrophes and environmental changes is growing and needs attention and support. Conflicts and war impoverish the population on all sides, and an important way to support the poor will be to work for peaceful solutions.

As a church, we are called to support the poor and challenge the rich. To begin to alleviate poverty, we support such policies as: adequate income maintenance, quality education, decent housing, job training, meaningful employment opportunities, adequate medical and hospital care, humanization and radical revisions of welfare programs, work for peace in conflict areas and efforts to protect creation's integrity. Since low wages are often a cause of poverty, employers should pay their employees a wage that does not require them to depend upon government subsidies such as food stamps or welfare for their livelihood.

Because we recognize that the long-term reduction of poverty must move beyond services to and employment for the poor, which can be taken away, we emphasize measures that build and maintain the wealth of poor people, including asset-building strategies such as individual development savings accounts, micro-enterprise development programs, progams enabling home

¶ 163

ownership, and financial management training and counseling. We call upon churches to develop these and other ministries that promote asset-building among the poor. We are especially mindful of the Global South, where investment and micro-enterprise are especially needed. We urge support for policies that will encourage equitable economic growth in the Global South and around the world, providing a just opportunity for all.

Poverty most often has systemic causes, and therefore we do not hold poor people morally responsible for their economic state.

F) Foreign Workers—For centuries people have moved across borders in search of work. In our global world this is still a relevant and increasing form of immigration. Improved wages, better working conditions, and jobs available are reasons for immigration due to work opportunities. Workers from other countries are in many societies an important resource to fill the society's need of workers. But foreign workers too often meet exploitation, absence of protecting laws, and unreasonable wages and working conditions.

We call upon governments and all employers to ensure for foreign workers the same economic, educational, and social benefits enjoyed by other citizens.

Foreign workers also need a religious fellowship, and we call for the churches to include these in their care and fellowships and to support them in their efforts for better conditions.

G) Gambling—Gambling is a menace to society, deadly to the best interests of moral, social, economic, and spiritual life, destructive of good government and good stewardship. As an act of faith and concern, Christians should abstain from gambling and should strive to minister to those victimized by the practice. Where gambling has become addictive, the Church will encourage such individuals to receive therapeutic assistance so that the individual's energies may be redirected into positive and constructive ends. The Church acknowledges the dichotomy that can occur when opposing gambling while supporting American Indian tribal sovereignty and self-determination. Therefore, the Church's role is to create sacred space to allow for dialogue and education that will promote a holistic understanding of the American Indians' historic quest for survival. The Church's prophetic call is to promote standards of justice and advocacy that would make it unnecessary and undesirable to resort to commercial gambling—including public lotteries, casinos, raffles, Internet gambling, gambling with an emerging wireless technology, and other games of chance—as a recreation, as an escape, or as a means of producing public revenue or funds for support of charities or government.

H) Family Farms—The value of family farms has long been affirmed as a significant foundation for free and democratic societies. In recent years, the survival of independent farmers worldwide has been threatened by various factors, including the increasing concentration of all phases of agriculture into the hands of a limited number of transnational corporations. The concentration of the food supply for the many into the hands of the few raises global questions of justice that cry out for vigilance and action.

We call upon the agribusiness sector to conduct itself with respect for human rights primarily in the responsible stewardship of daily bread for the world, and secondarily in responsible corporate citizenship that respects the rights of all farmers, small and large, to receive a fair return for honest labor. We advocate for the rights of people to possess property and to earn a living by tilling the soil.

We call upon governments to revise support programs that disproportionately benefit wealthier agricultural producers, so that more support can be given to programs that benefit medium- and smaller-sized farming operations, including programs that build rural processing, storage, distribution, and other agricultural infrastructure; which link local farmers to local schools; and which promote other community food security measures.

We call upon our churches to do all in their power to speak prophetically to the matters of food supply and the people who grow the food for the world and to develop ministries that build food security in local communities.

I) Corporate Responsibility—Corporations are responsible not only to their stockholders, but also to other stakeholders: their workers, suppliers, vendors, customers, the communities in which they do business, and for the earth, which supports them. We support the public's right to know what impact corporations have in these various arenas, so that people can make informed choices about which corporations to support.

We applaud corporations that voluntarily comply with standards that promote human well-being and protect the environment.

¶ 163

J) Finance—Financial institutions serve a vital role in society. They must guard, however, against abusive and deceptive lending practices that take advantage of the neediest among us for the gain of the richest. Banking regulations must prevent the collection of usurious interest that keeps people in cycles of debt. Personal-credit-issuing institutions must operate with responsibility and clarity that allow all parties to understand the full terms of agreements.

K) Trade and Investment—We affirm the importance of international trade and investment in an interdependent world. Trade and investment should be based on rules that support the dignity of the human person, a clean environment and our common humanity. Trade agreements must include mechanisms to enforce labor rights and human rights as well as environmental standards. Broad-based citizen advocacy and participation in trade negotiations must be ensured through democratic mechanisms of consultation and participation.

L) Graft and Corruption—God's good creation, the fullness of its bounty, and the loving, nurturing relationships that bind all together are intended by God to be enjoyed in freedom and responsible stewardship. To revere God's creation is a sacred trust that enables us to fashion just, equitable, sustainable relationships and communities. The strength, stability, security, and progress of such relationships and communities depend on the integrity of their social, economic, political, and cultural processes, institutions, and stakeholders. Graft, referring to unfair or illegal means of acquiring money, gain, or advantage, especially by abusing one's position in politics, business, and social institutions, transgresses human dignity and violates human rights. Corruption, referring to dishonest and undue exploitation of power for personal gain, subverts God's intention for the fullness of life and creation. Graft and corruption tangle the social thread of communities, erode the moral fiber of human relationships, and sully the reputation of social institutions. Legislative and judicial mechanisms, including a strong, just criminal justice system, must deal with graft and corruption at every level of society. Good, just political governance characterized by transparency, accountability, and integrity is crucial to the eradication of graft and corruption. Societies that are graft-ridden and plagued with corruption are needful of God's pardoning love and redeeming grace.

M) Public Indebtedness—The huge budget deficits produced by years of overspending by governments around the world is of great concern. We acknowledge that for a limited time in a nation's history governmental deficits are sometimes necessary. However, long periods of excessive overspending by governments have produced huge deficits and significant economic challenges for many nations. Such wanton carelessness cannot continue. Therefore, we call upon all governments to reduce budget deficits and to live within their means. We ask the governments and institutions that lend money to reduce significantly the interest rates on the money borrowed. We ask that public officials, when making financial adjustments, remember first and foremost obligations that promote the well-being of society such as the funding of schools and other opportunities that foster the growth of the individual, as well as agencies that care for the poor, the elderly, the disabled, and the disenfranchised.

We recognize that, if deficits are not brought under control, future generations will be shackled with a burden of public indebtedness that will force societies to live under the specter of coerced repayments, rising inflation, mass unemployment, and despair. Thus, this is not just a financial issue, but an issue of justice for those who are yet to be born. Wise stewardship is needed today to provide for future generations. We call on church leadership throughout the connection to encourage public officials to reduce public indebtedness and to begin the process toward balanced and fair budgets.

¶ 163

THE ECONOMIC COMMUNITY
THE RESOLUTIONS

CONSUMPTION

4021. Tobacco Marketing

As people of faith in the living God, we are reminded that Jesus spoke out for justice for the poor, the disenfranchised and the powerless and called us to love one another. The Bible reminds us that our bodies are "temples of the Holy Spirit" (1 Corinthians 6:19; also see vv. 13-20) and since we are created in God's own image, we are then called by God to perfect our bodies in God's image. Moreover, we are called by God to ensure that all of God's creation has access to the knowledge of God's love and God's concern for our well-being and welfare. Through our historic Wesleyan heritage and by John Wesley's words, we are reminded as United Methodists that "the world is our parish," and we are called to minister in and throughout the whole world.

The United Methodist Church and its predecessor denominations have a long history of witness against the use and marketing of tobacco products. There is overwhelming evidence linking cigarette smoking with lung cancer, cardiovascular diseases, emphysema, chronic bronchitis, and related illnesses. Alarming statistics point to the impact of tobacco companies and their marketing practices to entice people to smoke. The World Health Organization in its 2009 Report on Tobacco says tobacco use already kills 5.4 million people a year across the globe and the epidemic is worsening, especially in the developing world where more than 80 percent of tobacco-caused deaths will occur in the coming decades. "Unless urgent action is taken, one billion people will die worldwide from tobacco use this century," the report states. "Tobacco use is so devastating to the human body that it is a risk factor for six of the eight leading causes of death in the world."

We are outraged by the use of marketing techniques aimed at young people (children, youths, and young adults) worldwide and legal mechanisms used by leading cigarette manufacturers to loosen regulations and reverse laws enacted by countries and US states to restrict tobacco marketing. These practices are in direct conflict with the global tobacco treaty, The Framework Convention on Tobacco Control, which outlines the most effective policy in controlling tobacco in the interest of public health. The primary US companies who have used deceptive marketing strategies aimed at young people are Altria/Philip Morris, which sells Marlboro cigarettes, and RJR Nabisco, which sells Camel cigarettes.

Therefore, as people of faith who believe our bodies are temples of the Holy Spirit (1 Corinthians 6:13-20), we:

1. direct the General Board of Church and Society to collect and share information about Altria/Philip Morris, RJR Nabisco, and other major tobacco companies so that United Methodists are made aware of other products that provide indirect support of the tobacco industry and financial strategies the tobacco industry implements that unduly influence governments, elected officials, and community leaders.

2. commend the General Board of Pension and Health Benefits for its long-standing exclusion of tobacco manufacturers from its investment portfolio and ask it to challenge public media in its portfolio not to carry advertisements and promotion of tobacco products;

3. ask all United Methodist agencies and related institutions to take into account the church's Social Principles and tobacco concerns and, specifically, to consider the role of Altria/Philip Morris and RJR Nabisco in tobacco marketing as a factor in any decision concerning purchasing food products manufactured by them;

4. request the United Methodist general agencies to communicate, interpret, and advocate for this concern with their affiliated institutions;

5. ask local churches and annual conferences to educate their membership about the tobacco industry's marketing tactics aimed at young people. It is equally important we understand the connection between our purchasing food products and our indirect support of the tobacco industry;

6. request the General Board of Church and Society to explore productive measures aimed at stopping tobacco companies from marketing cigarettes and other tobacco products to young people and, if necessary, organize a boycott; and

7. direct the General Board of Church and Society to communicate this resolution to tobacco companies, serve as a continuing advocate of the United Methodist position within The United Methodist Church and with the companies, and monitor the implementation of this resolution for report at the next General Conference.

ADOPTED 1996
AMENDED AND READOPTED 2004, 2012
RESOLUTION #4021, 2008, 2012 *BOOK OF RESOLUTIONS*
RESOLUTION #198, 2004 *BOOK OF RESOLUTIONS*
RESOLUTION #189, 2000 *BOOK OF RESOLUTIONS*

See Social Principles, ¶ 163D.

EDUCATION

4031. The Methodist Global Education Fund for Leadership Development

Reaffirmation and Reauthorization of the World Service Special Gift—#05-06-04

WHEREAS, the 2004 General Conference of The United Methodist Church approved the Global Education Fund and authorized the General Board of Higher Education and Ministry to raise $4 million under the World Service Special Gift (#05-06-04) during the 2005-2008 quadrennium for the purpose of developing a new generation of principled Christian leaders who will inspire and transform the people of the world, and lead The United Methodist Church to become a truly global church through the worldwide cooperative network of Methodist schools, colleges, universities, and theological schools; and

WHEREAS, the General Board of Higher Education and Ministry has been engaging in infrastructure and capacity building of United Methodist and Methodist-related schools, colleges, universities, and theological schools in Africa, Asia, Europe, Latin America, and the United States; and

WHEREAS, at a request of the General Board of Higher Education and Ministry, the General Council of Finance and Administration, and the Connectional Table of The United Methodist Church, approved the name change from the "Global Education Fund" to the "Methodist Global Education Fund for Leadership Development" in September, 2006; and

WHEREAS, leadership development is recognized as one of The United Methodist Church's most prominent and galvanizing issues and needs, and the Methodist Global Education Fund for Leadership Development is a dynamic mechanism for leveraging the connectional resources of The United Methodist Church to address its leadership crisis and to support the Church's global mission; and

WHEREAS, the General Board of Higher Education and Ministry serves as the lead program board for leadership development; and

WHEREAS, continuing to reaffirm the resolution for the Methodist Global Education Fund for Leadership Development and reauthorizing the raising of $4 million under the World Service Special Gift by the 2012 General Conference, are absolutely necessary to undertake this initiative;

Therefore, be it resolved, that the 2012 General Conference of The United Methodist Church reaffirms the Methodist Global Education Fund for Leadership Development and reauthorizes the General Board of Higher Education and Ministry to raise $4 million under the World Service Special Gift during the 2013-2016 quadrennium; and

Be it further resolved, that said fund will be raised and administered under the leadership of the General Board of Higher Education and Ministry; and

Be it finally resolved, that this resolution be recorded in the *Book of Resolutions* of the 2012 General Conference.

Voted on by the General Board of Higher Education and Ministry, August, 2011.

ADOPTED 2008
AMENDED AND READOPTED 2012
RESOLUTION #4031, 2008, 2012 *BOOK OF RESOLUTIONS*

See Social Principles, ¶ 163.

4033. The Black College Fund

WHEREAS, since 1866 when Rust College was established to address the educational needs of freed slaves, and over the next 150 years, the mission to empower African Americans through education continued with the founding of Bennett College, Bethune-Cookman University, Claflin University, Clark Atlanta University, Dillard University, Huston Tillotson University, Meharry Medical College, Paine College, Philander Smith College, and Wiley College, The Methodist Church's commitment to higher education has been unequivocal; and

WHEREAS, since the founding of these colleges, they have added value to our society, educating some of the world's great teachers, scientists, bishops, doctors, ministers, politicians, and professionals in other walks of life, and some of the world's best and brightest students are today enrolled in these schools and are receiving a quality education through the work of dedicated and committed faculties and staffs; and

WHEREAS, since 1972, the Black College Fund has been an apportioned item and continues to provide necessary funds for daily operation, capital improvements, and academic program enhancement at these schools, and this funding is a critical investment in the dreams of young people and all those who thirst for knowledge; and

WHEREAS, these institutions are and have been since their founding, open to people of all ethnicities, races, creeds and nationalities, and all are treated with dignity and respect, and therefore the mission and ministry of these schools is still vital and important; and

WHEREAS, many annual conferences are going the extra mile to pay their 100 percent apportionments and this commitment and faithfulness to this important cause continues to make a difference;

Now, therefore, be it resolved, that the General Conference reaffirms its commitment to the ministry of the eleven church-related historically black colleges and universities;

Be it further resolved, that the General Conference reaffirms its commitment to the Black College Fund and expresses its intention to continue the Black College Fund as an apportioned item for the 2017-2020 and 2021-2024 quadrennia.

ADOPTED 2008
AMENDED AND READOPTED 2016
RESOLUTION #4033, 2008, 2012 *BOOK OF RESOLUTIONS*

See Social Principles, ¶ 163.

GAMBLING

4041. Gambling

The Social Principles state that, "Gambling is a menace to society, deadly to the best interests of moral, social, economic, and spiritual life, [and] destructive of good government. . . . As an act of faith and concern, Christians should abstain from gambling and should strive to minister to those victimized by the practice. Where gambling has become addictive, the Church will encourage such individuals to receive therapeutic assistance so that the individual's energies may be redirected into positive and constructive ends. The Church should promote standards and personal lifestyles that would make unnecessary and undesirable the resort to commercial gambling—including public lotteries —as a recreation, as an escape, or as a means of producing public revenue or funds for support of charities or government" (¶ 163G).

When asked which commandment is first of all, Jesus answered, "Hear, O Israel: the Lord our God, the Lord is one; you shall love the Lord your God with all your heart, with all your soul, and with all your mind, and with all your strength" (Mark 12:29-30 NRSV). Gambling feeds on human greed and invites persons to place their trust in possessions rather than in God. It represents a form of idolatry that contradicts the first commandment. Jesus said: "You shall love your neighbor as yourself" (Mark 12:31b NRSV). In relating with compassion and love to our sisters and brothers, we are called to resist those practices and systems that exploit them and leave them impoverished and demeaned. The apostle Paul wrote in 1 Timothy 6:9-10a: "Those who want to get rich fall into temptation and a trap and into many foolish and harmful desires that plunge people into ruin and destruction. For the love of money is a root of all kinds of evil" (NIV).

Gambling, as a means of acquiring material gain by chance and at the neighbor's expense, is a menace to personal character and social morality. Gambling fosters greed and stimulates the fatalistic faith in chance. Organized and commercial gambling is a threat to business, breeds crime and poverty, and is destructive to the interests of good government. It encourages the belief that work is unimportant, that money can solve all our problems, and that greed is the norm for achievement. It serves as a "regressive tax" on those with lower income. In summary, gambling is bad economics; gambling is bad public policy; and gambling does not improve the quality of life.

We oppose the growing legalization and promotion of gambling.

Dependence on gambling revenue has led many governments to exploit the weakness of their own citizens, neglect the development of more equitable forms of taxation, and thereby further erode citizen confidence in government.

We oppose the legalization of pari-mutuel betting, for it has been the opening wedge in the legalization of other forms of gambling that has fostered the growth of illegal bookmaking. We deplore the establishment of lotteries and their use as a means of raising public revenues. The constant promotion and the wide advertising of lotteries have encouraged large numbers of persons to gamble for the first time.

We express our concern for the increasing development of the casino enterprises, which have taken captive entire communities and corrupted many levels of government with its fiscal and political power.

Public apathy and a lack of awareness that petty gambling feeds organized crime have opened the door to the spread of numerous forms of legal and illegal gambling.

We especially express our deep concern at the rapid growth of two forms of gambling:

Internet/Digital Gambling: Internet/Digital gambling—encompassing online, mobile, and digital TV based gambling services—is available in the privacy of one's home and even in churches. Easy access to Internet/Digital gambling greatly increases the potential for addiction and abuse. Internet/Digital gambling is an international problem and it is virtually unregulated, which leads to corruption, money laundering, and funding of terrorist organizations. Individuals and local churches should seek to educate themselves on the easy access to Internet/Digital gambling. The social cost of addiction to Internet/Digital gambling is great and leads to bankruptcy, suicide, and family discord. Young adults and senior citizens are among the most vulnerable populations at risk to gambling addiction. Parents and caregivers should take steps to ensure that children and the elderly with access to electronic devices and digital media not be exposed to Internet/Digital gambling. Local churches and annual conferences should provide educational resources for parents and caregivers on the dangers of Internet/Digital gambling and enact strict oversight of church-owned electronic devices and digital media, including computers.

US Tribal Gambling: We grieve over the expansion of gambling onto tribal reservations and lands. Gambling expansion on tribal lands has fostered racism and hate crimes, has caused discord between and among tribal members, and has led to divisions in churches and families. While we support tribal self-determination and self-governance, resorting to gambling as a form of economic development is regrettable. We acknowledge and recognize the dichotomy created when the Church's positions oppose gambling and at the same time support tribal self-determination. We urge annual conferences and local churches, which reside near tribal casinos or are facing expansion of tribal gambling ventures, to build partnerships with churches on reservations and Indian lands to foster mutual trust and understanding of tribal history and of the United Methodist position on gambling without resorting to diminishing tribal sovereignty.

The church has a key role in fostering responsible government and in developing health and moral maturity that free persons from dependence on damaging social customs. We urge national, tribal, state, and local governments to read, analyze, and implement the recommendations of the National Gambling Impact Study report released by the United States in 1999. We encourage tribal governments to wean themselves from gambling as a form of economic development; and we encourage and fully support tribal efforts to diversify economically away from gambling.

We support the strong enforcement of antigambling laws and the repeal of all laws that give gambling an acceptable and even advantageous place in our society.

It is expected that United Methodist churches abstain from the use of raffles, lotteries, bingo, door prizes, other drawing schemes, and games of chance for the purpose of gambling or fundraising. United Methodists should refrain from all forms of gambling practices and work to influence community organizations and be supportive of American Indian tribes in developing forms of funding that do not depend upon gambling. Furthermore, it is incumbent upon local churches to reach out with love to individuals who are addicted, compulsive, or problem gamblers and support efforts at recovery and rehabilitation. We oppose coalitions, groups, organizations, and campaigns that claim opposition to gambling, yet at the same time undermine or oppose tribal sovereignty, which fosters a climate of hate and racism. An alarming trend is the attempt to use local churches in order to increase support for this destructive agenda. We believe that these groups operate contrary to Christian teachings. Therefore we strongly discourage United Methodist members and local churches from participating in such efforts.

The General Board of Church and Society will provide materials to local churches and annual conferences for study and action to combat gambling and to aid persons addicted to gambling. The General Board of Church and Society, annual conferences, and local churches shall work with coalitions and grassroots organizations (such as the National Coalition Against Legalized Gambling) that are compatible with the position of The United Methodist Church (Social Principles ¶ 163).

ADOPTED 1980
AMENDED AND READOPTED 1996, 2004, 2008, 2016
RESOLUTION #4041, 2008, 2012 *BOOK OF RESOLUTIONS*
RESOLUTION #203, 2004 *BOOK OF RESOLUTIONS*
RESOLUTION #193, 2000 *BOOK OF RESOLUTIONS*

See Social Principles, ¶ 163G.

GLOBAL ECONOMIC JUSTICE

4051. The United Methodist Church, Food, Justice, and World Hunger

Isn't this the fast I choose: releasing wicked restraints, untying the ropes of a yoke, setting free the mistreated, and breaking every yoke? Isn't it sharing your bread with the hungry, and bringing the homeless poor into your house, covering the naked when you see them, and not hiding from your own family? Then your light will break out like the dawn, and you will be healed quickly. Your own righteousness will walk before you, and the Lord's glory will be your rear guard (Isaiah 58:6-8).

I. The Scope and Causes of World Hunger and Food Insecurity

Although globally enough food is produced to feed everyone, 805 million people are undernourished, 791 million (98%) of them in the developing world (State of Food Insecurity in the World

2014, FAO). Children and elderly are particularly at risk. Nearly half of all deaths in children under five are attributable to under-nutrition. This translates into the unnecessary loss of about 3 million young lives a year (http://www.data.unicef.org/nutrition/malnutrition#sthash.9k0zPUqe.dpuf).

It is estimated that 80% of the world's hungry live in rural areas and are largely dependent on agriculture for their livelihoods; approximately 50% are smallholder farmers cultivating marginal lands prone to natural disasters like drought or flood, 20% are landless families working on other people's land and 10% depend on herding, fishing or forest resources (World Food Program: <http://www.wfp.org/hunger/who-are>).

Over 2 billion people suffer from micronutrient deficiencies or "hidden hunger." Micronutrient deficiencies occur when diets fail to provide sufficient amounts of micronutrients such as iodine, iron, zinc, and vitamin A. Micronutrient deficiencies increase morbidity and mortality, impair cognitive development, reduce learning ability and productivity, and reduce work capacity in populations as a result of higher rates of illness and disability—resulting in a tragic loss of human potential. For example, around 50% of pregnant women in developing countries are iron deficient. Lack of iron means 315,000 women die annually from hemorrhage at childbirth (World Food Program: <http://www.wfp.org/hunger/who-are>).

The reasons for this continuing tragedy are complex and inter-related. Some causes of world hunger are:

- poverty, greed, drought and other weather-related problems, dwindling water sources, and environmental degradation;
- inequitable distribution of wealth and unjust economic systems;
- insufficient food production in developing nations;
- lack of access to basic means of production (seeds, tools, land, water) or the credit to obtain them;
- insecure tenure or title to productive land;
- high incidence of waterborne diseases due to lack of access to and use of safe water sources and adequate hygiene and sanitation facilities;
- food loss and waste—globally, roughly one-third of the food produced for human consumption, about 1.3 billion tons per year, are lost or wasted;

- use of arable land for nonfood and cash crops such as tobacco;
- increasing emphasis on export-oriented agriculture from poorer countries;
- overfishing of the oceans;
- population growth;
- displacement of people;
- production of unnecessary goods and services that waste resources, and wasteful consumerism in richer countries;
- militarism, war, and civil unrest;
- HIV/AIDS pandemic;
- corruption in governments;
- lending policies of the World Bank (IBRD) and the International Monetary Fund (IMF);
- use of farm subsidies in richer nations that export to poor countries causing poorer countries to reject their own products;
- lack of participation in decision-making processes and access to land, training, and agricultural inputs by women; and
- poor regulation of multinational corporations.

It is especially important to note that the causes of hunger are intricately related to the problems of poverty and greed. Hunger cannot be dissociated from people and systems that keep people in poverty.

II. Theological Bases for Action

The Bible reveals that, from the earliest times, God's faithful community has been concerned about hunger and poverty. Helping those in need was not simply a matter of charity, but of responsibility, righteousness, and justice (Isaiah 58:6-8; Jeremiah 22:3; Matthew 25:31-46). For example, the Israelites were commanded to leave the corners of their fields and the gleanings of harvests for the poor and aliens (Leviticus 19:9-10). Jesus taught that whatever people do to "the least of these," they also do him (Matthew 25:31-46). That Jesus was born to a poor, unmarried woman who was living in a small nation, occupied and oppressed by a mighty foreign empire, concretely reveals God's full identification with poor, powerless, and oppressed people.

As Christians, a key question that we must ask ourselves is: What does God require and enable us individually and corporately to do? We know that God loves and cares for all creation. Jesus stressed that the two greatest commandments were to love God and to love our neighbors as ourselves (Matthew 22:34-40). He also challenged the rich young ruler, who said he was keeping all of the commandments, to sell all of his possessions and give his money to the poor (Matthew 19:16-26).

Jesus' own concern for human need in his ministry is a model for the church's concern. His opposition to those who would ignore the needs of the neighbor makes clear that we grossly misunderstand and fail to grasp God's grace if we imagine that God overlooks, condones, or easily tolerates our indifference to the plight of our neighbors, our greed and selfishness, or our systems of injustice and oppression.

We believe that God's Holy Spirit continues to move today, refashioning lives, tearing down unjust structures, restoring community, and engendering faith, hope, and love. The work of the Holy Spirit impels us to take action, even when perfect solutions are not apparent. We engage in the struggle for bread and justice for all in the confidence that God goes before us and guides us. That struggle includes examination of our personal and congregational lives in the light of God's love and concern for all and Jesus' question, "Who is your neighbor?"

As United Methodists, we also look to our ongoing tradition of social concern. Methodism's founder, John Wesley, preached and wrote about the importance of simpler lifestyles. He emphasized ethical stewardship of time, money, and resources as important means to enable ministry with those suffering from hunger and poverty. Wesley preached the gospel to people who were poor, visited them, and lived with them. He donated most of the money that he earned—not just a tithe (10 percent of his income)—to the church and charitable ends.

In faithfulness to our understanding of God's good intentions for all peoples, we, as members of The United Methodist Church, set for ourselves, our congregations, institutions, and agencies no lesser goals than repentance for the existence of human hunger and increased commitment to end world hunger and poverty.

III. A Call for United Methodists

Change is not easy. Movement toward the abolishment of hunger, injustice, and poverty requires commitment and stamina. All nations, particularly the developed nations, must examine and modify those values, attitudes, and institutions that are the basic causes of poverty and underdevelopment, the primary sources of world and economic hunger and disease. United Methodists must act corporately and individually.

1. We call for The United Methodist Church to engage in an educational effort that would provide information about the scale of world and domestic hunger and its causes, and to engage in study and effort to integrate the church's missional programs into a coherent policy with respect to a just, sustainable, and participatory development.

2. We call for The United Methodist Church to develop effective public policy strategies and educate the constituency on hunger issues, through its appropriate agencies, that would enable church members to participate in efforts to:

a. decrease mother/child morbidity and mortality;

b. support community-based economic development that engages and empowers community members; creates sustainable livelihoods; recycles money within communities; provides low-cost, high-quality services to meet basic human needs; and combats unemployment and underemployment;

c. facilitate access to safe drinking water, sustainable water resource management systems, and dignified hygiene and sanitation facilities;

d. facilitate access to basic health information and care;

e. promote environmental justice, biodiversity, and sustainable practices for using and restoring natural resources;

f. support community organizing to effect change in systems that keep people poor and powerless;

g. ensure that women, youth, indigenous peoples, and other marginalized groups have equal access to the means of production, training, and economic opportunities.

h. organize and work to retain programs such as Women, Infants, and Children (WIC), Supplemental Nutrition Assistance Programs (SNAP), and food co-ops;

i. develop and implement policies that enable family farms to thrive, provide just wages and working conditions for farm workers, and provide incentives that enable and promote sustainable agriculture and equitable access to land by all;

    j. protect craftspeople and artisans from exploitative trade practices;

    k. become advocates for reduction of military spending and reallocation of resources to programs that provide human services, convert military facilities to provide for civilian needs, and protect and restore the environment; and

    l. become advocates of trade policies that alleviate economic disparities between rich and poor countries while protecting labor and human rights; environmental, health, and safety standards; and respecting the need for agricultural and food security.

3. We specifically call upon each local church, cooperative parish, district, and conference to:

    a. increase support of church and community agencies dedicated to empowering and training people to sustainably meet their food and economic needs at home and abroad;

    b. become involved in Fair Trade activism through efforts such as purchasing fair trade products from fair trade companies such as SERVV International, participating In UMCOR's Coffee Project through Equal Exchange, and asking grocery and specialty stores to carry fair trade coffee and other fair trade items. (more ideas are on Global Exchange's Web site at: http://www.globalexchange.org); and

    c. promote World Food Day, which is observed on October 16 (*see* http://www.worldfooddayusa.org or http://fao .org/world-food-day).

4. We call on United Methodists to strive for "Christian perfection" and to recover the Wesleyan tradition of simpler lifestyles and generosity in personal service and financial giving. Therefore, individuals are encouraged to:

    a. study and discuss John Wesley's sermons (and related scripture passages) that address "acts of mercy" and Christian stewardship, including "The More Excellent Way," "The Use of Money," "On the Danger of Riches," "On the Danger of Increasing Riches," "On Dress," and "On Visiting the Sick." (These sermons are available in books and online at http://uncmission.org/Find-Resources /John-Wesley-Sermons/John-Wesley-Sermons.)

    b. simplify their lifestyles, moving away from consumerism and toward caring;

    c. compost, recycle, conserve energy, practice or support organic gardening, and participate in other environment-friendly practices;

    d. commit themselves to give more of their time and money to programs that address hunger and poverty, including United Methodist Advance projects and UMCOR's World Hunger/Poverty Advance (#982920); and

    e. participate in projects such as "The Souper Bowl of Caring" and Bread for the World's annual "Offering of Letters."

5. We urge the General Board of Church and Society and the General Board of Global Ministries to:

    a. work with the Food and Agriculture Organization, the International Fund for Agricultural Development, International development organizations, and grassroots small farmer and peasant organizations for the right of everyone to have access to adequate safe and nutritious food acceptable within their culture. This would require many countries to implement genuine agrarian reforms that allow for the fair distribution of incomes, new management models which place human needs before profits, and access for the poor to land, natural resources, capital, and markets. Many developed countries would have to reform their agricultural subsidies programs.

    b. work with other churches and agencies in the United States and internationally:

        1) for the achievement of the United Nations Sustainable Development Goals that will succeed the United Nations Millennium Development Goals (MDGs) and will set targets for developing nations to contribute to substantial improvements in the developing world in the areas of basic education, infant and maternal mortality, clean water supplies and sanitation, gender equity, food and nutrition security, poverty reduction, environmental sustainability, and climate change adaptation; and

        2) to continue to urge governments to support the creation of an International Finance Facility (IFF) (beyond the smaller IFF that already exists to support immunizations) that would facilitate

transfer of private sector investment funds from industrialized nations to developing nations as a catalyst for quicker progress in achieving United Nations Sustainable Development Goals. The concept is that, in addition to regular aid flows, these private investments flowing from industrialized countries would be treated as a liabiliy of the countries from which the investment flowed, rather than a liability of the recipient country, and would be repaid eventually from the aid budget of the country from which the investment flowed. This approach will avoid increasing the debt burden of the poorer recipient nations and facilitate sustainable development (see, e.g., http://www .leadinggroup.org/rubrique179.html).

ADOPTED 2004
READOPTED 2008
AMENDED AND READOPTED 2016
RESOLUTION #4051, 2008, 2012 *BOOK OF RESOLUTIONS*
RESOLUTION #205, 2004 *BOOK OF RESOLUTIONS*

See Social Principles, ¶ *164A*.

4053. Global Debt Crisis: A Call for Jubilee

I. Introduction

Since the inception of the global Jubilee Campaign in 2000, we can celebrate important strides. The debt of 36 nations to the International Monetary Fund and the World Bank has been wiped out, with the proceeds going to fight poverty in these nations. Despite this important step, the global debt crisis continues to cripple poor countries. Countries in Africa, Asia, the Pacific, Latin America, and the Caribbean owe over $6 trillion, with debt in the poorest countries that received debt relief growing rapidly again. The global financial crisis of 2008-09 and the ensuing policy responses had and continue to have negative spillovers for the debt of developing countries. For many countries left behind by world leaders, the burden of repaying the debt continues to prevent them from providing adequate health care, education, and food for their people. This debt burden—often incurred illegitimately by dictators—inhibits the social and economic change that is needed to lift people out of poverty. Throughout the world there is a call for Jubilee, a call for debt cancellation in a Sabbath Year.

II. Biblical Foundation

Scriptures mandate periodically overcoming structural injustice and poverty and for restoring right relationships by forgiving debt and reforming land holding. In the earliest Sabbath traditions, consumption and exploitation of the land were limited by the Sabbath and the Sabbath year. People and animals were to rest every seventh day (Exodus 23:10-12). In the Sabbath year, there was to be release from debts and slavery and during the jubilee year, every fiftieth year, a restoration of all family lands (Leviticus 25). Fulfilling these commandments proclaims "the year of the LORD's favor" (Isaiah 61:1-2), and anticipates "a new heaven and a new earth" (Isaiah 65:17-25).

Jesus emphasized this jubilee vision of proclaiming good news to the poor, release of the captives, sight to the blind, and liberation of the oppressed (Luke 4:16-19). He taught his disciples to pray for the forgiveness of debts (as we forgive our debtors) (Matthew 6:12 NRSV). Pentecost results in the voluntary sharing of possessions, so that "there were no needy persons among them" (Acts 4:34; Deuteronomy 15:4).

The Sabbath tradition of the jubilee vision is as relevant today as it was thousands of years ago. Debt bondage by the poorest countries to rich nations and financial institutions is today's new slavery. The accelerating concentration of wealth for a few in the richest countries and the devastating decline in living standards in the poorest countries call for correction along the lines of the ancient Sabbath and Jubilee cycles. The social, political, and ecological costs of the debt crisis are intolerable and must be challenged and stopped. Only when we have implemented the Sabbath-Jubilee mandate can we "turn to God" and "rejoice in hope."

III. Causes of the Debt Crisis

The causes of the debt crisis are complex. Colonialism tied the developing world's economies to the export of agricultural, mineral, and other raw materials while creating a dependence on manufactured imported goods with higher and more stable prices than raw materials. When prices of raw materials are down, countries whose economies depend heavily on them for exports build debts to pay for basic imports. When they are up—as it has been the case recently—their apparently improved prospects lead them to contract large borrowing that cannot be paid back by relying on commodity exports alone and expose them to more debt when commodity prices swing back down again.

Another cause of the debt is the lack of transparency, accountability, and democratic processes in lending and borrowing practices. A growing number of governments is undertaking official audits to assess the legitimacy of debts. Odious debts can also result. When debts result from loans contracted without the knowledge or consent of the population, government officials used the money for personal purposes or to oppress their people, and these are facts that creditors knew or should have known, the resulting debts may be considered odious and creditors cannot legitimately expect their repayment. Examples of odious debt are money from loans stolen by the ruling elite of the then-Indonesian dictator Suharto; debts contracted by the apartheid regime of South Africa; and debts accrued during the dictatorial rule of Mobbutu Sese Seko in the Democratic Republic of Congo, Ferdinand Marcos in the Philippines, and the military junta in Argentina.

IV. Consequences of the Global Crisis—Everyone Loses

The World Bank and International Monetary Fund (IMF), the two main international financial institutions, lend money and reschedule the debt of poor countries. These loans to highly indebted poor countries come with conditions previously known as Structural Adjustment Programs (SAPs), however, and today most commonly referred as austerity. SAPs consisted of measures designed to help a country repay its debts by earning more hard currency, i.e., increasing exports and decreasing imports, and cutting budget deficits. While a few countries appear to have been helped by SAPs, poverty and inequality have increased in most countries due to the externally imposed programs. This is because, in order to obtain more foreign currency and cut budget deficits, governments implementing such policies usually must:

- reduce government spending, resulting in cuts in health care, education, and social services, forcing many people to go without;
- reduce inflation by limiting the money supply, oftentimes with contractionary effects on employment, credit and growth
- reduce or eliminate transportation and food subsidies — because of this, prices of essentials soar out of the financial reach of many citizens;
- reduce jobs and wages for workers in government industries and services;
- encourage privatization of public industries, which benefits the country's business elite and foreign investors;
- broaden the tax base often by introducing regressive tax reforms, such as sales taxes or taxes on the poorest informal sector; and
- shift agricultural and industrial production from food staples and basic goods for domestic use to commodities for export, which results in a transfer of land holdings from small subsistence farmers to large-scale agribusiness, leaving many farmers with no land to grow their own food and few are employed on these new cash-crop farms.

Children and women bear the full costs of debt repayment. In addition, by concentrating on exports in order to repay their debts, poor countries strip forests and overexploit land and non-renewable resources, further aggravating serious environmental problems. Reports on the impact of debt repayment show that many indebted governments spend two to four times as much money "servicing," that is, making timely interest and principal payments, their international debt as they spend on health care, such as basic medicines and clean water, and education combined.

These IMF and World Bank policies, by taking away indebted country's sovereignty, undermine accountability by debtor governments, which in turn erodes local democratic institutions.

Today, a growing part of the debt is owed to private, commercial lenders, which adds to the debt burden and its impoverishing impacts on people. Crises in countries like Argentina, several Caribbean and European nations, notably Greece, show that the world lacks adequate tools to properly restructure these types of debts. The consequences of private-led debt crises are no different from the crises that were driven by credits provided by public international financial institutions.

The debt burden carried by impoverished nations hurts everyone, including citizens of rich nations such as the United States. The environmental damage magnified by indebtedness, such as destruction of forests, has global repercussions. Growing poverty worsened by the debt is linked to the spread of disease. Indebted countries are forced to use scarce dollars for debt payments instead of importing goods and services. This directly affects jobs and incomes in the rich countries. Indebtedness creates the climate that fosters the production and trafficking of illicit drugs. Debt also causes an increase of economic migration. It should trouble the conscience of citizens of rich nations that people living in misery have to spend their money for debt servicing that they need for their own survival.

V. Principles to Guide Debt-Crisis Solutions

As Christians, our love of God and neighbor must be reflected by our actions within the global family. Thus, we affirm the following policies and principles as necessary to ensure a just resolution to the debt crisis:

We need to examine patterns of greed that may cause us as individuals and nations to become debtors and lenders. Debt cancellation and relief should be fashioned in a way that benefits the poor and helps move debtor nations to sustainable human development.

The poor should not bear the burden of repayment and structural adjustment. Living standards of those least responsible and most vulnerable should not be sacrificed in order to meet external obligations. As put by the Guiding Principles on Foreign Debt and Human Rights, adopted by the Human Rights Council in 2012, "Debtor States should ensure that their level of debt servicing is not so excessive or disproportionate relative to their financial capacity and other resources as to amount to a diversion of their resources away from the provision of social services to all persons living in their territory and under their jurisdiction, including those pertaining to economic, social and cultural rights" (Principle 48).

Developing countries have the right to choose their own development paths without military or economic interference from outside. They should not be forced to surrender their right to political or economic self-determination in exchange for relief.

The debt burden should be shared equitably among credit institutions and the debtor governments, corporations, banks, and elites that incurred the debt. Factors adding to and perpetuating the debt problem but beyond the control of debtor countries, such as previous US budget deficits, high interest rates, unfair commodity prices, and trade barriers, should be alleviated.

Long-term solutions should promote a more just international economic system and the restoration of revenues for poor populations through curbing illicit financial flows and corporate tax avoidance, in order to prevent such crises from recurring. New structures and mechanisms, involving participation and dialogue between creditors and debtors, including civil-society groups such as community and faith-based organizations are critically needed.

There is a need for a new just process of arbitration for international debt cancellation, such as the introduction of an international sovereign insolvency law that ensures creditors share in the burden of responsibility for losses and debtors can get sufficient debt relief.

New mechanisms involving civil society must produce ethical, mutually responsible, and transparent solutions that not only satisfy requirements for economic efficiency, but also for the protection of basic human needs and rights as well as protecting of the environment.

Where funds are released through debt cancellation or other relief measures, civil-society organizations must be enabled to take part in determining how monies are reallocated for social priorities.

VI. Recommended Actions for The United Methodist Church

The United Methodist Church, as a covenant community committed to Christian discipleship and advocacy with the poor, must work toward "measures that would reduce the concentration of wealth in the hands of a few" (¶ 163, 2008 *Book of Discipline*). Thus, the General Conference of The United Methodist Church:

1. celebrates the worldwide movement to cancel the crushing debt of the world's poorest countries and the participation of the General Board of Church and Society and the General Board of Global Ministries in the campaign;

2. recognizes even with the progress made to cancel the debt of impoverished countries, much more remains to be done: as debts are accumulating faster than they are being cancelled;

3. calls for the United States, governments of other leading industrial nations, private commercial lending institutions, and international financial institutions such as the World Bank and IMF to:

    a. cancel the debts of the poorest countries to enable them to meet human development goals, beginning with the Sustainable Development Goals;

    b. audit their lending portfolios, including loans made to middle-income countries, in order to assess the legitimacy of these loans;

    c. support measures to promote accountability of debtor countries when debts are relieved; these measures must be determined and monitored by local community organizations, including churches, and other communities of faith, and representative organizations of civil society, to ensure that debt cancellation leads to a more just distribution of wealth;

    d. promote the orderly resolution of debtor-creditor disputes in cases of crises, through mechanisms similar to a bankruptcy process;

    e. use their powers to ensure that funds illegitimately transferred to secret foreign bank accounts are returned to debtor nations; and

    f. engage, in consultation with civil society, in a process of global economic reform toward the development of responsible financing standards for a more just distribution of wealth and prevention of new cycles of debt;

    g. promote progressive, transparent and accountable tax systems backed by fully supportive international-tax cooperation.

4. urges the General Board of Church and Society and the General Board of Global Ministries to:

    a. work with annual and central conferences to become advocates for the above actions; and

    b. develop and distribute resources to annual conferences and local congregations.

5. urges United Methodist theological seminaries to include Christian responsibility for economic justice, including the global debt crisis, as a necessary part of education for ministry; and

6. urges the General Board of Church and Society and the General Board of Global Ministries to continue public policy work for major reforms of the International Monetary Fund, the World Bank, the World Trade Organization, and other international financial institutions to promote equitable development through poverty alleviation, protection of the environment, openness, democracy, and human rights.

ADOPTED 1988
REVISED AND READOPTED 2000, 2008, 2016
RESOLUTION #4053, 2008, 2012 *BOOK OF RESOLUTIONS*
RESOLUTION #207, 2004 *BOOK OF RESOLUTIONS*
RESOLUTION #198, 2000 *BOOK OF RESOLUTIONS*

See Social Principles, ¶ 163D, E.

4056. Greed

God's vision of abundant living is a world where we live out of a theology of "enough," a theology based in the knowledge that we are grounded in Christ, that our sense of personal value and esteem grows from our Christ-centered life. (The *Book of Resolutions* 2000, #188)

Scripture calls us to be compassionate and just stewards of our wealth and warns us of the sin of greed and its devastating effects. The Law ensured that the basic needs and rights of the poor were protected from the greedy (Exodus 23:6-11; Leviticus 25:35-55). The prophets warned that an economic system based on greed is contrary to God's will and leads to society's ruin (Amos 8:4-7; Jeremiah 22:13-17). Echoing the Law and the prophets, Jesus condemned the rich for the hypocrisy of greed and the barriers greed creates to attaining salvation (Luke 6:24; 16:1-15; Matthew 18:16-22). He taught that in God's economy that everyone would have enough (Matthew 13:31-32; 20:1-16). The early church rejected greed by sharing their wealth among their members (Acts 2:44-45). When their salvation was jeopardized by greed, Paul warned them that "the love of money is the root of all kinds of evil" (1 Timothy 6:6-10).

In our Wesleyan tradition, greed is an impediment to holiness. John Wesley taught and practiced that excessive wealth, absent of effective stewardship and radical charity, prevents a believer from growing in grace and cultivates sinful actions and attitudes.

Wesley said that greed is "destructive of that faith which is of the operation of God; of that hope which is full of immortality; of love of God and of our neighbor, and of every good word and work." ("The Danger of Riches" I.11)

Therefore, we follow in this Methodist tradition and oppose public policies that have encouraged speculation; and tax policies that have concentrated wealth. We oppose "free trade agreements that strengthen the movement of money and goods but do not permit the free movement of labor across borders. International trade agreements without strong, just systems for corporate accountability have often decimated local cultures and their social support systems and have deeply affected environmental and economic sustainability. The proposed Trans-Pacific Partnership also has weak environmental, community, and labor protections. We also support efforts to revise tax structures so that the wealthiest pay enough for all to have guaranteed social protections (Social Principles, ¶ 163; see also the 2012 *Book of Resolutions*, #4052, "Economic Justice for a New Millennium").

Call to Action:

At the General Church Level:

1. That the General Board of Global Ministries, the General Board of Church and Society, and United Methodist Women support national and international measures that reject trade agreements that encourage the free flow of capital across national lines without environmental, economic, and social regulations or provisions for labor migration. That we support policies that promote the social, economic, and political self-determinations of all nations and peoples.

2. That The United Methodist Church support progressive taxation to more equitably distribute income and wealth across all income brackets. This includes a focus on taxing income and property rather than taxes on items of daily consumption. Taxes on daily consumption disproportionately impact people with low incomes.

3. That The United Methodist Church increase its efforts toward debt cancellation for nations of the Global South and challenge usurious loan practices in the United States that push interest on those unable to pay, intensifying poverty.

4. That the General Board of Global Ministries, the General Board of Church and Society, and United Methodist Women work

with partners to support public policy that regulates global financial industry's currency speculation that has had a devastating impact on both developed and developing nations.

At the Local Church Level:

1. That local congregations challenge "overconsumption" in a culture that does not take into consideration the consequences of such consumption including disproportionate resource use and waste.

2. That local congregations examine their investments and endowment funds to determine how they can be better invested in underserved and impoverished communities with regards to community development, coops, credit unions, and projects concerning the affordability and accessibility of housing, healthy foods, and energy.

3. That local congregations advocate for just tax structures that ensure that all people have adequate resources for housing, affordable healthy food, clean water, energy, health care, and public transportation.

4. That the people called United Methodists search the Scriptures concerning systemic greed, pray for forgiveness where appropriate, and develop relationships of mutuality and reconciliation across class, status, race, gender, ability, sexual orientation, and age while advocating for a system that, like the early Christians and John Wesley, values a just distribution of our common resources.

ADOPTED 2004
READOPTED 2008
AMENDED AND READOPTED 2016
RESOLUTION #4056, 2008. 2012 *BOOK OF RESOLUTIONS*
RESOLUTION #211, 2004 *BOOK OF RESOLUTIONS*

See Social Principles, ¶ 163*A*, *D*, *E*

4057. Protecting Health Care, Labor, and Environment in Trade Negotiations

Since the time of the prophet Ezekiel (34:4), Scripture has clearly affirmed nations' obligation to heal the sick and bind up the injured. In addition, Scripture has condemned the exploitation of the poor and those who use judicial systems to crush the needy (Proverbs 22:22-23).

Under the World Trade Organization (WTO) and its General Agreement on Trade in Services (GATS) first negotiated in 1994, the concept of free trade has moved beyond the lowering of trade barriers at a country's borders, focusing now on what are called "internal barriers to trade." But what appear to trade interests to be barriers to trade are often laws and regulations passed by national, regional, and local legislatures to protect health care, labor, and the environment. Past WTO decisions have compromised Ontario's ability to discourage the sale of alcoholic beverages, Guatemala's ability to promote breast feeding in preference to use of infant formula, and Europe's ability to support public health by restricting the sale of hormone-treated beef. In negotiations for the Trans-Pacific Partnership in 2014, the United States continued to promote provisions permitting tobacco companies to sue countries that legislate against tobacco marketing in the interest of public health. Under existing trade agreements, tobacco companies have sued Australia's plain packaging law and Uruguay's tobacco health warnings. The United Methodist Church supports economic development around the globe, but we insist that economic development be sustainable, safeguard human beings and the environment, support the health of workers and communities, and provide a safety net for the most vulnerable among us.

We call upon governments around the world to take steps to protect the right of legislatures at all levels—national, regional, and local—to safeguard the health care, environment, and labor of their citizens. In countries like the United States where "fast track" legislation permits Congress to only give a yes or no to new trade legislation, Congressional leaders must involve themselves more in the trade negotiations or be prepared to vote no to the entire trade package when it is presented.

We call upon the General Board of Church and Society to represent these concerns before the US Congress, the United Nations, and the WTO, and to assist United Methodists in all nations to seek attention of their own governments to health care, labor, and environmental issues when trade issues are negotiated.

ADOPTED 2004
READOPTED 2008
AMENDED AND READOPTED 2016
RESOLUTION #4057, 2008, 2012 *BOOK OF RESOLUTIONS*
RESOLUTION #212, 2004 *BOOK OF RESOLUTIONS*

See Social Principles, ¶ 163I, J.

4058. Privatization

"The earth and its fullness are the Lord's" (1 Corinthians 10:26 NRSV). The Lord's people have been given enough-an abundance of all of the things we need for life.

"We believe [that] governments have the responsibility, in the pursuit of justice and order under law, to provide procedures that protect the rights of the whole society as well as those of private ownership" (Social Principles, ¶ 163A).

One of our values as Christians is to provide an economy that serves God's vision of abundance to all. Ecclesiastes 3:22 states, "So I saw that there is nothing better than that all should enjoy their work, for that Is their lot" (NRSV); Luke 10:7 and 1 Timothy 5:18 state "the laborer deserves to be paid" (NRSV). And it is written in Matthew 20:8, "Call the laborers and give them their pay" (NRSV).

Jesus singled out the poor, the sick, and the imprisoned for special care and made them the special responsibility of the faithful. Under many privatization schemes, responsibility by the public has been abandoned to private enterprise. Our responsibility to the sick and poor and imprisoned has been left to the devices of private profit. Privatized prisons, nursing homes, hospitals, welfare programs, and other social services have sometimes been less dedicated to service and rehabilitation than to cutting service and increasing profits (Resolution 4052, "Economic Justice for a New Millennium," *The Book of Resolutions of the United Methodist Church, 2008*).

"We are called to see that all life has a sufficient share of the resources of nature." (Resolution 1026, "Environmental Stewardship": Right to Abundant and Clean Water, *Book of Resolutions, 2008*).

Introduction

Corporate interests are rushing to privatize many of the resources of the earth—water, energy, education, natural plants, human and animal genes, cultures and public services such as social security, health care and public safety. Everything from prescription drugs to prisons to welfare programs is considered fair game for corporate profit-making. Wall Street, according to the Economic Policy Institute, is fighting hard for a privatized Social

Security system because it would reap an estimated 240 billion dollars in fees for managing these funds during the first twelve years of such a system.

Private Control

Supporters of privatization accuse government of inefficiency and claim that, if allowed to make a profit, these same corporations could control resources more effectively and efficiently, saving public money and delivering better services. The expectation of privatization is that government would continue to collect taxes from the citizens and then provide that tax money to corporate CEOs who would manage salaries, resources, and functions better. Those who favor privatization argue that they would earn a profit, benefit the economy, and be less encumbered by inefficient bureaucracy and public controls.

The World Bank is actively subsidizing the privatization of public resources worldwide. The World Trade Organization (WTO) has been quietly renegotiating and expanding the General Agreement on Trade in Services (GATS). The range of services on the negotiating table is vast, covering such vital areas as water and energy, banking, communications and retail services. Eighty additional countries have been targeted by the European Union for this invasion by foreign corporations. If governments refuse to cooperate, they may be faced with world trade disputes claiming "barriers to free trade."

Public Control

Opponents of privatization point to corporate abuses and criminality in the management of pensions, energy, and communications systems.

Those who favor continued public control and regulation of these common resources and services argue that, when private forces take control, there is less accountability to the citizens. They claim that ever-growing profits are the primary interest of the corporations. They also note that worker salaries and working conditions are usually forfeited in the name of efficiency and private profits. Loss of well-paid public sector jobs is a burden to society in many ways, including reduced tax revenues and increasing the need for social welfare programs.

People worldwide are challenging the privatization of commonly held resources such as native seeds and plants under intellectual property rules established under international financial institutions such as the WTO. Many are calling for public control of resources such as water and the drugs necessary for eradicating some of the world's most devastating diseases.

Discernment

There may be instances where privatization is appropriate. However, the role of Christians requires us to honor the earth's resources and to protect our God-given common heritage. The public must be vigilant to regulate and control the privatization and the profiteering of public resources.

New Laws to Protect Our Common Property

We have rules that protect our private property and our personal property. We also need strong, ethical governments and new laws to protect our common property—the resources that God has asked us to be stewards of and the common services that constitute the basis of human dignity, protected by human rights. Responsive governments must be strengthened and supported to provide protection for all, particularly in the most exploited and impoverished nations, but also those marginalized communities in wealthy nations. These are necessary as preconditions for all persons to experience the abundant life provided by God.

There are efforts by the international financial institutions to impose new rules that increase the private invasion of common property. The sovereignty of underdeveloped countries has been undermined by Rule 11 of NAFTA and will be further undermined by other free trade agreements such as the proposed Trans-Pacific Partnership (TPP) trade agreement. These trade rules strengthen the ability of private interests to force local communities to allow their free trade operations and privatization of common resources without effective regulation. Under Rule 11, if the governments move to regulate the activities of the corporations on behalf of their own workers or their own environment, they face multi-million dollar penalties in private trade courts unattended and unregulated by the public. These rules are increasing the poverty and devastation of communities worldwide.

The Need for Effective Governments

Effective and democratic governments worldwide must be strengthened in order to function on behalf of the interest of their citizens. Our common resources do not belong to government or market, but responsible and effective government is essential for protecting those public properties. Privatization of common property rights should be viewed as a "form of taking" from the people. For decades a body of international rules has been developing led by corporations that would challenge the rights of governments to protect their workers and their natural resources from corporate exploitation.

Call to Action

The United Methodist Church and its predecessors have always had a history of public witness on matters of economic justice. Faced with protecting and securing the common resources and services needed by all humanity, the General Conference calls upon:

1. The General Board of Global Ministries to develop an educational program on the issues posed by privatization worldwide and join in challenging privatization where it endangers public interest.

2. The boards and agencies of The United Methodist Church to create and disseminate materials explaining proposed trade agreements and oppose them when they violate United Methodist ideals supporting a just economy.

3. The General Board of Global Ministries and the General Board of Church and Society to continue to invigorate efforts to acquire national publicly-provided health care for everyone in the United States and that the issue of worldwide health care be put on the agenda for increased support.

4. Members of The United Methodist Church to urge our governments to challenge and change the International Monetary Fund (IMF), World Bank, and WTO rules supporting massive privatization.

5. The United Methodist Church to question the IMF investment of billions of public dollars into support for the efforts of private corporations to take over public services and public resources in countries that are impoverished.

6. The General Board of Global Ministries and the General Board of Church and Society to study ways of supporting world

trade rules that would protect our commons from the growing trend of "takings" by private entrepreneurs.

7. The General Board of Global Ministries and the General Board of Church and Society to lead an effort to discern the societal effects of privatized services and resources on marginalized communities and nations, with special attention paid to both the beneficiaries of such privatization and those individuals and groups whose quality of life is dramatically diminished. Focusing on the violence in the Democratic Republic of the Congo over resource management or the water crisis in Detroit, Michigan, would provide important case studies.

8. The General Board of Church and Society to provide studies and actions on the importance of responsible government and ways to enact good governance.

9. United Methodists to study and act in support of our local governments by insisting that the Federal budget provide for adequate tax money for running public services and regulating private service initiatives for the benefit of all.

ADOPTED 2004
READOPTED 2008
AMENDED AND READOPTED 2016
RESOLUTION #4058, 2008, 2012 *BOOK OF RESOLUTIONS*
RESOLUTION #361, 2004 *BOOK OF RESOLUTIONS*

See Social Principles, ¶ 163*I*

4061. Enabling Financial Support for Domestic Programs

The United Methodist Church has a long history of advocacy for causes that support the well-being of all, including women, children, and people of all races. Since the earliest of our Social Creeds, we have affirmed these shared values. Our Christian faith has always compelled us to carry special concern for people living in poverty, from Deuteronomy's commands to care for the widows and orphans to Jesus' shocking revelation that we are caring for him when we care for the "least of these" in our midst (Matthew 25).

The United Methodist Church also has a long history of teaching and advocating for peace, and for resistance to the violence of war. Our Social Principles clarify that we find war to be "incompatible with the teachings of Jesus Christ," as revealed in Matthew 5:38-42 and Isaiah 2:4.

Contemporary challenges in all our nations would be served by governmental spending in areas that address immediate and long-term human need and invest in solutions that overcome inequalities currently based on dividing characteristics like race, socioeconomic level, and region. Unemployment—particularly among minority ethnic groups—lack of access to education and educational inequalities among racial and ethnic groups and the poor, and lack of access to health care are all too common tragic consequences of current funding priorities.

Concurrently, alarming portions of resources in many of our nations are devoted to military spending. Everywhere around the world, we caution our nations in their use of national resources for the proliferation of weapons and the preparation for war.

Particularly, we lament the dedication of vast federal funding in the United States to fund ongoing wars and interventions in foreign countries, and the ever-increasing dependence of the industrial sector on military spending. Additionally, we note the continuing practice of funding US military action with deficit spending, a policy that borrows from future generations and threatens long-term stability.

We call upon our governments to reduce spending on militaries. Particularly, we call on the US government to take significant measures in reducing military spending, both on wars and on its ongoing operations.

We call upon our governments to reapportion national revenue diverted from military spending, prioritizing domestic programs that invest in the needs of a nation's people and invest in the future by providing opportunities and services to those people. We support programs that increase the quality of educational offerings in public school systems, improve access to health care for all, create affordable housing, and support creation of employment opportunities and training programs. In particular, we urge governments to support these domestic programs whether they be government programs or private programs funded in part by government funds in ways that will reduce social inequalities based on gender, race, ethnicity, background, or any other factor.

ADOPTED 2012
RESOLUTION #4061, 2012 *BOOK OF RESOLUTIONS*

See Social Principles, ¶ 163.

4062. Create a Worldwide Peace Economy

The United Methodist Church supports a Peace Economy for every country on planet earth.

We recognize as the Honorable Dwight D. Eisenhower stated, "Every gun that is made, every warship launched, every rocket fired signifies, in the final sense, a theft from those who hunger and are not fed, those who are cold and are not clothed. This world in arms is not spending money alone. It is spending the sweat of its laborers, the genius of its scientists, the hopes of its children. . . . This is not a way of life at all in any true sense. Under the cloud of threatening war, it is humanity hanging from a cross of iron."

We remember the prophecy of the Rev. Dr. Martin Luther King, Jr., "When a nation continues year after year to spend more money on military defense than on programs of social uplift, it is approaching spiritual death."

We understand the preaching of this truth by Jesus, who is called the Prince of Peace, ". . . all those who use the sword will die by the sword" (Matthew 26:52*b*).

Therefore,

1. We call upon world leaders to order a thorough review of weapons systems and other military spending programs with the objective of bringing about at least a 25 percent reduction in financial expenditures and the number of armed forces without cuts that harm veterans and their families.

2. We call upon world leaders to reinvest those financial resources, which derive from taxes and borrowing, in societal improvement programs such as food security, health care, clean energy, housing, education, and the development of infrastructure.

3. We call upon the leaders of our congregations such as lay leaders to advocate for such a Peace Economy as they lead their congregations.

4. We call upon congregations to network with local peace, environmental, health care, educators, and other groups to lobby their local and national leaders to create a Peace Economy.

ADOPTED 2012
RESOLUTION #4062, 2012 *BOOK OF RESOLUTIONS*

See Social Principles, ¶ 163.

4063. A Call for Just Tax Structures

Biblical and Theological Foundation

The Law of Moses expresses God's expectation that society should care for its most vulnerable members both by refraining from exploiting them and by providing for their basic needs. The prophet Amos reminds the covenant community of God's expectations and rebukes his society for oppressing, trampling, and even crushing the poor and needy (Amos 2:6-8; 4:1, and 8:4-6). Amos gives voice to God's demand for just and equitable taxation as he cries out: "Because you crush the weak, / and because you tax their grain, / you have built houses of carved stone . . . / I know [you who are] afflicting the righteous, / taking money on the side, / turning away the poor who seek help" (Amos 5:11-12).

In the early church, all participants brought their gifts to the community with the understanding that everything should be shared according to everyone's needs (Acts 4:32-35). While this was voluntary behavior that was not implemented everywhere as the Christian movement expanded, the principle/value remains valid to Christian understanding of living in community with each other.

In today's world, we recognize and affirm the vital role of governments in ordering society and enabling us to do together that which none of us could do alone. Tax laws enable us to embody our Judeo-Christian values of equal opportunity for all and care for the poor. They are necessary to provide adequate revenue that supports our shared commitment to a just society, including the maintenance of a safety net of services and opportunities for those most in need. (See the work of United Methodist layperson, Susan Pace Hamill, professor of law at the University of Alabama.) Taxation allows us to create systems that prevent our societies from descending to the tempting sin of greed. Unfortunately, current tax structures often have perpetuated rather than addressed economic injustices and have failed to provide sufficient revenue for the health, safety, educational, and welfare needs of our communities. Recent economic research ties unregulated market forces to increased inequality, justifying government tax interventions to more equitably distribute economic gains (Thomas Piketty, *Capital in the Twenty-First Century*).

Current Concerns

The gap between the rich and poor continues to widen world-wide. The eighty-five richest people in the world control as much wealth as the poorest half of the world (source: Oxfam). As our Companion Litany to Our Social Creed states: "God cries with the masses of starving people, despises growing disparity between rich and poor. . . . And so shall we."

The challenges of establishing fair and just tax systems are global. While some nations offer stronger social safety nets funded through more equitable tax systems, everywhere the forces of power and privilege seek to change structures to their benefit, oftentimes at the expense of our poorest and most vulnerable brothers and sisters. In our world economy, too often those individuals and corporations with the most wealth are most able to avoid the social responsibility of taxes by finding exemptions in local tax law or by using varied nations' tax regulations.

Given the clear injustice of many tax structures and growing disparity between rich and poor, we affirm the need to reform these tax structures. Our Social Principles state our support for "efforts to revise tax structures and to eliminate governmental support programs that now benefit the wealthy at the expense of other persons" (¶ 163).

Principles for Tax Reform

The United Methodist Church calls for changes to current tax systems to better embody the following faithful principles:

Protecting the Poor and Vulnerable: All tax decisions must be judged by their impact on children, low-income families, the elderly, people with disabilities, and other vulnerable populations. Taxes should be applied to a market activity that causes cost upon others or upon a public good (for example, clean air). Additional taxes should be levied on products that are damaging, such as tobacco, alcohol, and weapons.

Community: Systems should strengthen and uphold values of our common life together. Any nation's well-being is dependent on that of all its members. Tax and revenue systems enable governments to provide for the needs of the common good and should not give privilege to wealth earned through investment over wealth earned by labor.

Justice: Each government should ensure that both the burdens and the benefits of a nation's common life are shared equitably and proportionally among its citizens. Laws should address inequalities not institutionalize them.

We call for a global treaty to prevent transnational avoidance of taxation.

ADOPTED 2016

See Social Principles, ¶ 163.

4064. A Call for Faithful Lending Practices

Biblical and Theological Foundation

The Bible is consistent in its witness that God desires humans to live together in authentic community: in an economy of abundance in which neighbors love and care for each other and no one lives in scarcity. God created humankind to inhabit the good earth on which God amply supplied the needs of all creatures (Genesis 1). In the Sinai covenant, God commanded the people of Israel to refrain from usury and to care for the most vulnerable among them (Exodus 22:25; Deuteronomy 26:12). Isaiah, Amos, Micah, and other prophets warned the people of Israel to honor God by seeking justice for the poor. Jesus Christ taught his followers to treat others as they would want to be treated (Matthew 7:12), and he warned against measuring the abundance of life by possessions (Luke 12:15). The earliest Christian community lived with "all things in common" (Acts 2:44).

In the General Rules, John Wesley warned Methodists against doing harm by greedy or self-indulgent behaviors, including "the giving or taking things on usury," and "borrowing without a probability of paying; or taking up goods without a probability of paying for them" (United Methodist *Book of Discipline*, ¶ 104).

Current Concerns

Today's global economy is premised on credit involving individuals, businesses, and institutions that exchange goods and services with the promise of future payment. This credit market has enhanced efficiency and brought many consumer benefits. These markets have also given rise to abusive and predatory practices, however, that challenge the conscience of Christians. Among our most pressing concerns are contemporary financial practices and business models that entrap people in cycles of debt. These practices are exacerbated by lenders employing tactics to exempt themselves from banking regulation and traditional usury laws.

These practices include:

- Operations that profit by charging unconscionable rates of interest, often disguising the costs as "fees" rather than "interest," thereby exempting themselves from financial oversight and effectively extracting very high rates of return at the expense of the borrower;
- Bank and credit agency fees that entrap consumers into schedules of penalties that charge the equivalent of interest rates up to 1,000 percent for "services"; and
- Plans in which consumers are enrolled without knowledge or consent. In addition, consumers are burdened with hidden transfer charges, inappropriately large late fees, and sudden-rising interest rates.

Credit card marketing practices and convoluted contract agreements lack transparency and clarity on full pricing, fees, and alterations to the terms of agreement.

Our history of concern for the poor calls us to be attentive to these alternative banking systems that are often the way people living closer to the economic margins find space to participate in our economy. We call our congregations to investigate the current situations in their communities, states, and nations. We call our congregations to demand that our systems be regulated in a way that does not profit the rich at the expense of the poor, that benefits both parties involved in the transaction, and that has integrity in that it is characterized by honesty, disclosure, equal access, and equal power to begin or end the transaction. We advocate the establishment of bankruptcy laws that provide a full opportunity to be released from debilitating debt and enable individuals or families to restore financial stability.

We call on United Methodist members, churches, institutions, and agencies to adhere to and advocate for the following faithful principles:

- Promoting honesty, clarity, transparency, and evenhandedness. All sides should have the same opportunity to understand and negotiate a contract. Kickbacks and fees should be eliminated that distort lender and broker incentives to deal fairly with customers.

- Prohibiting unconscionable rates of interest. Usury caps should be reinstated to address abusive lending.
- Holding lenders accountable for only funding loans that borrowers have a reasonable ability to repay.
- Establishing equity in credit across communities. Practices must be ended that particularly burden communities of color or low-income communities.
- Limiting fee-based penalties and business models that depend on consumer overspending and recurrent indebtedness. Penalties against repaying debts early should be eliminated.

ADOPTED 2016

See Social Principles, ¶ 163J.

INVESTMENTS

4071. Investment Ethics

Churches in the Wesleyan tradition have a long history of witness for justice in the economic order. John Wesley and the early Methodists, for example, were firmly opposed to the slave trade, to smuggling and to conspicuous consumption. Beginning in 1908, social creeds adopted by our predecessor churches focused attention especially on working conditions and child labor.

For decades, the Church has promoted safe and humane working conditions and the right to organize and bargain collectively. It has opposed discrimination in the workplace based on race, ethnic background, gender, age, or disability as well as investing in companies whose products and services violate United Methodist values. Recently, the Church has promoted sustainable and socially responsible corporate environmental practices and heightened stewardship of the natural world.

Because every financial investment has ethical dimensions with consequences that are both fiscal and social, The United Methodist Church believes that social justice concerns must be given consideration together with financial security and financial yield in the investment of funds by individuals, churches, agencies, and institutions in the United Methodist family.

Consequently, General Conference has instructed all Church-related investors to "make a conscious effort to invest in institutions, companies, corporations, or funds whose practices are consistent with the goals outlined in the Social Principles. . . ." This values-aligned investment philosophy is based soundly on the biblical concept that all resources are God-given and may be used to promote the reign of God on earth both now and into the future.

In recent years, leaders across The United Methodist Church have identified four areas of focus to continue and deepen the transforming work of Methodism in the world (Engaging in Ministry with the Poor, Improving Global Health, Developing Principled Christian Leaders, Creating New and Renewed Congregations). Investors in the Church community are well-positioned to promote the Church's ministry in two of the focus areas: Engaging in Ministry with the Poor and Improving Global Health

Preamble

The United Methodist Church strongly urges all of its member institutions to invest in a sustainable and socially responsible manner, which is an investment discipline that integrates environmental, social, and corporate governance (ESG) factors to achieve suitable financial returns and positive societal and environmental impact. Investing sustainably demands that United Methodist investors consider the moral and ethical dimensions, as specified in the Social Principles, of the policies and practices of the institutions in which they invest. They must also be cognizant of their fiduciary obligations as stipulated in the *Book of Discipline*.

Trustees, individuals, and committees responsible for the oversight of United Methodist assets are first legally bound to execute their responsibilities in a prudent manner. This responsibility is broadly referred to as "fiduciary duty." The *Book of Discipline* is consistently clear in its directive to local churches, boards, and agencies at all levels of the denomination that these entities must discharge their fiduciary duties in conformity with the laws of the country, state, or like political unit in which they are located.

However, fiduciaries must also be mindful of ¶ 717 of the *Book of Discipline* that states it shall be the policy of The United Methodist Church that these same denominational entities *"make a **conscious*** *effort* (emphasis added) *to invest in institutions, companies, corporations, or funds whose practices are consistent with the goals outlined in the Social Principles. . . ."* This two-tier directive presents both unique challenges and opportunities to those responsible for investing United Methodist assets.

Socially Responsible Investment Policy Goals for The United Methodist Church's Investment Community

The United Methodist Church aspires to have members of its investment community pursue the following investment policy goals, reflecting Church values and financial responsibilities:

1.   avoid investments in companies whose products and/or services are not aligned with the Social Principles of The United Methodist Church;

2.   seek investments in corporations, companies, institutions, funds, or ventures making a positive contribution to the realization of the goals outlined in the Social Principles and the *Book of Resolutions*;

3.   promote sustainable and socially responsible investment practices by integrating environmental, social, and governance (ESG) factors into the investment decision-making process;

4.   influence corporations to manage ESG issues in their operations and to be transparent in monitoring and documenting these practices in public reports;

5.   seek investments in corporations, companies, institutions, funds, or ventures whose policies and practices help protect the natural world by, among other things, recycling, eliminating toxic chemicals and materials, and reducing greenhouse gas emissions; and pursue investments in companies that provide products, technology, and services that seek to increase energy efficiency and mitigate and/or adapt to climate change.

6.   pursue investments in corporations, companies, institutions, funds, or ventures with positive records in hiring and promoting women and persons of color and/or that are owned by women, racial and ethnic persons, or other underrepresented segments of society;

7.   pursue investments in financial institutions, non-gambling-related economic enterprises and development projects that

support and/or are owned by Native American and indigenous communities;

8. pursue investments in underserved communities through affordable housing and community development projects;

9. seek investments in corporations, companies, institutions, funds, or ventures that respect international human rights and labor standards by avoiding the manufacture, or purchase through subcontracting, of products made with sweatshop, forced, or child labor and adhering to business practices detailed in the Universal Declaration of Human Rights, the United Nations Global Compact, the United Nations Guiding Principles on Business and Human Rights (also known as the Ruggie Principles), and the International Labour Organization's core labor standards; and encourage companies that have not adopted the foregoing standards to do so;

10. encourage companies to promote the responsible use of their products and encourage them to raise concerns with the customers who knowingly use their products in a manner not aligned with United Methodist values;

11. seek investments in companies that publish and enforce supplier codes of conduct and hold suppliers accountable for any breaches of conduct;

12. seek investments in corporations, companies, institutions, funds, or ventures located in or dedicated to alleviating poverty in developing countries, provided that those countries respect human and labor rights and have a record of pursuing improvements in national living standards while working to maintain ecological integrity;

13. pursue opportunities to encourage companies to work in partnerships to address major health challenges, including treatment for HIV/AIDS, tuberculosis, and malaria and to promote access to medicines and global health care;

14. endeavor to commend corporations for their transparency, disclosure, sustainable and socially responsible business practices, and efforts to raise industry standards on ESG issues that are of major concern to The United Methodist Church; and

15. actively evaluate external consultants, investment advisors, and funds regarding their commitment to sustainable and socially responsible investment practices and diversity within their workforce and governance structure.

Investment Strategies

The United Methodist Church's investment community is encouraged to use widely practiced sustainable and socially responsible investment strategies to fulfill its investment policy goals. These include:

1. Avoidance ("Screening" or "Ethical Exclusions")

United Methodist investors should endeavor to exclude from their investment portfolios companies whose products or services do not align with longstanding Church values and/or ethical considerations in accordance with ¶ 717 of the *Book of Discipline*.

2. Advocacy ("Engagement" or "Active Ownership")

The Social Principles (*Book of Discipline* ¶ 163I) recognize that "corporations are responsible not only to their stockholders, but also to other stakeholders: their workers, suppliers, vendors, customers, the communities in which they do business, and for the earth, which supports them." Companies may meet the broad investing guidelines of the Church but still fall short of the goals outlined in the Social Principles and the *Book of Resolutions*.

United Methodist investors, therefore, should endeavor to be active owners, engaging the companies in which they invest to manage ESG issues and exhibit high standards of corporate responsibility.

Engagement with companies may take many forms, including written communications, dialogues (including face-to-face meetings), proxy voting, and the filing of shareholder resolutions.

Sustainable and socially responsible investment is also dependent on actions beyond engagement with individual corporations and may involve influencing public policy and regulatory bodies where the long-term sustainability of investment funds can be enhanced and priority ESG issues can be addressed.

3. Positive Impact Investments

Some investments may be designed to achieve specific positive outcomes, such as the construction of affordable housing, the renewal of neighborhoods or the provision of clean energy. United Methodist investors are encouraged to pursue such opportunities around the world.

4. Strategic Partnerships

Working in collaboration with like-minded partners strengthens and magnifies sustainable and socially responsible investment voice. Strategic partners may include United Methodist boards, agencies, foundations and universities, other faith-based investors, domestic and global nongovernmental organizations, and other global sustainable and socially responsible investors, such as signatories to the the United Nations Principles for Responsible Investment (PRI).

5. Divestment

Divestment is a strategy available to investors but it should be considered an investment strategy of last resort. Shareholder advocacy/engagement—though it takes time—generally is a more effective and constructive way to influence corporate decision-making.

Investing Guidelines for Program Agencies

The General Council on Finance and Administration (GCFA) is responsible for preparing and distributing the investment guidelines that are to be used by all general agencies receiving general Church funds. GCFA shall review and update these guidelines periodically, inviting the input of the agencies and other interested sectors of the Church. GCFA encourages investing agencies to be involved actively in the overview of sustainable and socially responsible investing as described in this policy.

Each general agency receiving general Church funds shall provide GCFA with a copy of its investment policy. The policy shall be made available upon request to any interested member of the Church.

All organizations affiliated with The United Methodist Church, including annual conferences, local churches, foundations, healthcare systems, colleges, and universities, are strongly urged to follow these guidelines and to make public, either on the Internet or by request, their specific investing policies. Investing organizations may want to consider disclosing all of their sustainable and socially responsible investing activities on publicly accessible websites.

Where financial considerations preclude immediate exclusion of securities held in violation of the above policies, the affected boards, agencies, and institutions of The United Methodist Church shall develop a plan for complying with the guidelines no later than the 2020 General Conference.

All United Methodist investors and users of financial services, whether institutional or individual, are strongly encouraged to use these guidelines.

ADOPTED 1992
AMENDED AND ADOPTED 2000
AMENDED AND READOPTED 2004, 2008, 2012, 2016
RESOLUTION #4071, 2008, 2012 *BOOK OF RESOLUTIONS*
RESOLUTION #213, 2004 *BOOK OF RESOLUTIONS*
RESOLUTION #202, 2000 *BOOK OF RESOLUTIONS*

See Social Principles, ¶ 163D.

POVERTY

4094. Support of NETWorX

Whereas, poverty continues to abound in the USA, especially in the rural areas where the average national rate is 18.4 percent, and in the urban areas where the rate is 15.4 percent compared to the national average of 14.5 percent (USDA Economic Research Service);

Whereas, The United Methodist Church has had as one of its four Areas of Ministry Focus: Engaging in Ministry with the Poor;

Whereas, this focus emphasizes "with"—standing with those who are regarded as "the least of these," listening to them, understanding their needs and aspirations, and working with them to achieve their goals;

Whereas, United Methodists believe working side by side with those striving to improve their situation is more effective long term than top-down charity;

Whereas, the Council of Bishops at the May 2015 meeting in Berlin affirmed the intent to build on and extend the Four Areas of Focus adopted in 2008 and for 2017-2020 would provide a missional direction for the next quadrennium, which includes partnering with schools to help end poverty;

Whereas, for the past eight years, beginning in 2007, Rural Faith Development CDC as an affiliate of the Western North Carolina Annual Conference has been in engaged with transformational ministry with the poor across NC;

WHEREAS, at the request of other conferences and with leadership from across the USA, RFD has created a Wesleyan informed initiative with a measurable outcome of well-being of abundance that is measured in many dimensions: cognitive, physical, emotional, social, spiritual, and financial;

WHEREAS, the very being of NETworX is encompassed in a mutual commitment to the core values of

Love—The foundational value for NETworX is love—love of neighbor,

Transformation—A belief in transformation and the importance of faith further define the power of this love; and

WHEREAS, these values are acted out with accountability, transparency, authenticity, acceptance, and inclusiveness; now,

Therefore, be it resolved, that General Conference encourages bishops, annual conferences, and agencies to support local groups of United Methodist congregations to work or be in ministry with the poor and to consider NETworX initiatives.

ADOPTED 2016

See Social Principles, ¶ 163E.

STEWARDSHIP ISSUES IN THE CHURCH

4101. Living Wage Model

Throughout Scripture, God commands us to treat workers with respect, dignity, and fairness. Exploitation or underpayment of workers is incompatible with Christ's commandment to love our neighbor—a love that extends to all persons in all places, including the workplace. The Old Testament and New Testament include explicit warnings to those who would withhold fair pay to workers. "How terrible for [him] . . . working his countrymen for nothing, refusing to give them their wages" (Jeremiah 22:13). "Listen! Hear the cries of the wages of your field hands. These are the wages you stole from those who harvested your fields. The cries of the harvesters have reached the ears of the Lord of heavenly forces" (James 5:4).

A century ago, the Methodist Episcopal Church, in adopting the first social creed, responded to this call for worker justice by proclaiming support for "a living wage in every industry" (1908 Social Creed). In the global community of the twenty-first century, the Church has no choice but to be concerned about and involved in issues of globalization including the impact of changing global economic structures on workers. A living wage in a safe and healthy workplace with reasonable hours of work is a universal right not restricted by national borders. Therefore, The United Methodist Church reaffirms its historic support for the living wage movement and calls upon businesses and governments to adopt policies to ensure employees are paid sufficient wages to afford shelter, food, clothing, health care, and other basic expenses, according to local costs of living. United Methodists will work in partnership with persons, communities, and governments everywhere around the world to bring about the creation of conditions that encompass fundamental workers' rights, fair wages, a safe and healthy workplace, reasonable hours of work, decent living standards, support for community infrastructure, and commitment to community economic development.

In calling for a living wage in every industry, The United Methodist Church recognizes its own responsibility to model fair and faithful compensation. To this end, The United Methodist Church adopts the living wage as a model for justice in the world and in the household of faith, holding all levels of the church accountable to adjust compensation for all employees, including support staff, to effect the following:

- reflect the local cost of living;
- reduce disparity between top and bottom wage earners;
- provide for adequate health coverage for employees and their dependents;
- provide mechanisms for training, promotion, and advancement for all United Methodist employees at all levels; and
- ensure that fair and consistently applied personnel policies pertain to all employees of The United Methodist Church and its agencies.

ADOPTED 2000
REVISED AND READOPTED 2008, 2016
RESOLUTION #4101, 2008, 2012 *BOOK OF RESOLUTIONS*

RESOLUTION #217, 2004 *BOOK OF RESOLUTIONS*
RESOLUTION #210, 2000 *BOOK OF RESOLUTIONS*

See Social Principles, ¶ 163*B, C.*

WORKERS' RIGHTS

4134. Rights of Farm Workers in the US

The cries of the harvesters have reached the ears of the Lord of heavenly forces.

—James 5:4*b*

Throughout Scripture we are taught the importance of respecting and rewarding work. The prophets decried economic systems that denied workers fair compensation and dignity and Christ's ministry was centered on those individuals marginalized by society. Today, workers whose hands gather the fruits of God's good earth are among the most marginalized—both economically and socially—in our communities. As the cries of the harvesters continue, we are called as a church to respond.

Farm workers are the men, women, and children who climb for our apples, oranges, and peaches, stoop for our cucumbers and strawberries, and dig for our sweet potatoes. The overwhelming majority of fruits and vegetables in the United States are hand-picked by some of the nation's most vital workers, essential to the economic well-being of the United States. While conditions have improved for some farm workers through successful, and long-fought, organizing campaigns, the majority of farm workers continue to struggle with low wages, minimal legal protections, and unhealthy work environments.

The average income of the nearly two million farm workers in the United States is between $10,000 and $12,499 (Source: National Farm Worker Ministry and National Agricultural Survey). In some areas workers earn significantly less, often paid by piece rate, earning as little as forty cents per bucket of tomatoes or sweet potatoes collected. Women may receive less pay than men for the same work and face sexual discrimination, harassment, and abuse by crew leaders who control their jobs.

Agriculture is consistently ranked as one of the most dangerous occupations in the United States. Farm workers face pesticide risks and suffer from the highest rate of toxic chemical injuries and skin disorders of any workers in the country. Children in the fields are particularly susceptible to the hazards of pesticides, and women who work in the fields have given birth to babies with severe birth defects, attributed by many to pesticide exposure. In recent years, workers across the United States have died in fields nationwide from heat exposure combined with lack of drinking water, shade, or breaks.

Farm workers face numerous obstacles to receiving health care including lack of transportation, lack of paid sick leave and risk of job loss if they miss work. Only a small number of them are covered by health insurance. Most farm workers are immigrants who have come to the United States to seek a better life for their families. Many here today were once farmers in their own countries who have been driven from their land, unable to compete with the price of subsidized crops from the United States. The majority of farm workers are undocumented and with strict enforcement of the southern US border, many have not seen their families for years. An increasing number of farm workers arrive through the H2-A agricultural guest worker program, some from as far away as Thailand. Isolated in remote labor camps without transportation, these workers are in particular need of outreach, support, and ministry from the community.

Farm workers were excluded from federal laws passed in the 1930's to protect workers, such as the National Labor Relations Act and those mandating overtime pay and minimum wage. Few states require overtime pay for farm workers and minimum wage statutes apply to workers on large farms only. Laws designed to protect farm workers are often not enforced. Furthermore, workers often fear firing or deportation if they speak up about abuses.

When asked what farm workers expected from churches, Cesar Chavez responded, "We wanted the church to be present with us, beside us, willing to sacrifice for justice, ready to be Christ among us."

Farm workers call on us to stand in solidarity with them to change unjust conditions and scripture calls us to respond. As Christians, we cannot sit silently as our brothers and sisters are exploited and abused, but rather following the teachings of Christ we must ensure that the men and women who harvest our food are invited to share fully in the fruits of their labor.

The United Methodist Church:

- publicly denounces any and all mistreatment of farm workers and repents of any complicity that we hold as consumers and often-silent participants in and beneficiaries of an exploitive food production and distribution system;
- demands that employers treat farm workers and their families with dignity and respect; and that corporate processors, food retailers, and restaurants take responsibility in proportion to the power they possess for the treatment of the farm workers in their supply chains;
- advocates for policies that ensure the workers who harvest food for US families are not separated from their own families;
- calls on the General Board of Church and Society, the General Board of Global Ministries, annual conferences, and local churches to support state and federal legislation, particularly initiatives developed by farm-worker organizations, that would strengthen the laws protecting farm workers' rights and provide the funding necessary for adequate enforcement of laws protecting farm workers' rights, health, and safety;
- celebrates that farm worker organizing campaigns have resulted in labor agreements producing significant change in farm workers' lives, including wage increases, benefits, pesticide protection, and treatment with respect;
- commits itself to work in cooperation with the National Farm Worker Ministry whose primary mission is supporting farm workers organizing for justice and empowerment;
- urges annual conferences, especially where farm workers live and work, to use personal and institutional resources to encourage recognition of farm workers' rights to a voice in the agricultural industry, including representation and good faith bargaining;
- urges local churches to identify and reach out to farm workers in their communities, including those in the H2-A guest worker program;

- urges local faith communities, through worship, education, and calls to action, to remember and honor farm workers for the work they do and the hope they offer us through their courage, persistence, and faith; and
- urges the United Methodist Committee on Relief to consider the needs of farm workers when administering relief efforts.

ADOPTED 2008
AMENDED AND READOPTED 2016
RESOLUTION #4134, 2008, 2012 *BOOK OF RESOLUTIONS*
RESOLUTION #236, 2004 *BOOK OF RESOLUTIONS*
RESOLUTION #223, 2000 *BOOK OF RESOLUTIONS*

See Social Principles, ¶ 163H.

4135. Rights of Workers

I. Biblical/Theological Background

Human beings, created in the image of God, have an innate dignity (Genesis 1:27). Commanding human beings to farm and take care of the earth, God granted dignity to the work of human hands (Genesis 1:28, 2:15). Work remains a means of stewardship and God-given creativity.

Throughout Scripture, God orders life together based on right relationships, shared resources, and economic justice. In the very act of creation, God demonstrates time for work and rest. The Hebrew prophets decry the growing disparities of wealth and poverty. The Book of Acts describes an early Christian community that shared its goods with one another. The basic principles are clear: All human beings should be treated with respect and dignity. Thus, those who work should earn wages that sustain themselves and their families. Employers have a particular responsibility to treat workers fairly and empower them to organize to improve conditions.

The concern of The United Methodist Church for the dignity of workers and the rights of employees to act collectively is stated in the Social Principles. Both employer and union are called to "bargain in good faith within the framework of the public interest" (¶ 163B). In response to the increasing globalization of the economic system, the widening disparity between rich and poor, and attempts to deprive workers of their fundamental rights, the church reaffirms its position in support of workers and their right to organize.

II. Historic Witness of The United Methodist Church

Historically, The United Methodist Church has been concerned about the plight of working men and women. In the United States, we were among the first supporters of the labor movement where both lay and clergy members played leadership roles in supporting garment workers, textile workers, farm workers, and factory workers and advocating passage of the Fair Labor Standards Act and the National Labor Relations Act. From our beginnings and across the globe, we have led the way in seeking improved conditions and stronger unions for workers. Through public policy work, shareholder advocacy, and consumer power, the Church and its members have sought to influence political and corporate decisions affecting working conditions around the world.

III. Supporting Workers in the International Economy

Although the phenomenon of globalization has been occurring for hundreds of years, the pace of globalization has increased dramatically with the widespread mobility of capital and labor. Companies are no longer subject to the rules of one country and search the globe for resources, cheap labor, and access to markets. Although there are social, economic, and educational benefits to globalization, workers face many challenges in the new global economy. The rapid process of unchecked globalization in many countries has produced sweatshops, encouraged the contracting out of skilled workers to richer nations, undermined local food production, exacerbated child labor and forced labor, and drawn young people out of rural areas to urban ones or to other countries. Too few multinational corporations have taken leadership in setting higher standards for wages, benefits, and working conditions, and fewer still have supported international workers' right to organize. Workers, governments, and the Church must challenge the negative aspects of rapid globalization and improve working conditions around the world.

Despite the challenges and complexities of engaging in the international arena, The United Methodist Church is a participant in the global economy and thus must witness for justice in the international labor arena. To this end, The United Methodist Church:

1. supports the conventions of the International Labor Organizations that advance safety in the workplace; freedom from bonded or forced labor; the elimination of discrimination in respect to employment and occupation; effective abolition of child labor; fair compensation; just supervision; and the right of collective action for employees in all nations. The United Methodist Church shall continue to seek ratification and enforcement of these conventions;

2. encourages the General Board of Pension and Health Benefits to continue to invest in companies that set high standards for treatment of workers throughout the world and to file or join shareholder resolutions that encourage such high standards;

3. urges the General Board of Church and Society and the General Board of Global Ministries to partner with United Methodists around the globe and international advocacy organizations such as International Labor Rights Fund to challenge unjust working conditions;

4. urges governments to protect the rights of migrant workers through the ratification of the International Convention on the Rights of Migrant Workers and Their Families;

5. encourages United Methodist youth groups and mission trips to meet with sweatshop workers, factory workers, farm workers or trade unions to learn about working conditions and how they can improve conditions through personal actions and advocacy; and

6. lifts up workers in prayer and reaffirms our belief in workers' rights on the Sunday nearest Labor Day or May Day.

IV. Supporting Living Wages and the Sharing of Prosperity

Since 1908, the church has advocated for a living wage in every industry (1908 Social Creed) and continues to support the rights of workers to share fully in the prosperity of society. Unfortunately, too many workers earn poverty wages with few benefits, and disparities are growing between high-wage earners and low-wage earners. Despite rising productivity and profits in recent years, these gains have not been shared by a majority of workers. Therefore, The United Methodist Church:

1. encourages all employers—and especially employers who are United Methodist—to share prosperity with workers and seek ways to reduce disparity between top and bottom wage earners;

2. supports efforts by governments to ensure living wages indexed to inflation, expand health care benefits to workers, expand and protect worker pension programs, set core national standards for workers for paid sick days and paid vacation days, and limit mandatory overtime;

3. calls upon government agencies to expand targeted investigations of industries that routinely violate wage and hour laws, partner with workers' centers and congregations that are in ministry with low-wage and immigrant workers, and develop new print and online resources for educating workers about their rights in the workplace;

4. affirms efforts by governments to explore new mechanisms and policies to improve standards for wages, benefits and conditions for workers in low-wage jobs;

5. asks United Methodist seminaries to expose seminary students to worker concerns through teaching, internships, and field placement opportunities; and

6. urges the General Board of Church and Society and the General Board of Global Ministries to partner with organizations such as the National Farm Worker Ministry and Interfaith Worker Justice to engage United Methodists in education and advocacy to improve wages, benefits and working conditions for workers in low-wage jobs.

V. Supporting Workers' Right to Organize and Bargain Collectively

The United Methodist Church through its Social Principles recognizes and supports the right of workers to organize into unions of their own choosing and to bargain collectively regarding hours, wages, and conditions of employment (Social Principles ¶163B). Workers around the world are finding it harder and harder to form labor unions to achieve economic and social justice in the workplace. Many employers interfere with employees' efforts to exercise their right to unionize by firing or retaliating against union supporters, threatening to close their facilities, or speciously challenging bargaining units or election results.

Affirming its historic position and in response to new challenges facing workers, The United Methodist Church:

1. calls upon United Methodist institutions and organizations to exemplify the teachings found in the Social Principles and to support the right of their employees to organize for collective bargaining;

2. calls upon United Methodist agencies and congregations to use their purchasing and contracting dollars to support employers who pay living wages and support workers' right to organize;

3. encourages all employers to respect workers' right to organize and recognize the inherent power that employers have over workers in most workplaces. This power over workers' livelihoods means that employers must be especially careful not to bully or threaten employees, if workers are indeed to experience freedom of association. In particular, employers are encouraged to clearly communicate to their employees that they are neutral on their employees' choice and will deal fairly with any union they select; abide by their employees' decision when a majority has indicated their desire to be represented by a union, and refrain from using hearings, elections, and appeals as a means for delaying or avoiding representation for their employees. The United Methodist Church is particularly concerned about the unethical practices of locking workers out of their workplaces and permanently replacing striking workers;

4. expresses additional concern about the erosion of worker rights and supports policies to strengthen the power of workers to challenge unjust working conditions and guarantee their right to organize.

ADOPTED 2008
AMENDED AND READOPTED 2016
RESOLUTION #4135, 2008, 2012 *BOOK OF RESOLUTIONS*
RESOLUTION #237, 2004 *BOOK OF RESOLUTIONS*
RESOLUTION #224, 2000 *BOOK OF RESOLUTIONS*

See Social Principles, ¶ 163B, C.

¶ 164. V. THE POLITICAL COMMUNITY

While our allegiance to God takes precedence over our allegiance to any state, we acknowledge the vital function of government as a principal vehicle for the ordering of society. Because we know ourselves to be responsible to God for social and political life, we declare the following relative to governments:

A) Basic Freedoms and Human Rights—We hold governments responsible for the protection of the rights of the people to free and fair elections and to the freedoms of speech, religion, assembly, communications media, and petition for redress of grievances without fear of reprisal; to the right to privacy; and to the guarantee of the rights to adequate food, clothing, shelter, education, and health care. Blockades and embargoes that seek to impede the flow or free commerce of food and medicines are practices that cause pain and suffering, malnutrition, or starvation with all its detrimental consequences to innocent and noncombatant civilian populations, especially children. We reject these as instruments of domestic and foreign policy regardless of political or ideological views. The form and the leaders of all governments should be determined by exercise of the right to vote guaranteed to all adult citizens. We also strongly reject domestic surveillance and intimidation of political opponents by governments in power and all other misuses of elective or appointive offices. The use of detention and imprisonment for the harassment and elimination of political opponents or other dissidents violates fundamental human rights. Furthermore, the mistreatment or torture, and other cruel, inhumane, and degrading treatment or punishment of persons by governments for any purpose violates Christian teaching and must be condemned and/or opposed by Christians and churches wherever and whenever it occurs.

The Church regards the institution of slavery, the practice and commission of genocide, war crimes, crimes against humanity, and aggression as infamous and atrocious evils. Such evils are destructive of humanity, promote impunity, and therefore must be unconditionally prohibited by all governments and shall never be tolerated by the Church.

B) *Political Responsibility*—The strength of a political system depends upon the full and willing participation of its citizens. The church should continually exert a strong ethical influence upon the state, supporting policies and programs deemed to be just and opposing policies and programs that are unjust.

C) *Church and State Relations*—The United Methodist Church has for many years supported the separation of church and state. In some parts of the world this separation has guaranteed the diversity of religious expressions and the freedom to worship God according to each person's conscience. Separation of church and state means no organic union of the two, but it does permit interaction. The state should not use its authority to promote particular religious beliefs (including atheism), nor should it require prayer or worship in the public schools, but it should leave students free to practice their own religious convictions. We believe that the state should not attempt to control the church, nor should the church seek to dominate the state. The rightful and vital separation of church and state, which has served the cause of religious liberty, should not be misconstrued as the abolition of all religious expression from public life.

D) *Freedom of Information*—Citizens of all countries should have access to all essential information regarding their government and its policies. Illegal and unconscionable activities directed against persons or groups by their own governments must not be justified or kept secret, even under the guise of national security.

E) *Education*—We believe that every person has the right to education. We also believe that the responsibility for education of the young rests with the family, faith communities, and the government. In society, this function can best be fulfilled through public policies that ensure access for all persons to free public elementary and secondary schools and to post-secondary schools of their choice. Persons should not be precluded by financial barriers from access to church-related and other independent institutions of higher education. We affirm the right of public and independent colleges and universities to exist, and we endorse public policies that ensure access and choice and that do not create unconstitutional entanglements between church and state. We believe that colleges and universities are to ensure that academic freedom is protected for all members of the academic community and a learning environment is fostered that allows for a free exchange of ideas. We affirm the joining of reason and faith; therefore, we urge colleges and universities to guard the expression of religious life on campus.

F) Civil Obedience and Civil Disobedience—Governments and laws should be servants of God and of human beings. Citizens have a duty to abide by laws duly adopted by orderly and just process of government. But governments, no less than individuals, are subject to the judgment of God. Therefore, we recognize the right of individuals to dissent when acting under the constraint of conscience and, after having exhausted all legal recourse, to resist or disobey laws that they deem to be unjust or that are discriminately enforced. Even then, respect for law should be shown by refraining from violence and by being willing to accept the costs of disobedience. We do not encourage or condone any form of violent protest as a legitimate exercise of free speech or civil disobedience. We offer our prayers for those in rightful authority who serve the public, and we support their efforts to afford justice and equal opportunity for all people. We assert the duty of churches to support those who suffer because of their stands of conscience represented by nonviolent beliefs or acts. We urge governments to ensure civil rights, as defined by the International Covenant on Civil and Political Rights, to persons in legal jeopardy because of those nonviolent acts.

G) The Death Penalty—We believe the death penalty denies the power of Christ to redeem, restore, and transform all human beings. The United Methodist Church is deeply concerned about crime throughout the world and the value of any life taken by a murder or homicide. We believe all human life is sacred and created by God and therefore, we must see all human life as significant and valuable. When governments implement the death penalty (capital punishment), then the life of the convicted person is devalued and all possibility of change in that person's life ends. We believe in the resurrection of Jesus Christ and that the possibility of reconciliation with Christ comes through repentance. This gift of reconciliation is offered to all individuals without exception and gives all life new dignity and sacredness. For this reason, we oppose the death penalty (capital punishment) and urge its elimination from all criminal codes.

¶ 164

H) Criminal and Restorative Justice—To protect all persons from encroachment upon their personal and property rights, governments have established mechanisms of law enforcement and courts. A wide array of sentencing options serves to express community outrage, incapacitate dangerous offenders, deter crime, and offer opportunities for rehabilitation. We support governmental measures designed to reduce and eliminate crime that are consistent with respect for the basic freedom of persons.

We reject all misuse of these mechanisms, including their use for the purpose of revenge or for persecuting or intimidating those whose race, appearance, lifestyle, economic condition, or beliefs differ from those in authority. We reject all careless, callous, or discriminatory enforcement of law that withholds justice from persons with disabilities and all those who do not speak the language of the country in which they are in contact with the law enforcement. We further support measures designed to remove the social conditions that lead to crime, and we encourage continued positive interaction between law enforcement officials and members of the community at large.

In the love of Christ, who came to save those who are lost and vulnerable, we urge the creation of a genuinely new system for the care and restoration of victims, offenders, criminal justice officials, and the community as a whole. Restorative justice grows out of biblical authority, which emphasizes a right relationship with God, self, and community. When such relationships are violated or broken through crime, opportunities are created to make things right.

Most criminal justice systems around the world are retributive. These retributive justice systems profess to hold the offender accountable to the state and use punishment as the equalizing tool for accountability. In contrast, restorative justice seeks to hold the offender accountable to the victimized person, and to the disrupted community. Through God's transforming power, restorative justice seeks to repair the damage, right the wrong, and bring healing to all involved, including the victim, the offender, the families, and the community. The Church is transformed when it responds to the claims of discipleship by becoming an agent of healing and systemic change.

I) Military Service—We deplore war and urge the peaceful settlement of all disputes among nations. From the beginning, the Christian conscience has struggled with the harsh realities of violence and war, for these evils clearly frustrate God's loving purposes for humankind. We yearn for the day when there will be no more war and people will live together in peace and justice. Some of us believe that war, and other acts of violence, are never acceptable to Christians. We also acknowledge that many Christians believe that, when peaceful alternatives have failed, the force of arms may regretfully be preferable to unchecked aggression, tyranny, and genocide. We honor the witness of pacifists who will not allow us to become complacent about war and violence. We also respect those who support the use of force, but only in extreme situations and only when the need is clear beyond reasonable doubt, and through appropriate international organizations. We urge the establishment of the rule of law in international affairs as a means of elimination of war, violence, and coercion in these affairs.

We reject national policies of enforced military service as incompatible with the gospel. We acknowledge the agonizing tension created by the demand for military service by national governments. We urge all young adults to seek the counsel of the Church as they reach a conscientious decision concerning the nature of their responsibility as citizens. Pastors are called upon to be available for counseling with all young adults who face conscription or who are considering voluntary enlistment in the armed forces, including those who conscientiously refuse to cooperate with a system of conscription.

¶ 164

We support and extend the ministry of the Church to those persons who conscientiously oppose all war, or any particular war, and who therefore refuse to serve in the armed forces or to cooperate with systems of military conscription. We also support and extend the Church's ministry to all persons. This includes those who conscientiously choose to serve in the armed forces or to accept alternative service. When persons choose to serve in the armed forces, we support their right to adequate care for injuries suffered, and advocate for sufficient resources to meet their physical and mental health needs, both during and after their service. We are aware that we can become guilty both by military action and by conscientious objection, and that we all are dependent on God's forgiveness.

THE POLITICAL COMMUNITY
THE RESOLUTIONS

CHURCH AND STATE

5012. Church-Government Relations

In Luke 20:20-26, the teachers of the law and the scribes sent "spies" to watch Jesus closely hoping to entrap him in either a theological or political error. They asked him whether or not it was right to pay taxes to Caesar. Considering that taxes were a means of Roman oppression and the inscription on the coin represented submission to Caesar, this is a dangerous question for Jesus. For the Israelites suffering under Roman imperialism, to answer in the affirmative would imply that Roman colonization is an appropriate form of governance and that God's people should accept whatever form of government, no matter how repressive, they find themselves under. However, we know that Jesus did not uphold the right of government to oppress its people because he was brought before Pilate on charges of treason, which he never refuted (Luke 23:1-2). If Jesus had answered the question negatively he would have been openly calling for revolt against the ability of Rome to tax its people. In Jesus' answer to an earlier provocation, "Give to Caesar what belongs to Caesar, and to God what is God's," he refuses to incriminate himself through the questions of those out to trap him (Luke 20:25). We know that Scripture presents various examples and ways for the people of God to relate with the governing authorities. Jesus does not call his followers to open revolt although there are times when biblical faithfulness will necessitate civil disobedience to the ruling authorities (Acts 4:1-20). Jesus does not call his followers to submit blindly to all governing authorities although there are times when biblical faithfulness necessitates compliance (Romans 13:5-6).

While declaring our ultimate allegiance is to God, Scripture recognizes that faithfulness to God requires political engagement by the people of God. The nature of this engagement is determined by the particular situation and biblical faithfulness. The Social Principles of The United Methodist Church assert: "We believe that the state should not attempt to control the church, nor should the church seek to dominate the state. . . . Separation of church and state means no organic union of the two, but it does permit interaction" (¶ 164C). "The church should continually exert a strong ethical influence upon the state, supporting policies and programs deemed to be just and opposing policies and programs that are unjust" (¶ 164B).

As we consider the religious protections of the First Amendment of the US Constitution—the free exercise and nonestablishment of religion—we are profoundly grateful for the major statement made by the 1968 General Conference on "Church/Government Relations." In recognizing that debt, we reaffirm the substance of that declaration.

A Statement Concerning Church-Government Relations and Education

The fundamental purpose of universal public education at the elementary and secondary levels is to provide equal and adequate educational opportunities for all children and young people, and thereby ensure the nation an enlightened citizenry.

We believe in the principle of universal public education, and we reaffirm our support of public educational institutions. At the same time, we recognize and pledge our continued allegiance to the US constitutional principle that citizens have a right to establish and maintain private schools from private resources so long as such schools meet public standards of quality. Such schools have made a genuine contribution to society. We do not support the expansion or the strengthening of private schools with public funds. Furthermore, we oppose the establishment or strengthening of private schools that jeopardize the public school system or thwart valid public policy.

We specifically oppose tuition tax credits, school vouchers, or any other mechanism that directly or indirectly allows government funds to support religious schools at the primary and secondary level. Persons of one particular faith should be free to use their own funds to strengthen the belief system of their particular religious group. They should not, however, expect all taxpayers, including those who adhere to other religious belief systems, to provide funds to teach religious views with which they do not agree.

To fulfill the government's responsibility in education, sometimes government and nonpublic educational institutions need to enter a cooperative relationship. But public funds should be used only in the best interests of the whole society. Extreme caution must be exercised to ensure that religious institutions do not receive any aid directly or indirectly for the maintenance of their religious expression or the expansion of their institutional resources. Such funds must be used for the express purpose of fulfilling a strictly public responsibility, and should be subject to public accountability.

By providing a setting for contact at an early age between children of vastly different backgrounds, public schools have often been an important unifying force in modern pluralistic society. We recognize in particular that persons of all religious backgrounds may have insight into the nature of ultimate reality, which will help to enrich the common life. It is therefore essential that the public schools take seriously the religious integrity of each child entrusted to their care. Public schools may not properly establish any preferred form of religion for common exercises of worship, religious observance, or study. At the same time, however, education should provide an opportunity for the examination of the various religious traditions of humankind.

We believe that every person has a right to an education, including higher education, commensurate with his or her ability. It is society's responsibility to enable every person to enjoy this right. Public and private institutions should cooperate to provide for these educational opportunities.

Freedom of inquiry poses a risk for established ideas, beliefs, programs, and institutions. We accept that risk in the faith that all truth is of God. Colleges and universities can best perform their vital tasks of adding to knowledge and to the perception of truth in an atmosphere of genuine academic freedom.

We affirm the principle that freedom to inquire, to discuss, and to teach should be regulated by the self-discipline of scholarship and the critical examination of ideas in the context of free public dialogue, rather than by censorship by supervisors, school boards, or any control imposed by churches, governments, or other organizations. In the educational process, individuals have the right to appropriate freely for themselves what they believe is real, important, useful, and satisfying.

Experience has demonstrated that freedom to inquire, to discuss, and to teach is best preserved when colleges and universities are not dependent upon a single base or a few sources of support. When an educational institution relies upon multiple sources of financial support, and where those sources tend to balance one another, the institution is in a position to resist undue pressures toward control exerted from any one source of support. In the case of church-related colleges and universities, we believe that tuitions; scholarships; investment return; bequests; payments for services rendered; loans; government grants; and gifts from individuals, business corporations, foundations, and churches should be sought and accepted in as great a variety as possible. Care must be exercised to ensure that all support from any of these sources is free from conditions that hinder the college or university in the maintenance of freedom of inquiry and expression for its faculty and students.

We are very much aware of the dangers of church-sponsored colleges and universities being overly dependent upon government funding. However, we are also aware that given the independent thought of most college students today, there is little danger of using government funds to indoctrinate students with religious beliefs. Therefore, institutions of higher learning should feel free to receive government funds (except for religious teaching and structures for worship). At the same time, they should be eternally cognizant of the dangers of accompanying government oversight that might threaten the religious atmosphere or special independent character of church-sponsored educational institutions.

No church-sponsored higher education institution should become so dependent upon government grants, research projects, or support programs, that its academic freedom is jeopardized, its responsibility for social criticism (including criticism of governments) inhibited, or its spiritual values denied.

We recognize that the freedom necessary to the existence of a college or university in the classical sense may be threatened by forces other than those involved in the nature and source of the institution's financial support. Institutional freedom may be adversely affected by governmental requirements of loyalty oaths from teachers and students, by public interference with the free flow of information, or by accreditation and certification procedures and requirements aimed at dictating the content of college and university curricula.

With respect to church-related institutions of higher education, we deplore any ecclesiastical attempts to manipulate inquiry or the dissemination of knowledge, to use the academic community for the promotion of any particular point of view, to require ecclesiastical loyalty oaths designed to protect cherished truth claims, or to inhibit the social action activities of members of the academic community. We call upon all members of The United Methodist Church, in whatever capacity they may serve, to be especially sensitive to the need to protect individual and institutional freedom and responsibility in the context of the academic community.

We are persuaded that there may be circumstances or conditions in which the traditional forms of tax immunities granted to colleges and universities may be a necessary requirement for their freedom. Therefore, we urge a continuation of the public policy of granting reasonable and nondiscriminatory tax immunities to all private colleges and universities, including those that are related to churches.

We believe that colleges and universities should consider the benefits, services, and protections that they receive from the community and its governmental agencies and should examine their obligations to the community in the light of this support. We believe it is imperative that all church-related institutions of higher education determine on their own initiative what benefits, services, and opportunities they ought to provide for the community as a whole, as distinct from their usual campus constituencies.

A Statement Concerning Church-Government Relations and Governmental Chaplaincies

We recognize that military and public institutional chaplaincies represent efforts to provide for the religious needs of people for whom both churches and governments are responsible. We recognize that in such a broad and complex undertaking there are bound to exist real and serious tensions that produce genuine uneasiness on the part of government officials as well as church leaders. Great patience and skill are required to effect necessary accommodations with understanding and without compromising religious liberty.

We believe that there are both ethical and constitutional standards that must be observed by governments in the establishment and operation of public chaplaincies. At a minimum, those standards are as follows:

First, the only obligation that governments have is to ensure the provision of opportunities for military personnel, patients of hospitals, and inmates of correctional institutions to engage in religious worship or have access to religious nurture.

Second, participation in religious activities must be on a purely voluntary basis; there must be neither penalties for nonparticipation nor any rewards for participation.

Third, no preferential treatment should be given any particular church, denomination, or religious group in the establishment and administration of governmental chaplaincies.

Fourth, considerable care should be exercised in the role assignments of chaplains so they are not identified as the enforcers of morals. Precaution should also be taken to avoid chaplains being given duties not clearly related to their primary tasks.

Standards should be maintained to protect the integrity of both churches and governments. The practice of staffing governmental chaplaincies with clergy personnel who have ecclesiastical endorsement should be continued. The practice of terminating the services of such personnel in any instance where it becomes necessary for ecclesiastical endorsement to be withdrawn should also be continued. Supervision of clergy personnel in the performance of their religious services in governmental chaplaincies should be clearly effected through ecclesiastical channels with the cooperation of the public agencies and institutions involved. In the performance of these administrative functions, churches and agencies of government have an obligation to be fair and responsible and to ensure that due process is observed in all proceedings.

The role of a governmental chaplain should be primarily pastoral but with important priestly, prophetic, and teaching roles. The chaplain has an obligation to perform these ministries in as broad an ecumenical context as possible. A chaplain is responsible for the spiritual welfare and religious life of all the personnel of the military unit or the public institution to which he or she is assigned.

There are many persons, and some groups, whose personal religious practices or whose church's rules make it impossible for them to accept the direct ministry of a particular chaplain. In such instances, the chaplain, to the full extent of his or her powers, has an obligation to make provision for worship by these persons or groups. A chaplain is expected to answer specific questions by members of faith groups other than his or her own. Chaplains must know the basic tenets of their denominations in order to protect such members in the expression and development of their faith. The absence of parochialism on the part of a chaplain is more than an attitude; it necessitates specific, detailed, and accurate knowledge regarding many religions.

The churches should strive to make public chaplaincies integral expressions of their ministry and to face the implications of this for supervision and budget. The chaplain represents the church by affirming the dignity of all persons in military service through the chaplain's function in upholding their freedom of religion and conscience. Every person exists within a broader set of values than those of the military, and within a broader spectrum of responsibilities than those created by military orders. The chaplain is a bearer of the gospel to affirm the freedom of the individual and represents The United Methodist Church at that point of tension. Whether the freedom of the gospel is compromised or limited may be a result of either external pressures or internal submission, or both. Failure to sustain the freedom of the gospel lies within any human system or any individual. It is the task of the church to confront prophetically institutions or chaplains who compromise the gospel. The United Methodist Church provides presence, oversight, and support to chaplains who risk ministry in such a setting.

There are degrees of tension in present arrangements whereby a chaplain is a commissioned officer of the armed forces or an employee of a public institution. As such, he or she is a member of the staff of the military commander or of the director of the public institution involved. Government regulations and manuals describe him or her as the adviser on religion, morals, morale, and welfare. Therefore, we believe it is the chaplain's duty in faithfulness to his or her religious commitments to act in accordance with his or her conscience and to make such viewpoints known in organizational matters affecting the total welfare of the people for whom the chaplain has any responsibility. The chaplain has the obligation and should have the opportunity to express his or her dissent within the structures in which the chaplain works, in instances where he or she feels this is necessary. With respect to such matters, it is the obligation of religious bodies to give the chaplain full support.

Churches must encourage chaplains who serve in the armed forces to resist the exaltation of power and its exercise for its own sake. They must also encourage chaplains who serve in public institutions to maintain sensitivity to human anguish. Churches and chaplains have an obligation to speak out conscientiously against the unforgiving and intransigent spirit in people and nations wherever and whenever it appears.

A Statement Concerning Church-Government Relations and Tax Exemption

We believe that governments recognize the unique category of religious institutions. To be in this unique category is not a privilege held by these institutions for their own benefit or self-glorification but is an acknowledgment of their special identity designed to protect their independence and to enable them to serve humankind in a way not expected of other types of institutions.

We urge churches to consider at least the following factors in determining their response to the granting of immunity from property taxes:

1. responsibility to make appropriate contributions for essential services provided by government; and

2. the danger that churches become so dependent upon government that they compromise their integrity or fail to exert their critical influence upon public policy.

A Statement Concerning Church Participation in Providing Social Services

We believe that all the organizations and resources of the private sector, as well as those of governments, should be taken into account in the formulation and execution of social welfare policies.

We recognize that appropriate government bodies have the right to prescribe minimum standards for all public and private social welfare agencies. We believe that no private agency, because of its religious affiliations, ought to be exempted from any of the requirements of such standards.

Governmental provision of material support for church-related agencies inevitably raises important questions of religious establishment. In recognition, however, that some health, education, and welfare agencies have been founded by churches without regard to religious proselytizing, we consider that such agencies may, under certain circumstances, be proper channels for public programs in these fields. When government provides support for programs administered by private agencies, it has the most serious obligation to establish and enforce standards guaranteeing the equitable administration of such programs and the accountability of such agencies to the public authority. In particular, we believe that government resources should not be provided to any church-related agency unless it meets the following minimum criteria:

1. The services to be provided by the church-related agency shall meet a genuine community need.

2. The services of the agency shall be designed and administered in such a way as to avoid serving a sectarian purpose or interest.

3. The services to be provided by the agency shall be available to all persons without regard to race, color, national origin, creed, or political persuasion.

4. The services to be rendered by the agency shall be performed in accordance with accepted professional and administrative standards.

5. Skill, competence, and integrity in the performance of duties shall be the principal considerations in the employment of personnel and shall not be superseded by any requirement of religious affiliation.

6. The right to collective bargaining shall be recognized by the agency.

We recognize that all of the values involved in the sponsorship of a social welfare agency by a church may not be fully expressed if that agency has to rely permanently on access to government resources for its existence. We are also aware that under certain circumstances, sponsorship of a social welfare agency by a church may inhibit the development of comprehensive welfare services in the community. Therefore, the church and the agency should choose which pattern of service to offer: (1) channeling standardized and conventional services supplied or supported by government, or (2) attempting experimental or unconventional ministries and criticizing government programs when they prove inadequate. We believe that these two patterns are difficult, if not impossible, to combine in the same agency, and that the choice between them should be made before dependence upon government resources makes commitment to the first pattern irreversible. In their efforts to meet human needs, churches should never allow their preoccupation with remedial programs under their own direction to divert them or the larger community from a common search for basic solutions. In dealing with the elimination of the conditions of poverty and hunger, churches should have no stake in programs that contribute to promote dependency or embody attitudes and practices that fail to promote self-sufficiency.

We believe that churches have a moral obligation to challenge violations of the civil rights of the poor and marginalized. They should direct their efforts toward helping the poor overcome the powerlessness that makes such violations of civil rights possible. Specifically, churches should protest such policies and practices by welfare personnel as unwarranted invasions of privacy and oppose any requirement of attendance at church activities in order to qualify for social services.

A Statement Concerning Church Participation in Public Affairs

We recognize that churches exist within the body politic, along with numerous other forms of human association. Like other social groups, their existence affects, and is affected by, governments. We believe that churches have the right and the duty to speak and act corporately on those matters of public policy that involve basic moral or ethical issues and questions. Any concept of, or action regarding, church-government relations that denies churches this role in the body politic strikes at the very core of religious liberty.

The attempt to influence the formation and execution of public policy at all levels of government is often the most effective means available to churches to keep before humanity the ideal of a society in which power and order are made to serve the ends of justice and freedom for all people. Through such social action churches generate new ideas, challenge certain goals and methods, and help rearrange the emphasis on particular values in ways that facilitate the adoption and implementation of specific policies and programs that promote the goals of a responsible society.

We believe that any action that would deny the church the right to act corporately on public policy matters threatens religious liberty. We therefore oppose inclusion of churches in any lobby disclosure legislation.

This does not mean, in any way, that we wish to hide actions taken by the church on public issues. On the contrary, we are usually proud of such actions. It does recognize, however, that the church is already responding to members who request information with respect to church action on public policy questions. In effect, in accordance with legislation enacted by the 1976 General Conference, The United Methodist Church already has its own lobby disclosure provisions in place.

It is quite another matter, however, for the government to insist that it must know everything about what a church is saying in its private communications with its own members.

When the US Supreme Court acted in the 1971 landmark case of *Lemon* v. *Kartzman* (403 US 602, 612-13), the Court applied a test to determine the constitutionality of legislation on First Amendment grounds as it deals with religion. Among its three criteria were these two: (1) its principal or primary effect must neither advance nor inhibit religion; (2) the statute must not foster an excessive government entanglement with religion.

Lobby disclosure legislation before the US Congress over the last several years has required: (1) extremely burdensome record keeping and reporting of all legislative activity; (2) reporting of contributions of churches giving $3,000 or more annually to a national body if a part of this is used for legislative action; (3) criminal penalties with up to two years in jail for violations; and (4) unwarranted subpoena powers to investigate church records.

Legislation that passed the House in 1978 would have required detailed records of expenditures of twenty-two items. As such, it would have been burdensome and would inhibit religion in that The United Methodist Church would have been severely handicapped in implementing its Social Principles due to being neutralized by minutia.

Furthermore, if the government insists on knowing everything the church is doing on public policy questions over a five-year period (as was required) and imposes a criminal sentence for violations, this could inhibit religion to the extent that the church might be tempted to limit severely its activity to avoid noncompliance.

If the government is going to require that religious groups keep burdensome records and make voluminous reports, and there is some question as to whether the churches are complying, federal authorities would be authorized to step in and check church records and files. Such action would undoubtedly represent an unconstitutional excessive government entanglement with religion.

The United Methodist Church would have great difficulty in complying with the provision that all organizational contributions of $3,000 annually be reported if some of these funds are used for lobbying. Since local churches contribute generously to the World Service Fund, and a small portion of those funds is used for legislative action, this brings our church under coverage of this provision. Such a requirement could mean that reports of contributions of some 30,000 United Methodist churches would have to be made to the government shortly after the close of each year. This could not be done, and we would be in violation, having knowingly omitted material facts required to be disclosed. As a result, church officials would be subject to criminal penalties of up to two years in prison.

For these reasons, we oppose lobby disclosure measures for the churches. In its most stringent form, legislation such as this would inhibit our free exercise of religion. It would be impossible for the church to comply with certain provisions, thus subjecting our church leaders to criminal penalties.

We believe that churches must behave responsibly in the arena of public affairs. Responsible behavior requires adherence to ethically sound substantive and procedural norms.

Churches should seek to enlarge and clarify the ethical grounds of public discourse and to identify and define the foreseeable consequences of available choices of public policy.

In participating in the arena of public affairs, churches are not inherently superior to other participants; hence the stands that they take on particular issues of public policy are not above question or criticism.

Responsible behavior in the arena of public affairs requires churches to accept the fact that in dealing with complex issues of public policy, good intentions and high ideals need to be combined with as much practical and technical knowledge of politics and economics as possible.

Another norm of responsible behavior derives from the fact that no particular public policy that may be endorsed by churches at a given point in time should be regarded as an ultimate expression of Christian ethics in society. Churches should not assume that any particular social pattern, political order, or economic ideology represents a complete embodiment of the Christian ethic.

When churches speak to government, they also bear the responsibility to speak to their own memberships. Cultivation of ethically informed public opinion is particularly crucial in local congregations. It is essential to responsible behavior that procedures be established and maintained to ensure full, frank, and informed discussion by religious groups within the arena of public affairs. In the present period of human history, attention should be given to the dignity of every person, and appeal should be made to the consciences of all persons. Churches must acknowledge and respect the role of the laity as well as the clergy in determining their behavior in the arena of public affairs.

Because of their commitment to unity, and in the interest of an effective strategy, churches should, to the maximum extent feasible, coordinate their own efforts and, where appropriate, cooperate with other organizations when they seek to influence properly the formation and execution of public policy at all levels of government.

Finally, churches should not seek to utilize the processes of public affairs to further their own institutional interests or to obtain special privileges for themselves.

United Methodism is a part of the universal church. In the formulation and expression of the United Methodist voice in public affairs, we must listen to the concerns and insights of church members and churches in all nations. It is imperative that our expressions and actions be informed by participation in the universal church.

With particular reference to The United Methodist Church and public affairs, we express the following convictions: Connectional units of the denomination (such as General Conference, jurisdictional conference, annual conference, local congregation, or general board or agency) should continue to exercise the right to advocate government policies that involve basic moral or ethical issues or questions. In exercising this right, each such connectional unit, or any other official group within The United Methodist Church, should always make explicit for whom or in whose name it speaks or acts in the arena of public affairs. Only the General Conference is competent to speak or act in the name of The United Methodist Church.

(The provisions of Resolution 5012 shall be effective at the conclusion of the 2012 General Conference.)

ADOPTED 1980
AMENDED AND READOPTED 2000, 2008, 2012
RESOLUTION #5012, 2008, 2012 *BOOK OF RESOLUTIONS*
RESOLUTION #242, 2004 *BOOK OF RESOLUTIONS*
RESOLUTION #228, 2000 *BOOK OF RESOLUTIONS*

See Social Principles, ¶ 164*A, E.*

CRIMINAL JUSTICE

5031. Humanizing Criminal Justice

The biblical view of the criminal justice system is one that should be characterized by accessibility to all (Deuteronomy 1:17; 16:18), impartiality (Exodus 23:1-3), honesty (Exodus 23:7), integrity (Exodus 23:6, 8), and fairness to all without regard to status (Leviticus 19:15). God exhorts God's people, "Justice, and only justice, you shall pursue" (Deuteronomy 16:20 NRSV).

It is later in the narrative of God's people when justice has become subverted by greed and self-indulgence that God prescribes corrective action, as described by prophets such as Isaiah and Amos. When justice is distorted God desires for the cause of the widow and the orphan, those most vulnerable to the injustice of the affluent and powerful, to be defended (Isaiah 1:17). When injustice is committed against the poor and marginalized, authentic justice as described here is prevented from being experienced and God's people are alienated from God (Amos 5:7, 10-13, 21-24). God is just and those who follow God must be just as well.

A justice system that reflects God's desires for the world is one that is healing and restorative. Those who have been victimized by crime and the communities in which they reside need healing. Healing can come as safety and security are restored and the broken bonds of mutuality and shared existence are mended. Those who commit crimes must be held accountable through making amends to those they have caused to suffer, and they must be given the opportunity to return to their full place in society and community.

Since crimes are so often linked to a lack of access to resources, gaining access to resources is a necessary part of this return. As United Methodists we "support measures designed to remove social conditions that lead to crime, and we encourage continued positive interaction between law enforcement officials and members of the community at large" (¶ 164H).

A justice system must be first and foremost about humanization since God's justice always works to bring reconciliation. Systems of retribution breed only violence and isolation. Indeed, "we cannot punish our way to a healthy society" (Laura Magnani and Harmon Wray, *Beyond Prisons: A New Interfaith Paradigm for Our Failed Prison System*. Minneapolis, MN: Fortress Press [p. 5]).

Retributive systems of justice form barriers to the realization of the vision of restorative justice because they are tainted with explicit and implicit racial and ethnic bias, they punish children as harshly as adults, and they accommodate a two-tiered system that serves those with wealth and subjugates those without. Indeed, most justice systems do not seek healing and restoration for the people affected by crime or for those who commit crimes. Too many social and political obstacles blocking our path to achieving equal justice and safety for all God's children exist, including:

- Misinformed and biased public perceptions of racial and ethnic minorities that justify excessively punitive policies;
- Inadequate public health systems that neglect serious mental illness and treatment for addictions;
- Limited assistance and social services for victims of crime, and for children living in poverty and those with incarcerated parents;
- Justice systems that measure success by increasing numbers of arrests, prosecutions, and incarcerations over ensuring fair and impartial justice;
- Outdated public policies that equate crime reductions only with increased incarceration and longer sentences, and inadequately support rehabilitative programming; and
- Inferior or absent legal representation for defendants without financial means to hire counsel.

Crime Prevention and Criminal Proceedings

Communities plagued by high rates of violent and nonviolent crime need the attention of the Church and government to heal their pain. These communities are often disproportionately poor, disenfranchised, and populated by racial and ethnic minority peoples. Sometimes victims have also committed crimes and support services are unavailable to them. The Church believes that all people have sacred worth, including those who commit crimes and those impacted by it, and deserve our attention and support in order to limit recidivism and the intergenerational cycle of crime.

Racial and ethnic profiling is never an acceptable law enforcement tool. Police and prosecutors must be trained to avoid its use even unconsciously. Special care must be exercised in the selection of persons who serve as police officers, prosecutors, and court personnel. They should be persons who possess good judgment, sound discretion, and proper temperament.

Moreover, police encounters with people who break the law must not always end in arrest. In certain circumstances diversion to a mental-health or treatment provider, homeless shelter, or outreach to a parent in the case of a child are more effective strategies to combat criminal behavior, reduce costs to the criminal-justice system, and avoid a stigmatizing arrest record.

These kinds of restorative-justice practices should be utilized within the community as a first response to criminal behavior.

Young people under the age of eighteen who commit a criminal offense should not be adjudicated within the adult criminal-justice system. A special diversion program and/or court system centered on family solutions to addressing youth behavior is most appropriate.

When the arrest of adults is warranted, criminal defendants should have access to appropriate legal representation even in circumstances when he or she cannot afford to pay for representation. Prosecutors and the court system should use utmost scrutiny in determining whether or not sufficient evidence exists to charge a defendant. Decisions about guilt or innocence are best decided by a jury of peers within a court of law. All trials and the sentencing of those convicted under criminal laws must be conducted in a public courtroom.

The United Methodist Church urges the following recommendations in the area of crime prevention and criminal proceedings:

- Police departments publicly establish standards of police conduct and policies for promotion that incorporate training in peacekeeping, life-protecting, other service roles, and law enforcement. The standards must include strict limits on the deadly use of force;
- The composition of police agencies should reflect the communities that they serve, including geographic residence, diversity in race, ethnicity, gender, sexual orientation, etc.;
- Law enforcement agencies should be held accountable by the communities they serve. We encourage churches to coordinate events with these agencies to allow for open dialogue with the community and to safely air grievances and concerns to authorities in order to ensure a culture of trust and transparency;
- Fair and adequate compensation for police officers, public defenders, prosecutors, and other court and law-enforcement personnel should be provided to these valuable public servants;
- Train judges of juvenile and criminal courts in the use of non-incarcerating community sanctions whenever the offense does not involve persistent violence;
- Encourage local churches to set up court-monitoring panels to observe court operations and proceedings. Such panels may well adopt a role of friends of the court or of advocacy on behalf of accused persons and/or on behalf of crime victims. They may adopt other appropriate procedures in the interest of restorative justice, including close scrutiny of plea bargaining and/or evidence of unequal imposition of sentences;
- Develop appropriate jury selection procedures that would ensure the most inclusive representation, including representatives of the socioeconomic class and ethnic group of the defendants and of the crime victims; and
- Adoption by all courts of: (a) speedy trial provisions; and (b) a presumption that a person accused of a crime should be released on personal recognizance unless an evidentiary-based determination is made that personal recognizance will not reasonably assure future appearance or represents a risk of imminent physical harm to others. Financial bond should be used as a last resort. A

monetary bond can create an undue burden on individuals accused of crimes who have limited financial means and results in unnecessarily prolonged periods of pretrial detention.

Criminal Laws and Penalties

Persons convicted of criminal offenses should be subject to penalties proportional to the harm caused by the offense. In cases involving limited victim impact or no violence, opportunities to address wrongdoing within a restorative-justice framework, and outside the criminal-justice system, are most appropriate. Penalty decisions must allow for consideration of a multitude of factors in the circumstances of a case, including but not limited to a defendant's age, intellectual capacity, mental and physical health, prior history of criminal behavior and/or victimization. Conversely, a defendant's race, ethnicity, religion, familial status, political affiliation, sexual orientation or economic status should not be considered in sentencing decisions.

Criminalization of personal behaviors or conditions perpetuates unfair racial disparity, class discrimination, stigmatization, and wastes resources needed for other purposes. Therefore, the Church supports the repeal of laws that criminalize personal conditions or behaviors. Examples include vagrancy, homelessness, personal gambling, public drunkenness, drug use, prostitution, and real or perceived sexual orientation or consensual sexual activity. Moreover, individuals forced or coerced into criminal behavior should not be criminalized. The Church also opposes extreme sentences, including the death penalty and life imprisonment with no consideration for release, particularly for people under the age of eighteen. These extreme sentences are inherently cruel and leave out any opportunities for redemption or rehabilitation among people who commit crime.

Penal codes should prescribe a range of penalty options for courts to consider at sentencing with an emphasis on utilizing non-incarceration community sanctions wherever consistent with community protection. Furthermore, court-determined sentences that consider the unique circumstances of each case are most appropriate, rather than mandatory sentences prescribed by policymakers unaffiliated or unfamiliar with the nuances of specific criminal proceedings.

Judges and juries issuing penalties should issue publicly accessible statements to the court detailing the reasons for selecting a particular penalty for a defendant. When fines are assessed, they should be scaled to the magnitude of the crime and the ability of a defendant to pay.

Governmentally regulated programs of compensation for reimbursement of financial loss incurred by victims of crime should be encouraged, particularly as an alternative to incarceration.

Conditions of Confinement

More than 10 million people are held in penal institutions throughout the world, according to data compiled in 2013. The Church is concerned for the health and well-being of all detained and incarcerated people. Those confined in institutions, regardless of the length of their mandated stay, have basic human rights that must be protected by administrators and government officials. All confinement facilities must provide:

- Safe and sanitary living conditions, which incorporate a zero tolerance in policy and practice for violence, including sexual violence, committed by staff or other incarcerated individuals, and a bar on solitary confinement except in extraordinary situations where the safety of an individual or individuals is in jeopardy and then only for the briefest time possible;
- Medical and mental health care treatment services that meet community standards;
- Nutritious foods;
- Opportunities for compensated employment, education, recreation, and other rehabilitative programming;
- Fair and responsive grievance systems;
- Regular access to family, friends, clergy, legal representation, and the media.

Exiting Incarceration

People leaving incarceration to return to their home communities require special assistance during their transition. Communities benefit if people leaving incarceration are successful in their reintegration and do not return to criminal behavior. Families may also need aid in preparing to welcome home loved ones, particularly children who disproportionately feel the burden of a parent's absence. The Church has a powerful role to play in the reentry process and should utilize its resources to ensure successful transitions for those leaving incarceration and the families and neighborhoods to which they return.

Discrimination against people with criminal records must not be tolerated. Stereotypes about people who have been incarcerated can result in unemployment and homelessness because of a desire to exclude people with criminal records from businesses and housing. Laws that forbid professional licenses to persons with a criminal record, regardless of the relevance of the person's criminal history to the occupation, should be repealed. In addition, persons who commit no new offenses after a short time deserve an opportunity to expunge or erase a criminal record permanently. Moreover, laws that exclude any persons with a criminal record from the normal benefits and rights of citizenship, including publicly financed income assistance and housing, student loans, and voting rights should be ended.

United Methodist churches are encouraged to build relationships with returning citizens in their communities and congregations. Healing Communities is a framework for ministry for United Methodist congregations to mobilize existing resources within the congregation for ministry with the families of those impacted by crime and the criminal-justice system. By fostering reciprocal relationships and removing stigma and shame within congregations, Healing Communities emphasizes that good theology is an engaged missiology. Healing Communities engages in ministry with those directly impacted by the criminal-justice system and their families, and mobilizes congregations to join in advocating for "the creation of a genuinely new system" (¶ 164H).

We call upon the General Board of Church and Society to mobilize United Methodist churches to advocate for legislation that will eliminate racism and classism in the criminal-justice system; ensure equality, transparency, and fairness; and protect the human rights of all adults and children by:

- promoting equity and transparency in courts by instituting legal representation of equal quality, regardless of financial ability, and public scrutiny of decisions to pursue criminal charges, convictions, and sentencing;

- reassessing incarceration guidelines and reducing sentences of incarceration of persons guilty of nonviolent crimes, and eliminating extreme sentences, including capital punishment and life imprisonment with no opportunity for parole;
- ensuring adequate government funding to support the prevention of crime, including anti-poverty measures, strong public-education systems and universal access to medical and mental-health care, services for victims of crime, services for incarcerated people and those leaving incarceration and their families;
- protecting children from the severity of the adult criminal justice system, and ensuring the punishment of youths takes into full account the science of youth brain development and youth's still immature impulse control and decision-making capacity;
- creating laws prohibiting discrimination against people with criminal records; and
- restoring voting rights for people with criminal records.

ADOPTED 2016

See Social Principles, ¶ 164H.

5037. Texas Death Penalty

WHEREAS, The United Methodist Church strongly opposes capital punishment; and

WHEREAS, in the state of Texas:
- over 515 persons have been put to death since the state resumed executions in 1982 as of 2015 (http://www.tdcj .state.tx.us/death_row/dr_executed_offenders.html);
- among the persons executed since 1982 at least nine had intellectual or developmental disabilities (http://www .deathpenaltyinfo.org/list-defendants-mental-retarda tion-executed-united-states), at least 20 percent of the 290 people on death row suffered from mental illness in 2013 alone (http://www.texasmonthly.com/story/trouble mind/page/0/1), and thirteen were juveniles when their crimes were committed;

- among those executed 108 African Americans were put to death for crimes against white victims (http://www.deathpenaltyinfo.org/), and only 4 white persons were executed for crimes against African Americans (http://www.deathpenaltyinfo.org/);
- twelve persons sentenced to die have later been proven innocent and removed from death row (http://www.deathpenaltyinfo.org/innocence-and-death-penalty?did=412&scid=6#inn-st);
- capital trials have at times been characterized by "unreliable witnesses, lack of evidence, incorrect experts, official misconduct, and inadequate defense attorneys";
- the Innocence Project of Texas has pointed to the likelihood that one or more innocent persons have been executed (http://www.innocenceproject.org/Content/Cameron_Todd_Willingham_Wrongfully_Convicted_and_Executed_in_Texas.php); and

WHEREAS, over 250 organizations of all kinds, including religious, civic, political, legal, and humanitarian groups, have officially called either for a moratorium on executions or for the abolition of the death penalty in Texas; and

WHEREAS, at least ten major newspapers in Texas have endorsed either a moratorium on executions or the abolition of capital punishment in the state;

Therefore, be it resolved, that the 2008 General Conference of The United Methodist Church, meeting in Fort Worth, Texas:

- express its deepest appreciation to all those organizations and individuals in the state of Texas who have valiantly struggled and continue to struggle for a more humane society in which the death penalty is rare or nonexistent;
- call upon the Texas Legislature either to abolish the death penalty completely or to stop executions in the state until such time as all capital cases can be tried in a completely equitable way;
- call upon the Texas Pardon and Parole Board and the governor to commute the sentences of persons currently on death row to life in prison without parole or to life in prison; and
- instruct the secretary of the General Conference to have copies of this resolution sent immediately to all members of the Texas Legislature, to each member of the Pardon

and Parole Board, to the governor of Texas, to the Texas Conference of Churches, and to the Texas Coalition to Abolish the Death Penalty.

ADOPTED 2008
AMENDED AND READOPTED 2016
RESOLUTION #5037, 2008, 2012 *BOOK OF RESOLUTIONS*

See Social Principles, ¶ 164*G*, *H*.

5038. Caring for Victims of Crime

In the parable of the good Samaritan (Luke 10:25-37), Jesus illustrates for his listeners the importance of caring for those who have been victims of crime. The way in which the Samaritan cares for the man who was robbed, beaten, and left for dead was specific as to the areas of need and lovingly generous. The Samaritan personally bandages his wounds, shares his wine and oil for healing, shares his animal so that the beaten man can ride to the inn, stays with him and cares for him during the night, and then covers all of his expenses while promising to return to check back in. Jesus defines a neighbor as the outpouring of mercy on this man by the Samaritan. For us to be neighbors today means that we must follow this example. We too must care for victims of crime.

Many people are victims of crime. Victims and their families suffer shock and a sense of hopelessness. In addition to financial loss, there is a spiritual and emotional trauma and often a lack of support and direction. Many victims feel frustrated because there often seems to be no provision for them to be heard. Their injuries are not redressed, and they are not always notified of the court procedures. Victims should have a greater voice within the criminal-justice system.

The United Methodist Church believes in healing through the ministries of restorative justice. As stated in the *Book of Discipline*, "restorative justice grows out of biblical authority, which emphasizes a right relationship with God, self, and community. When such relationships are violated or broken through crime, opportunities are created to make things right" (¶ 164*H*). Making restitution to those who have been victimized is at the heart of restorative justice. Judges and criminal-justice officials are urged to consider this when appropriate to help make victims of crime as financially whole again as possible.

For United Methodist congregations to effectively live out Jesus' call to be a neighbor to those who are victims of crime there are strategic ways in which congregations can act. These include:

- prayers by congregations for the healing of victims of crime and their families,
- funeral assistance,
- congregational care groups assigned to care for the crime victim,
- participation in, support of, and utilization of advocacy groups for victims of crime,
- referral to individual counselors and support groups that help crime victims as well as provide space for support groups to meet,
- help for the victim to understand how the criminal-justice system works,
- transportation getting to and from court,
- child care for young children while the victim is in court,
- good writers available to help the victim write their victim impact statement, and
- financial aid to help those with financial losses or the losses that occur from missed periods of work.

Congregations can be advocates for the rights of crime victims. Victims of crime should know these rights include:

- the right to participate and be heard at all phases of the criminal-justice process,
- the right to be treated with dignity and compassion and respect by criminal-justice and church officials,
- the right to be notified about the criminal case dispositions,
- the right to disclosable information about the case, and
- the right to request compensation that includes state victims compensation, restitution in the courts and paroling authorities, and civil-justice tort claims.

Therefore, The United Methodist Church calls for:

- Congregations to embrace and care for victims of crime by identifying leaders and necessary resources both within the congregation and the local community;
- Pastors and congregations to study the biblical basis of restorative justice and discuss how their church might engage in restorative-justice ministries. Some resources for this study include *Changing Lenses: A New Focus for Crime and Justice* by Howard Zehr, *Ambassadors of Recon-*

ciliation: New Testament Reflections on Restorative Justice and Peacemaking by Elaine Enns and Ched Myers, *Restorative Justice: Moving Beyond Punishment* by Peggy Hutchison and Harmon Wray, *Redeeming the Wounded* by B. Bruce Cook, and *Criminal Justice: Retribution vs. Restoration* by Eleanor Hannon Judah and the Rev. Michael Bryant; and

- The General Board of Church and Society to advocate for the recognition of the needs and rights of victims of crime.

ADOPTED 2016

See Social Principles, ¶ 164*H*.

POLITICAL RESPONSIBILITY

5071. Electoral Campaign Finance Reform

Campaign finance reform is a moral matter for the religious community. The temptation to buy favors is an ancient and unjust one addressed often in Scripture. The prophet Amos thundered against those merchants in Israel who "have sold the innocent for silver, and those in need for a pair of sandals . . . and push the afflicted out of the way . . ." (Amos 2:6-7). Psalm 15 defines upright persons as those who ". . . [keep] their promise even when it hurts . . . who won't accept a bribe against any innocent person" (vv. 4-5).

The pouring of large sums of money into political campaigns in order to buy special influence with legislators is a scandal. Too often citizens forsake participation in the political process because they believe policies are shaped by money from special interests, not by the national interest or the needs of the people.

The issue of campaign financing is far more than a political matter. It goes to the heart of the ethical and moral life of a nation.

Many elected officials continually court monied special interests in order to finance their next election campaign. If politicians are to focus on the well-being of the people and the nation, they must be able to depend on public financing rather than pursuing special-interest money.

It is time to free electoral politics from this corrupting pressure. A system of public campaign financing would take government away from special interests and return it to the people.

We commend those politicians of all parties who are working to achieve real campaign financing reform.

We call upon all United Methodists to work within their own countries to build support for measures that would end the flood of special-interest monies to political campaigns and restore integrity to decision making.

ADOPTED 1996
AMENDED AND READOPTED 2004, 2012
RESOLUTION #5071, 2008, 2012 *BOOK OF RESOLUTIONS*
RESOLUTION #269, 2004 *BOOK OF RESOLUTIONS*
RESOLUTION #253, 2000 *BOOK OF RESOLUTIONS*

See Social Principles, ¶ 164A, B.

UNITED STATES LEGISLATIVE ISSUES

5083. Right to Privacy

Theological Statement

The Christian faith stresses the dignity of and respect for human personality and the need to protect its privacy. Our human right to privacy has an importance in this age of electronic communication and information data bases that it did not have in the days when our Scriptures were written. The right to privacy, however, and the corollary duty to protect the privacy of others, are not without mention in the Bible.

Jesus tells us to give our alms in secret so that God may bless us (Matthew 6:4). What God commands us to do, we surely must have a right to do. And with that right, comes a duty. We are to protect the secrets of others and not disclose them, for doing so will bring us both shame and ill repute (Proverbs 25:9-10). Vulnerability is closely linked with our need for privacy and we have a positive duty to make the vulnerable less vulnerable; when we see the naked, we are to cover them (Isaiah 58:7), and by extension, when we encounter information which is better kept private, we are to keep it from going farther.

The ability to respect the privacy of others is a virtue: he who is trustworthy in spirit keeps a thing hidden (Proverbs 11:13). Conversely, because gossip leads to the invasion of others' privacy and the revelation of their secrets, gossips are viewed as destructive people, and a careful steward of private information will not let oneself become vulnerable to them (Proverbs 20:19).

At the same time, our Scriptures recognize that privacy can be abused. Employing privacy to slander another in secret is an offense against God, who will destroy the violator (Psalm 101:5). Delilah abuses her relationship with Samson to learn the secret of his strength, then violates his privacy, jeopardizing his life by sharing his secret with his enemies (Judges 16:9). The Bible recognizes that privacy can be abused in the service of oppression; the poor are devoured in secret, Habakkuk (3:14) reminds us, for frequently evil is the result of conspiracies undertaken in secret. The prophets of Israel denounced the repression of the poor, widows, orphans, and others of their society, and our Lord's ministry began with the announced purpose to set at liberty the poor and disadvantaged.

Privacy takes on special meaning in the context of our spirituality. The psalmist identifies privacy with inwardness; "You want truth in the most hidden places; you teach me wisdom in the most secret space" (Psalm 51:6). Privacy is an attribute of God, who owns secrets (Deuteronomy 29:29), and who creates humanity in secret (Psalm 139:15). We have no privacy, however, from God, from whom no secret is hidden (Ezekiel 28:3, Mark 4:22), and who will reveal all secrets (Luke 8:17). The secrets of our heart are disclosed to God (1 Corinthians 14:25) who judges these secrets by Christ (Romans 2:16). These scriptural roots claim our attention in several areas of modern life.

Privacy as a Civil Liberty

Because privacy is a human right, it is also a civil liberty. Privacy is meaningless if it does not include privacy from the intrusion of government bodies. Implicit in the right to privacy is the assumption that humans are the owners of their private information, and it is from that position of ownership that the right to choose whether or not to disclose flows. The power to control one's own information is the mark of a free person rather than a slave.

We recall among the many offenses of slavery how slaves were exhibited naked on the auction block so that potential buyers might examine them as a commodity. Invasion of the privacy of an ordinary citizen of society negates this dignity and respect.

Further, the Christian faith is supportive of a society that elicits hope and trust, not a society that foments fear and threatens with oppression. The packaging and sale in today's world of information about persons represents a commodification of their humanity and is an offence against their freedom.

We recognize that many of the obligations of government necessitate the collection of personal information by the government. Every instance of such collection must be justified through due process where challenge is possible.

The Social Principles of The United Methodist Church affirm that "illegal and unconscionable activities directed against persons or groups by their own governments must not be justified or kept secret, even under the guise of national security" (¶ 164D). "We . . . strongly reject domestic surveillance and intimidation of political opponents by governments in power and all other misuses of elective or appointive offices" (¶ 164A).

Law Enforcement

We recognize that privacy can be abused for idolatry and murder (Deuteronomy 27:24), for political intrigue (2 Samuel 15:10), and for treachery (Judges 3:19). The psalmist prays that God will protect us from the secret plots of the wicked (Psalm 64:2) and Psalm 10:9 warns its readers of the wicked who lurk in secret like a lion.

We therefore recognize that law enforcement in particular requires the collection and presentation of data to prove a defendant's guilt. We affirm, however, the principle that all are innocent until proven guilty, and, as innocent persons, enjoy the right to privacy.

Medical Privacy

The purpose of health care, whether provided by physicians or other professionals, whether provided by solo practitioners or large institutions, is to restore the health of individual human beings. Persons who seek healing entrust medical practitioners and institutions with their private information, which remains their property.

We therefore support the understanding that patient records and the information in them are the property of the patients to whom the individual pertains and are not the property of the medical institutions which maintain the records. Institutions are trustees of such information and must use it for its intended purpose, namely the restoration to health of the affected individuals and, where appropriate, for the health of the public.

We oppose the use of private medical information to promote the products of commercial enterprises. We oppose the provision of private medical information to employers or creditors without the consent of the persons who own the information. We oppose the use of private medical information in legal situations without the person's consent, as this amounts to involuntary self-incrimination.

We oppose the use of private medical information without the owner's permission, to discriminate against the owner of the information in employment, in housing, in the provision of credit.

Genetic Privacy

We are particularly opposed to the use of genetic information concerning an individual in order to discriminate in the provision of credit, employment, and various forms of insurance.

We support genetic privacy and nondiscrimination legislation that seeks to prohibit discrimination on the basis of genetic information with respect to life insurance, health insurance, employment, and other areas of life in which genetic information can be used for injustice and oppression.

National Security and Government Privacy

Governments are comprised of human beings and it is understandable that governments will have the same desire for privacy that individual humans will have. In addition, governments have responsibilities for national security that individuals do not have and have a legitimate right to keep certain information secret, whose transmission could leave a nation vulnerable. In Isaiah 39, the king of Judah unwisely allowed the Babylonians information on both the treasure and the defense of Judah; this information was then used by Babylon to defeat Judah. We oppose, however, the extension of government's legitimate need for security to include information which is of little value to an enemy, but which might be embarrassing to the government, or might subject the government to greater accountability from a concerned public.

Citizens of all countries should have access to all essential information regarding their government and its policies. Openness is a redemptive gift of God, calling for trust and honesty between various segments of the community. Justice is the cornerstone of that trust we have come to expect in our elective and appointive representatives of the community. Communal wholeness is attained through the concerted use of these elements.

We support laws in all nations similar to the Freedom of Information Act in the United States and the extension of the protection of *habeas* data such as exist in Latin American nations and the Philippines. We support "sunshine laws," which require that the business of government not be conducted in secret. We recognize that agencies charged with public and national security need information in order to discharge their duties. We believe that when government needs private information, there must be clear communication between the government and the people and the agreement of all parties involved that the public need for this information outweighs the private right of the individual to privacy. Additionally, governments should have in place legal protections to ensure proper oversight of these programs.

We strongly oppose warrantless intrusions into private communications by telephone, mail, and e-mail, and the secret searching of bank records and other records. This includes the provisions of laws like the USA Patriot Act in the United States and similar laws in the Philippines.

Revelations that, in many nations, government intelligence agencies, local police, the tax services, and military organizations have, over a number of years, developed a domestic espionage apparatus involving the gathering of information about the lawful political activities of millions of citizens is a continuing cause for concern.

It is deplorable that in a society that is democratic in theory and structure there are signs of increasing repression: dragnet arrests; police and the intelligence community's harassment of minority leaders; charges of conspiracy; summary acquittals of police accused of brutality; the rising militancy of rank-and-file police; support for the use of preventive detention; the utilization of wiretaps; censorship of journalism in educational and correctional institutions; heavy punitive action against dissidents; the confinement of those who protested within the military forces; the utilization of grand juries for the purpose of harassment rather than indictment; and the use of church members, clergy, and missionaries for secret intelligence purposes by local police departments, the Federal Bureau of Investigation, and the Central Intelligence Agency.

We call for restoration of legal protections against any kind of wiretapping without a warrant of a court and restraint in the use of wiretapping and electronic surveillance. Surveillance creates an air of suspicion throughout the whole society and contributes to the insecurity of law-abiding American citizens.

We affirm the many civil, school, and church authorities who are working toward the elimination of these abuses through their work and example; and we note that many of the most flagrant of these acts of repression no longer occur. Congress, the press, and the American people have begun watching agency activities more closely and with a greater demand for public accountability.

This vigilance must not be relaxed, for if it is, there may be renewed acts of repression and fresh attempts to curtail the rights of citizens whenever redress is sought for economic and social grievances.

We are particularly appalled when the promotion of fear appears to be a means of undermining our civil liberties including the right to privacy. We agree with Benjamin Franklin in his statement that, "They who would give up an essential liberty for temporary security, deserve neither liberty nor security."

Sexual Privacy

Of all topics related to privacy, the Bible is most clear regarding our right to sexual privacy. In the biblical narrative, privacy is addressed in the very first pages of Genesis. Immediately upon eating the fruit of the tree of good and evil, Adam and Eve cover their loins (Genesis 3:7), a recognition not only that human beings need privacy, but that it is in the area of sexual relationship that human beings are most vulnerable to each other, and that we legitimately seek a degree of privacy in the area of sex and reproduction that exceeds what we require in other areas.

Subsequent statements of the Hebrew Scriptures emphasize the primacy of sexuality in matters of privacy. When identification is made of those for whom sexual relationships are forbidden, what is forbidden is described in euphemisms of privacy: one must not "uncover the nakedness" of those with whom sexual intercourse is forbidden (Leviticus 18:6-19; see 20:18-19; Deuteronomy 22:30). By extension, one must also not "uncover the nakedness" of those for whom sexual intercourse is protected. We therefore support the privacy rights of men and women regarding reproductive health decisions. The Scriptures also acknowledge our need for privacy in meeting our bodies' needs; the servants of Eglon, king of Moab, do not rush into his chamber after his murder, thinking that he is relieving himself (Judges 3:19).

We therefore maintain the appropriateness of a greater degree of privacy regarding sexuality than in other areas.

We oppose strip searches by law enforcement personnel of the opposite sex. We oppose the employment of prison guards of the opposite sex where prisoners have no privacy for dressing, undressing, or the performance of bodily functions. We support the right of medical patients to have a chaperone of the same sex present when being examined by a practitioner of the opposite sex. It is in the deprivation of the right to sexual privacy that the most degrading forms of dehumanization occur in our society.

Charge

We call upon:

- The General Board of Church and Society to represent this perspective to American legislators in Washington and to the global community at the United Nations in New York. We respectfully request the Congress of the United States to:
    1. enact comprehensive charter legislation for all of the intelligence agencies that would prohibit them from engaging in surveillance or disruption of lawful political activity. We oppose any charter provision that permits intelligence agencies to recruit and use as agents clergy or missionaries;
    2. place statutory limitations upon the demand by governmental bureaus and agencies for personal information about any citizen or family for statistical purposes. When such requests by agencies are for information not required by law, the respondent should be informed that compliance is voluntary.

Restrictions should be placed by law on private agencies in gathering, storing, and disseminating personal information; and

3. retain the Freedom of Information Act as it is, in support of the right of all citizens to know the actions of their government.

- The General Board of Discipleship to include in its curricula an understanding of the biblical bases for the right to privacy. They have influence, both personally and as members of church congregations.

- All church members and leaders to continue to be sensitive to this situation in their local community and in the nation by:

1. seeking to understand and undergird responsible institutions and agencies of the community and being supportive of measurements that will improve them and upgrade their personnel; and

2. establishing programs in the community sponsored by local churches to:
   - educate church members and their wider community about the potential for repression in the institutions of society;
   - study and affirm the biblical and constitutional basis for justice under law;
   - work in legislatures to bring about just and responsible criminal code revisions that do not reinforce repressive elements in our nation's life;
   - oppose forms of legislation that would legalize repression; support legislation that would prohibit intelligence agencies from conducting surveillance or disruption of lawful political activities or otherwise violating constitutional rights;
   - develop an awareness of the rights and protection citizens should expect; and
   - work for institutional change in situations where rights are not respected and protection is not furnished.

ADOPTED 2008
AMENDED AND READOPTED 2016
RESOLUTION #5083, 2008, 2012 *BOOK OF RESOLUTIONS*

RESOLUTION #276, 2004 *BOOK OF RESOLUTIONS*
RESOLUTION #258, 2000 *BOOK OF RESOLUTIONS*

See Social Principles, ¶ 164*A*.

5086. Voting Representation for People in the District of Columbia

The District of Columbia was established on the first Monday in December, 1800, by an Act of Congress as a seat for the national government under authority granted to the Congress by Article 1, Section 8, of the US Constitution, under which the Congress has the power to "exercise exclusive legislation in all cases whatsoever, over such District." At no time since has the federal legislature passed any provision for voting representation for the residents of the District of Columbia. Yet, throughout our nation's history, citizens of the District of Columbia have given their undivided allegiance to the United States: fighting and dying in wars, paying their full measure of taxes, and providing labor and resources to the federal government.

Therefore, because we recognize:

- that governments derive their "just powers from the consent of the governed" in order to secure the people's rights "endowed by their Creator";
- the Social Principles contained in *The United Methodist Book of Discipline* state that the "form and the leaders of all governments should be determined by exercise of the right to vote guaranteed to all adult citizens";
- the Social Principles also state that "the strength of a political system depends on the full and willing participation of its citizens" (¶ 164*B*);
- it has been the enduring tradition and history of the Methodist movement, from the time of Wesley to the present day, to support the rights of the individual, to provide relief to the disenfranchised, and to champion the equality of all persons before God and before the law; and
- in Scripture the importance of full participation of all people in the life of the society can be found throughout, including Exodus 18:13-27 when Jethro instructs Moses, his son-in-law to appoint "officers over thousands, hundreds, fifties, and tens" (v. 25 NRSV). In addition to pro-

viding some respite for Moses, this ensures that every person has equal access to those who rule over them. Similarly, in Acts 6:1-7, at the birth of the New Testament Church, a dispute arose over the distribution of food between Hellenist widows and Hebraic widows. To settle the dispute and to ensure both equal access and distribution, seven servants were appointed over the food distributed. Unfortunately, for residents in the District of Columbia today, there is no equal access to representative government.

The United Methodist Church agrees that the continuing disenfranchisement of the citizens of the District of Columbia is an egregious moral wrong that must be rectified.

Therefore, the General Conference of The United Methodist Church declares its full support, on moral grounds that citizens of the District of Columbia are entitled to political rights equal to those of other United States citizens, including voting representation in both houses of Congress. We call on the President and the Congress of the United States of America to take action to provide congressional representation to the citizens of Washington, DC.

We call on all United Methodist congregations throughout the United States to support the people of the District of Columbia in this cause by calling upon their elected representatives in Congress to demand democratic rights for the District of Columbia.

ADOPTED 1980
REVISED AND ADOPTED 2000
REVISED AND READOPTED 2008, 2016
RESOLUTION #5086, 2012 *BOOK OF RESOLUTIONS*
RESOLUTION #5088, 2008 *BOOK OF RESOLUTIONS*
RESOLUTION #280, 2004 *BOOK OF RESOLUTIONS*
RESOLUTION #262, 2000 *BOOK OF RESOLUTIONS*

See Social Principles, ¶ 164*B*.

¶ 165. VI. THE WORLD COMMUNITY

God's world is one world. The unity now being thrust upon us by technological revolution has far outrun our moral and spiritual capacity to achieve a stable world. The enforced unity of humanity, increasingly evident on all levels of life, presents the Church as well as all people with problems that will not wait for answers: injustice, war, exploitation, privilege, population, international ecological crisis, proliferation of arsenals of nuclear weapons, development of transnational business organizations that operate beyond the effective control of any governmental structure, and the increase of tyranny in all its forms. This generation must find viable answers to these and related questions if humanity is to continue on this earth. We commit ourselves as a Church to the achievement of a world community that is a fellowship of persons who honestly love one another. We pledge ourselves to seek the meaning of the gospel in all issues that divide people and threaten the growth of world community.

A) Nations and Cultures—As individuals are affirmed by God in their diversity, so are nations and cultures. We recognize that no nation or culture is absolutely just and right in its treatment of its own people, nor is any nation totally without regard for the welfare of its citizens. The Church must regard nations as accountable for unjust treatment of their citizens and others living within their borders. While recognizing valid differences in culture and political philosophy, we stand for justice and peace in every nation.

B) National Power and Responsibility—Some nations possess more military and economic power than do others. Upon the powerful rests responsibility to exercise their wealth and influence with restraint. We will promote restorative justice strategies to support positive social change and peace building. We affirm the right and duty of people of all nations to determine their own destiny. We urge the major political powers to use their nonviolent power to maximize the political, social, and economic self-determination of other nations rather than to further their own special interests. We applaud international efforts to develop a more just international economic order in which the limited resources of the earth will be used to the maximum benefit of all nations and peoples. We urge Christians in every society to encourage the governments under which they live and the economic entities within their societies to aid and work for the development of more just economic orders.

C) War and Peace—We believe war is incompatible with the teachings and example of Christ. We therefore reject war as an instrument of national foreign policy. We oppose unilateral first/ preemptive strike actions and strategies on the part of any government. As disciples of Christ, we are called to love our enemies, seek justice, and serve as reconcilers of conflict. We insist that the first moral duty of all nations is to work together to resolve by peaceful means every dispute that arises between or among them. We advocate the extension and strengthening of international treaties and institutions that provide a framework within the rule of law for responding to aggression, terrorism, and genocide. We believe that human values must outweigh military claims as governments determine their priorities; that the militarization of society must be challenged and stopped; that the manufacture, sale, and deployment of armaments must be reduced and controlled; and that the production, possession, or use of nuclear weapons be condemned. Consequently, we endorse general and complete disarmament under strict and effective international control.

D) Justice and Law—Persons and groups must feel secure in their life and right to live within a society if order is to be achieved and maintained by law. We denounce as immoral an ordering of life that perpetuates injustice and impedes the pursuit of peace. Peoples and nations feel secure in the world community when law, order, and human rights are respected and upheld.

Believing that international justice requires the participation of all peoples and nations, we endorse the United Nations, its related bodies, the International Court of Justice, and the International Criminal Court as the best instruments now in existence to achieve a world of justice and law. We commend the efforts of all people in all countries who pursue world peace through law. We endorse international aid and cooperation on all matters of need and conflict. We urge acceptance for membership in the United

Nations of all nations who wish such membership and who accept United Nations responsibility. We urge the United Nations to take a more aggressive role in the development of international arbitration of disputes and actual conflicts among nations by developing binding third-party arbitration. Bilateral or multilateral efforts outside of the United Nations should work in concert with, and not contrary to, its purposes. We reaffirm our historic concern for the world as our parish and seek for all persons and peoples full and equal membership in a truly world community.

¶ 165

THE WORLD COMMUNITY
THE RESOLUTIONS

EDUCATION

6001. Africa University

WHEREAS, the Africa University initiative formally began by the inspiring address delivered by Bishop Emilio de Carvalho of Angola at the General Board of Higher Education and Ministry of The United Methodist Church in October, 1984; and

WHEREAS, Bishop de Carvalho was joined by Bishop Arthur Kulah of Liberia, Bishop F. Herbert Skeete, then president of the General Board of Higher Education and Ministry, Bishop Felton E. May, then president of the General Council on Ministries, and other members in discussing the educational needs of Africa and ways the denomination might respond to this challenge; and

WHEREAS, the African central conferences of The United Methodist Church asked the General Board of Higher Education and Ministry and the General Board of Global Ministries to assist them in developing significant post-secondary institutions of learning for the churches of Africa; and

WHEREAS, in St. Louis, Missouri, the 1988 General Conference of The United Methodist Church overwhelmingly approved the establishment of a university on the continent of Africa to be built in Zimbabwe and authorized an apportionment of $10 million over a four-year period and an additional $10 million to be raised through World Service Special Gifts; and

WHEREAS, the official groundbreaking for the university occurred on site in Old Mutare in 1991, and Africa University opened in 1992 with two faculties (schools) and forty students representing six nations on the African continent; and

WHEREAS, Africa University's enrollment reached a significant milestone in 2014 with its student population reaching 1,474 representing 23 African nations; and

WHEREAS, Africa University is committed to the education of African women with young women comprising 53.5 percent of the student population in 2014; and

WHEREAS, the number of faculties has grown from the initial two in 1992 to now six, plus the Institute of Peace, Leadership, and Governance; and

WHEREAS, more than 5,000 Africa University alumni have been deployed across the African continent in fulfillment of the university's mission to train new leaders for the nations of Africa—new leaders like Walter Manyangawirwa, who was in the first graduating class at Africa University and who is now on the Africa University faculty and is one of Africa's few doctoral-level entomologists; and

WHEREAS, the support and enthusiasm of United Methodists worldwide for Africa University are demonstrated in the apportionments remitted annually, the second-mile givings, and contributions from churches and individuals for the Africa University Endowment Fund; and

WHEREAS, each local church is called upon to pay the full Africa University apportioned line item and give generously to the Africa University Endowment Fund;

Therefore, be it resolved, that the General Conference affirms that Africa University is a dynamic and important mission project of The United Methodist Church; affirms the leadership of all those involved in the continuing development and day-to-day operations of the university; and commends the Africa University Board of Directors and advisory Development Committee for their persistence, diligence, and visionary leadership in overcoming the obstacles and barriers to fulfilling the dream; and,

Be it further resolved, that the 2016 General Conference make Africa University a priority and allocate an apportionment of $10 million over a four-year period and an additional $10 million to be raised through World Service Special Gifts to continue development, construction, and endowment of Africa University as outlined in the planning process determined by the General Board of Higher Education and Ministry and the Africa University Board of Directors.

ADOPTED 2004
REVISED AND READOPTED 2008
AMENDED AND READOPTED 2016
RESOLUTION #6001, 2008, 2012 *BOOK OF RESOLUTIONS*
RESOLUTION #304, 2004 *BOOK OF RESOLUTIONS*
RESOLUTION #284, 2000 *BOOK OF RESOLUTIONS*

See Social Principles, ¶ 165A.

GLOBAL INTERRELIGIOUS RELATIONS

6006. Our Muslim Neighbors

Christians are called to initiate and promote better relationships between Christians and Muslims on the basis of informed understanding, critical appreciation, and balanced perspective of one another's basic beliefs.

The Historical Context

United Methodists, seeking to be faithful neighbors and witnesses to other members of the human family, recognize with respect peoples of the religion of Islam.

Christians and Muslims acknowledge common roots, along with Jews, in the faith of Abraham, Sarah, and Hagar. As members of one of the monotheistic world religions, Muslims worship and serve the one God with disciplined devotion. Both Christians and Muslims believe that God is ever-inclined toward humankind in justice and mercy. Based on this common ground, we celebrate where Christians and Muslims are working together to make God's justice a reality for all people. The two faiths sometimes understand differently the particular ways in which God deals with human beings, but they agree that the proper human response to the Almighty is a life of humble obedience, including repentance, faith, and good works. Muslims believe that the Qur'an sets forth the principles for righteous conduct and a harmonious life in society. The following verses from the Qur'an show that these principles are similar to the ones found in the Christian Scriptures:

O believers, be steadfast witnesses for God with justice. Do not let the hatred of a people make you act unjustly. Be just, for justice is next to piety (5:8).

Worship only God; be good to parents and kindred, to orphans and the poor; speak kindly to others (92:83).

Do not mix truth with falsehood, nor knowingly conceal the truth (2:42).

O believers, fulfill your obligations (5:1).

Hold to forgiveness and enjoin good; turn aside from the foolish (7:199).

It may be that God will bring about friendship between you and those whom you hold to be your enemies (60:7).

The Need for Understanding

United Methodists live together with Muslims in many countries of the world and in a variety of social environments. Indeed, in the United States of America, Muslims comprise one of the most rapidly growing religious communities. In places around the world, Muslims may constitute the majority of the population, and in other places, Christians may be the majority. As believers of the two religions build their lives in the same general area, they are often affected by patterns of religious antagonism inherited from the past history of disputes and misunderstanding between the two.

Also, Muslims and Christians experience varying degrees of political and social discrimination, depending on the particular circumstances of each country. In certain areas of tension believers in the two faiths are caught up in struggles for economic, political, and human rights.

We believe that sustained and ever-renewed initiatives of open discussion and sharing of concerns in interfaith settings contribute to the achievement of social justice.

By this statement, we express solidarity with those of either religion who suffer oppression or discrimination.

By this statement, we make a step toward more hospitable and cooperative relationships and encourage dialogical relations.

Basic United Methodist Documents

A. Called to Be Neighbors

A clear biblical basis for discussion in interfaith settings is set forth in Guidelines for Interreligious Relationships:

In conversation with a lawyer (Luke 10:25), Jesus reminded him that his neighbor, the one to whom he should show love and compassion, included a stranger, a Samaritan. Today, Christ's call to neighborliness (Luke 10:27) includes the "stranger" of other faiths. It is not just that historical events have forced us together. The Christian faith itself impels us to love our neighbors of other faiths and to seek to live in contact and mutually beneficial relationship, in community with them.

B. The Social Community

In our United Methodist Social Principles, we affirm all persons as equally valuable in the sight of God and determine to work toward societies in which each person's value is recognized, maintained, and strengthened.

Religious persecution has been common in the history of civilization. We urge policies and practices that ensure the right of every religious group to exercise its faith free from legal, political, or economic restrictions. In particular, we condemn anti-Semite, anti-Muslim, and anti-Christian attitudes and practices in both their overt and covert forms, being especially sensitive to their expression in media stereotyping.

C. Our Theological Task

In our United Methodist Doctrinal Standards, our relationship with adherents of other living faiths of the world is set in the context of our ecumenical commitment. We are encouraged to enter into serious interfaith encounters and explorations between Christians and adherents of other living faiths of the world. Scripture calls us to be both neighbors and witnesses to all people. Such encounters require us to reflect anew on our faith and to seek guidance for our witness among neighbors of other faiths.

When Christians enter into such dialogue, they come to it consciously as they seek to live as one people, under the living God who is the Creator of all humankind, the One "who is above all and through all and in all" (Ephesians 4:6 NRSV).

This theological understanding compels us to a particular kind of dialogue, one in which we reflect critically upon our Christian tradition, gain accurate appreciation of the traditions of others, and engage with love and generosity of spirit as we seek "to raise all such relationships to the highest possible level of human fellowship and understanding."

Christian-Muslim Discussions

The long-standing commitment of The United Methodist Church to social justice, to theological inquiry, and to just and open relationships places a particular responsibility on its members to develop discussions between Christians and Muslims. Mutual respect requires the church to recognize and affirm that, although individuals may move from one religion to another, we do not enter into formal interfaith dialogue with the intent to convert the Muslim community to Christianity. Although the movement is still small, there is increasing evidence that groups of Christians and Muslims are coming together to witness to their faith and acknowledge the power of God in their lives, to identify problems that challenge all on the deepest theological and moral level, and to try to understand better the complex factors that determine the crucial decisions being made by governments around the world.

Through such interactions, Christians and Muslims are finding that working for better exchange of information and for ways to cooperate in solving mutual problems and concerns often leads to discovery and growth, adding to the depth and understanding of each tradition.

If we observe the unfolding of events in today's world and assess Islamic movement as only reactionary and threatening, we will hinder the advancement of justice and peace and neither gain from nor contribute to mutual understanding.

If we develop friendships with Muslims as members of the human community from whom and with whom we have much to learn, we will increase our respect for Islam as a way of life that calls its millions of followers to the highest moral ideals and satisfies their deepest spiritual aspirations.

In the aftermath of September 11, 2001, The United Methodist Church has intentionally explored what it means to be in relationship with the Muslim community. The United Methodist Church stands in solidarity with Muslims in the struggles for economic, political, and human rights.

Action Statement

Local congregations and United Methodist agencies are encouraged to develop ongoing relationships with Muslims and their respective organizations. They are urged to initiate conversations, programs, and dialogues leading to the understanding of both Islam and Christianity, and appreciation of their particular gifts, while discovering commonalities and differences; and seeking areas of mutual cooperation. They are also urged to exchange information and discuss ways to cooperate when they address common problems and concerns.

Recommendations

We request the Council of Bishops to support, participate in, and assist United Methodists in implementing this resolution.

We call upon United Methodist Women to promote a program of ongoing relationships with Muslim women, seeking areas of mutual concern about how to live ethically, morally, and responsibly in today's world and to join in common struggles for peace and justice.

We urge the General Board of Church and Society to work with Muslims in activities designed to achieve common political, social, economic, and ecological goals.

We urge that the General Board of Global Ministries and the General Board of Church and Society develop advocacy programs on behalf of religious freedom and minority rights, particularly regarding nations that are experiencing crisis in Christian-Muslim conflict in which religious minorities are harassed or persecuted.

We recommend that the Office of Christian Unity and Interreligious Relationships, as it initiates and engages in dialogue with representatives of Islam, remain mindful of the evangelism imperatives of the gospel and the gospel mandate to seek justice for those who are oppressed.

We recommend that United Methodist Communications monitor and call attention to discrimination against Muslims in both the religious and secular media.

We urge United Methodist members, local churches, and agencies to take the following specific actions:

1. Learn more about Islam, using the resolution "Called to be Neighbors and Witnesses: Guidelines for Interreligious Relationships," this resolution, and other resources which the Office of Christian Unity and Interreligious Relations can recommend.

2. Initiate dialogue with Muslims, utilizing as our guide the resolution of the 2016 General Conference entitled "Called to Be Neighbors and Witnesses: Guidelines for Interreligious Relationships" (p. 293), and models of dialogue developed by the Office of Christian Unity and Interreligious Relationships. The dialogue

will address theological and justice issues, related to the particular contexts in which those dialogues occur.

3. Develop awareness of the concerns of particular Muslim populations through implementation of other applicable General Conference Resolutions in the 2000 *Book of Resolutions*, such as "Prejudice Against Muslims and Arabs in the USA."

4. Promote understanding between Christians and Muslims in local communities through:

- arranging visits to local mosques;
- developing and participating in cultural exchanges with Muslims;
- inviting Muslims to social occasions;
- seeking Muslim participation in local interfaith councils and interfaith worship;
- sending messages of greeting and good will to Muslims upon the occasion of their religious festivals;
- encouraging authorities of schools, hospitals, prisons, factories, and places of business and government to respect particular features of Muslim life;
- upholding the dignity of individuals, families, and communities; and
- seeking to remedy situations in which Muslims encounter misunderstanding, prejudice, stereotyping, or even hostility from the neighborhood or population when they desire to express their faith in everyday life.

ADOPTED 1992
AMENDED AND READOPTED 2004
ADOPTED 2016
RESOLUTION #6061, 2008 *BOOK OF RESOLUTIONS*
RESOLUTION #315, 2004 *BOOK OF RESOLUTIONS*
RESOLUTION #299, 2000 *BOOK OF RESOLUTIONS*

See Social Principles, ¶ 165*A, B, C.*

JUSTICE AND LAW

6024. Global Racism and Xenophobia: Impact on Women, Children, and Youth

The General Conference of The United Methodist Church affirms the United Nations principles relating to global racism, tribalism, and xenophobia.[1]

The General Conference reaffirms the principles of equality and nondiscrimination in the Universal Declaration of Human Rights and encourages respect for human rights and fundamental freedoms for all without distinction of any kind such as race, color, sex, language, religion, political, tribe, or other opinion, national or social origin, property, birth, or other status.

We, the General Conference, affirm that all peoples and individuals constitute one human family, rich in diversity. "So now you are no longer strangers and aliens. Rather, you are fellow citizens with God's people, and you belong to God's household" (Ephesians 2:19).

We recognize the fundamental importance of nations in combating racism, racial discrimination, xenophobia, tribalism, and related intolerance and the need to consider signing, ratifying or acceding to all relevant international human rights instruments, with a view to international adherence.

We recognize that religion, spirituality, and belief can contribute to the promotion of the inherent dignity and worth of the human person and to the eradication of racism.

We recognize that racism reveals itself in a different manner for women and girls and can be among the factors leading to deterioration in their living conditions, poverty, violence, multiple forms of discrimination, and the limitation or denial of their human rights.

We recognize the need to develop a more systematic and consistent approach to evaluating and monitoring racial discrimination against women, children, and youth.

Therefore, we, the General Conference, urge that, in light of these affirmations and principles, each nation in which The United Methodist Church is established:

- adhere to the principles and programs contained in the opening statements;
- incorporate a gender perspective in all programs of action against racism, tribalism, and xenophobia;
- undertake detailed research on racism, tribalism, and xenophobia, especially in respect to its effect on women, children, and youth;

1. Principles can be found on the United Nations website in various reports including "Declarations World Conference against Racism, Racial Discrimination, Xenophobia and Related Intolerance, Durban, South Africa, 31 August to 8 September 2001."

- address the burden of such discrimination on women, children, and youth and promote their participation in the economic and productive development of their communities, especially in respect to:
  * the increased proportion of women migrant workers, human rights violations perpetrated against them, and the contribution they make to the economies of their countries or their host countries;
  * the large number of children and young people, particularly girls, who are victims of racism, tribalism, and xenophobia;
  * the rights of children belonging to an ethnic, religious, linguistic minority or indigenous community and their right individually or in community to enjoy their own culture, their own religion, and their own language;
  * child labor and its links to poverty, lack of development, and related socioeconomic conditions that can perpetuate poverty and racial discrimination disproportionately, denying children a productive life and economic growth;
  * education at all levels and all ages.
- involve women, children, and youth in decision-making at all levels related to the eradication of racism, tribalism, and xenophobia;

Therefore, we further resolve that the General Commission on Religion and Race, the General Commission on the Status and Role of Women, in consultation with United Methodist Women, assess evidences of racism, tribalism, and xenophobia in programs for and with women, children, and youth;

- all mission institutions, schools, and institutions of higher education, annual conferences, and general agencies evaluate current and projected programs to determine their impact in reducing racism, tribalism, and xenophobia in programs for women, children, and youth; and
- a report be prepared and presented to each General Conference by the General Commission on Religion and Race, the General Commission on the Status and Role of Women, in consultation with United Methodist Women,

related to the status of women, children, and youth impacted by racism, tribalism, and xenophobia.

ADOPTED 2004
READOPTED 2008
AMENDED AND REDOPTED 2016
RESOLUTION #6024, 2008, 2012 *BOOK OF RESOLUTIONS*
RESOLUTION #286, 2004 *BOOK OF RESOLUTIONS*

See Social Principles, ¶ 165.

6025. Globalization and Its Impact on Human Dignity and Human Rights

> *What are human beings that you think about them;*
> *what are human beings that you pay attention to them?*
> *You've made them only slightly less than divine,*
> *crowning them with glory and grandeur.*
> —Psalm 8:4-5

> *Human rights are what make us human. They are the principles by which we create the sacred home for human dignity. Human rights are what reason requires and conscience commands.*
> —Kofi Annan, United Nations Secretary-General

Our Globalized World

In an age of globalization, the recognition of human dignity and the struggle to protect human rights has become even more complex and challenging. While protections for human rights are increasingly enacted by governments and international bodies like the United Nations, grave threats to and gross violations of human rights are also on the rise.

The world's financial capital is ever more integrated, and wealth is ever more centralized in the hands of financial elites and corporate institutions. Realizing social and economic rights, especially eradicating hunger and reducing unemployment, is becoming increasingly difficult. Bringing conflicts to a just and durable resolution is more daunting with the increased capacity of individuals, governments and their military forces, and other entities, including paramilitary and extremist groups, to organize and unleash violence. These groups have access to more sophisticated communications technology and more deadly instruments of war than ever before.

Ending violence and wars, and checking impunity and disregard for international human rights and humanitarian laws will require more than political will and moral courage. Concrete programs and mechanisms are needed to realize the totality of human rights: civil, political, social, economic, and cultural. We must offer peace by advocating for its concrete manifestations in the availability of nutritious food to eat and clean water to drink, for decent work and living wage for everyone, and health, housing and education for all.

Our Christian tradition shows us an alternative to globalization. It is a "counter-globalization" that empowers God's people to "do justice, embrace faithful love, and walk humbly with your God" (Micah 6:8b). What must be globalized is a culture of peace that institutes peace with justice in ways that are visible and tangible in the lives of peoples and communities. We are challenged to globalize an ethos that respects and protects human life with human rights so that all "could have life—indeed, . . . live life to the fullest" (John 10:10b) as God intends.

Biblical and Theological Grounding

The psalmist exclaims: "What are human beings / that you think about them; / what are human beings / that you pay attention to them? / You've made them only slightly less than divine [divine beings, or angels], / crowning them with glory and grandeur" (Psalm 8:4-5). Every human being bears the likeness of our just, gracious, and loving God: "God created human beings, in the image of God they were created; male and female were created" (Genesis 1:27, adapted).

Human dignity is the foundation of all human rights. It is inherent and inborn. We do not legislate human dignity; we only need to recognize and affirm each human being who bears it. Human dignity is the image of God in each human being. Human dignity is the sum total of all human rights.

We protect human dignity with human rights. Human rights are the building blocks of human dignity. They are indivisible and interdependent. It is God's gift of love for everyone. Human rights, being the expression of the wholeness and fullness of human dignity, are indivisible and interdependent.

Human rights, expressed in affirmations and declarations, treaties and conventions, laws and statutes, are products of struggles to affirm and fulfill the wholeness and fullness of life. As peoples and governments increase the catalogue of rights that are recognized and protected, protections not only increase, but so do our approximation of and striving for human dignity. To be engaged in the human rights struggle is to accept God's gift of love in Jesus Christ who has come to affirm all God's people as they are: as individuals and people in community together.

But human rights do not affect humanity alone. The integrity of God's creation is possible only with the affirmation of both the dignity of all persons and the integrity of the whole ecological order. Human rights cannot be enjoyed in an environment of pillage and decay. The health of human beings is intricately connected to the health of the planet and the entire cosmos.

Human dignity is the common bond that affirms the individuality of each human being while celebrating the plurality and variety of communities to which each belongs, including the diverse social economic, civic, political, religious, ideological, racial, class, gender, and ethnic identities each represents.

The United Methodist Church and Human Rights

The United Methodist Church's Social Principles provide foundational understanding of rights and freedoms. These principles affirm both the sovereignty of God over all of creation and the duties and responsibilities of each person for the natural and nurturing world, and the social, economic, political, and world communities. At their spring 1998 meeting, and on the occasion of the fiftieth anniversary of the Universal Declaration of Human Rights, the Council of Bishops called on "United Methodists across the connection worldwide [to] join in . . . safeguarding the worth and dignity of peoples and the integrity and sacredness of all of God's creation."

"As Christians," the bishops said, "loving our God and loving our neighbor together advance the imperatives of human rights. Human rights enable us to express in concrete ways our love for one another by assuring that each person's value is recognized, maintained, and strengthened." Human rights are safeguards of peoples and communities against violations of their rights and infringements on their freedoms. To this end, the General

Conference called on all governments to accept their obligation to uphold human rights by refraining from repression, torture, and violence against any person and to ratify and implement international conventions, covenants, and protocols addressing human rights in the context of justice and peace.

Arenas for Human Rights Work

Today's global context is ever more complex, not in the least through the institutions and agents that mark an unprecedented globalization that we are experiencing, if not, participating in. At the same time that we witness the rapid change in local and global processes, we also see the rise and increasing participation of peoples' and citizens' organizations in leading the establishment of just, participatory, and sustainable communities. These are communities that will prosper a culture of peace and human rights as a way of life. Through the work and presence of nongovernmental organizations and other civic community formations, in all levels of governance—local, national, regional, global—globalization is challenged in multiple ways. Human-rights monitors, themselves a threatened group of defenders, have increased in the ranks of civil society. Their work must be protected and safeguarded.

We lift the following arenas for human-rights work to all United Methodists worldwide, and to the attention of all general agencies, particularly the General Board of Church and Society and the General Board of Global Ministries of The United Methodist Church. We also support the work of the Pan-Methodist Commission and their work with children.

A. Children's Rights and Well-Being: Receiving the Reign of God as a Little Child

"'Allow the children to come to me,' Jesus said. 'Don't forbid them, because the kingdom of heaven belongs to people like these children'" (Matthew 19:14).

The Social Principles strongly support children and children's rights. It says: "Once considered the property of their parents, children are now acknowledged to be full human beings in their own right, but beings to whom adults and society in general have special obligations. . . . All children have the right to quality education. . . . Moreover, children have the rights to food, shelter, clothing, health care, and emotional well-being as do adults, and these rights we affirm as theirs regardless of actions or inactions of their parents or guardians. In particular, children must be protected from economic, physical, and sexual exploitation and abuse" (¶ 162C).

The United Nations Convention on the Rights of the Child expresses this same concern for all the children of the world. United Methodists celebrate the ratification of this convention by 195 nations even as it urges the United States to ratify it soonest. The convention extends the basic concept of protection to the level of human rights. The convention affirms that the rights described in the Universal Declaration of Human Rights are rights that belong also to children. Children's rights are human rights. United Methodists worldwide must continue to urge their governments to implement the convention, and its related protocols.

The proliferation of and easy access to small arms have a devastating effect on our children. Children must never have access to or opportunity to use guns. Both the children killed and those wounded by small arms are victims of a culture of violence that denies human rights, snuffs out precious human life, and debases human dignity.

The United Methodist Church is called to join the international campaign to prevent the proliferation and unlawful use of small arms. The campaign raises our awareness of the need for emergency measures to save the lives of children, in our schools, in inner cities, and in many parts of the world, particularly those countries and communities that are highly militarized and governed by national security laws.

Children in situations of conflict and war test our commitment to the future. There is something wrong in our sense of the moral when children are put in harm's way. No boy or girl must be sent to the front lines of war, battles, and conflict. The field of play must not be replaced with the field of combat. War games are not child games. Playgrounds are for children; battlegrounds are not.

The United Methodist Church must oppose the recruitment and use of child soldiers. We must support the call of the United Nations Commission on Human Rights (Resolution 1999/80) to raise the current minimum age limit set by Article 38 of the Convention on the Rights of the Child on the recruitment into the armed forces or participation of any person in armed conflicts from 15 to 18. The General Conference of the International Labor

Organization (ILO), through Convention 182 (1999), prohibits forced or compulsory recruitment of children under the age of 18 for use in armed conflict. ILO also recommends (Recommendation 190) that governments prohibit the use, procuring or offering of a child for activities that involve the unlawful carrying or use of firearms or other weapons.

Human trafficking involves the illegal trade in human beings for purposes that include commercial sexual exploitation, forced labor, or a modern-day form of slavery. Children must be especially protected from the ills that a growing global sex industry peddles. The recruitment and trafficking of girls and boys for child labor, prostitution, sexual slavery, forced marriage, as child soldiers, and even for organ trading are predatory and must be condemned. We must actively seek the ratification by all countries of the United Nations Convention against Transnational Organized Crime, which includes the Protocol to Prevent, Suppress and Punish Trafficking in Persons, especially Women and Children (also referred to as the Trafficking Protocol).

B. Migrant Workers: Entertaining Angels Unawares

"Do not deprive the foreigner or the fatherless of justice, or take the cloak of the widow as a pledge" (Deuteronomy 24:17 NIV).

"Keep loving each other like family. Don't neglect to open up your homes to guests, because by doing this some have been hosts to angels without knowing it" (Hebrews 13:1-2).

A complex of factors—civil conflicts, human rights abuse, extreme poverty, environmental degradation, militarization, political persecution and misguided development schemes—have produced in many countries around the world an unprecedented number of people in situations of forced and enforced movement, including migrants and migrant workers looking for jobs and security beyond their national borders.

While globalization heralded the swift movement of capital across national borders, the movement of laborers seeking work in richer countries of the world while steadily growing has been increasingly restricted, securitized, racialized, gendered and sexualized. Transnational corporations have moved to poor countries where labor is much cheaper and workers' organizing is either weak, suppressed, or altogether banned.

Regional and international collaborators of Churches Witnessing With Migrants (CWWM), including the General Board of

Church and Society, assert in their Advocacy Paper (dated October 1 and 2, 2013, and referred to below) that "the well-being, safety and sustainability of migrants becomes as urgent as their fight for justice." CWWM asserts that "(b)ilateral and multilateral negotiations all too often focus on the management of migration for the maintenance of economic prosperity and security of destination countries. These conditions have resulted in restrictive migration and immigration legislations, including job and wage conditions that are far from decent and sustainable, thus violating migrants' rights."

"Managing migration for development perpetuates global and structural inequalities and obscures the unjust international trade, investment and financial regime set by the advanced countries. This regime leads to the destruction of livelihoods and forms the basis for unsustainable development in poor countries, forcing millions of working people to seek economic opportunities in foreign lands. The negotiations largely ignore centuries of colonial and neo-colonial exploitation and plunder that have consigned countries to perpetual bouts of extreme poverty internally and economic dependence externally."

Migrant workers continue to be discriminated against and abused, especially those who are undocumented in their host countries. Women migrants are particularly vulnerable to exploitation especially when they work in gender-specific jobs that consign them to various forms of sexual, domestic, and menial work. Studies show that the majority of migrants are uprooted because of the lack of jobs at home, or because jobs pay extremely low wages. While globalization has spawned more capital and spurred greater production, workers' wages have been kept low and below a livable wage even in those countries whose governments have a prescribed minimum wage.

Migrants' rights are human rights. It is tragic when migrants, whose rights have already been violated in their home countries, find their human rights also violated in their foreign host countries. Invoking host-country laws rarely works in their favor. United Methodists should urge their governments to ratify and implement the United Nations International Convention on the Protection of the Rights of All Migrant Workers and Members of Their Families (also called International Migration Convention). This Convention is designed to protect, secure, and ensure the human rights of migrant workers and their families.

As a worldwide presence and structure, The United Methodist Church plays an important and influential role in prospering the human rights of migrants and migrant workers among whom are its members and many who collaborate in its global mission work. The worldwide church has a special opportunity in its work with and among migrants to make visible a theology, mission and church structure that is migrant-inclusive and sensitive.

The church must advocate in all economic, social, and political arenas for justice, human rights, and hospitality. Such advocacy is about the abundance of life and of God's grace: lived in plenitude, never in scarcity. In this regard, our advocacy may take these into consideration (These considerations are adopted from the Advocacy Paper and Stockholm Affirmations of Churches Witnessing With Migrants [CWWM], an international platform for common advocacy of migrants, migrant advocates, churches and ecumenical bodies. The General Board of Church and Society participates actively in CWWM. CWWM believes that migrants are human beings who cannot be reduced to mere commodities to be traded and exchanged in the global market. It affirms that freedom of movement of peoples is a human right and that forced migration is a violation of that right. It works for development justice as a general framework for advocacy. The pillars of development justice—redistributive justice, economic justice, social justice, environmental justice and accountability to the people—are co-constitutive and indivisible and form part of CWWM advocacadvocacy work. These pillars are simultaneously global and local in character.):

- the development of a protocol of how migrants, migrants organizations, and church and ecumenical institutions, respond to urgent situations of life and death facing migrant communities today;
- the facilitation with like-minded groups of a collective shadow report to be submitted to the United Nations Human Rights Council's Universal Periodic Review and to the Committee on Migrant Workers monitoring implementation of the International Migration Convention;
- the continuation of collective analysis of the root causes of forced migration, and the churches' role in seeking development justice; and the articulation and advancement of an alternative narrative informed by faith-based perspectives based on the understanding that "migrants

are truly the ones who speak best about their hopes and aspirations and about how to advance and protect their rights and interests."

C. Indigenous Peoples: Toward Self-Determination

"All will sit underneath their own grapevines, / under their own fig trees. / There will be no one to terrify them; / for the mouth of the LORD of heavenly forces has spoken" (Micah 4:4).

Globalization threatens the human rights of indigenous peoples, including their aspirations for self-determination. Exploration and colonization have led to rapid appropriation of indigenous peoples' lands and natural resources, and the destruction of their sciences, ideas, arts, and cultures.

Indigenous peoples struggle against the industries encroaching on their sacred lands. They are fighting for sovereignty over their ancestral lands in the face of systematic campaigns of extermination. They face population transfers, forced relocation, and assimilation, often because of the aggressive development interests of big business.

Indigenous peoples demand respect of their right to their culture, spirituality, language, tradition, forms of organization, ways of knowing and doing, and their intellectual properties. Indeed, it will be hard for indigenous peoples all over the world to exercise their fundamental human rights as distinct nations, societies, and peoples without the ability to control the knowledge and resources they have inherited from their ancestors and reside in their ancestral domains.

The 1992 General Conference urged The United Methodist Church to "place itself at the vanguard of the efforts to undo and correct the injustices and the misunderstandings of the last 500 years" of colonialism. It raised the church's awareness of "the shameful stealing of the Native's land and other goods and the cruel destruction of their culture, arts, religion, the environment, and other living things on which their lives depended."

In the 2012 General Conference, our worldwide church demonstrated its commitment to indigenous peoples through an Act of Repentance Toward Healing Relationships with Indigenous Peoples. Its significance for the church is described in this manner: "The Act of Repentance not only addresses the communities and tribal nations of Native Americans in the United States. It encompasses the indigenous communities and tribal/nation entities of the various countries around the world where The United Methodist Church has spread its blanket. Taken together, the similarities are real and palpable. They reflect issues of self-determination, sovereignty, cultural integrity and how Native and indigenous peoples embrace The United Methodist Church as truth carriers of the Good News, declaring the Gospel of Jesus Christ with no other allegiances." (The Rev. Dr. Thom White Wolf Fassett on the Act of Repentance of The United Methodist Church, published by the Office of Christian Unity and Interreligious Relationships of the Council of Bishops)

Religious intolerance is one form of human-rights violation perpetrated on indigenous peoples around the world. The experience of forced relocation by the Dineh (Navajo) of Black Mesa in Arizona is an example of religious intolerance. The Dineh consider their ancestral lands as sacred. For them, to be uprooted is to be exterminated as a people. In this light, we must continue support for the work and mandate of the U.N. Special Rapporteur on Religious Intolerance as well as the U.N. Special Rapporteur on the Rights of Indigenous Peoples.

Big mining companies have been responsible in the destruction of livelihood, sacred sites, and ancestral homelands of indigenous peoples. Indigenous peoples' rights are human rights. Extractive mining, a form of development aggression, is opposed by indigenous peoples for destroying their lands and resources and wreaks havoc on the unity and health of their peoples and communities. United Methodists are urged to support the United Nations Declaration on the Rights of Indigenous Peoples. UNDRIP, as it is commonly called, was adopted on September 7, 2007, by the General Assembly of the United Nations, with the overwhelming support of 143 countries. Troubling, however, were the abstentions by Australia, Canada, New Zealand, and the United States, homes of many indigenous peoples.

We must call as a worldwide church for the universal adoption of this important instrument that the United Nations Human Rights Council hails as "a universal framework of minimum standards for the survival, dignity, well-being and rights of the world's indigenous peoples." The Council asserts: "The Declaration addresses both individual and collective rights; cultural rights and identity; rights to education, health, employment, language, and others. It outlaws discrimination against indigenous peoples and promotes their full and effective participation in all matters that concern them. It also ensures their right to remain distinct and to pursue their own priorities in economic, social, and cultural development. The Declaration explicitly encourages harmonious and cooperative relations between States and indigenous peoples."

United Methodists must support the Permanent Forum of Indigenous Issues. This Forum, established by the United Nations Economic and Social Council in July 2000, formally integrated indigenous peoples into the U.N. system and was mandated to "address indigenous issues related to economic and social development, culture, the environment, education, health and human rights." We remain in support of the appointment of a Special Rapporteur on Indigenous Populations within the aegis of the United Nations.

Indigenous peoples' self-determination, sovereignty, and spirituality are at the core of our support for their historic claim to their cultures, histories, and spiritual traditions, and to their historic rights to specific lands, territories, and resources. Colonialism eroded these claims and extinguished their rights. The process of decolonization is an unfinished business at the United Nations and in many social institutions. The role of religion and the church in the colonization of peoples and nations, including Native nations and indigenous peoples, is part of this hard and painful process of decolonization. It is part of an act of repentance that truly honors what indigenous people feel about how they have been wronged and where the restitution and forgiveness might come from, and what it will look like and entail.

D. Impunity: The Case for an International Criminal Court

"You must not act unjustly in a legal case. Do not show favoritism to the poor or deference to the great; you must judge your fellow Israelites fairly" (Leviticus 19:15).

A culture of peace must be globalized today. The prevailing culture of repression, oppression, and exploitation has no place in this culture of peace. Only the pursuit of a just peace, which includes the search for truth and justice for victims, will bring about forgiveness, reconciliation, and healing in many rural villages, towns, cities, nations, and regions of the world that are scarred by conflict and war.

The establishment of an International Criminal Court (ICC), as provided for in a treaty adopted in Rome in June 1998 by the United Nations Diplomatic Conference of Plenipotentiaries on the Establishment of an International Criminal Court, provides an important step in ending impunity. This court, whose charter called the Rome Statute was adopted in July 1998, and entered into force in July 2002 with the 60th country ratification, continues today to hear cases against war crimes, genocide, crimes against humanity, and crimes of aggression.

Faith-based and religious groups, working together with the Coalition for an International Criminal Court (CICC), identified several moral and ethical imperatives for the importance of the ICC. These imperatives remain true and urgent today: "Desirous that the quest for justice includes retributive justice whose purpose is the prosecution and punishment of offenders while insuring the rights of the accused to fair trials, restorative justice whose purpose is that of reparation, restitution and rehabilitation for the victims, and redemptive justice which must be seen as the enablement of communities to deal with the truths of the past in ways which will allow and enable social reconstruction and reconciliation, and the ending of cycles of violence;

"Recognizing that adjudication of crimes of international concerns that have transcended national boundaries are often beyond the scope of national criminal-justice systems, and that crimes whose immediate victims have occurred within national contexts are often beyond the competence or ability of national judicial systems;

"Noting the basic principles of justice for victims of crime and the abuse of power approved by the United Nations General Assembly;

"Therefore, establish the International Criminal Court."

United Methodists all over the world must urge all governments to sign and ratify the treaty to establish the court. As of today, there are at least 123 parties to the Rome Statute of the ICC. These parties do not yet include countries like the United States, Israel, Kuwait, Mozambique, Russian Federation, Sudan, Syrian Arab Republic, Ukraine, Yemen, Zimbabwe, and a few more which have signed the statute but have not ratified it. The work of the CICC and the Washington Working Group on the International Criminal Court, which focuses on getting the US to ratify the treaty, must be supported. In their support, United Methodists must preserve and strengthen the unprecedented provisions of the Rome Statute calling for an end to impunity for crimes committed against women and children.

E. Religious Liberty: The Case Against Intolerance

"For the law of the Spirit of life in Christ Jesus has made me free from the law of sin and death" (Romans 8:2 NKJV).

Religious liberty forms part of the pantheon of human rights. The Universal Declaration of Human Rights provides: "Everyone has the right to freedom of thought, conscience and religion: this right includes freedom to change his religion or belief, freedom, either alone or in community with others and in public or private, to manifest his religion or belief in teaching, practice, worship and observance" (Art. 18).

The United Methodist Church maintains that "religious persecution has been common in the history of civilization" and therefore urges for "policies and practices that ensure the right of every religious group to exercise its faith free from legal, political or economic restrictions." The Church also asserts that "all overt and covert forms of religious intolerance" must be condemned (2012 Social Principles, ¶ 162B).

Religious liberty continues to be denied and violated in many parts of the world. Concerns about religious persecution have been raised by almost every religious group, especially in places where one particular religion or belief is in a minority position. Religious intolerance, of both the established as well as "nontraditional" religions, is growing both in new and established democracies. The rise in religious extremism of all sorts and from all of the established and nontraditional religions has been convenient pretext for the curtailment of the exercise of religious liberty by many governments around the world.

The United Methodist Church must continue to foster further cooperation among spiritual, religious, and ecumenical bodies for the protection of religious freedom and belief. It must enter into healthy dialogues with peoples of differing faiths and ideologies, including Native and indigenous peoples, in the search for shared spiritual, social, and ethical principles that engender peace and justice.

The United Methodist Church is committed to uphold the minimum standards of the right of belief that are contained in the provisions of the United Nations Declaration on the Elimination of All Forms of Intolerance and of Discrimination Based on Religion or Belief. This declaration enunciates that "freedom of religion and belief should also contribute to the attainment of the goals of world peace, social justice and friendship between peoples and to the elimination of ideologies or practices of colonialism and racial discrimination."

United Methodists must urge their governments and encourage civil society to enter into dialogues about racism and discrimination and resolve to address especially those concerns that have institutionalized religious bases. The United Methodist Church urges global support for the Durban Declaration and Program of Action Against Racism, Racial Discrimination, Xenophobia and Related Intolerance.

F. Peace and Peacebuilding: Support for the United Nations and the Case for a Culture of Peace

"God will judge between the nations / and settle disputes of mighty nations, which are far away. / They will beat their swords into iron plows / and their spears into pruning tools. / Nation will not take up sword against nation; / they will no longer learn how to make war" (Micah 4:3).

"For he himself is our peace, who has made the two groups one and has destroyed the barrier, the dividing wall of hostility" (Ephesians 2:14 NIV).

In this era of globalization, the icons of war are more prominent and the arsenal of killing machines is more lethal than ever before. Our images of peace and the implements that make for a just peace most often are stymied by these icons and arsenals.

The resolution of conflicts and the establishment of a just and durable peace proceed from a just and liberating practice of governance on all levels of life: local and global. Just governance thrives not on wars and rumors of wars, but in the advancement of a world order that protects human rights, develops sustainable communities, cultivates a culture of peace, empowers people and their associations, and promotes a just and participatory democracy. It is imperative for human rights to be the foundational principle for a just and durable peace. The United Methodist Church must participate in building communities that prioritize the eradication of poverty and the elimination of hunger; the ending of wars and the resolution of conflicts, and the overcoming of ignorance, curing of diseases, and healing of enmities.

The United Nations remains the single most important international institution to achieve these ends. The United Methodist Church must continue to support the United Nations (¶ 165D).

Our participation in its many activities allows us to participate in making it a responsible and effective global force in peacekeeping, peacemaking and peacebuilding, and in the recognition of human dignity and the protection of human rights.

The resolve to stem the increasing forms, acts and agents of extremism and terrorism, including rooting out the drivers and causes for such, must be located within the bounds of multilateral mechanisms and transnational institutions, under the leadership of the United Nations. Our Social Principles guides us in this resolve: "We advocate the extension and strengthening of international treaties and institutions that provide a framework within the rule of law for responding to aggression, terrorism and genocide" (¶ 165C).

The United Methodist Church supports The Hague Agenda for Peace and Justice for the 21st Century which it joined in shaping. This agenda, produced by a historic conference in The Hague in May of 1999, encompasses fifty areas of concern highlighting the: 1) root causes of war and the culture of peace; 2) international humanitarian and human rights law and institutions; 3) the prevention, resolution, and transformation of violent conflict; and 4) disarmament and human security.

The United Methodist Church understanding of a culture of peace and the importance of multilateral cooperation in advancing peace, justice, and security based on human rights and sustainable development issues stems from its support for the Pillars of Peace for the 21st Century, a policy statement in support of the United Nations for the National Council of the Churches of Christ in the USA. The seven pillars state that peace rooted in justice requires:

1. increased political collaboration and accountability among governments within the United Nations system, among regional bodies, governments, local authorities, people's organizations, and global economic structures to seek the common good and equality for all;

2. increased moral, ethical, and legal accountability at all levels from governments, financial institutions, multilateral organizations, transnational corporations, and all other economic actors to seek a just, participatory, and sustainable economic order for the welfare and well-being of all people and all creation;

3. a comprehensive international legal system, capable of change as conditions require, in order to prevent and resolve conflicts, to

protect rights, to hold accountable those who disturb peace and violate international law, and to provide fair and effective review and enforcement mechanisms;

4. the participation of vulnerable and marginalized groups, seeking to promote justice and peace, in those mechanisms capable of redressing the causes and consequences of injustice and oppression;

5. the nurturing of a culture of peace in homes, communities, religious institutions, and nations across the world, including the use of nonviolent means of resolving conflict, appropriate systems of common security, and the end of the unrestrained production, sale, and use of weapons worldwide;

6. respect for the inherent dignity of all persons and the recognition, protection, and implementation of the principles of the International Bill of Human Rights, so that communities and individuals may claim and enjoy their universal, indivisible, and inalienable rights; and

7. a commitment to the long-term sustainability of the means of life, and profound reorientation of economic systems and individual lifestyles to support ecological justice for human communities in harmony with the whole of creation.

The United Methodist Church must also continue its support for the campaign to ban landmines by urging all governments to ratify and implement the landmine-ban treaty that prohibits the use, production, stockpiling and transfer of antipersonnel land mines. This treaty also calls on parties to increase landmine clearance and victim assistance efforts around the world.

United Methodists must also urge their governments to ratify the Comprehensive Nuclear Test Ban Treaty. Counter globalization happens when we ban landmines, abolish nuclear weapons, and prevent wars from continuing to fester or being waged.

G. Economic, Social, and Cultural Rights: That the Hungry May Be Filled

"When you give a banquet, invite the poor, crippled, lame, and blind" (Luke 14:13).

The Lord our God commanded us "to do justice, and to love kindness, and to walk humbly" (Micah 6:8 NRSV).

Justice, kindness, and humility underscore society's obligations to its people. But even with the indivisibility of civil, political, economic, social, and cultural rights, global hunger and poverty challenge our priorities. It is a challenge that confronts and addresses our concern for lifting the poor and marginalized among us.

In this era of globalization, poverty is defined as the inability of a human being to take advantage of global and market opportunities that are supposed to be booming and soaring. This globalization process deifies the market even as it commodifies the earth and its resources, if not even people themselves, who become pawns to economic production. One's worth and dignity in this globalization process is measured by one's ability to contribute to the gains of the market.

But gain or loss, in this era of globalization, it is the poor, the marginalized, and the vulnerable who suffer from price increases, reductions in government support for needed social and environmental programs, business disruptions, higher unemployment levels, and increased human rights violations.

The indivisibility of human rights underscores the understanding that freedom is hollow without food, that justice without jobs is like a clanging cymbal, and that liberty is a sham when people do not have land to inhabit and farm. The right to food and the right to employment are fundamental economic human rights. Societies become peaceful when the demands of justice are met. Justice becomes not only a dream but also a reality when implements of war give way to implements of peace. Food and jobs, also, are implements of peace. Would that indeed, at the end of the day, no child, no woman, and no one, goes to bed with an empty stomach.

United Methodists must continue to urge their governments to ratify the International Covenant on Economic, Social, and Cultural Rights and for these governments to make these rights a reality.

The Millennium Development Goals (MDGs), which we have supported as a church, we now deem to have largely faltered, especially because human rights was abandoned as a core principle. The economic challenges of unbridled globalization, especially widespread economic recession, coupled with indecisive action on climate change, did not help to attain the lofty goals of this millennial initiative. The inadequate attention to inequality, discrimination and exclusion of marginalized groups doomed the MDGs, whose targets were not fully achieved before they expired in 2015.

Another chance at targeting the root causes of development problems, not the least extreme poverty and hunger, is presented to the world community through another listing of sustainable development goals (SDGs) negotiated again under the auspices of the United Nations. Human rights, which affirms sacred and human worth at their core, must be foundational to any development agenda, always and in any timeline, post-2015 and beyond.

Our support for a new set of SDGs is predicated on the recognition of God-given human dignity and the protection of human rights. It recognizes the health and wholeness of human beings as much as that of the planet and the cosmos. It also includes the recognition of the requirements of development justice that addresses historic inequalities brought about by slavery and colonialism, as well as modern forms of pillage and plunder brought about by unbridled globalization and historic degradation of planet earth.

U.N. Secretary-General Ban Ki-moon put the sustainable development challenge thus: "Our globalized world is marked by extraordinary progress alongside unacceptable and unsustainable levels of want, fear, discrimination, exploitation, injustice and environmental folly at all levels. We also know, however, that these problems are not accidents of nature or the results of phenomena beyond our control. They result from actions and omissions of people, public institutions, the private sector and others charged with protecting human rights and upholding human dignity."

In this era of globalization, where profit and profit making at the expense of the needs and welfare of the poor and the vulnerable and where unbridled pursuit of wealth and power have trampled upon and denied human rights of peoples, peace rooted in God's justice will bring about the true globalization that will heal the wounds and scars of wars and conflict that peoples and nations have waged against each other. Peace rooted in God's justice will help bring about forgiveness and wholeness for all God's people and the whole of creation. Peace rooted in God's justice will provide sustenance for God's people and sustainability for God's earth. God's reign on earth, as it is in heaven, is, in the end, the true globalization we must long and work for.

ADOPTED 2000
AMENDED AND READOPTED 2004
READOPTED 2008
AMENDED AND READOPTED 2016
RESOLUTION #6025, 2008, 2012 *BOOK OF RESOLUTIONS*
RESOLUTION #309, 2004 *BOOK OF RESOLUTIONS*
RESOLUTION #289, 2000 *BOOK OF RESOLUTIONS*

See Social Principles, ¶ 165.

6026. International Day of Prayer

As Paul writes of the interrelatedness of the body of Christ to the Corinthians saying that when "one part suffers, all the parts suffer with it" (1 Corinthians 12:26), so we recognize the presence of religious persecution throughout the world. As The United Methodist Church condemns religious intolerance and persecution of all faith groups, we heed Paul's words and acknowledge the interconnectedness we have with members of the body of Christ throughout the world who endure persecution because of their faith.

Since The United Methodist Church opposes injustice, intolerance, and bigotry and believes in the power of prayer, we encourage United Methodist congregations to observe in November an International Day of Prayer for the Persecuted Church. It is through our earnest prayers that we grow in our sense of unity with Christians around the world, as well as with all members of religious groups who endure persecution. We become more aware of the needs of our brothers and sisters who suffer because of their faith, as we defend the religious freedoms of all faith communities.

ADOPTED 2000
REVISED AND READOPTED 2008
READOPTED 2016
RESOLUTION #6026, 2008, 2012 *BOOK OF RESOLUTIONS*
RESOLUTION #311, 2004 *BOOK OF RESOLUTIONS*
RESOLUTION #292, 2000 *BOOK OF RESOLUTIONS*

See Social Principles, ¶ 165A.

6028. Global Migration and the Quest for Justice

"Ways must be found to share more equitably the resources of the world."
—Social Principles, ¶ 163E, The United Methodist Church
Global migration is a historical and current concern of The United Methodist Church, addressed in the Social Principles and frequently by General Conference action. The Social Principles frame the issue in theological and humanitarian contexts:

1. "We commit ourselves as a Church to the achievement of a world community that is a fellowship of persons who honestly love one another. We pledge ourselves to seek the meaning of the

gospel in all issues that divide people and threaten the growth of world community" (¶ 165).

2. "In order to provide basic needs such as food, clothing, shelter, education, health care, and other necessities, ways must be found to share more equitably the resources of the world" (¶ 163E).

3. "We advocate for the rights of all migrants and applaud their efforts toward responsible self-organization and self-determination" (¶ 163F, 2004 *Book of Resolutions*).

I. Introduction

Human migration is as old as human history. Individuals, families, tribes, and nations have been on the move since the days of Abraham and Sarah and before. Throughout the centuries, political and economic factors, including wars; health and environmental challenges; and racism, xenophobia, and religious discrimination have at times uprooted people and at others lured them to new venues across deserts, rivers, continents, oceans, and national and ethnic boundaries.

Today, migration is a critical international and at times a pressing national issue; a matter of last resort and no other choice for millions of human beings, and a desperate alternative to many who would rather stay where they are if conditions could permit safety and essentials for survival. In general terms, migrants today are those who by force or choice leave their regions of origin because of armed conflict, natural disaster, institutional or gang violence, development projects, human trafficking (including labor, sexual or drug trafficking) or extreme economic deprivation. Contemporary migration involves the linked realities of abundance and poverty and racial/ethnic/religious identities and exclusion. It often reflects a global system that expects many people to live in poverty, or have their nations torn by conflict, or their natural resources exploited, so that others may live in abundance. That many people will resist poverty and war through migration is an ancient and modern fact of human existence. As a consequence, elaborate national and international systems of containment and classification based on national origin have been developed over the past quarter-century with regard to migrants (see below).

Global migration as a factor in the quest for justice is a major priority of The United Methodist Church as a denomination that is global in its vision, mission, and ministries. This concern is rooted in both a biblical mandate for justice and a commitment to the future of the church. Many migrants and potential migrants today are Methodists; some are welcomed in new places, bringing new vigor to old congregations, while others face discrimination and exploitation in new places. Migration today is inextricably linked to the issues of Christian community, evangelism, new church development, the nurturing of church leadership, and ministry WITH the poor. Migrants in the future will increasingly enrich United Methodist understanding and practice of mission, church life and organization, intergroup relations, and concepts of the universal love of God.

This resolution addresses the varieties, contexts, and responses to global migration in the first quarter of the twenty-first century. It reflects concern for the right to stay where one is, for safe passage in migration, and for a welcome that can lead to a sense of belonging in a new place.

II. *Contemporary Migration*

Environmental catastrophe, organized violence, political chaos, economic desperation, human trafficking, and ecological exploitation are among the most common causes of contemporary migration. To respond to and keep track of massive movements of people, the international community has instituted categories of migrants. The four traditional categories are:

- Refugees—persons outside of their country of origin who are unable or unwilling to return for fear of persecution based on race, religion, ethnicity, political affiliation, or opinion; official "refugees" are so recognized by the United Nations High Commissioner for Refugees (UNHCR), which is charged by the international community to oversee service to, and protection of, refugees. As of 2014, UNHCR listed 51 million displaced people; in 2015, some 3.8 million Syrian refugees.
- Asylum seekers—a type of refugee, persons who have left their homeland to petition for refuge in the country to which they have fled; asylum seekers must be so recognized by the countries whose protection they seek. More than a million people requested asylum in 2013, according to the UNHCR, including large numbers in transit. Others were Central American refugees in Mexico and the United States, and Africans in Italy. Many asylum

seekers find no protection and are jailed or returned to dangerous situations.

- Internally displaced persons—those who are displaced within their own country because of military, economic, and social upheaval, and natural disasters such as famine, earthquake, and flood; they are generally not protected by the international community and must depend for protection and assistance primarily on their country of residence, which may be implicit in the cause of displacement. In 2014, some 33.3 million people lived uprooted in their own countries.

- Economic migrants—people who move from one country to another to find work. Most frequently they seek to flee from poverty and often permanently relocate so they may feed their families. Some are allowed into more affluent nations as immigrants; some enter without documentation and may be welcomed in times of labor shortages and deported in times of economic downturn or public disapproval. Such migrants are among the most vulnerable in any society; many are women and children who become the objects of abuse and brutality. One subcategory in this classification consists of migratory or itinerant workers, people who move from place to place, often with the agricultural cycle, to find employment. Large numbers of such workers are technically short-term contract laborers, or "guest workers," although they may stay a lifetime, renewing short-term contracts under circumstances that are at best precarious. Some return on a periodic or eventually permanent basis to their homelands; others make domestic and other ties in places of employment and wish to remain. The number of current economic migrants is difficult to calculate. In 2015, the International Labor Organization (ILO) placed the global estimate of migrant workers at 232 million, including 53 million domestic workers, focused in affluent regions such as North America, Japan, Australia, the Gulf States, and Europe.

III. A Context of Migration

Virtually all groups of today's migrants and refugees are battered by the divide between the rich and the poor, a divide rooted in nineteenth and twentieth century colonialism and directly caused by rapid corporate globalization in agriculture, industry, and commerce. Trade policies and arms deals enrich the rich and undercut economies in the global South without providing new contexts for prosperity or hope. These realities, along with armed conflict, environmental spoilage, and natural disasters force people to find new homes within their own countries or across national borders. The entire planet is affected in some way by the global economic divide.

Yet, while money and products may flow with relative ease across borders, the movement of people is increasingly restricted, leading to concentrations of the poor along borders and, often, to the building of literal and figurative walls of exclusion, notably around the rich nations of the northern hemisphere and the affluent enclaves in Asia, Latin America, Africa, the Middle East, and the Pacific. While the legal and physical walls seek to exclude flows of undocumented migrants, in fact, there is growing demand in wealthier nations for cheap labor. Millions of migrants do enter— through formal guest worker programs or through informal business networks that actively seek undocumented workers while maintaining them in an exploitative, noncitizen underclass. Many of those who are shut out or who migrate without legal status are at the bottom of racial, ethnic, and caste hierarchies. They are often poor women and children. On either side of the divide, families are relegated to intense human suffering, inadequate nutrition and health service, lack of educational opportunities, and the reverberating, debilitating experience of oppression. Ironically, and horribly, with regard to economic migrants, the rich say, "Come in, do our dirty work at low wages, and then go away."

The global South is particularly concerned with the loss of young generations to other countries, the departures dictated either by economic need or wooing by affluent societies seeking to fill jobs with cheap labor. Such émigrés often do not want to leave; they may feel pressured by promises of education, jobs, and economic security for themselves and their families. They become entrapped in unjust global systems that drain the resources of poor, Southern countries for the benefit of the affluent societies of the global North.

IV. Biblical Perspectives: Justice and Shared Resources

Attitudes toward and treatment of migrants are usually conditioned today, even within the church, by nation-state considerations expressed in the language of "us" and "them"—or "we" the homefolks and "they" the intruder/alien. A beneficent attitude sometimes prevails: "'We'" will allow X number of 'them' to come among 'us' provided they acknowledge our generosity and become like us; so long, of course, as they do not threaten our comfort."

There are more biblically and theologically sound perspectives for Christians. In the biblical understanding, it is not about us and them, but about one people of God, called to seek justice and share equitably, at the very core of spiritual and physical survival.

The prophet Isaiah put the matter in context and posed the daunting question: "On your fast day you do whatever you want, / and oppress all your workers. / . . . You shouldn't fast as you are doing today / if you want to make your voice heard on high. / . . . Isn't this the fast I choose: / releasing wicked restraints, untying the ropes of a yoke, / setting free the mistreated, / and breaking every yoke? / Isn't it sharing your bread with the hungry / and bringing the homeless poor into your house?" (Isaiah 58:3-7). Not only does God's understanding of faithfulness entail the achievement of justice, but for the comfortable, the promise of healing and salvation depends on that action. It was only when the people turned from false religiosity to operative justice that they would receive the promise of spiritual wholeness.

The Hebrew Scriptures contain many references to "strangers" and "sojourners" among the people of Israel and to provisions for treatment that reflect a tribal framework that had stipulated rules for hospitality and also limits on the outsiders. However, in the Books of the Law, and to an even greater extent in the prophetic literature, concern for the stranger focuses on justice and the sharing of resources that flow from the bounty of God. Ezekiel anticipated a time when foreigners would share with the ancient Jewish nation all the blessings of the land, which was understood to belong to God alone (Leviticus 25:23). In a real sense, the ancient scriptures understand both the people of Israel and sojourners to be aliens since the people of Israel had been sojourners in Egypt. God's providence for Israel extends to others (Psalm 146:9; Malachi 2:5), and everything, and everyone, belongs to God (Psalm 24:1-2).

Christians do not approach the issue of migration from the perspective of tribe or nation, but from within a faith community of love and welcome, a community that teaches and expects hospitality to the poor, the homeless, and the oppressed. The Christian community at its best not only welcomes and embraces migrants but can be led by them toward clearer understandings of justice and hospitality. Christians rejoice in welcoming migrants who are also Christian, brothers and sisters of the same baptism, gathered around the same sacramental table. And people beyond the Christian community deserve no less hospitality than Christians extend to themselves.

The breadth of God's love permeates the New Testament; that love incorporates the faith community and goes beyond it. This is clearly emphasized in a short passage in 1 Thessalonians (3:12), where Paul prays that God will provide the grace for Christians to "increase and enrich your love for each other and for everyone."

United Methodists should harbor no doubt about their responsibility to all those who live here on the earth, especially the poor, the homeless, and the mistreated. John Wesley's concern for the poor and outcast was constant and extended far beyond acts of charity. He worked for just systems in which persons could with dignity stand on their own feet. Wesley advocated just relationships within the social order. When some have great abundance while others are homeless and hungry, the biblical task is not merely to help those in need, but to seek justice—to shift resources and opportunity so that all are at the table, all are fed, all experience the abundance of God's love, both physically and spiritually.

V. Critical Issues Relating to Migration Today

United Methodists and all Christians face numerous critical situations, causes, and effects relating to migration today, especially in regard to war and economic systems and policies that perpetuate poverty. As a denomination with a global mission, The United Methodist Church experiences the dilemmas of nations that "send," "transit," and "receive" migrants. Citizens and undocumented immigrants are within the Church's membership, as are employers and migrant workers, police and detainees, and affluent and poor families. The United Methodist family is a microcosm of migrant issues, a church that through God's grace seeks to respond to the needs of the most physically vulnerable and traumatized, but also address the spiritual needs of the privileged.

The following are among the critical issues demanding attention:

1. The volume of refugees, asylum seekers, and persons displaced within their own countries is growing, as are the numbers of economic migrants with and without documentation.

2. Wealthy nations, especially those with decreasing populations, are increasingly dependent upon migrants to maintain their current economies. They seek both highly skilled professionals and low-wage workers for jobs in construction, health care, agriculture, meat packing, and domestic service.

3. The critical loss of skilled workers and potential leaders in "sending" countries undermines the future economic and social advancement of those societies. Doctors from poorer nations can often earn more in the US as a nurse than as a physician in their country of origin. The "brain drain," often deliberately encouraged by rich countries for their own benefit, affects teachers, engineers, medical personnel, researchers, and technicians. Large numbers of persons, including young, unaccompanied children, traverse the corridors of "transit" countries, on the move from their homes to other places. In Mexico, nearly half a million Central Americans ride the freight trains known as "La Bestia" (The Beast) as the trains head north to deliver goods for export. Since there are no passenger cars, people ride atop the moving trains on a perilous trek.

Those who survive are faced with extortion and violence at the mercy of gangs and organized crime that control the migrant corridors. People often die along the route, unidentified, with their families often never knowing the fate of their loved ones. Another dangerous and recurring intersection for migrants is off the coast of Italy, near the island of Lampedusa. Shipwreck catastrophes have occurred involving migrants from Libya, Eritrea, Somalia, Ghana, Palestine, and Syria. Traffickers torture and rape migrants who have paid thousands of dollars to gangs that move people across the Sahara to Libya.

4. Old wars and territorial occupations have left a critical migration crisis and new wars add to the problem. This can be illustrated in the Middle East, where many Palestinians remain as refugees more than a half century since they lost their homes in Israel. In recent years, millions of Iraqis and Syrians have fled their countries, adding to the displaced population of the greater Middle East.

5. The passage of stricter enforcement of anti-immigrant legislation and the building of exclusionary walls, often in response to increased migration, intensifies cultural tensions, marked by racial, class, and religious "backlash." Restrictive policies also intensify migrant resistance based on fear of arrest and deporta-

tion, substandard wages, physical and mental abuse, and even death for crossing a border. Migrants fall prey to trafficking for economic or sexual purposes and sometimes become virtual slaves in their new place of residence.

6. An increasing percentage of migrant women now make up almost half of the international migrant population. Many of these women are domestic workers, who may raise other peoples' children while being separated from their own. Some migrant women and girls are subjected to physical and sexual abuse and fear reprisals if they complain. Human trafficking is growing globally, especially in the area of forced labor, which includes the sex trade, the primary reason. The 2014 report of the UN Office of Drugs and Crime indicates that women and girls account for 70 percent of all trafficking victims. One in three victims is a child and two out of three are girls.

7. Migration policy and practice divide families across generations. Filipino contract workers in Saudi Arabia may serve in those countries for their entire careers, and then watch their own children, who they hardly know, step into their roles as they retire. Families are also divided by the deportation of the undocumented parents who leave behind children holding citizenship.

8. Remittances (sending "home" the paycheck) have become major sources of financing for poor countries; revenues that threaten to undercut aid assistance from rich nations. The monies migrants send home is massive, an estimated $650 billion in 2015, according to the World Bank. Some nations, including the Philippines, Bangladesh, and El Salvador, depend on remittances to support their financial system. In an effort to escape responsibility for the sharing of resources, some officials in the global North tout remittances as replacements for development aid. This attitude violates the spirit of the Sustainable Development Goals and other United Nations accords. Through international instruments, northern nations have set the goal of providing 0.7 percent of their gross national product in development aid to poor nations, as well as to cancel some debt and alter trade policies in ways that benefit poor nations.

VI. Response of the Church

The United Methodist Church commits itself to:

1. provide support and opportunities for refugees, asylees, and migrants, including annual conference and local church ministries

that promote the Right to Stay in traditional sending countries, Safe Passage in countries of transit, and training for Welcoming and Belonging in receiving locales;

2. engage in strong, coordinated advocacy on migration issues that seeks to overcome poverty, war and other causes leading to the displacement and marginalization of people; and

3. organize through institutional channels and prepare educational resources for the achievement of these objectives; support leadership development programs for migrants, especially for those within The United Methodist Church.

Assistance includes:

1. work with global mission partners to equip personnel to provide direct services that help persons and families live safely and with dignity in their places of origin; or if they must leave, that help keep them safe in transit, and that support programs that welcome migrants, giving them a sense of security in a new locale. Relief to refugees and displaced persons around the world, including the resettlement, when possible, of refugees through congregations and through economic development programs both for those who permanently resettle and those who may return to homelands;

2. congregational and annual conference programs (US and central conferences) that humanely respond to migrants within their borders—defending human rights, advancing just immigration policies by national governments, and tending to their spiritual, material, and legal needs as required, with the General Boards of Global Ministries and Church and Society, and other partners, helping to equip conferences and congregations to engage in these ministries;

3. education of church members and communities on the causes and realities of migration, including international treaty commitments, the issues of economic and environmental justice, and the obstacles to a just, peaceable world created by anti-immigrant racism and xenophobia;

4. bridge building between diverse races, ethnicities, religions, and cultures, opposing violence against and abuse of migrants;

5. strengthen migrant congregations in new locales and/or integrate migrant faith communities into existing congregations; facilitate local, national, and international dialogue of those on the

front lines of migrant ministries for the sake of sharing best practices and promoting collaboration;

6. work with civic and legal organizations to help communities alleviate social conditions caused by harsh immigration laws and heavy-handed national security measures; and

7. recognize the right of sanctuary in any United Methodist local church for migrants subject to detention or deportation by government security forces.

Advocacy includes promotion of:

1. just and equitable trade and development policies that support human rights and counteract the root causes of migration such as war and militarization, environmental spoilage, and corporate greed;

2. engagement with other Christian and religious organizations in North-South dialogues, study of international economic policies, and joint action;

3. training young clergy and laity for leadership in migrant communities or those receiving migrants;

4. protection for uprooted women and children from all forms of violence and abuse, including full legal protection of children in situations of armed conflict;

5. unification of families divided by borders and legal status wherever this occurs;

6. denunciation of xenophobic, Islamophobic, and racist reactions against newcomers;

7. defense of civil liberties and social protections regardless of the legal status of persons;

8. abolition of governmental anti-terrorism policies and practices that criminalize or profile refugees and immigrants as threats to national security; and

9. adoption by all nations of the United Nations International Convention on the Protection of the Rights of All Migrant Workers and their Families, and mobilize to promote compliance with the terms of the convention.

Institutional organization includes:

1. Continuation of a United Methodist Immigration Task Force to lead the church in a prophetic response to refugee and migrant issues by interpreting official policy in light of current realities, coordinating vision, analysis, education and action. Said task

force will be convened by one or more bishops designated by the Council of Bishops. It will be comprisedof representatives from all appropriate general agencies, as well as persons from jurisdictions, central conferences, annual conferences, partner churches, denominational ethnic/racial caucuses, and ethnic and language ministry plans. General agencies will each bear the cost of their participation in the task force and those agencies may underwrite the costs of non-agency participation as needs require and resources permit.

2. Establishment of the third Sunday of February as an annual Migrant Sunday in congregations throughout the denomination, following the lead of the Methodist Church of Mexico. This observance will provide an opportunity for worship, education, and mission action, and advocacy on behalf of migrant ministries.

3. Dissemination and study of the 2013 report of the Human Rights and Investment Task Force convened by the General Board of Global Ministries and General Board of Pension and Health Benefits, which seeks to align denominational investment policy and practice with mission objectives, and takes account of violations of the human rights of migrants.

4. Continuation of migration as one specific component of the denomination focus area on Ministry WITH the Poor.

5. Engagement in research on migrants and existing and emerging migrant ministries within The United Methodist Church.

ADOPTED 2008
AMENDED AND READOPTED 2016
RESOLUTION #6028, 2008, 2012 *BOOK OF RESOLUTIONS*

See Social Principles, ¶ 165A, D.

6031. Holy Land Tours

For many years, some Palestinian Christians have expressed deep dismay that too many United Methodists and other Christian groups traveling to Israel/Palestine, also called the Holy Land, have missed an extraordinary opportunity for ecumenical fellowship and sharing with other followers of the Prince of Peace. Our Christian sisters and brothers indigenous to the area continue to wonder why they are so often ignored by Christian pilgrims to the region. Why, they ask, do travelers tend to honor the inanimate stones that testify to Jesus' life and ministry while ignoring the "living stones," the indigenous Christians who represent an unbroken line of discipleship to Jesus in the land that he called home?

In December 2009, Palestinian Christian leaders from all the church families present in the Holy Land, launched a Kairos Palestine document: "A moment of truth: a word of faith, hope and love from the heart of Palestinian suffering." (See kairospalestine .ps>)

In Kairos Palestine, which the 2012 General Conference commended as a study resource, Palestinian Christians have issued an invitation to all sisters and brothers: "In order to understand our reality, we say to the Churches: Come and See. We will fulfill our role to make known to you the truth of our reality, receiving you as pilgrims coming to us to pray, carrying a message of peace, love and reconciliation." See <http://www.kairospalestine.ps /content/come-and-see-call-palestinian-christians-journey -peace-justice-guidelines-christians>.

Travelers to this land have the opportunity to be ambassadors of unity and concern to the rapidly dwindling churches and Christians in a troubled land. They also have an opportunity to share in the vocation of peacemaking and to learn from the spiritual traditions of the churches indigenous to the Middle East. Further, they have a special opportunity to discover firsthand the realities of a region of deep meaning and vital importance to Christians, as well as to Jews and Muslims.

We recognize the tragic history that Christians share with Jews, and the complex relationships between particular nations and the state of Israel. We encourage dialogue between Christians, Jewish, and Muslim religious leaders.

Therefore, The United Methodist Church:

1. strongly affirms the resolution of the 1984 General Conference, offering "encouragement of all leaders of and participants in 'Holy Land tours' to contact indigenous Christian leaders in the Middle East, and to hear the concerns of both the Israelis and Palestinians who live there, as well as visit the biblical and historical sites" ("The Arab-Israeli Conflict," *The Book of Resolutions, 1984;* page 280);

2. asks the bishops, clergy, members, agencies, and congregations of The United Methodist Church, as they plan visits to the Holy Land, to devote significant program time to contact with indigenous Christian leaders and to hearing the concerns

of Palestinians and Israelis on the current crisis of Palestinian self-determination;

3. urges all United Methodists planning, organizing, and/or participating in a trip to the Holy Land to apply to their Holy Land trip planning the guidelines outlined in the General Conference resolution 6030, "Responsible Travel" [see 2012 *Book of Resolutions*];

4. recommends that United Methodists planning individual or group tours to Israel/Palestine consult with the United Methodist Liaison Office in Jerusalem to seek opportunities to worship with indigenous Christian congregations, to include overnight stays in Bethlehem, and to visit United Methodist-supported mission sites;

5. supports the purchase of local Palestinian-made fair trade products and crafts in keeping with the guidelines in the General Conference resolution on "Responsible Travel" [see 2012 *Book of Resolutions*];

6. asks the General Board of Global Ministries and the General Board of Church and Society to prepare specific recommendations regarding preparation, participation in, and follow-up education and advocacy actions for United Methodists traveling in the Middle East and other sensitive regions of the world;

7. recommends that United Methodist-sponsored tours use the denomination's seminar program in predeparture seminars for the travelers;

8. urges that travelers use, as advance study materials, positions adopted by General Conference and by general church agencies relating to the Middle East, as well as resources such as "*Working for a Just and Lasting Peace in Israel and Palestine*" (an advocacy packet prepared by the boards of Church and Society and Global Ministries, http://umc-gbcs.org/content/general /Advocacy Packet_Fall_2013.pdf); the Kairos Palestine document, http://www.kairospalestine.ps/content/kairos-document; and other peacemaking resources;

9. urges seminaries and United Methodist-related colleges to apply the guidelines in this resolution to any school-sponsored trips, internships, and/or semesters of study in Palestine/Israel;

10. extends sincere appreciation to those United Methodists who have facilitated the implementation of the above recommendations in tours they have sponsored or participated in since the adoption of this resolution;

11. expresses deep concern that many tours sponsored or arranged by United Methodist bishops, pastors, and laity do not schedule program time for participants to enter into relationship with the indigenous Christians so that they may "Walk With the Living Stones" in their strides toward Palestinian self-determination, their rich spiritual heritage, and their faithful contemporary witness;

12. expresses deep concern that Christian presence in the land of Jesus continues to decline in numbers through economic, social, and political pressures, which have greatly diminished the numbers and percentage of Christians in the Holy Land. United Methodist bishops and other organizers of Holy Land tours have a special responsibility to strengthen the witness of the remaining Palestinian disciples of the living Lord;

13. affirms the presence of The United Methodist Church, the Methodist Church of Britain, and the World Methodist Council in Jerusalem through our Methodist Liaison Office and through our ongoing partnership with Palestinian and Israeli organization working for reconciliation and to establish equal rights for all under international law;

14. encourages tour leaders to consult with the General Board of Global Ministries and the Methodist Liaison Office in Jerusalem in order to facilitate adherence to these recommendations;

15. instructs annual conferences and general agencies to monitor and report to the General Conference regarding the implementation of this resolution;

16. urges close cooperation with the Jerusalem Interchurch Center and other indigenous Christian groups to facilitate informed, alternative travel opportunities to the region; and

17. commends all who initiate visits to the Bible lands that explore issues of justice and peace among all participants in the region, with special emphasis upon the concerns of our Palestinian Christian colleagues.

ADOPTED 1992
AMENDED AND READOPTED 1996, 2000, 2008, 2016
RESOLUTION #6031, 2008, 2012 *BOOK OF RESOLUTIONS*
RESOLUTION #292, 2004 *BOOK OF RESOLUTIONS*
RESOLUTION #271, 2000 *BOOK OF RESOLUTIONS*

See Social Principles, ¶ 165A, B, D.

6032. Eradicating Modern-Day Slavery

"How terrible for [him], who builds his house with corruption / and his upper chambers with injustice, / working his countrymen for nothing, / refusing to give them their wages" (Jeremiah 22:13).

"But people who are trying to get rich fall into temptation. They are trapped by many stupid and harmful passions that plunge people into ruin and destruction. The love of money is the root of all kinds of evil. Some have wandered away from the faith and have impaled themselves with a lot of pain because they made money their goal" (1 Timothy 6:9-10).

While the transatlantic slave trade—Africans kidnapped and taken to work as slaves in the United States, Latin America, and the Caribbean—was abolished around 1807 (Ngwe, Job Elom and O. Oko Elechi. (2012). Human Trafficking: Modern Day Slavery in the 21st Century. *African Journal of Criminology and Justice Studies*: AJCJS, Vol.6, #s1&2), modern-day slavery has become the fastest-growing transnational criminal enterprise, earning an estimated $150 billion (U.S.) in illegal profits annually while enslaving 21 million people around the world (International Labour Organization, www.ilo.org <http://www.ilo.org>). "[T]here are essentially three aspects of modern slavery according to Craig, et al (2007), namely, that they involve (1) severe economic exploitation; (2) the absence of any framework of human rights; and (3) the maintenance of control of one person over another by the prospect or reality of violence" (p. 12) (Ngwe, Job Elom and O. Oko Elechi. (2012). Human Trafficking: Modern Day Slavery in the 21st Century. *African Journal of Criminology and Justice Studies*: AJCJS, Vol.6, #s1&2.)

Slavery exists in several forms, including the "descent slavery" (slaves and children of slaves passed down as property to one's descendants) practiced in some African countries such as Mali and Mauritania; "bonded labor, serfdom, debt bondage, sexual slavery, child labor and enforced participation in armed conflict" as noted by Craig, et al (2007). Slavery has endured despite its abhorrence by . . . societies because of the critical role of labor as a factor of production. Some governments have either actively or tacitly participated in the exploitation of other peoples' labor (or even their citizens' labor) for economic benefits" (Ngwe, Job Elom and O. Oko Elechi. (2012). Human Trafficking: Modern Day Slavery in the 21st Century. *African Journal of Criminology and Justice Studies*: AJCJS, Vol.6, #s1&2).

Due to globalized communication, currency exchange, migration, and trading, human trafficking has become the predominant means by which people are enslaved. The United Nations defines trafficking to be "the recruitment, transportation, transfer, harboring, or receipt of persons, by means of the threat or use of force or other forms of coercion, of abduction, of fraud, of deception, of the abuse of power or of a position of vulnerability or of the giving or receiving of payments or benefits to achieve the consent of a person having control over another person, for the purpose of exploitation. Exploitation shall include, at a minimum, the exploitation of the prostitution of others or other forms of sexual exploitation, forced labor or services, slavery or practices similar to slavery, servitude. . . ."

One of the challenges in the abolition of modern-day slavery is that "[t]here is no consistent face of a trafficker. Traffickers include a wide range of criminal operators, including individuals, small families or businesses, loose-knit decentralized criminal networks, and international organized criminal syndicates" (Polaris Project, www.polarisproject.org <http://www.polarisproject.org>). In addition, trafficking is low risk and high profit because victims are isolated and often deemed "disposable" (Stop the Traffik UK, www.stopthetraffik.org <http://www.stopthetraffik.org>). It is estimated that 95 percent of trafficking victims experience physical and/or sexual violence while trafficked (The Health Risks and Consequences of Trafficking in Women and Adolescents. (2003). London School of Hygiene & Tropical Medicine).

A report from the Australian Institute of Criminology referred to reports of Chinese female migrants who, under the control of traffickers, were raped while family members were listening on the phone in order to persuade families to pay off debts (The Health Risks and Consequences of Trafficking in Women and Adolescents. (2003). London School of Hygiene & Tropical Medicine).

Industries where people are trafficked include: agriculture, domestic labor, hotels, landscaping, forestry, day labor, garment factories, manufacturing, warehousing, nail salons, meat/seafood processing, mining, brothels, massage parlors, construction, canning, door-to-door sales/street vendors, restaurants and bars, tourism, entertainment, carnivals, disaster cleanup, strip clubs, sex trade, child soldiers, pornography, and fishing.

The majority of source countries of trafficking are on the continents of Africa and Asia, and the destination countries are often in Europe and North America. Colonization and an increasing globalized economy are two leading factors promoting human trafficking. As large groups of people were removed from their land in order to grow cash crops and mine, urban centers became overcrowded, joblessness increased and poverty swelled. People were no longer able to sustain themselves because economic and trade policies that allowed raw materials and resources to move from the continents of Africa, South America, and Asia did not allow the people of those same lands to move with the resources. This transfer of wealth continues to destabilize governments, as do wars seeking to return indigenous peoples to leadership and fighting among tribes or factions to gain control of lucrative natural resources. Failing economies and resulting budgetary constraints often inhibit the enforcement of national and international anti-trafficking laws and can lead to corruption of new governments and law enforcement entities who benefit from money earned through trafficking enterprises.

Jesus' ministry focused on standing with people who were most vulnerable. The reasons that children and adults fall prey to traffickers rest at individual, cultural, institutional, and governmental levels. There is a significant gap in wealth between urban and rural areas that creates a deep yearning to escape poverty. Abusive interpersonal relationships and unfair treatment, cultural practices and norms, institutional policies, and business practices at country level and beyond continue to deny the sacred worth of women and girls, and perpetuate gender inequality resulting in a disproportionate percentage of women and children living in poverty around the world. The United Nations Development Program reports that in many places women lack access to paid work and/or the ability to get a loan; thus, women make up 50 percent of the world's population but own only 1 percent of the world's wealth. Parents and children, who are often deceived by promises of education, citizenship in a more prosperous country, or love, send their children or leave with traffickers without knowing of the exploitation and abuse awaiting their children or them, respectively. This disparity in wealth and opportunity is mirrored in the percentages of women (70 percent) and children (50 percent) who are victims of trafficking. Human trafficking is particularly dangerous to children in disaster zones. Eva Biaudet of the Organization for Security and Cooperation in Europe said: "When there are catastrophes—when the state fails, when there are no systems—children are extremely at risk for not only being abandoned . . . but also for abuse and exploitation. It's a very good place for traffickers to be when the state fails" (<http://www.humantrafficking.org>).

According to the Polaris Project, "Human trafficking is a market-based economy that exists on the principles of supply and demand. It thrives due to conditions that allow for high profits to be generated at low risks." International conventions have been ratified and country-level laws have been passed by numerous countries around the world. The laws provide necessary tools for governments, law enforcement, and nongovernmental organizations to raise awareness about trafficking, prosecute traffickers, and require governments to ensure the rescue and rehabilitation of trafficking survivors. These initiatives primarily focus on reducing the supply side of this economic equation. People of faith must lead the efforts to decrease the demand for cheap labor, goods, and services that drive modern-day slavery.

Jesus' ministry recognizes the sacred worth of every person and directly challenges the exploitation and abuse of people. In John 10:10, Jesus says, "I came so that they could have life—indeed, so that they could live life to the fullest." John Wesley, the founder of Methodism, condemned slavery as wrong and incompatible with Christ's teachings in numerous instances, including a tract entitled "Thoughts on Slavery" and a sermon, "The Use of Money." Like all people, women and girls are promised the abundant life offered by Christ. Far too often, experiences such as these are recounted by trafficking survivors:

"Constance" was trafficked from the Middle East to the United States by a family that kept her as a domestic worker. She was a survivor of female genital mutilation and was physically, sexually, and emotionally abused by her employer. By the time she escaped and found help from a service provider, she was vomiting blood, experienced daily headaches, and suffered from severe stomach pain. Eventually, her pelvic pain was mitigated with the use of hormonal contraceptives (Trafficking in Persons Report, US Department of State [2012]).

People of faith must work to change attitudes, beliefs, policies, and practices at all levels of society that dehumanize and promote the exploitation and abuse of women and girls. "Women with equal rights are better educated, healthier and have greater access to land, jobs and financial resources" (United Nations Development Program, Gender and Poverty Reduction, www.undp.org <http://www.undp.org>).

The United Methodist Social Principles state; "Consumers should exercise their economic power to encourage the manufacture of goods that are necessary and beneficial to humanity . . ," and call "[c]onsumers [to] avoid purchasing products made in conditions where workers are being exploited because of their age, gender, or economic status" (¶ 163D). Through the United Methodist Committee on Relief's partnership with Equal Exchange, individuals and United Methodist entities are able to purchase chocolate, cocoa, coffee, tea, and other goods that are fair trade, guaranteeing that no slave labor is involved in the production of such goods. Economic pressure and advocacy by United Methodists and other people of faith has led some major chocolate companies to commit to removing child slave labor from their supply chains in coming years. This is an important step; however, there are many more industries that need to eradicate slave labor from their business practices. For example, "Children from ages four to 14 are subjected to forced labor, working as many as 18 hours a day to weave rugs destined for export markets such as the U.S. and Europe" (Trafficking in Persons Report, US Department of State [2012]).

In order to eradicate modern-day slavery, we call on United Methodists, local churches, campus ministries, colleges, universities, seminaries, annual conferences, general agencies and commissions, and the Council of Bishops to:

1. affirm human rights and dignity of all peoples who are on the move, asserting the right to freedom of movement, and resisting violations and curtailments of such rights through forced migration, including trafficking in persons;

2. advocate for economic and trade policies that facilitate job development that is accessible to all sectors of societies, with wages that allow all persons to thrive according to God's will;

3. actively champion anti-slavery efforts by petitioning the United Nations and the legislative bodies of all countries in

which The United Methodist Church has an organized ecclesiastical structure, to demand the freeing of all persons subjected to modern-day forms of enslavement and bonded labor;

4. petition the United Nations and governments around the world to abolish slavery through the use of nonmilitary options such as negotiations leading to agreements with binding obligations and corollary sanctions;

5. encourage swift resolution to civil strifes and armed conflicts and engage in coordinated responses to mitigate disasters to prevent traffickers from preying on children;

6. officially support stock/mutual fund divestment campaigns that urge people to remove funds from organizations and corporations whose actions profit from and contribute to slavery's existence;

7. create environments that model safe, healthy, and violence-free communities in order to raise children who do not accept violence as normative;

8. implement children's ministries that bolster self-esteem and provide educational and economic opportunities for women and children who are especially vulnerable to traffickers;

9. build a new generation of male leaders across the Church who model nonviolent, emotionally healthy masculinity, serving as positive change-makers in society.

10. educate pastors, lay leaders, children and families, teachers, health-care providers, and outreach workers about fraudulent promises of traffickers and the resulting exploitation and abuse;

11. advocate for local, regional, national, and international laws and funds that ensure trafficking victims have access to services that enable them to heal from the trauma, including counseling, reproductive health care, education/job training, legal services and shelter;

12. commit to interrupting the demand for slaves by purchasing fair trade products, including coffee, tea, chocolate, T-shirts, athletic equipment, and other goods for personal and ministry-related activities; and,

13. demand that corporations eliminate exploitative labor in their business practices and use their influence to eradicate all slavery from their supply chains.

As Ambassador Melanne Verveer of Global Women's Issues 2009-2013 implores in the documentary *Not My Life,* "[I]f we address women's needs in terms of accessing education, being free from violence, being economic participants, our world will be better for everybody."

ADOPTED 2016

See Social Principles, ¶ 165.

US POWER AND RESPONSIBILITY IN THE WORLD

6043. Guidelines for the Imposition of Sanctions

The parable of the good Samaritan invites us to see the fundamental character of God's love as unconditional and overflowing. In the face of death and in death-dealing situations, aid and succor are the hallmarks of Christian response. In this parable the neighbor in need and the good neighbor were not known for their friendly relations. They were strangers and historical enemies to one another. In the time of need, however, compassion flowed and care was ultimately ensured by the good neighbor's request of an innkeeper: "'Look after him, . . . and when I return, I will reimburse you for any extra expense you may have' (Luke 10:35 NIV). This provision of care was unconditioned by tribe, class, kinship, gender, religion, race, and economic or political status. Jesus' command was plain but bold: "Go and do likewise" (Luke 10:37 NIV). And our prayer echoes the prayer of the psalmist, "How long will you defend the unjust / and show partiality to the wicked? / Defend the weak and the fatherless; / uphold the cause of the poor and the oppressed. / Rescue the weak and the needy; / deliver them from the hand of the wicked" (Psalm 82:2-4 NIV).

Sanctions as political and economic tools of pressure and leverage can play a critical role in the mitigation and deterioration of conflicts. It is in this sense that sanctions are sometimes seen as a more tolerable alternative to war, but in no case should they impede the ability of people to have adequate access to food, water, and medicine.

Sanctions, in whatever form, however, lay conditions on the extension of humanitarian aid and succor; thus, they fall short of the gospel imperative for unconditional love. Bearing in mind the limitations of sanctions, we must provide guidelines for their imposition and implementation so that we may be reminded of the compassion in which we should always act.

A 2006 Church World Service and Witness (CWSW) study defines sanctions as "a menu of possible diplomatic, communications and economic measures used by governments, intergovernmental bodies, and nongovernmental entities to force changes in policies and behavior (usually but not exclusively on the part of a government)." The study continues: "Sanctions cover a wide variety of measures from moratoria on diplomatic contacts to trade embargoes. Consumer boycotts and disinvestments programs are related measures." (See report: http://www.ncccusa.org/98ga /sancpol.html, 2006-04-23)

The CWSW study notes that "sanctions can be limited and targeted, such as sports boycotts or restrictions on air travel, or they can be comprehensive, as in the case of trade embargoes. Sanctions can be unilateral (involving a single government) or multilateral (involving more than one)." The term *sanction* is most frequently associated with economic measures intended to inflict economic damage and thereby force a government or other entity to change its behavior and its policies. The effective use of sanctions lies in the political will of the imposer and is to be measured by the positive effects of the sanctions on the desired outcomes.

At the heart of the conflictive character of sanctions is the concern for possible adverse effects of sanctions on the most vulnerable segments of the population as well as added strain on the already struggling economies of developing countries. Thus, the cautioned use of sanctions arises out of a fundamental ethical and moral dilemma to protect: the innocent, and noncombatants in situations of disaster, conflict, and emergency. Those countries and entities who impose sanctions of any kind must always take care to protect the suffering and the innocents by means of the basic, uncompromised modicum of international human rights and humanitarian laws. We must guarantee the right to protection of human life, human rights, and civil liberties; sanctions should not be imposed at the expense of the vulnerable. Therefore the Christian community must insist that any and all sanctions provide humanitarian exemptions for the provision of care—which includes food, medicine, medical supplies and equipment, basic school supplies, and agricultural inputs and implements—to those in dire need under circumstances of disaster, conflict, and emergency.

Humanitarian exemptions in the case of sanctions are embodied by the concept of the responsibility to protect. Responsibility to protect (R2P) is defined as an international security and humanitarian norm that calls the international community to protect innocent civilians and noncombatants in the face of war crimes, genocide, ethnic cleansing, and other crimes against humanity. We acknowledge that God's mercy happens not when one is suffering, however, but at the point where people are still empowered to act, a prior state in which one is capable of deciding for and producing for their own needs as well as the needs of their children and loved ones.

Thus, the responsibility to protect arises out of a failure of prevention. The responsibility to prevent calls us to address the root causes of internal conflict and other crises that put marginalized populations at risk. We must begin to foster an ethic of prevention—as additional to and foremost of protection—to ensure that people live "in peaceful dwelling places, in secure homes, in undisturbed places of rest," in assurance that peace is the fruit of justice and righteousness (Isaiah 32:16-18 NIV). (See World Council of Churches publication entitled *The Responsibility to Protect: Ethical and Theological Reflections,* 2005. See also www.responsibilitytoprotect.org and December 2001 Report of the International Commission on Intervention and State Sovereignty entitled *The Responsibility to Protect.*)

The CWSW study on the effectiveness of sanctions as an alternative to war concluded with recommendations that include the establishment of decision-making criteria for the imposition of sanctions based on the following guidelines:

- Sanctions must be a part of a broader strategy of peacemaking and an alternative to warfare.
- Sanctions should be adopted only in circumstances of flagrant and persistent violations of international law.
- Sanctions should have a clearly defined purpose.
- Sanctions have their greatest legitimacy and moral authority when authorized by a competent multilateral authority.
- The good achieved must not be exceeded by anticipated harm.
- There must be a reasonable prospect that their stated purpose of effecting political change will be achieved.
- Sanctions are effective only to the extent that they are consistently and thoroughly applied.

There must also be operational criteria to sanction impositions:

- Sanctions should be directed as precisely as possible to those bodies and leaders most responsible for the violation. Humanitarian assistance should be made available to the general population.
- The progress and effects of sanctions should be continually monitored by an independent and impartial multilateral monitoring body.
- Enforcers should be prepared to address the hurts and needs of victims in the sanctioned country and affected third countries.
- Open communication should be maintained with government leaders and civic groups in the sanctioned country.

United Methodists are called to:

- request that all governments employ and subscribe to already available indicators to assess potential humanitarian impacts prior to imposing sanctions and for monitoring impacts once sanctions are in place; especially those developed by multilateral institutions such as the United Nations;
- request that all governments seek to develop a list of humanitarian exceptions in cases in which no previous precedent as developed by the United Nations and other multilateral institutions exists and to incorporate those exemptions in any and all sanctions regimes;
- call for systematic monitoring of sanctions by independent expert observers;
- call for consensus to be required on a regular basis, before the United Nations imposes and/or continues Security Council sanctions;
- ensure in our advocacy efforts that sanctions and embargoes meet the requirements of available international human rights and humanitarian laws, including the provisions of the Statute of the International Criminal Court;
- commit ourselves and our humanitarian aid efforts as United Methodists, especially through UMCOR, to be carried out with awareness of the limited effectiveness of sanctions and similar enforcement tools in achieving their stated political goals and while also fostering and imple-

menting an ethic of protection and more importantly prevention such that the dignity and human rights of the most vulnerable are preserved; and

- call on the General Board of Church and Society to advocate for policies in national and international arenas that embody the understanding of sanctions and their implications that is contained in this resolution.

ADOPTED 2004
READOPTED 2008 AND 2016
RESOLUTION #6043, 2008, 2012 *BOOK OF RESOLUTIONS*
RESOLUTION #296, 2004 *BOOK OF RESOLUTIONS*

See Social Principles, ¶ 165A, B, D.

6051. United States-China Political Relations

Our Political Understandings

In late 1978, the governments of the United States and the People's Republic of China (PRC) reached agreement establishing full diplomatic relations. The United States ended official relations—diplomatic and military—with the authorities on Taiwan. The United States recognized the People's Republic of China as the "sole legal government of China" but reserved the right, over PRC objections, to sell "defensive" weapons to Taiwan. At the time of normalization, the PRC refused to rule out the possibility of reunifying with the island of Taiwan by force but offered to allow Taiwan to maintain the political, economic, and military status quo if Taiwan were to recognize PRC sovereignty.

This normalization agreement ended a thirty-year period in which formal American commitments to the authorities on Taiwan blocked closer relations with the People's Republic of China. It laid the foundations for a framework of cooperation and exchanges that continues to develop. Highlights include:

- government-to-government agreements covering consular relations and embassies, civil aviation, scientific and technical cooperation, educational exchange, trade and credit, fisheries, and a wide range of other fields;
- extensive private and government economic and technological investments;

- substantial expansion of tourism and specialized visits;
- educational programs facilitating tens of thousands of scholars and teachers resident in the other country;
- numerous governmental and private institutional exchange agreements in education, the fine and performing arts, cinema, publishing, and so forth;
- state-province and city-to-city agreements calling for various kinds of cooperation; and
- extensive cooperation on international platforms relating to economic, health, environmental concerns, and so forth.

The rapid growth and elaboration of these bilateral relations has been a positive indicator of a maturing relationship between the United States and the PRC that has become multi-dimensional and interdependent. Yet, because the PRC and US systems are so different, misperceptions and misunderstandings are all too common on both sides, even on basic principles.

Recommendations on US-China Political Relations

The United Methodist Church:

1. recognizes the necessity for China to continue sustained economic and social development and urges US cooperation to that end within the context of peace and stability;

2. feels the long-term basis of US-China relations should emphasize people-to-people, educational, social, and responsible economic and technological development, including the adoption of clean energy initiatives;

3. opposes the sale of US military equipment to the PRC;

4. endorses a peaceful approach to ending the long-standing conflict between the governments in the People's Republic of China and in Taiwan while recognizing that the resolution of the status of Taiwan is a matter for the People's Republic of China and for Taiwan and in that context opposes the sale of US military equipment to Taiwan;

5. declares our continuing concern regarding the human rights of all people on both sides of the Taiwan Straits; and

6. recognizes that US-PRC relations have an important influence on the peace and stability of the Asian region, particularly in Southeast Asia; and urges the United States and the People's

Republic of China and Taiwan to seek peaceful means to contribute to the peace and stability of the region.

ADOPTED 1984
AMENDED AND READOPTED 2000, 2008, 2012
RESOLUTION #6051, 2012 *BOOK OF RESOLUTIONS*
RESOLUTION #6045, 2008 *BOOK OF RESOLUTIONS*
RESOLUTION #301, 2004 *BOOK OF RESOLUTIONS*
RESOLUTION #281, 2000 *BOOK OF RESOLUTIONS*

See Social Principles, ¶ 165C, D.

6057. Political Status of Puerto Rico

The United States Congress, other entities of the United States government, and different groups in Puerto Rico have long been studying the relationship between the United States and Puerto Rico. This topic is a hot and divisive issue in Puerto Rico with many diverse and strong opposing views. The Church enters into this discussion because of its mandate to be a prophetic voice that intends to assist in finding ways that are in accordance with the values of the reign of God. There are certain principles that need to be emphasized:

1. We believe that all human beings are God's creatures and therefore of equal value and dignity.

2. We recognize that the church must take into consideration the following historical facts as it develops its theological thinking regarding the political status of Puerto Rico:

   a. Puerto Rico officially came to be subject to the United States of America as result of the Treaty of Paris on December 10, 1898, through which Spain surrendered its colonies to the United States. At that point Puerto Rico began to be governed by United States military authorities.

   b. The Foraker Act approved by the US Congress in 1900 put an end to the US military government of Puerto Rico. The President of the United States appointed a governor of Puerto Rico and the administration of the island came to be under the US Department of the Interior.

   c. In 1917 the Jones Act was approved by the United States granting United States citizenship to all Puerto Ricans.

   d. In 1947 the United States Congress approved a law allowing the people of Puerto Rico to elect their own governor.

e. The United States authorities have persecuted and acted against the Puerto Rico pro independence movements all along. There was even a period when it was forbidden to raise the Puerto Rican flag or to display the shield of arms that served as an emblem of Puerto Rico or to speak of advocating for the independence of Puerto Rico.

f. The people of Puerto Rico, as permitted by the appropriate United States authorities, approved in 1952 the constitution of the "Commonwealth of Puerto Rico" known in Spanish as "Estado Libre Asociado de Puerto Rico." The relationship is described as a pact. The people of Puerto Rico continue to be subjugated to the authorities of the United States of America.

The present economic crisis in Puerto Rico has served to highlight how problematic is the territorial or colonial condition of Puerto Rico in subordination to the United States of America. The government of Puerto Rico approved a local bankruptcy law to enable public authorities to have a mechanism to work in an orderly fashion with their lack of funds to cover all their financial obligations. The Federal Court, District of Puerto Rico ruled that the law approved by the government of Puerto Rico was unconstitutional given that federal laws cover bankruptcy situations. The government of Puerto Rico appealed to Boston and the aforementioned court affirmed the determination of the Federal Judge in Puerto Rico. The government of Puerto Rico then tried to be covered under the US bankruptcy laws, but this was not accepted, leaving Puerto Rico without the possibility of bankruptcy protection for the public authorities.

The present status of Puerto Rico as a nonincorporated territory of the United States, with a clear subordination to the United States, moves us to take the following position from a moral and ethical perspective according to the traditions and teachings of our Church:

1. We firmly believe in self-determination for all peoples. Clearly Puerto Rico is a country with its own idiosyncrasy, cultural expressions, and that treasures its Spanish language which has survived under the remnants of a colonial system.

2. We believe that Puerto Rico's political problem is not just a problem for Puerto Ricans; but also a problem for the people of the United States of America, and therefore, the United States should act to facilitate a real self-determination process that is in agreement with criteria accepted by the international community. The active participation of different

social and political entities in the United States is needed to solve the problem.

Therefore, we call upon the churches to be educated about the political situation of Puerto Rico without promoting a particular political partisan perspective. We affirm that truth will set us free. We affirm that God has created us equal and with the same dignity. The subordination of a people by another people is contrary to our Church's teachings.

As a Church we confess that for too long we have kept ourselves uninvolved in this and other important issues for the sake of avoiding conflicts and divisions. Now we recognize that this is contrary to the prophetic tradition of our faith.

We call upon the authorities of the United States government to foster a true process of self-determination for the people of Puerto Rico in which the United States Congress participates in working out alternatives and definitions that achieve a nonterritorial formula. The United States government should clearly define which are the vested rights of Puerto Ricans as United States citizens that will not change regardless of the political formula selected to solve the territorial problem.

We also call upon the United States government to free the Puerto Rican political prisoners in United States prisons and to drop pending charges against other persons related to their struggle for the independence of Puerto Rico. It is important for the United States to show that the era of persecution has come to an end and that we are at the beginning of a new journey where there will be space for dialogue with all the groups representing different ideologies.

ADOPTED 2008
REVISED AND READOPTED 2012
AMENDED AND READOPTED 2016
RESOLUTION #6057, 2012 *BOOK OF RESOLUTIONS*
RESOLUTION #6047, 2008 *BOOK OF RESOLUTIONS*

See Social Principles, ¶ 165A, B, D.

6058. US Policy in Vieques

Historical Background

Vieques is a small island about eight miles east of the island nation of Puerto Rico. In 1938 the US Navy began using the island-municipality of Vieques for military practices. In 1941, during the height of WWII, the United States initiated a campaign of expropriation of territory (evicting over 3,000 people), which ended in the Navy's control of over two-thirds of the island's most arable land. Thousands of families were displaced and those remaining were jeopardized in their basic means of subsistence. The net effect of these policies was the clustering of the entire civilian population into a small strip of land right in the middle of the island. Only 25 percent of the island remained under civilian control.

One of the effects of 60 years of bombing has been the degradation, and in some cases destruction, of Vieques' delicate ecosystems. Hundreds of species of plants and animals have been killed as a result of the direct impact of projectiles during military practices. These bombings and military maneuvers have led to serious contamination of the environment due to toxic residues and other contaminants.

Conclusion

The United Methodist Church has been a key supporter of the struggle in Vieques. The voice of our Church joined with the voices of many organizations in Puerto Rico and around the world to halt the Navy's maneuvers on the island. The Navy's military presence finally ended on May 1, 2003, which the 2004 General Conference celebrated. Justice, however, is not complete.

Over twelve years have passed since the end of the bombing and other military practices in Vieques. Nevertheless, the waters surrounding the former target practice area still filled with unexploded bombs and contaminants from the target area continue to be allowed to go into the sea causing great damage to the ecosystem. It is imperative that these issues be addressed as soon as possible not only because of the clear environmental justice concerns but also for bringing about economic justice and full respect for human rights that continue to elude new generations of Puerto Ricans.

The removal of thousands of live bombs in the area is being done by exploding them on site, in the open air. This produces an additional quantity of contaminants that enter different ecosystems and continue to have an adverse impact on the food chain and on the health of the people of Vieques. The cleanup process is going too slow and many times is not done in ways that protect the residents of Vieques from further contamination.

Therefore be it resolved, that The United Methodist Church:

1. request of the appropriate agencies of the United States government that the cleaning of all the contaminants produced by the US Navy activities or activities allowed by the US Navy be done using methods that will keep to a minimum the release of toxic agents into the environment. The health of the residents of Vieques must be protected. Diverse sources have published information on the availability of equipment and methodology that make possible the removal of explosive artifacts without detonating them in open air spaces;

2. urge the US Congress to appropriate sufficient funds to decontaminate Vieques such that the land is again suitable for agriculture, environmental tourism, and other social uses;

3. call upon the United States government to assign funds to enable the people of Vieques to have access to new health programs directed to reduce the high incidence of different types of cancer, to provide treatment to all the persons with toxic chemicals in their bodies, and to treat and reduce the high incidence of respiratory diseases;

4. urge Congress and the government of Puerto Rico to establish mechanisms to promote the reconstruction and sustainable economic development of Vieques;

5. call upon the Environmental Protection Agency and all other government agencies responsible for the cleaning to also expedite the cleaning of the island of Culebra, Puerto Rico, that was also contaminated as a result of military maneuvers.

ADOPTED 2004
REVISED AND READOPTED 2008, 2012, 2016
RESOLUTION #6058, 2012 *BOOK OF RESOLUTIONS*
RESOLUTION #6048, 2008 *BOOK OF RESOLUTIONS*
RESOLUTION #294, 2004 *BOOK OF RESOLUTIONS*
RESOLUTION #274, 2000 *BOOK OF RESOLUTIONS*

See Social Principles, ¶ 165B.

6060. Lift the US Embargo of Cuba

WHEREAS, The United Methodist Church and the Methodist Church of Cuba share a long history of joint ministry and service and a common mission; and

WHEREAS, we, United Methodists, join the international community in celebrating the dialogue and negotiation process between Cuba and the United States that led to the reestablishment of diplomatic relations between the two countries and the reopening of the Cuban Embassy in Washington, DC in July, 2015, and the reopening of the US Embassy in La Habana in August, 2015; and,

WHEREAS, The United Methodist Church has spoken through Resolutions approved by the 2004, 2008, and 2012 General Conferences stating that "from its Christian and humanitarian perspective, inspired by the love of God and historic Methodist commitment to peace and social justice, . . . hereby petitions the President and the Congress of the United States to lift its economic embargo against Cuba and any other regulations, practices or measures enforcing the embargo law" (p. 770, Resolution #6059, 2012 *Book of Resolutions*); and,

WHEREAS, the economic embargo has for over fifty-five years created unnecessary suffering and many hardships on the people of Cuba while preventing US citizens from traveling freely to Cuba in the exercise of their constitutional rights and curtailing the ability of churches to provide missional support freely to its sisters and brothers on the island; and

WHEREAS, the long-standing embargo has provided the Cuban government with a ready-made argument of external aggression to justify its lack of respect for the human and civil rights of dissidents at home; and

WHEREAS, the General Assembly of the United Nations has voted almost unanimously year after year to condemn the US Economic Embargo of Cuba; and

WHEREAS, many religious organizations and churches, like the Council of Evangelical Methodist Churches of Latin America and the Caribbean (CIEMAL), the Caribbean Council of Churches, the United Church of Christ, the Presbyterian Church, the American Baptist churches, and most recently by Pope Francis himself, among others, have also passed resolutions and spoken asking for the end of the embargo against Cuba;

Therefore, be it resolved, that the General Conference of The United Methodist Church commends President Barack Obama for the reestablishment of diplomatic relations between the two countries and the partial easing of travel restrictions; and,

Be it further resolved, that the General Conference of The United Methodist Church requests the US Congress to officially lift the economic embargo against Cuba, which as noted above, has been asked for many years by a great number of religious organizations and the United Nations, and most recently by the President of the United States.

ADOPTED 2016

See Social Principles, ¶ 165*A*, *D*.

6066. Atomic Testing on the Marshall Islands: A Legacy

WHEREAS, in the Old Testament the Lord spoke to Moses saying: "Tell the Israelites: When a man or a woman commits any sin against anyone else, thus breaking faith with the LORD, that person becomes guilty. Such persons will confess the sin they have done. Each will make payment for his guilt, add one-fifth more, and give it to the injured party" (Numbers 5:5-7). And in the New Testament Zacchaeus stood there and said to the Lord, "Look, Lord, I give half of my possessions to the poor. And if I have cheated anyone, I repay them four times as much" (Luke 19:8).

WHEREAS, evidence from declassified US government reports and studies shows that many more Marshall Islanders were exposed to nuclear fallout from the 67 US atomic and nuclear tests, which were detonated between 1946 and 1962, than American negotiators admitted when the compensation package in the compact was negotiated in the early 1980s; and

WHEREAS, the Marshall Islands government has indicated that information on the health of its people exposed to radiation from atomic and nuclear testing by the United States in the Marshalls requires more just compensation and expansion of medical care than the $150 million trust fund provided in the Compact of Free Association; and

WHEREAS, declassified documents show that the United States knew the anticipated power of the explosion of "Castle Bravo," which at 15 megatons was 1,000 times more powerful than the bomb dropped on Hiroshima, Japan, in 1945 (See *Newsweek* article "Marshall Islands Nuclear Lawsuit Reopens Old Wounds"); and

WHEREAS, many questions are arising about the accuracy of medical research done by US government labs on Marshall Islanders who were exposed to fallout from atomic and nuclear testing; and

WHEREAS, although the US government provided full compensation to American citizens living in Nevada, Utah, and Arizona, downwind of the Nevada Test Site, not one of the more than 2,000 Marshall Islanders, who received awards from the Nuclear Claims Tribunal were paid 100 percent of their compensation; and

WHEREAS, the US government provided full compensation to American citizens living in a significantly larger area compared to the Marshall Islands, despite the fact that the total tonnage of US tests in the Marshall Islands was almost 100 times greater than the yield of tests at the Nevada test site; and

WHEREAS, more than one-third of the total number of Marshall Islands recipients of nuclear test awards has died without receiving full compensation; and

WHEREAS, documents now show that the people of Ailuk and other nearby atolls and islands were exposed to dangerous amounts of radiation, yet purposely were not evacuated despite information that prevailing wind would blow fallout over a number of inhabited islands; and

WHEREAS, the Marshall Islanders are increasingly becoming aware that islanders were not evacuated because they were likely being used as "guinea pigs" in radiation studies; and

WHEREAS, the March 1, 1954, "Castle Bravo" hydrogen bomb test at Bikini Atoll was detonated despite weather reports the previous day that winds were blowing to the east toward the inhabited atolls of Rongelap, Utrik, Ailuk and others; and

WHEREAS, US government representatives deceived the people of Bikini Atoll by telling them that their island would be used "for the benefit of mankind" and evoking other Christian parables; and

WHEREAS, the atomic testing and nuclear fallout has caused high levels of cancer, genetic defects, radiation burns, and thyroid disorders among the Marshallese peoples and many have not been awarded personal injury compensation; and

WHEREAS, while the negative adverse health impacts of "Castle Bravo" and other nuclear bombs have great significance, the destruction of the cultural, environmental, and emotional well-being of the Marshallese peoples is critical, which includes forced resettlement and uninhabitable land; and

WHEREAS, the US government has not yet apologized to the Marshallese people for the death of Marshallese citizens and for the damage done to their homeland, waters and people; and

WHEREAS, the economic provisions of a Compact of Free Association implemented in 1986 expired in 2001 and prohibited Marshall Islanders from "seeking future redress in US courts" (See *Newsweek* article cited previously); and

WHEREAS, the $150 million trust fund provided in a Compact of Free Association with the Marshall Islands is woefully inadequate, and not just compensation for the health injuries and deaths caused by US nuclear testing to the population, and the loss of the use of 20 atolls and single islands because of radiation contamination; and

WHEREAS, US funding for medical surveillance and treatment programs is inadequate to meet the needs of the exposed population in the Marshall Islands; and

WHEREAS, the Republic of the Marshall Islands filed a series of lawsuits in the International Court of Justice on April 24, 2014, against the United States, United Kingdom, France, Russia, China, India, Pakistan, Israel, and North Korea with the claim that these nuclear powers have violated their nuclear-disarmament obligations under the Non-Proliferation Treaty (NPT) and customary international law applying to all states (See the Lawyers Committee on Nuclear Policy November 2014 statement, The Marshall Islands' Nuclear Zero Cases in the World Court: Background and Current Status); and

WHEREAS, only "three of the nine states possessing nuclear arsenals—the UK, India, and Pakistan—have accepted the compulsory jurisdiction of the Court when the opposing state has done so, as the Marshall Islands has,"

Therefore, be it resolved, that this General Conference call upon The United Methodist Church through the General Board of Church and Society and the General Board of Global Ministries to work closely with the Marshallese people and our ecumenical partners, to bring about an official apology and full redress, including all necessary funding from the US government as well as urge the US government to accept the compulsory jurisdiction of the International Court of Justice and perform their obligations under the Nuclear Non-proliferation Treaty to disarm and pursue the cessation of the nuclear arms race; and

Be it further resolved, that copies of this resolution be sent to the US Attorney General, the Secretary of the Department of Energy, the Secretary of Defense, the Secretary of State, with copies to the

Republic of the Marshall Islands Embassy Office in Washington, DC, and to the people in the Marshall Islands.

ADOPTED 2000
READOPTED 2008
AMENDED AND READOPTED 2016
RESOLUTION #6066, 2012 *BOOK OF RESOLUTIONS*
RESOLUTION #6050, 2008 *BOOK OF RESOLUTIONS*
RESOLUTION #288, 2004 *BOOK OF RESOLUTIONS*
RESOLUTION #267, 2000 *BOOK OF RESOLUTIONS*

See Social Principles, ¶ 165B.

6072. United States-Mexico Border

The United States-Mexico border is a 2,000-mile-long area where negative socioeconomic dynamics within two interactive cultures have had an impact on the quality of life of adjoining populations. This adverse situation has been exacerbated by domestic and international policies espoused by the US and Mexican governments.

The border region is characterized by:

- drastic economic disparity between segments of the population;
- constant deterioration of the health conditions, particularly those affecting the poor;
- high incidence of crime, drug trafficking, and human trafficking for the exploitation of children and adults;
- high rates of unemployment and underemployment; and
- increased militarization of the border that further alienates the US and Mexico separating families and leading to the tragic deaths of people.

Confronted by this human suffering along the United States-Mexico border region, we recognize that the vision of "a new heaven and a new earth" (Revelation 21) will be only an illusion as long as "one of the least of these" (Matthew 25) continues to suffer.

We are particularly concerned about the following conditions:

1. Environmental:

   a. the constant indiscriminate use of pesticides in the growing and harvesting of agricultural products, a problem on both sides of the border; and the export of banned or restricted pesticides across the border;

b. water contamination caused by corporations dumping industrial toxic waste and the flushing of poisonous compounds into the Rio Grande, the Colorado, and other rivers; and

c. growing air pollution on both sides of the border.

2. Health:

a. a high rate of birth defects and other health problems among industrial workers, many of whom have neither been given proper equipment nor been informed of the hazards of the toxic materials they have been exposed to;

b. the high incidence of dysentery, tuberculosis, and hepatitis especially among children in the Colonias (rural unincorporated areas), caused by lack of adequate water treatment facilities and a lack of food and fresh water;

c. the growing number of unsafe, crowded barracks and shanty towns without sanitation and other basic facilities due to a lack of adequate, affordable housing for workers; and

d. the lack of access to health, education, and welfare services, already overburdened by the volume of need, perpetuating the cycle of poverty and dehumanization.

3. Economic:

a. wages kept low by repressing workers' bargaining rights, which keeps the border region below the average of Mexican industrial wage levels, despite the fact that the Maquiladoras are the second largest producers of export income (after oil), and the largest source of income for the Mexican border region;

b. the lack of long-range economic and industrial development strategies, making both the United States. and the Mexican economies more dependent on quick economic fixes such as Maquiladoras, quick cash crops, tourism, and services that can help temporarily and superficially, but ignore the needs of most of the present and future generations;

c. the trade agreements (such as the North American Free Trade Agreement), which worsen existing economic dependencies and foster the exploitation of human and natural resources; and

   d. the region's low level of educational attainment, high incidence of illiteracy, the high dropout rate, and the availability and influx of drugs, which have a greater impact on the low-income population along the border.

4. *Civil and Human Rights:*

   a. heightened anxieties of Americans who perceive immigrants as unwelcomed foreigners who threaten US social, political, and economic security;

   b. strategies devised by US governmental agencies and groups to harass, intimidate, and repress legal and foreign entrants into the US territory; and

   c. the poor administration of justice; the cultural insensitivity of border patrol agents; the high incidence of illegal use of force; and the constant violation of the civil and human rights of those detained or deported. These situations create an atmosphere of tension and distrust that adds to the polarization between Mexicans and US residents and transients.

These detrimental conditions affect the constant influx of thousands of refugees and undocumented persons coming to the United States seeking safe haven or better economic conditions. Also, these situations create pain and suffering among millions of children, women, and men residing on both sides of the border. The impact of these dynamics reaches well into the interiors of both countries. As Christians and United Methodists, we express our sorrow and indignation about this human suffering and accept the responsibility to use our resources toward the elimination of the root causes creating this tragic human problem. We are urged by God through Christ to love our neighbor and to do what we must to bring healing in the midst of pain, and to restore to wholeness those whose lives are shattered by injustice and oppression.

Therefore, we recommend and urge the Mexican and US governments to:

- develop national and international policies that bring more economic parity between the two countries, as an integral part of any trade agreement;

- develop binational and multilateral agreements that improve the quality of life; safeguard water rights; and prevent the contamination of air, water, and land of both sides of the border;

- develop binding and enforceable mechanisms with respect to: labor and human rights; agriculture, including farm workers; environmental standards; and health and safety standards for both nations and in any agreements to which they are a party;
- develop and support national and international policies, such as the UN Convention on the Protection of the Rights of all Migrant Workers and Members of their Families, that facilitate the migration and immigration of peoples across the border while respecting their rights and aspirations; and
- find alternative and creative ways to reduce the foreign debt of Mexico.

We further recommend that the General Board of Church and Society, with churches in Mexico, the United States, and Canada, seek ways to network on fair trade, labor and human rights, agricultural, and environmental concerns.

ADOPTED 1992
AMENDED AND READOPTED 1996, 2000, 2004
READOPTED 2008, 2012
AMENDED AND READOPTED 2016
RESOLUTION #6072, 2012 *BOOK OF RESOLUTIONS*
RESOLUTION #6052, 2008 *BOOK OF RESOLUTIONS*
RESOLUTION #302, 2004 *BOOK OF RESOLUTIONS*
RESOLUTION #282, 2000 *BOOK OF RESOLUTIONS*

See Social Principles, ¶ 165.

6073. Border Ministry in the Western Jurisdiction

WHEREAS, there is an unprecedented number of deportations taking place today that dramatically affect the lives of millions of people in the US and Mexico, The United Methodist Church needs to partner with the Methodist Church of Mexico in ministry to these deportees left in the border towns with no resources to relocate to their places of origin. From January 2009 to July of 2011, there had been 1,107,415 deportations [Downloaded September 13, 2011 from <http://www.ice.gov/doclib/about/offices/ero /pdf/ero-removals.pdf>]. Because the crossing to the US without the proper documentation has become a titanic effort, our neighbors from the south receive a massive number of deportees every week; and

WHEREAS, migrants around the world are forced to leave their homes for economic reasons and foreign policies of developed countries aggravate their already affected economic status, with more than 240 million of them moving around the world continually in search of a better life, and an estimated of 23 percent of the world's migration arrives in North America; and

WHEREAS, the numbers of deaths of undocumented migrant workers wanting to cross to the US has reached an unprecedented number, with an average of 200 deaths recorded every year in the Arizona desert and between 1995 and 2004 more than 2,640 migrants have died intending to cross the United States and Mexico border, and since 2004 more than one undocumented migrant has died per day in the effort to cross; and

WHEREAS, the number of deportations (from 2009 to July of 2011 deportations equaled 1,107,415: 389,834 in 2009, 392,862 in 2010, and 324,719 in 2011, more than the number of deportations combined in the last ten years) continues to impact both sides of the US and Mexico border as US families are being separated from family members; our neighbors from the southwest receive a massive number of deportees every week, estimating that 1,000 of them wander around the border of Tijuana every day with no help, and the programs trying to address this need are too few to provide help for so many of them; and

WHEREAS, the growing fear of terrorist attacks has mobilized the Department of Homeland Security to make the crossing of the border for undocumented migrant workers a Herculean effort, for there are almost 21,000 border patrol agents at this moment, more than twice as many as there were in 2004, working to stop undocumented migration; as of May of 2011, 17,659 of them stationed along the southwest border with Mexico, which is the contributing factor to the steady decline in the flows of undocumented migration in recent years (the November 2006 annual report made by the Office of Immigration Statistics reported that apprehensions, detentions of foreign nationals has been drastically reduced from 1,291,000 in 2005 [Downloaded September 14, 2011 from http://www.dhs.gov/xlibrary/assets/statistics/year book/2005/Enforcement_AR_05.pdf] to 517,000 in 2010 [Downloaded September 14, 2011 from http://www.dhs.gov/xlibrary /assets/statistics/publications/enforcement-ar-2010.pdf]) forcing undocumented crossers to walk the Arizona desert where they lose their life; and

WHEREAS, our Methodist tradition based on the Judeo-Christian values reminds us that we are to care for the immigrants by loving them as ourselves and providing for their welfare instead of oppressing them (Leviticus 19:30), just as Jesus modeled for us and identified with them and calls us to provide hospitality to immigrants (Matthew 25:38-40), for he says: "When you have done it for one of the least of these brothers and sisters of mine, you have done it for me" (Matthew 25:40); and by doing so we spread scriptural holiness throughout the land and participate in our own salvation; and

WHEREAS, without addressing immigration reform, the crackdown, criminalization, imprisonment, and deportation of productive undocumented migrants, will continue to occur, separation of families, death in the desert, division of communities, and frustration of the future of so many talented Dreamers will continue to take place;

Therefore, the General Conference requests that the Interagency Task Force and specific general agencies named below, having demonstrated deep commitment to and success in addressing immigration issues generally, mobilize and respond to the impacts of deportation outside of the United States and specifically in Mexico including but not limited to the following measures:

1. The Interagency Task Force on Immigration, representing the Council of Bishops, agencies and racial/ethnic caucuses:
   a) Include the impact of deportation on the Mexican side of the border by intentionally planning and providing resources to respond to the needs of families that are trapped in the border struggle.
   b) Work to challenge the criminalization of migrants by law enforcement agents in Mexico resulting from the bad propaganda originating in the US that only migrants with criminal records are deported.

2. The General Board of Church and Society, the General Commission on Religion and Race, the General Board of Global Ministries, and United Methodist Women:
   a) Work with national and international civil rights, human rights, and migrant rights organizations to develop resources and advocacy materials for use in border cities in Mexico that are impacted by the unprecedented number of deportations.
   b) Mobilize congregations to support programs outside the US that are responding to the deportation impact.

c) Work in collaboration with CONAM (Comisión Nacional de Asuntos Migratorios) of the Methodist Church of Mexico to educate and advocate for the rights of women, men, and children who face the challenges of adapting to a new way of life as a result of their deportation.

ADOPTED 2012
RESOLUTION #6073, 2012 *BOOK OF RESOLUTIONS*

See Social Principles, ¶ 165.

NATIONS AND CULTURES

6081. Africa Growth and Development

We applaud international efforts to develop a more just international economic order in which the limited resources of the earth will be used to the maximum benefit of all nations and peoples. We urge Christians in every society to encourage the governments under which they live and the economic entities within their societies to aid and work for the development of more just economic orders. (Social Principles, ¶ 165B)

The continent of Africa is gradually moving from crisis to peace, economic growth, and development. Decades of inter- and intra-state conflicts that left much of Africa's social, political, and economic life in a shambles are being replaced by a new dispensation marked by growth and signs of development. Six of the world's ten fastest growing economies of the past decade are in sub-Saharan Africa. A clutch of countries have enjoyed growth in income per person of more than 5% a year since 2007. Based on UN reports, the continent is expected to have 5% to 7% income increase in years to come. One of the challenges facing Africa currently is to transform economic growth into development, job creation, and into improved well-being of its citizens. Despite significant economic growth, Africa is still braced with catastrophic diseases like HIV, malaria, tuberculosis, and Ebola. The 2014 United Nations Conference on Trade and Development report indicates that:

"Despite Africa's relatively strong economic growth performance over the past decade, many countries in the continent are grappling with several development challenges ranging from food insecurity, high unemployment, poverty, and inequality, to commodity dependence, lack of economic transformation, environmental degradation, and low integration of the continent in the global economy. Since the dawn of the new millennium, African governments and the international community have adopted various initiatives aimed at addressing these development challenges and improving living conditions on the continent. At the continental level, African Heads of State and Government adopted the New Partnership for Africa's Development (NEPAD), which emphasizes African ownership of the development process and outcome, and calls for interventions in the following priority areas: agriculture and food security, regional integration and infrastructure, climate change and environment, human development, economic governance, and capacity development and women empowerment."

Africa is blessed with people of remarkable energy, spirit, and ingenuity. The continent is rich in natural resources needed by the entire world. The spread of democracy and the growing strength of African civil society offer a real chance to tackle the root causes of poverty and conflict. Social movements and organizations throughout the continent have developed to hold governments accountable and to build societies where public institutions and policies will guarantee cultural, economic, political, and social rights of all citizens. There is a call for alternative development programs based on the fundamental principles of democracy, human rights, gender equality and social justice.

The United Methodist Church in Africa is continuing to grow rapidly and is a transforming presence in many countries, influential beyond its numbers, engaging in a holistic Wesleyan ministry of outreach, evangelism, and humanitarian service. The church in Africa is part of civil society and has a strong witness to make in participating in community development; in promoting conflict resolution, reconciliation, and justice ministries; in humanitarian assistance ; and in public health and diseases prevention, including malaria, HIV/AIDS, and Ebola. The church in the United States and in Europe has a strong role to play in advocating respect for the rights of African governments and peoples to define their economic policies and priorities and for continuing to support— among other things—debt cancellation, increased humanitarian and development aid, removal of trade barriers which discourage African exports, and funding to overcome HIV/AIDS, malaria, tuberculosis, Ebola, and other preventable diseases.

As Christians, our faith is in the God of Jesus Christ, who stands with the most vulnerable and oppressed people in our societies. Their well-being must serve as a guidepost for justice. God, sovereign over all nations, has made of one blood all the peoples of the earth. United Methodists, therefore, remain ever-vigilant, listening more attentively than ever to churches and movements around the world, as they struggle for social, political, economic, and spiritual development.

Therefore, we call upon the United Methodist people, local churches, and agencies to:

1. encourage United Methodist churches to increase their participation in programs of missionary support, pastors' salary supplementation, emergency relief, aid to refugees, reconstruction, and development through the appropriate units of the General Board of Global Ministries, regional councils of churches and the World Council of Churches;

2. encourage United Methodists to participate in Volunteers in Mission programs and other volunteer-based projects; and educate themselves (through orientation, cultural sensitivity, and contingency planning) for working alongside African brothers and sisters to, for example, construct more schools, clinics, and churches. There is a need to emphasize the importance of preparation for the cross-cultural experience by volunteers and receiving partners. Orientation and training for both are available through the Jurisdictional VIM Coordinators and the Mission Volunteers Program of the General Board of Global Ministries. In addition, the United Methodist Seminar Program on National and International Affairs in Washington, DC, and New York City provides educational opportunities for United Methodists to learn about significant issues affecting Africa;

3. urge United Methodist churches in Africa to advocate with government leaders in every country as to the need for people and justice to be at the center of any concerted national and international efforts toward the eradication of poverty and sustainable and equitable development on the continent of Africa. Advocacy for appropriate exploration and usage of natural resources must be undertaken so that a sustainable growth and development is guaranteed in the long run;

4. urge United Methodists to persuade their governments to ratify the United Nations Convention to Combat Desertifica-

tion in Those Countries Experiencing Serious Drought and/or Desertification;

5. be supportive of civil society in Africa as it seeks to continually review, assess and offer constructive suggestions to government leaders implementing the objectives of the New Partnership for Africa's Development (NEPAD). Urge the General Board of Global Ministries and the General Board of Church and Society to stay abreast of the issues involved, be ready to offer resources and opportunities for United Methodist churches and the ecumenical movement in Africa to gather, study and debate the concerns;

6. urge the General Board of Church and Society to develop a grassroots public policy action network to:

    a. address good governance and democratization issues, including electoral rights and peaceful co-existence of political parties;

    b. support efforts aimed at promoting the development and implementation of policies that guarantee equitable distribution of resources.

7. continue and further develop the General Board of Global Ministries' commitment to health care in Africa through comprehensive, community-based primary health care and public health, recognizing the role that poverty, lack of awareness, and poor sanitation play in the spread of communicable diseases across the continent. Support AIDS, malaria, and Ebola prevention training through the UMC health boards, annual conferences health coordinators, and other partners working on health issues;

8. monitor all programs of relief and development, with special attention to these criteria:

    a. give priority to women and children, who suffer the most during times of social unrest and war;

    b. involve full consultation with African United Methodists, relying upon their experience, wisdom, and resourcefulness/local assets;

    c. design programs to alleviate the root causes of poverty, oppression, and social unrest;

    d. seek resources for program support from beyond the church to augment the church's contribution to African social, economic, and political development;

    e. implement methods to demonstrate financial transparency and accountability in all development programs and projects; and

f. program for sustainability, both in terms of ecological integrity and appropriate technologies that do not require continuing input of resources from other countries, and capacity building for local hand-off of sustainable size and scale of projects.

> *God bless Africa . . .*
> *Guard her children . . .*
> *Guide her leaders . . .*
> *And give her peace.*

ADOPTED 1996
READOPTED 2000, 2004, 2008
AMENDED AND READOPTED 2016
RESOLUTION #6081, 2012 *BOOK OF RESOLUTIONS*
RESOLUTION #6062, 2008 *BOOK OF RESOLUTIONS*
RESOLUTION #303, 2004 *BOOK OF RESOLUTIONS*
RESOLUTION #283, 2000 *BOOK OF RESOLUTIONS*

See Social Principles, ¶ 165A.

6082. Democratic Republic of Congo: Hope for a Radiant Future

> *Violence will no longer resound throughout your land,*
> *nor devastation or destruction within your borders.*
> *You will call your walls Salvation,*
> *and your gates Praise.*

(Isaiah 60:18)

The people of the Democratic Republic of Congo (DRC) have not seen peace since its independence in 1960. Decades of a corrupt dictatorial government, backed by the US and other Western powers, and war have been their history. A war over the country's vast resources involving nine countries broke out in 1998. Cruelties and atrocities have been inflicted upon its people. Children and young people were forcibly recruited by militias operating in the East and South regions of the country. Sexual violence has been used as a weapon of war against females, both young girls and older women. It is estimated that 4 million died, largely from disease and hunger, or have disappeared without a trace. The war is one of the bloodiest in modern times.

In 2006, the Congolese people elected a president, Joseph Kabila, and a National Assembly. The newly elected administration, which is the first elected in over 40 years, has taken steps toward the building of democracy and infrastructure. The DRC has a new constitution and security in parts of the country has improved dramatically, except the challenging eastern and southern regions still preyed upon by intransigent militias who assault innocent people and government symbols. The elections and regional security are milestones in the restoration of stability in the Congo and show there is hope for the future of the country.

We pray for the rebirth of the nation and end to war and conflict.

Life for the Congolese People

The vast majority of the people live in poverty, despite the country's rich natural resources and having the second largest rainforest in the world. Only 20 percent of the population has access to safe water, 70 percent has little or no access to health care, 16 million have critical food needs, and the country has the highest infant mortality rate in Africa. Very few social services are provided to the population by the government. The conflict has caused the displacement of millions of people. Children have experienced extreme hardships—lifelong physical and psychological harm—due to the war. Each year, more children die in DRC than in China, a country with 23 times the population, and than in all the Latin American countries combined, according to a 2006 UNICEF report. According to the 2013 Human Development Index the Democratic Republic of the Congo has a low level of human development, ranking 186 out of 187. According to the World Bank, with 80 million hectares of arable land and over 1,100 minerals and precious metals, the DRC has the potential to be one of the richest countries on the African continent and a driver of African growth.

Challenges for the New Government

The challenges facing the new government are vast. It must consolidate the peace process, rebuild the government's administrative capacity, and restore its authority at all levels throughout the entire country, overcome corruption, insure freedom of assembly and free speech for its citizens, unify and consolidate its armed forces, and institute an impartial and credible judiciary system.

The government has developed an economic development plan for reconstruction. The success of the plan requires reform and enforcement of laws on the extraction, production, and use of the country's natural resources. The government and its international partners must implement the independent mechanism to monitor the implementation of contracts and ensure transparent and fair management of mining resources.

The country's development cannot be achieved without political stability, accountability, and the active participation of its citizens. Nongovernmental organizations need to be strengthened and given a real voice in the future of their country.

Congolese need and deserve support to consolidate peace, construct democracy, save lives, and rebuild their country. Celebrating with the Congolese people in the rebirth of their nation, the General Conference urges United Methodists to:

1. support the peoples and the mission of The United Methodist Church in the DRC through Advance Special giving, covenant relationship between annual conferences, and other mission funding. We also urge United Methodists and all Methodist peoples to join in prayer and solidarity for the people, leaders, and churches of the DRC;

2. work with The United Methodist Church in the DRC and with nongovernmental organizations in rebuilding the country, its churches and seminaries, and the repatriation, resettlement, and provision of shelter for displaced persons, child soldiers, and other war victims;

3. encourage the government of the DRC to continue to implement and move forward with reforms, including freedom of assembly and free speech; security; economic and mining; judiciary; education; and communications; and to implement an economic platform that promotes entrepreneurship and investment to help poor communities; encourages fair play; and environmental protection;

4. encourage all parties involved in the conflict to eliminate all forms of sexual violence;

5. request governments and international institutions to provide economic assistance for reconstruction and development and debt cancellation to the government of the DRC;

6. engage multinational corporations, especially mining companies and neighboring countries, to respect the sovereignty and integrity of the DRC; and

7. support the continued presence of MONUSCO, the UN peacekeeping force in the DRC, in order to neutralize militias operating in the eastern and southern regions and train Congolese security forces.

The situation in the Democratic Republic of the Congo is applicable to other countries in crisis in Africa.

ADOPTED 2008
AMENDED AND READOPTED 2016
RESOLUTION #6081, 2012 *BOOK OF RESOLUTIONS*
RESOLUTION #6063, 2008 *BOOK OF RESOLUTIONS*

See Social Principles, ¶ 165*A, B, D.*

6083. Bringing Justice to Gatumba Genocide

WHEREAS, during the night of August 13, 2004, in a refugee camp in Burundi, Africa, called Gatumba, 166 innocents from the Democratic Republic of the Congo (DRC) were mercilessly slaughtered by armed factions and 116 other victims were maimed and injured; and

WHEREAS, almost all the 166 people killed and the 116 people injured were members of the Banyamulenge tribe that had earlier been forced from their homes in the southern Kivu region of the DRC; and

WHEREAS, the report S/2004/821 of October 5, 2004, of the United Nations peacekeeping mission in DRC concluded that the massacres of Banyamulenge in the camp of Gatumba were planned and only the Congolese Tutsi were targeted. The report of human rights declared also that the massacres of Banyamulenge in the camp of Gatumba were planned, consequently only Banyamulenge ethnic were targeted; and

WHEREAS, Pasteur Habimana, FNL-PALIPEHUTU's spokesman of Agathon Rwasa, recognized the responsibility of this movement in the massacres of Banyamulenge refugees; and

WHEREAS, there is evidence that the massacres were perpetuated by FNL-PALIPEHUTU, FDLR composed by Interahamwe that committed genocide in Rwanda, and Mai-Mai; and

WHEREAS, there has been no one brought to justice by the DRC, government of Burundi, or the International Criminal Court; and

WHEREAS, there is still violence in the form of killing, burning houses, rape, and terror being perpetrated against the Banyamulenge people; and

WHEREAS, the International Rescue Committee released a study in January 2008, which found that conflict and humanitarian crisis in Congo has claimed the lives of over 5 million people since 1998; and

WHEREAS, that the people of The United Methodist Church cannot remain silent when faced with acts of genocide; and

WHEREAS, that the people of The United Methodist Church cannot remain silent when there is violence perpetrated against innocent men, women, and children; and

WHEREAS, that although the seeking of justice for the Gatumba genocide will not address all the current issues of violence in the region, it will encourage the tracking down of the perpetrators of similar atrocities in the region, and the bringing of them to justice;

Therefore, be it resolved, that the Global Young People's Convocation and Legislative Assembly meeting in Berlin, Germany, calls upon the International Criminal Court, the government of Burundi, and the government of the Democratic Republic of the Congo to investigate the August 13, 2004, attack on the Gatumba refugee camp, to name the individuals and groups responsible, and to bring these individuals to justice; and

Be it further resolved, that The United Methodist Church calls upon the International Criminal Court, the governments of Burundi and the Democratic Republic of the Congo to collaborate in the continued investigation of the August 13, 2004, attack on the Gatumba refugee camp.

ADOPTED 2012
RESOLUTION #6083, 2012 *BOOK OF RESOLUTIONS*

See Social Principles, ¶ 165C, D.

6084. Liberia

Our Lord is great and so strong!
God's knowledge can't be grasped!
The LORD *helps the poor,*
but throws the wicked down on the dirt!

(Psalm 147:5-6)

Violence will no longer resound throughout your land,
nor devastation or destruction within your borders.
You will call your walls Salvation,
and your gates Praise.

(Isaiah 60:18)

In 2005, the people of Liberia "seized the moment" to elect new political leaders after a 14-year civil war that left the country in ruins. Ellen Johnson Sirleaf, a United Methodist, was elected as the first woman president of an African country. The people of Liberia expect the new government to tackle the national ills of bad governance, corruption, poverty, illiteracy, diseases, unemployment, and mediocrity.

During the 14-year civil war more than 270,000 Liberians were killed and over 500,000 were forced to flee their homes. Entire communities were uprooted. Economic activity declined sharply. Poverty increased sharply. Agricultural production dropped as people fled their farms. Exports nearly ceased. Mining and timber industries shut down. The infrastructure of the country was destroyed. Government finances collapsed. More than 75 percent of Liberians now live below the poverty line of $1 a day. Unemployment is as high as 85 percent.

Since President Sirleaf's inauguration in January 2006, Liberia has begun the long journey to recovery. The new government has resettled tens of thousands of refugees and begun training new security forces, increased government revenues, partially restored electricity and water to part of the capital, substantially increased primary school enrollment, and has begun to rebuild roads and attempts have been made for the rebuilding of other critical infrastructure.

The government developed a plan for the reconstruction and development of the country. A key element of the plan is restoring and strengthening basic human rights and further empowering the Liberian people. The reconstruction and development strategy is based on four pillars: 1) expanding peace and security; 2) revitalizing economic activity; 3) strengthening governance and the rule of law; and 4) rebuilding infrastructure and providing basic services. The success of the plan must be based on how well it alleviates poverty and empowers people.

In 2014, Ebola devastated Liberia, Sierra Leone, and other countries in West Africa. It killed almost half of the people it affected. Fear gripped the countries. Government offices, businesses, and schools were closed. Streets were completely deserted. Economic development was stalled. The entire health sector collapsed, thus leaving the population vulnerable.

Given this dreadful disease we, as United Methodists, remain steadfast in our support of the Liberian people in their journey for a new future. We commit ourselves to:

1. support the peoples and mission of the Liberian people through Advance Special giving, covenant relationships between annual conferences, and through other mission funding. We also urge all Methodist and United Methodist peoples to join in prayer and solidarity for the people, leaders, and churches of Liberia;

2. urge governments to provide economic assistance for reconstruction and development to the government of Liberia and should hold multinational corporations and other big businesses operating in Liberia accountable for any breach of national and international laws with respect to the United Nations Guiding Principles on Business and Human Rights;

3. support and strengthen Liberian civil society so that all Liberians will be able to fully participate in public life, where government is at the service of its people, and where human rights and the rule of law is respected;

4. urge the United Nations and nongovernmental organizations to join in the effort to help stabilize and rebuild Liberia;

5. provide humanitarian assistance, including medical services for Ebola, HIV/AIDS and other illnesses, food, and water;

6. provide financial assistance to pastors and their families;

7. rebuild churches, parsonages, and church-related institutions;

8. repatriate, resettle, and provide shelter for displaced persons and war victims;

9. assist young people to become responsible citizens by developing their skills in career development through the resources of counseling, vocational and general education;

10. engage in reconciliation and healing at the grassroots level between and among various ethnic groups;

11. train pastors to be agents of reconciliation, peace, and healing;

12. set up counseling and education programs to help children, women, and others traumatized by war; and

13. urge multinational corporations investing in Liberia to be good corporate citizens by respecting labor laws, training workers, protecting the environment, and supporting value-added production (i.e., rubber products) to the country's present exports.

The United Methodist Church in Liberia is committed to prioritizing ministries on human rights, peace-building, conflict resolution, and reconciliation. We stand with you on this mission.

ADOPTED 2008
AMENDED AND READOPTED 2016

RESOLUTION #6084, 2012 *BOOK OF RESOLUTIONS*
RESOLUTION #6064, 2008 *BOOK OF RESOLUTIONS*

See Social Principles, ¶ 165*A, B, D.*

6094. East Turkistan Self-Determination and Independence

Be it resolved, that The United Methodist Church supports self-determination and independence of the people and land of East Turkistan (Xinjiang Uyghur Autonomous Region, People's Republic of China); and

Be it further resolved, that The United Methodist Church supports the United Nations' efforts to protect the human rights of all Uyghurs and other peoples of East Turkistan (Xinjiang) (including political prisoners) wherever they live and to preserve the distinct religious, cultural, and linguistic heritage of the people of East Turkistan; and

Be it further resolved, that the general boards and agencies of The United Methodist Church continue to monitor this situation and provide opportunities for United Methodist church members to advocate for justice for the people of East Turkistan (Xinjiang), including political prisoners.

ADOPTED 2012
RESOLUTION #6094, 2012 *BOOK OF RESOLUTIONS*

See Social Principles, ¶ 165.

6095. Relations With Democratic People's Republic of Korea

- The United Methodist Church supports a peaceful diplomatic engagement between the United States (USA) and the Democratic People's Republic of Korea (DPRK) to end the Korean War.
- The USA and the DPRK enter into a peace treaty and normalize their relations.
- The USA supports the process of healing and reconciliation between the two Koreas for peaceful reunification with mutually acceptable ways.
- The USA cooperates with other nations in the process of developing a viable and long-lasting peace regime in the Far East and Pacific Rim.

ADOPTED 2012
RESOLUTION #6095, 2012 *BOOK OF RESOLUTIONS*

See Social Principles, ¶ 165.

6101. Haiti Reconstruction and Development

> *When the very bottom of things falls out,*
> *what can a righteous person possibly accomplish?*
> —Psalm 11:3

The history of Haiti is one of both spirit and struggle. Haiti became the first independent Black republic and remains the first and only country to win independence from slavery. Centuries of foreign imposition, dictatorship, and debt contributed to a weakening of the nation's infrastructure, inadequate social services, and persistent conditions of impoverishment. Seeking employment, many people migrated from the countryside to the capital city, and hundreds of thousands of Haitians re-established life and livelihoods on other shores.

These conditions all contributed to the massive destruction that resulted when on January 12, 2010, a 7.0 earthquake struck Haiti. The disaster took the lives of more than 300,000 people, including 17 percent of government employees, and destroyed nearly every government building. More than 300,000 people were injured, increasing the pressure on an already fragile healthcare system. More than one million were left without homes. People throughout Haiti and the Haitian Diaspora continue to grapple with the impacts and are paving the way forward for healing.

In the midst of crisis are opportunities to change the cycles that have contributed to Haiti's struggles. The Haitian people are Haiti's greatest strength. The earthquake, in spite of its tragic dimensions, has obliged them and the international community to examine the causes of Haiti's chronic underdevelopment and impoverishment. It provides an opportunity for the Haitian people to demand and work toward a different future, the fruit of seeds sown and partnerships forged today.

The United Methodist Church is deeply committed to a long-term relationship with the Eglise Méthodiste d'Haiti (EMH) and other organizations that lasts beyond the season of immediate relief needs. We continue to partner with Haitians and the global community in providing humanitarian assistance and economic empowerment. In the year following the earthquake, United Methodists contributed generously and sacrificially toward the reconstruction of Haiti. The funds are being invested in rebuilding Haiti in a way that strengthens the capacity of the people and to develop a sustainable infrastructure.

As we partner with the people of Haiti, we embrace the faith and hope depicted by the prophet Isaiah: "The LORD will guide you continually and provide for you, even in parched places. He will rescue your bones. . . . They will rebuild ancient ruins on your account; the foundations of generations past you will restore. You will be called Mender of Broken Walls, Restorer of Livable Streets" (Isaiah 58:11a, 12).

To this end, the General Conference of The United Methodist Church:

1. Shares in the sorrow for all the lives lost in the earthquake and continues to pray with the Haitian people for continued strength of spirit. With gratitude we remember the lives of Sam Dixon and Clint Rabb, staff of the General Board of Global Ministries.

2. Recognizes the need for Haitians to lead the reconstruction efforts of their country and calls on governments, the United Nations, and multilateral institutions to work with the Haitian government, Haitian civil society, and the Haitian Diaspora, to rebuild the country in a way that is stronger than it was before the earthquake.

3. Encourages financial support through The Advance to ensure that 100 percent of the funds are used for long-term relief and development efforts in an accountable and responsible manner.

4. Urges governments and multilateral institutions that have not forgiven debts owed by Haiti to do so and to give grants rather than loans for the reconstruction.

5. Urges nongovernmental and peacekeeping organizations working for development in Haiti to use a Rights-Based Approach, respecting the dignity of all people; strengthening governmental, corporate, and community sectors; and giving equal voice and value to women, children, and young people.

6. Ensures that women play meaningful, sustained, and formal roles in the long-term reconstruction efforts and in the design, implementation, and monitoring of aid programs; measures should be taken to protect women from sexual violence, particularly in temporary settlements; enable grassroots and other wom-

en's organizations to build their capacity to function effectively as development and social justice promoters.

7. Calls on the US government to create an expedited Haitian Family Reunification Parole Program to allow thousands of Haitians who reside legally in the US, many as US citizens, to bring their family members from Haiti to the US (as part of the Church's overall call to support reunifying families, see "Welcoming the Migrant to the U.S." 2008 *Book of Resolutions* #3281).

8. Urges United Methodists to create local programs that deepen the awareness and understanding of Haiti, its history and culture and to engage members of the US Haitian Diaspora in these programs.

9. Invites those who seek to accompany our brothers and sisters in Haiti in responding directly to the needs in Haiti to discuss strategies for recovery with Global Ministries and coordinate efforts through EMH and in cooperation with the United Methodist Committee on Relief and United Methodist Volunteers in Mission.

10. Urges The United Methodist Church and its congregations to collaborate with the EMH, Grace Children's Hospital, Global Health Action, and other partners to increase the long-term capacity of the health-care infrastructure of the country.

ADOPTED 2012
RESOLUTION #6101, 2012 *BOOK OF RESOLUTIONS*

See Social Principles, ¶ 165*A, B*.

6102. Violence Against Children in Latin America and the Caribbean

WHEREAS, millions of children in Latin America and the Caribbean struggle daily to survive in the midst of the violence that forces them to migrate out of their homes, cities, and country in search of safety and better living conditions; and

WHEREAS, the root causes of migration and immigration are:

- violence of armed conflict;
- scarce resources taken from children's health and educational needs to support inordinately large military budgets;
- poverty linked to the massive concentration of wealth in a very small percentage of the population; high unemployment; and lack of affordable education opportunities;

- hunger;
- culture of violence permeating television and other mass media;
- lack of medical facilities accessible to the general population, leading to high child mortality;
- violence created by organized crime engaged in the traffic of illegal drugs en route to the US;
- violence caused by gangs (maras) infiltrated by drug cartels who recruit children as young as eight years of age in Honduras, El Salvador, and other countries;
- widespread domestic violence;
- ecological violence that is destroying and polluting the natural world and all live creatures;
- HIV-Aids, with the second highest incidence in the world in many Caribbean nations, destroying children's lives from birth;
- very high infant mortality.

Therefore, be it resolved, that MARCHA's petition to the 2016 General Conference to request the United Methodist Women (UMW), the General Board of Global Ministries (GBGM), the General Board of Church and Society (GBCS), the General Board of Higher Education and Ministry (GBHEM), and the General Board of Discipleship (GBOD) to develop programs, in cooperation with the member churches of CIEMAL, to address the grave crisis of children struggling to survive in the midst of violence and poverty.

Be it further resolved, that the Council of Bishops and the General Council on Finance and Administration (GCFA) support the implementation of these programs.

ADOPTED 2004
READOPTED 2008
AMENDED AND READOPTED 2016
RESOLUTION #6102, 2012 *BOOK OF RESOLUTIONS*
RESOLUTION #6071, 2008 *BOOK OF RESOLUTIONS*
RESOLUTION #324, 2004 *BOOK OF RESOLUTIONS*

See Social Principles, ¶¶ 162C, 164A, and 165.

6111. Opposition to Israeli Settlements in Palestinian Land

We join with Palestinian Christians as well as our Jewish and Muslim brothers and sisters in feeling a deep sense of rootedness to the land that has special meaning for our three religious traditions. We celebrate the diversity of religious customs and traditions throughout the Middle East.

Jerusalem is sacred to all the children of Abraham: Jews, Muslims, and Christians. We have a vision of a shared Jerusalem as a city of peace and reconciliation, where indigenous Palestinians and Israelis can live as neighbors and, along with visitors and tourists, have access to holy sites and exercise freedom of religious expression. The peaceful resolution of Jerusalem's status is crucial to the success of the whole process of making a just and lasting peace between Palestinians and Israelis.

We seek for all people in the Middle East an end to military occupation, freedom from violence, and full respect for the human rights of all under international law.

WHEREAS, the prophet Isaiah cautioned against coveting the lands and homes of one's neighbors: "Doom to those who acquire house after house, who annex field to field until there is no more space left and only you live alone in the land" (Isaiah 5:8); and

WHEREAS, the continuing confiscation of Palestinian land for construction of settlements and the building of a separation wall violates human rights, subverts the peace process, destroys the hope of both Israelis and Palestinians who are working for and longing for peace, and fosters a sense of desperation that can only lead to further violence; and

WHEREAS, continued and often intensified closures, curfews, dehumanizing check points, home demolitions, uprooted trees, bulldozed fields, and confiscation of Palestinian land and water by the government of Israel have devastated economic infrastructure and development in the West Bank and Gaza, have caused a massive deterioration of the living standards of all Palestinians . . . and an increasing sense of hopelessness and frustration; and

WHEREAS, targeted assassinations, suicide bombings, and attacks against civilians by both Israelis and Palestinians heighten the fear and suffering of all, and have led to many deaths of Palestinian and Israeli children; and

WHEREAS, people in the United States, through their taxes, provide several billion dollars in economic and military assistance to the State of Israel each year, which allows for the building of bypass roads and settlements that are illegal according to the Fourth Geneva Convention; and

WHEREAS, a number of Israeli and international companies profit from the building and maintaining of Israeli settlements on Palestinian land in a variety of ways, and many churches and Christians have funds invested in some of these companies; and

WHEREAS human rights organizations have documented that private foreign donors, including Jewish and Christian individuals and nonprofit organizations, have provided financial support for settlements and that some of these donations are tax-deductible; and

WHEREAS, the Church continues to work with ecumenical and interfaith bodies to advocate for Palestinian self-determination and an end to Israeli occupation; to affirm Israel's right to exist within secure borders; to affirm the right of return for Palestinian refugees under international law; to call for region-wide disarmament; to urge Israelis and Palestinians to stop human rights violations and attacks on civilians, such as targeted assassinations and suicide bombings; and to urge the US government to initiate an arms embargo on the entire Middle East region;

Therefore, be it resolved, that The United Methodist Church opposes continued military occupation of the West Bank, Gaza, and East Jerusalem, the confiscation of Palestinian land and water resources, the destruction of Palestinian homes, the continued building of illegal Jewish settlements, and any vision of a "Greater Israel" that includes the occupied territories and the whole of Jerusalem and its surroundings.

In our call for an end to the Israeli occupation we affirm the Church's commitment to nonviolent responses to the Israeli-Palestinian conflict, and acknowledge the need to hear the voices of all those—Muslim, Christian, and Jewish—harmed by the conflict, including the Palestinian Christians as voiced in the Kairos Palestine document.

Be it further resolved, that we urge the US government to end all military aid to the region, and second to redistribute the large amount of aid now given to Israel and Egypt; to support economic development efforts of nongovernmental organizations throughout the region, including religious institutions, human rights groups, labor unions, and professional groups within Palestinian communities.

The United Methodist Church requests that all governments, especially that of the United States, work in cooperation with the United Nations to urge the State of Israel to:

1. cease the confiscation of Palestinian lands and water for any reason;

2. cease the building of new, or expansion of existing, settlements and/or bypass roads in the occupied territories including East Jerusalem;

3. lift the closures and curfews on all Palestinian towns by completely withdrawing Israeli military forces to the Green Line (the 1948 ceasefire line between Israel and the West Bank);

4. dismantle that segment of the Wall of Separation constructed since May 2002 that is not being built on the Green Line but on Palestinian land that is separating Palestinian farmers from their fields.

We also urge the Palestinian Authority and all Palestinian religious leaders to continue to publicly condemn violence against Israeli civilians and to use nonviolent acts of disobedience to resist the occupation and the illegal settlements.

We further call on all nations to prohibit:

1. any financial support by individuals or organizations for the construction and maintenance of settlements; and

2. the import of products made by companies in Israeli settlements on Palestinian land.

We ask all companies that profit from and/or support settlements through their business activities to examine these and stop any business that contributes to serious violations of international law, promotes systemic discrimination, or otherwise supports ongoing military occupation.

The United Methodist Church does not support a boycott of products made in Israel. Our opposition is to products made by Israeli companies operating in occupied Palestinian territories.

We urge all United Methodists in the US to:

1. advocate with the US administration and Congress to implement the aforementioned steps;

2. urge the US government to examine the role played by donations from tax-exempt charities in support of discriminatory and other illegal aspects of Israeli settlements, and develop recommendations to ensure that tax-exempt funds do not support illegal settlements and other violations of international law.

We urge all United Methodists to:

1. read about the suffering of Israelis and Palestinians and nonviolent ways of ending the Israeli/Palestinian conflict from the perspective of all faith communities including the Kairos Palestine document; and

2. encourage members of each congregation to study the Israeli-Palestinian conflict from all perspectives by inviting speakers to

church events, reading books, using audiovisual resources in educational forums, and getting information from websites. We especially commend the 2010 British Methodist Church's call "on the Methodist people to support and engage with [a] boycott of Israeli goods emanating from illegal settlements," as well as a call for nonviolent actions issued by several annual conferences.

3. provide financial support to the Palestinian people through contributions to the General Board of Global Ministries;

4. support, and participate in, the work of international peace and human rights organizations, such as the Ecumenical Accompaniment Program in Palestine & Israel and Christian Peacemaker Teams, to provide protection for Palestinians and Israelis seeking nonviolently to end the occupation; and

5. reach out to local synagogues, mosques, and Christian faith groups by engaging in interfaith and ecumenical dialogue on nonviolent ways to promote justice and peace in the Holy Land; and

That the General Board of Global Ministries, working together with the General Board of Church and Society and interfaith organizations, develop advocacy packets for use in local congregations to promote a just and lasting peace and human rights for all in the region.

ADOPTED 2004
READOPTED 2008
AMENDED AND READOPTED 2012
RESOLUTION #6111, 2012 *BOOK OF RESOLUTIONS*
RESOLUTION #6073, 2008 *BOOK OF RESOLUTIONS*
RESOLUTION #312, 2004 *BOOK OF RESOLUTIONS*

See Social Principles, ¶ 165.

6112. United Nations Resolutions on the Israel-Palestine Conflict

WHEREAS, negotiations between the State of Israel and the Palestinian National Authority still have not achieved a just and lasting peace for the Palestinian people; and

WHEREAS, the United Nations Security Council and General Assembly have passed numerous resolutions since UN Resolution 181, the Partition Plan, first adopted in November 1947, including Resolutions 242 and 338, that outline a framework for a just and lasting peace; and

WHEREAS, The UMC in the Social Principles recognizes and affirms the role of the United Nations in the just and lasting resolution of conflict, "Believing that international justice requires the participation of all peoples and nations, we endorse the United Nations, its related bodies, the International Court of Justice and the International Criminal Court as the best instruments now in existence to achieve a world of justice and law" (¶ 165D); and

WHEREAS, Security Council Resolution 242, unanimously adopted in 1967, declares "the inadmissibility of the acquisition of territory by war and the need to work for a just and lasting peace in which every State in the area can live in security"; and

WHEREAS, the security of every State depends on it having defined borders and not occupying the territory of its neighbors, and

WHEREAS, the 10th commandment in the Bible states, "Do not desire your neighbor's house . . . or anything that belongs to your neighbor" (Exodus 20:17); and

WHEREAS, for more than 40 years the government of Israel has continued its military occupation of East Jerusalem, the West Bank, and Gaza and the seizing of more and more Palestinian land for illegal settlements in direct violation of UN resolutions as well as United Methodist General Conference resolutions; and

WHEREAS, since its creation, Israel has faced armed resistance that refuses to acknowledge Israel's right to exist; and

WHEREAS, the International Court of Justice, on July 9, 2004, issued an advisory opinion that declared that Israel's security barrier or wall built on occupied Palestinian territories violates international law; that it must be dismantled; and that compensation must be provided to Palestinians for loss of land and livelihood; and

WHEREAS, Israel's government has continued to build the wall on Palestinian land in ongoing violation of international law, which greatly increases Palestinian suffering as well as heightens the insecurity of both Palestinians and Israelis; and

WHEREAS, May 2012 marks over 60 years since the establishment of the State of Israel as well as the dispossession of 750,000 to 900,000 Palestinians who are still seeking their full human rights; and

WHEREAS, ongoing military occupation and armed resistance heightens violence and insecurity for Palestinians and Israelis alike; and

WHEREAS, The United Methodist Church opposes all violence against civilians and considers "war is incompatible with the teachings and example of Christ" (Social Principles, ¶ 165C); and

WHEREAS, the United States' use of its veto more than 30 times in the UN Security Council to block actions by the international community to criticize and prevent the killing of Palestinian civilians has contributed to a climate of impunity and exacerbated the cycle of violence affecting both Palestinians and Israelis;

Therefore, be it resolved, that The United Methodist Church calls upon Israel, the Palestinian National Authority, and all States to abide by and uphold UN resolutions, International Court of Justice rulings, and international law as the basis for just and lasting peace in Palestine/Israel; and

Be it further resolved, that The United Methodist Church calls upon the United States, as a permanent member of the UN Security Council, to accept the authority of Security Council resolutions to refrain from vetoing resolutions, and abide by Security Council Resolutions 242 and 338, as well as all other relevant UN resolutions and International Court of Justice rulings, that provide a framework for bringing this conflict to a just and permanent end.

ADOPTED 2000
REVISED AND READOPTED 2008
AMENDED AND READOPTED 2012
RESOLUTION #6112, 2012 *BOOK OF RESOLUTIONS*
RESOLUTION #6074, 2008 *BOOK OF RESOLUTIONS*
RESOLUTION #323, 2004 *BOOK OF RESOLUTIONS*
RESOLUTION #305, 2000 *BOOK OF RESOLUTIONS*

See Social Principles, ¶ 165*A, B, C, D*.

6114. A Pathway for Peace in Palestine and Israel

WHEREAS, The United Methodist Church has committed itself to peacemaking, as well as to affirming "the right and duty of people of all nations to determine their own destiny" (Social Principles, ¶ 165*B*); and

WHEREAS, in spite of strong support from many for a two-State solution involving Israel and Palestine, the conflict between the two peoples remains an enduring one that has not been resolved over many years and continues to negatively impact the lives of all those in the region in substantial ways; and

WHEREAS, after years of occupation and violence, a deep and fundamental lack of trust exists between many Israelis and Palestinians, requiring the difficult work of genuine reconciliation in order for a just and lasting peace to be sustained; and

WHEREAS, the Church has been called to practice restorative justice wherever it may do so in order to bring about healing and trust, particularly where there has been very little in the past; and

WHEREAS, true peace must reveal itself in both the spiritual and temporal aspects of the life and culture of both Israel and Palestine, where both parties may see themselves as the victims and the other as the aggressors/offenders;

Therefore, be it resolved, that this General Conference of The United Methodist Church affirms strategies including favorable trade and shipping arrangements, student and work-related visa policies, and diplomatic initiatives that will engage both Israelis and Palestinians in an effort to understand the fears, hopes, and aspirations of each other. Such strategies should actively seek a way to promote a just and lasting peace and cooperation that will lead to a two-State solution within two years, an end to the current occupation and violence, and the creation of a viable Palestinian state living side by side in peace with Israel, and

Be it further resolved, that the General Conference fully supports commitments by the General Board of Pension and Health Benefits and United Methodist foundations to research and identify investment opportunities that support the Palestinian economy, as well as joint ventures between Israelis and Palestinians that can help to build trust and reconciliation, and

Be it further resolved, that the General Conference encourages our members around the world to develop a balanced understanding of the concerns and perspectives of both Palestinians and Israelis, being careful to lift up the voices of those victims of violence and injustice across the region, and rejecting oversimplified efforts to simply "blame" one side or the other, even as we encourage United Methodists to join in prayer for "the peace of Jerusalem" (Psalm 122:6) and all of those who call it home.

ADOPTED 2016

See Social Principles, ¶ 165B.

6115. Condemnation of Terrorist Acts of ISIL

The United Methodist Church condemns terrorist acts of the Islamic State in Iraq and the Levant, commonly referred to as

ISIL, also known as Daesh or ISIS, that violate The United Methodist Church's principles found in the *Book of Resolutions* against minorities based on religious or political differences. The violent acts of ISIL are evil and The United Methodist Church calls for all nations to oppose, dismantle, and disarm ISIL. The United Methodist Church does not condone any attempt to declare or recognize ISIL as a State, with diplomatic relations, and supports the continued effort to bring relief to the captive people of that region to restore a viable and sustainable society.

ADOPTED 2016

See Social Principles, ¶ 165.

6116. Palestinian Land Rights and Access to Water and Electricity

The General Conference of The United Methodist Church calls upon the nation of Israel to provide the same access to water and electricity in the West Bank as settlers in the Israeli settlements in the area receive and to recognize existing titles to land within the West Bank which Palestinians hold. We ask the USA to respect international law and use its influence to demand equal access to water and electricity, and recognition of land titles.

ADOPTED 2016

See Social Principles, ¶ 165.

6117. End Impunity in the Philippines

"Indeed, the extra-judicial killings, enforced disappearances and other forms of human rights violations were conducted with impunity as the perpetrators remain free and exempted from justice while the victims are vilified and dismissed as subversives and undeserving of any of form of justice. . . . People have been offended, profaned, and outraged by an artist's work. Yet, what greater offense, profanity, and outrage can there be than the violation and destruction, with impunity, of that most real and live image of God—the human being? The effects of impunity will continue to scar the people of this country, impairing seriously family and community relations now and in the future, be they the children, relatives, and friends of the victims or the children, relatives, and friends of those who perpetrate human rights abuses. We have seen and continue to see its tragic results on our social fiber—broken community relations, the forced migration of our people, the destruction of our natural resources and sovereignty and national dignity seriously compromised. It must be stopped." Father Rex R. B. Reyes, Jr.—General Secretary of National Council of Churches in the Philippines.

"President Aquino's avowed commitment for human rights is starting to unravel. While the record of former president Macapagal-Arroyo remains unbeaten, I am afraid that President Aquino's record could turn out worse given the rise in human rights abuses under his watch," he said.

"Former president Gloria Macapagal-Arroyo would do well to answer the many questions regarding her accountability not only for the massive corruption and fraud under her administration, but also on her responsibility for the gross human rights violations under her watch," said Cristina Palabay, convenor of the End Impunity Alliance.

Under the Arroyo administration, Karapatan says it has documented 1,206 victims of extrajudicial killings, 206 victims of enforced disappearances and thousands more victims of other forms of abuses.

Since Aquino assumed office on July 1, 2010, up to July 21, 2011, Karapatan says it has already documented 50 cases of extrajudicial killings, eight cases of enforced disappearances, and more than a hundred cases of illegal arrests and detentions.

"Impunity prevails because no one has been put behind bars for the violations up to the present. Thus, it is important that freedom-loving individuals call on the Aquino administration to decisively stop human rights violations in the country and end the reigning climate of impunity by ensuring justice is rendered to victims."

(Source: <http://www.ucanews.com/2011/08/18/activists -launch-impunity-campaign/>)

Therefore, be it resolved, for The United Methodist Church to urge Philippine President Benigno "Noynoy" Aquino, Jr., to end impunity and stop human rights violations in the Philippines.

Be it further resolved, for The United Methodist Church to urge Philippine President Benigno "Noynoy" Aquino, Jr., to order the landowners (Cojuangcos, Arroyos, Ayalas, Sys, etc.) to return the land to their rightful owners, the farmers.

Be it further resolved, for The United Methodist Church to support, endorse, and help promote IBON Foundation's "Challenges for Democracy":

- Investigate former President Gloria Macapagal-Arroyo/ allies for electoral fraud, corruption, along with military/ police for serious human rights violations
- Independent probe of May 10, 2010 elections
- Review Visiting Forces Agreement
- Immediately resume and genuinely advance formal peace talks with NDFP and MILF.

ADOPTED 2012
RESOLUTION #6117, 2012 *BOOK OF RESOLUTIONS*

See Social Principles, ¶ 165D.

6118. Philippines: Democratic Governance, Human Rights, and the Peace Process

Justice is pushed aside; / righteousness far off, / because truth has stumbled in the public square, / and honesty can't enter. / Truth is missing; / anyone turning from evil is plundered. / The LORD looked and was upset at the absence of justice. / Seeing that there was no one, / and astonished that no one would intervene. . . .

(Isaiah 59:14-16)

"Jerusalem, Jerusalem! You who kill the prophets and stone those who were sent to you. How often I wanted to gather your people together, just as a hen gathers her chicks under her wings. But you didn't want that."

(Matthew 23:37)

"An injustice does not only affect the people against whom the injustice is committed, but threatens every one of us and the life we share together as an ordered society. It is a Christian imperative that we are vigilant in defending the rights of every person at all times. Long before human rights were formulated in law, they were inscribed in the being of every person, for it is in the very image of God that we are created. For human rights to have meaning they need to be vigilantly defended, where possible the dignity of those denied their rights needs to be restored, and those who are responsible for violations, be they states or individuals need to be made accountable. In our Philippine society we have seen the institutionalization of a culture of impunity, where those who violate the human rights of others, are able to escape investigation and prosecution" (Rev. Fr. Rex R. B. Reyes, General Secretary, National Council of Churches in the Philippines).

Our Concern: Intensifying Impunity Amidst
Increasing Militarization in the Philippines

The United Methodist Church continues to be alarmed by and concerned about the unabated and egregious violations of human rights in the Philippines. Such violations that take place within the perpetual framework of US counterinsurgency and military doctrine, take the form of extrajudicial killings, summary executions, abductions, torture, arbitrary and prolonged political detentions, and enforced disappearances. Since the beginning of Philippine President Benigno Aquino III's term in office, victims of human rights violations include over 226 extrajudicial killings and 26 forced disappearances, 693 illegally arrested and detained, and 491 political prisoners (KARAPATAN Report, December 2014).

The Philippines persists in officially collaborating with the United States-sanctioned war on terror, willingly subordinating itself to interests of U.S. militarism. The Philippines has adopted the US Counterinsurgency Program of 2009 as its blueprint for counterinsurgency, a methodology demonstrably dismissive of human rights. Criticisms directed at the Armed Forces of the Philippines about its dismal human rights record since 2007 have been defended by the defense establishment as falling within the frame of counterinsurgency. Such frame is inherently flawed and fundamentally at odds with the genuine pursuit of peace and the protection of human rights.

Very alarming and disturbing is the increasingly militarized approach of both the Philippine and US governments to the economic development of and humanitarian crises in the Philippines. This approach follows the 2012 announcement of plans by the US Department of Defense to "pivot to Asia" (See http://www .defense.gov/news/Defense_Strategic_Guidance.pdf). The Asia pivot heralds the Pentagon's strategy to shift at least 60 percent of its military forces to the Asia Pacific, including the Philippines.

It is a US bid to protect and expand the United States' market and military interests in the region. This military, defense, and foreign policy focus on Asia benefits the advancement of free-trade partnerships and agreements in Asia. Most notable for its disturbing features is the Trans-Pacific Partnership, otherwise called TPP Agreement (https://ustr.gov/tpp and http://en.wikipedia.org /wiki/Trans-Pacific_Partnership. Accessed February 2, 2015). This partnership agreement is modeled after the North American Free Trade Agreement (NAFTA) that has devastated the economies of Mexico and Central America, triggering an exponential increase in the migration of people fleeing poverty and violence. This neoliberal economic strategy seeks to further open markets in the Philippines and throughout Asia, ultimately making the fragile economies of the region even more vulnerable to intrusion and domination by foreign multinational corporations.

The Backdrop of United Methodist and Ecumenical Witness in the Philippines

There is expressed opposition of the ecumenical community in the Philippines to the TPP. In a statement dated August 24, 2014, the National Council of Churches in the Philippines (NCCP) stated: "The President's attempt to reopen the issue of Charter change is related to influence being exerted by the U.S. government, large corporations and some developed countries in the region to pave the way for the entry of the Philippines into a massive 'free-trade' agreement referred to as the Trans-Pacific Partnership (TPP). The TPP negotiations that were a central discussion point during the recent visit of U.S. President [Barack] Obama have been shrouded in secrecy.

"The TPP threatens to raise the legal status of large corporation to effective equality with sovereign nations, and to undermine the sovereign rights of participant nations to establish their own financial and product standards regulative regimes. The Philippines is currently on the sidelines of the TPP negotiations because our current Constitution does not conform to TPP requirements. The Constitution is a basic protection of our national sovereignty, and it is inappropriate for any other country, even when acting behind the scenes, to exert pressure for Constitutional change."

Intimidation and violence have met the opposition by Filipino peoples to the economic impositions by foreign powers such as the TPP, and the violation of their human rights, especially the human rights of indigenous peoples, farm workers, and land tillers in rural areas. Philippine military, paramilitary forces, private armies and vigilante groups of warlords, and big landlords and multinational corporations have been documented to be in collusion (<http://www.hrw.org/asia/-philippines>).

Under the terms of the 1999 Visiting Forces Agreement (VFA) between the US and the Philippines, since 2006 over 600 American special-operations forces have been on "permanent rotation" in resource-rich areas on the southern island of Mindanao. Joint training exercises involving several thousands of US and Philippine military personnel are conducted dozens of times every year on Philippine air, land, and water. Such exercises serve as a not-so-subtle reminder of the military muscle backing up both the Philippine military and US business interests in the region.

When Typhoon Haiyan, the strongest typhoon in recorded history to hit land, struck the Philippines in 2013, the enormity of destruction to human lives, infrastructure, and property was staggering. More than 6,000 people were confirmed dead, nearly four million people were displaced, and 1,600 were declared missing. The immediate response of the US government was to send military support to the Philippines. The US "pivot to Asia Pacific" meant sending ships, weapons, and soldiers, in stark contrast to other countries that provided medical professionals, engineers, aid workers, and food.

This militarized and securitized approach to humanitarian aid was cemented in a new agreement called Enhanced Defense Cooperation Agreement (EDCA), which was signed by the US and the Philippines a mere five months after Typhoon Haiyan. As the Visiting Forces Agreement (VFA) and numerous Status of Forces and Mutual Logistics Support Agreements before it, forged between the US and other states after, the EDCA is also an access agreement. It grants the US the ability and flexibility to station its war material, Special Operations Forces, and forces to handle "housekeeping" matters, such as logistics support, administration, and military justice. The aim is to wage asymmetrical warfare against anyone: governments, "rogue states," but also activists. The activists who are opposed to the economic and security interests of the US are casually branded as terrorists.

EDCA also protects the interests of the oil, mining, agribusiness, banking and technology corporations that depend on the

US military to protect US investments and operations on foreign soil. Such protection extends to the water and airways that serve as the shipping lanes for global commodities, even when such protections have contributed to the destruction in the Philippines of livelihoods and properties of over 13,000 people and the displacement of nearly 50,000 people during Benigno Aquino III's presidency.

Retired Chief Justice of the Supreme Court of the Philippines, Hon. Reynato Puno, who was the first Filipino United Methodist to hold this high position, said in a university commencement speech: "One visible result of the scramble to end terrorism is to take legal shortcuts and legal shortcuts always shrink the scope of human rights. . . . These shortcuts have scarred the landscape of rights in the Philippines. . . . The escalation of extrajudicial killings in the Philippines has attracted the harsh eye of advocates of human rights. . . . Their initial findings do not complement our Constitutional commitment to protect human rights. . . . If there is any lesson that we can derive from the history of human rights, it is none other than these rights cannot be obliterated by bombs but neither can they be preserved by bullets alone. Terrorism is a military/police problem but its ultimate solution lies beyond the guns of our armed forces. . . . The apathy of those who can make a difference is the reason why violations of human rights continue to prosper. The worst enemy of human rights is not its nonbelievers but the fence sitters who will not lift a finger despite their violations."

Patronage politics, an economy controlled by oligarchies, and a tightening space for democratic speech and organizing to air grievances against powerful political and economic forces characterize the Philippine situation today. This situation has led to prophetic and forthright witness by United Methodist leaders and members in the country, asserting it as a moral response. Speaking to the accountability of Philippine government officials in the way they disburse and use funds from the public coffers, United Methodist bishops of the Philippines and the leaders of the Philippines Central Conference Board of Church and Society asserted:

"[O]ur country has been governed by an oligarchy of big business people and big landlords who effectively influence all the branches of government and have succeeded in preserving their selfish interest at the expense of the greater interest of the people. The amassing of immoral wealth dog[s] the heels of the ancient shepherds/rulers who disregarded their flock. . . . The present outcry against PDAF [Priority Development Assistance Fund] and DAP [Disbursement Acceleration Program] is all about misappropriating the people's money while shrugging off any responsibility especially to the poor of the land, and then shifting that burden to those who create those resources. Taxes and other revenues are all managed and manipulated by the unholy alliance of political and economic elites for their own benefit and to the neglect of the hungry sheep who are deprived of those resources" (Statement by Philippines Central Conference, The Filipino People Deserve Servant Leaders and Righteous Governance!).

The Human Rights Situation Is Appalling

Many international groups—religious bodies, nongovernmental organizations, foreign governments, and intergovernmental organizations such as the United Nations—have pressed the Philippine government to do more to stop the many disturbing forms of human rights violations in the Philippines, urging the government to fulfill its constitutional and international law obligations. These human rights violations continue unabated and are escalating with impunity. Calls to stop them are contained in detailed, credible, and substantiated reports from various sources. Such reports were issued by the UN Special Rapporteur on Extrajudicial, Summary or Arbitrary Executions; the US State Department, in particular its Country Report on Human Rights Practices, from 2007 to the present; Amnesty International; Human Rights Watch; Human Rights First; and the Asian Human Rights Commission.

The Armed Forces of the Philippines (AFP), paramilitary units under its control, and the Philippine National Police (PNP) continue to be implicated in EJKs, enforced disappearances, torture, and illegal arrests and detention. One hundred ninety of the 226 victims of EJKs were peasant activists and indigenous peoples. The targeting of these specific populations reveals the victimization of people actively resisting economic exploitation, land grabbing, and forced displacement. (Many EJKs were conducted with impunity through the very familiar and visible method involving two men on a motorcycle with hidden or missing license plates, faces covered, driving up and shooting the victim or victims with a handgun, and then speeding off to evade identification and arrest.)

The US State Department 2013 Human Rights Report states, "The most significant human rights problems [continue] to be extrajudicial killings and enforced disappearances undertaken by security forces; a dysfunctional criminal justice system notable for poor cooperation between police and investigators, few prosecutions, and lengthy procedural delays; and widespread official corruption and abuse of power."

In 2013, from January to October, the Office of the Ombudsman, an independent agency in the Philippines responsible for investigating and prosecuting charges of public abuse and impropriety, received 306 cases involving military and law enforcement officers accused of committing human-rights abuses. These cases included killings, injuries, unlawful arrest, and torture. Most were filed against low-ranking police and military officials. As of October 2014, some 302 cases were dismissed due to insufficiency of evidence, and eight are under investigation. There are no recorded convictions of high-ranking police or military officials.

Many of the victims of human-rights violations are themselves human-rights defenders, also labor leaders, peasant leaders, environmentalists, journalists, and others fighting against graft and corruption, and for peace and justice. They are frequently vilified as "enemies of the state" by the police and military establishments, tagged as supporters of a 45-year-long armed struggle conducted by the National Democratic Front of the Philippines (NDFP) and its armed wing, the New Peoples Army. Their vilification has been used by paramilitary forces under the control of the police and military as some sort of license to arrest, even kill, these ordinary citizens and their community leaders.

Harassment by military and paramilitary forces is rampant among indigenous peoples who are protesting against dislocation from their ancestral lands. Forced dislocations have happened due to increased operation of extractive mining companies that have sprung up in many parts of the country, but mostly in indigenous peoples' lands. A hearing on the killing of four members of the B'laan tribe in Mindanao, who protested against the large Tampakan copper-gold mine being proposed and developed by Sagittarius Mines Inc., disclosed that the mining company has paramilitary-armed men on its payroll who are under the nominal command of the AFP.

In the case of Manobo tribes of Southern Mindanao, armed paramilitary units operate in their indigenous communities and are pitted against their own tribes who are opposed to large-scale logging, mining and other foreign-funded projects like hydroelectric power plants that encroach into their ancestral lands.

Hamleting, food blockades, food rationing, and establishing curfew hours are just some of the harassment they commit to force these indigenous peoples into submission.

Those who dare resist are threatened and many of them eventually become victims of extrajudicial killings. In situations where entire communities protest the encroachment, massive military operations have been undertaken, causing dislocations of entire villages such as the evacuation of 118 families of the Talaingod-Manobos in 2014. The schooling of indigenous children is compromised, even stopped, under these situations. A campaign to spare schools from combat and to declare the schools as zones of peace is of paramount importance. (This area of Mindanao where the Manobos have their ancestral lands has been visited five times between 2010 and 2014 by a group organized under the auspices of the Philippines Task Force of the California-Pacific Annual Conference and leads hosting in the Philippines by Panalipdan-Southern Mindanao, a broad alliance of environmentalists and people's organizations with a strong human-rights advocacy, and the Davao Episcopal Area of The United Methodist Church.)

Persistence in Peace Negotiations

The past 46 years have been marked by two armed conflicts waged separately against the Government of the Philippines (GPH) by the National Democratic Front of the Philippines (NDFP) and the Moro Islamic Liberation Front (MILF). Through the process of peace negotiations, the GPH and the MILF forged an agreement to end formally their armed hostilities. The two parties signed the Comprehensive Agreement on the Bangsamoro in 2014. The peace talks between GPH and NDFP remain stalled.

The Filipino people's clamor for peace with justice is a fervent desire. The National Council of Churches in the Philippines (NCCP) has called for ". . . principled negotiations to thresh out the issues, unearth and address the root causes of the conflict." The NCCP asserted, "The peace negotiation is a way to just and lasting peace," stating, "it is a way to end the armed conflict that has claimed the lives of thousands of Filipinos, combatants and non-combatants alike."

Peace negotiations aimed to pave decisively the way to a just, sustainable, and durable peace must resume and aim for completion. It must focus on resolving the conditions that have provoked the past 46 years of armed conflict throughout the Philippines. Solving this long-term conflict, including ending the AFP counterinsurgency program that has been prosecuted with so many human-rights violations committed, is vital to achieving a lasting and durable peace and beginning a solid regime of human rights and human dignity.

Building peace requires building trust. Between 2002 and 2003, the US made a deal with the GPH whereby upon GPH joining the "Coalition of the Willing" to invade Iraq, the US would add the Communist Party of the Philippines–New People's Army (CPP-NPA) to the list of Foreign Terrorist Organizations (FTO), even though the CPP-NPA does not fit the State Department's definition of FTO.

The listing of the CPP-NPA has been a significant contributing factor to the deteriorating environment for concluding a peace agreement with this insurgent group. Still, 27 years of sporadic yet persistent negotiations have produced more than 10 significant peace agreements aimed at addressing the lingering root causes of the Philippine crisis.

The call for peace with justice is an international call and the resolution of the Philippine crisis must involve the international community. The support of the Government of Norway in helping broker the peace negotiations between the GPH and the NDFP is most commendable.

The time is ripe and the moment is urgent. Both GPH and NDFP must proceed to implement in earnest and with good faith the agreements they have already negotiated between them. Among these agreements are The Hague Joint Declaration of 1992, the Joint Agreement on Safety and Immunity Guarantees (JASIG, 1995), and The Comprehensive Agreement on Respect for Human Rights and International Humanitarian Law (CARHRIHL, 1998).

There are palpable challenges to the peace process. Thousands of grievances have been filed against the AFP and PNP for violating the JASIG and CARHRIHL. The peace talks are derailed by the imprisonment of registered NDFP peace-negotiation consultants on false charges. There are the EJKs, disappearances, and illegal arrest and torture of NPA sympathizers. These governmental acts undermine the peace process and must be stopped at all costs.

The reported success of the December 2014 meetings of special teams from both the GPH and NDFP to discuss compliance with past agreements, along with the release of prisoners of war by the NDFP, augurs well for the resumption of peace talks. The resumption shows the readiness amongst various parties to come to the negotiating table for more needed steps in the peace process. The peace negotiations must resume as soon as possible.

The Filipino People Deserve Our Solidarity and Action

We welcome the release of "Let the Stones Cry Out: An Ecumenical Report on Human Rights in the Philippines and a Call to Action" released by the ecumenical and nongovernmental community in the Philippines, led by the National Council of Churches in the Philippines, whose production and distribution was led and supported by a couple of general agencies of The United Methodist Church.

We share with the ecumenical community in the Philippines the perspective posed and the burden of the question raised in the ecumenical report's preface: "Something is wrong when members of the clergy and lay missionaries are being silenced when they are deeply engaged in missions that address the concerns of their constituencies—and the Philippine society as a whole. Something is wrong when members of the church and faith institutions are killed, go missing or are arrested while pursuing their calling to bring about justice closer to the poor, to fight for their rights, and advocate peace in a society that is torn asunder by armed conflicts fueled by structural problems. Of greater alarm is that the gross and systematic attacks on these pilgrims of peace and servants of God are forcing their institutions to an inevitable clash with the State."

We issue this statement not only to support the ecumenical report from the Philippines and the direction in which its call to action points. We issue this statement because the struggle for human rights in the Philippines is at a point when our solidarity and accompaniment, as we have expressed in many ways and many times in the past, are crucial and needed even more so today.

We Commit to Action with Resolve and Dispatch

Filipino faith communities and citizens continue to address the situation in the Philippines. General boards and agencies of The United Methodist Church have addressed the human-rights situation in the Philippines in a variety of ways and venues, including providing to the Philippine Working Group (PWG) of the Asia Pacific Forum of US and Canadian church and ecumenical staff executives, which helped produce the ecumenical human-rights report and supported the itineration in Canada, US, and Europe, of a Philippine ecumenical delegation called "Ecumenical Voice for Human Rights and Peace in the Philippines." This ecumenical voice has briefed US House of Representatives members and testified at a US Senate hearing on March 14, 2007. This ecumenical voice was submitted numerous reports to, and addressed the sessions of, the UN Human Rights Council in Geneva, engaging this global-human rights body in its Universal Periodic Review of the Philippines. This ecumenical voice has since expanded its membership, and its voice is ever more heard and its perspective ever more sought, in the Philippines and abroad.

Our denomination also helped secure meetings with the US State Department and key congressional offices to raise concerns about the Philippine human-rights situation. Our denomination, through a number of its boards and agencies, also accompanied the ecumenical delegation in submitting the ecumenical report to a variety of United Nations-related offices in Geneva, Switzerland, especially the UN Human Rights Council, the Office of the UN High Commissioner for Human Rights, and the UN Special Rapporteurs on Indigenous Peoples, and on the promotion and protection of human rights while countering terrorism.

Other annual conferences in the United States, such as California-Nevada, Pacific Northwest, Desert Southwest, California-Pacific, and Northern Illinois, have also addressed these issues, including conducting fact-finding, solidarity, and mission trips to the Philippines. In all these visits, Philippine church leaders and church workers showed them the appalling human-rights situation and in turn the visitors voiced their concern with government and military officials, and expressed their solidarity with church and community leaders.

We Commit to Work on the Following Actions:

We will submit this statement to concerned governmental and intergovernmental offices to convey our call to the Philippine government to stop immediately illegal arrests and prolonged detention; stop the killings, disappearances, torture, forced displacement; and stop all the other forms of human-rights violations.

We also call on the Philippine government to take effective measures to bring to justice members of its security forces and their agents for whom there is credible evidence of human-rights violations, to comply with its obligations under international human-rights and humanitarian laws, to rescind national security policies that make no distinction between combatants and noncombatants, to hold free and fair elections, and to investigate any allegations of electoral fraud.

We call on the Philippine government to stop the practice of listing peace and human-rights advocates in its watch lists of individuals banned from entering or leaving the Philippines and to expunge such record of names already listed.

We call on other governments, but especially the governments of the United States of America, the European Union, the Association of Southeast Asian Nations, and significant development aid and trading partners like Japan, to look into these human-rights violations and pressure the Philippine government to stop them. To this end, we also support moves within the US Congress calling for a review of official development aid, and trade and economic arrangements to examine whether these do or do not further exacerbate human-rights violations.

We support the call to require the Department of Defense of the United States to file Environmental Impact Assessment (EIA) reports, including social impacts, with every US military or resource deployment in the Philippines, to prevent environmental damages, as well as remediation of environmental damages caused US military activities.

We especially call for any military appropriations and official development assistance to the Philippine government to be withheld unless the Philippine government demonstrates strict adherence to international laws and standards of human rights and good governance, and thereby supports the development and use of benchmarks that will guide and measure the Philippine government's adherence to the same.

Since human rights thrive under democratic, just, and peaceful conditions we therefore call for the resumption and full engagement of peace talks by the government, without preconditions, with all of the Philippine rebel groups. With the successful completion of negotiations the civil, political, social, economic, and cultural problems that beset the Philippines may yet result in just and durable peace.

We call on the United Nations and its agencies to continue investigating human-rights violations in the Philippines, and to offer help to the Philippine government in meeting its international obligations, including non-interference, empowerment, and capacity-building of nongovernmental organizations in their work of monitoring Philippine government compliance and promotion of human rights.

We call for the termination of military agreements between the US and the Philippines that prioritize profits over people and foster conditions that abet the culture of impunity in the Philippines.

Lastly, we call on our general boards, agencies, annual conferences, and local churches in the US and throughout the global connection, including the National Association of Filipino American United Methodists, to work with Philippine annual conferences, ecumenical bodies, and nongovernmental organizations in joint undertakings to address the peace and human-rights situation in the Philippines.

Eyes on the Prize: Truth, Justice, and Peace

The Human Rights Watch (HRW) World Report 2015 called on Philippine President Aquino to "take decisive action against torture and extrajudicial killings by the police and other state security forces." In his introductory essay of that report, HRW Executive Director Kenneth Roth, urged "governments to recognize that human rights can offer an effective moral guide in turbulent times, and that violating rights can spark or aggravate serious security challenges. The short-term gains of undermining core values of freedom and non-discrimination are rarely worth the long-term price" (Press Release by Human Rights Watch, "Philippines: End Police Torture, Killings," Manila, January 29, 2015).

We must keep our eyes on the prize even as we struggle for the recognition of each one's human dignity and fight for each one's human rights.

"These are the things you should do: Speak the truth to each other; make truthful, just, and peaceable decisions within your gates. Don't plan evil for each other. Don't adore swearing falsely, for all of these are things that I hate, says the LORD." (Zechariah 8:16-17)

ADOPTED 2008
AMENDED AND READOPTED 2016
RESOLUTION #6118, 2012 *BOOK OF RESOLUTIONS*
RESOLUTION #6078, 2008 *BOOK OF RESOLUTIONS*

See Social Principles, ¶ 165*A, B, D*.

PEACEMAKING

6126. A Call for Peacemaking

God's earth is aching for peace. Domestic strife, interpersonal violence and abuse, civil conflict, ethnic and racial clashes, religious schism and interfaith rivalry, terrorist attacks, wars between nations, and threatened use of nuclear, chemical, and biological weapons—all of these prevent us from achieving God's shalom. In response we who are disciples of Jesus Christ are called to be peacemakers for the transformation of the world.

The biblical foundation for peacemaking is the Sermon on the Mount where Jesus taught, "Happy are people who make peace" (Matthew 5:9), "Don't react violently against the one who is evil" (Matthew 5:39, Scholars Version*), "Love your enemies and pray for those who harass you" (Matthew 5:44), and pray to forgive those who trespass against us (Matthew 6:12, 14-15). Paul echoed Jesus' teaching when he instructed Christians in Rome, "Don't be defeated by evil, but defeat evil with good" (Romans 12:21; see also vv. 14-21). He told the church in Corinth that through Christ we have a "ministry of reconciliation" (2 Corinthians 5:17-18).

For The United Methodist Church, peacemaking is an essential task for achieving success in other initiatives. Working with the poor to eliminate poverty, caring for children, and conducting global health initiatives can be most successful in stable and just

*The Five Gospels: The Search for the Authentic Words of Jesus. New Translation and Commentary by Robert W. Funk, Roy W. Hoover, and the *Jesus Seminar* [also known as the Scholars Version]; Robert W. Funk, et al. (New York: Macmillan, 1993).

societies free from armed conflict. To have sufficient resources for these tasks requires global peace and disarmament in order to redirect vast amounts of public funds now spent on armed forces and weaponry. Moreover, a strong concern for peace and justice is a necessary feature of vital congregations.

Therefore, the 2012 General Conference of The United Methodist Church calls upon:

- United Methodist children, youth, and adults—as devoted disciples of Jesus Christ—to become peacemakers wherever they are—at home, school, work, in the local community and the wider world—and to show the love, compassion, and concern for justice that Jesus taught and lived;
- local congregations—as an expression of Wesleyan social holiness—to teach and practice peacemaking, to study underlying causes of conflict among social groups and nations, to seek positive remedies and become instruments of peace;
- annual conferences to undergird congregations through training, encouragement, and active support for peacemaking activities and to be voices for peace, justice, and reconciliation within the conference area and beyond; and
- bishops to encompass peacemaking in teaching what it means to live the United Methodist way, engage in conflict resolution where appropriate, and offer a prophetic voice for peace and justice.

The 2012 General Conference calls upon boards and agencies to incorporate peacemaking into their regular programs and budgets, including but not limited to the following:

- The General Board of Discipleship to develop, publish, and distribute Christian education material on the biblical basis of peace and justice and ways in which children, youth, and adults can be peacemakers and seekers of justice; and to publish devotional material for peacemakers.
- The General Board of Church and Society to serve as public policy advocate for actions that promote peace and oppose war, to provide resources on peacemaking to annual conferences and local congregations, and to facilitate training for nonviolence that applies Jesus' teaching in the Sermon on the Mount.
- The General Board of Global Ministries and United Methodist Women to both continue and augment peacemak-

ing activities in their ministries in the United States and around the globe.

- The General Board of Higher Education and Ministry to work with United Methodist seminaries and Africa University for encouragement of research, teaching, and publications on the theology of peace and methods of peacemaking and peace building with justice.
- United Methodist seminaries to teach the theology of peace to students, clergy, and laity and provide training for peacemaking.
- JUSTPEACE: Center for Mediation and Conflict Transformation to promote a culture of just peace in the church and in the world and to provide training for peacemaking practitioners within annual conferences and local congregations.
- The Office of Christian Unity and Interreligious Relationships and the General Commissions on Religion and Race, the Status and Role of Women, and United Methodist Men to illuminate causes of injustice and inter-group tension, engage in advocacy for peace and justice, provide training for conflict resolution, and become instruments of peace.
- The Connectional Table to facilitate cooperation among United Methodist boards, agencies, conferences, and congregations on peacemaking endeavors.

ADOPTED 2008
AMENDED AND READOPTED 2012
RESOLUTION #6126, 2012 *BOOK OF RESOLUTIONS*
RESOLUTION #6091, 2008 *BOOK OF RESOLUTIONS*

See Social Principles, ¶ 165C.

6128. Seeking Peace in Afghanistan

Neither by power, nor by strength,
but by my spirit, says the LORD *of heavenly forces.*

—Zechariah 4:6

US military involvement in Afghanistan now represents the longest war in US history. The involvement of North American

Treaty Organization (NATO) forces constitutes the largest military operation outside of its role in Europe. For Afghans, the current war involving more than 100,000 foreign military troops is simply the latest in a long history of foreigners trying to impose by military might their own agenda in Afghanistan.

While generals and government officials all acknowledge that there is "no military solution" in Afghanistan, they continue to place their primary trust in weapons. Yet the psalmist reminds us, "A warhorse is a bad bet for victory;/it can't save despite its great strength" (Psalm 33:17).

Tragically, the situation on the ground has worsened. The number of US/NATO foreign troops in Afghanistan has tripled since 2008,[1] and so has the number of improvised explosive devices (IEDs). Consequently, civilian casualties have escalated significantly, with many going unreported. The majority of the public in the United States and NATO countries opposes ongoing war and troop involvement. Most Afghans want an end to decades of war and for foreign troops to leave.

Since 2006, the steady increase of troops has fanned popular resentment at foreign troops and the corrupt Afghan government officials they support. More troops—both foreign and Afghan—has increased the number of violent attacks by insurgents and coalition forces alike and devoted precious resources to weapons rather than health care, education, and community development.

The war has expanded to Pakistan as well. Armed insurgent groups operate on both sides of the Afghanistan-Pakistan border, and the United States has greatly increased unmanned drone strikes in remote Pakistani villages. Very little effort is made to account for civilian casualties from these strikes, and some bombings are based on faulty intelligence. Such remote bombings—especially in noncombat zones—create widespread resentment among the families and communities hit, making them a recruiting tool for armed groups. These attacks in noncombat zones are similar to targeted assassinations or extrajudicial killings that are

1. Elisabeth Bumiller, "Troops in Afghanistan Now Outnumber Those in Iraq," New York Times, May 25, 2010, available: http://atwar.blogs.nytimes .com/2010/05/25/troops-in-afghanistan-now-outnumber-those-in-iraq/. The total number of NATO troops as of November 2010 is 130,930—BBC News, "Afghan Troop Map: U.S. and NATO Deployments," November 19, 2010, available www.bbc .co.uk/news/world-south-asia-11795066. The total number of NATO trips in 2009 was 55,100—International Security Assistance Force, North American Treaty Organization, "ISAF Regional Commands and PRT Locations," January 12, 2009, available: www.nato.int/isaf/docu/epub/pdf/placemat_archive/isaf_placemat_090112.pdf.

strongly prohibited under international law and sharply criticized by the United Nations Special Rapporteur on Extrajudicial killings and numerous human rights advocates. It sets a disturbing precedent for governments to take the law into their own hands.

For more than 30 years, governments and armed groups have pumped billions of dollars in weapons into Afghanistan with bitter consequences for the people. The continuing militarization of Afghan society has taken significant resources away from diplomatic and development work in a deeply impoverished, war-torn land. United Methodists have long expressed concern that those who suffer the most in war are women and children. Indeed, Afghanistan has one of the highest infant[2] and maternal mortality[3] rates, and average life expectancy is mid-40s. While each year the United States and other governments devote over $100 billion dollars to weapons and soldiers,[4] one in four Afghan children still will not reach the age of 5.[5] By contrast, for more than 45 years United Methodists and other humanitarian organizations, in partnership with local Afghans, have supported health care and community development work in Afghanistan.

The United Methodist Social Principles recognize that "Conflicts and war impoverish the population on all sides, and an important way to support the poor will be to work for peaceful solutions" (¶ 163E). United Methodists also recognize that women have long taken the lead in calling and working for peace. In October 2001, Women's Division directors adopted a resolution that asked United Methodist Women to: "Urge the president to use diplomatic means to bring the perpetrators of terrorist acts to justice and to end the bombing of Afghanistan."

We recall the words of US representative Barbara Lee (California) in September 2001, who was the lone voice at that time in the US government to question military action against Afghanistan. She warned in a House of Representatives floor speech on

2. Department of Economic and Social Affairs, Population Division, *World Population Prospects: The 2006 Revision*, New York: United Nations, 2007, available: www.un.org/esa/population/publications/wpp2006/WPP2006_Highlights_rev .pdf, see Table A.18.

3. World Health Organization, *Trends in Maternal Mortality: 1990 to 2008*, Geneva, Switzerland: WHO, 2010, available: <http://whqlibdoc.who.int/publica tions/2010/9789241500265_eng.pdf>, see Annex 1.

4. Amy Belasco, *The Cost of Iraq, Afghanistan, and Other War on Terror Operations Since 9/11*, Washington, DC: Congressional Research Service, 2011, available: www.fas.org/sgp/crs/natsec/RL33110.pdf , see Table 1, p. 3.

5. *World Population Prospects*, see Table A.19.

September 14, 2001, "If we rush to launch a counterattack, we run too great a risk that women, children, and other noncombatants will be caught in the crossfire. . . . [W]e must be careful not to embark on an open-ended war with neither an exit strategy nor a focused target. We cannot repeat past mistakes."

We confess that years of war and pumping of weapons into Afghanistan, along with years of silence by too many of us in churches, has not served the needs of people—in Afghanistan or at home—but rather prolonged a cycle of militarism, violence, and suffering. Today the United States as 5 percent of the world's population devotes almost the same amount of resources to military spending as the other 95 percent of the world combined.[6] Forty-five years ago, the Rev. Dr. Martin Luther King, Jr. warned that "a nation that continues year after year to spend more money on military defense than on programs of social uplift is approaching spiritual death" ("Beyond Vietnam" speech, April 4, 1967). We are haunted by the prophet Habakkuk's lament, "Their own might is their god!" (Habakkuk 1:11 NRSV). May we find the courage to join with Afghans and neighboring Pakistanis and all who seek to transform today's glut of swords into iron plows.

In November 2009, 79 United Methodist bishops signed an open letter to the US president calling on him to turn from military escalation "to set a timetable for the withdrawal of all coalition forces by the end of 2010." Our long-standing conviction that "war is incompatible with the teachings and example of Christ" and our call into discipleship as peacemakers have led us in our Social Principles to declare, "We oppose unilateral first/preemptive strike actions and strategies on the part of any government" (*The Book of Discipline of The United Methodist Church, 2008,* ¶ 165C).

Now in the ongoing war in Afghanistan we must also challenge any preemptive arguments for prolonging war and militarization of the society. The argument that more than $100 billion per year should be devoted to waging war in the hopes of "denying a future safe haven to terrorists" when those same funds devoted to meeting the Millennium Development Goals in health care would save tens of thousands of lives across the globe is neither moral, sustainable, nor realistic.

6. Christopher Hellman and Travis Sharp, "The FY 2009 Pentagon Spending Request," Center for Arms Control and Non-Proliferation, February 22, 2008, available: http://armscontrolcenter.org/policy/securityspending/articles/fy09_dod_request_global.

We offer the following points for reflection and action as we seek to live out our Christian vocation as peacemakers:

1. Urge prompt and complete withdrawal of US/NATO forces as a necessary step toward demilitarizing the region and promoting Afghan-led peace talks among all parties. We urge an immediate unilateral cease-fire, an end to night raids, and an end to bombings as initial confidence-building steps toward demilitarization and reconciliation. We support peace that includes Afghan women in all negotiations in a substantive way.

2. We call for an immediate end to drone strikes in Afghanistan and Pakistan, which have escalated exponentially since 2008. We support full and independent investigations into all such bombings to account for civilian casualties.

3. End the militarization of Afghanistan. Most US foreign aid to Afghanistan currently goes to training, equipping, and funding the Afghan National Army, the Afghan National Police, and to private security contractors. Foreign aid has helped train several hundred thousand Afghan men as soldiers and police while funding training for only 2,500 Afghan midwives.[7] This is neither just nor sustainable in the short or long term. Lasting human security and stability in Afghanistan will come through diplomacy, education, and health care, not more weapons, more police, and more soldiers. We urge an end to all arms shipments from all sources.

4. Shifting resources from military spending and training to health and education, where many more women work, is one of the best ways of supporting and empowering Afghan women's leadership. We recognize and commit our support to the creative ways Afghan women are organizing and working in their communities despite war and conflict.

5. Ongoing war in Afghanistan costs $100+ billion per year. It costs $1 million per year for each US soldier serving in Afghanistan.[8] These funds are beating plowshares, classrooms, and hospitals into weapons. Teachers, firefighters, and other public employees are facing layoffs in part because the US government keeps redirecting tax dollars from local communities

7. Abby Sugrue, "Afghan Mothers Delivered into Good Hands," USAID Frontlines, January 2011, available: www.usaid.gov/press/frontlines/fl_jan11/FL_jan11_AFmothers.html.

8, Christopher Drew, "High Costs Weigh on Troop Debate for Afghan War," *New York Times*, November 14, 2009, available: www.nytimes.com/2009/11/15/us/politics/15cost.html.)

to war overseas. Each dollar spent on war in Afghanistan is taken from women and children and communities in the United States and around the world. War spending endangers civilians in Afghanistan, Pakistan, and the home countries of US/NATO forces.

6. Military spending should be shifted to humanitarian work that is not at all connected with any military forces. Humanitarian work should be nonpolitical and not connected with any of the warring parties. Nongovernmental organizations report that health and education work in highly militarized areas is now far more dangerous for internationals and Afghans alike, and many parts of the country are no longer accessible for aid workers. We call for an end to Provincial Reconstruction Teams and a strict separation of humanitarian work from military operations as called for in the International Red Cross and Red Crescent Code of Conduct.

7. The apostle Paul reminds us, "God is not mocked. A person will harvest what they sow" (Galatians 6:7). Corruption is best challenged by "first examining the log in our own eye" (Matthew 7:3, paraphrase). We urge cutting off the source of funds for bribes. The huge amounts of foreign money flowing into Afghanistan are largely diverted by warlords and private contractors (both international and Afghan). US forces end up subcontracting warlords to secure the vast military supply line. According to US Representative John Tierney's (Massachusetts) June 2010 congressional report "Warlord, Inc.: Extortion and Corruption Along the U.S. Supply Chain in Afghanistan," $400 million per year of US security funding ends up in the hands of the Taliban—more than they get from drug sales. Military contractors and defense corporations (e.g., Blackwater/Xe Services LLC, Dyncorp, Halliburton, Lockheed, etc.) are among the most unaccountable actors in Afghanistan. Cut off funding for private security contractors, as it masks the level of US war spending and personnel in Afghanistan, Iraq, and elsewhere.

ACTIONS

Urge all United Methodists to:

1. Call for a "swords into iron plows" approach in government spending and to develop church and peacemaker alliances with local governments to press national governments to redirect money from war spending to meet human needs.

2. Many young people facing unemployment are being targeted by the military for recruitment. Support peace education, provide counseling on selective conscientious objection, and offer alternative service education options for all high school students, with an emphasis on impoverished communities.

3. Support veterans, families of veterans, and Afghan civilians facing post-traumatic stress disorder (PTSD). It has been reported that in 2009 and 2010 more US veterans and active duty soldiers died from suicide than were killed in combat. Raise awareness about the high number of suicides, the increase in domestic violence, and other destructive behaviors brought on by war-related trauma. Support full funding of health care, especially mental health care and traumatic brain injury (TBI), for all affected by war.

4. The war has been used to justify ongoing war spending and increasing repressive measures that stifle dissent and encourage racial profiling of Arab and Muslim people in many countries (see other General Conference resolutions: "Taking Liberties: On the Stifling of Dissent" and "Prejudice Against Muslims and Arabs in the USA"). We call on United Methodists to stand with communities facing discrimination and urge all governments to restrain their use of measures that increase racial profiling and scapegoating.

5. Support regional negotiations and diplomacy throughout Central/South Asia with all parties to build cooperation. We support and encourage our partners to monitor that women's leadership is central in these negotiations; women must be involved in all peace negotiations, and this participation must be real and not simply a token gesture. The United Nations Security Council Resolution 1325 adopted on October 31, 2000, directly calls for women to participate equally and fully in all levels of peacemaking and decision making, from conflict prevention and mitigation to postconflict recovery and transformation. It also calls to end impunity against those who commit violence against women. Durable peace, security, and reconstruction in Afghanistan will not occur without the direct participation of all in the society, including women, who represent half of the population.

ADOPTED 2012
RESOLUTION #6128, 2012 *BOOK OF RESOLUTIONS*

See Social Principles, ¶ 165C.

6129. The United Methodist Church and Peace

Then justice will reside in wild lands, / and righteousness will abide in farmlands. / The fruit of righteousness will be peace, / and the outcome of righteousness, / calm and security forever. / Then my people will live in a peaceful dwelling, / in secure homes, in carefree resting places. (Isaiah 32:16-18)

For he himself is our peace, who has made the two groups one and has destroyed the barrier, the dividing wall of hostility. (Ephesians 2:14 NIV)

Christ is our peace. He is the Prince of Peace (Isaiah 9:6). Yet we know that the peace of Christ, the peace that passes all understanding, has not always ruled our lives and swayed our actions as peoples, institutions, or nations. We have not always followed God's will for peace evidenced by the many conflicts and wars waged throughout human history. We have not always sought counsel from the Christ whose words assure us justice and peace, compassion and forgiveness, and yes, salvation and liberation, even in our wayward and non-peaceful ways.

The Bible makes justice the inseparable companion of peace (Isaiah 32:17; James 3:18). Both point to right and sustainable relationships in human society, the vitality of our connections with the earth, the well-being and integrity of creation. To conceive peace apart from justice is to compromise the hope that justice and peace shall embrace (Psalm 85:10). When justice and peace are lacking we need to reform our ways.

Peace is God's will and must be done. Christ's true disciples must work for peace: build it and not just keep it; live it and not just aspire for it. If Christ is our peace, then peace must be imperative. In the end, war and conflict will not triumph over the Prince of Peace.

Even God's people, however, do not always see and acknowledge the peace of Christ and God's justice. As the prophets have done, God's people must be reminded and warned of their collusion with destruction and with injustice and non-peace. The United Methodist Church, whose commitment to peace is rooted in its obedience to the Prince of Peace, must recognize the things that make for peace.

The Council of Bishops asserted in 2009 that God's people "have neglected the poor, polluted our air and water, and filled our communities with instruments of war. We have turned our backs on

God and one another. By obstructing God's will, we have contributed to pandemic poverty and disease, environmental degradation, and the proliferation of weapons and violence" ("A Call of the Council of Bishops of The United Methodist Church to Hope and Action for God's Good Creation," 2009).

The bishops' call was prefaced by an assertion that God's creation is in crisis and that our neglect, selfishness, and pride have fostered a trio of "threats to life and hope." The gravity of these threats prompted the bishops to call for a comprehensive response that urged United Methodists and "people of goodwill" to offer themselves as instruments of God's renewing Spirit in the world.

"God calls us and equips us to respond," the bishops exhorted. They reminded us of God's offer of redemption to all creation and reconciliation to all things, "whether on earth or in heaven" (Colossians 1:20 NRSV). The bishops made us recognize again that God's Spirit is always and everywhere at work in the world fighting poverty, restoring health, renewing creation, and reconciling peoples.

The bishops' collective prayer is that God will accept and use our lives and resources that we rededicate to a ministry of peace, justice, and hope to overcome poverty and disease, environmental degradation, and the proliferation of weapons and violence. The bishops' 2009 call for hope and action built on their 2004 document, "In Search of Security." The 2004 document asserted that "the longing for safety is a feeling that all human beings share with one another. . . . The way to real peace and security is reconciliation. We will not attain full reconciliation between all peoples before God's final consummation because the forces of evil and destruction are still at work in the hearts of human beings and in their relationships. But we are called to be peacemakers and ministers of reconciliation until our Lord comes ("In Search of Security," Council of Bishops Task Force on Safety and Security, 2004).

The 2009 call for hope and action also recalled the bishops' 1986 study document, "In Defense of Creation: The Nuclear Crisis and a Just Peace." The 2009 document described "In Defense of Creation" as "an urgent message to all United Methodists and the Church at large on the growing threat of nuclear war and of the extinction of life on the planet through a 'nuclear winter.'" The bishops reasserted that "the nuclear crisis threatens 'planet earth itself,' that the arms race 'destroys millions of lives in conventional wars, repressive violence, and massive poverty,' and that the 'arms race is a social justice issue, not only a war and peace issue.'"

"Peace is not simply the absence of war, a nuclear stalemate or combination of uneasy ceasefires. It is that emerging dynamic reality envisioned by prophets where spears and swords give way to implements of peace (Isaiah 2:1-4); where historic antagonists dwell together in trust (Isaiah 11:4-11); and where righteousness and justice prevail. There will be no peace with justice until unselfish and informed life is structured into political processes and international arrangements" (Bishops' Call for Peace and the Self-Development of Peoples).

The mission of Jesus Christ and his church is to serve all peoples regardless of their government, ideology, place of residence, or status. Surely the welfare of humanity is more important in God's sight than the power or even the continued existence of any state. Therefore, the church is called to look beyond human boundaries of nation, race, class, sex, political ideology, or economic theory and to proclaim the demands of social righteousness essential to peace.

The pursuit of peace is a universal longing. It is a fervent prayer of all religions. It is the pilgrimage that the ecumenical community continues to embark on. At the 10th Assembly of the World Council of Churches in Busan, Korea, Christian leaders asserted in their "Statement on the Way to Peace": "Those who seek a just peace seek the common good. On the way of just peace, different disciplines find common ground, contending worldviews see complementary courses of action, and one faith stands in principled solidarity with another. Social justice confronts privilege, economic justice confronts wealth, ecological justice confronts consumption, and political justice confronts power itself. Mercy, forgiveness and reconciliation become shared public experiences. The spirit, vocation and process of peace are transformed."

The following are interrelated areas that must be dealt with concurrently in a quest for lasting peace in a world community.

I. Disarmament

"In that day I will make a covenant for them / with the beasts of the field, the birds in the sky / and the creatures that move along the ground. / Bow and sword and battle / I will abolish from the land, / so that all may lie down in safety" (Hosea 2:18 NIV).

The arms race goes on. "After many decades and millions of dollars, we are no more secure or peaceful in our world with a larger number of nations in the 'nuclear club,'" the Council of Bishops said.

While the exact number of the world's combined stockpile of nuclear warheads is not known, all respectable institutions monitoring and reporting such numbers agree that they remain at unacceptably high levels. (See "World Nuclear Stockpile Report," Updated August 28, 2014. Ploughshares Fund. http://www.ploughshares.org/world-nuclear-stockpile-report accessed on January 12, 2015. See also "Worldwide Nuclear Arsenals," Fact Sheet by Union of Concerned Scientists, http://www.ucsusa.org/sites/default/files/legacy/assets/documents/nwgs/Worldwide-Nuclear-Arsenals-Fact-Sheet.pdf accessed on January 12, 2015. Also, "Nuclear Weapons: Who Has What at a Glance: Fact Sheets and Briefs," http://www.armscontrol.org/print/2566 accessed on January 12, 2015.)

The illicit trading in small arms, light weapons and ammunition remains a worldwide scourge even as the Arms Trade Treaty took effect December 14, 2014. With less reliable data compared to nuclear weapons, small arms remain a worldwide scourge, according to the United Nations Office for Disarmament Affairs (http://www.un.org/disarmament/convarms/salw/, accessed January 12, 2015).

If there is any concern in the international community where international law intersects with ethics and morality, it is the legality of the threat or use of nuclear weapons. In an advisory opinion sought by the UN General Assembly in 1996, the International Court of Justice (ICJ) ruled: "The threat or use of nuclear weapons would generally be contrary to the rules of international law applicable in armed conflict, and in particular the principles and rules of humanitarian law. . . . There exists an obligation to pursue in good faith and bring to a conclusion negotiations leading to nuclear disarmament in all its aspects under strict and effective international control."

In spite of the ICJ ruling, billions of dollars in research, development, maintenance, and deployment continue to be spent on nuclear weapons. International law bans chemical and biological weapons, including landmines and cluster munitions, for being excessively cruel and indiscriminate. This has been proven in Hiroshima and Nagasaki, and yet nuclear weapons, remain outside of this classification.

The danger of a nuclear holocaust remains as long as nations maintain nuclear weapons, however. Many more people will be maimed and killed as long as small arms are easy to acquire and readily available for use in domestic quarrels, street fights, or in wars and conflict zones.

Wars and rumors of wars are not unique in our time. What is new is the sophistication with which they are waged. High-precision technologies exist side-by-side with conventional weapons. For example, drones and other robotic weapons systems are progressively developed and increasingly employed. Their use to select and strike at targets without human intervention when operating in fully autonomous mode must be banned. These instruments of destruction fracture the fragility of peace. They are not under the control of nations only. They are also in the hands of non-state actors, therefore making possible unregulated, indiscriminate, and unpredictable use. Their use falls under the judgment of a God whose design is of a world of peaceful, caring, and loving relationships.

Current expenditures on weapons are distorting priorities in national budgeting. Because of fear of unemployment, desire for profits, and contributions to the national balance of payments, the arms industry engenders great political power. Arms-producing nations seek to create markets, then vie with one another to become champions among the arms merchants of the world. We must advocate for the reallocation of national military budgets for purposes that are humanitarian and sustainable, and promote civilian peacebuilding and conflict transformation.

Disarmament is related to military spending and is possible and sustainable when defense funding in national budgets does not overshadow and underfund the social and welfare needs of people. Meaningful disarmament will happen when countries like the United States, China, Russia, Saudi Arabia, France, Japan, United Kingdom, Germany, India, and Brazil, which lead the world in military spending (according to 2013 report by Stockholm International Peace Research Institute), start to redirect their defense budgets to peaceful and sustainable purposes.

National budgets are moral documents. They are a testament to national priorities. May it be that such budgets invest in life-giving and life-sustaining priorities, indeed, the things that make for peace.

We support initiatives in every part of the world that move toward the goal of disarmament. This demands a radical reordering of priorities coupled with an effective system of international peacemaking, peacekeeping, and peacebuilding. The Church must constantly keep that goal before peoples and governments. In particular, we support the abolition of nuclear weapons.

Food, health, social services, jobs, and education are vital to the welfare of nations. Yet the overriding priority given by governments to "defense" constantly threatens their availability. Millions starve and development stagnates. Repeatedly, regional tensions grow, conflicts erupt, and outside forces intervene to advance or protect their interests without regard to international law or human rights.

Our bishops' historic position remains sound and clear: "We say a clear and unconditional 'NO' to nuclear war and to any use of nuclear weapons. We conclude that nuclear deterrence is a position that cannot receive the church's blessing" ("In Defense of Creation").

We affirm the prophetic position of our bishops who said in their statement "In Defense of Creation": "We say a clear and unconditional 'NO' to nuclear war and to any use of nuclear weapons. We conclude that nuclear deterrence is a position that cannot receive the church's blessing."

Accordingly, we reject the possession of nuclear weapons as a permanent basis for securing and maintaining peace. Possession can no longer be tolerated, even as a temporary expedient. We call all nations that possess nuclear weapons to renounce these vile instruments of mass destruction and to move expeditiously to dismantle all nuclear warheads and delivery vehicles. As a first step, we support all movement to ban the "first strike" policy from all North Atlantic Treaty Organization (NATO) doctrine.

We support the Comprehensive Nuclear Test Ban Treaty and the Nuclear Non-Proliferation Treaty. We call upon all nations to sign and ratify these important treaties and to abide by their provisions. These treaties form part of a non-nuclear proliferation regime under the purview of the United Nations. The ratification of the New Start Treaty by the United States and Russia in 2010 is to pave the way for the reduction of strategic nuclear missile launchers by half. It is, though, only a beginning. Far more agreements need to be signed not just by these two powers but also by other nuclear and non-nuclear states alike. Beyond nuclear proliferation itself, the threat of nuclear terrorism must inform the move for global disarmament.

Deterrence comes from international controls on materials used to make bombs. We support the concept of nuclear-free zones where governments or peoples in a specific region band together to bar nuclear weapons from the area either by treaty or declaration.

As Christian people committed to stewardship, justice, and peacemaking, we oppose and condemn the use of the Pacific for developing, testing, storage, and transportation of nuclear weapons and weapons-delivery systems and the disposal of radioactive wastes. We further affirm the right of all indigenous peoples to control their health and well-being.

Disarmament deals with not only non-conventional weapons, such as nuclear weapons, but also conventional weapons, particularly small firearms and light weapons. In this regard, we must support the continued review of implementation of the UN Program of Action to Prevent, Combat and Eradicate the Illicit Trade in Small Arms and Light Weapons in All Its Aspects.

The agreement moves forward the goal of making the Middle East a zone free of nuclear and other weapons of mass destruction. We must help diminish the perceived political and military value of nuclear weapons that is prevalent in security doctrines. A humanitarian approach is crucial to understanding nuclear weapons as cruel, inhumane instruments of mass murder and environmental destruction. True security puts human security over any other national security consideration.

World public opinion justly condemns the use of chemical or biological weapons. Governments must renounce the production and use of these particularly inhumane weapons as part of their national policy. We support universal application of the Chemical Weapons Convention and the Biological Weapons Convention.

We support treaty efforts to ban the development, trade, and use of weapons that are inhumane, are excessively injurious, and have indiscriminant effects. Such weapons include landmines, booby traps, weapons with non-detectable fragments, incendiary weapons, dirty bombs, cluster bombs, and blinding laser weapons.

We join religious leaders, physicians, veterans, humanitarian activists, environmentalists, and human-rights advocates in calling governments to sign and ratify the Convention on the Prohibition of the Use, Stockpiling, Production, and Transfer of Anti-Personnel Mines and on Their Destruction, also called the Ottawa Treaty, or simply the Mine Ban Treaty.

Antipersonnel land mines are a growing threat to human community and the environment, kill or maim hundreds of people every week, bring untold suffering and casualties to mostly innocent and defenseless civilians and especially children, obstruct economic development and reconstruction, inhibit the repatriation of refugees and internally displaced persons, and have other severe consequences for years after emplacement. The United States, Russia, and China are among 34 countries that are not signatories to the Mine Ban Treaty. They refuse to halt production of antipersonnel land mines.

Since 2008, the General Conference has condemned the use of cluster bombs. We reiterate this call, urging all governments to stop its production, use, transfer, and stockpiling. Cluster bombs are often scattered indiscriminately in wide areas. Like landmines, they remain a lethal threat to anyone in the area for decades. Their small size and curious shapes make them particularly appealing to children, who make up a large proportion of casualties. Cluster bombs kill and injure people. The almost perpetual threat of explosion prevents people from safely using their land for sustainable and productive, including agricultural, uses. This situation makes rebuilding lives and communities after a conflict more difficult and challenging. We therefore call all countries to sign, accede, and ratify the Convention on Cluster Munitions, which provides for a legal and regulatory framework to address the humanitarian consequences and unacceptable harm to civilians caused by cluster munitions.

We are also concerned about the use of inhumane weapons by civilian or military police. The increasing use of military-grade weapons and munitions, and military-style tactics, by civilian police is troubling. The militarization of police departments does not augur well for ethnic relations and domestic harmony.

Hollow-point ("dumdum") or other bullets designed to maim are not acceptable weapons for use by civilian or military forces. We support measures that outlaw use of such weapons at all levels.

Progress in disarmament must be monitored so that declarations to disarm are truly matched by action. We support five criteria to use in assessing progress in disarmament:

1. Verification—A state's unilateral declaration that it does not have nuclear weapons must be confirmed by highly reliable sources and by objective means;

2. Irreversibility—Confidence in compliance grows if controls are sufficient to make it extremely difficult, if not impossible, for a state to abandon a disarmament commitment and build or construct a nuclear arsenal;

3. Transparency—It is essential to have hard facts about the size of nuclear arsenals and concrete progress made in eliminating them;

4. Universality—Any agreement to achieve global nuclear disarmament must be fully "global" in geographic scope, with no exceptions; and

5. Legally binding—The world community expects commitments to disarmament to be legally binding.

We affirm peoples' movements directed to abolition of the tools of war. Governments must not impede public debate on this issue of universal concern.

Nongovernmental Organizations (NGOs) play important roles in the campaign for global disarmament. Their presence and advocacy at every Review Conference of the NPT as well as in the UN conferences dealing with small arms and light weapons are crucial. NGOs dealing with international humanitarian law, human-rights protection and environmental justice must work together to form a strong foundation for an effective, universal, comprehensive nuclear weapons convention. The convention would outlaw and ban development, possession, use, and threat of use of nuclear weapons.

To realize our commitment to disarmament, we call The United Methodist Church to a ministry of justice and peacebuilding. In particular, we call on the General Board of Global Ministries, nongovernmental organizations, and all governments to increase resources for humanitarian de-mining, mine awareness programs, and increased resources for landmine victim rehabilitation and assistance. We also call on the General Board of Church and Society to advocate for the signature and ratification of all disarmament-related treaties and conventions cited herein.

II. Multilateral Cooperation Among Nations
for Democracy, Freedom, and Peace

"Turn from evil and do good;
seek peace and pursue it." (Psalm 34:14 NIV)

Millions of people still live under oppressive rule and various forms of exploitation. Millions more live under deplorable conditions of racial, sexual, religious, and class discrimination. In many countries, many persons, including Christians, are suffering repression, imprisonment, and torture as a result of their efforts to speak truth to those in power.

Action by governments to encourage liberation and economic justice is essential. Such action must be supported by parallel action on the part of private citizens and institutions, including the churches, if peaceful measures are to succeed. Unless oppression and denial of basic human rights are ended, violence on an increasing scale will continue to erupt in many nations and may spread throughout the world. The human toll in such conflicts is enormous, for it results in new oppression and further dehumanization. We are concerned for areas where oppression and discrimination take place.

We, as United Methodists, must build the conditions for peace through development of confidence and trust between peoples and governments. We are unalterably opposed to those who instill hate in one group for another. Governments or political factions must not use religious, class, racial, or other differences as the means to achieve heinous political purposes. This concern extends to all situations where external commercial, industrial, and military interests are related to national oligarchies that resist justice and liberation for the masses of people. It is essential that governments which support or condone these activities alter their policies to permit and enable people to achieve genuine self-determination.

Democracy thrives under a rule of law founded on human rights and fundamental freedoms. The UN General Assembly World Summit of 2005 reaffirmed democracy as "a universal value based on the freely expressed will of people to determine their political, economic, social and cultural systems, and their full participation in all aspects of their lives." The UN Democracy Fund was established at this summit. The large majority of the fund is intended for local organizations whose projects aim to strengthen the voice of civil society, promote human rights, and encourage the participation of all groups in democratic processes. United Methodists must promote this fund and help grassroots groups to access it.

Graft and corruption erode the credibility of governments. (See ¶ 163L.) Transparency and accountability are pillars of a democratic system and are checks upon graft and corruption. Much of today's anger vented against governments arises from graft and corruption, and from economic fraud and exploitation. The United Nations Convention Against Corruption must be supported. This international law deals with promoting prevention, criminalization, law enforcement, international cooperation, asset recovery, technical assistance, and information exchange. It also includes mechanisms for implementation against corruption.

Peace and societal harmony are greatly enhanced when peoples and nations cooperate to address global concerns for economic and environmental justice, for peace and security, and for human dignity and human rights. Addressing these in a manner that invites all peoples and nations to just, participatory, and democratic processes is the hallmark of international law and cooperation, which are the cornerstones of multilateralism. (See Resolution #6133, 2012 *Book of Resolutions*.) The United Nations is a primary venue for multilateral cooperation and remains to be the best instrument now in existence to pursue these mechanisms and frameworks. (See Social Principles, ¶ 165D.)

III. World Trade, Economic Justice, and Sustainable Development

"Everyone will sit under their own vine and under their own fig tree, and no one will make them afraid, for the LORD Almighty has spoken" (Micah 4:4 NIV).

The gap between rich and poor countries continues to widen. When the surpluses of some arise in part as a result of continued deprivation of others, human rights are bound to be denied. This growing inequity exists in our own communities and in all our nations. Globalization has exacerbated these inequities when plentiful resources are not equitably shared and sustainably used. Past efforts to alleviate these conditions have failed. Too often these efforts have been limited by our own unwillingness to act with the posture of kindness and the ethical attitude of sharing in abundance rather than out of scarcity. Sometimes efforts have been frustrated by private interests and governments striving to protect the wealthy and the powerful.

Debate is growing on why Gross Domestic Product (GDP) as a measure of economic success is failing to represent national well-being even as the two are increasingly interconnected. Economic development is heavily dependent on investment in human capacity development. To proponents, the shift must move from simply measuring economic production to measuring the well-being of people. Such a shift moves in the direction of a more equitable, sustainable future (Center for Partnership Studies, "The State of Society: Measuring Economic Success and Human Well-Being," 2010).

To eliminate inequities in the control and distribution of the fruits of God's good earth, which are the common goods of humanity, we are called to join the search for more just, equitable international economic structures and relationships. We seek a society that will assure all persons and nations the opportunity to achieve their maximum potential.

Sustainable development is development that is people-centered, human rights-based, and justice-oriented. Such is the concept of development justice that must define our support for sustainable development and serves as a framework to support as well as critique development agendas developed at the United Nations and other international arenas. According to the Campaign for People's Goals for Sustainable Development (see http://peoplesgoals.org/), development justice is "a transformative development framework that aims to reduce inequalities of wealth, power, and resources between countries, between rich and poor, and between men and women. Development justice places people, the majority poor and the marginalized, at the front and center of development. It is a paradigm for development that upholds people as the primary agents and subjects of change. Development justice upholds that development will, and should be, designed and adapted in response to the aspirations of the people and their available resources, and not imposed by technocrats and so-called high-level experts for all time and for all peoples."

In working toward that purpose, we believe these steps are needed:

1. Conceive, develop, and structure economic systems designed to cope with the needs of the world's peoples and the increased demand on limited and nonrenewable natural resources. Such systems must consider the debilitating effects of climate change on our ecological system and its ability to respond to the increased demands of development and by the population.

2. Implement measures that will free peoples and nations from reliance on financial arrangements that place them in economic bondage. In this regard, we support the creation of a Global Economic Council. This council was one of the recommendations of the Commission of Experts of the President of the UN General

Assembly on Reforms of the International Monetary and Financial System. Such a council, when created, would become the main forum within the United Nations for setting the agenda for worldwide economic and financial policy.

3. Develop policies and practices that establish just prices and avoid damaging fluctuations in price for the exchange of commodities and rare and raw materials. Policies must be developed and supported to stop manipulation and marketing of commodities and rare and raw materials for illegal and unregulated uses, including so called "conflict minerals" used in funding wars and conflicts.

4. Development agencies and international financial institutions must operate with great transparency, accountability, and democratic participation. They must be free from the domination of industrialized economies under the aegis of the Group of 8 or Group of 20 countries. Control of international monetary facilities must be more equitably shared by all the nations, including the needy and less powerful. We support efforts to make the Bretton Woods institutions, namely the International Monetary Fund and the World Bank, and other international financial institutions more representative, transparent, and democratic, including being accountable within the United Nations framework.

5. The resources of the seabed, subsoil, outer space, and those outside a specific national jurisdiction are the heritage of humanity and should be accepted by all nations as part of the global commons. Their use and protection must be governed by agreements that affirm the common heritage principle. We support UN efforts to develop international law to govern the sea through the Convention on the Law of the Sea and to ensure that the world's common resources will be used cooperatively and equitably for the welfare of humankind.

6. We urge the appropriate boards and agencies of The United Methodist Church to continue and expand efforts to bring about peace and justice in cooperative and multilateral action between peoples and governments of all countries. Multilateral, rather than bilateral, assistance programs should be encouraged for secular as well as religious bodies. They must be designed to respond to the growing desire of the "developing" countries to become self-reliant and sustainable.

7. Nations that possess less military and economic power than others must be protected through international agreements from

loss of control of their own resources and means of production to either transnational enterprises or other governments.

These international policies will not narrow the rich-poor gap within nations unless the disenfranchised poor are enabled to take control of their own political and economic destinies. The internationally accepted principle of free, prior, and informed consent is a great measure to adopt.

Economic and political turmoil within many developing nations has been promoted and used by other powers as an excuse to intervene through subversive activities or military force in furtherance of their own national interests. We condemn this version of imperialism that often parades as international responsibility. The concept and practice of responsibility to protect (R2P) and an evolving counterpart responsibility to prevent are twin measures that deserve our attention and call for the harmonious coexistence of peoples and nations who endeavor to prevent wars and end conflicts.

IV. Peace Research, Education, and Action

"Would that you, even you, had known on this day the things that make for peace! But now they are hidden from your eyes" (Luke 19:42 ESV).

The 1960 General Conference established the landmark study "The Christian Faith and War in the Nuclear Age." That study said, "The Christian Church and the individual must accept responsibility for the creation of a climate of opinion in which creative changes can occur." It called work for these creative alternatives "our mission field as we live as disciples of the Prince of Peace."

The study, "In Search of Security" issued by the Council of Bishops Task Force on Safety and Security in June 2004, asserted: "Fear causes us to accumulate weapons and to devote all too much of our resources to the goal of deterring our supposed enemy. Paradoxically enough, it is the special temptation of the strong and the rich to overreact in this way. This blocks resources that could be used much more creatively for development and social justice around the world."

The living out of peace prospers in a climate of mutual understanding, tolerance, and the acknowledgment of the inherent dignity and self-realization of every human being, indeed of every child of God. Peace, security, and human rights help realize sustainable development and social justice in the world.

For true peace and security to take root in the lives of people and in the relations of nations, we call upon The United Methodist Church, especially those engaged in informal and formal learning from primary to higher education, in the light of its historical teachings and its commitment to peace, human rights, and self-development of peoples, to:

1. Seek the establishment of educational institutions and the development of programs and curricula devoted to the learning and living out of peace and human rights;

2. Develop alternatives to vocations that work for peace, and support individuals in their quest;

3. Explore and apply ways of resolving domestic and international differences that affirm human fulfillment and tolerance, rather than exploitation and violence;

4. Affirm and employ methods that build confidence and trust between peoples and countries, including training in multicultural understanding and appreciation of differences, rejecting all promotion of hatred and mistrust;

5. Continue to develop and implement the search for peace through educational experiences, including immersion and educational exchange programs, church school classes, schools of Christian mission, and other settings throughout the church;

6. Encourage local churches and members to take actions that make for peace and to act in concert with other peoples and groups of goodwill toward the achievement of a peaceful world; and

7. Develop study and action materials that incorporate the understanding and practice of peacekeeping actions that keep the peace through law and order, peacemaking actions that make for peace in personal, institutional, and social relations, and peace-building infrastructures fostering values that secure peace and constitute justice.

8. Commend to study the following international documents that engender peace and justice, including religious and cultural harmony: "Promotion of Interreligious Dialogue" (United Nations General Assembly Resolution, hereinafter UN GA/RES /59/23), "Promotion of religious and cultural understanding, harmony and cooperation" (UN GA/RES/59/142), "Global Agenda for Dialogue Among Civilizations" (UN GA/RES/56/6), "International Decade for a Culture of Peace and Non-Violence for the Children of the World (UN GA/RES/53/25), "International Day

of Peace" (UN GA/RES/55/282), "Program of Action on a Culture of Peace" (GA/RES/53/243 B), UNESCO Director-General's report to the 59th Session of the UN General Assembly "Promotion of religious and cultural understanding, harmony and cooperation" (UN GA/RES/58/128), and the Hague Agenda for Justice and Peace and its Global Campaign for Peace Education.

ADOPTED 1984
AMENDED AND READOPTED 2000, 2008, 2016
RESOLUTION #6129, 2012 *BOOK OF RESOLUTIONS*
RESOLUTION #6094, 2008 *BOOK OF RESOLUTIONS*
RESOLUTION #338, 2004 *BOOK OF RESOLUTIONS*
RESOLUTION #318, 2000 *BOOK OF RESOLUTIONS*

See Social Principles, ¶ 165B, C.

6130. A Call for Peace March

WHEREAS, the *Book of Resolutions* contains "Korea: Peace, Justice, and Reunification," a comprehensive resolution on Korea's peace, first adopted in 1988 and then amended and readopted in 2000, 2004, and 2008; and

WHEREAS, the year 2013 marks the 60th anniversary of the armistice of the Korean War; and

WHEREAS, the cycle of 60 years marks a new beginning in Asia, a concept similar to the biblical Jubilee;

Be it resolved, that The United Methodist Church proclaim the message of God's peace and reconciliation in the Korean Peninsula on July 27, 2013 on the 60th anniversary of the armistice of the Korean War and recommend the following actions:

a. Organize a peace march at the Demilitarized Zone in Korea on July 27, 2013, led by United Methodist episcopal leaders.

b. Organize a peace march in Washington DC on July 27, 2013.

c. Seek the support for these peace marches from the Korean Methodist Church, the World Methodist Council, the National Council of the Churches of Christ in the USA, and the World Council of Churches.

d. Organize a task force for peace in Korea to prepare for these peace marches.

ADOPTED 2012
RESOLUTION #6130, 2012 *BOOK OF RESOLUTIONS*

See Social Principles, ¶ 165.

6135. Korea: Peace, Justice, and Reunification

For he is our peace; in his flesh he has made both groups into one and has broken down the dividing wall, that is, the hostility between us (Ephesians 2:14 NRSV).

Our Faith Commitment to Peace and Reconciliation

At the 10th General Assembly of the World Council of Churches held in Busan, South Korea, in late 2013, the delegates declared in a statement the following, which could also serve as a faith statement of our commitment to peace and reconciliation:

"As a global body of believers in Jesus Christ, we confess our sins in having given in to the powers and principalities of the world in their wars and military conflicts full of hate and enmity, armed with nuclear arsenals and weapons of mass destruction targeting humanity and the whole of God's creation. Also we lament our failure to adequately acknowledge the Korean people's long suffering, caused by external powers fighting for colonial expansion and military hegemony. We hereby join the Christians in Korea in their confession of faith in Jesus Christ, who came to this world as our Peace (Ephesians 2:13-19); who suffered, died upon the Cross, was buried, and rose again to reconcile humanity to God, to overcome divisions and conflicts, and to liberate all people and make them one (Acts 10:36-40); who, as our Messiah, will bring about a new Heaven and new Earth (Revelation 21–22). With this confession, we join in firm commitment with the Christians of Korea, both North and South, especially in Korean churches' faithful actions to work towards peace, healing, reconciliation and reunification of their people and their land" (WCC Statement on Peace and Reunification of the Korean Peninsula).

The Tragedy of Division and the Urgency of Peace

Christians in Korea have spoken about the urgency of the reunification of their nation. Celebrating one hundred years of Korean Methodism in 1985, the Korean Methodist Church, in its Centennial Statement, said:

"Faced as we are with the forty years' tragic division of the Korean Peninsula, we express our longing for unification of the nation in any form possible through peaceful means in the earliest possible time. This must be done through establishing a democratic political structure based upon freedom and human rights, and must be fulfilled by working toward the establishment of a just society built for the sake of the people. Therefore, we reject any form whatever of dictatorship. Deploring the long history of our nation in which the reality has been the sacrifice of our country's political life, and now with a definite sense of national self-determination which rejects any domination by the superpowers, we disavow any form of war or the taking of life, and commit the whole strength of the Korean Methodist Church to the peaceful reunification of our country."

For the nation of Korea, divided for more than sixty-six years, justice, peace, and reconciliation are tragically overdue. In 1945, just before the end of World War II, the United States proposed and the Soviet Union agreed to the division of Korea, which resulted in the Korean War with more than 3 million lives lost and millions of families separated. The tragedy of the Korean people continued because the Korean War did not end with a Peace Treaty. Instead, the Armistice Treaty was signed in 1953 leaving the Korean Peninsula under a state of war and tension for more than sixty years. This resulted in the separation of families, many of whom never saw each other again.

The enmity between the superpowers has been played out in the Korean tragedy of war and death, dictatorship and militarization, separation of one people into two hostile camps, and divided families with no contact at all. All members of the body of Christ have a responsibility to support the Korean people in their attempts to build democracy, reduce tension, create trust on the Korean Peninsula, heal the divisions, and reunite their country. The threat to peace remains critical with the world's fifth and sixth largest armies facing each other across the Demilitarized Zone.

North-South Reconciliation Efforts

In many ways, the Korean people, north and south, have expressed their strong desire for reunification. Since 1984, there have been official contacts and conversations on economic and humanitarian issues between the Republic of Korea (ROK, also known as South Korea) and the Democratic People's Republic of Korea (DPRK, also known as North Korea). Emergency assistance by the DPRK and ROK following devastating floods in the south and floods and drought in the north was offered and accepted by each other.

The first government-sponsored exchange of visits between divided family members occurred in 1985. Thousands of overseas Koreans were able to visit their family members in the DPRK. Christians from north and south met in 1986 in Glion, Switzerland, as part of an ecumenical process on peace and the reunification of Korea led by the World Council of Churches. In 1987, both sides offered proposals to lower military tensions on the peninsula.

In June 2000, an unprecedented historic summit between North and South Korean leaders took place in Pyongyang, DPRK. ROK President Kim Dae Jung and DPRK Chairman Kim Jong Il pledged themselves to work toward Korean reunification. Since the summit, both Koreas have had numerous exchanges such as reunions of separated families, ministerial-level talks, and other economic, social, cultural, and sports exchanges including reconnection of railways and roads through the Demilitarized Zone.

The two Koreas marched together in the opening ceremony of the 2004 Olympic Games in Sydney, Australia, carrying the Korean unification flag. In 2007, the late President Roh Moo Hyun urged US President George W. Bush to resolve the Korean War by signing a peace treaty with North Korea. At the second summit between leaders of North and South Korea, President Roh and Chairman Kim Jong Il committed to resolving disputes in the West Sea surrounding the Northern Limit Line.

The relationship between the United States and the DPRK, however, has deteriorated due to the issues related to the DPRK's withdrawal from the nuclear nonproliferation treaty, its violation of the 1994 Agreed Framework, and threats by the United States of pre-emptive strikes on North Korea.

In 1991, the Agreement on Reconciliation, Non-aggression, Exchanges and Cooperation was adopted by the Republic of Korea and DPRK; and in 1992, both countries signed a joint declaration on the denuclearization of the Korean Peninsula. In 1994, the United States and DPRK signed the Agreed Framework whose objective "was the freezing and replacement of North Korea's indigenous nuclear power plant program ... and the step-by-step normalization of relations between the U.S. and the DPRK" (http://en.wikipedia.org/wiki/Agreed_Framework, accessed Feb. 1, 2015). The agreement stipulated that funds would be provided to the DPRK from the United States, Japan, and ROK for the construction of two light-water electric power reactors. In addition, the US agreed to provide 500,000 tons of heavy oil annually to the DPRK. In return, the DPRK agreed to forgo any further accumulation of fuel rods, which could be used to produce atomic bombs.

Over time, the mandates of the Agreement were violated by both sides. It is most desirable that the United States and the DPRK, through direct negotiations, redraft or update the 1994 Agreement encompassing all vital matters of interest to both sides, including DPRK's nuclear-proliferation issues, and US recognition of the sovereignty and security of the DPRK.

The Agreed Framework remains an important stabilizing element in US-DPRK relations. It is one of the key tools of engagement by which DPRK uses incentives rather than threats to build inter-Korean and regional cooperation.

Historic Role of the Ecumenical Community for Peace in the Korean Peninsula

In 1986, as a result of consultations in Korea, North and South, with Christians and government representatives, the National Council of the Churches of Christ in the USA (NCCCUSA) adopted an important policy statement on "Peace and the Reunification of Korea." United Methodist representatives participated fully in the development of this statement, in consultations on peace and reunification, and in an official ecumenical delegation to North and South Korea in the summer of 1987.

The WCC Assembly of 2013, adopted the "Statement on Peace and Reunification of the Korean Peninsula" urging churches to "call upon all stakeholders in the region to participate in a creative process for building peace on the Korean Peninsula by halting all military exercises on the peninsula, by ceasing foreign intervention, withdrawing foreign troops and reducing military expenditures." The statement called on ecumenical partners to be peacemakers and bridge builders for the two Koreas and the world, and to embark upon a universal campaign for a Peace Treaty to replace the Armistice of 1953, bringing an end to the state of war and paving the path toward reconciliation and peace.

In an international ecumenical consultation held in May of 2013, United Methodist groups, including the United Methodist Korean American National Association Committee on Korean Reunification & Reconciliation and the National Council of Churches in Korea, issued the "Call for Peace and Reconciliation on the Korean Peninsula," stating in part: "For too long, the Korean people have been divided and suffered from political brinkmanship, the wall of ideology, and the scourge of militarism.

The Armistice Agreement of 1953 only temporarily halted the war that claimed 4 million lives and divided 10 million families. This lingering state of war on the Korean Peninsula is a major contributor to tension and instability, both regionally and globally, and contravenes the spirit of United Nations Resolution 39/11, which recognizes a people's right to peace. We Christians of different communions, gathered together in the common cause of peace, are deeply concerned about the growing tensions on the Korean Peninsula over recent nuclear testing in North Korea and US-South Korea joint military exercises. We join with the Korean people, both in North and South Korea, in yearning for reconciliation, reunification and sustainable peace. Replacing the Armistice Agreement with a Peace Treaty is and should be the first step in establishing a lasting and sustainable peace on the Korean Peninsula."

Current Plan and Actions Taken by Agencies and Caucuses of The UMC

The Reunification Committee of Korean United Methodist Churches, in close collaboration with other United Methodist churches, agencies, and the ecumenical community, has initiated a four-year Korea Peace Movement project in 2013 in response to "A Call for Peace March," a petition adopted by General Conference of 2012 (*Book of Resolutions* #6130):

- To promote the awareness for peace and reconciliation in the Korean Peninsula;
- To build an ecumenical advocacy movement to replace the Armistice of 1953 with a peace treaty;
- To build a coalition of peace workers among US churches as well as churches in the Korean Peninsula; and
- To prepare Christian leaders and churches for the work of reconciliation and peace in the Korean Peninsula and the world,

For these purposes, the Committee and its coalition developed a four-year plan:

- A petition campaign for a peace treaty in the Korean Peninsula, to officially end the Korean War, an ecumenical effort from May 2013 to May 2016.
- The Korea Peace Conference: In May 2013, this event was attended by more than 120 participants from US and South Korea, including representatives from NCC Korea.

- The Korea Peace March and Advocacy: July of 2014 in Washington, DC, attended by 300 participants from across the US.
- Peace visits to the Korean Peninsula, both North and South Korea, in the summer and fall of 2015.
- A Conference for Peace and Reconciliation for youths and young adult Christians in 2015.

Recommendations for Action

In support of the Korean people and in cooperation with partner Christian groups, it is recommended that The United Methodist Church, its members, local churches, annual conferences, and agencies undertake the following actions through intercession, education, public advocacy, and support of programs furthering justice, peace, and reconciliation:

1. Engage in prayer of penitence and petition with the Korean people and with Christians in the north and south, scarred and pained by the division of their nation and yearning for reunion, and establish working, collaborative, and supportive relationships with the Korean Methodist Church, the National Council of Churches in Korea (ROK), and the Korean Christian Federation (DPRK) to seek peace and reconciliation.

2. Commend for study and action, the "Statement on Peace and the Reunification of the Korean Peninsula" adopted by the 10th WCC Assembly which called on churches to commit to, among others, the following:

   a) Work with our governments to mandate the UN Security Council to initiate new efforts for peacebuilding across the Korean Peninsula and to lift the existing economic and financial sanctions imposed on the Democratic People's Republic of Korea;

   b) Embark upon a universal campaign for a peace treaty to replace the Armistice Agreement of 1953, bringing an end to the state of war;

   c) Call upon all foreign powers in the region to participate in a creative process for building peace on the Korean Peninsula by halting all military exercises on the Korean Peninsula, by ceasing their interventions, and by reducing military expenditures;

   d) Ensure the complete, verifiable, and irreversible elimination of all nuclear weapons and power plants in northeast

Asia, by taking steps to establish a Nuclear-free World and simultaneously joining the emerging international consensus for a humanitarian ban on nuclear weapons in all regions of the world, so that life is no longer threatened by nuclear dangers anywhere on earth;

e) Urge the governments in both North and South Korea to restore human community with justice and human dignity by overcoming injustice and confrontation, and to heal human community by urgently addressing the humanitarian issue of separated families, by establishing a sustainable process allowing confirmation of the whereabouts of family members and free exchanges of letters and visits, and by offering the support of international agencies where necessary; and

f) Work with the governments of the Democratic People's Republic of Korea and Republic of Korea in providing international cooperation to maintain a truly Demilitarized Zone (DMZ) and transform it into a zone of peace. (http://www.oikoumene.org/en/resources/documents /assembly/2013-busan/adopted-documents-statements /peace-and-reunification-of-the-korean-peninsula).

3. Engage in a worldwide campaign for a Peace Treaty to replace the Armistice Agreement of 1953.

4. Urge all governments that have relations with the ROK or the DPRK, or both, to exercise their influence to further mediation, interchange, peace, and reunification.

5. Urge all governments involved to forthright commitment to the following policy directions in support of Korean efforts for peace and reunification:

a. The peaceful reunification of Korea should be a formal US policy goal.

b. A peace treaty should be signed among the nations involved to eliminate the threat of war, establish an enduring peace, and minimize tension in the Korean Peninsula. The peace treaty, replacing the existing armistice treaty, should be based on the conditions of a non-aggression pact between the Republic of Korea and the Democratic People's Republic of Korea, with the full participation of the United States and the People's Republic of China, as well as other related countries.

c. ROK and DPRK contacts should be encouraged;

d. Bilateral diplomatic and human contacts between the United States and the DPRK should be enhanced.

e. The US should negotiate to end the war and to seek a comprehensive peace settlement in Korea.

6. Encourage continued humanitarian aid to the DPRK through agencies like the UN World Food Program (WFP). This aid is directed to those persons most at risk and is monitored carefully. The WFP has developed productive working relationships with its DPRK counterparts and continues to push for more open access to the food distribution process.

7. Increase communication, dialogue and exchange of delegations, with church and ecumenical representatives, with ROK and DPRK. Political, economic, social, and religious delegations are a high priority with DPRK leaders. They provide Korean middle management with experience outside their country and a greater perspective regarding the situation between the Korean Peninsula and outside it. Delegations from DPRK can also be matched with exchange delegations to DPRK, which allows people from around the world to see and understand the country, share ideas, and have personal contact with Korean peoples.

8. Advocate for removal of economic sanctions against DPRK. Sanctions limit the engagement of DPRK in the regional and global economy. Removing sanctions will also facilitate foreign investment in improving the DPRK production infrastructure. Because of economic and legal obstacles, development of foreign investment will be a difficult and long-term process, even without sanctions. Removing sanctions is a high priority with DPRK leaders.

9. Continue to redraft or update policies to comply with the Agreed Framework, of which the most positive element is US-DPRK relations, by supplying heavy fuel oil and supporting ROK and Japanese financing for the Korea Peninsula Energy Development Office (KEDO) light-water reactors.

10. Encourage a consistent, bipartisan, and long-range policy formulation regarding both North and South Korea by governments around the world, but especially the US, China, Russia, Japan, and the European Union. Policies that engage the ROK and DPRK governments effectively and promote change and moderation will stand a greater chance of resolving the current crisis and bringing every party, including the DPRK, to relate according to agreed international norms and mechanisms.

11. Urge the United Nations to look into the North Korean refugee situation arising from political and economic needs, as thousands of North Koreans are crossing the border seeking asylum in neighboring countries. The United Nations should declare them refugees, assist them as they seek asylum, and provide humanitarian assistance.

12. Urge continued humanitarian assistance to North Korea, at the same time calling on the North Korean government to work with the United Nations to abide by all internationally agreed principles of human rights and humanitarian law, principles that must guide all parties addressing the resolution of the crisis in the Korean Peninsula.

When these approaches can be taken, and most of them depend on US government policy decisions, there are still no guarantees that the crisis can be resolved. But it is quite clear that a US policy of isolation, sanctions, and military buildup directed against DPRK will stimulate North Korea to rely more on its military, even at the expense of the lives of its population, and may lead to another catastrophic war on the Korean Peninsula. Continued engagement, steadfast negotiation, and careful cultivation of cooperative relationships with appropriate DPRK organizations provide the only real opportunity for a positive resolution of the Korean stalemate.

ADOPTED 1988
AMENDED AND READOPTED 2000, 2004
READOPTED 2008
AMENDED AND READOPTED 2016
RESOLUTION #6135, 2012 *BOOK OF RESOLUTIONS*
RESOLUTION #6100, 2008 *BOOK OF RESOLUTIONS*
RESOLUTION #328, 2004 *BOOK OF RESOLUTIONS*
RESOLUTION #309, 2000 *BOOK OF RESOLUTIONS*

See Social Principles, ¶ 165*B, C.*

6137. Interfaith Advocacy in Support of Israel/Palestine Peace

WHEREAS, it is the position of The United Methodist Church that all United Methodists should reach out to local synagogues, mosques, and Christian faith groups by engaging in interfaith and ecumenical dialogue on how to promote justice and peace in the Holy Land ("Opposition to Israeli Settlements in Palestinian Land"; *The Book of Resolutions of The United Methodist Church, 2008*, pg. 832); and

WHEREAS, in order to be productive, any such interfaith and ecumenical dialogue designed to lead to action relating to any specific advocacy position must take place in an atmosphere of mutual understanding and trust; and

WHEREAS, establishing such mutual understanding and trust can, at times, appear almost unattainable inasmuch as various constituencies, even within The United Methodist Church as well as within other faith groups, support such a wide range of specific and often divergent advocacy steps designed to bring about a just peace in Israel/Palestine; and

WHEREAS, mutual understanding and trust can be established, however, when all parties recognize that, from a moral and ethical standpoint, there is a single universal standard of human rights that applies to all stakeholders in every situation; and

WHEREAS, interfaith and/or ecumenical dialogue on how best to promote justice and peace in the Holy Land can be most productive when it engages particular committees, task forces, or boards within faith communities that are committed to this universal standard of human rights and that are open to the principle of supporting an end to military aid to any country and/or group that commits human rights abuses;

Therefore, be it resolved, that, in order to promote justice and peace in the Holy Land, the 2012 United Methodist General Conference supports the efforts of existing or newly formed conference-wide and/or locally based United Methodist and/or interfaith or ecumenical committees, task forces, boards, or agencies that are committed to engaging in ecumenical and interfaith dialogue leading to achieving common goals relating to Israel/Palestine. Such goals to include the recognition of a single universal standard of human rights that applies to all stakeholders and support for an end of military aid by any country, to those parties in the conflict that commit human rights abuses.

ADOPTED 2012
RESOLUTION #6137, 2012 *BOOK OF RESOLUTIONS*

See Social Principles, ¶ 165C.

6138. Pursue Formal Peace Talks in Philippines

The Philippine Ecumenical Peace Platform (PEPP), the broadest ecumenical formation of church leaders advocating for the formal peace negotiations between the Government of the Philippines (GPH) and the National Democratic Front of the Philippines (NDFP), is alarmed over recent pronouncements of both sides that may not augur well for the continuation of the formal peace talks.

After the spark of hope that was brought about by the GPH-NDFP formal peace talks last February, which produced the February 21, 2011, Oslo Joint Statement, the recent pronouncements to the media from both GPH Peace Panel Chair Atty. Alex Padilla and NDFP Peace Panel Spokesperson, Fidel Agcaolli, bodes for another postponement of the formal talks. The talk was postponed already last June and they feel that another postponement may truly derail the peace negotiations.

The PEPP also encourages both sides to abide by their own reaffirmation of the validity and binding effect of all previous bilateral agreements as stated in the February Joint Statement.

One of the major developments last February was the setting up of a timetable for the negotiations. For advocates, the schedules indicated in the timetable can be guideposts to peace. They call on both panels to work hard in order to meet the proposed schedules. If both sides abide by this, and try to build bridges instead of hurdles, and they reiterate this—through principled negotiations—our country will enjoy what the psalmist promised, "a future awaits those who seek peace" (Psalm 37:37 NIV).

(Source: Most Rev. DEOGRACIAS S. INIGUEZ, JR., D.D.— Head of the Secretariat; Archbishop ANTONIO J. LEDESMA, SJ, DD Ms. SHARON ROSE JOY RUIZ-DUREMDES—Co-chairpersons, August 28, 2011)

Therefore, be it resolved, for The United Methodist Church to urge the president and executive branch of the Philippine government to order the immediate continuation and genuinely advance formal peace talks with NDFP and MILF.

Be it further resolved, for The United Methodist Church to urge the president and executive branch of the Philippine government to consider accepting the "10-Point Proposal for a Concise Agreement for an Immediate Just Peace":

1. Unite the Filipino people through a broad alliance of patriotic and progressive forces and a clean and honest coalition government for genuine national independence and democracy against any foreign domination or control and against subservience.
2. Empower the toiling masses of workers and peasants by respecting their democratic rights and providing for their sig-

nificant representation in organs of the coalition government and for assistance to the organizations, programs, and projects of the toiling masses.

3. Uphold economic sovereignty, carry out Filipino-owned national industrialization and land reform and oppose imperialist plunder and bureaucratic and military corruption in order to develop the national economy.

4. Cancel the foreign debt and reduce the appropriations for the military and other armed organizations of the GRP in order to provide adequate resources and savings for economic development, improvement of the means of livelihood, the alleviation of poverty, the realization of gender equality, promotion of children's rights and welfare and healthy environment.

5. Promote and support a patriotic, scientific, and pro-people culture through the educational system, mass media, and mass organizations, cherish the cultural heritage of the Filipino nation and all the ethno-linguistic communities in the country.

6. Recognize the right to self-determination and autonomy of national minorities, ensure proportionate representation in organs of the coalition government and institutions and provide for affirmative action to countervail long running discrimination and wrongs.

7. Investigate and try government officials who are liable for treason, corruption, and human rights violations.

8. Carry out a truly independent foreign policy for world peace and economic development, oppose imperialist acts of plunder and foreign aggression and intervention, and prevent the basing and stationing of foreign troops and weapons of mass destruction in the country.

9. Maintain normal trade and diplomatic relations with all countries and develop the closest of relations with other ASEAN countries, China, South and North Korea, Japan, and Russia, emphasizing equable exchange of goods, acquiring goods for industrialization, and guaranteeing energy supply.

10. Inaugurate a truce between the warring forces of the GRP and NDFP for the purpose of alliance and other constructive purposes as stated above.

ADOPTED 2012
RESOLUTION #6138, 2012 *BOOK OF RESOLUTIONS*

See Social Principles, ¶ 165C.

6139. Peace With Justice Sunday and Special Offering

Background: From Despair to Hope

Today our world is facing crises on an unprecedented scale: war, genocide, poverty, hunger, disease, and global warming. Saddened by the state of the world, overwhelmed by the scope of these problems, and anxious about the future, we believe God calls us and equips us to respond.

Harsh economic conditions have made it impossible for the world's poor to break the ongoing cycle of despair and exploitation. The disparity between rich and poor has grown. Global financial improvement has not affected many of those living on the margins of society.

Ongoing wars and intractable conflicts and political strife and repressive conditions have led to the disregard for international law and the breakdown of international cooperation. Human rights continue to be violated and disregarded. These and related changes taking place in our global community diminish our hope for potential future reductions in military expenditures. Global military spending, totaling $1.75 trillion in 2013 (Stockholm International Peace Research Institute Yearbook), drains resources of money and talent that might be used for meeting urgent social needs, long-term sustainable social and human development, and protecting God's creation.

We have realized that we live in a broken world. We are challenged by acts of intolerance and aggression, by acts of racism and xenophobia, by acts of classism, sexism, ageism, and gender discrimination. God's beautiful universe and all that was good in creation are in danger of extinction by unsafe and unsound environmental practices. HIV/AIDS continues to escalate to pandemic proportions. Malaria and tuberculosis remain urgent concerns, even as new and deadly viruses like Ebola ravage communities around the world.

We must renew our call for a social transformation, for the quest to open the doors of opportunity for all, to distribute resources more equitably, and to provide better care for persons in need.

Peace with Justice is a faithful expression of shalom in the Bible. It calls the church to strengthen its capacity to advocate publicly in communities and nations throughout the world. It aims to make shalom visible and active in people's lives and communities by setting people free from bondage. We will celebrate Peace with Justice when all people have access to adequate jobs, housing, education, food, health care, income support, and clean water. We will further celebrate when there is no more economic exploitation, war, political oppression, and cultural domination.

Biblical Basis for Response

The United Methodist Church, with its historic commitment to peace and justice, can and should provide leadership to this social transformation. This heritage is expressed in the Social Principles and the Social Creed. It was articulated by the United Methodist Council of Bishops foundation document "In Defense of Creation: The Nuclear Crisis and a Just Peace," which offers a well-grounded biblical analysis for Peace with Justice. The bishops wrote:

"At the heart of the Old Testament is the testimony to *shalom*, that marvelous Hebrew word that means peace. But the peace that is *shalom* is not negative or one-dimensional. It is much more than the absence of war. *Shalom* is positive peace: harmony, wholeness, health, and well-being in all human relationships. It is the natural state of humanity as birthed by God. It is harmony between humanity and all of God's good creation. All of creation is interrelated. Every creature, every element, every force of nature participates in the whole of creation. If any person is denied *shalom*, all are thereby diminished. . . .

"The Old Testament speaks of God's sovereignty in terms of *covenant*, more particularly the 'covenant of peace' with Israel, which binds that people to God's *shalom* (Isaiah 54:10; Ezekiel 37:26). In the covenant of shalom, there is no contradiction between justice and peace or between peace and security or between love and justice (Jeremiah 29:7). In Isaiah's prophecy, when 'the Spirit is poured upon us from on high,' we will know that these laws of God are one and indivisible:

"'Then justice will dwell in the wilderness, and righteousness abide in the fruitful field. And the effect of righteousness will be peace, and the result of righteousness, quietness and trust forever. My people will abide in a peaceful habitation, in secure dwellings, and in quiet resting places' (Isaiah 32:16-18).

"*Shalom*, then, is the sum total of moral and spiritual qualities in a community whose life is in harmony with God's good creation" ("In Defense of Creation," pp. 24, 25-26).

Paul's letters announce that Jesus Christ is "our peace." It is Christ who "broke down the barrier of hatred that divided us," creating one humanity, overcoming enmity, so making peace (Ephesians 2:14-19). It is Christ who ordains a ministry of reconciliation. Repentance prepares us for reconciliation. Then we shall open ourselves to the transforming power of God's grace in Christ. Then we shall know what it means to be "in Christ." Then we are to become ambassadors of a new creation, a new Kingdom, a new order of love and justice (2 Corinthians 5:17-20).

In their 2010 pastoral document, "God's Renewed Creation: Call to Hope and Action," the Council of Bishops reminds us:

"No matter how bad things are, God's creative work continues. Christ's resurrection assures us that death and destruction do not have the last word. Paul taught that through Jesus Christ, God offers redemption to all of creation and reconciles all things, 'whether on earth or in heaven' (Colossians 1:20). God's Spirit is always and everywhere at work in the world fighting poverty, restoring health, renewing creation, and reconciling peoples."

This is the foundation of faith that enables us in The United Methodist Church to offer hope to those who despair and to bring forth joy to replace sadness. We can join hearts in the traditional prayer of Saint Francis of Assisi that we act in the spirit of Christ, so we too can sow love where there is hatred, can dispense pardon where there is injury, can cast light where there is darkness. As instruments of peace and justice, we can seek to replace discord with harmony and to repair the brokenness that shatters the wholeness of shalom.

Program Activities

The General Board of Church and Society will carry out the following "Peace with Justice" activities:

1. implement the "Policies for a Just Peace" as specified in the Council of Bishops' "In Defense of Creation," the Council's "God's Renewed Creation: Call to Hope and Action," and the resolutions on "The United Methodist Church and Peace," "Globalization and Its Impact on Human Dignity and Human Rights," as well as other resolutions on war, peace, disarmament, and terrorism;

2. participate in the pilgrimage of Justice and Peace as our contribution to realizing the call of the 10th assembly of the World Council of Churches in 2013 held in Busan, South Korea.

3. work with the World Council of Churches, interfaith and ecumenical bodies, and secular organizations for social-justice policies and programs that seek the wholeness of shalom for all of God's people, and

4. work to eradicate attitudinal and systemic behavior patterns that perpetuate the sin of racism and gender discrimination as it is lived out in the areas of peace, justice, and the integrity of creation.

To achieve these objectives, the General Board of Church and Society may:

a. assist annual conferences, districts, and local churches to organize and carry out Peace with Justice activities and to promote the Peace with Justice Special Sunday Offering in coordination with United Methodist Communications;

b. provide a regular flow of information on public issues to local churches, districts, and annual and central conferences;

c. strengthen its capacity to act as a public-policy advocate of measures that improve global relations and move toward just peacemaking and measures that provide jobs, housing, education, food, health care, income support, and clean water to all;

d. assist annual and central conferences and/or local churches to assess and respond to the disproportionate effect of injustices on racial and ethnic persons in the world; and

e. assist annual conference Peace with Justice coordinators to carry out their duties.

For the purpose of financing activities (a) to achieve the "Policies for a Just Peace" contained in the Council of Bishops' "In Defense of Creation" and "God's Renewed Creation: Call to Hope and Action," and (b) to pursue other justice and peace objectives contained within the vision of shalom in this same document, revenue shall come from the Peace with Justice Special Sunday offering and other possible sources in accordance with the 2012 *Book of Discipline* ¶ 263.5 and World Service Special gifts.

Assignment

The Peace with Justice Sunday and Special Offering shall be assigned to the General Board of Church and Society.

ADOPTED 2016

See Social Principles, ¶ 165C, D.

WAR AND THE MILITARY

6144. Respect of the People in Okinawa

Won't God provide justice to his chosen people who cry out to him day and night? Will he be slow to help them? (Luke 18:7).

This cry of despair can be found in the voice of the people of Okinawa, Japan. In the November 2014 elections, the residents of Okinawa reaffirmed their demand that the U.S. military base in Okinawa be closed. The elected governor ran for office on closing the base and opposition of a new base off the sea of Henoko.

In recognition of the great investment that The United Methodist Church has made in the mission of the Church in Okinawa (Japan) since the turn of the [twentieth] century, with the arrival of the first Methodist missionary, this resolution is presented to request the support of United Methodist congregations for one of the urgent issues in mission of the Okinawa District of The United Church of Christ in Japan, the Christian body with which The United Methodist Church has a cooperative mission relationship.

In accordance with the US-Japan Mutual Security Treaty, which grants the US use of facilities and areas in Japan, the United States military forces occupy a substantial amount of the land area of Okinawa Island, in addition to having exclusive use of designated air and sea space for military training. This vast military presence greatly hinders the development of Okinawa and threatens the livelihood of Okinawan citizens.

Even after Allied occupation ended on the Japanese mainland in 1952, Okinawa remained under complete US military administration for twenty years, until 1972, when the islands reverted to Japanese jurisdiction

Private property requisitioned by the US military to construct the vast military bases after the war is still held today, denying some 30,000 families the right to live on and utilize their own land. Military aircraft produce ear-splitting noise on a daily basis. Military drills endanger the lives of citizens and destroy the natural environment.

Since 1972, the date of Okinawa's reversion to Japan, US military personnel have committed thousands of crimes. These crimes, which include robbery, murder, and rape, imperil the fundamental human rights of the Okinawan people. The residents of Okinawa living around the bases become the primary targets of this violence, with women and children being especially vulnerable.

In its July 8, 2001, statement, the Okinawa District of the United Church of Christ in Japan demanded "1) apology, mental and physical care, and compensation to the victim, and 2) removal of military bases from Okinawa in order to establish sovereignty and to protect dignity of Okinawan people."

The Okinawa District considers militarization to be an issue that the church is called on to address in its mission of peacemaking.

In light of the above, the General Conference of The United Methodist Church continues to join with Okinawan Christians in urging the following four appeals to the governments of the United States and Japan:

1. a thorough investigation of all crimes and acts of violence committed by US military personnel stationed on US military bases in Okinawa, and an apology and compensation to the victims of the crimes;

2. an immediate cessation of all military exercises that destroy the environment and threaten the daily life of Okinawans;

3. an immediate review of the US-Japan Mutual Security Treaty (AMPO) which completely ignores the laws of Japan, imposing great hardship on the people of Okinawa; and

4. establishment of a peace not based on military power, and the removal of all US bases from Okinawa.

Therefore, be it resolved, that the 2004 General Conference support the prefectural government of Okinawa and the vast majority of the Okinawan people in their strong, unceasing efforts to achieve the complete removal or substantial reduction of US military bases and US military personnel on the island of Okinawa and other islands in Okinawa Prefecture of Japan, and the return of those lands for peaceful, constructive purposes; and that a copy of this petition be sent to the President of the United States, the US Secretary of State, and the US Secretary of Defense for consideration and action, as well as to the Governor of Okinawa and the Prime Minister of Japan for their information.

ADOPTED 2004
READOPTED 2008
AMENDED AND READOPTED 2016
RESOLUTION #6144, 2012 *BOOK OF RESOLUTIONS*
RESOLUTION #6114, 2008 *BOOK OF RESOLUTIONS*
RESOLUTION #331, 2004 *BOOK OF RESOLUTIONS*

See Social Principles, ¶ 165*B, C.*

6147. The Abolition of Torture

Remember those who are in prison, as though you were in prison with them; those who are being tortured, as though you yourselves were being tortured (Hebrews 13:3 NRSV).

Torture is a grave sin that inflicts severe moral injury not only to victims, their families, and communities, but also to any society that remains silent whenever the evil acts of torture occur. The biblical mandate is clear that evil must cease and evil deeds must stop. "[C]ease to do evil,/learn to do good;/seek justice,/rescue the oppressed,/defend the orphan,/plead for the widow" (Isaiah 1:16-17 NRSV). The Social Principles remind United Methodists that the "use of detention and imprisonment for the harassment and elimination of political opponents or other dissidents violates fundamental human rights. Furthermore, the mistreatment or torture, and other cruel, inhumane, and degrading treatment or punishment of persons by governments for any purpose violates Christian teaching and must be condemned and/or opposed by Christians and churches wherever it occurs" (Social Principles ¶ 164A).

The United Nations Convention against Torture and Other Cruel, Inhuman or Degrading Treatment or Punishment came into force June 26, 1987. The Convention is a key tool to fight torture and other forms of ill-treatment and protect the rights of the survivors, the women, children, and men in every country. By early 2015, 157 governments had ratified the Convention but in 131 countries there were cases of torture and ill-treatment by security forces, police, and other state authorities, according to Amnesty International. (Amnesty International Report 2014/15: The State of the World's Human Rights, <https://www.amnesty.org/en/documents/pol10/0001/2015/en/>).Torture is defined as ". . . any act by which severe pain or suffering, whether physical or mental, is intentionally inflicted on a person for such purposes as obtaining from him or a third person information or a confession, punishing him for an act he or a third person has committed or is suspected of having committed, or intimidating or coercing him or a third person, or for any reason based on discrimination of any kind, when such pain or suffering is inflicted by or at the instigation of or with consent or acquiescence of a public official or other person acting in an official capacity. It does not include pain or suffering arising only from, inherent in or incidental to lawful sanctions" (Part I, Article 1 of the Convention against Torture and other Cruel, Inhuman or Degrading Treatment or Punishment, adopted and opened for signature, ratification and accession by General Assembly resolution 39/46 of 10 December 1984, entry into force 26 June, 1987, in accordance with article 27 (1)-Office of the High Commissioner for Human Rights, <http://www.ohchr.org>).

Each year, the 26th of June is lifted up as the International Day in Support of Victims of Torture. It reminds us what the writer of Hebrews urged long ago, that we are first and foremost called to offer compassion for all victims of torture as if it were ourselves. We seek societies based on the golden rule that would never condone the use of torture that we would never want imposed on ourselves. The International Federation of Action by Christians for the Abolition of Torture (FIACAT) on June 26, 2014, joined together in calling on all States to take up three key actions:

- Prevent torture by ensuring respect for all human rights, by training government agents, by cooperating with international and regional institutions and by making their populations aware of torture and other forms of cruel, inhuman and degrading punishment or treatment;
- Condemn any act of torture by criminalizing it in their legislation, by systematically prosecuting those responsible for acts of torture and by fighting against impunity;
- Support victims of torture and ill-treatment by offering them protection and by putting into place mechanisms for reparation and compensation.

(International Federation of Action by Christians for the Abolition of Torture, Statement on International Day in Support of Victims of Torture: FIACAT celebrates 30 years of the UN Convention against Torture. See www.fiacat.org <http://www.fiacat.org>.)

In the United States the religious community's struggle against torture is interreligious. The National Religious Campaign Against Torture (NRCAT) has a membership of over 320 religious organizations including Christians (Catholic, evangelical, mainline Protestant, and Orthodox), Unitarians, Bahai, Buddhist, Jewish, Muslim and Sikh communities. NRCAT works for an end to torture in four areas:

1. To ensure that US-sponsored torture of detainees never happens again.

2. To end the use of torture in US prisons and detention facilities, in particular the use of prolonged solitary confinement.

3. To end US support (direct or indirect) of any country that engages in torture and to work for US policies that help other nations stop their torture practices.

4. To end the bigotry and hatred that promotes the practice and acceptance of torture against religiously, ethnically and other targeted groups. Since the fall of 2010, NRCAT has worked for an end to anti-Muslim bigotry. (National Religious Campaign Against Torture (NRCAT) WHAT IS NRCAT? See web site: www. nrcat.org <http://www.nrcat.org>. Note: Both the Board of Global Ministries and Board of Church and Society of The United Methodist Church belong to NRCAT.)

On June 26, 2007, the United Nations International Day to Remember the Victims of Torture, several religious leaders, representing member organizations of NRCAT, spoke. Dr. Ingrid Mattson, President of the Islamic Society of North America, noted, "Torture is a major transgression of God's limits. The impact of such a transgression is not just on the victim, but on the souls of those engaged in and complicit in the evil act." Rabbi Gerry Serrota, Chair of the Board of Rabbis for Human Rights-North America, joined her, ". . . torture shatters and defiles God's image . . . meaning that torture violates the tortured human being, who was created in the likeness of God, as well as the torturer's human soul, which is inevitably defiled and compromised in dishonoring the image of God in his victim." And, Dr. Charles Gutenson, an evangelical leader and Professor at Asbury Theological Seminary, adds, "Jesus not only commanded, but also modeled a way of life that refused to repay evil with evil. When his enemies came for him, he embodied that call to love our enemies. How then can we who seek to imitate this Jesus ever see torture as a legitimate tool wielded to serve our own purposes?" (NRCAT Press Release— June 26, 2007, Religious Leaders' Message to Congress: Restore Habeas Corpus, Abolish Torture.)

Increasingly governments are using prolonged solitary confinement as a form of punishment. According to the Vera Institute, roughly 80,000 incarcerated adults and youth are held in solitary confinement each day in the United States. The UN Special Rapporteur on Torture, Juan Mendez, in a 2011 report found that "where the physical conditions and the prison regime of solitary confinement cause severe mental and physical pain or suffering, when used as a punishment, during pretrial detention, indefinitely, prolonged, on juveniles or persons with mental disabilities, it can amount to cruel, inhuman or degrading treatment or punishment and even torture. In addition the use of solitary confinement increases the risk that acts of torture and other cruel, inhuman or degrading treatment or punishment will go undetected and unchallenged." (See <http://solitaryconfinement.org /uploads/SpecRapTortureAug2011.pdf>)

The UN Special Rapporteur, international human rights organizations, and the National Religious Campaign Against Torture are all calling for: an end to prolonged solitary confinement beyond 15 days; abolishing the use of solitary confinement for pretrial detainees, individuals with mental illnesses, youth under the age of 18, pregnant women, and immigrants detained on immigration charges.

Therefore:

1. The United Methodist Church must continue to publicly condemn and oppose torture wherever it occurs through legislative and other means. The Council of Bishops and all agencies of the church must work together to develop resources and find ways to keep the information about torture, its perpetrators, the victims, their families, and their communities continuously in the consciousness of United Methodists.

2. United Methodists must take time in their churches, women's, youth, and men's groups to study, reflect, and pray about how to abolish torture and live out the biblical mandate to "love our neighbors" even in the midst of a "war on terror." (Paraphrase from Letter to the United Methodist Women on Torture, May 11, 2005, sent by Kyung Za Yim, President, Women's Division, Global Ministries, United Methodist Church, and Jan Love, Deputy General Secretary, Women's Division.)

3. United Methodists must seek to ensure the ratification by and compliance of their governments with the provisions of the Convention against Torture and all internationally accepted norms and standards on the prevention of torture; fully support the work of the International Criminal Court (ICC) and honor their international obligations to prosecute alleged perpetrators of torture.

4. United Methodists should join international efforts to end the use of solitary confinement.

5. United Methodists must express their solidarity with churches and peoples everywhere in the common struggle to have the provisions of the Covenant on Civil and Political Rights and

the Convention against Torture strictly applied in all countries. And, United Methodists should organize or join events and join in prayer on the 26th of June, the United Nations International Day to Remember the Victims of Torture.

6. United Methodists should seek access to places of detention and interrogation centers in order to ensure that persons held are not mistreated. Treatment of prisoners should not be contrary to the Geneva Convention Relative to Treatment of Prisoners of War (1949) particularly Articles 13, 14, 15, 17, 18. (Geneva Convention relative to the Treatment of Prisoners of War, adopted on 12 August 1949 by the Diplomatic Conference for the Establishment of International Conventions for the Protection of Victims of War, held in Geneva from 21 April to 12 August 1949, entered into force: 21 October 1950, Office of the United Nations High Commissioner for Human Rights: Web site: <http://www.ohchr.org>.)

7. United Methodists should join ecumenical and interfaith efforts to ensure the inalienable right of survivors of torture to rehabilitation, access to adequate reparations, including medical and psychological rehabilitation, restitution, compensation, satisfaction, and the guarantee of nonrepetition. It is recommended that The United Methodist Church work in partnership with international organizations, such as the Center for Victims of Torture, which have for many years developed the skills to care for victims of torture. Most organizations have Centers around the world sensitive to the language and culture of the victims and their families.

8. United Methodists should urge governments to fully fund the United Nations Voluntary Fund for Victims of Torture which was established in 1981 for humanitarian, legal, and financial aid to persons who have been tortured and to members of their families. (Fact Sheet No. 4, Methods of Combating Torture, Office of High Commissioner for Human Rights.)

ADOPTED 2008
AMENDED AND READOPTED 2016
RESOLUTION #6147, 2012 *BOOK OF RESOLUTIONS*
RESOLUTION #6119, 2008 *BOOK OF RESOLUTIONS*

See Social Principles, ¶ 165C, D.

X. OTHER RESOLUTIONS

8002. A Commitment to Unity in Mission and Ministry

WHEREAS, the mission of The United Methodist Church is to make disciples of Jesus Christ for the transformation of the world;

WHEREAS, the Council of Bishops has expressed a vision of mission and ministry that articulates the aspirations and ministries prevalent across the United Methodist connection and the general agencies have responded by identifying four areas of focus that live out the vision for the current quadrennium and beyond;

WHEREAS, the spirit of collaboration and shared ministry through the Council of Bishops, the Connectional Table, the general agencies, and the annual conferences is infusing new energy and recommitment to assure vitality and effectiveness across the connection;

WHEREAS, the following four areas of focus provide crucial avenues for shared labor and witness:

1. leader development with particular focus on leading the United Methodist way of discipleship,
2. new church starts and congregational vitality,
3. ministry with the poor with particular attention to caring for and protecting children,
4. global health by confronting the diseases of poverty and health care access for all,

Therefore, be it resolved, that we, the General Board of Discipleship (Discipleship Ministries),

- Commit ourselves to work in a spirit of unity with all across the Connection and with our ecumenical partners to give form to new expressions of shared mission and ministry;
- Commit ourselves to equip United Methodist Christians to perform mission and ministry as disciples of Jesus Christ;

- Commit ourselves to intentionally and collaboratively address the four areas of focus of congregational vitality, leader development, ministry with the poor, and global health as we prepare in planning and budgeting for mission and ministry in 2017-2020.

ADOPTED 2008
AMENDED AND READOPTED 2016
RESOLUTION #8002, 2008, 2012 BOOK OF RESOLUTIONS

8006. Ethics of Embryonic Stem Cell Research

Preamble

The following statement addresses the ethical implications of using human embryos as a source of stem cells for research. It also examines in vitro fertilization procedures, as they are the source of most of the embryos that are presently used for research. This statement does not explore in detail other kinds of stem cell research, but finds no moral objections to research involving stem cells derived from adult cells or umbilical cord blood. The United Methodist Church has made a commitment to consider all issues in light of concerns for the welfare of all people and the just distribution of resources. In light of that, we wish to state at the outset our conviction that Christians are called to use their resources to meet the basic health care needs of all people.

Description of In Vitro Fertilization

In vitro fertilization (IVF) is a clinical practice in which a woman's ovaries are hyper-stimulated to release several eggs, which are extracted and subsequently fertilized in a laboratory dish. This is for the purpose of creating embryos to be introduced into the uterus in the hope of implantation, gestation, and eventual birth. Current practice usually involves the extraction of up to 15-16 eggs for fertilization. The resulting embryos that are judged most viable are either introduced into the womb in the initial attempt or frozen and stored for possible later use. Some of the embryos are judged to be less viable than others and are discarded. (Those stored embryos that are not later used become the "excess embryos" whose use as a source of embryonic stem cells is currently under discussion.)

Concerns Regarding the Status of Human Embryos

A human embryo, even at its earliest stages, commands our reverence and makes a serious moral claim on us. For this reason we should not create embryos with the sole intention of destroying them.

We recommend the following guidelines for clinicians and couples considering IVF:

- We call for rigorous standards of informed consent regarding the procedures, the physical and emotional risks, and the associated ethical issues be applied to all reproductive technologies.
- We urge clinicians and couples to make the determination of how many eggs to fertilize and implant on a case-by-case basis.

Some Judgments Regarding the Use of Existing Embryos for Stem Cell Research

There has been a great deal of scientific interest recently generated by research on human stem cells. These are the cells that give rise to other cells. There are a number of potential sources for stem cells, including adult tissues, fetal remains, umbilical cord blood, and human embryos. The use of adult stem cells and stem cells derived from umbilical cord blood raises few moral questions. The use of human embryos as a source for stem cells has been the subject of intense moral debate.

Given the reality that most, if not all, excess embryos will be discarded, we believe that it is morally tolerable to use existing embryos for stem cell research purposes. This position is a matter of weighing the danger of further eroding the respect due to potential life against the possible, therapeutic benefits that are hoped for from such research. The same judgment of moral tolerability would apply to the use of embryos left from future reproductive efforts if a decision has been made not to introduce them into the womb. We articulate this position with an attitude of caution, not license. We reiterate our opposition to the creation of embryos for the sake of research. (See *Book of Resolutions*, 2000, p. 254)

The Issue of "Therapeutic Cloning"

The United Methodist Church supports persons who wish to enhance medical research by donating their early embryos remaining after in vitro fertilization (IVF) procedures have ended, and urges national governments to pass legislation that would authorize funding for derivation of and medical research on human embryonic stem cells that were generated from IVF embryos and remain after fertilization procedures have been concluded, provided that:

1. these early embryos are no longer required for procreation by those donating them and would simply be discarded;

2. those donating early embryos have given their prior informed consent to their use in stem cell research;

3. the embryos were not deliberately created for research purposes; and

4. the embryos were not obtained by sale or purchase.

National health agencies are urged to establish an interdisciplinary oversight body for all research in both the public and private sectors that involves stem cells from human embryos, adult stem cells that have been made pluripotent, parthenotes, sperm cells, or egg cells, and cells that produce sperm or eggs.

ADOPTED 2004
REVISED AND READOPTED 2008, 2016
RESOLUTION #8006, 2012 *BOOK OF RESOLUTIONS*
RESOLUTION #8003, 2008 *BOOK OF RESOLUTIONS*
RESOLUTION #366, 2004 *BOOK OF RESOLUTIONS*

8007. Study of Ecclesiology

The Committee on Faith and Order proposes a period of study to stimulate and aid theological reflection throughout the church on the identity and mission of the United Methodist Church.

The study and response process in the coming quadrennium will involve these elements:

1. A teaching document on ecclesiology will be made available electronically through www.umc.org, www.gbhem.org, and www.gbod.org along with a brief study and response guide to facilitate study of the document. These documents will be translated into the language of the General Conference.

2. Each resident bishop will be asked to arrange for congregationally based studies of United Methodist ecclesiology between

June 2016 and December 2017 involving approximately ten percent of both the laity and clergy of her or his episcopal area. Resources for the study will be provided by the Committee on Faith and Order.

3. Responses will be solicited from specific groups who may have particular expertise in ecclesiology, including: faculty from United Methodist seminaries and schools of theology, general agency staff, pan-Methodist theologians and officials, and other selected ecumenical partners.

4. All United Methodists will be invited and encouraged to offer feedback on United Methodist ecclesiology.

5. The Committee on Faith and Order will design processes to solicit and receive these responses.

6. The Committee on Faith and Order will be responsible for evaluating the study process, considering the responses received, and will offer appropriate action to the 2020 General Conference. The Committee on Faith and Order will send to the 2020 General Conference a theological teaching document on ecclesiology for adoption as an official document of the church, comparable to *By Water and the Spirit* and *This Holy Mystery*.

ADOPTED 2016

8008. Task Force on Israel and Palestine

WHEREAS, it is God's will that all people enjoy peace/*shalom*/ *salaam*, i.e., peace, security, prosperity, and right relationships with one another and the earth; and

WHEREAS, the psalmists call us to pray for the peace of Jerusalem (Psalm 122:6), and to "seek peace and pursue it" (Psalm 34:14); and

WHEREAS, we affirm Israel's right to permanent, recognized, and secure borders, and Palestinians' rights to self-determination and formation of a viable state; and,

WHEREAS, the 2012 *Book of Resolutions* states "we seek for all people in the Middle East region an end to military occupation, freedom from violence, and full respect for the human rights of all under international law" (Resolution #6073, 2008 *Book of Resolutions*, amended and readopted in 2012 [R6111]); and

WHEREAS, "The United Methodist Church opposes continued military occupation of the West Bank, Gaza, and East Jerusalem, the confiscation of Palestinian land and water resources, the destruction of Palestinian homes, the continued building of illegal Jewish settlements, and any vision of a 'Greater Israel' that includes the occupied territories and the whole of Jerusalem and its surroundings" (Resolution #6111: "Opposition to Israeli Settlements in Palestinian Land," 2012 *Book of Resolutions*); and,

WHEREAS, we are called to support members of Christ's church around the world, including Palestinian Christians who are being forced to leave the Holy Land due to Israel's confiscation of their property and the severe hardships of living under occupation; and,

WHEREAS, the Palestinian Christian community, through the Kairos Palestine document, has requested the support of the wider Church (Kairos Palestine. "A Moment of Truth: A Word of Faith, Hope and Love from the Heart of Palestinian Suffering" <http://www.kairospalestine.ps/content/kairos-document> Web. December 2009); and,

WHEREAS, Palestinian Christian leaders have specifically requested the support of The United Methodist Church (Letter to The United Methodist Church from Rifat Odeh Kassis, General Coordinator, Kairos Palestine, November 28, 2014 <https://www.kairosresponse.org/Rifat_Kassis.html>. Web. January 2015); and,

WHEREAS, the 2012 General Conference reiterated the call to end the occupation, through boycotts of goods produced in the occupied territories (Resolution #6111: "Opposition to Israeli Settlements in Palestinian Land," 2012 *Book of Resolutions*); and,

WHEREAS, all UMC missionaries serving in the Holy Land over the last twenty-five years support concrete actions by our denomination to show our support of Palestinian rights (United Methodist Missionaries Support Divestment from the Israeli Occupation, https://www.kairosresponse.org/UMC_Missionar ies_Divestment.html. Web. January 2015 <https://www.kairosre sponse.org/UMC_Missionaries_Divestment.html.%20Web.%20 January%202015>).

Therefore, be it resolved, that the General Board of Church and Society together with the General Board of Global Ministries shall create a diverse and representative task force to review and research actions that can be taken to respond to these requests by our UMC missionaries and our Palestinian sisters and brothers in Christ, and formulate and publish recommendations for annual conferences, local churches, and members, including helping organize Holy Land Tours that are consistent with the 2008 resolution #6031 "Holy Land Tours," as revised and readopted, *The Book of Resolutions, 2016*, that provides guidelines for travel in Israel/Palestine.

Be it further resolved, that the 2016 General Conference of The United Methodist Church calls on the US government, the government of Israel, and the elected Palestinian leadership to work for diplomatic and nonviolent solutions to the problems of the region, to respect the equality and dignity of all the region's people, and to forge solutions based on the principles of international law and human rights.

ADOPTED 2016

8011. Biblical Language

Whereas, The United Methodist Church affirms the use of biblical language and images in worship and in our common life together, and affirms the use of language that reflects the long-standing commitment to the inclusiveness and diversity of United Methodist members and constituencies; and

Whereas, the use of metaphors of color, darkness, ability, and age in negative ways has had a harmful effect;

Therefore, be it resolved, that United Methodist clergy and laity be encouraged to use diverse biblical images and titles for God, including masculine/feminine metaphors; use language for humans that reflects both male and female; use metaphors of color, darkness, ability, and age in positive ways; and

Be it further resolved, that we affirm the use of biblical language and images in all their forms as appropriate for use in hymns, liturgy, teaching, and in all areas of our common life together; and

Be it further resolved, that publications, audiovisual media, online resources, and other communication materials of The United Methodist Church shall reflect the diverse biblical metaphors and the diversity and inclusiveness of humanity.

ADOPTED 1988
REVISED AND ADOPTED 2000, 2008
READOPTED 2016
RESOLUTION #8011, 2012 *BOOK OF RESOLUTIONS*
RESOLUTION #8006, 2008 *BOOK OF RESOLUTIONS*
RESOLUTION #344, 2004 *BOOK OF RESOLUTIONS*
RESOLUTION #321, 2000 *BOOK OF RESOLUTIONS*

8012. Use of the Name: The United Methodist Church in Periodicals and Advertisements

The 1980 United Methodist General Conference, sympathetic toward Evangelical United Brethren, moved Heritage Sunday from the anniversary of John Wesley's Aldersgate experience (the former Aldersgate Sunday) to the anniversary of the Uniting Conference and passed a resolution on the "Proper Use of the Name: The United Methodist Church."

We call our members to a more thorough understanding of the joint heritage of our Methodist and Evangelical United Brethren forebears, and we call on our members and agencies to implement with energy and enthusiasm, the 1980 resolution on the "Proper Use of the Name: The United Methodist Church."

We call on our church periodical editors, where contributors omit the word "United" from "United Methodist" to correct this usage—both in articles and in letters to the editor. With direct quotations, they should insert "United" in brackets. They should further instruct advertisers that advertisements that refer to "Methodist" without "United" are unacceptable.

We further direct the General Council on Finance and Administration and the General Commission on Communication, when they become aware of the omission of "United" from "United Methodist" in the church or secular press, to notify the responsible parties that this is unacceptable usage and to report to the Church annually in *The Interpreter* of its compliance with this directive.

ADOPTED 2004
AMENDED AND READOPTED 2012
RESOLUTION #8012, 2012 BOOK OF RESOLUTIONS
RESOLUTION #8007, 2008 *BOOK OF RESOLUTIONS*
RESOLUTION #352, 2004 *BOOK OF RESOLUTIONS*

8013. Meeting Times

WHEREAS, The United Methodist Church recognizes the leadership of young people within the Church; and

WHEREAS, young people of The United Methodist Church are called by God to serve in leadership roles at the local, district, and conference levels; and

WHEREAS, a churchwide effort in recruiting and retaining young people's participation is growing; and

WHEREAS, the time constraints of young people through school, career, and family are great, making accessibility to leadership roles difficult;

Therefore, be it resolved, that in choosing dates and times for all meetings of United Methodist Church boards and agencies, utmost importance is given to the consideration of times, dates, and places between all conferences that will make young people's participation as great as possible.

Be it further resolved, that in choosing dates and times for district, annual/central, and General Conference meetings that utmost importance is given to the consideration of allowing as many youth and young adult delegates to actively participate as is possible.

ADOPTED 2008
READOPTED 2012
RESOLUTION # 8013, 2012 *BOOK OF RESOLUTIONS*
RESOLUTION #8008, 2008 *BOOK OF RESOLUTIONS*

8014. Church Participation by a Registered Child Sex Offender

The Social Principles of The United Methodist Church declare: "We recognize that family violence and abuse in all its forms— verbal, psychological, physical, sexual—is detrimental to the covenant of the human community. We encourage the Church to provide a safe environment, counsel, and support for the victim. While we deplore the actions of the abuser, we affirm that person to be in need of God's redeeming love" (Social Principles ¶ 161G [2012 *Discipline*]).

Churches are faced with a dilemma in their attempt to be faithful to both of the last two sentences above. Assuring the safety of children in our care, our facilities and our programs is a sacred duty. We must weigh that duty in the balance with what often seems the conflicting value of participation in the life of the church by a convicted child abuser. Being part of a worshiping community is not the only way for a person to experience God's redeeming love, but it is an important one.

Ongoing studies suggest a low likelihood that pedophiles can or will change. Without extensive professional treatment, virtually all child sexual offenders will re-offend. Repentance, prayer, and pastoral support, always in combination with lifelong professional treatment, can be crucial in helping to change behavior but, in themselves, offer slim hope of changing the behavior of perpetrators. Thorough awareness, careful planning, and ongoing monitoring must accompany welcoming a child sex offender into a congregation.

A convicted and/or registered sex offender who wishes to be part of a church community should expect to have conditions placed on his or her participation. Indeed, offenders who have been in treatment and are truly committed to living a life free of further abuse will be the first to declare that, in order to accomplish that, they must structure a life that includes ongoing treatment, accountability mechanisms, and lack of access to children.

The following steps should be taken in order to be faithful to the Social Principles' commitment both to safety from abuse and to ministry with abusers:

A. Local churches should:

- hold discussions in the church council and in adult education settings about the possibility of facing the situation of a convicted sex offender returning to or joining the church. These discussions should be held and general agreements reached about actions to be taken should the church find itself in this circumstance;

- develop a carefully constructed and openly negotiated covenant between the offender and the church community. The covenant should include agreements in the following areas: participation in a professional counseling program for at least the entire time of church membership or participation; adult "covenant partners" to accompany the offender while on church property or attending church activities; areas of church facilities that are "off limits"; restrictions on leadership in or on behalf of church; no role in church that includes contact with children or youth; any additional conditions for presence or participation; restrictions on use of church-related media; and

- assure that the covenant is maintained by having it written and signed by the offender, the pastor(s), and the chairperson of the church council. While confidentiality of victims should be respected, the covenant should not be secret. Monitoring of the covenant should be taken seriously as a permanent responsibility.

B. *Annual conferences should:*

- develop similar plans and covenant for situations in which a convicted and/or registered sexual offender is involved or seeks involvement in the conference, its activities or facilities;
- include information about this concern and assistance with implementation of this resolution in its training and resourcing of clergy and local church lay leaders;

C. *The General Board of Discipleship and the General Board of Global Ministries should:*

- cooperatively develop and promote a process and specific guidelines to assist congregations in the education and covenant tasks outlined above.

ADOPTED 2004
READOPTED 2008
AMENDED AND READOPTED 2012
RESOLUTION #8014, 2012 *BOOK OF RESOLUTIONS*
RESOLUTION #8009, 2008 *BOOK OF RESOLUTIONS*
RESOLUTION #355, 2004 *BOOK OF RESOLUTIONS*

8015. Guidelines: The UMC and the Charismatic Movement

Introductory Statement

In 1976 General Conference approved *"Guidelines: The United Methodist Church and the Charismatic Renewal."* These Guidelines served the church well. At the 2004 General Conference the GBOD was assigned the responsibility to review and revise the Guidelines, while retaining their general focus and purpose.

Glossary

Terminology associated with the charismatic movement is confusing because of varying usage.

Pentecostal. This term refers to the movement whose roots began late in the nineteenth century, resulting in the formation of a number of pentecostal denominations in the early years of the twentieth century. Classic pentecostalism affirms what is sometimes spoken of as initial evidence, which includes the concept of requisite "baptism in the Holy Spirit," that every Christian must experience the "baptism in the Holy Spirit" that is accompanied by *glossolalia* or speaking in tongues as an "initial evidence." Pentecostals also emphasize strongly the full recovery of the gifts of the Holy Spirit.

Charismatic. The word *charismatic* comes from the Greek word *charismata*, meaning "gifts." The root words in Greek mean grace and joy. By definition, a charismatic should be a joyful, grace-gifted Christian. Charismatic Christians emphasize the need to recover the empowerment and the gifts of the Spirit for ministry today. They affirm the importance of all the "gifts of the Spirit."

Charismatic Movement. Throughout this report the term *charismatic movement* is used to identify the movement that began about 1960 in mainline Christian bodies, both Protestant and Roman Catholic. This movement emphasizes the central importance of the "baptism of the Holy Spirit," but without the elevation of "speaking in tongues" as the initial evidence. A focus is placed on the need to recover the Holy Spirit's empowering and gifts for ministry today. These gifts include prophecy, healing, tongues, and interpretation of tongues, because these gifts are perceived to have been neglected by the Church.

In a biblical sense there is no such person as a "noncharismatic Christian," since the term *charismata* refers to the gracious gifts of God bestowed upon all Christians to equip them for ministry: "A demonstration of the Spirit is given to each person for the common good" (1 Corinthians 12:7).

Pentecostals and *Charismatics* emerged out of Christianity in the West, where for long periods Christianity neglected the importance of the gifts of the Holy Spirit in the life of the church. However, the activity of the Holy Spirit is not merely restricted to Western Christianity. Indeed, when the gospel reached different parts of the non-Western world, many Christians learned of the Holy Spirit's work in the Bible. In simple faith they believed, and many began exercising the gifts of the Spirit. Although the ministries of such individuals and churches are similar to those of the Pentecostals and the Charismatics in many ways, they do not owe their origins to these Western sources. Rather, they sprang up entirely on their own under the direct leading of the Spirit.

Neo-charismatics, or Third Wave (the Pentecostals being the first wave and the Charismatics being the second wave). These are

Christians who, unrelated or no longer related to the Pentecostal or Charismatic renewals, have become filled with the Spirit, are energized by the Spirit, and exercise gifts of the Spirit without recognizing a baptism in the Spirit separate from conversion. Speaking in tongues is considered optional or unnecessary. Signs and wonders, supernatural miracles, and power encounters are emphasized. Third-wavers form independent churches and do not identify themselves as either Pentecostals or Charismatics (Synan, p. 396).

Guidelines

We believe the church needs to pray for a sensitivity to be aware of and to respond to manifestations of the Holy Spirit in our world today. We are mindful that the problems of discerning between the true and fraudulent are considerable, but we must not allow the problems to paralyze our awareness of the Spirit's presence; nor should we permit our fear of the unknown and the unfamiliar to close our minds against being surprised by grace. We know the misuse of mystical experience is an ever-present possibility, but that is no reason to deny spiritual experiences.

In facing the issues raised by charismatic experiences, we plead for a spirit of openness and love. We commend to the attention of the church the affirmations of Paul on the importance of love in First Corinthians 13 and of Wesley—"In essentials, unity; in nonessentials, liberty; and, in all things, charity" (love that cares and understands). Without an active, calm, objective, and loving understanding of the religious experience of others, however different from one's own, harmony is impossible.

The criteria by which we understand another's religious experience must include its compatibility with the mind and the spirit of our Lord Jesus Christ, as revealed in the New Testament. If the consequence and quality of a reported encounter with the Holy Spirit leads to self-righteousness, hostility, and exaggerated claims of knowledge and power, then the experience is subject to serious question. However, when the experience clearly results in new dimensions of love, faith, joy, and blessings to others, we must conclude that this is "what the Lord hath done" and offer God our praise. "You will know them by their fruit" (Matthew 7:20).

Guidelines for All

1. Be open and accepting of those whose Christian experiences differ from your own.

2. Continually undergird and envelop all discussions, conferences, meetings, and persons in prayer.

3. Be open to new ways in which God by the Spirit may be speaking to the church.

4. Seek the gifts of the Spirit that enrich your life and your ministry, as well as the life of the church.

5. Recognize that although spiritual gifts may be abused in the same way that knowledge or wealth or power may be abused, this does not mean that they should be prohibited.

6. Remember that, like other movements in church history, the charismatic renewal has a valid contribution to make to the ecumenical church.

7. Remember the lessons of church history that when God's people rediscovered old truths the process was often disquieting and that it usually involved upheaval, change, and a degree of suffering and misunderstanding.

8. Always be mindful of the spiritual needs of the whole congregation.

9. In witnessing, teaching, or preaching, the wholeness of all aspects of the gospel must be presented.

For Pastors Who Have Had Charismatic Experiences

1. Combine with your charismatic experience a thorough knowledge of and adherence to United Methodist theology, polity, and tradition. Remember your influence will, in large part, be earned by your loving and disciplined employment of the gifts, by your conduct as a pastor of your entire congregation, and by your participation as a responsible pastor.

2. Seek a deepening and continued friendship with your clergy colleagues regardless of their charismatic experience.

3. Remember your ordination vow to "love, serve, and pray for all the people among whom you work . . . to serve rather than to be served . . . to look after the concerns of Christ above all." (*The United Methodist Book of Worship*, "The Order for the Ordination of Elders," 675)

4. Avoid the temptation to force your personal views and experiences on others. Seek to understand those whose spiritual experiences differ from your own.

5. Seek to grow in your skills as a biblical exegete, a systematic theologian, and a preacher in all the fullness of the gospel.

6. Pray for the gifts of the Spirit essential for your ministry; continually examine your life for the fruits of the Spirit.

7. Let your personal experience demonstrate the power of the Spirit in "works of piety" and "works of mercy" as understood and practiced in the Wesleyan tradition.

For Pastors Who Have Not Had Charismatic Experiences

1. Continually examine your understanding of the doctrine and experience of the Holy Spirit, so you can communicate this with clarity.

2. Remember the lessons of church history when God's people rediscover old truths—the process is often disquieting, that it usually involves upheaval, change, and a degree of suffering and misunderstanding.

3. Seek firsthand knowledge of what the charismatic renewal means to those who have experienced it. Keep your mind open until this firsthand knowledge is obtained. Then observe and respond as a loving Christian, as a United Methodist minister, and as a sympathetic, conscientious pastor. Keep to scriptural teaching regarding all the gifts of the Holy Spirit.

4. When speaking in tongues occurs, seek to understand what it means to the speaker in his or her private devotional life and what it means when used for intercessory prayer, especially in group worship.

5. Seek to understand the meaning of the other "gifts of the Spirit" in the charismatic experience, such as the utterance of wisdom, knowledge, faith, healing, miracles, and prophecy.

6. United Methodist pastors should be intentional about the benefits to be derived by a mutual sharing of a variety of experiences that have biblical foundation. Accordingly, the pastor should seek to keep all meetings called for prayer and fellowship open to all interested members of the congregation.

For Laity Who Have Had Charismatic Experiences

1. Remember to combine with your enthusiasm a thorough knowledge of and adherence to the United Methodist form of church government. The charismatic movement is closely related to the holiness movement and to the Wesleyan tradition. Consult with your pastor(s) and if they have not also had your experience, help him or her understand what it means to you. Invite your pastor(s) to attend your worship services and prayer meetings.

2. Pray that the Spirit will help you to maintain fellowship with all United Methodists.

3. Strive for a scholarly knowledge of scriptural content in combination with your spiritual experiences. "Seek to unite knowledge and vital piety" (Wesley). Strive to integrate your experiences with the theological traditions of our church.

4. Avoid undisciplined, undiplomatic enthusiasm in your eagerness to share your experiences with others. Resist the temptation to pose as an authority on spiritual experiences. Failure in this area may cause your fellow Christians to interpret your behavior as spiritual pride.

5. Be intentional about keeping your prayer meetings and other gatherings open to all members of your congregation. When those who do not share your experiences do attend, discuss with them the purpose of the meeting with an interpretation of the significance of the content.

6. Remember that there are many types of Christian experiences that lead to spiritual growth; charismatic experience is one of these.

7. Accept opportunities to become personally involved in the work and mission of your own congregation. Let the results of your experience be seen in the outstanding quality of your church membership and service to others. Be an obvious, enthusiastic supporter of your congregation, its pastor, and its lay leadership and of your district, your annual conference, the General Conference, and mission of each. This may well be the most effective witness you can offer to the validity and vitality of your charismatic experience.

8. Remember Paul's injunction that when the gift of tongues is spoken to the body in a group context, there must be interpretation to ensure proper order (1 Corinthians 14:27, 40). If the gift is exercised in a worship setting or group prayer, be careful that it does not hinder worship or cause distraction for others.

9. Keep your charismatic experience in perspective. No doubt it has caused you to feel that you are a better Christian. Remember that this does not mean you are better than other Christians but that you are, perhaps, a better Christian than you were before. Jesus commanded us to love one another (John 13:34).

For Laity Who Have Not Had Charismatic Experiences

1. We believe God is constantly seeking to renew the church, including The United Methodist Church. Pray that God may make known to you your own place in the process of renewal. The advent of the charismatic movement into our denomination is only one aspect of renewal.

2. If there are members of your congregation who have had charismatic experiences, accept them as brothers and sisters. Jesus commanded us to love one another (John 13:34).

3. Be aware of the tendency to separate ourselves from those who have experiences that differ from our own. Observe personally the charismatics in their prayer meetings, in your congregation, and in the mission of your church. Examine scriptural teaching about this. Pray about it. Discuss your concern with your pastor. The United Methodist Church is theologically diverse.

4. Do not be disturbed if your experience is not the same as others. The work and mission of a healthy congregation calls for many gifts (1 Corinthians 12–14). Each Christian is a unique member of the body of Christ and should seek to discover his or her gifts and role.

5. Should your pastor emphasize charismatic experiences, help her or him to be mindful of the spiritual needs of the entire congregation, to be a pastor and teacher to all. Encourage her or him in preaching to present the wholeness of all aspects of the gospel. Be open to what God would say to you through your pastor about the Holy Spirit.

For Connectional Administration

1. Refer prayerfully and thoughtfully to the other sections of these Guidelines.

2. Remember your pastoral responsibilities toward ordained persons and congregations within the connection, particularly toward those whose spiritual experience differ from your own.

3. Each administrator should consider whether any teaching or practice regarding the charismatic movement involving an ordained minister of a congregation is for the edification of the church.

4. If there is division involved in a particular situation, make as careful an evaluation as possible, remembering that there are other kinds of issues that may divide our fellowship—a lack of openness to something new or an unwillingness to change, for example. Sometimes tensions and conflicts may result in the edification and growth and maturity of the church and therefore need to be handled wisely and prayerfully by all concerned.

5. Administrators and connectional bodies will be required to deal with expressions of the charismatic movement. We urge all involved to seek firsthand information and experience about the movement, its meaning for those involved in it, and its value to the particular congregation.

6. Care should be taken that persons whose theology and experiences align with those of the Charismatic Renewal are not discriminated against in appointments or as candidates for ordination.

7. Where an ordained person seems to overemphasize or de-emphasize some charismatic doctrines/practices, she or he should be counseled to preach the wholeness of the gospel, to minister to the needs of all of the congregation, and as a pastor to grow in understanding of our polity in the mission of the particular annual conference.

8. Annual conferences may also be faced with a situation where there is a charismatic group within a congregation whose pastor or whose lay leadership or both may be hostile to or ignorant of the charismatic movement. The annual conference Board of Ordained Ministry, the bishop, and the district superintendent have a pastoral responsibility to mediate and to guide in reconciliation, using these guidelines.

9. Pray continuously for sensitivity to the will and the leading of the Holy Spirit.

Historical Perspective:

The Ministry of the Holy Spirit in Church History

The Holy Spirit in the New Testament Period

The Holy Spirit came upon Mary (Luke 1:35), descended upon Jesus at his baptism (Luke 3:22) and filled Jesus before the temptation in the wilderness (Luke 4:2ff). Jesus claimed that the Spirit was upon him when he stood up to preach (Luke 4:18*ff*) and that the Spirit empowered him to cast out demons (Matthew 12:28). John the Baptist and Jesus both indicated the importance of the power of the Spirit (Luke 3:15-19; John 7:37-39; Acts 1:5, 8).

The coming of the Holy Spirit ushered in the beginning of the Church (Acts 2) and empowered the disciples to be witnesses (Acts 1:8, Acts 2:4*ff*). Paul writes about the gifts of the Spirit in his letters (Romans 12:6-8; 1 Corinthians 12:4-11, 27-31; Ephesians 4:11) and describes his missionary outreach to the Gentiles as "by what I've said and what I've done, by the power of signs and wonders, and by the power of God's Spirit" (Romans 15:18-19; see also 1 Corinthians 2:4-5; 1 Thessalonians 1:5).

The Holy Spirit in John Wesley's Life and Ministry

John Wesley and his followers were bearers of Scriptural Christianity. Their ministry testifies to the dynamic work of the Spirit in early Methodism.

To begin with, Wesley's Aldersgate experience of the assurance of his salvation on 24 May 1738 was certainly a work of the Spirit. He relates in his journal how as he heard of "the change which God works in the heart through faith in Christ, I felt my heart strangely warmed . . . and an assurance was given that he had taken away my sins." Some months later, he was at prayer with seventy others, including his brother Charles and also George Whitefield, on the night of 1 January 1739. In the early hours of the next morning, the Holy Spirit was poured on them in a most powerful manner. He writes: "About three in the morning . . . the power of God came mightily upon us insomuch that many cried out for exceeding joy and many fell to the ground. As soon as we were recovered a little from that awe and amazement at the presence of His majesty, we broke out with one voice, 'We praise Thee, O God, we acknowledge Thee to be the Lord.'"

"On the basis of Scripture, Wesley taught that the Holy Spirit is present and active in *every major stage of Christian experience*." (Stokes, 46) Careful study of Wesley's writings shows clearly that spiritual gifts, including healing and deliverance of the demonized, were clearly manifested in his ministry and that of his coworkers. There were also reported cases of people falling to the ground under the power of the Holy Spirit due to a variety of reasons, including deliverance from demonization, deep conviction of sin and subsequent release, or simply being overcome by the Spirit (Davies, *Methodism*, pp. 60f; Heitzenrater, *Wesley and the People Called Methodists*, pp. 100f, 319). One study has shown that, "a careful study of Wesley's *Works* and particularly of the lives of the early Methodist preachers reveals evidence that all the spiritual gifts listed in 1 Corinthians 12:8-10 were exercised, with the one exception of the interpretation of tongues" (Davies and Peart, *The Charismatic Movement and Methodism*, 2).

Finally, Wesley himself has noted that the spiritual gifts were not generally exercised after the first two or three centuries after Christ. But the reason for this was not that these gifts were not available. Rather, as he noted, "The real cause was 'the love of many,' almost all Christians, was 'waxed cold,' because the Christians were turned Heathens again, and had only a dead form left" (Sermon LXXXIX, "The More Excellent Way," *Works*, Vol. 7, 26-27). And Wesley wrote, "I do not recollect any scripture wherein we are taught that miracles were to be confined within the limits either of the apostolic or the Cyprianic age, or of any period of time, longer or shorter, even till the restitution of all things" ("Principles of a Methodist Farther Explained," *Works*, Vol. 8, 465).

The Pentecostal and Charismatic Movements and the Wesleyan Framework

It is impossible to speak of Pentecostalism and the Charismatic Renewal apart from their roots in Methodism. It was, after all, the Wesleyans who first applied the title "pentecostal" to their movement and to a variety of their publications. The Methodists were also first to coin the phrase *baptism of the Holy Spirit* as applied to a second and sanctifying grace (experience) of God. (Cf. John Fletcher of Madeley, Methodism's earliest formal theologian.) The Methodists meant by their "baptism" something different from the Pentecostals, but the view that this is an experience of grace separate from and after salvation was the same. However, the roots of Pentecostalism in Methodist soil go much deeper than titles and phrases. While the phenomenon of speaking in tongues, commonly associated with Pentecostalism, was not an experience sought or promoted by early Methodists, other equally startling manifestations of the Spirit did abound. This was particularly so as Methodism spread across the American frontier. When asked once why the gifts of the Spirit, manifest in the early church, had disappeared, as if the church had no more need for them, Mr. Wesley responded: "It should not be reasoned that the absence of such in the church (eighteenth-century Church of England) reflects the reluctance of God to give, rather the reticence of the church to receive" (Tuttle, 106). Methodism then, at its inception, invited God's people to expect and receive whatever blessing God would give "for the common good" (1 Corinthians 12:7). It is not surprising that many of the first Pentecostal leaders were originally Methodists. Pentecostalism has continued to be what Francis Asbury wanted Methodism to remain, a pliable movement more than a static institution. Whether Methodism claims it or not, Pentecostalism is an offspring and will perhaps be its greatest legacy. Conservative estimates of the number of classical denominational Pentecostals run 200 million. Combined with the millions of charismatics and neo-pentecostals or third-wavers and those in house churches, that number now stands at 500 million (Synan, 2) to 700 million (Rutz, 44-46), making this the second largest group of Christians in the world, second only to the Roman Catholic Church as a whole. This group is estimated to be growing worldwide by 8 percent a year (Rutz, 15).

Charismatics should interpret their gifts and experiences in light of their own traditions. When this does not occur, division and/or exploitation sets in. When United Methodist charismatics adopt a classical pentecostal line, they are no longer United Methodist—at least in the Wesleyan sense. United Methodist Charismatics need to recognize that, properly understood within the context of our own tradition, their charismatic gifts and experiences can be considered as fresh wind of the Spirit.

Wesley's theology of grace is in fact a theology of the Holy Spirit. He believed that Reformation theology was built upon the cardinal doctrine of original sin and that it is God's sovereign will to reverse our "sinful, devilish nature" by the work of the Holy Spirit. He called this activity of God prevenient, justifying, and sanctifying grace. Bound by sin and death, one experiences almost from the moment of conception the gentle wooing of the Holy Spirit—*prevenient grace*. This grace "prevents" one from wandering so far from God that when a person finally understands what it means to be a child of God the Holy Spirit enables us to say Yes to this relationship. For Wesley, this Yes was a heartfelt faith in the merit of Christ alone for salvation. It allows the Holy Spirit to take the righteousness that was in Christ and attribute or impute it to the believer—*justifying grace*. For Wesley this begins a *lifelong movement* from imputed to imparted righteousness in which the Holy Spirit moves the believer from the righteousness of Christ attributed through faith to the righteousness of Christ realized within the individual—*sanctifying grace*.

To understand Wesley's experience of "entire sanctification" is to know how far the pentecostal baptism of the Holy Spirit falls short if there are not continuing works of grace. Grace is continual, though we may not always perceive it. It is essential that we do not confuse being "filled with the Holy Spirit" with Wesley's mature doctrine of sanctification. The Spirit-filled life is, rather, a sustained journey of gifts, experiences, and divine support, beginning with conversion, constantly moving us toward the goal of sanctification.

Many charismatics have come to believe that being filled with the Holy Spirit is an experience that begins with justification and continues as a lifelong process of growth in grace. For the charismatic, Spirit-baptism bestows not one but many gifts and not one but many experiences intended to sustain one day after day. Being baptized in the Spirit (Acts 1:4-5) and being continually filled with the Spirit (Ephesians 5:18) and walking with the Spirit (Galatians 5:25) are important parts of the *journey* toward Christ-likeness, but they are only *parts* of the journey. Thus, United Methodist charismatics, within the context of our own rich tradition, can never interpret gifts and experiences as signs of superior spirituality, making them better than others. Rather, the power of God being sustained within them makes them better than they were and able to "pursue . . . the prize of God's upward call in Christ Jesus" (Philippians 3:14).

The Charismatic Renewal has been instrumental in providing many gifts to the Church of Christ Jesus and has made a profound impact upon present-day United Methodism.

Methodists throughout history have always worshiped God in a variety of styles—never more so than today. In addition worship itself—from openly free to highly liturgical—is now more broadly and correctly understood as a personal offering from the body rather than simply the service of worship that one attends. "*God is spirit, and it is necessary to worship God in spirit and truth*" (John 4:24).

Contemporary Christian music—a hallmark of the charismatic renewal—fills many of our churches each Sunday, enriches the spiritual life of individuals and enhances small group meetings.

There are a variety of healing services offered in *The United Methodist Book of Worship*. In addition, the church offers a number of helpful resources for beginning and sustaining healing ministries within the local church.

Spiritual formation is now considered an integral part of planning for annual conferences and important in the continuing education for clergy.

The renewing work of the Holy Spirit within The United Methodist Church has supported the *Lay Witness Movement*, the *Walk to Emmaus*, and the *Academy for Spiritual Formation*. In 1978, Aldersgate *Renewal Ministries* (whose purpose is to "encourage United Methodists to be filled, gifted, empowered and led by the Holy Spirit in ministry to the world" became an affiliate of the General Board of Discipleship. These ministries have been used by God to bring thousands of people around the world into a new or deeper relationship with the Lord.

United Methodist charismatics and noncharismatics alike should be encouraged. In fact, the term *noncharismatic* Christian is a misnomer. All Christians have gifts. *Charismatic*, as earlier defined, refers to those who more explicitly acknowledge and emphasize teaching concerning the power of the Holy Spirit at work within them and the church through such gifts.

Bibliography

Davies, Rupert E. *Methodism*. London: Epworth, 1976. This is a standard reference work written by a British Methodist scholar.

Davies, William R. and Peart, Ross. *The Charismatic Movement and Methodism*. Westminster, UK: Methodist Home Mission, 1973. This resource written by clergy within the Charismatic tradition of the British Methodist Church.

DeArteaga, William. *Quenching the Spirit: Discover the Real Spirit behind the Charismatic Controversy*. Lake Mary, FL: Creation House 2002. This volume contains a historical overview of spiritual gifts from the early church to the date of publication. It also provides the history of opposition to spiritual gifts. www.creationhouse.com <http://www.creationhouse.com>.

Heitzenrater, Richard P. *Wesley and the People Called Methodists*. Nashville: Abingdon, 1995. This is a standard reference work written by a United Methodist scholar in the USA. www.cokesbury.com <http://www.cokesbury.com>.

"The Holy Spirit and Revival." The Methodist Church in Malaysia, August 2006. This document was recently approved in Malaysia and represents a more global and biblical perspective on spiritual gifts.

Hyatt, Eddie L. *2000 Years of Charismatic Christianity*. Lake Mary, FL: Charisma House, 2002. This book traces the history of Charismatic Christianity from the early church to the present time with significant attention to Methodism. www.charismahouse.com <http://www.charismahouse.com>.

Jennings, Daniel R. *The Supernatural Occurrences of John Wesley*. Sean Multimedia 2005. This resource gathers information from John Wesley's writings on spiritual gifts and the supernatural. www.seanmultimedia.com <http://www.seanmultimedia.com>.

Moore, Gary L. *Life in the Spirit Seminar*. Franklin, TN: Providence House, 2003. This resource is the manual for local church *Life in the Spirit* seminars. It also can be used for small group bible studies on the Holy Spirit from a Wesleyan perspective. www.aldersgaterenewal.org <http://www.aldersgaterenewal.org>.

Rutz, James. *Mega Shift*. Colorado Springs: Empowerment Press, 2005. This resource describes the miraculous work of God around the world through ordinary people and the house-church movement.

Stokes, Mack B. *The Holy Spirit in the Wesleyan Heritage*. Nashville: Abingdon Press, 1985, 1993. This is a standard work by a bishop of The United Methodist Church.

Synan, Vinson. *The Century of the Holy Spirit: 100 Years of Pentecostal and Charismatic Renewal*. Nashville: Thomas Nelson, 2001. This book traces the development of the Pentecostal, Charismatic, and Third Wave movements from 1901 to 2001 including references to Methodism.

Tuttle, Robert G. *Sanctity without Starch*. Anderson, IN: Bristol Books, 1992. A standard work by a United Methodist theologian within the Charismatic tradition.

ADOPTED 2008
READOPTED 2016
RESOLUTION #8015, 2012 *BOOK OF RESOLUTIONS*
RESOLUTION #8010, 2008 *BOOK OF RESOLUTIONS*

8016. Proper Use of Information Communication Technologies

We affirm that the right to communicate and to access information is a basic human right, essential to human dignity and to a just and democratic society.

Our understanding of communication is grounded in Scripture. God is a communicating God.

Christians believe that the creation of the world is rooted in the spoken Word of God.

God made all persons in the divine image. God created the world and all living things for relationship.

The Bible is the inspired Word of God about communication and a God who created the world and all living things for relationship.

The biblical account of the tower of Babel presents a classic example of the integral relationship between communication and being human.

This theme repeats itself in the story of Pentecost, the birthplace of the church. Being filled with the Holy Spirit and in communion with God and one another, the people of God spoke and heard the divine message of God in their own languages. We acknowledge that every right brings with it responsibilities. The whole community—owners, managers, and consumers—is responsible for the functioning of communication in society.

Christians have an obligation to advocate that mass media and communication technologies are operated to serve the public good rather than merely commercial interests.

Most peoples of the world have no access to even the most rudimentary communication technologies—telephones, radio—much less the digital, satellite, and other technologies that are rapidly expanding in the developing world.

These technologies allow their owners to manage information and resources at increasingly remote distances from the local cultures and economies affected. The instantaneous nature of global data transmission means that economic powers often have access to information before others do. The global-technological nature of the economy gives tremendous fiscal power to these same developed world and transnational interests.

This system works to advance the cause of the global market and promote commercial values aimed only at profit, often neglecting the aspects of communication and culture that promote the common good. Media companies, as producers and carriers of information, have a far-reaching effect on value formation.

Issues of justice in local and national development cannot be addressed without a consciousness of the role of communication, nor can any people do so without the tools with which to make their views known.

Information Communication Technologies (ICTs) offer enormous benefits. They enable global contact and, when made available for human uses and to address human needs, can significantly enhance life, development, and global consciousness.

Such uses will not become widespread unless concrete enabling steps are taken. Therefore the church's voice is crucial.

The church continues its mission and ministry amid this enormous revolution in communication.

The church quickly embraced the first communication revolution, the invention of the printing press, and used the printed word to disseminate the written word and to teach literacy to millions who were otherwise considered unfit to learn, empowering them to fully engage in the world.

The education of his neighbors was a matter close to John Wesley's heart, and his efforts gave many the education necessary to read and understand the gospel of Jesus Christ and to interpret the events of their world in the light of the gospel.

The Church carries a responsibility for helping its members achieve media literacy, not only to read and understand the gospel but also to discern from the flood of information an understanding of the events of our world today. Citizens cannot get responsible political information without media literacy. The current media revolution challenges all people to resist becoming mere consumers of messages that are created and controlled by a relatively small number of super-powerful transnational media corporations.

Media technologies have great potential to bind the world together, when not beholden entirely to transnational commercial interests.

Therefore, The United Methodist Church commits to:

A. Change of the Church

- Encourage leaders to preach and teach about the impact of media on the quality of life and values of individuals and society and to suggest ways congregations and individuals can both work with the positive forces and resist the negative.
- Use the available ICTs of local churches and other UMC entities to provide training in communication technologies to persons in their communities, particularly children, youth, and the poor, so that they might become active creators of story and culture rather than simply passive consumers.

- Assist members of United Methodist churches, our clergy, seminarians, and those who serve in the Church to become literate and committed to using ICTs for ministry and advocacy. As part of becoming aware of the power of the media, we particularly suggest the study of the Principles of Christian Communication developed by the World Association of Christian Communication.

- Encourage United Methodist institutions of higher education, particularly communication and theology faculties, to address societal communication issues.

- Reevaluate the church's work at every level of the United Methodist connection, including allocation of resources, decisions about programs, ministries, and missions, in light of the vital need to affirm the dignity of all persons by ensuring them equal opportunity to be heard, to have voice in the shaping of the church and of the world, and to communicate their story.

B. Change of Society

- Devote serious attention to the economic, political, and cultural forces that constrain the press and other communication media, challenging the use of communication as a force that supports the powerful, victimizes the powerless, and marginalizes minority opinion.

- Use ICTs for acts of love that liberate.

- We will work to preserve the right to communication for oppressed and persecuted communities, to oppose efforts to deny citizens the right of information, and to develop communication technologies that can be used to protect children from exploitation and psychological harm.

- Advocate for uses of media and communication technologies that promote peace, understanding, cooperation, and multiculturalism and oppose those uses of media that encourage violence, factionalism, militarism, and ethnic strife.

- Advocate for technologies that allow consumers to exclude unwanted commercial messages.

- Encourage the production and broadcast of independently owned media, particularly those of developing nations, which encompass artistic and entertainment programming as well as news and information.

C. Change of the World

- Develop methods to educate persons about the impor-tance of communication as a basic right for all persons and advocate for public policies that promote fair and equitable access to ICTs through educational, advocacy, and communications ministries.

- Identify and eliminate the hindrances to communication technologies with a view toward assisting those with-out those technologies to acquire, access, and use them. In this context the Church supports the development of open source software (General Public License systems). Its availability in the public domain helps overcome some of the digital divide between the developed and develop-ing countries.

- Work through annual conferences and the general boards and agencies with regional, national, and international bodies to provide support for such activities as:

  1. scholarships and training of persons, especially women, in developing countries in communica-tion policy issues and communication manage-ment in order that they may be fully prepared to participate in planning for the communica-tions policy, programs, and infrastructure in their respective nations;

  2. participation in communication efforts that offer alternatives to the mass media.

- Integrate sustained work for both domestic and global communications justice into current peace and justice advocacy agendas.

- Work through shareholder groups to persuade compa-nies to respect nations' attempts to protect their cultural sovereignty.

Global communications justice, in the end, is about communi-cation that is just and participatory, equitable and sustainable.

ADOPTED 2004
READOPTED 2008, 2016
RESOLUTION #8016, 2012 *BOOK OF RESOLUTIONS*
RESOLUTION #8011, 2008 *BOOK OF RESOLUTIONS*
RESOLUTION #362, 2004 *BOOK OF RESOLUTIONS*

8017. Cultural Competency Training

WHEREAS, The United Methodist Church is an increasingly diverse denomination that seeks to be the effective and inclusive body of Christ; and

WHEREAS, historical realities of social oppression and church practices that reflect and favor dominant cultures, frequently lead to a lack of effective participation in all levels of conference leadership; and

WHEREAS, cultural competency is a leadership skill that can be learned and The United Methodist Church has a responsibility to resource and support annual conference leadership in their responsibilities for the effective participation of all members and most especially those members of historically marginalized communities;

Therefore, be it resolved, the chairpersons of all annual conference boards, agencies, committees, and commissions, and the full membership of the Committee on Nominations and the Board of Laity are strongly urged to participate in cultural competency training; and the annual conference is encouraged to provide such cultural competency training in order to better ensure the effective and full participation of all committee members with the support and resourcing of the General Commission on Religion and Race; self-assessment tools are encouraged for use as part of the training and may include but not be limited to, the Intercultural Development Inventory [IDI] and the Intercultural Effectiveness Scale [IES];

Therefore, be it further resolved, such trainings ideally would take place each year within the first six months after annual conference and reports of the completion of trainings shared with the chairperson of the annual conference Commission on Religion and Race or its equivalent body; and the responsibility for encouraging that the actions and values of this resolution are implemented shall be that of the resident bishop and/or his or her designee.

ADOPTED 2012
RESOLUTION #8017, 2012 *BOOK OF RESOLUTIONS*

8018. Support for Clergywomen

WHEREAS, United Methodist churches have not always supported clergywomen; and

Whereas, clergywomen have gifts and graces that have enriched the witness of this denomination; and

Whereas, clergywomen have been supportive of United Methodist Men as expressed in scouting ministry and men's ministry,

Therefore, be it resolved, that United Methodist men be expected to welcome women to the pulpits of their churches, and

Be it further resolved, that clergywomen be invited to share in the studies and activities of local chapters of United Methodist Men.

ADOPTED 2012
RESOLUTION #8018, 2012 *BOOK OF RESOLUTIONS*

8019. Expanding Outreach to Men and Youth

Whereas, membership in The United Methodist Church has declined every year since the 1968 merger of The Methodist Church with The Evangelical United Brethren Church; and

Whereas, an ABC poll found that only 32 percent of American men attend church compared to 44 percent of American women, and 13 million more women than men attend church in the US; and

Whereas, 25 percent of married women attend church without their husbands; and

Whereas, a Gallup poll shows declining interest among young people with only 47 percent of young adults indicating that religion is important in their lives compared to 75 percent of persons over 75 years of age answering in the same manner; and

Whereas, only 10 percent of US churches maintain vibrant men's ministry programs, and most congregations struggle to find ways to minister to men and reach young people;

Therefore, be it resolved, that churches be encouraged to expand their ministries to all men in the church and the community. The group of men that meets monthly for study, worship, and fellowship serves an important purpose; but it should be only a fraction of a local church's effort to deepen the spiritual lives of men and to minister to men and young people without church homes; and

Be it further resolved, that all churches are encouraged to charter a United Methodist Men's organization. Pastors and superintendents are encouraged to utilize DVDs, online training, lay-speaking courses, the services of men's ministry specialists, and other resources provided by the General Commission on United Methodist Men to expand the ministry to all men within and beyond the congregation; and

Be it further resolved, that United Methodist churches be encouraged to charter Scout troops and to add other youth-serving ministries as a way to reach unchurched youth and as a way to minister to young people within their faith communities; and

Be it further resolved, that local churches encourage members to become scouting ministry specialists as a way to expand their ministries through youth-serving agencies; and

Be it further resolved, that local churches are encouraged to provide funding to enable one or more of their members to become men's ministry specialists and to utilize the services and resources of those already accredited as men's ministry specialists.

Be it further resolved, that one of the most effective means of making disciples takes place when men meet in weekly groups, using the "Class Meeting" model of Wesley as described in the book by Dr. Kevin Watson with the same title. These meetings can be either face-to-face or in an e-meeting format. Here men don't talk about a "historical" relationship with Jesus, but answer transformational questions as to where they have intersected with Christ in the last week.

ADOPTED 2012
AMENDED AND READOPTED 2016
RESOLUTION #8019, 2012 BOOK OF RESOLUTIONS

8020. Effectively Recruiting and Retaining Young Clergy of Color

Be it resolved, that The United Methodist Church in all of its United States annual conferences will actively recruit and retain clergy of color, with particular efforts to recruit and retain young clergy of color, using empirically supported, culturally relevant employment practices for African American, Native American, Latina/o, and Asian American/Pacific Islander clergy.

Be it further resolved, that each United States conference shall actively educate its clergy and lay members about institutional racism in accordance with ¶ 162A of the Social Principles of The United Methodist Church.

Be it further resolved, that each United States conference shall include a report of its racial diversity clergy recruitment and retention practices and progress in its annual conference journal.

ADOPTED 2016

8021. Functions of an Annual Conference COSROW or Related Committee

Focusing on a general call to make disciples of all people, annual conferences fulfill the responsibilities of the *Book of Discipline* ¶ 644 through various creative structures and forms of institutional support. When it comes to advocating for the full participation of women in the total life of the Church, some annual conferences maintain an independent Conference Commission on the Status and Role of Women, while others include this work within other structures established to address interrelated concerns. Such an adaptive and flexible model provides an opportunity for identifying how each annual conference will participate in the work of ensuring that disciple making at all levels of the Church is gender sensitive and inclusive, encouraging cooperation between all people with respect for the unique gifts of each person.

Conferences with active and effective existing ministries should continue these programs and regularly relate to the General Commission on the Status and Role of Women around their work and the status of women in the annual conference. The below recommended actions are not intended to replace already existing programs or effective ministries but to guide in planning regardless of the particular conference structure.

1. *Host annual gatherings for the support of women and education about pertinent issues* including but not limited to work-life balance, domestic violence, pay equity, leadership development, cooperative leadership, maternity and paternity leave, education, and other relevant topics.

2. *Discuss and encourage attention to issues of sexual ethics.* Find out if the annual conference has policies and procedures in place to address instances of sexual misconduct, including practices to care for victims and affected communities (e.g., through the use of response teams). Using the General Commission on the Status and Role of Women and umsexualethics.org <http://umsexualeth ics.org> as resources, sponsor education and training events and work to establish and strengthen policies aimed at fair process, healing, and reconciliation.

3. *Arrange meetings with conference leadership,* e.g., conference

lay leader, Board of Laity, Committee on Nominations, Board of Ordained Ministry, cabinet, and bishop. The purpose of these meetings may include recommending any strategies, programs, or resources for the continued effort to improve the full participation of women in the life of the church with awareness of the unique gifts and struggles brought on by race, ethnicity, age, ability, and status.

4. *Send at least two participants* to leadership development events sponsored by the General Commission on the Status and Role of Women including Do No Harm sexual ethics summit. Annual conferences are advised to provide as much support as possible to assist with travel costs and registration.

5. *Recruit and identify women* for recommendation to the annual conference Board of Laity, Committee on Nominations, and other leadership. This may take place by requesting recommendations from all local church lay leaders, district lay leaders, United Methodist Women and United Methodist Men district offices, and other persons in local leadership.

6. *Provide at least one monitoring, research, or other report on the status of women to the annual conference.* Highlight areas of progress and concern to guide strategic planning and future ministry development. The methods and goal of such reports should be established in consultation with conference leadership, General Commission on the Status and Role of Women staff, and women lay and clergy leaders of the conference.

7. *Use the General Commission on the Status and Role of Women as a regular resource.*

The General Commission on the Status and Role of Women will provide resources and recommendations for trainings for conference-wide events. Toolkits for meetings with conference leadership, fact sheets about women's issues, the most recent research, and information about the General Commission on the Status and Role of Women leadership convocation will be made available at gcsrw.org.

ADOPTED 2016

8031. By Water and the Spirit:
A United Methodist Understanding of Baptism

A Report of the Baptism Study Committee

Contemporary United Methodism is attempting to recover and revitalize its understanding of baptism. To do this, we must look to our heritage as Methodists and Evangelical United Brethren and, indeed, to the foundations of Christian tradition. Throughout our history, baptism has been viewed in diverse and even contradictory ways. An enriched understanding of baptism, restoring the Wesleyan blend of sacramental and evangelical aspects, will enable United Methodists to participate in the sacrament with renewed appreciation for this gift of God's grace.

Within the Methodist tradition, baptism has long been a subject of much concern, even controversy. John Wesley retained the sacramental theology which he received from his Anglican heritage. He taught that in baptism a child was cleansed of the guilt of original sin, initiated into the covenant with God, admitted into the church, made an heir of the divine kingdom, and spiritually born anew. He said that while baptism was neither essential to nor sufficient for salvation, it was the "ordinary means" that God designated for applying the benefits of the work of Christ in human lives.

On the other hand, although he affirmed the regenerating grace of infant baptism, he also insisted upon the necessity of adult conversion for those who have fallen from grace. A person who matures into moral accountability must respond to God's grace in repentance and faith. Without personal decision and commitment to Christ, the baptismal gift is rendered ineffective.

Baptism for Wesley, therefore, was a part of the lifelong process of salvation. He saw spiritual rebirth as a twofold experience in the normal process of Christian development—to be received through baptism in infancy and through commitment to Christ later in life. Salvation included both God's initiating activity of grace and a willing human response.

In its development in the United States, Methodism was unable to maintain this Wesleyan balance of sacramental and evangelical emphases. Access to the sacraments was limited during the late eighteenth and early nineteenth centuries when the Methodist movement was largely under the leadership of laypersons who were not authorized to administer them. On the American frontier where human ability and action were stressed, the revivalistic call for individual decision making, though important, was subject to exaggeration. The sacramental teachings of Wesley tended to be ignored. In this setting, while infant baptism continued not only to be practiced, but also to be vigorously defended, its significance became weakened and ambiguous. Later toward the end of the nineteenth century, the theological views of much of Methodism were influenced by a new set of ideas which had become dominant in American culture. These ideas included optimism about the progressive improvement of humankind and confidence in the social benefits of scientific discovery, technology, and education. Assumptions of original sin gave way before the assertion that human nature was essentially unspoiled. In this intellectual milieu, the old evangelical insistence upon conversion and spiritual rebirth seemed quaint and unnecessary.

Thus the creative Wesleyan synthesis of sacramentalism and evangelicalism was torn asunder and both its elements devalued. As a result, infant baptism was variously interpreted and often reduced to a ceremony of dedication. Adult baptism was sometimes interpreted as a profession of faith and public acknowledgment of God's grace, but was more often viewed simply as an act of joining the church. By the middle of the twentieth century, Methodism in general had ceased to understand baptism as authentically sacramental. Rather than an act of divine grace, it was seen as an expression of human choice.

Baptism was also a subject of concern and controversy in the Evangelical and United Brethren traditions that were brought together in 1946 in The Evangelical United Brethren Church. Their early pietistic revivalism, based upon belief in the availability of divine grace and the freedom of human choice, emphasized bringing people to salvation through Christian experience. In the late nineteenth and early twentieth centuries, both Evangelical and United Brethren theologians stressed the importance of baptism as integral to the proclamation of the gospel, as a rite initiating persons into the covenant community (paralleling circumcision), and as a sign of the new birth, that gracious divine act by which persons are redeemed from sin and reconciled to God. The former Evangelical Church consistently favored the baptism of infants. The United Brethren provided for the baptism of both infants and adults. Following the union of 1946, The Evangelical United Brethren Church adopted a ritual that included services of baptism for infants and adults, and also a newly created service for the dedication of infants that had little precedent in official rituals of either of the former churches.

The 1960-64 revision of *The Methodist Hymnal,* including rituals, gave denominational leaders an opportunity to begin to recover the sacramental nature of baptism in contemporary Methodism. The General Commission on Worship sounded this note quite explicitly in its introduction to the new ritual in 1964:

> In revising the Order for the Administration of Baptism, the Commission on Worship has endeavored to keep in mind that baptism is a sacrament, and to restore it to the Evangelical-Methodist concept set forth in our Articles of Religion. . . .
> Due recognition was taken of the critical reexamination of the theology of the Sacrament of Baptism which is currently taking place in ecumenical circles, and of its theological content and implications.

The commission provided a brief historical perspective demonstrating that the understanding of baptism as a sacrament had been weakened, if not discarded altogether, over the years. Many in the church regarded baptism, both of infants and adults, as a dedication rather than as a sacrament. The commission pointed out that in a dedication we make a gift of a life to God for God to accept, while in a sacrament God offers the gift of God's unfailing grace for us to accept. The 1964 revision of the ritual of the sacrament of baptism began to restore the rite to its original and historic meaning as a sacrament.

In the 1989 *United Methodist Hymnal,* the Services of the Baptismal Covenant I, II, and IV (taken from the 1984 official ritual of the denomination as printed in *The Book of Services*) continue this effort to reemphasize the historic significance of baptism. These rituals, in accenting the reality of sin and of regeneration, the initiating of divine grace, and the necessity of repentance and faith, are consistent with the Wesleyan combination of sacramentalism and evangelicalism.

United Methodism is not alone in the need to recover the significance of baptism nor in its work to do so. Other Christian communions are also reclaiming the importance of this sacrament for Christian faith and life. To reach the core of the meaning and practice of baptism, all have found themselves led back through the life of the church to the Apostolic Age. An ecumenical convergence has emerged from this effort, as can be seen in the widely acclaimed document *Baptism, Eucharist, and Ministry* (1982).

Established by the General Conference of 1988 and authorized to continue its work by the General Conference of 1992, the Committee to Study Baptism is participating in this process by offering a theological and functional understanding of baptism as embodied in the ritual of The United Methodist Church. In so doing, the broad spectrum of resources of Scripture, Christian tradition, and the Methodist-Evangelical United Brethren experience has been taken into account. The growing ecumenical consensus has assisted us in our thinking.

We Are Saved by God's Grace

The Human Condition. As told in the first chapters of Genesis, in creation God made human beings in the image of God—a relationship of intimacy, dependence, and trust. We are open to the indwelling presence of God and given freedom to work with God to accomplish the divine will and purpose for all of creation and history. To be human as God intended is to have loving fellowship with God and to reflect the divine nature in our lives as fully as possible.

Tragically, as Genesis 3 recounts, we are unfaithful to that relationship. The result is a thorough distortion of the image of God in us and the degrading of the whole of creation. Through prideful overreach or denial of our God-given responsibilities, we exalt our own will, invent our own values, and rebel against God. Our very being is dominated by an inherent inclination toward evil which has traditionally been called original sin. It is a universal human condition and affects all aspects of life. Because of our condition of sin, we are separated from God, alienated from one another, hostile to the natural world, and even at odds with our own best selves. Sin may be expressed as errant priorities, as deliberate wrongdoing, as apathy in the face of need, as cooperation with oppression and injustice. Evil is cosmic as well as personal; it afflicts both individuals and the institutions of our human society. The nature of sin is represented in Baptismal Covenants I, II, and IV in *The United Methodist Hymnal* by the phrases "the spiritual forces of wickedness" and "the evil powers of this world," as well as "your sin." Before God all persons are lost, helpless to save themselves, and in need of divine mercy and forgiveness.

The Divine Initiative of Grace. While we have turned from God, God has not abandoned us. Instead, God graciously and continuously seeks to restore us to that loving relationship for which we were created, to make us into the persons that God would have us be. To this end God acts preveniently, that is, before we are aware of it, reaching out to save humankind. The Old Testament records the story of God's acts in the history of the covenant community of Israel to work out the divine will and purpose. In the New Testament story, we learn that God came into this sinful world in the person of Jesus Christ to reveal all that the human mind can comprehend about who God is and who God would have us be. Through Christ's death and resurrection, the power of sin and death was overcome and we are set free to again be God's own people (1 Peter 2:9). Since God is the only initiator and source of grace, all grace is prevenient in that it precedes and enables any movement that we can make toward God. Grace brings us to an awareness of our sinful predicament and of our inability to save ourselves; grace motivates us to repentance and gives us the capacity to respond to divine love. In the words of the baptismal ritual: "All this is God's gift, offered to us without price" (*The United Methodist Hymnal,* page 33).

The Necessity of Faith for Salvation. Faith is both a gift of God and a human response to God. It is the ability and willingness to say "yes" to the divine offer of salvation. Faith is our awareness of our utter dependence upon God, the surrender of our selfish wills, the trusting reliance upon divine mercy. The candidate for baptism answers "I do" to the question "Do you confess Jesus Christ as your Savior, put your whole trust in his grace, and promise to serve him as your Lord . . . ?" (*The United Methodist Hymnal,* page 34). Our personal response of faith requires conversion in which we turn away from sin and turn instead to God. It entails a decision to commit our lives to the Lordship of Christ, an acceptance of the forgiveness of our sins, the death of our old selves, an entering into a new life of the Spirit-being born again (John 3:3-5; 2 Corinthians 5:17). All persons do not experience this spiritual rebirth in the same way. For some, there is a singular, radical moment of conversion. For others, conversion may be experienced as the dawning and growing realization that one has been constantly loved by God and has a personal reliance upon Christ.

John Wesley described his own experience by saying, "I felt my heart strangely warmed. I felt I did trust in Christ, Christ alone for salvation; and an assurance was given me that he had taken away my sins, even mine, and saved me from the law of sin and death."

The Means by Which God's Grace Comes to Us

Divine grace is made available and effective in human lives through a variety of means or "channels," as Wesley called them. While God is radically free to work in many ways, the church has been given by God the special responsibility and privilege of being the body of Christ which carries forth God's purpose of redeeming the world. Wesley recognized the church itself as a means of grace—a grace-filled and grace-sharing community of faithful people. United Methodism shares with other Protestant communions the understanding that the proclamation of the Word through preaching, teaching, and the life of the church is a primary means of God's grace. The origin and rapid growth of Methodism as a revival movement occurred largely through the medium of the proclaimed Gospel. John Wesley also emphasized the importance of prayer, fasting, Bible study, and meetings of persons for support and sharing.

Because God has created and is creating all that is, physical objects of creation can become the bearers of divine presence, power, and meaning, and thus become sacramental means of God's grace. Sacraments are effective means of God's presence mediated through the created world. God becoming incarnate in Jesus Christ is the supreme instance of this kind of divine action. Wesley viewed the sacraments as crucial means of grace and affirmed the Anglican teaching that "a sacrament is 'an outward sign of inward grace, and a means whereby we receive the same.'" Combining words, actions, and physical elements, sacraments are sign-acts that both express and convey God's grace and love. Baptism and the Lord's Supper are sacraments that were instituted or commanded by Christ in the Gospels.

United Methodists believe that these sign-acts are special means of grace. The ritual action of a sacrament does not merely point to God's presence in the world, but also participates in it and becomes a vehicle for conveying that reality. God's presence in the sacraments is real, but it must be accepted by human faith if it is to transform human lives. The sacraments do not convey grace either magically or irrevocably, but they are powerful channels through which God has chosen to make grace available to us. Wesley identified baptism as the initiatory sacrament by which we enter into the covenant with God and are admitted as members of Christ's church. He understood the Lord's Supper as nourishing and empowering the lives of Christians and strongly advocated frequent participation in it. The Wesleyan tradition has continued to practice and cherish the various means through which divine grace is made present to us.

Baptism and the Life of Faith

The New Testament records that Jesus was baptized by John (Matthew 3:13-17), and he commanded his disciples to teach and baptize in the name of the Father, Son, and Holy Spirit (Matthew 28:19). Baptism is grounded in the life, death, and resurrection of Jesus Christ; the grace which baptism makes available is that of the atonement of Christ which makes possible our reconciliation with God. Baptism involves dying to sin, newness of life, union with Christ, receiving the Holy Spirit, and incorporation into Christ's church. United Methodists affirm this understanding in their official documents of faith. Article XVII of the Articles of Religion (Methodist) calls baptism "a sign of regeneration or the new birth"; the Confession of Faith (EUB) states that baptism is "a representation of the new birth in Christ Jesus and a mark of Christian discipleship."

The Baptismal Covenant. In both the Old and New Testaments, God enters into covenant relationship with God's people. A covenant involves promises and responsibilities of both parties; it is instituted through a special ceremony and expressed by a distinguishing sign. By covenant God constituted a servant community of the people of Israel, promising to be their God and giving them the Law to make clear how they were to live. The circumcision of male infants is the sign of this covenant (Genesis 17:1-14; Exodus 24:1-12). In the death and resurrection of Jesus Christ, God fulfilled the prophecy of a new covenant and called forth the church as a servant community (Jeremiah 31:31-34; 1 Corinthians 11:23-26). The baptism of infants and adults, both male and female, is the sign of this covenant.

Therefore, United Methodists identify our ritual for baptism as "The Services of the Baptismal Covenant" (*The United Method-*

ist Hymnal, pages 32-54). In baptism the church declares that it is bound in covenant to God; through baptism new persons are initiated into that covenant. The covenant connects God, the community of faith, and the person being baptized; all three are essential to the fulfillment of the baptismal covenant. The faithful grace of God initiates the covenant relationship and enables the community and the person to respond with faith.

Baptism by Water and the Holy Spirit. Through the work of the Holy Spirit—the continuing presence of Christ on earth—the church is instituted to be the community of the new covenant. Within this community, baptism is by water and the Spirit (John 3:5; Acts 2:38). In God's work of salvation, the mystery of Christ's death and resurrection is inseparably linked with the gift of the Holy Spirit given on the Day of Pentecost (Acts 2). Likewise, participation in Christ's death and resurrection is inseparably linked with receiving the Spirit (Romans 6:1-11; 8:9-14). The Holy Spirit who is the power of creation (Genesis 1:2) is also the giver of new life. Working in the lives of people before, during, and after their baptisms, the Spirit is the effective agent of salvation. God bestows upon baptized persons the presence of the Holy Spirit, marks them with an identifying seal as God's own, and implants in their hearts the first installment of their inheritance as sons and daughters of God (2 Corinthians 1:21-22). It is through the Spirit that the life of faith is nourished until the final deliverance when they will enter into the fullness of salvation (Ephesians 1:13-14). Since the Apostolic Age, baptism by water and baptism of the Holy Spirit have been connected (Acts 19:17). Christians are baptized with both, sometimes by different sign-actions. Water is administered in the name of the triune God (specified in the ritual as Father, Son, and Holy Spirit) by an authorized person, and the Holy Spirit is invoked with the laying on of hands in the presence of the congregation. Water provides the central symbolism for baptism. The richness of its meaning for the Christian community is suggested in the baptismal liturgy which speaks of the waters of creation and the flood, the liberation of God's people by passage through the sea, the gift of water in the wilderness, and the passage through the Jordan River to the promised land. In baptism we identify ourselves with this people of God and join the community's journey toward God. The use of water in baptism also symbolizes cleansing from sin, death to old life, and rising to begin new life in Christ. In United Methodist tradition, the water of baptism may be administered by sprinkling, pouring, or immersion. However it is administered, water should be utilized with enough generosity to enhance our appreciation of its symbolic meanings.

The baptismal liturgy includes the biblical symbol of the anointing with the Holy Spirit—the laying on of hands with the optional use of oil. This anointing promises to the baptized person the power to live faithfully the kind of life that water baptism signifies. In the early centuries of the church, the laying on of hands usually followed immediately upon administration of the water and completed the ritual of membership. Because the laying on of hands was, in the Western church, an act to be performed only by a bishop, it was later separated from water baptism and came to be called confirmation (*see* pp. 720-722). In confirmation the Holy Spirit marked the baptized person as God's own and strengthened him or her for discipleship. In the worship life of the early church, the water and the anointing led directly to the celebration of the Lord's Supper as part of the service of initiation, regardless of the age of the baptized. The current rituals of the baptismal covenant rejoin these three elements into a unified service. Together these symbols point to, anticipate, and offer participation in the life of the community of faith as it embodies God's presence in the world.

Baptism as Incorporation into the Body of Christ. Christ constitutes the church as his Body by the power of the Holy Spirit (1 Corinthians 12:13, 27). The church draws new persons into itself as it seeks to remain faithful to its commission to proclaim and exemplify the gospel. Baptism is the sacrament of initiation and incorporation into the body of Christ. An infant, child, or adult who is baptized becomes a member of the catholic (universal) church, of the denomination, and of the local congregation (*see* pp. 720-722). Therefore, baptism is a rite of the whole church, which ordinarily requires the participation of the gathered, worshiping congregation. In a series of promises within the liturgy of baptism, the community affirms its own faith and pledges to act as spiritual mentor and support for the one who is baptized. Baptism is not merely an individualistic, private, or domestic occasion. When unusual but legitimate circumstances prevent a baptism from taking place in the midst of the gathered community during its regular worship, every effort should be made to assemble representatives of the congregation to participate in the celebration. Later, the baptism should be recognized in the public assembly of worship in order that the congregation may make its appropriate affirmations of commitment and responsibility.

Baptism brings us into union with Christ, with each other, and with the church in every time and place. Through this sign and seal of our common discipleship, our equality in Christ is made manifest (Galatians 3:27-28). We affirm that there is one baptism into Christ, celebrated as our basic bond of unity in the many communions that make up the body of Christ (Ephesians 4:4-6). The power of the Spirit in baptism does not depend upon the mode by which water is administered, the age or psychological disposition of the baptized person, or the character of the minister. It is God's grace that makes the sacrament whole. One baptism calls the various churches to overcome their divisions and visibly manifest their unity. Our oneness in Christ calls for mutual recognition of baptism in these communions as a means of expressing the unity that Christ intends (1 Corinthians 12:12-13).

Baptism as Forgiveness of Sin. In baptism God offers and we accept the forgiveness of our sin (Acts 2:38). With the pardoning of sin which has separated us from God, we are justified—freed from the guilt and penalty of sin and restored to right relationship with God. This reconciliation is made possible through the atonement of Christ and made real in our lives by the work of the Holy Spirit. We respond by confessing and repenting of our sin, and affirming our faith that Jesus Christ has accomplished all that is necessary for our salvation. Faith is the necessary condition for justification; in baptism, that faith is professed. God's forgiveness makes possible the renewal of our spiritual lives and our becoming new beings in Christ.

Baptism as New Life. Baptism is the sacramental sign of new life through and in Christ by the power of the Holy Spirit. Variously identified as regeneration, new birth, and being born again, this work of grace makes us into new spiritual creatures (2 Corinthians 5:17). We die to our old nature which was dominated by sin and enter into the very life of Christ who transforms us. Baptism is the means of entry into new life in Christ (John 3:5; Titus 3:5), but new birth may not always coincide with the moment of the administration of water or the laying on of hands. Our awareness and acceptance of our redemption by Christ and new life in him may vary throughout our lives. But, in whatever way the reality of the new birth is experienced, it carries out the promises God made to us in our baptism.

Baptism and Holy Living. New birth into life in Christ, which is signified by baptism, is the beginning of that process of growth in grace and holiness through which God brings us into closer relationship with Jesus Christ and shapes our lives increasingly into conformity with the divine will. Sanctification is a gift of the gracious presence of the Holy Spirit, a yielding to the Spirit's power, a deepening of our love for God and neighbor. Holiness of heart and life, in the Wesleyan tradition, always involves both personal and social holiness.

Baptism is the doorway to the sanctified life. The sacrament teaches us to live in the expectation of further gifts of God's grace. It initiates us into a community of faith that prays for holiness; it calls us to life lived in faithfulness to God's gift. Baptized believers and the community of faith are obligated to manifest to the world the new redeemed humanity which lives in loving relationship with God and strives to put an end to all human estrangements. There are no conditions of human life (including age or intellectual ability, race or nationality, gender or sexual identity, class or disability) that exclude persons from the sacrament of baptism. We strive for and look forward to the reign of God on earth, of which baptism is a sign. Baptism is fulfilled only when the believer and the church are wholly conformed to the image of Christ.

Baptism as God's Gift to Persons of Any Age. There is one baptism as there is one source of salvation—the gracious love of God. The baptizing of a person, whether as an infant or an adult, is a sign of God's saving grace. That grace—experienced by us as initiating, enabling, and empowering—is the same for all persons. All stand in need of it, and none can be saved without it. The difference between the baptism of adults and that of infants is that the Christian faith is consciously being professed by an adult who is baptized. A baptized infant comes to profess her or his faith later in life, after having been nurtured and taught by parent(s) or other responsible adults and the community of faith. Infant baptism is the prevailing practice in situations where children are born to believing parents and brought up in Christian homes and communities of faith. Adult baptism is the norm when the church is in a missionary situation, reaching out to persons in a culture which is indifferent or hostile to the faith. While the baptism of infants is appropriate for Christian families, the increasingly minority status of the church in contemporary society demands more attention to evangelizing, nurturing, and baptizing adult converts.

Infant baptism has been the historic practice of the overwhelming majority of the church throughout the Christian centuries. While the New Testament contains no explicit mandate, there is ample evidence for the baptism of infants in Scripture (Acts 2:38-41; 16:15, 33) and in early Christian doctrine and practice. Infant baptism rests firmly on the understanding that God prepares the way of faith before we request or even know that we need help (prevenient grace). The sacrament is a powerful expression of the reality that all persons come before God as no more than helpless infants, unable to do anything to save ourselves, dependent upon the grace of our loving God. The faithful covenant community of the church serves as a means of grace for those whose lives are impacted by its ministry. Through the church, God claims infants as well as adults to be participants in the gracious covenant of which baptism is the sign. This understanding of the workings of divine grace also applies to persons who for reasons of disabilities or other limitations are unable to answer for themselves the questions of the baptismal ritual. While we may not be able to comprehend how God works in their lives, our faith teaches us that God's grace is sufficient for their needs and, thus, they are appropriate recipients of baptism.

The church affirms that children being born into the brokenness of the world should receive the cleansing and renewing forgiveness of God no less than adults. The saving grace made available through Christ's atonement is the only hope of salvation for persons of any age. In baptism infants enter into a new life in Christ as children of God and members of the body of Christ. The baptism of an infant incorporates him or her into the community of faith and nurture, including membership in the local church. The baptism of infants is properly understood and valued if the child is loved and nurtured by the faithful worshiping church and by the child's own family. If a parent or sponsor (godparent) cannot or will not nurture the child in the faith, then baptism is to be postponed until Christian nurture is available. A child who dies without being baptized is received into the love and presence of God because the Spirit has worked in that child to bestow saving grace. If a child has been baptized but her or his family or sponsors do not faithfully nurture the child in the faith, the congregation has a particular responsibility for incorporating the child into its life.

Understanding the practice as an authentic expression of how God works in our lives, The United Methodist Church strongly advocates the baptism of infants within the faith community: "Because the redeeming love of God, revealed in Jesus Christ, extends to all persons and because Jesus explicitly included the children in his kingdom, the pastor of each charge shall earnestly exhort all Christian parents or guardians to present their children to the Lord in Baptism at an early age" (1992 *Book of Discipline*, ¶ 221). We affirm that while thanksgiving to God and dedication of parents to the task of Christian child-raising are aspects of infant baptism, the sacrament is primarily a gift of divine grace. Neither parents nor infants are the chief actors; baptism is an act of God in and through the church.

We respect the sincerity of parents who choose not to have their infants baptized, but we acknowledge that these views do not coincide with the Wesleyan understanding of the nature of the sacrament. The United Methodist Church does not accept either the idea that only believer's baptism is valid or the notion that the baptism of infants magically imparts salvation apart from active personal faith. Pastors are instructed by *The Book of Discipline* to explain our teaching clearly on these matters, so that parent(s) or sponsors might be free of misunderstandings.

The United Methodist Book of Worship contains "An Order of Thanksgiving for the Birth or Adoption of a Child" (pages 585-87), which may be recommended in situations where baptism is inappropriate, but parents wish to take responsibility publicly for the growth of the child in faith. It should be made clear that this rite is in no way equivalent to or a substitute for baptism. Neither is it an act of infant dedication. If the infant has not been baptized, the sacrament should be administered as soon as possible after the Order of Thanksgiving.

God's Faithfulness to the Baptismal Covenant. Since baptism is primarily an act of God in the church, the sacrament is to be received by an individual only once. This position is in accord with the historic teaching of the church universal, originating as early as the second century and having been recently reaffirmed ecumenically in *Baptism, Eucharist, and Ministry*.

The claim that baptism is unrepeatable rests on the steadfast faithfulness of God. God's initiative establishes the covenant of grace into which we are incorporated in baptism. By misusing our God-given freedom, we may live in neglect or defiance of that covenant, but we cannot destroy God's love for us. When we repent and return to God, the covenant does not need to be remade, because God has always remained faithful to it. What is needed is renewal of our commitment and reaffirmation of our side of the covenant.

God's gift of grace in the baptismal covenant does not save us apart from our human response of faith. Baptized persons may have many significant spiritual experiences, which they will desire to celebrate publicly in the worship life of the church. Such experiences may include defining moments of conversion, repentance of sin, gifts of the Spirit, deepening of commitment, changes in Christian vocation, important transitions in the life of discipleship. These occasions call not for repetition of baptism, but for reaffirmations of baptismal vows as a witness to the good news that while we may be unfaithful, God is not. Appropriate services for such events would be "Confirmation or Reaffirmation of Faith" (*see* Baptismal Covenant I in *The United Methodist Hymnal*) or "A Celebration of New Beginnings in Faith" (*The United Methodist Book of Worship*, pages 588-90).

Nurturing Persons in the Life of Faith. If persons are to be enabled to live faithfully the human side of the baptismal covenant, Christian nurture is essential. Christian nurture builds on baptism and is itself a means of grace. For infant baptism, an early step is instruction prior to baptism of parent(s) or sponsors in the gospel message, the meaning of the sacrament, and the responsibilities of a Christian home. The pastor has specific responsibility for this step (the 1992 *Book of Discipline*, ¶ 439.1*b*). Adults who are candidates for baptism need careful preparation for receiving this gift of grace and living out its meaning (the 1992 *Book of Discipline*, ¶ 216.1).

After baptism, the faithful church provides the nurture which makes possible a comprehensive and lifelong process of growing in grace. The content of this nurturing will be appropriate to the stages of life and maturity of faith of individuals. Christian nurture includes both cognitive learning and spiritual formation. A crucial goal is the bringing of persons to recognition of their need for salvation and their acceptance of God's gift in Jesus Christ. Those experiencing conversion and commitment to Christ are to profess their faith in a public ritual. They will need to be guided and supported throughout their lives of discipleship. Through its worship life, its Christian education programs, its spiritual growth emphases, its social action and mission, its examples of Christian discipleship, and its offering of the various means of grace, the church strives to shape persons into the image of Christ. Such nurturing enables Christians to live out the transforming potential of the grace of their baptism.

Profession of Christian Faith and Confirmation. The Christian life is a dynamic process of change and growth, marked at various points by celebrations in rituals of the saving grace of Christ. The Holy Spirit works in the lives of persons prior to their baptism, is at work in their baptism, and continues to work in their lives after their baptism. When persons recognize and accept this activity of the Holy Spirit, they respond with renewed faith and commitment.

In the early church, baptism, the laying on of hands, and Eucharist were a unified rite of initiation and new birth for Christians of all ages. During the Middle Ages in Western Europe, confirmation was separated from baptism in both time and theology. A misunderstanding developed of confirmation as completing baptism, with emphasis upon human vows and initiation into church membership. John Wesley did not recommend confirmation to his preachers or to the new Methodist Church in America. Since 1964 in the former Methodist Church, the first public profession of faith for those baptized as infants has been called Confirmation. In the former Evangelical United Brethren Church, there was no such rite until union with The Methodist Church in 1968. With the restoration of confirmation—as the laying on of hands—to the current baptismal ritual, it should be emphasized that confirmation is what the Holy Spirit does. Confirmation is a divine action, the work of the Spirit empowering a person "born through water and the Spirit" to "live as a faithful disciple of Jesus Christ."

An adult or youth preparing for baptism should be carefully instructed in its life-transforming significance and responsibilities. Such a person professes in the sacrament of baptism his or her faith in Jesus Christ and commitment to discipleship, is offered the gift of assurance, and is confirmed by the power of the Holy Spirit (*see* Baptismal Covenant I, sections 4, 11, and 12). No separate ritual of confirmation is needed for the believing person.

An infant who is baptized cannot make a personal profession of faith as a part of the sacrament. Therefore, as the young person is nurtured and matures so as to be able to respond to God's grace, conscious faith and intentional commitment are necessary. Such a person must come to claim the faith of the church proclaimed in baptism as her or his own faith. Deliberate preparation for this event focuses on the young person's self-understanding and appropriation of Christian doctrines, spiritual disciplines, and life of discipleship. It is a special time for experiencing divine grace and for consciously embracing one's Christian vocation as a part of the priesthood of all believers. Youth who were not baptized as infants share in the same period of preparation for profession of Christian faith. For them, it is nurture for baptism, for becoming members of the church, and for confirmation.

When persons who were baptized as infants are ready to profess their Christian faith, they participate in the service which United Methodism now calls Confirmation. This occasion is not an entrance into church membership, for this was accomplished through baptism. It is the first public affirmation of the grace of God in one's baptism and the acknowledgment of one's acceptance of that grace by faith. This moment includes all the elements of conversion-repentance of sin, surrender and death of self, trust in the saving grace of God, new life in Christ, and becoming an instrument of God's purpose in the world. The profession of Christian faith, to be celebrated in the midst of the worshiping congregation, should include the voicing of baptismal vows as a witness to faith and the opportunity to give testimony to personal Christian experience. Confirmation follows profession of the Christian faith as part of the same service. Confirmation is a dynamic action of the Holy Spirit that can be repeated. In confirmation the outpouring of the Holy Spirit is invoked to provide the one being confirmed with the power to live in the faith that he or she has professed. The basic meaning of confirmation is strengthening and making firm in Christian faith and life. The ritual action in confirmation is the laying on of hands as the sign of God's continuing gift of the grace of Pentecost. Historically, the person being confirmed was also anointed on the forehead with oil in the shape of a cross as a mark of the Spirit's work. The ritual of the baptismal covenant included in *The United Methodist Hymnal* makes clear that the first and primary confirming act of the Holy Spirit is in connection with and immediately follows baptism.

When a baptized person has professed her or his Christian faith and has been confirmed, that person enters more fully into the responsibilities and privileges of membership in the church. Just as infants are members of their human families, but are unable to participate in all aspects of family life, so baptized infants are members of the church—the family of faith—but are not yet capable of sharing everything involved in membership. For this reason, statistics of church membership are counts of professed/confirmed members rather than of all baptized members.

Reaffirmation of One's Profession of Christian Faith. The life of faith which baptized persons live is like a pilgrimage or journey. On this lifelong journey there are many challenges, changes, and chances. We engage life's experiences on our journey of faith as a part of the redeeming and sanctifying body of Christ. Ongoing Christian nurture teaches, shapes, and strengthens us to live ever more faithfully as we are open to the Spirit's revealing more and more of the way and will of God. As our appreciation of the good news of Jesus Christ deepens and our commitment to Christ's service becomes more profound, we seek occasions to celebrate. Like God's people through the ages, all Christians need to participate in acts of renewal within the covenant community. Such an opportunity is offered in every occasion of baptism when the congregation remembers and affirms the gracious work of God which baptism celebrates. "Baptismal Covenant IV" in *The United Methodist Hymnal* is a powerful ritual of reaffirmation which uses water in ways that remind us of our baptism. The historic "Covenant Renewal Service" and "Love Feast" can also be used for this purpose (*The United Methodist Book of Worship,* pages 288-94 and 581-84). Reaffirmation of faith is a human response to God's grace and therefore may be repeated at many points in our faith journey.

Baptism in Relation to Other Rites of the Church

The grace of God which claims us in our baptism is made available to us in many other ways and, especially, through other rites of the church.

Baptism and the Lord's Supper (Holy Communion or the Eucharist). Through baptism, persons are initiated into the church; by the Lord's Supper, the church is sustained in the life of faith. The services of the baptismal covenant appropriately conclude with Holy Communion, through which the union of the new member with the body of Christ is most fully expressed. Holy Communion is a sacred meal in which the community of faith, in the simple act of eating bread and drinking wine, proclaims and participates in all that God has done, is doing, and will continue to do for us in

Christ. In celebrating the Eucharist, we remember the grace given to us in our baptism and partake of the spiritual food necessary for sustaining and fulfilling the promises of salvation. Because the table at which we gather belongs to the Lord, it should be open to all who respond to Christ's love, regardless of age or church membership. The Wesleyan tradition has always recognized that Holy Communion may be an occasion for the reception of converting, justifying, and sanctifying grace. Unbaptized persons who receive communion should be counseled and nurtured toward baptism as soon as possible.

Baptism and Christian Ministry. Through baptism, God calls and commissions persons to the general ministry of all Christian believers (*see* 1992 *Book of Discipline,* ¶¶ 101-07). This ministry, in which we participate both individually and corporately, is the activity of discipleship. It is grounded upon the awareness that we have been called into a new relationship not only with God, but also with the world. The task of Christians is to embody the gospel and the church in the world. We exercise our calling as Christians by prayer, by witnessing to the good news of salvation in Christ, by caring for and serving other people, and by working toward reconciliation, justice, and peace, in the world. This is the universal priesthood of all believers.

From within this general ministry of all believers, God calls and the church authorizes some persons for the task of representative ministry (*see* 1992 *Book of Discipline,* ¶¶ 108-110). The vocation of those in representative ministry includes focusing, modeling, supervising, shepherding, enabling, and empowering the general ministry of the church. Their ordination to Word, Sacrament, and Order or consecration to diaconal ministries of service, justice, and love is grounded in the same baptism that commissions the general priesthood of all believers.

Baptism and Christian Marriage. In the ritual for marriage, the minister addresses the couple: "I ask you now, in the presence of God and these people, to declare your intention to enter into union with one another through the grace of Jesus Christ, who calls you into union with himself as acknowledged in your baptism" (*The United Methodist Hymnal,* page 865). Marriage is to be understood as a covenant of love and commitment with mutual promises and responsibilities. For the church, the marriage covenant is grounded in the covenant between God and God's people into which Christians enter in their baptism. The love and fidelity which are to characterize Christian marriage will be a witness to the gospel, and the couple are to "go to serve God and your neighbor in all that you do."

When ministers officiate at the marriage of a couple who are not both Christians, the ritual needs to be altered to protect the integrity of all involved.

Baptism and Christian Funeral. The Christian gospel is a message of death and resurrection, that of Christ and our own. Baptism signifies our dying and rising with Christ. As death no longer has dominion over Christ, we believe that if we have died with Christ we shall also live with him (Romans 6:8-9). As the liturgy of the "Service of Death and Resurrection" proclaims: "Dying, Christ destroyed our death. Rising, Christ restored our life. Christ will come again in glory. As in baptism *Name* put on Christ, so in Christ may *Name* be clothed with glory" (*The United Methodist Hymnal*, page 870).

If the deceased person was never baptized, the ritual needs to be amended in ways which continue to affirm the truths of the gospel, but are appropriate to the situation.

Committal of the deceased to God and the body to its final resting place recall the act of baptism and derive Christian meaning from God's baptismal covenant with us. We acknowledge the reality of death and the pain of loss, and we give thanks for the life that was lived and shared with us. We worship in the awareness that our gathering includes the whole communion of saints, visible and invisible, and that in Christ the ties of love unite the living and the dead.

Conclusion

Baptism is a crucial threshold that we cross on our journey in faith. But there are many others, including the final transition from death to life eternal. Through baptism we are incorporated into the ongoing history of Christ's mission, and we are identified and made participants in God's new history in Jesus Christ and the new age that Christ is bringing. We await the final moment of grace, when Christ comes in victory at the end of the age to bring all who are in Christ into the glory of that victory. Baptism has significance in time and gives meaning to the end of time. In it we have a vision of a world recreated and humanity transformed and exalted by God's presence. We are told that in this new heaven and new earth there will be no temple, for even our churches and services of worship will have had their time and ceased to be, in the presence of God, "the first and the last, the beginning and the end" (Revelation 22:13; see also chapters 21-22).

Until that day, we are charged by Christ to "go and make disciples of all nations, baptizing them in the name of the Father and of the Son and of the Holy Spirit, teaching them to obey everything that I've commanded you. Look, I myself will be with you every day until the end of this present age" (Matthew 28:19-20).

Baptism is at the heart of the gospel of grace and at the core of the church's mission. When we baptize we say what we understand as Christians about ourselves and our community: that we are loved into being by God, lost because of sin, but redeemed and saved in Jesus Christ to live new lives in anticipation of his coming again in glory. Baptism is an expression of God's love for the world, and the effects of baptism also express God's grace. As baptized people of God, we therefore respond with praise and thanksgiving, praying that God's will be done in our own lives:

> *We your people stand before you,*
>   *Water-washed and Spirit-born.*
> *By your grace, our lives we offer.*
>   *Re-create us; God, transform!*
> —Ruth Duck, "Wash, O God, Our Sons and Daughters"
> (*The United Methodist Hymnal*, 605); Used with permission.

ADOPTED 1996
READOPTED FOR 2005-2008
AND 2009-2012 QUADRENNIA
READOPTED FOR 2013-2016
AND 2017-2020 QUADRENNIA
RESOLUTION #8031, 2012 *BOOK OF RESOLUTIONS*
RESOLUTION #8013, 2008 *BOOK OF RESOLUTIONS*
RESOLUTION #343, 2004 *BOOK OF RESOLUTIONS*
RESOLUTION #320, 2000 *BOOK OF RESOLUTIONS*

8032. This Holy Mystery

WHEREAS, the 2000 General Conference directed the General Board of Discipleship in collaboration with the General Board of Higher Education and Ministry, the General Commission on Christian Unity and Interreligious Concerns (now the Office of Christian Unity and Interreligious Relationships), and the Council of Bishops, to develop a comprehensive interpretive document on the theology and practice of Holy Communion in United

Methodism and report their findings and recommendations to the 2004 General Conference; and

WHEREAS, in developing its report the Holy Communion Study Committee took intentional steps to heed our United Methodist heritage and history, remain sensitive to the ecumenical church, and hear the voices of United Methodists in the United States as well as in central conferences in the Philippines, Africa, and Europe; and

WHEREAS, the General Conference adopted This Holy Mystery: A United Methodist Understanding of Holy Communion in 2004 as an authoritative contemporary statement of its understanding of Holy Communion; and

WHEREAS, The United Methodist Church has used this document to strengthen our interpretation and practice of the Lord's Supper in its congregations and ministries and as a basis for deepening our ecumenical conversations and relationships with other denominations;

Therefore, be it resolved, that *This Holy Mystery: A United Methodist Understanding of Holy Communion* be continued in the *Book of Resolutions* as an official interpretive statement of theology and practice in The United Methodist Church for the next two quadrennia (2013-2016 and 2017-2020); and

Be it further resolved, that *This Holy Mystery: A United Methodist Understanding of Holy Communion* be used by the Council of Bishops, Church School Publications of The United Methodist Publishing House, the General Board of Higher Education and Ministry, and the General Board of Discipleship as a guide for teaching and formation of both clergy and laity in relation to Holy Communion; and

Be it further resolved, that *This Holy Mystery* be used by the Office of Christian Unity and Interreligious Relationships and the Council of Bishops in interpreting United Methodist understandings and practices in ecumenical dialogue; and

Be it further resolved, that the 2012 General Conference commend to the Church the principles, background, and practices in *This Holy Mystery: A United Methodist Understanding of Holy Communion* for the interpretation and use of the services of Word and Table in our hymnals and *The United Methodist Book of Worship*; and

Be it further resolved, that *This Holy Mystery* be published in the *Book of Resolutions*, and that the General Board of Discipleship offer it online and in study editions with a leader's guide.

This Holy Mystery:

A United Methodist Understanding
of Holy Communion

Part One: There Is More to the Mystery

The story is told of a little girl whose parents had taken her forward to receive Holy Communion. Disappointed with the small piece of bread she was given to dip in the cup, the child cried loudly, "I want more! I want more!" While embarrassing to her parents and amusing to the pastor and congregation, this little girl's cry accurately expresses the feelings of many contemporary United Methodist people. We want more! We want more than we are receiving from the sacrament of Holy Communion as it is practiced in our churches.

According to the results of a survey conducted by the General Board of Discipleship prior to the 2000 General Conference, there is a strong sense of the importance of Holy Communion in the life of individual Christians and of the church. Unfortunately, there is at least an equally strong sense of the absence of any meaningful understanding of Eucharistic theology and practice. United Methodists recognize that grace and spiritual power are available to them in the sacrament, but too often they do not feel enabled to receive these gifts and apply them in their lives. Many laypeople complain of sloppy practice, questionable theology, and lack of teaching and guidance. Both clergy and laity recognize the crucial need for better education of pastors in sacramental theology and practice. The concern for improved education is coupled with a call for accountability. Bishops, district superintendents, and other annual conference and general church authorities are urged to prepare their pastors better and to hold them accountable for their sacramental theology, practice, and teaching. Many of the people surveyed are plainly resentful of the lack of leadership they believe they are receiving in these areas. These results are troubling and must provoke the church to reexamination and recommitment.

These results are also exciting and challenging! They reveal a deep hunger for the riches of divine grace made available to us through Holy Communion, for real communion with Jesus Christ and with Christian people. They show that United Methodists want our faith to be enlivened and made more relevant to our daily lives. How can our church best respond to the wonderful hunger of its people for "this holy mystery" ("A Service of Word and Table I," *BOW*; page 39)?

United Methodists share with many other Christians an increased interest in the study and celebration of the sacraments. For the last several decades we have been actively seeking to recover and revitalize appreciation of Holy Baptism and Holy Communion. Our current services of the Baptismal Covenant and Word and Table are the fruit of a long process of development that began in the 1960's and culminated in their adoption by the 1984 General Conference and publication in *The United Methodist Hymnal* approved in 1988. The change in location of these sacramental rituals from the back to the front of the *Hymnal* is an intentional expression of their significance in the life of the community of faith. In 1996, the General Conference approved *By Water and the Spirit: A United Methodist Understanding of Baptism* as an official interpretive and teaching document for the church. *This Holy Mystery: A United Methodist Understanding of Holy Communion* is submitted to the 2004 General Conference with the same purpose. Both of these documents reflect United Methodism's efforts to reclaim its sacramental heritage and to be in accord with ecumenical movements in sacramental theology and practice.

This Holy Mystery is characterized by the effort to avoid rigidity on the one hand and indifference on the other. Neither extreme is true to our heritage nor faithful to the Spirit who leads the church forward in the work of making disciples living toward the new creation. The document is made up of two main parts. The expository introduction titled "Part One: There Is More to the Mystery" describes the document's development and provides grounding in historical tradition and sacramental theology. "Part Two: Christ Is Here: Experiencing the Mystery" is organized by principles. Under each principle, "Background" provides an explanation for the principle, while "Practice" provides guidelines for applying the principle. The principles make assertions that are truthful and doctrinally clear. They honor the historic and ecumenical center of the Christian church's theology and practice. The committee has endeavored to explain in the "Background" sections how the principles are rooted in the theology and practice of Christians past and present, particularly United Methodist Christians. In the

"Practice" sections we have applied the principles to contemporary sacramental practices of the church in the various contexts of United Methodism.

The church is always universal and particular, catholic and local, united and diverse. United Methodists vary geographically, racially, and culturally. *This Holy Mystery* invites United Methodists to share common understandings while allowing for appropriate, faithful applications. Some United Methodist practices differ from those of other Christian traditions. Being truthful about these differences recognizes our ties and responsibility to the wider church while claiming God's work in leading us to affirm distinctive understandings and practices. Both within our own United Methodist community and in fellowship with other traditions, we reject cavalier or arrogant attitudes. We seek to strengthen the bond of unity by "speaking the truth with love" (Ephesians 4:15) as, with humility and openness, we acknowledge our principles, explain our backgrounds, and affirm our practices.

Names of the Sacrament

Several terms naming the sacrament are used in past and present Christianity. In *This Holy Mystery* some are used more than others, but all are largely synonymous. *The Lord's Supper* reminds us that Jesus Christ is the host and that we participate at Christ's invitation. This title suggests the eating of a meal, sometimes called the Holy Meal, and makes us think of the meals that Jesus ate with various people both before his death and after his resurrection. The term *the Last Supper* is not appropriately used for the sacrament, but it does encourage us to remember the supper that Jesus ate with his disciples on the night when he was arrested. This emphasis is especially meaningful around Maundy Thursday. The early church appears to have referred to their celebrations as breaking bread (Acts 2:42).

The term *Holy Communion* invites us to focus on the self-giving of the Holy God, which makes the sacrament an occasion of grace, and on the holiness of our communion with God and one another. *Eucharist*, from the Greek word for thanksgiving, reminds us that the sacrament is thanksgiving to God for the gifts of creation and salvation. The term *Mass*, used by the Roman Catholic Church, derives from the Latin word *missio*, literally "sending forth," and indicates that this celebration brings the worship service to a close by sending forth the congregation with God's blessing to live as

God's people in the world. *The Divine Liturgy* is a name used mostly by churches in the tradition of Eastern Orthodoxy. All of these names refer to the same practice: the eating and drinking of consecrated bread and wine in the worshiping community.

Background

As early as the Emmaus experience on the day of Resurrection, recorded in Luke 24:13-35, Christians recognized the presence of Jesus Christ in the breaking of bread. The traditional Jewish practice of taking bread, blessing and thanking God, and breaking and sharing the bread took on new meaning for them. When followers of Christ gathered in Jesus' name, the breaking of bread and sharing of the cup was a means of remembering his life, death, and resurrection and of encountering the living Christ. They experienced afresh the presence of their risen Lord and received sustenance for their lives as disciples. As the church organized itself, this custom of Eucharist became the characteristic ritual of the community and the central act of its worship.

Over the centuries, various understandings and practices of Holy Communion have developed. Roman Catholicism teaches that the substance of bread and wine are changed (although not visibly) into the actual body and blood of Christ (sometimes called transubstantiation). Protestant Reformers in the sixteenth century rejected this teaching but had diverse ideas among themselves. Lutherans maintain that Christ's body and blood are truly present in and with the elements of bread and wine in the celebration (sometimes erroneously called corporeal presence or consubstantiation). Ulrich Zwingli, a Swiss reformer, taught that the Lord's Supper is a memorial or reminder of Christ's sacrifice, an affirmation of faith, and a sign of Christian fellowship. Although his name may be unfamiliar, Zwingli's views are widely shared today, especially within evangelical churches. Denominations in the Reformed tradition, following John Calvin, maintain that although Christ's body is in heaven, when Holy Communion is received with true faith, the power of the Holy Spirit nourishes those who partake. The Church of England affirmed a somewhat similar view in its Catechism and Articles of Religion. These understandings (stated here very simplistically) suggest the range of ideas that were available to John and Charles Wesley and the early Methodists.

United Methodist Heritage

Early Methodism

The Methodist movement in eighteenth-century England was an evangelical movement that included a revival of emphasis on the sacraments. The Wesleys recognized the power of God available in the Lord's Supper and urged their followers to draw on that power by frequent participation. The grace available in and through the sacrament was active in conviction, repentance and conversion, forgiveness, and sanctification. John Wesley described the Lord's Supper as "the grand channel whereby the grace of his Spirit was conveyed to the souls of all the children of God" ("Sermon on the Mount—Discourse Six," III.11). During the years in which Methodism was beginning and growing, Wesley himself communed an average of four to five times a week. His sermon "The Duty of Constant Communion" emphasizes the role of the sacrament in the lives of Christians in ways that are keenly meaningful today. The Wesley brothers wrote and published a collection of 166 *Hymns on the Lord's Supper*, which was used for meditation as well as for singing. The Wesleys understood and taught the multifaceted nature of the Lord's Supper. They wrote about love, grace, sacrifice, forgiveness, the presence of Christ, mystery, healing, nourishment, holiness, and pledge of heaven. They knew that Holy Communion is a powerful means through which divine grace is given to God's people. Our sacramental understandings and practices today are grounded in this heritage.

Evangelical and United Brethren Roots

The movements that developed into the Church of the United Brethren in Christ and the Evangelical Church began in the late eighteenth century and early nineteenth century in America. From the beginning, relationships between these groups and the Methodists were close and cordial. The beliefs and practices of the three churches were similar. Francis Asbury and Philip William Otterbein were close friends, and Otterbein participated in Asbury's consecration as a Methodist Episcopal bishop. Conversations about possible union began at least as early as 1809 and continued intermittently until the churches finally merged in 1968 to form The United Methodist Church.

Unfortunately, Otterbein and Martin Boehm—founders of the United Brethren—left little written material. The same is true of Evangelical founder Jacob Albright. Therefore, we can make comparatively few references to their theology and practice of Holy Communion. The *Journal* of Christian Newcomer (d. 1830), third United Brethren bishop, records so many occasions of administering and participating in the sacrament that its significance in the life of the church is apparent.

American Methodism

The early American Methodists, who began arriving in the 1760's, were at first able to receive the sacraments from Anglican churches of which they were considered a part. But the situation soon changed, and Methodists began to reject the English church. As rising tensions between the colonies and England led to the Revolutionary War, most Anglican priests left the country. By the mid 1770's, most Methodists had no access to the sacraments. The missionary preachers sent by John Wesley were laymen, as were the Americans who became preachers. They had no authority to baptize or to offer Holy Communion. Methodists were longing for the sacraments, and it was this need that motivated Wesley to take actions to provide ordained elders for America. In 1784, the Methodist Episcopal Church was created and some preachers were ordained. Still, the number of elders was too small to offer the sacraments regularly to the rapidly increasing number of Methodists. During the decades of the circuit riders, most Methodists were able to receive the Lord's Supper quarterly, at best, when the ordained elder came to their community. The camp meetings of the period were also sacramental occasions where large numbers of people communed. By the late nineteenth century and throughout the twentieth, many Methodist churches were served by ordained elders, but the habit of quarterly Holy Communion remained strong.

American Methodists considered Holy Communion a sacred and solemn event. The tone of the ritual was deeply penitential, calling upon people to repent and having less emphasis on celebration of God's grace. During the nineteenth and twentieth centuries the rich Wesleyan understandings of Eucharist were largely lost, and the sacrament became understood only as a memorial of the death of Christ. In many congregations attendance on Communion Sunday was low. Revitalization of the Lord's Supper in

Methodism, and in the Evangelical and United Brethren churches, started in the mid-twentieth century when the churches began to reclaim their sacramental heritage and create new rituals to express it.

As Methodism spread to other parts of the world, ritual and practice established in America were followed. Over the years, however, there have been certain influences from surrounding Christian traditions. These are to some extent reflected in Holy Communion practice in the central conferences (those beyond the geographic area of the United States).

Grace and the Means of Grace

Today Holy Communion must be viewed within the larger context of United Methodist theology. In accord with biblical and Christian teaching, we believe that we are sinners, constantly in need of divine grace. We believe that God is gracious and loving, always making available the grace we need. Grace is God's love toward us, God's free and undeserved gift. Several words describe how grace works in our lives. Prevenient grace is that which "comes before" anything we can do to help ourselves. Although we are all bound by our sinful nature, grace gives us enough freedom of will to be able to respond to God. In truth, all grace is prevenient—we cannot move toward God unless God has first moved toward us. God seeks us out, pursues us, calls us to come into the loving relationship that we were created to enjoy. Convicting grace makes us conscious of our sinfulness and urges us to repentance. Justifying grace forgives and puts us into right relationship with God. Sanctifying grace enables us to grow in holiness of life. Perfecting grace molds us into the image of Christ. The grace of God is made available to us through the life, death, and resurrection of Jesus Christ and works in our lives through the presence and power of the Holy Spirit.

While divine grace reaches us any time and in any way that God chooses, God has designated certain means or channels through which grace is most surely and immediately available. John Wesley expressed it this way: "By 'means of grace' I understand outward signs, words, or actions, ordained of God, and appointed for this end, to be the ordinary channels whereby he might convey to men [and women], preventing, justifying, or sanctifying grace" ("The Means of Grace," II.1). In the General Rules, Wesley listed these means of grace as, "The public worship of God. The ministry of the Word, either read or expounded. The Supper of the Lord. Family and private prayer. Searching the Scriptures. Fasting or abstinence" (*BOD*; ¶ 103; page 74). Elsewhere Wesley added Christian conferencing, by which he meant edifying conversation and meeting together in groups for nurture and accountability. These means are not to be understood as ways of earning salvation, for that is an unmerited gift. They are, rather, ways to receive, live in, and grow in divine grace. The Wesleyan tradition has continued to emphasize the practice of these means of grace throughout our salvation process.

The Theology of Sacraments

The Greek word used in the early church for sacrament is *mysterion*, usually translated "mystery." It indicates that through sacraments, God discloses things that are beyond human capacity to know through reason alone. In Latin the word used is *sacramentum*, which means a vow or promise. The sacraments were instituted by Christ and given to the church. Jesus Christ is himself the ultimate manifestation of a sacrament. In the coming of Jesus of Nazareth, God's nature and purpose were revealed and active through a human body. The Christian church is also sacramental. It was instituted to continue the work of Christ in redeeming the world. The church is Christ's body—the visible, material instrument through which Christ continues to be made known and the divine plan is fulfilled. Holy Baptism and Holy Communion have been chosen and designated by God as special means through which divine grace comes to us. Holy Baptism is the sacrament that initiates us into the body of Christ "through water and the Spirit" ("The Baptismal Covenant I," *UMH*; page 37). In baptism we receive our identity and mission as Christians. Holy Communion is the sacrament that sustains and nourishes us in our journey of salvation. In a sacrament, God uses tangible, material things as vehicles or instruments of grace. Wesley defines a sacrament, in accord with his Anglican tradition, as "an outward sign of inward grace, and a means whereby we receive the same" ("Means of Grace," II.1). Sacraments are sign-acts, which include words, actions, and physical elements. They both express and convey the gracious love of God. They make God's love both visible and effective. We might even say that sacraments are God's "show and tell," communicating with us in a way that we, in all our brokenness and limitations, can receive and experience God's grace.

The Meaning of Holy Communion

In the New Testament, at least six major ideas about Holy Communion are present: thanksgiving, fellowship, remembrance, sacrifice, action of the Holy Spirit, and eschatology. A brief look at each of these will help us better comprehend the meaning of the sacrament.

Holy Communion is Eucharist, an act of thanksgiving. The early Christians "broke bread in their homes and ate together with glad and sincere hearts, praising God and enjoying the favor of all the people" (Acts 2:46-47a, NIV). As we commune, we express joyful thanks for God's mighty acts throughout history—for creation, covenant, redemption, sanctification. The Great Thanksgiving ("A Service of Word and Table I," *UMH*; pages 9-10) is a recitation of this salvation history, culminating in the work of Jesus Christ and the ongoing work of the Holy Spirit. It conveys our gratitude for the goodness of God and God's unconditional love for us.

Holy Communion is the communion of the church—the gathered community of the faithful, both local and universal. While deeply meaningful to the individuals participating, the sacrament is much more than a personal event. The first person pronouns throughout the ritual are consistently plural—*we, us, our*. First Corinthians 10:17 explains that "since there is one loaf of bread, we who are many are one body, because we all share the one loaf of bread." "A Service of Word and Table I" uses this text as an explicit statement of Christian unity in the body of Christ (*UMH*; page 11). The sharing and bonding experienced at the Table exemplify the nature of the church and model the world as God would have it be.

Holy Communion is remembrance, commemoration, and memorial, but this remembrance is much more than simply intellectual recalling. "Do this in remembrance of me" (Luke 22:19; also see 1 Corinthians 11:24-25) is *anamnesis* (the biblical Greek word). This dynamic action becomes re-presentation of past gracious acts of God in the present, so powerfully as to make them truly present now. Christ is risen and is alive here and now, not just remembered for what was done in the past.

Holy Communion is a type of sacrifice. It is a re-presentation, not a repetition, of the sacrifice of Christ. Hebrews 9:26 makes clear that "he has now appeared once at the end of the ages to get rid of sin by sacrificing himself." Christ's atoning life, death, and resurrection make divine grace available to us. We also present ourselves as sacrifice in union with Christ (Romans 12:1; 1 Peter 2:5) to be used by God in the work of redemption, reconciliation, and justice. In the Great Thanksgiving, the church prays: "We offer ourselves in praise and thanksgiving as a holy and living sacrifice, in union with Christ's offering for us . . ." (*UMH*; page 10).

Holy Communion is a vehicle of God's grace through the action of the Holy Spirit (Acts 1:8), whose work is described in John 14:26: "The Companion, the Holy Spirit, whom the Father will send in my name, will teach you everything and will remind you of everything I told you." The *epiclesis* (biblical Greek meaning "calling upon") is the part of the Great Thanksgiving that calls the Spirit: "Pour out your Holy Spirit on us gathered here, and on these gifts of bread and wine." The church asks God to "make them be for us the body and blood of Christ, that we may be for the world the body of Christ, redeemed by his blood. By your Spirit make us one with Christ, one with each other, and one in ministry to all the world . . ." (*UMH*; page 10).

Holy Communion is eschatological, meaning that it has to do with the end of history, the outcome of God's purpose for the world—"Christ has died; Christ is risen; Christ will come again" (*UMH*; page 10). We commune not only with the faithful who are physically present but with the saints of the past who join us in the sacrament. To participate is to receive a foretaste of the future, a pledge of heaven "until Christ comes in final victory and we feast at his heavenly banquet" (*UMH*; page 10). Christ himself looked forward to this occasion and promised the disciples, "I won't drink wine again until that day when I drink it new with you in my Father's kingdom" (Matthew 26:29; Mark 14:25; also see Luke 22:18). When we eat and drink at the Table, we become partakers of the divine nature in this life and for life eternal (John 6:47-58; Revelation 3:20). We are anticipating the heavenly banquet celebrating God's victory over sin, evil, and death (Matthew 22:1-14; Revelation 19:9; 21:1-7). In the midst of the personal and systemic brokenness in which we live, we yearn for everlasting fellowship with Christ and ultimate fulfillment of the divine plan. Nourished by sacramental grace, we strive to be formed into the image of Christ and to be made instruments for transformation in the world.

Toward a Richer Sacramental Life

Like the little girl who was disappointed with what she received, United Methodist people are looking and hoping for something more in their Eucharistic experience. As we move toward a richer sacramental life, including weekly celebration of Holy Communion, we ask what spiritual benefits we receive from it. What do divine love and power do in and for us through our participation in the sacrament? The answers to this question involve forgiveness, nourishment, healing, transformation, ministry and mission, and eternal life.

We respond to the invitation to the Table by immediately confessing our personal and corporate sin, trusting that, "If we confess our sins, he is faithful and just to forgive us our sins and cleanse us from everything we've done wrong" (1 John 1:9). Our expression of repentance is answered by the absolution in which forgiveness is proclaimed: "In the name of Jesus Christ, you are forgiven!" (*UMH*; page 8). This assurance is God's gift to sinners, enabling us to continue striving to live faithfully. Wesley wrote, "The grace of God given herein confirms to us the pardon of our sins by enabling us to leave them" ("The Duty of Constant Communion," I.3).

We receive spiritual nourishment through Holy Communion. The Christian life is a journey, one that is challenging and arduous. To continue living faithfully and growing in holiness requires constant sustenance. Wesley wrote, "This is the food of our souls: This gives strength to perform our duty, and leads us on to perfection" ("The Duty of Constant Communion," I.3). God makes such sustenance available through the sacrament of Eucharist. In John 6:35, Jesus tells the crowd: "I am the bread of life. Whoever comes to me will never go hungry, and whoever believes in me will never be thirsty." As we return to the Table again and again, we are strengthened repeatedly. We go out empowered to live as disciples, reconcilers, and witnesses. In the words of the prayer after Communion, "Grant that we may go into the world in the strength of your Spirit, to give ourselves for others . . ." (*UMH*; page 11).

As we encounter Christ in Holy Communion and are repeatedly touched by divine grace, we are progressively shaped into Christ's image. All of this work is not done in a moment, no matter how dramatic an experience we may enjoy. It is, instead, a lifelong process through which God intends to shape us into people motivated by love, empowered and impassioned to do Christ's work in the world. The identity and ministry that God bestows on us in our baptism are fulfilled as we continue to be transformed into disciples who can respond to God's love by loving God and others (Romans 12:1-2).

Through Eucharist, we receive healing and are enabled to aid in the healing of others. *Sozo*, the root of the Greek word used in the New Testament for "healing," is also translated as "salvation" and "wholeness." Much of this healing is spiritual, but it also includes the healing of our thoughts and emotions, of our minds and bodies, of our attitudes and relationships. The grace received at the Table of the Lord can make us whole. As those who are being saved, we seek to bring healing to a broken world. *The United Methodist Book of Worship* describes this well: "Spiritual healing is God's work of offering persons balance, harmony, and wholeness of body, mind, spirit, and relationships through confession, forgiveness, and reconciliation. Through such healing, God works to bring about reconciliation between God and humanity, among individuals and communities, within each person, and between humanity and the rest of creation" (page 613). Holy Communion can be a powerful aspect of the services of healing provided in the *Book of Worship* (pages 615-623).

The grace we receive at the Lord's Table enables us to perform our ministry and mission, to continue his work in the world-the work of redemption, reconciliation, peace, and justice (2 Corinthians 5:17-21). As we commune, we become aware of the worth and the needs of other people and are reminded of our responsibility. We express the compassion of Christ through acts of caring and kindness toward those we encounter in our daily lives. In our baptism, we have vowed to "accept the freedom and power God gives [us] to resist evil, injustice, and oppression in whatever forms they present themselves" (*UMH*; page 34). But, in the words of the prayer of confession, we acknowledge our failures: "We have rebelled against your love, we have not loved our neighbors, and we have not heard the cry of the needy" (*UMH*; page 8). Remembering the revolutionary Jesus, we are impelled to challenge unjust practices and systems that perpetuate political, economic, and social inequity and discrimination (Matthew 23; Luke 4:16-21; 14:7-11).

The loving God who meets us at the Table gives us the gift of eternal life. Jesus' presentation of himself as the spiritual bread of life in John's Eucharistic account (6:25-58) makes clear the connection: "Whoever eats my flesh and drinks my blood has eternal life, and I will raise them up at the last day" (6:54). This life in union with Christ is life eternal. It is not only the promise of our being with Christ after physical death. It is also our being in dynamic loving relationship with Christ here and now. It is life that never ends because it is grounded in the everlasting love of God who comes to us in the sacraments.

> *O Thou who this mysterious bread*
> *didst in Emmaus break,*
> *return, herewith our souls to feed,*
> *and to thy followers speak.*
>
> Charles Wesley
> *The United Methodist Hymnal*, 613

Part Two: Christ Is Here: Experiencing the Mystery

The Presence of Christ

Principle:

Jesus Christ, who "is the light of God's glory and the imprint of God's being" (Hebrews 1:3), is truly present in Holy Communion. Through Jesus Christ and in the power of the Holy Spirit, God meets us at the Table. God, who has given the sacraments to the church, acts in and through Holy Communion. Christ is present through the community gathered in Jesus' name (Matthew 18:20), through the Word proclaimed and enacted, and through the elements of bread and wine shared (1 Corinthians 11:23-26). The divine presence is a living reality and can be experienced by participants; it is not a remembrance of the Last Supper and the Crucifixion only.

Background:

Christ's presence in the sacrament is a promise to the church and is not dependent upon recognition of this presence by individual members of the congregation. Holy Communion always offers grace. We are reminded of what God has done for us in the past, experience what God is doing now as we partake, and anticipate what God will do in the future work of salvation. "We await the final moment of grace, when Christ comes in victory at the end of the age to bring all who are in Christ into the glory of that victory" (*By Water and the Spirit: A United Methodist Understanding of Baptism*, in *BOR*; page 875), and we join in feasting at the heavenly banquet table (Luke 22:14-18; Revelation 19:9).

The Christian church has struggled through the centuries to understand just how Christ is present in the Eucharist. Arguments and divisions have occurred over the matter. The Wesleyan tradition affirms the reality of Christ's presence, although it does not claim to be able to explain it fully. John and Charles Wesley's 166 *Hymns on the Lord's Supper* are our richest resource for study in order to appreciate the Wesleyan understanding of the presence of Christ in the Eucharist. One of these hymns expresses well both the reality and the mystery: "O the Depth of Love Divine," stanzas 1 and 4 (*The United Methodist Hymnal*, 627):

> O the depth of love divine,
> the unfathomable grace!
> Who shall say how bread and wine
> God into us conveys!
> How the bread his flesh imparts,
> how the wine transmits his blood,
> fills his faithful people's hearts
> with all the life of God!
>
> Sure and real is the grace,
> the manner be unknown;
> only meet us in thy ways
> and perfect us in one.
> Let us taste the heavenly powers,
> Lord, we ask for nothing more.
> Thine to bless, 'tis only ours
> to wonder and adore.

Article XVI of The Articles of Religion of The Methodist Church describes the sacraments as "certain signs of grace, and God's good will toward us, by which he doth work invisibly in us, and doth not only quicken, but also strengthen and confirm, our faith in him" (*BOD*; page 63).

Article XVIII describes the Lord's Supper as "a sacrament of our redemption by Christ's death; insomuch that, to such as rightly, worthily, and with faith receive the same, the bread which we break is a partaking of the body of Christ; and likewise the cup of blessing is a partaking of the blood of Christ" (*BOD*; page 64). (*See* section "The Communion Elements" in this paper [p.761] for related material.)

Article VI of The Confession of Faith of The Evangelical United Brethren Church speaks similarly of the sacraments: "They are means of grace by which God works invisibly in us, quickening, strengthening and confirming our faith in him. . . . Those who rightly, worthily and in faith eat the broken bread and drink the blessed cup partake of the body and blood of Christ in a spiritual manner until he comes" (*BOD*; page 68).

United Methodists, along with other Christian traditions, have tried to provide clear and faithful interpretations of Christ's presence in the Holy Meal. Our tradition asserts the real, personal, living presence of Jesus Christ. For United Methodists, the Lord's Supper is anchored in the life of the historical Jesus of Nazareth, but is not primarily a remembrance or memorial. We do not embrace the medieval doctrine of transubstantiation, though we do believe that the elements are essential tangible means through which God works. We understand the divine presence in temporal and relational terms. In the Holy Meal of the church, the past, present, and future of the living Christ come together by the power of the Holy Spirit so that we may receive and embody Jesus Christ as God's saving gift for the whole world.

Practice:

Because Jesus Christ has promised to meet us there (1 Corinthians 11:23-26), Christians approach the Communion Table with desire and expectation, with awe and humility, and with celebration and gratitude.

Pastors need to be trained and formed (in seminary, course of study, licensing school, and continuing education) in the theology, spirituality, history, and tradition of the sacraments and in how to most effectively utilize proclamation, ritual, gestures, postures, and material signs in order to convey their full meaning.

Christ Is Calling You

Invitation to the Lord's Table

Principle:

The invitation to the Table comes from the risen and present Christ. Christ invites to his Table those who love him, repent of sin, and seek to live as Christian disciples. Holy Communion is a gift of God to the church and an act of the community of faith. By responding to this invitation we affirm and deepen our personal relationship with God through Jesus Christ and our commitment to membership and mission in the body of Christ.

Background:

The Invitation to Holy Communion in "A Service of Word and Table I" and "A Service of Word and Table II" proclaims, "Christ our Lord invites to his table all who love him, who earnestly repent of their sin and seek to live in peace with one another" (*UMH*; pages 7, 12). The more traditional wording in "A Service of Word and Table IV" invites, "Ye that do truly and earnestly repent of your sins, and are in love and charity with your neighbors, and intend to lead a new life, following the commandments of God, and walking from henceforth in his holy ways: Draw near with faith . . ." (*UMH*; page 26). "A Service of Word and Table V," for use with people who are sick or homebound, says that Christ invites "all who love him and seek to grow into his likeness" (*BOW*; page 51).

Practice:

When Holy Communion is celebrated, it is important to always begin with the words of Invitation, including Confession and Pardon. If these are omitted, all those present may not understand either the openness of the Table of the Lord or the expectation of repentance, forgiveness, healing, and entrance into new life in Christ.

The church community has a responsibility to provide ongoing age-appropriate nurture and education about the sacrament of Holy Communion to all its people. Those who are baptized as infants need continual teaching as they mature in faith. Those who come into membership later in life also need ongoing instruction about the significance of the sacrament in their personal faith journey and in the life of the congregation and larger Christian community. All who seek to live as Christian disciples need formation in sacramental spirituality.

Bishops, elders, deacons, pastors, Sunday school teachers, parents and guardians, seminary professors, and others have responsibility for faithfully teaching understandings and practices of Holy Communion. Teaching about the sacraments should emphasize United Methodist positions and practices but should also encourage knowledge of and respect for those of other Christian traditions.

Principle:

All who respond in faith to the invitation are to be welcomed. Holy Baptism normally precedes partaking of Holy Communion.

Holy Communion is a meal of the community who are in covenant relationship with God through Jesus Christ. As circumcision was the sign of the covenant between God and the Hebrew people, baptism is the sign of the new covenant (Genesis 17:9-14; Exodus 24:1-12; Jeremiah 31:31; Romans 6:1-11; Hebrews 9:15).

Background:

Baptism is the nonrepeatable rite of initiation into the body of Christ, while the Lord's Supper is the regularly-repeated celebration of communion of the body of Christ.

Beginning early in its history, the Christian church divided its worship services into the Liturgy of the Word, in which all participated, and the Liturgy of the Faithful, which was the celebration of Holy Communion. Those who were not yet baptized were dismissed before the celebration of the sacrament (*Didache* 9; Justin Martyr, *First Apology*, 66; *The Apostolic Constitutions*, Book VIII; *The Liturgy of St. Basil*).

John Wesley stressed that baptism is only a step in the salvation process and must be followed by justifying faith and personal commitment to Christ when one reaches an age of accountability. He referred to Holy Communion as "a converting ordinance" (Journal from November 1, 1739, to September 3, 1741; Friday, June 27, 1740). In eighteenth-century England, Wesley was addressing people who, for the most part, although baptized as infants and possessing some degree of faith had not yet experienced spiritual rebirth. Therefore, the conversion Wesley spoke of was transformation of lives and assurance of salvation.

Soon after the merger of The Evangelical Church and the United Brethren in Christ, The Evangelical United Brethren *Discipline* of 1947, reads, "We invite to [the Lord's Supper] all disciples of the Lord Jesus Christ who have confessed him before men and desire to serve him with sincere hearts" (page 447).

The United Methodist Book of Worship says, "All who intend to lead a Christian life, together with their children, are invited to receive the bread and cup. We have no tradition of refusing any who present themselves desiring to receive" (page 29). This statement means that in practice there are few, if any, circumstances in which a United Methodist pastor would refuse to serve the elements of Holy Communion to a person who comes forward to receive.

By Water and the Spirit affirms: "Because the table at which we gather belongs to the Lord, it should be open to all who respond to Christ's love, regardless of age or church membership. The Wesleyan tradition has always recognized that Holy Communion may be an occasion for the reception of converting, justifying, and sanctifying grace" (*BOR;* pages 873-74).

Practice:

Invitation to partake of Holy Communion offers an evangelical opportunity to bring people into a fuller living relationship with the body of Christ. As means of God's unmerited grace, Holy Baptism and Holy Communion are to be seen not as barriers but as pathways. Pastors and congregations must strive for a balance of welcome that is open and gracious and teaching that is clear and faithful to the fullness of discipleship.

Nonbaptized people who respond in faith to the invitation in our liturgy will be welcomed to the Table. They should receive teaching about Holy Baptism as the sacrament of entrance into the community of faith—needed only once by each individual—and Holy Communion as the sacrament of sustenance for the journey of faith and growth in holiness—needed and received frequently. "Unbaptized persons who receive communion should be counseled and nurtured toward baptism as soon as possible" (*By Water and the Spirit*, in *BOR;* page 874).

Principle:

No one will be turned away from the Table because of age or "mental, physical, developmental, and/or psychological and neurological" capacity (*BOD*, ¶ 162G) or because of any other condition that might limit his or her understanding or hinder his or her reception of the sacrament.

Background:

According to *By Water and the Spirit,*

"The services of the baptismal covenant appropriately conclude with Holy Communion, through which the union of the new member with the body of Christ is most fully expressed. Holy Communion is a sacred meal in which the community of faith, in the simple act of eating bread and drinking wine, proclaims and participates in all that God has done, is doing, and will continue to do for us in Christ. In celebrating the Eucharist, we remember the grace given to us in our baptism and partake of the spiritual food necessary for sustaining and fulfilling the promises of salvation" (*BOR*; page 873).

The concluding rubrics of the services make clear that this applies to people of all ages.

The theological basis for baptism of infants and people of varying abilities applies as well to their participation in Holy Communion:

"Through the church, God claims infants as well as adults to be participants in the gracious covenant of which baptism is the sign. This understanding of the workings of divine grace also applies to persons who for reasons of disabilities or other limitations are unable to answer for themselves the questions of the baptismal ritual. While we may not be able to comprehend how God works in their lives, our faith teaches us that God's grace is sufficient for their needs and, thus, they are appropriate recipients of baptism" ("By Water and the Spirit," in *BOR*; page 868).

Likewise, the grace given through Holy Communion is offered to the entire church, including those who are unable to respond for themselves. Children are members of the covenant community and participants in the Lord's Supper.

Practice:

Young children and people with handicapping or incapacitating conditions may need special consideration as the elements are served. Pastors and congregations should develop plans for providing assistance that maintains the dignity and affirms the worth of those receiving.

Children of all ages are welcome to the Table and are to be taught and led to interpret, appreciate, and participate in Holy Communion. Adults need training to help them explain the sacrament to children.

When worship spaces are constructed or renovated, attention needs to be given to providing physical access to the Communion Table for all.

Principle:

The Lord's Supper in a United Methodist congregation is open to members of other United Methodist congregations and to Christians from other traditions.

Background:

"A baptized or professing member of any local United Methodist church is a member of the global United Methodist connection and a member of the church universal" (*BOD*; ¶ 215).

The United Methodist Church recognizes that it is only one of the bodies that constitute the community of Christians. Despite our differences, all Christians are welcome at the Table of the Lord.

Practice:

As a part of the directions before the invitation, it is customary to announce that all Christians are welcome to participate in the sacrament in United Methodist congregations.

Response to the invitation is always voluntary, and care needs to be taken to ensure that no one feels pressured to participate or conspicuous for not doing so.

When Holy Communion is served as part of a service of Christian marriage or a service of death and resurrection, "It is our tradition to invite all Christians to the Lord's table, and the invitation should be extended to everyone present; but there should be no pressure that would embarrass those who for whatever reason do not choose to receive Holy Communion" (*BOW*; page 152). It is not appropriate for only the couple or family to commune.

The Issue of "Unworthiness"

Principle:

Any person who answers in faith the invitation "Christ our Lord invites to his table all who love him, who earnestly repent of their sin and seek to live in peace with one another" (*UMH*; page 7) is worthy through Christ to partake of Holy Communion. Christians come to the Lord's Table in gratitude for Christ's mercy toward sinners. We do not share in Communion because of our worthiness; no one is truly worthy. We come to the Eucharist out of our hunger to receive God's gracious love, to receive forgiveness and healing.

Background:

Some deeply committed United Methodist people who hesitate or even refuse to partake of Holy Communion do so because of their sense that they are unworthy. This problem is largely based upon misinterpretation and false fears. Within the United Methodist tradition, people who participate in the sacrament are assured of the forgiveness of their sins and of pardon through their participation in the Invitation and the Confession and Pardon.

Paul's words of warning in 1 Corinthians 11:27-32 have long been a source of confusion and concern. Some people are fearful of communing "in an unworthy manner" (NRSV) and, sometimes out of genuine Christian humility, believe that their participation would be improper. John Wesley addressed this problem in his sermon "The Duty of Constant Communion": "God offers you one of the greatest mercies on this side of heaven, and commands you to accept it. . . . You are unworthy to receive any mercy from God. But is that a reason for refusing all mercy? . . . Why do you not obey God's command? . . . What! unworthy to obey God?" (II.7-8).

Wesley went on to explain that unworthiness does not apply to the people who are to commune, but to the manner in which the consecrated elements are consumed: "Here is not a word said of being unworthy to eat and drink. Indeed he [Paul] does speak of eating and drinking unworthily; but that is quite a different thing. . . . In this very chapter we are told that by eating and drinking unworthily is meant, taking the holy Sacrament in such a rude and disorderly way, that one was 'hungry, and another drunken' [1 Corinthians 11:21]" (II.9).

First Corinthians 11:29 is a word of judgment against "those who eat and drink without correctly understanding the body." A footnote to this passage in *The New Oxford Annotated Bible* (NRSV) explains that this is a reference to "the community, one's relation to other Christians" (page 242). Paul is speaking against those who fail to recognize the church—the body of Christ—as a community of faith within which Christians relate to each other in love.

Practice:

Pastors and other leaders can alleviate most of these concerns about worthiness through patient counseling, faithful teaching, and prayers for healing. These efforts can be focused on study of the cited passage in First Corinthians, with clear explanation of what it meant in its first-century context and what it means today.

The Basic Pattern of Worship: A Service of Word and Table

Principle:

The complete pattern of Christian worship for the Lord's Day is Word and Table—the gospel is proclaimed in both Word and sacrament. Word and Table are not in competition; rather they complement each other so as to constitute a whole service of worship. Their separation diminishes the fullness of life in the Spirit offered to us through faith in Jesus Christ.

Background:

In *The United Methodist Book of Worship* (pages 13-14), the Basic Pattern of Worship is traced to its Jewish roots:

The Entrance and the Proclamation and Response—often called the Service of the Word or the Preaching Service—are a Christian adaptation of the ancient synagogue service. The Thanksgiving and Communion, commonly called the Lord's Supper or Holy Communion, is a Christian adaptation of Jewish worship at family meal tables. . . . Christians held an adapted synagogue service and broke bread when they gathered on the first day of the week (Acts 20:7).

The practice of the Christian church from its earliest years was weekly celebration of the Lord's Supper on the Lord's Day. The Didache, a source from the late first century or early second century says, "On every Lord's Day—his special day—come together and break bread and give thanks . . ." (14). Justin Martyr, writing around A.D. 150, relates, "And on the day called Sunday there is a meeting . . . bread is brought, and wine and water, and the president similarly sends up prayers and thanksgivings . . ." (Chapter 67). Most Christian traditions have continued this pattern.

John Wesley was highly critical of the infrequency of Holy Communion in the Church of England of his day. He exhorted his followers to practice "constant communion" because Christ had so commanded and because the spiritual benefits are so great ("The Duty of Constant Communion"). In his 1784 letter to American Methodists, Wesley counseled, "I also advise the elders to administer the supper of the Lord on every Lord's day" ("Letter to Dr. Coke, Mr. Asbury, and Our Brethren in North America").

For decades the scarcity of ordained pastors made it difficult if not impossible for churches in the Wesleyan tradition to observe the Lord's Supper as a part of regular Sunday worship. The custom of celebrating the sacrament at least quarterly, when an ordained elder was present, ensured the opportunity for regular if infrequent participation. With the introduction of new liturgical texts for the Lord's Supper in 1972, United Methodism has been recovering the fullness of Word and Table as the pattern for weekly worship on the Lord's Day.

The *Journal* of Christian Newcomer, third bishop of the United Brethren in Christ, is filled with references to frequent celebrations of Holy Communion. He rejoiced in the "sacramental festivals" that he led and in which he participated.

Recent theology and practice of worship stress both the proclamation of the gospel enacted through Holy Communion and the sacramental power of Christ's presence through preaching. Partaking of Holy Communion is a response to and continued participation in the Word that has been proclaimed. Those seeking to live as Christian disciples have constant need of the nourishment and sustenance made available through both the Word and the sacrament of Holy Communion.

Practice:

Congregations of The United Methodist Church are encouraged to move toward a richer sacramental life, including weekly celebration of the Lord's Supper at the services on the Lord's Day, as advocated by the general orders of Sunday worship in *The United Methodist Hymnal* and *The United Methodist Book of Worship*. The sacrament can also be celebrated appropriately on other occasions in the life of the church from the congregational to the denominational level. However, occasions of worship that might not always include Communion are revivals, services of daily praise and prayer, love feasts, and services on days other than Sunday.

Attention should be given to the special needs of churches whose pastoral leadership is neither ordained nor licensed. Cooperative parishes and ecumenical shared ministries (*BOD*; ¶¶ 206.2 and 207) may offer patterns through which such congregations could receive regular sacramental ministry.

The Gathered Community

The Whole Assembly

Principle:

The whole assembly actively celebrates Holy Communion. All who are baptized into the body of Christ Jesus become servants and ministers within that body, which is the church. The members are claimed by God as a royal priesthood, God's own people (1 Peter 2:9). The one body, drawn together by the one Spirit, is fully realized when all its many parts eat together in love and offer their lives in service at the Table of the Lord.

Background:

Those baptized are called "Christ's royal priesthood" in the United Methodist services of the Baptismal Covenant ("The Baptismal Covenant I," *BOW;* page 92). We are "royal" because we belong to Christ, the sovereign. As priests, each of us can have access to God without any human intermediary. This priesthood means, especially, that we are to be priests to each other as together we seek to live as Christians. The exchange of words of forgiveness between pastor and congregation is an example in the ritual of this role (*UMH;* page 8).

All Christians share in the ministry of the church. Our diverse abilities and callings are gifts from God that together form the unity of the body of Christ and carry out its mission (Romans 12:3-8; 1 Corinthians 12:4-30; Ephesians 4:1-16). There is no more powerful expression of this reality than the participation of the whole gathered community in the celebration of Eucharist.

Practice:

All in the congregation are participants in the ministry of offering praise and worship to God and in the servant work of mutual ministry. The terms "presiding minister" and "assisting minister" describe the work of those who lead and assist the congregation.

The Prayer of Great Thanksgiving

Principle:

The prayer of Great Thanksgiving is addressed to God, is prayed by the whole people, and is led by the presiding minister. The prayer is shaped by our Trinitarian understanding of the nature of God. It includes an introductory dialogue, thankful remembrance of God's mighty acts of creation and the salvation made possible through Jesus Christ, the institution of the Lord's Supper, invoking of the present work of the Holy Spirit, and concluding praise to the Trinity. The prayer recognizes the fullness of God's triune nature, expresses the offering of ourselves in response, and looks toward the joy of sharing in God's eventual victory over sin and death.

Background:

The Trinitarian structure is evident in the Great Thanksgiving in the Word and Table services of *The United Methodist Hymnal* (pages 6-16). Following the introductory exchange between presiding minister and people in the Great Thanksgiving, prayer is addressed to "Father [God] Almighty, creator of heaven and earth." Following the Sanctus ("Holy, holy, holy . . ."), the work of the second person of the Trinity is proclaimed: ". . . and blessed is your Son [Child] Jesus Christ." The presence and work of the Holy Spirit are invoked in the portion beginning "Pour out your Holy Spirit on us gathered here and on these gifts . . . ," words historically known as the *epiclesis*. Throughout the Great Thanksgiving the congregation prays actively but silently and speaks its responses aloud at designated points in the service.

In their *Hymns on the Lord's Supper*, John and Charles Wesley make clear that divine presence and power come into the Eucharistic experience through the action of the Holy Spirit. Hymn 72 in that collection is a good example:

Come, Holy Ghost, Thine influence shed,
And realize [make real] the sign;
Thy life infuse into the bread,
Thy power into the wine.
Effectual let the tokens prove,
And made, by heavenly art,
Fit channels to convey Thy love
To every faithful heart.

Biblical worship was expressed in gestures and bodily movements, including bowing (Micah 6:6), lifting the cup of salvation (Psalm 116:13), lifting hands (Psalm 141:2), clapping (Psalm 47:1), and dancing (Psalm 149:3). The Gospels tell of Jesus' characteristic actions at meals that include taking bread, blessing or giving thanks, breaking the bread, and giving the bread. In Luke, the disciples who walked with Jesus on the way to Emmaus without recognizing him had their eyes opened "after he took his seat at the table with them" and "he took the bread, blessed and broke it, and gave it to them" (Luke 24:30).

Practice:

The prayer of Great Thanksgiving includes the voices of both the presiding minister and the people. The congregation's responses, which may be spoken or sung, include adoration, acclamation, and affirmation.

The whole assembly might join in parts of the Great Thanksgiving that speak for them: (a) the memorial acclamation, beginning, "And so, in remembrance . . ."; (b) an expression of intention to serve the world, beginning, "Make them be for us . . ."; (c) the concluding doxology, beginning, "Through your Son Jesus Christ. . . ." Congregational responses of "Amen" are the affirmation by the people of what has been prayed.

Presiding at Holy Communion involves bodily action as well as verbal communication. Gestures evoke and lead physical and visual participation by the congregation and aid worshipers in recognizing that the action at the Lord's Table is more than reading a script. For the presiding ministers, such gestures may include making welcoming gestures with arms or hands during the Invitation, raising arms or hands to God in praise or supplication, opening arms and hands to indicate including the entire body of Christ, and holding arms and hands over the elements as blessing.

Different postures are appropriate at different points in the ritual. The presiding minister and those in the whole assembly who are physically able appropriately stand throughout the Great Thanksgiving (*BOW*; page 28). Those unable to stand might participate with other gestures of praise as they desire. Standing communicates an attitude of respect and reverence; kneeling and bowing signify humility and confession; hands raised and open express praise and receptivity. The sign of the cross affirms our baptismal identity and the centrality of the cross to our faith. The ancient biblical use of hands and arms in expressing prayer and thanksgiving to God (arms uplifted, called *orans*; see 1 Timothy 2:8) and other gestures are recommended in *The United Methodist Book of Worship*, pages 36-39 and 46-79.

The Community Extends Itself

Principle:

The Communion elements are consecrated and consumed in the context of the gathered congregation. The Table may be extended, in a timely manner, to include those unable to attend because of age, illness, or similar conditions. Laypeople may distribute the consecrated elements in the congregation and extend them to members who are unavoidably absent (*BOD*; ¶¶ 340.2.a and 1117.9). An elder or deacon should offer appropriate training, preparation, and supervision for this important task (¶ 340.2.a).

Background:

In his description of worship practices of the early church, second-century writer Justin Martyr noted that consecrated bread and wine were carried to Christians who were unable to attend the service (*First Apology*; 67).

"Since the earliest Christian times, communion has been brought as an extension of the congregation's worship to sick or homebound persons unable to attend congregational worship" (*BOW*; page 51).

Practice:

When Holy Communion is extended to those unable to attend, the liturgy should include the reading of the Scripture Lesson(s), the Invitation, Confession and Pardon, the Peace, the Lord's Prayer, distribution, and post-Communion prayer. Elders, deacons, and laity may use this liturgy. A prayer of Great Thanksgiving should not be repeated, since this service is an extension of the Communion service held earlier (*BOW*; page 51).

If Holy Communion is to be celebrated with people who are homebound on a day when the congregation has not gathered at Table, "A Service of Word and Table V" (*BOW*; pages 51-53), which includes the Great Thanksgiving, should be used by an elder or another who is authorized to preside.

The Lord's Supper is to be made available to people who are in hospitals and hospices; nursing, convalescent, and rehabilitation facilities; correctional and custodial institutions; or other situations that make it impossible for them to gather with the community of faith. If a person is unable to eat or drink, one or both of the elements may be touched to his or her lips.

Both "self-service" Communion, where people help themselves, and "drop-in" Communion, where the elements are available over a period of time, are contrary to the communal nature of the sacrament, which is the celebration of the gathered community of faith.

The Ritual of the Church

Principle:

As stewards of the gifts given by God to the church, pastors have a responsibility to uphold and use the texts for Word and Table of The United Methodist Church found in *The United Methodist Hymnal*; *Mil Voces Para Celebrar: Himnario Metodista*; *Come, Let Us Worship: The Korean-English United Methodist Hymnal*; *The United Methodist Book of Worship*; and other liturgical material approved by central conferences in accordance with the *Book of Discipline*, ¶ 544.13. These liturgies, arising from biblical, historical, and ecumenical sources, are expressions of the Christian faith and the worship of God.

Background:

Article XXII of The Articles of Religion of The Methodist Church affirms some diversity of "rites and ceremonies" but rebukes "whosoever, through his private judgment, willingly and purposely doth openly break the rites and ceremonies of the church" (*BOD*; page 65).

The *Book of Discipline* specifies in ¶ 1114.3 that "the ritual of the Church is that contained in *The United Methodist Hymnal* (1989), *The United Methodist Book of Worship* (1992), *Mil Voces Para Celebrar: Himnario Metodista* (1996), and *Come, Let Us Worship: The Korean-English United Methodist Hymnal* (2000)."

In the Order for the Ordination of Elders, candidates promise to "be loyal to The United Methodist Church, accepting its order, liturgy, doctrine, and discipline" (*BOW*; page 676).

The preface to "An Order of Sunday Worship Using the Basic Pattern" in *The United Methodist Book of Worship* (page 16) states,

"While the freedom and diversity of United Methodist worship are greater than can be represented by any single order of worship, United Methodists also affirm a heritage of order and the importance of the specific guidance and modeling that an order of worship provides. . . . Acts of worship that reflect racial, ethnic, regional, and local customs and heritages may be used appropriately throughout this order."

The ritual officially approved by The United Methodist Church represents the decisions of the church about the theology and practice of Holy Communion. This ritual expresses the unity of the universal church of Jesus Christ and exemplifies our connection within The United Methodist Church. It had its origin in the early Christian community and has evolved in the practice of the church through the centuries. Our ritual is in accord with those currently used in most Christian bodies.

At its best, United Methodist liturgy combines the order and beauty of established ritual with the vitality and freshness of creative expression. The richness of tradition developed through two thousand years of Christian history can be faithfully adapted for present times and situations.

Practice:

Bishops, pastors, and congregations are expected to use the services of Word and Table in the official United Methodist hymnals and books of worship. Knowledgeable use of these resources allows for a balance of flexibility to meet contextual needs and order that reflects our unity and connectional accountability.

"An Order of Sunday Worship Using the Basic Pattern" (*UMH*; pages 3-5) offers flexibility for response to the activity of the Holy Spirit as well as the specifics of events and settings. In attending to the season, day, or occasion, presiders may insert words of their own composition or selections taken from fuller ritual texts as indicated in "A Service of Word and Table II" and "A Service of Word and Table III." (See *UMH*, "A Service of Word and Table II," pages 12-15; "A Service of Word and Table III," pages 15-16; musical settings, pages 17-25.) Pastors using *Mil Voces Para Celebrar* or *Come, Let Us Worship* may apply these directions to the use of the respective rituals in those books. Material from different regions and cultures may also enrich our celebrations.

Pastors and congregations in ecumenical shared-ministry settings will necessarily need to incorporate and use the rituals of the denominations comprising those parishes in ways that are responsible and respectful, both of United Methodist understandings and practices and of those of the other traditions represented.

In accord with our commitments to the pursuit of Christian unity and seeking shared Communion, bishops, pastors, and congregations are encouraged to use the Word and Table ritual from other denominations. Such use is to be compatible with our Basic Pattern of Worship and with United Methodist liturgical and theological commitments.

Servants at the Table

Presiding Ministers: Elders and Licensed Local Pastors

Principle:

An ordained elder or a person authorized under the provisions of the *Book of Discipline* presides at all celebrations of Holy Communion.

Background:

In accord with the practice of the church throughout Christian history, God calls and the church sets apart certain people for leadership within the body of Christians. We believe that the Holy Spirit gives to such people the grace and gifts they need for leadership in obedience to their call. The meaning and purpose of ordination are described in ¶¶ 301-303 in the *Book of Discipline*.

Elders are ordained to a lifetime ministry of service, word, sacrament, and order (*BOD*; ¶ 332) and charged to "administer the sacraments of baptism and the Lord's Supper and all the other means of grace" (*BOD*; ¶ 340.2.a).

John Wesley drew a sharp distinction between the preaching ministry, which was open to lay men and women, and the priestly ministry of administering the sacraments, which was to be exercised only by those ordained as elders. Recounting the 1744 preachers' conference, Wesley wrote, "None of them dreamed, that the being called to preach gave them any right to administer sacraments. . . . 'You are to do that part of the work which we appoint.' But what work was this? Did we ever appoint you to administer sacraments; to exercise the priestly office? Such a design never entered into our mind; it was the farthest from our thoughts" ("The Ministerial Office"). Wesley insisted that there could be no sacramental ministry without ordination as elder. This conviction ultimately determined his decision to perform "extraordinary" ordinations himself.

"The authority of the ordained minister," according to *Baptism, Eucharist, and Ministry* (World Council of Churches, 1982), "is rooted in Jesus Christ who has received it from the Father (Matt. 28:18), and who confers it by the Holy Spirit through the act of ordination. This act takes place within a community which accords public recognition to a particular person" (page 22). Elders administer the sacraments as authorized representatives of the church.

Under the terms of the *Book of Discipline*, several groups of people are authorized to preside at Eucharist in the charges to which they are appointed. These include associate member deacons, deacons ordained under the provisions of the 1992 *Book of Discipline*, licensed local pastors, and commissioned ministers licensed for pastoral ministry (*BOD*; ¶¶ 315, 316, 339, 340). Some of these provisions have been in effect since 1976 in order to enable the sacraments to be served regularly in many small congregations that do not have elders as their pastors. The church continues to seek the best ways to meet this need and still uphold the historic linkage of ordination and administration of the sacraments.

Practice:

Bishops and district superintendents are elders who are assigned and appointed to exercise the ministry of superintending (*BOD*; ¶¶ 403 and 404) as an expression of the connectional nature of The United Methodist Church. To embody the connectional nature of the church and its sacramental life, a bishop or district superintendent who is present may be invited to preside at Holy Communion.

An elder or a person authorized under the provisions of the *Book of Discipline* presides at all celebrations of Holy Communion. While some portions of the order of worship may be led by others, an elder or authorized pastor leads the congregation in praying the Great Thanksgiving, in which the whole assembly takes an active role. (*See* the Sanctus, the memorial acclamation, and the Amen, all printed in bold type, in *UMH*, pages 9-10.)

Elders who are in extension ministries and retired elders may be asked to preside when they are needed in local churches or on other sacramental occasions. "All conference members who are elders in full connection, including those in extension ministries, shall be available and on call to administer the sacraments of baptism and the Lord's Supper as required by the *Discipline*

(¶ 340.2.a) and requested by the district superintendent of the district in which the appointment is held" (*BOD*; ¶ 344.3.a). Those in the Order of Elders are encouraged to make every effort to be available for presiding when Holy Communion is needed or desired.

All elders or deacons who are present may be invited to participate in leadership of the service, stand with the presider at the table, and assist in distributing the elements.

All who lead Holy Communion should be knowledgeable and prepared in Eucharistic theology, spirituality, and practice, including the roles of those assisting. This ministry is under the supervision of district superintendents and pastoral mentors (*BOD*; ¶ 316.4).

Assisting Ministers: Deacons and Laity

Principle:

Deacons are ordained to the ministry of word and service (*BOD*; ¶ 329) and charged to "give leadership in the Church's life" in, among other ways, "assisting the elders in the administration of the sacraments" and "in the congregation's mission to the world" (¶ 328).

Background:

"Within the church community, there are persons whose gifts, evidence of God's grace, and promise of future usefulness are affirmed by the community, and who respond to God's call by offering themselves in leadership as ordained ministers" (*BOD*; ¶ 301.2). Deacons, as well as elders, are ordained to the ministry of leadership in The United Methodist Church.

This ordination of a deacon is to a life of linking the church's worship to Christ's service in the world. In worship it is appropriate for deacons to lead, or recruit and support others to lead, those parts of the liturgy that manifest the connection between our worship and Christian witness in daily life.

Practice:

In continuity with historic and ecumenical practice (*Baptism, Eucharist, and Ministry*), the role of deacon in services of Word and Table appropriately includes reading the Gospel lesson; leading the concerns and prayers for the world, the church, and the needy; receiving the elements and preparing the table before the Great Thanksgiving; assisting the elder in serving the Communion elements; setting the table in order; and dismissing the people to serve before the elder offers God's blessing. Further, deacons have a significant role in preparing for the service by organizing, assembling the necessary elements and containers, and making assignments for other participants, including those taking the meal to those unable to attend. Deacons are designated to serve as links between the church and the world. Their ministry appropriately includes taking the consecrated elements from their congregations and serving them in their places of ministry.

Deacons need training and preparation for their diverse roles in Eucharistic ministry.

Principle:

All members of Christ's universal church are, through their baptism, called to share in the Eucharistic ministry that is committed to the whole church (*BOD*; ¶ 220). Lay people assist the presider in leading the whole congregation to celebrate the Lord's Supper.

Background:

In the section titled "The Ministry of All Christians," the *Book of Discipline* says, "All Christians are called through their baptism to this ministry of servanthood in the world to the glory of God and for human fulfillment" (¶ 125).

In depicting the church as a body of many parts, Paul declares in 1 Corinthians 12:7: "A demonstration of the Spirit is given to each person for the common good." This diversity of ministry requires cooperation within the body of Christ, since it is only through such cooperation that the body is complete (1 Corinthians 12:12-31). It is important for liturgical celebrations to embody the active participation of all those gathered, as a demonstration of the full ministry of the body of Christ in the world.

As each layperson fulfills his or her vital ministry in worship, some will be called to exercise various leadership roles. "The United Methodist tradition has recognized that laypersons as well as ordained persons are gifted and called by God to lead the Church. The servant leadership of these persons is essential to the mission and ministry of congregations" (¶ 132). The whole of Part III of the *Book of Discipline* elaborates on this idea.

Practice:

Pastors and other leaders facilitate the full and active engagement of the ministry of all laity in celebrations of Holy Communion. As part of this general liturgical ministry of all Christians, laypeople exercise leadership of worship by reading Scripture, leading prayers, preparing the table, providing and preparing the elements, distributing the elements, and helping with other parts of the service.

At the appropriate point in the service, laity representing the whole congregation may bring the elements forward to the Table as a part of the offering. The entire congregation responds in unison as indicated throughout the ritual. Laypeople may take the consecrated elements to members who are unable to attend the congregational celebration.

Laypeople need instruction and training for this leadership, under the supervision of pastors and deacons.

Setting the Table

The Holy Communion Table

Principle:

The people and leaders gather around the elements for Holy Communion. The place where the elements are set is the Holy Communion table.

Background:

In the Old Testament, sacrifice was offered on an altar. In the Gospel narratives of the Last Supper, Jesus "took his place at the table, and the apostles joined him" (Luke 22:14). Through time, the church increasingly understood the Eucharist as a repetition of Christ's sacrifice on the cross, and the Table came to be seen as an altar of sacrifice. It was moved against the wall of the sanctuary and priests stood before the altar, with their backs to the congregation, to offer sacrifice to God.

The more radical Protestant reformers abandoned altars, preferring simple tables and reenactment of the Last Supper of Jesus with his disciples. Others, including the Church of England, of which John Wesley was a priest, retained the altar against a wall.

A twentieth-century international liturgical renewal movement, expressed in the changes of the Second Vatican Council of the Roman Catholic Church, made major reforms in worship. These reforms included moving the table into an open space so that the priest could stand behind it, giving the assembly a sense of meeting around it. The United Methodist Church, along with many other mainline churches, adopted revised rituals that call for the presiding minister to stand behind the Lord's Table, facing the people, from the offertory through the breaking of the bread (*BOW*; page 36).

In a church building, the place where the elements are set is sometimes called the altar, but the terms *altar-table* and *Lord's Table* are preferable.

The rail that in some churches is located between the congregation and the chancel area, while not properly called the altar, is a sacred area for kneeling to receive Communion. People may also come to one or more stations where the elements are served and receive them standing, with an option of kneeling at the rail for prayer.

Practice:

In our churches, the Communion table is to be placed in such a way that the presider is able to stand behind it, facing the people, and the people can visually if not physically gather around it. The table should be high enough so that the presider does not need to stoop to handle the bread and cup. Adaptations may be necessary to facilitate gracious leadership.

While architectural integrity should be respected, it is important for churches to carefully adapt or renovate their worship spaces more fully to invite the people to participate in the Holy Meal. If "altars" are for all practical purposes immovable, then congregations should make provisions for creating a table suitable to the space so that the presiding minister may face the people and be closer to them.

The Communion Elements

Principle:

In accordance with the words of Christ and Christian tradition, the church uses bread in celebrations of Holy Communion.

Background:

Bread is used in both the Old and New Testaments to signify God's sustenance of human beings and the importance of our eating together. When God liberated the Hebrew people from slavery in Egypt, they carried their bread with them. The Jews have celebrated this exodus throughout the centuries as Passover. The provision of manna and the showbread (bread of the Presence) kept in the Tabernacle are examples of God's sustenance from the time of Israel's wandering in the wilderness (Exodus 16; 25:23-30). In the New Testament, Jesus shared meals frequently with his disciples and with others (Matthew 9:9-11 and similar passages). He fed the multitudes (Matthew 14:13-21 and parallels) and used bread to signify his identity and mission (John 6). On the eve of his crucifixion, Jesus ate the Last Supper with his disciples (Matthew 26:26-29 and parallels). After his resurrection, he broke bread with the travelers to Emmaus (Luke 24:13-35) and with his disciples on the seashore (John 21:9-14).

Practice:

It is appropriate that the bread eaten in Holy Communion both look and taste like bread. The use of a whole loaf best signifies the unity of the church as the body of Christ and, when it is broken and shared, our fellowship in that body (1 Corinthians 10:16-17).

Historical continuity with the practice of the universal church is important; however, worship planners should be sensitive to local situations. Bread may be made from any grain according to availability. In ecumenical and other settings, wafers may be an appropriate choice.

The loaf should be plain bread (no frostings, nuts, raisins, artificial coloring, or other additions). Leavened or unleavened bread is equally acceptable. In congregations where there are people with gluten allergies, gluten-free bread may be offered. The loaf broken at the table is to be the bread distributed to the people. As appropriate to the dignity of the occasion, care should be taken to avoid excessive crumbling of the bread and to remove large pieces that fall to the floor.

Principle:

In accordance with Scripture and Christian tradition, the historic and ecumenical church uses wine in celebrations of Holy Communion.

Background:

Throughout the Old Testament story of God's relationship with the Hebrew people, blood was the sign of covenant ratification (Exodus 12:12-28; 24:1-8). At his last meal with the disciples, Jesus spoke of the wine as his blood-the blood of the new covenant (Jeremiah 31:31-34) between God and God's people, made possible through Christ's death and resurrection (Revelation 5:9). Jesus also spoke of the wine as a sign of the heavenly banquet that he will celebrate with the church in the future (1 Corinthians 11:23-26; Matthew 26:26-29).

The juice of the red grape in a common cup represents the church's covenant with Christ, established through his atoning death (Hebrews 9:15-28; 13:20-21), and fulfills Christ's commands at the Last Supper (Matthew 26:27-29; Mark 14:23-24; Luke 22:19-20).

Roman Catholicism, Eastern Orthodoxy, and many Protestant denominations have always used wine in the Eucharist. During the movement against beverage alcohol in the late nineteenth century, the predecessor bodies of The United Methodist Church turned to the use of unfermented grape juice. This continues to be the position of the denomination (*BOR,* 2000; page 838). (The term *wine* is used in this document because of its biblical and historical antecedents, although United Methodists customarily serve unfermented grape juice in Holy Communion.)

The use of a common cup dates back to the Last Supper where Jesus takes a single cup of wine, blesses it, and gives it to the disciples. It is a powerful symbol of the unity of the body of Christ gathered at the Lord's Table.

Practice:

Variations may be necessary in cultural contexts where the juice of the grape is unavailable or prohibitively expensive.

A single cup or chalice may be used for intinction—dipping the bread into the wine—or for drinking. The use of a common chalice best represents Christian unity, but individual cups are used in many congregations. In these situations, unity can be effectively symbolized if each person's cup is filled from a pouring chalice.

Principle:

The consecrated elements are to be treated with reverent respect and appreciation as gifts of God's creation that have, in the words of the Great Thanksgiving, become "for us the body and blood of Christ" (*UMH*; page 10).

Background:

We do not worship the consecrated elements nor reserve them for adoration. We respect the elements because God is using them for holy purposes—reconstituting the assembly as the body of Christ, conveying grace, forgiving sin, foreshadowing heaven, and strengthening the faithful for the journey of salvation. Although they have undergone no substantive (physical) change, the elements have been consecrated—set apart for sacred use.

While, in the history of the church, reverence for the consecrated elements has sometimes led to superstition, proper respect for the elements helps Christians grow in authentic sacramental piety.

As Article XVIII of The Articles of Religion of the Methodist Church makes clear, United Methodism rejects any suggestion that the bread and wine used in Communion are transformed or transubstantiated into other substances:

"Transubstantiation, or the change of the substance of bread and wine in the Supper of our Lord, cannot be proved by Holy Writ, but is repugnant to the plain words of Scripture, overthroweth the nature of a sacrament, and hath given occasion to many superstitions. The body of Christ is given, taken, and eaten in the Supper, only after a heavenly and spiritual manner. And the mean whereby the body of Christ is received and eaten in the Supper is faith" (*BOD*; page 64).

(The United Methodist Church notes that the anti-Roman Catholic tone of Article XVIII reflects the "bitterly polemical" relationships of past centuries and "rejoice[s] in the positive contemporary relationships that are being developed . . . at levels both official and unofficial" [*BOR*; pages 272-273].)

The Book of Worship directs, "What is done with the remaining bread and wine should express our stewardship of God's gifts and our respect for the holy purpose they have served" (page 30).

Practice:

The practice of consecrating elements ahead of time for the convenience of the pastor not having to go to small or remote congregations, weekend camps, or other such occasions is inappropriate and contrary to our historic doctrine and understanding of how God's grace is made available in the sacrament (Article XVIII, The Articles of Religion, *BOD*; page 64). If authorized leadership is not available for celebrating the Lord's Supper, other worship services such as love feasts, agape meals, or baptismal reaffirmations are valid alternatives that avoid the misuse of Communion elements.

The consecrated elements of bread and wine are used for distribution to the sick and others who wish to commune but are unable to attend congregational worship. If any bread and wine remain, they should always be disposed of by (1) the pastor and/or others at the pastor's direction consuming them in a reverent manner following the service; (2) returning them to the earth by pouring (2 Samuel 23:16), burying, scattering, or burning.

Hygiene and Table Setting

Principle:

Those who prepare the elements and give them to the people are to demonstrate care that the bread and cup are administered so as to minimize contamination.

Background:

In administering the elements to the people, both perception and reality of hygiene are important. The people have justifiable health concerns that the signs of the body and blood of Christ given to them at the Holy Meal are handled carefully and with concern for hygiene.

This need for care and hygiene should be considered along with scientific studies that make it clear that those who partake in Holy Communion have no higher incidence of illness than those who do not.

Concern and planning are necessary in situations of serious illness and for accommodating at the Table those whose immune systems are compromised. The counsel of Romans 14 and 15 can guide our practice.

Practice:

Those who will prepare and serve the elements should wash their hands. This can be done simply and without creating an additional layer of ceremony in the service.

The piece of bread given should be sizeable enough to be a generous sign and to be able to be dipped in the cup without the fingers of the recipient dipping into the liquid.

Extending the Table

Holy Communion and Evangelism

Principle:

The Lord's Supper forms the church into a community of evangelism that reaches out to preach, teach, baptize, and make new disciples of Christ (Matthew 28:19-20).

Background:

Immediately after his account of the institution of the Lord's Supper in 1 Corinthians 11-12, Paul moves into an extended discussion of the body of Christ composed of many members whose gifts for ministry are diverse. Paul understood the sacrament of Holy Communion to form and shape the church for its mission of redeeming the world. In 2 Corinthians 5:16-6:10, he describes more fully "the ministry of reconciliation" that is the work of the church as "ambassadors for Christ."

United Methodists have inherited a tradition that emphasizes that spiritual benefits are not received for ourselves alone but also to prepare and propel us for the work of evangelism. In our prayer after Communion, we give thanks for what we have received and ask God to "grant that we may go into the world in the strength of your Spirit, to give ourselves for others" (*UMH*; page 11).

The *Book of Discipline* emphasizes the imperative of evangelism: "The people of God, who are the church made visible in the world, must convince the world of the reality of the gospel or leave it unconvinced. There can be no evasion or delegation of this responsibility; the church is either faithful as a witnessing and serving community, or it loses its vitality and its impact on an unbelieving world" (¶ 128).

Practice:

Through the grace received in continual participation in the Lord's Supper, the community of faith reaches beyond itself to proclaim and exemplify the good news of salvation in Jesus Christ.

In Christian education and congregational life, we teach about the significance and meaning of the sacraments so that the faithful appreciate their own spiritual journey and are empowered to be knowledgeable and hospitable guides to those who seek Christ.

As members of the congregation partake of the Lord's Supper, the bonds of love within are strengthened and the worshiping community is empowered to reach out in dynamic and meaningful ways to evangelize and to work for peace and justice.

Principle:

As followers of Jesus, who ate with sinners and reached out to the marginalized, the church must intentionally concern itself about those who are absent from Christ's Table—those who feel unworthy, the poor, the unconverted, victims of prejudice, and others who are oppressed or neglected.

Background:

One of the themes of the Gospels, most prominent in Luke, is Jesus' ongoing efforts to teach the disciples that God's love and favor are extended to all people, not just those of a certain ethnicity, status, economic or political standing, or gender. The Book of Acts records some of the attempts of the early Christian community to define its limits, and God's continued efforts to broaden its inclusiveness. Peter's vision in Acts 10 is a particularly dramatic example.

Early English Methodists were typically (with some notable exceptions) from the socioeconomic groups that we might today speak of as the working poor. Wesley realized that a community of people who lived according to his General Rules (*BOD*; pages 71-74) were inevitably going to rise in status. He preached fervently against the dangers of money and the spiritual weakness that often accompanies prosperity.

In "The Ministry of All Christians," the *Book of Discipline* asserts: "We are called to be faithful to the example of Jesus' ministry to all persons. Inclusiveness means openness, acceptance, and support that enables all persons to participate in the life of the Church, the community, and the world. Thus, inclusiveness denies every semblance of discrimination" (¶ 138).

Practice:

The church is to consciously identify and seek out those who feel unwelcome, even excluded, from its congregations and to invite them to become part of the body of Christ and join in its celebrations of Holy Communion.

Holy Communion and Ethical Christian Discipleship

Principle:

The sacraments are God's gifts to the gathered body of believers to form the church into Christ's body in ministry to the world. Through Holy Communion, the Holy Spirit works to shape our moral and ethical lives. In the ongoing process of conversion, we grow in personal and social holiness and are empowered to work for healing, compassion, reconciliation, justice, and peace.

Background:

The Old Testament prophets denounced the injustice and oppression that they saw around them. They proclaimed a God who acts in favor of the poor and powerless and calls God's people so to act. (Isaiah 1:16-17; 58:6-9; Amos 2:6-8; 5:11-15, 21-24; and Micah 6:6-8 are among a multitude of such passages.) When Jesus began his public ministry, he announced his mission: "The Spirit of the Lord is upon me, because the Lord has anointed me. He has sent me to preach good news to the poor, to proclaim release to the prisoners and recovery of sight to the blind, to liberate the oppressed, and to proclaim the year of the Lord's favor" (Luke 4:18-19; see also vv. 16-21). He associated with those who were stigmatized and despised. Much of his teaching addressed economic and social inequality. Following his example, the early Christian community tried to care for the needs of all people (Acts 4:32-35; James 1:27; 2:14-17).

The United Methodist Church has a heritage from John Wesley in which ethical discipleship was inextricably related to sacramental worship. From concern by the Holy Club for the imprisoned, through care of the sick by the societies, to Wesley's own lifelong giving away of most of his money, the early Wesleyan movement sought to ease the suffering of the needy. Wesley made the linkage explicit when he wrote, "The Gospel of Christ knows no religion but social, no holiness, but social holiness" (Preface to *Hymns and Sacred Poems*). Collection at the Lord's Supper of alms to be given to the poor is a historic practice that many congregations in our tradition continue.

By the early twentieth century, Methodists had begun to realize that holy living meant even more than acts of charity. Beginning with the Social Creed, American Methodists started to point out injustices caused by economic, social, and political structures and to call for the reform of such structures. The Social Principles in the *Book of Discipline* and the General Conference positions recorded in the *Book of Resolutions* show ongoing response to these concerns.

In carrying out our mission to make disciples of Jesus Christ, *The Book of Discipline* stipulates that the church is to "send persons into the world to live lovingly and justly as servants of Christ by healing the sick, feeding the hungry, caring for the stranger, freeing the oppressed, being and becoming a compassionate, caring presence, and working to develop social structures that are consistent with the gospel" (¶ 122).

Those who partake of Holy Communion are sent from the Table to be in ministry as Christ's presence in the world. God's people are sent to work compassionately for healing, reconciliation, justice, and peace. Such work requires prophetic, subversive actions: "renounc[ing] the spiritual forces of wickedness, reject[ing] the evil powers of this world, . . . accept[ing] the freedom and power God gives . . . to resist evil, injustice, and oppression in whatever forms they present themselves" (vows from the services of the Baptismal Covenant, *BOW*; for example page 88), claiming and making real the victory of the risen Christ over all evil, sin, and death. Such faithful living in the power of the Holy Spirit answers the prayer in the Great Thanksgiving "that we may be for the world the body of Christ" and the petition "your kingdom come, your will be done" in the Lord's Prayer (*UMH*; page 10). Celebrations of Holy Communion are, therefore, a foretaste of the realm of God, when God's future breaks into our present world. Here the church enacts the words of Jesus, "People will come from east and west, north and south, and sit down to eat in God's kingdom" (Luke 13:29).

Practice:

Holy Communion is to be conducted in ways that make apparent the inherent link between the Table and holy living, both individual and corporate. Participation in the Eucharist bears fruit in the world in attitudes and actions of personal and social holiness.

Communing with others in our congregations is a sign of community and mutual love between Christians throughout the church universal. The church must offer to the world a model of genuine community grounded in God's deep love for every person. As we eat and drink, we are motivated to act compassionately for those whose physical, emotional, and spiritual needs are unmet.

Receiving the bread and wine as products of divine creation reminds us of our duties of stewardship of the natural environment in a time when destruction and pollution imperil the earth and unjust distribution of the planet's resources destroys the hopes and lives of millions.

As we gratefully receive God's abundant grace, we are challenged to accept fully our responsibility and accountability for renewal of the social order, liberation for the oppressed, and the coming of the realm of God.

Holy Communion and the Unity of the Church

Principle:

Holy Communion expresses our oneness in the body of Christ, anticipates Jesus' invitation to feast at the heavenly banquet, and calls us to strive for the visible unity of the church.

Background:

In its Constitution, The United Methodist Church affirms its ecumenical commitment: "As part of the church universal, The United Methodist Church believes that the Lord of the church is calling Christians everywhere to strive toward unity; and therefore it will seek, and work for, unity at all levels of church life" (*BOD*; ¶ 6).

In "Our Doctrinal Heritage" in the *Book of Discipline* (pages 41-43), the church affirms:

"United Methodists share a common heritage with Christians of every age and nation. This heritage is grounded in the apostolic witness to Jesus Christ as Savior and Lord, which is the source and measure of all valid Christian teaching. . . . With Christians of other communions we confess belief in the triune God—Father, Son, and Holy Spirit. This confession embraces the biblical witness to God's activity in creation, encompasses God's gracious self-involvement in the dramas of history, and anticipates the consummation of God's reign."

In the quest for greater visible unity, United Methodism has undertaken numerous concrete actions that express its commitment and promote ecumenical sharing:

1. Since the 1960's, the church has been involved with partners through Churches Uniting in Christ, formerly called the Consultation on Church Union. Throughout most of that history United Methodists have joined the partner churches in Holy Communion using liturgy approved by those churches for celebration together.

2. United Methodists across the world have entered into ecumenical agreements enhancing the unity of the church through recognition and reconciliation of ministries and sacraments.

3. Ecumenical representatives have been invited and encouraged to participate in United Methodist services of Holy Communion.

4. United Methodists have participated in the Eucharist services of other traditions when invited to do so, as an affirmation and reflection of our commitment to the church universal.

Baptism, Eucharist, and Ministry affirms the significance of the sacrament for all Christians:

It is in the Eucharist that the community of God's people is fully manifested. Eucharistic celebrations always have to do with the whole Church, and the whole Church is involved in each local Eucharistic celebration. In so far as a church claims to be a manifestation of the whole Church, it will take care to order its own life in ways which take seriously the interests and concerns of other churches (page 14).

For churches such as the Orthodox and Roman Catholic, sharing the Eucharist between churches that are not in full agreement with one another is unacceptable because the Eucharist is itself a sign that unity and full agreement have been achieved. For other churches, including The United Methodist Church, the Eucharist can be a means to express the unity in Christ that already exists as a gift from God in spite of our failure to manifest it.

Practice:

United Methodists are encouraged to continue participating in ecumenical services that include Holy Communion. Special care is to be given to the use of commonly approved texts or the development of liturgy that reflects the beliefs and practices of the different traditions. If bishops or superintendents are present, it is appropriate for them to be invited to preside.

Church members can practice hospitality by participating in each others' liturgies with attitudes of respect and openness to learning. United Methodists are encouraged to receive Communion in other churches when they are invited to do so.

Churches need to address, within official dialogues, the theological barriers to full Eucharistic sharing. Materials already available from the official dialogues shall be part of the study resources of the denomination.

United Methodists need to study and work to answer questions that are critical to ecumenical conversation and sensitive to ecumenical concerns—the presence of Christ ("real presence"), frequency of celebration, who presides at the Table, use of grape juice, and baptism in relation to Eucharist, among others.

Principle:

United Methodists enter into the ecumenical conversation about Eucharist grounded in several historic sources of authority and relate most authentically to other Christian bodies as we remain faithful to these sources.

Background:

Most prominent among United Methodism's sources of authority are the Scriptures of the Old and New Testaments; the hymns and writings of John and Charles Wesley (especially the Standard Sermons, the General Rules, and *Explanatory Notes Upon the New Testament*); the Constitution, Articles of Religion, Confession of Faith, and other doctrinal standards; the writings and traditions emerging from the evangelical experience, through the Wesleyan, Evangelical, and United Brethren movements; and current ecumenical developments and statements that have had United Methodist involvement, especially multilateral and bilateral agreements, some of which have been approved by the World Methodist Council and/or the General Conference.

"Our Doctrinal Heritage" points out some distinctive aspects of the United Methodist tradition:

"Although Wesley shared with many other Christians a belief in grace, justification, assurance, and sanctification, he combined them in a powerful manner to create distinctive emphases for living the full Christian life. The Evangelical United Brethren tradition, particularly as expressed by Phillip William Otterbein from a Reformed background, gave similar distinctive emphases.

"Grace pervades our understanding of Christian faith and life. By grace we mean the undeserved, unmerited, and loving action of God in human existence through the ever-present Holy Spirit. While the grace of God is undivided, it precedes salvation as 'prevenient grace,' continues in 'justifying grace,' and is brought to fruition in 'sanctifying grace'" (*BOD*; pages 45-46).

These distinctive emphases of United Methodists provide the basis for "practical divinity," the experiential realization of the gospel of Jesus Christ in the lives of Christian people. These emphases have been preserved not so much through formal doctrinal declarations as through the vital movement of faith and practice as seen in converted lives and within the disciplined life of the Church.

Devising formal definitions of doctrine has been less pressing for United Methodists than summoning people to faith and nurturing them in the knowledge and love of God. The core of Wesleyan doctrine that informed our past rightly belongs to our common heritage as Christians and remains a prime component within our continuing theological task (*BOD*; pages 49-50).

The General Commission on Christian Unity and Interreligious Concerns (now the Office of Christian Unity and Interreligious Relationships) spearheads the ecumenical work of the denomination by fulfilling its purpose: "To advocate and work toward the full reception of the gift of Christian unity in every aspect of the Church's life and to foster approaches to ministry and mission that more fully reflect the oneness of Christ's church in the human community" (2004 *BOD*; ¶ 1902.1).

In "Resolution of Intent: With a View to Unity," the 2000 General Conference declared it "our official intent henceforth to interpret all our Articles, Confession, and other 'standards of doctrine' in consonance with our best ecumenical insights and judgment" (2004 *BOR*; page 273).

Practice:

Within all discussions of Holy Communion, United Methodism must remain firmly anchored in its traditional sources of authority. We recognize and respect authorities that other church traditions hold dear. United Methodists remain open to greater Christian unity through the work of the Holy Spirit in response to Jesus' prayer that "they will be one" (John 17:21).

Committee Members:

L. Edward Phillips, Chairperson
Daniel T. Benedict, Jr.
Michael J. Coyner
Jerome King Del Pino
Gayle Carlton Felton
Thelma H. Flores
Barbara Thorington Green
Karen A. Greenwaldt
Susan W. Hassinger
Sally Havens
Dong Hyun (David) Kim
Jon E. McCoy
Sophie Pieh
Arturo L. Razon, Jr.
Bruce W. Robbins
Frank E. Trotter, Jr.
Karen Westerfield Tucker
Hans Växby
Josiah U. Young, III

Notes About This Document

Scripture quotations, unless otherwise indicated, are taken from the Common English Bible. Copyright © 2011 by the Common English Bible. All rights reserved. Used by permission. (www.CommonEnglishBible.com)

BOD, Discipline, and *Book of Discipline* refer to *The Book of Discipline of The United Methodist Church, 2004,* copyright © 2004 The United Methodist Publishing House.

UMH refers to *The United Methodist Hymnal,* copyright © 1989 The United Methodist Publishing House.

BOW refers to *The United Methodist Book of Worship,* copyright © 1992 The United Methodist Publishing House.

BOR refers to *The Book of Resolutions of The United Methodist Church, 2004,* copyright © 2004 The United Methodist Publishing House.

Quotations from John Wesley are from the Jackson edition of *The Works of John Wesley.*

ADOPTED 2004
AMENDED AND READOPTED 2012
FOR 2013-2016 AND 2017-2020 QUADRENNIA
RESOLUTION #8032, 2012 *BOOK OF RESOLUTIONS*
RESOLUTION #8014, 2008 *BOOK OF RESOLUTIONS*
RESOLUTION #353, 2004 *BOOK OF RESOLUTIONS*

[Editor's Note: Resolution 2044 has not expired, despite the indication in the 2012 *Book of Resolutions* that it was last revised and readopted in 2008. It was revised and readopted in 2012 by the General Conference, Calendar Item 388, page 2183 in the 2012 *Daily Christian Advocate*. The resolution will expire in 2020 if it is not readopted by the 2020 General Conference.]

2044. Sexual Misconduct Within Ministerial Relationships

The abuse of power occurs when we use power to gratify our own needs rather than to carry out God's sacred trust. It happens when we refuse to own the responsibility of guardianship that comes with the privilege of power . . . until we understand that power is the responsibility to give, instead of the opportunity to take, we will continue to abuse it."[1]

"There is little doubt that sexual misconduct in church and society is significant and troubling for our communities and congregations worldwide. This unwanted behavior damages the moral environment where people worship, minister, work, and learn. In 1996, the General Conference made a commitment to focus on sexual misconduct within the church and took action to address this brokenness and pain within The United Methodist Church" (*The Book of Resolutions, 1996*, p. 128; *2000*, p. 135; *2004*, p. 150).

Sacred Trust, Power, and Responsibility

The Book of Discipline, 2012, ¶ 161F, declares all human beings have equal worth in the eyes of God. As the promise of Galatians 3:26-29 states, "you are all God's children"; therefore, we as United Methodists support equity among all persons without regard to ethnicity, situation, or gender. In our congregations and settings for ministry, we seek to create an environment of hospitality for all persons, male or female, which is free from misconduct of a sexual nature and encourages respect, equality, and kinship in Christ.

Those in positions of authority in the church, both clergy and lay, have been given much responsibility, vested with a sacred trust to maintain an environment that is safe for people to live and grow in God's love. Misconduct of a sexual nature inhibits the

---

1. Ann Smith, *Alive Now*, Sept./Oct. 1996.

full and joyful participation of all in the community of God. Sexual misconduct in church and ministry settings impedes the mission of Jesus Christ. Ministerial leaders have the responsibility not only to avoid actions and words which hurt others, but also to protect the vulnerable against actions or words which cause harm.

As our children, youth, and adults come to worship, study, camps, retreats, and schools of mission, they bring a heightened awareness of the issues of sexual abuse, sexual harassment, incest, rape, and sexual assault. Ministerial leaders have the responsibility not only to avoid actions and words that hurt others, but also to protect the vulnerable against actions or words that cause harm. In the safety and sanctity of the church's settings, we as church leaders, both clergy and lay, paid and volunteer, must be held to the highest standard of conduct as we lead, provide guidance and support, and work with children, youth, and adults in ministry settings. Sexual misconduct in any form is a violation of the membership and ordination vows we take as laity and clergy in The United Methodist Church. Sexual abuse, sexual misconduct, and sexual harassment are chargeable offenses both for clergy and laity per *The Book of Discipline*, ¶ 2702.

Definitions

Sexual misconduct within ministerial relationships is a betrayal of sacred trust. It is a continuum of sexual or gender-directed behaviors by either a lay or clergy person within a ministerial relationship (paid or unpaid). It can include child abuse, adult sexual abuse, harassment, rape or sexual assault, sexualized verbal comments or visuals, unwelcome touching and advances, use of sexualized materials including pornography, stalking, sexual abuse of youth or those without capacity to consent, or misuse of the pastoral or ministerial position using sexualized conduct to take advantage of the vulnerability of another. In includes criminal behaviors in some nations, states, and communities.

Sexual harassment is a form of sexual misconduct and is defined in ¶ 161*I* (*Book of Discipline*, 2012) in the Social Principles. To clarify further, it is unwanted sexual or gender-directed behavior within a pastoral, employment, ministerial (including volunteers), mentor, or colleague relationship that is so severe or pervasive that it alters the conditions of employment or volunteer work or unreasonably interferes with the employee or volunteer's performance by creating a hostile environment that can include unwanted sexual jokes, repeated advances, touching, displays, or comments that insult, degrade, or sexually exploit women, men, elders, children, or youth.

Sexual abuse is a form of sexual misconduct and occurs when a person within a ministerial role of leadership (lay or clergy, pastor, educator, counselor, youth leader, or other position of leadership) engages in sexual contact or sexualized behavior with a congregant, client, employee, student, staff member, coworker, or volunteer (1996 *Book of Resolutions*, p. 130). It can include coerced or forced sexual contact (including those unable to give informed consent), sexual interaction or contact with children or youth, and sexual exhibitionism or display of sexual visuals or pornography.

Sexualized behavior is behavior that communicates sexual interest and/or content. Examples include, but are not limited to displaying sexually suggestive visual materials; use of pornography in church programs on or with church property, making sexual comments or innuendo about one's own or another person's body; touching another person's body; touching another person's body/hair/clothing; touching or rubbing oneself in the presence of another person; kissing; and sexual intercourse. Sexualized behavior can be a form of sexual misconduct when this behavior is unwanted by the recipient or witness, is a violation of society's or the Church's law, breaks the sacred trust in the ministerial role, or violates the vows taken at membership or ordination.

The continuum of behaviors called sexual misconduct within the ministerial relationship represents an *exploitation of power* and not merely "inappropriate sexual or gender-directed conduct." Sexual misconduct in any form is unacceptable in church and ministry settings whether it is clergy-to-lay, lay-to-clergy, clergy-to-clergy, lay-to-lay, staff-to-staff, staff-to-volunteer, volunteer-to-volunteer, or volunteer-to-staff. Anyone who works or volunteers under the authority or auspices of the Church must be held to the highest standards of behavior, free of sexual misconduct in any form.

Those in Ministerial Roles

Both laity and clergy fill ministerial roles in our Church. In addition to clergy or professional staff, any United Methodist may fill a ministerial role by participating in ministries including, but not limited to:

- leading and participating in lay servant ministries;
- counseling or leading events for children, youth, and adults;
- teaching and leading in church schools for children, youth, and adults;
- counseling victims of violence, domestic violence, or sexual abuse;
- counseling couples about marriage, divorce, or separation;
- leading in worship as speaker from the pulpit, liturgist, communion server, or usher;
- volunteering to chaperone trips, work camps, or special events;
- working in Walks to Emmaus and Chrysalis retreats;
- mentoring;
- supervising church staff members; and
- working with computers, websites, and the Internet in church property/programs.

Progress and Troubling Trends

The General Conference not only has mandated adoption of policies in our churches, conferences, agencies, and schools, it called for training, advocacy practices, and surveys of progress as a denomination conducted by the General Commission on the Status and Role of Women.

Now twenty years after General Conference first committed to the elimination of sexual misconduct in the Church (1988), good work has been done:

- Thirty-five annual conferences now assign oversight of sexual misconduct issues to a "team";
- Many conferences require sexual misconduct awareness training for all clergy, lay leadership, and appointees;
- The General Commission on the Status and Role of Women has provided support and counsel to victims and church officials in hundreds of cases.

Work remains to be done. Recent findings show the experiences of leadership of the Church on many levels—local church, seminary, annual and general conferences in particular:

- Awareness of the denomination's policy on sexual misconduct is high, but awareness of the resources for victims and congregations is much lower;
- Harassment is still a significant problem: well over three-fourths of the clergy (men and women) and half of the laywomen had experienced sexual harassment in the Church (about one third of laymen);
- Holding offenders accountable, removing errant pastors, lay staff, or volunteers as needed, and requiring counseling, training, and supervision before resumption of ministerial roles are remedial steps our episcopal and superintending leaders should use;
- Follow-up on situations of misconduct so that appropriate and effective remediation is achieved so that the behavior stops, does not reoccur, and relationships and ministry are returned to wholeness as much as possible;
- Placing justice for victims above protection of offenders, including pastors, is an equally pressing need;
- With this global *Internet age* and the growing use of computers by clergy and laity has come more frequent reports of the use of pornography and sexualized materials by laity and clergy within church programs or with church computers or property.

Progress in four areas is not adequate: prevention, education, intervention, and healing. Additional work is now needed:

1. resources for various constituencies addressing prevention, education, intervention, and healing after lay or clergy sexual misconduct (including the United Methodist website on sexual ethics www.umsexualethics.org);

2. updated training (initial, follow-up, and advanced) for the various constituencies within the church, including education on the prevention of the use of pornography, its destructive impact on users, and its potential for abuse in or with church programs or property;

3. implementation of models for intervention and healing in order to provide a consistent and thorough response when complaints are initiated;

4. development of a model for ongoing assessment of policies, practices, and responses of conferences;

5. appropriate handling of the presence and involvement of legally convicted sexual offenders in local congregational activities and ministry;

6. opportunities for annual conferences to share their resources and experience.[2]

Therefore be it resolved, that The United Methodist Church renews its stand in opposition to the sin of sexual misconduct within the Church worldwide. It further recommits all United Methodists to the eradication of sexual misconduct in all ministerial relationships, and calls for:

1. the General Commission on the Status and Role of Women to continue to convene and coordinate a cooperative interagency group to address the areas of prevention, education, intervention, and healing including a representative of the Council of Bishops, the General Boards of Discipleship, Higher Education and Ministry, Global Ministries, Church and Society, the General Council on Finance and Administration, the Division on Ministries with Young People, and representatives of annual conference Response/Crisis Teams and Safe Sanctuary Teams (each agency member responsible for his or her own expenses and a share of the expenses of the annual conference representatives);

2. the General Commission on the Status and Role of Women be provided resources sufficient to develop/distribute resources for leaders of lay events and programs within the church in order to help train and equip them to raise this important issue with laity (including lay servants, lay leaders, Christian educators, persons in mission, leaders in Schools of Christian Mission, Walks to Emmaus, Chrysalis, and leaders of events with young people);

3. the General Commission on the Status and Role of Women, through the interagency group, to ensure that resources for laity and clergy in ministerial roles are identified and promoted for use in conferences, districts or clusters, and local congregations;

4. the Council of Bishops to reaffirm its commitment to preventing and eradicating sexual harassment, abuse, and misconduct in the church through education, training, and sharing of resources. Each episcopal area will implement policies, procedures, and ongoing plans to coordinate persons involved in prevention and intervention, including but not limited to: district superintendents, boards of ordained ministry, boards of laity, advocates, intervention and healing teams, trained mediators, and staff-parish relations committees;

2. For more information, see the United Methodist Web site on Sexual Ethics, www.umsexualethics.org.

5. United Methodist-related schools of theology to provide training on the prevention and eradication of sexual harassment, abuse, and misconduct within the ministerial relationship;

6. annual conference boards of ordained ministry to provide education (entry level, follow-up, advanced) for all appointed clergy, local pastors, and commissioned members. Annual conferences are also encouraged to provide similar education and training for those employed in ministerial leadership;

7. episcopal areas to require that all clergy, local pastors, assigned laity, and commissioned members appointed in each annual conference have regular, up-to-date sexual ethics training to be in good standing for appointment;

8. the General Board of Church and Society to continue to advocate for just laws that address or counter sexual harassment and abuse in our larger societies.

ADOPTED 1996
REVISED AND READOPTED 2000, 2004, 2008, 2012
RESOLUTION #2044, 2008, 2012 *BOOK OF RESOLUTIONS*
RESOLUTION #36, 2004 *BOOK OF RESOLUTIONS*
RESOLUTION #30, 2000 *BOOK OF RESOLUTIONS*

See Social Principles, ¶ 161J.

Alphabetical List of Resolution Titles

Scripture References
in Resolutions

(Resolution numbers in **bold**)

Genesis 1—**3427, 4064**
Genesis 1:2—**8031**
Genesis 1:26, 28—**1001**
Genesis 1:27—**1035, 4135, 6025**
Genesis 1:28—**1002, 1033, 3361,**
4135
Genesis 1:31—**3202**
Genesis 2—**1033**
Genesis 2:7—**1001**
Genesis 2:15—**1003, 4135**
Genesis 3—**8031**
Genesis 3:7—**5083**
Genesis 9:9—**1033**
Genesis 9:9-10—**1002**
Genesis 15:15—**3202**
Genesis 17:1-14—**8031**
Genesis 17:9-14—**8032**
Genesis 18:1-11—**3281**
Genesis 21:19—**1029**
Genesis 24:15-21—**1029**
Genesis 34—**3427**
Genesis 35:16-20—**3203**

Exodus 1:9-10—**3379**
Exodus 12:12-28—**8032**
Exodus 12:21—**3024**
Exodus 12:38—**3379**
Exodus 16—**8032**
Exodus 18:13-27—**5086**

Exodus 20:17—**6112**
Exodus 22:21—**3281**
Exodus 22:25—**4064**
Exodus 23:1-3—**5031**
Exodus 23:6, 8—**5031**
Exodus 23:6-11—**4056**
Exodus 23:7—**5031**
Exodus 23:9—**3281**
Exodus 23:10-12—**4053**
Exodus 24:1-8—**8032**
Exodus 24:1-12—**8031, 8032**
Exodus 25:23-30—**8032**

Leviticus—**1025**
Leviticus 18:6-19—**5083**
Leviticus 19:9-10—**4051**
Leviticus 19:15—**5031, 6025**
Leviticus 19:30—**6073**
Leviticus 19:33-34—**3281**
Leviticus 19:34—**3281**
Leviticus 20:18-19—**5083**
Leviticus 25—**4053**
Leviticus 25:23—**6028**
Leviticus 25:35-55—**4056**

Numbers 5:5-7—**6066**
Numbers 20:9-11—**1029**

Deuteronomy 1:17—**5031**

New Resolutions

Deleted and Expired Resolutions

(2012 Resolution Numbers)

Abolition of Sex Trafficking—6023

Abuse of Older Adults—3021

Abusive Treatment Methods for Persons With Mental Disabilities—3301

Act of Repentance for Racism—3372

Adoption in a Global Climate—2021

Aging in the United States: The Church's Response—3022

Appalachia: A Call to Action—4001

Assisting Personal Mobility—3003

Ban Cluster Bombs—6152

Being the Church Amid Disagreement—2061

Black Leadership—3064

Bread for the World Covenant Church—4055

Call for Comprehensive Immigration Reform—5081

Call to Action on Alcohol, A—3045

Economic Justice for a New Millennium—4052

End Exploitation by United Nations Personnel—6029

End the US Embargo of Cuba—6059

Ending the Colonial Status of Puerto Rico—6056

Environmental Health and Safety in Workplace
   and Community—4132

Environmental Justice for a Sustainable Future—1023

Environmental Law: The Precautionary Principle—1024

Environmental Stewardship—1026

Equal Justice—5031

Equity in Access to High School Education—3163

Eradicating Abusive Child Labor—3083

Establish US Department of Peace—5082

Evolution and Intelligent Design—5052

Faith Communities on Campus—2002

Filipino Veterans Equity Act of 2007—5088

Food and Drug Administration (FDA) Regulation
   of Tobacco—5085

Girl Child, The—3089

Global Economy and the Environment—4059

Global Living Wage—4060

Global Ministries and Mission Society—6011

Seek Moratorium on Capital Punishment—5036

Smithfield Foods, Inc. and Union Organizing—4136

Society of St. Andrew—4093

Sons and Daughters of Our Fathers—3282

Statement Against Extrajudicial Killings in the Philippines—6119

Statement of Concern on Poverty—4092

Status of Women, The—3444

Stem Cell Research—3183

Stewardship Education for Small Membership Churches—4103

Strengthening Bridges—3146

Sudan: A Call to Compassion and Caring—6085

Support and Protection of Rural People—3393

Support and Services for US Military and Rebuilding Iraq—6142

Support Campus Ministers—2003

Support for All Who Minister in Rural Settings—3394

Support for the Land Mine Treaty—6151

Support for the Religious Coalition for Reproductive Choice—3204

Support Legislation Prohibiting Malicious Harassments—5084

Support of Taiwan—6092

Taiwan Security, Stability, and Self-Determination—6091

INDEX

A

AAMHC. *See* African American Methodist Heritage Center

abortion, 87–89, 144
gender-selective, 104–6
HIV and, 275
stress after, 317

abstinence, 135

abuse. *See also* sexual abuse
drug, 158, 366
family violence, 86, 385
of migrant workers, 533
substance, 276–77

ACA. *See* Affordable Care Act

Academy for Spiritual Formation, 695

access barriers, 238

access to health care, 238, 242, 316

Accessibility Audit for Churches, 306

accessibility/equal access, 306. *See also* disabilities
accessibility grants for churches, 147

ADA and Standard Rules on the Equalization of Opportunities for Persons With Disabilities, 148–49
Church and Deaf Ministries Steering Committee, 149–51

accountability, 534, 643, 646

Acquired Immune Deficiency Syndrome (AIDS). *See* HIV/AIDS

Act of Repentance Service for the Healing of Relationships with Indigenous Persons, 333, 535–36

Act of Repentance with Native Peoples, 326

ADA. *See* Americans with Disabilities Act

adopt-a-school programs, 221

adoption, 89
family support for, 95–97

adult baptism, 716–17, 720

Advance Specials, 154, 593

for opposing criminalization of
communities of color, 365–66
on peace, 447, 449, 634
for Peace with Justice, 663
for peacemaking, 625
privatization, 443
for racial justice, 350
on racism and economic injustice, 361–62
on religious conflict, 199
for reparations, 176
right to privacy, 502, 503
for sanctions guidelines, 566,
568
sexual privacy, 507–8
on SGBV, 389
on slavery, 560
speaking in tongues, 688
spiritual rebirth, 710
for stewardship and justice,
67–68
tax structures, 450
tobacco marketing, 417, 418
for torture abolition, 668
US energy policy and United
Methodist responsibility, 48
victim care, 499
for violence, 377–78
voter representation, 510, 511
water protection, 62
for women in church and society, 397, 399
workers' rights, 466
world hunger, 427–28
for world population, 344

Bikini Atoll, 579

Bill of Rights, 321

bioengineering, 226

Biological Weapons Convention,
640

biotechnology, 226

birth spacing, 257

bishops, 757. *See also* Council of
Bishops
women as, 398

Bishops' Initiative on Drugs and
Drug Violence, 159

B'laan tribe, 618

Black Americans, 168–76
African American Methodist
Heritage Center (AAMHC),
169–72
observance of Martin Luther
King Jr. Day and, 174–75
reparations for, 175–76
resourcing Black churches in
urban communities, 172–73

Black Church Week of Prayer for
the Healing of AIDS, 273

Black churches, resourcing,
172–73

The Black College Fund, 421

Black family life, 168

Black Mesa, 536

Black Methodists for Church
Renewal (BMCR), 170

blood, in Holy Communion,
763–64

BMCR. *See* Black Methodists for
Church Renewal

Board of Ordained Ministry, 364

Board of Temperance, Prohibition, and Public Morals, 159,
234

Boehm, Martin, 732

Covenant on Civil and Political Rights, 671

"Covenant Renewal Service," 722

Covenant to Care: Recognizing and Responding to the Many Faces of HIV/AIDS in the USA, 267–74

CPP-NPA. *See* Communist Party of the Philippines–New People's Army

creation, 224
caring for, 67–73

credit card marketing practices, 453

Criminal Alien Requirement program, 367

criminal justice
biblical reference and, 490
confinement conditions, 495
crime prevention and criminal proceedings, 492–94
criminal laws and penalties, 494–95
exiting incarceration, 495–97
humanizing, 490–91
restorative justice and, 474
Texas death penalty, 497–99
victim care, 499–501

criminals, sterilization laws and, 235

crystal meth, 164, 165

Cuba, lifting US embargo of, 576–78

cultural competency training, 701

cultural issues
church's response to ethnic and religious conflict, 198–200

expansion of inclusive language, 197
Holocaust Memorial Day, 200–201
in maternal health, 257–58
opposing English as official language, 194–97
prejudice against Muslims and Arabs in the USA, 202, 524
support for ethnic ministry plans, 197–98
use of diverse languages, 194–97

cultural rights, 542–44

culture, 513
health factors of, 249–50
identity and, 83

Cushman, Robert, 207

CWSW. *See* Church World Service and Witness

CWWM. *See* Churches Witnessing With Migrants

cyberbullying, 91–92

D

Dahill, Lisa E., 119

DAP. *See* Disbursement Acceleration Program

Darrow, Clarence, 234

Darwin, Charles, 232, 233

Darwin, Leonard, 233

de Carvalho, Emilio, 517

de facto nuclear waste dumps, 52

First 100 German Words

Berlitz Kids™

Berlitz Publishing Company, Inc.

Princeton   Mexico City   Dublin

Eschborn   Singapore

all
alle

All the frogs are green.

Die Frösche sind alle grün.

and
und

I have two sisters and two brothers.

Ich habe zwei Schwestern und zwei Brüder.

to ask
fragen

It is time to ask, "Where are my sheep?"

Es wird Zeit, dass du fragst: „Wo sind meine Schafe?"

aunt
die Tante

My aunt is my mom's sister.

Meine Tante ist die Schwester meiner Mutti.

3

black
schwarz

Zebras have
black stripes.

**Zebras haben
schwarze Streifen.**

blue
blau

The sky is blue.

**Der Himmel ist
blau.**

boy
der Junge

The boys are
brothers.

**Die Jungen sind
Brüder.**

brother
der Bruder

He is my brother.

Er ist mein Bruder.

cake
der Kuchen
She likes to eat cake.

Sie ißt gern Kuchen.

carrot
die Karotte
A carrot is orange.

Eine Karotte ist orange.

cat
die Katze
The cat sees the mouse.

Die Katze sieht die Maus.

chair
der Stuhl
He is sitting on a chair.

Er sitzt auf einem Stuhl.

dad
der Vati

My dad and I
look alike.

**Mein Vati und ich
sehen uns ähnlich.**

doctor
der Arzt

The doctor checks
the baby.

**Der Arzt untersuch
das Baby.**

dog
der Hund

The dog has a
funny hat.

**Der Hund hat
einen lustigen Hut.**

door
die Tür

What is behind
the door?

**Was ist hinter
der Tür?**

to eat
essen (people)
fressen (animals)

The bird likes
to eat worms.

**Der Vogel frißt
gern Würmer.**

eight
acht

He put eight celery
sticks in the salad.

**Er gab acht
Selleriestengel in
den Salat.**

everyone
jeder

Everyone here has
spots!

**Jeder hier hat
Flecken!**

everything
alles

Everything is purple.

Alles ist lila.

F

family
die Familie

This is a big family.

Dies ist eine große Familie.

five
fünf

The rabbit ate five carrots.

Der Hase aß fünf Karotten.

four
vier

I gave four pears to my grandma.

Ich gab meiner Großmutter vier Birnen.

Friday
der Freitag

On Friday, we go to the park.

Am Freitag gehen wir in den Park.

girl
das Mädchen

The girl is dancing.

Das Mädchen tanzt.

grandfather
der Großvater

I have fun with my grandfather.

Ich habe viel Spaß mit meinem Großvater.

grandmother
die Großmutter

My grandmother likes to bake.

Meine Großmutter backt gern.

green
grün

Grass is green.

Gras ist grün.

happy
fröhlich

This is a happy face.

Dies ist ein fröhliches Gesicht.

hello
Guten Tag

Hello. How are you?

Guten Tag. Wie geht es Ihnen.

hot
heiß

Fire is hot.

Feurer ist heiß.

house
das Haus

The house has many windows.

Das Haus hat viele Fenster.

ice
das Eis

We skate on ice.

Wir laufen auf dem Eis Schlittschuh.

ice cream
die Eiscreme

Clara likes ice cream.

Klara mag Eiscreme.

inside
drinnen

He is inside the house.

Er ist im Haus drinnen.

into
in

Do not go into that cave!

Geh ja nicht in diese Höhle!

11

jam
die Marmelade

Do you think she
likes bread and jam?

**Meinst du, sie mag
Brot mit Marmelade?**

job
die Arbeit

It is a big job.

Das ist viel Arbeit.

juice
der Saft
(...saft)

She is pouring a
glass of orange juice.

**Sie geißt ein Glas
Orangensaft ein.**

to jump
springen

The animal loves
to jump.

**Das Tier springt
sehr gern.**

key
der Schlüssel

Which key opens
the lock?

**Welcher Schlüssel
öffnet das Schloß?**

kind
freundlich

She is kind to animals.

**Sie ist freundlich
zu Tieren.**

kiss
der Kuß

Would you like to give
the monkey a kiss?

**Möchtest du dem
Affen einen Kuß
geben?**

kitten
das Kätzchen

A kitten is a baby cat.

**Ein Kätzchen ist ein
Katzenbaby.**

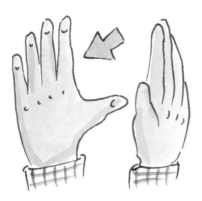

left

(der, die, das)

linke

This is your left hand.

Dies ist deine linke Hand.

library

die Bücherei

The library is full of books.

Die Bücherei ist voll mit Büchern.

to like

mögen

He is going to like the cake.

Er wird den Kuchen mögen.

love

die Liebe

Love is wonderful.

Liebe ist wunderschön.

me
mich
Look at me!
Schau mich an!

milk
die Milch
He likes milk.
Er mag Milch.

mom
die Mutti
She is the baby's mom.
**Sie ist die Mutti
des Babys.**

Monday
der Montag
On Monday,
we take baths.
**Am Montag nehmen
wir ein Bad.**

name
der Name

His name
begins with "R".

**Sein Name beginnt
mit „R".**

night
die Nacht

It is dark at night.

**In der Nacht ist
es dunkel.**

nine
neun

The pig ate nine ice
cream cones!

**Das Schwein aß
neun Eiswaffeln.**

no
nein

No, you may not go.

**Nein, du darfst
nicht gehen.**

ocean
der Ozean

This turtle swims in the ocean.

Diese Schildkröte schwimmt im Ozean.

o'clock
Uhr

It is one o'clock.

Es ist ein Uhr.

one
eins

I need one pineapple for this cake.

Ich brauche eine Ananas für diesen Kuchen.

orange
orange

Leaves turn orange in the fall.

Blätter verfärben sich im Herbst zu Orange.

paper
das Papier
Write on the paper!
Schreib auf das Papier!

pen
der Füller
The pen is leaking.
Der Füller läuft aus.

pencil
der Bleistift
A pencil is for drawing.
Ein Bleistift ist zum Zeichnen da.

purple
lila
I like purple grapes.
Ich mag lila Trauben.

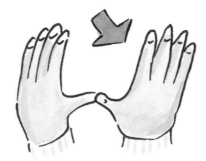

red
rot
A strawberry is red.
Eine Erdbeere ist rot.

right
(der, die, das)
rechte
This is your right hand.
Dies ist deine rechte Hand.

rose
die Rose
She likes roses.
Sie mag Rosen.

to run
laufen
You need feet to run!
Man braucht Füße, um zu laufen!

Saturday
der Samstag

On Saturday, we work together.

Am Samstag arbeiten wir zusammen.

seven
sieben

There are seven cherries for seven sundaes.

Es gibt sieben Kirschen für sieben Eisbecher.

sister
die Schwester

They are sisters.

Sie sind Schwestern.

six
sechs

My grandpa bought six watermelons.

Mein Großvati kaufte sechs Wassermelonen.

Sunday
der Sonntag

On Sunday, we eat
dinner with Grandma.

**Am Sonntag essen
wir mit Großmutter
zu Abend.**

ten
zehn

My mother uses ten
peppers for her pizza.

**Meine Mutter braucht
für ihre Pizza zehn
Paprikaschoten.**

three
drei

Do not put three chili
peppers in that sandwich!

**Lege keine drei
Paprikaschoten auf
das belegte Brot!**

Thursday
der Donnerstag

On Thursday, we
wash clothes.

**Am Donnerstag
waschen wir Wäsche.**

Tuesday
der Dienstag

On Tuesday, we
wash floors.

**Am Dienstag putzen
wir die Fußböden.**

two
zwei

She gave the teacher
two apples.

**Sie gab dem
Lehrer zwei Äpfel.**

umbrella
der
Regenschirm

She has a yellow
umbrella.

**Sie hat einen gelben
Regenschirm.**

uncle
der Onkel

My uncle is my dad's
brother.

**Mein Onkel ist der
Bruder meines
Vaters.**

walk
laufen

It is good to walk.

Es tut gut zu laufen.

we
wir

See us? We are all purple.

Siehst du uns? Wir sind alle lila.

Wednesday
der Mittwoch

On Wednesday, we go to work.

Am Mittwoch gehen wir zur Arbeit.

white
weiß

Clouds are white.

Wolken sind weiß.

yes
ja

Is he yellow?
Yes! He is.

Ist er gelb? Ja, er ist gelb.

yellow
gelb

A banana is yellow.

Eine Banane ist gelb.

you
du

You are reading this book.

Du liest dieses Buch.

your
dein

What color are your eyes?

Welche Farbe haben deine Augen?

zebra
das Zebra

You cannot have a
pet zebra!

**Du kannst kein
Zebra als Haustier
haben!**

zigzag
das Zickzack

The house has zigzags
on it.

**Das Haus hat ein
Zickzackmuster.**

zipper
der Reißverschluß

The zipper is stuck.

**Der Reißverschluß
klemmt.**

zoo
der Zoo

I can see many
animals at the zoo.

**Im Zoo kann ich
viele Tiere sehen.**

On the next few pages, write and draw your favorite German words.